W9-CTW-750

THE
WORLD
OF
RAV KOOK'S
THOUGHT

THE

WORLD

OF

RAV KOOK'S

THOUGHT

Presentations from an
AVI CHAI-Sponsored Conference Held
in Jerusalem August 19–22, 1985
(ELUL 2–5, 5745)
On the Occasion
of the 50th Anniversary of
Rav Kook's Death

TRANSLATED FROM THE HEBREW EDITION
YOVEL OROT

EDITORS OF THE HEBREW EDITION

Dr. Benjamin Ish Shalom
Professor Shalom Rosenberg

TRANSLATORS OF THE HEBREW EDITION

Rabbi Shalom Carmy
Rabbi Bernard Casper zt'l

ISBN: 0-9623723-2-3

Manufactured in the United States of America
2 4 6 8 9 7 5 3
First Edition

Editor's Note

In translating the articles in this book from the Hebrew original to English parlance there may be a loss of some of the nuances in terminology. Serious scholars should check the Hebrew edition, *Yovel Orot,* rather than relying solely on the accuracy of the English phraseology.

The reader should also note that the Hebrew letters "chet" and "chaf" are variably transliterated into English as *ch, h, ḥ, kh.* In the interest of consistency, throughout this volume *ch* is used for both of these letters with few exceptions.

Translator's Note

The full name of Rav Kook was Rav Avraham Yitzchak HaCohen, of which the acronym is HaReAYaH. In the text, often only this acronym is used. When the surname is used, it has become customary to write simply "Rav Kook." In the Hebrew text, the name "Rav Kook" is usually followed by the letters zt'l, which mean literally, "May the memory of the righteous be for a blessing." In the present English text, this epitaph has been omitted, and the name stands in the simple form by which it is generally known, i.e., Rav Kook.

Foreword

WHEN ONE EMBARKS on any endeavor, the first step sets the direction on the path to be taken. The first project that AVI CHAI sponsored as a philanthropic foundation was a conference that brought together scholars and philosophers of various perspectives to discuss the implications of the teachings of Rav Avraham Yitzchak HaCohen Kook zt'l as they apply to contemporary society. It is Rav Kook's vision of Judaism in harmony with modern life and his love for all the Jewish people, the land of Israel, the Torah of Israel and all of mankind, which inspires the work of AVI CHAI. It is our hope that increased understanding of his message by a broad spectrum of both scholars and laymen will have a meaningful impact on not only our communities but the entire world.

The concept of holding a conference on Rav Kook's philosophy in Jerusalem on the 50th anniversary of his passing was suggested by Samuel J. "Buddy" Silberman, a founding Trustee of AVI CHAI. The Board of AVI CHAI expresses its deep appreciation to Mr. Silberman, who from the outset believed the conference should be designed so that the proceedings could be published in several languages to enable those who were not in attendance to benefit from the mosaic of interpretations.

The presentations were adapted and originally published in a Hebrew volume entitled *Yovel Orot,* edited by Dr. Benjamin Ish Shalom and Professor Shalom Rosenberg. The English translation of that text, *The World of Rav Kook's Thought,* was begun by Rabbi Bernard Casper zt'l, distinguished former Chief Rabbi of South Africa, who passed away before its completion. AVI CHAI was honored to have Rabbi Casper participate in this project. Rabbi Shalom Carmy, noted scholar on Rav Kook, graciously undertook to complete the translation and did so with meticulous care.

The outline of the conference was originally discussed by a committee consisting of Zalman C. Bernstein, chairman of AVI CHAI, Arthur W. Fried, a founding Trustee of AVI CHAI, Rabbi Yochanan Fried, Rabbi Shlomo Riskin, Rabbi Daniel Tropper, and Haim Zohar. Each of these individuals contributed in significant ways to the program's actualization and quality. This committee selected Dr. Benjamin Ish Shalom as the conference organizer.

The World Congress of Jewish Thought on the 50th Anniversary of the Death of Rav Kook was held at the King David Hotel in Jerusalem, Israel, in Elul 5745 (August 19–22, 1985 C.E.), encompassing the 3rd of Elul, the exact *Yahrzeit* of Rav Kook. This event was conceived and funded by AVI CHAI, via its funds at P.E.F. Israel Endowment Fund, Inc. The World Zionist Organization, Department of Torah Education and Culture in the Diaspora, and the Ministry of Education and Culture, Torah Culture Department, of the Government of Israel were associated with AVI CHAI in this endeavor.

The opening ceremony of the conference took place at the residence of the president of Israel, Chaim Herzog. Greetings were expressed by Chief Rabbi Avraham Shapira, Mr. Arye Dulzin, chairman of the WZO, and Dr. Norman Lamm, president of Yeshiva University. The opening address was presented by Professor Ephraim A. Urbach, zt'l, president of the Israel Academy of Sciences and Humanities. Rabbi Moshe Zvi Neriah and Rabbi Yehuda Amital completed the presentation of the program on that occasion.

As an expression of AVI CHAI's desire to continue to promote Rav Kook's message, a collation was held for a *minyan* of ten key individuals on the first anniversary of the conference. This was an opportunity for AVI CHAI to express its appreciation to this *minyan.* Rabbi Yehoshua Zuckerman, a Rosh Yeshiva at Mercaz HaRav Kook, presented a *dra-*

sha on this occasion. Also in attendance, with their spouses, were Zalman C. Bernstein, Arthur W. Fried, Rabbi Yochanan Fried, Dr. Benjamin Ish Shalom, Yitzchak Mayer, Rabbi Shlomo Riskin, Professor Shalom Rosenberg, Samuel J. Silberman, Rabbi Daniel Tropper, Haim Zohar and Mrs. Yehoshua Zuckerman.

Contents

Avraham Yitzchak HaCohen Kook: A Biographical Profile*

Jacob Agus

RAV AVRAHAM YITZCHAK KOOK is a legendary figure in both Israel and the United States. The first chief rabbi of Palestine, though one of the leading authorities of Orthodox Judaism in the modern period, towered above ideological differences and the fires of partisanship, and concerned himself with all groups within the Jewish community. A philosophical and literary mystic of scope and profundity, he belonged to that company of rare souls for whom religion is not merely faith and conviction but direct experience and the essence of life itself. He drew his inspiration from Jewish sources, though he was not unfamiliar with the vision and sweep of classical and modern thought.

More than any of his contemporary colleagues, Rav Kook was aware of the need for adapting the tradition of Judaism to the temper of the new age, of endowing ancient doctrines and concepts with fresh life and relevancy to the problems of the day. To achieve this goal, however, he did not deem it necessary to compromise with Orthodoxy. On the contrary, he felt that what was needed was not the trimming down

*excerpted from *Great Jewish Thinkers of the Twentieth Century,* ed., Simon Noveck, Washington, D.C. 1986. B'nai B'rith Department of Continuing Jewish Education. Reprinted by permission.

or streamlining of Jewish theory or practice but rather its emotional vitalization and intellectual reinterpretation. Rav Kook also made a unique contribution to the development of modern Zionism by giving to the spirit of nationalism a more honored place in the divine scheme of things than any of his predecessors had done. He interpreted the whole range of Jewish religious practice from the prohibition of shaving to the observance of the Sabbath in terms of the nationalist ideology of Zionism.

All of his attitudes and ideas can be understood in reference to his deep and genuine mysticism. Contrary to the general impression, a mystic is not a monk, living in an isolated cell and guarding his soul in a shaded retreat so as to keep it "unspotted of the world." The great mystics were men of action. Certainly, Rav Kook took an active part in the major concerns and most important controversies of modern Jewish life. He emerges as a religious nationalist, and one of the most luminous personalities in twentieth-century Orthodox Judaism.

EARLY YEARS AND STUDY

Avraham Yitzchak Kook, born in 1865, was reared in northwestern Russia in the little Jewish community of Grieve, a typical self-enclosed shtetl isolated from the broad stream of history. The son of the local rabbi, a Hasid, and of a devout mother, herself descended from Mitnagged rabbis, he was plundered almost from birth into a G-d-centered pattern of life with piety and love of learning as its two central pillars. The great figures of Jewish history and legend were more real to him than the leading political and military figures of his time, and the past of his people was more alive than the present. Among his early memories were tales of his paternal great-grandfather, Rav Yitzchak, reputed to have been one of the first disciples of the Baal Shem Tov, the founder of Hasidism. Despite this illustrious ancestry, however, the dominant tradition in the Kook home was not the emotional and gentle piety of the Hasidim but rather the stern austerity of his maternal antecedents, the *Mitnaggdim.*

The ideal of Torah was intense, and Rav Kook was plunged at a very early age into the "sea of Talmud." From then on, his intellectual fare was restricted to the law and lore of that complex storehouse of Jewish learning. A phenomenal student, by the age of nine the boy had already

earned the name of *illuy* or child prodigy, and was no longer required
to attend *cheder.* Instead, he studied entirely on his own, in a corner
of the ancient synagogue, and was soon recognized as a *matmid,* i.e.,
an unusually diligent student. At fifteen, he went to study in Lutzin,
in keeping with the traditional principle of being "an exile to a place
of Torah." In that distant city, free from any family interference, he
could give single-minded devotion to learning. An account of young
Kook's life in Lutzin by a classmate describes him as "an exceedingly
diligent student, whose diligence was not the same type as that described by Chayyim Nachman Bialik in his famous poem 'The *Matmid.*' Bialik's *matmid* studied Torah in order to attain the scholarly
level of an *illuy* or a *gaon,* but the diligence of Avraham Yitzchak
derived entirely from a sense of piety; therefore, his ardor was all the
more remarkable. If he failed to study Torah for a short period of time,
he would feel genuine sorrow, real physical pain."

Until now Rav Kook's world was circumscribed, and his sense of
religious consecration so intense that he barely deigned to cast a glance
beyond the recognized limits of Orthodox studies. He lived the life of
Torah and dreamed of serving as a priest in the reestablished Holy
Temple on the sacred mountain in Jerusalem. He did not apparently
miss the larger world of secular studies, and he allowed his soul to
respond to the stringent disciplines of the Talmud with utter abandon.
But when, after a few years, he left the quiet little town of Lutzin and
moved to the metropolis of Smargon, he came into contact with Maskilim (students and lovers of secular learning), university students and
men of the world. During this period, young Avraham Yitzchak joined
the Musar movement, founded by Rav Yisrael Lipkin of Salant, which
held that the path to faith was long, winding, and narrow as the edge
of a knife. "Sinfulness" was the inevitable state of the human soul,
sorrow was the only proper mood of a sensitive person, salvation in the
hereafter the only worthwhile goal. His aim was to ward off the corro-
sive effects of the modern spirit by fortifying himself with the fundamental motivations and teachings of Judaism.

From Smargon, the young scholar went on to the famed Academy
of Volozhin, then under the leadership of the aged scholar Rav Naph-
tali Zvi Yehuda Berlin. This great institution was then the foremost
center of Talmudic learning in the world, with a student body of close
to five hundred. Rav Kook's piety, scholarship, and arduous manner of

praying soon won him a place as one of the outstanding scholars of the academy. "Every prayer that was uttered by Avraham Yitzchak," commented a former roommate, "was thoroughly soaked with tears."

During his stay in Volozhin, Rav Kook developed a predilection for speaking Hebrew to his friends instead of employing the Yiddish vernacular. Since the revival of Hebrew (as the basic vehicle for secular nationalism) was one of the ideals of the Maskilim, his comrades suspected him of being infected with the virus of Haskalah. Their suspicion was only partly justified; actually his use of Hebrew was an early manifestation of his way of meeting the manifold challenges of modernism by deepening his piety and incorporating into it the new values. He saw nothing strange in accepting Hebrew as part of his pattern of Jewish loyalties. Under the influences of his teachers, he was becoming more and more interested in Zionism, which was then a new movement, and in Palestine as the Land of Israel. He paid Rav Berlin the great compliment of saying that he felt at Volozhin "as if (he) were living in the Holy Land."

While still a student at Volozhin, Avraham Yitzchak was married to the daughter of Eliyahu David Rabinovitz-Tomin, the rabbi of Ponivesh. This marriage was not so much an affair of love, but, as in the case of Achad Haam, a recognition of the scholarly achievements of the young *yeshiva bachur.* Subsequently, his father-in-law preceded Rav Kook to the Holy Land, where he became the head of the *Bet Din* (religious court) of Jerusalem. He was to be a great influence on his young son-in-law, and was later largely responsible for the fact that Rav Kook was invited to become the rabbi of Jaffa.

After his marriage, Avraham Yitzchak, in the fashion of the day, lived with his bride's parents at Ponivesh, where he continued his Talmudic studies with even greater zeal than before. As was his habit, he wore tallit and tefillin all day while he studied, feeling that these holy objects helped to inspire within him the mood of consecration to the word of G-d. All this time, Rav Kook was becoming increasingly aware of the intense spiritual crisis confronting Judaism during the latter half of the nineteenth century. For the first time in his life, he was venturing beyond the limited sphere of the Talmud and attaining an acquaintance with the secular culture of his day. He read the literature of Haskalah in Hebrew, and also the works of Kant and Schopenhauer in German. As far as we know, his faith did not seem to falter even for a moment. His was a peculiarly selective mind, which intuitively drew from Western philosophy and literature only those elements that enriched and deepened his religious beliefs. Appalled by the apathy and utter lack of responsiveness to the burning issues of the day on the part of the official leaders of Russian Jewish Orthodoxy, he embarked on a one-man crusade to rouse public opinion. Certain that the truth was contained in the Torah and tradition of Israel, Avraham Yitzchak believed that the inroads of heresy into Jewish life could be stemmed only if an aggressive literary campaign were undertaken by the leaders of world Jewry. He himself, at twenty-three, sought to voice his opinions by publishing a rabbinical periodical called *Itur Sofrim.* Its purpose was to discuss not only "problems of ritual sanctity, halachic questions, and Midrashic interpretations, but also those problems that stand at the zenith of the world of Torah and Judaism; to clarify the multitude of great and important questions that concern the present life of our people, to discuss and to establish the right policy and the proper path for the solution of the great problems, upon which depend the honor of the nation, its fortunes and its revival." Though this bold venture into rabbinical journalism proved abortive, the young editor was able to enlist the cooperation of some of the leading rabbis of the time. His own reputation as a scholar had already spread far; in some quarters, despite his youthfulness, he was referred to as a *gaon.*

SPOKESMAN FOR ORTHODOXY

For some time, Avraham Yitzchak had rejected the advice of his father-in-law to become a practicing rabbi, and had sought to engage instead in some kind of commercial enterprise that would give him financial independence and at the same time leave him free to pursue his studies. During this period, he studied Talmud with Rav Yisrael Meir of Radin, better known by the name of his book *Chofetz Chayyim.* This saintly personality also urged him to enter the rabbinate, which he considered more important even than studying Talmudic law. He told him that a position was open in the town of Zoimel and persuaded Avraham Yitzchak to accept it. Since pastoral and preaching obligations in Zoimel were few and unexacting, Rav Kook was able to continue his studies with only minor interruptions. From time to time, he would go out on preaching tours to plead for more conscientious observance of the mitzvah of tefillin. Perhaps the outstanding event in his life during the six years he served in Zoimel was his acquaintance with Rav Solomon Eliashev of Shavell, the great Kabbalist, in whose company he stayed up many a night, poring over the books of Lurianic Kabbalah, the ancient lore of Jewish theosophy and mysticism. It was under the aegis of Kabbalah that his own philosophy was formed.

At the age of thirty, he became rabbi in the comparatively large city of Boisk, situated close to the border of the province of Kurland and within the sphere of German culture. Here Rav Kook was brought closer than ever before to the challenge of modernism. His brilliant sermons and essays on current problems, published in his rabbinical periodical *HaPeles*, brought him national recognition and fame. While his unquestioned piety and vast Talmudic erudition won him the reverence of the Orthodox, his original ideas and eloquent style were expertly attuned to the modern ear. In a short time, he became known as the outstanding spokesman for an awakened Orthodoxy.

CONCEPT OF ZIONISM

Rav Kook was also gaining notice at this time by his defense of Jewish nationalism as a mystical current of thought and sentiment that issued out of the sacred source of divine inspiration. It was his belief that along with the Books of the Torah, G-d has given the people of Israel certain unique endowments as well as the feeling of mutual solidarity. Divine revelation was in part the letter of the Law and in part the living spirit of the Jewish people. It followed for Rav Kook that all which is truly and genuinely Jewish was by the same token also truly divine.

Rav Kook's ascription of a high dimension of holiness to the sentiments and products of Jewish nationalism won for him the name of "the Orthodox Achad Haam," leader of the Orthodox "lovers of Zion," in distinction from the secularist or cultural Zionists who followed the leadership of Achad Haam. Rav Kook, however, never joined the Mizrachi (Orthodox branch of the World Zionist Organization) because he could not accept the secular interpretation of the nature of Jewish being, which lies at the base of the world Zionist movement. But he labored mightily to obtain the cooperation of the Orthodox masses toward the practical tasks involved in the upbuilding of the Holy Land.

Rav Kook's concept of Zionism was developed in his essay *The Mission of Israel and Its Nationhood,* which saw the dynamic creative urge of the Jewish people, which perpetually assumes new forms and creates new values, as holy in the highest sense of the word. While other Orthodox leaders regarded the new secularistic Hebraic art and literature emerging in Palestine as an impudent attempt to supplant the religious culture of Judaism, Rav Kook recognized it as a divine phenomenon and set the seal of divine approval on these products of the enlightenment and the national renaissance. As he saw it, secular nationalists like Achad Haam and Berdichevsky, who proclaimed their "liberation from the precepts of the Torah of Israel," were in reality doing the work of G-d, though unwittingly.

All the while, Rav Kook, of course, remained unimpeachably Ortho-dox, accepting the traditional conception of divine revelation. But at the same time, he showed an unusual willingness to assimilate modern ideas in a genuinely Orthodox frame of reference. He provided nation-alistic reasons for the precepts of Torah. He transcended the national-ists by exalting nationalism to the rank of a sacred principle, a divine creative ferment growing out of the inner mystical bond between Israel and Torah. Zionism emerged as the most important religious obligation of Orthodox Jews. "There is no doubt," Rav Kook wrote, "that we cannot fulfill our all-embracing mission unless we settle in the Holy Land, for only there can the spirit of our people develop and become a light for the world." In his view, nearness to G-d could in some measure be attained through the intensification of national feeling, which restores to the Jew the sense of being rooted in G-d's world and encourages him to be true to the deeper springs of his own soul.

THE HOLY LAND

In keeping with his Zionist philosophy, Rav Kook decided to settle permanently in Palestine, where, as he was to write later, the soul of a Jew regains its roots and vital force. Calls from such prominent communities as Vilna and Kaunas came to him, and some of the leading rabbis appealed to him to remain in Russia where the vast majority of the world's Jews were concentrated. But he preferred to accept the call to the city of Jaffa in Palestine, the Ashkenazic Jewish population of which was then scarcely larger than that of a village. He felt strongly that Palestine would eventually become the center of world Jewry. In the summer of 1904, therefore, in full awareness of the difficulties that would confront him, Rav Kook began the career that subsequently earned him the title "High Priest of Rebirth." He took up his post as the religious leader of Jaffa and the surrounding agricultural colonies.

It was not long before he was accepted as a man above all party differences. While the Orthodox were impressed by his profound piety and Talmudic learning, Maskilim were elated by the fact that he spoke fluent Hebrew, the language of national rebirth. Unlike other Orthodox leaders who decried the atheism of the colonists, he praised the *chalutzim* on the collective farms, most of whom had little or no use for Jewish ritual.

After only a few weeks in Palestine, he undertook to visit each of the kibbutzim or colonies on a preaching tour. The colonists, many of whom were former students of Russian universities, sophisticated intellectuals who scorned the morals as well as the rites of religion, became acquainted with a new type of rabbi, one who wore tallit and tefillin all day, but who spoke and thought in thoroughly modern terms. These first *chalutzim* had come to the fields and swamps of Palestine out of European classrooms, impelled by the desire to build a new life for themselves and lay a new foundation for the life of the Jewish people. They felt that the circumscribed little world of Orthodox Judaism was totally irrelevant to their problems and their vision of days to come. Rav Kook was, therefore, a complete revelation to them, impressing them as a saint who did not dwell in the mental atmosphere of the past, and who was human enough to join them in dancing the hora. Though they disagreed with his Orthodoxy, they could not ignore his sincere interest in their problems and his Zionist principles.

However, Rav Kook was severely criticized by other Orthodox leaders for his friendliness toward the *chalutzim*. When challenged to explain why the Lord should allow atheistic laborers to lead the way, if the upbuilding of Palestine is truly a divine undertaking, he answered that in ancient Israel there were degrees of holiness within the Holy Temple. The holiest portion, he said, was the so-called Holy of Holies, which only the high priest was allowed to enter. And even the high priest was permitted to do so only on the holiest day of the year, Yom Kippur, the Day of Atonement, after a weeklong period of preparation supervised by members of the Sanhedrin. Yet, when the Holy Temple needed to be rebuilt, ordinary workmen in working clothes were allowed to enter and do their jobs. The present time, he declared, was one of building, when the entrance of workmen into the Holy of Holies was altogether in order. In the future, pietists and priests would come.

Rav Kook's interest in the colonies was not confined to religious and educational matters. In a short time, he came to be recognized as their adviser and godfather. To improve their financial position, for example, he encouraged the colonists to plant *etrogim* (citrons used in the ritual of the Feast of Tabernacles), and he campaigned for the sale of the ritualistic fruit among Jewish communities the world over. He made strenuous efforts to get the rabbis of Russia to urge the use of Palestinian citrons in preference to those that were then being imported from the Greek Island of Corfu. In the same vein, he conducted an active correspondence with his colleagues in order to stimulate the sale of Palestinian wine.

As the religious authority for the colonists, Rav Kook was on one occasion confronted with the task of rendering the final decision on a question that had occupied the greatest halachic minds in the past generation—the question of *shemittah*, the law prohibiting agricultural work every seventh year. If the colonists were to be required to cease all work on their lands for a whole year, the infant settlements would be thrown into bankruptcy. Following the precedent of such earlier pro-Zionist rabbis as Mordechai Eliashberg and Samuel Mohilever, Rav Kook, despite opposition from many quarters, took the initiative in suspending the law. While he himself did not eat any of the products of the Sabbatical year, it was his hope, as it had been of his predecessors, that by granting this permission during these early years, the colonists would be strengthened, and the time would come when they would be able to observe the law. His argument was subtle enough, proceeding in the approved pathways of *pilpul* (Talmudic casuistry) and involving the subterfuge of "selling" land to a Gentile for the duration of the seventh year, but his real motive was to permit no obstacle to stand in the way of the progress of reconstruction of the Holy Land. Through activities of this sort, he gradually won the affection and esteem of all the colonists, who knew that in Rav Kook they had a friend who would procure whatever help was necessary.

Indeed, Rav Kook responded warmly to every aspect of life in Palestine, finding his every contact with it an exalted and ineffable religious experience.

He wrote:

The difference between Torah in Palestine and that of other lands is mighty and powerful. In Palestine, the flow of the Holy Spirit bursts forth, ready to invade the minds of the scholars who seek to study Torah for its own sake . . . the kind of sweetness and light of holiness that it offers in Palestine to scholars who seek G-d is not found at all in other lands. I can testify to this fact out of my own experience.

In this spirit, Rav Kook made all the problems of the community his intimate concern, seeing them in a total religious context. Less than a year after his arrival, he found it necessary to publish a circular letter criticizing the nationalistic atheists who clustered around the Hebrew enthusiast Eliezer Ben Yehuda, editor of the periodical *Hashkafah.* In a special pamphlet addressed to the *yeshiva bachurim* and other Talmud scholars, Rav Kook urged them to widen their horizons so as to meet the challenge of modern free thought. "It is our duty," he wrote, "to work with the living and for the living in order to sanctify life." He delivered daily lectures on the Talmud and the *Kuzari* in the local yeshivot, and founded a special trade school in which students might continue their Torah education while preparing themselves for the practice of a chosen trade.

EUROPEAN INTERLUDE

In 1914, Rav Kook traveled to Germany to attend the second conference of Agudat Israel, the non-Zionist Orthodox organization. When it was first organized in 1912, Rav Kook had hoped that it would subscribe to his own bold philosophy of nationalism and that it would be a unifying force in world Jewry. Though greatly disappointed in the organization's initial tendencies, he nevertheless decided to attend its second convention. Arriving in Berlin just a few days before World War I broke out, he was interned, at first, as an enemy alien, since he was a Russian citizen. Through efforts of several German rabbis, he was later given the opportunity to travel to Switzerland, where he attempted unsuccessfully to procure return passage to Palestine. After two years in Switzerland, he went to London, where he was able to help mobilize public opinion in favor of the Balfour Declaration. During these years, Rav Kook continued to write philosophical reflections on the nature of the religious consciousness, a work he had begun in Switzerland. A collection of these reflections, centering around the mystical significance of the Hebrew letters, vowel signs, and musical notes, and entitled *Resh Millin,* was published in London. This Kabbalistic little book, conceived and written in the intoxication of mystical ecstasy, was particularly precious to its author, who considered its conception an "undeserved gift from G-d."

Following the war, Rav Kook launched the "Banner of Jerusalem" *(Degel Yerushalayim)* movement of Orthodox Jews, dedicated to the upbuilding of Palestine. Detached from the official World Zionist movement, of which many observant Jews disapproved, this organization carried on an active campaign for the maintenance and growth of the spirit of religion in the Holy Land.

In 1919, after normalcy returned to Palestine following World War I, Rav Kook received and accepted an invitation from the Jewish community of Jerusalem to become its chief rabbi. He returned to the Holy Land and subsequently, in 1921, became chief rabbi of all Palestine.

CHIEF RABBI OF PALESTINE

The period of Rav Kook's leadership, 1919–35, coincided with the formative stage of the emergent Jewish commonwealth in the Holy Land. During that comparatively brief epoch, Palestine's Jewish population increased from 90,000 to 400,000, and the "old *Yishuv,*" formerly the dominant element, was reduced to a lesser position. The new settlements, consisting of young, idealistic pioneers, seethed with spiritual unrest and bristled with intellectual and physical energy. Palestine became the scene of a new birth, the reemergence on the political and cultural stage of history of one of the oldest peoples in the civilized world. In this drama, Rav Kook played the role of revered godfather.

The chief rabbi's first great achievement was the organization of the rabbinate of the Holy Land. A united and effective rabbinate was obviously essential if the religious character of the rapidly growing Jewish community was to be maintained. As it happened, the initial suggestion for its organization and possible unification came from the British government in Palestine, the office of which was then headed by Sir Herbert Samuel, the high commissioner. Chief Rabbi Kook responded to this challenge with great enthusiasm, seeing in it a long-hoped-for opportunity to introduce order and discipline in the inner life of the Jews residing in Palestine.

Subsequently, the Jewish community of Palestine, the so-called *Knesset Yisrael,* was organized with Chief Rabbi Kook at the head. The vast majority of Jews in Palestine were thereby rallied behind this beloved spiritual leader, who became the most respected rabbinic authority in world Jewry as well as the official representative of the Jewish religion before the Mandatory Government. The Orthodox and the secularists were brought to a common meeting ground and made to realize that the bonds of kinship between them were more significant than the doctrinal differences that kept them apart. On the one hand, the Orthodox were compelled to agree that nonobservant Jews were also entitled to the name and destiny of Israel. On the other hand, the secular nationalists had to concede that membership in the Jewish community entailed the obligation to respect the authority of the Torah and the rabbinate, though only in limited areas.

Despite this superficial harmony, however, Jewish Palestine was rent by differences, and the chief rabbi encountered many problems and conflicts. A group of ultra-Orthodox extremists, for example, headed by the Hungarian Rav Sonnenfeld, refused to recognize Rav Kook as chief rabbi or to abide by his religious authority. His supposed leniency in the interpretation of the Law was offensive to them, and his friendly attitude toward the secularists seemed to them sinful.

Party tension and strife reached its apex in Rav Kook's last years, when he found it more and more difficult to endure or harmonize the turbulent partisanship of Palestinian politics. During the notorious Stavsky trial, the chief rabbi was sorely abused. Chayyim Arlosorof, leader of *Histadrut,* the general Jewish workers' union, had been assassinated, and the murderers could not be found. Suspicion fell upon a small Revisionist clique, headed by Stavsky, who was arrested and brought to trial. The evidence presented at the trial was extremely meager, but the organs of the *Histadrut,* in the blind fanaticism of bitter partisanship, campaigned for conviction. Though the majority of Palestinian Jews prejudged the accused Revisionist, Chief Rabbi Kook regarded the whole trial as a mockery of true justice and the result of Palestine's unhealthy and poisonous politics. Accordingly, he took the side of the accused in a most forthright and crusading spirit. Daring the displeasure, abuse, and alienation of the Jewish workers and "leftists," he did not leave a stone unturned in his efforts to save the accused. A storm of protests descended upon the aged saint, but, when the dust kicked up by the bitter clamor of fratricidal strife cleared, there were few indeed who did not recognize the justice of his position.

As Ashkenazic chief rabbi of Palestine, Rav Kook had the opportunity to speak for the whole people of Israel during the trying days that began in 1929 with disputes over the Wailing Wall and a series of bloody riots. During all that troubled period, he represented his people with courage and dignity. Though many Zionists were willing to compromise regarding the Wailing Wall, he insisted that no Jewish individual or group had the right to sign away any part of the eternal possessions of the nation, and least of all the Wailing Wall, the symbol and remnant of the grandeur of ancient Judaism.

When, in spite of all the efforts of Zionist leadership, the Passfield White Paper was proclaimed in 1930, the chief rabbi urged the Jews throughout the world not to lose hope or to despair, but to remember that Israel's strength lay in the spirit that is eternal.

In the dark days of the thirties, when cynicism and despair enveloped Jewish communities, the chief rabbi was an inexhaustible fountain of faith. His home became a haven for worried and distraught Jewish leaders, and included Chayyim Nachman Bialik and M. M. Ussishkin as well as less famous figures of Palestine Jewry. The nonobservant as well as the Orthodox felt that his spirit was an inspiration to weary souls, radiating faith and hope in the future of Israel.

From every corner of the Jewish world, questions in Jewish law and thought were addressed to him. His replies comprise four big volumes, covering every aspect of Jewish life, including the right of workers to strike. Regarding himself as a servant of his people, he attended personally to a multitude of requests, large and small. He could be seen at all hours, walking in the fur hat and long gown, the dress of the East European religious Jew, which he always wore, visiting the sick and ministering to the diverse concerns of the community. As his son Zvi Yehuda Kook recalled:

He was always overburdened with the needs of the community. Everything was referred to him. A call from the High Commissioner asking his intervention in keeping the Jews from blowing the *shofar* at the Wailing Wall, or someone asking for help in getting a visa. And everything he liked to do personally. Even when he was sick in the last months of his life, I can remember his running through the streets to the Consulate to arrange some papers for somebody . . . the water bottles, which he carried to relieve his pain (he was afflicted with cancer), flapping about his body as he hurried. He always wanted to do things with his own hands.

Rav Kook, for example, always insisted, in spite of his inhumanly heavy load of work, on copying his own manuscripts to prepare them for the press, and on doing his own proofreading for his books. His reason was that since the *chalutzim* had to do so much "black work" in building the land, he also felt obliged to do some "black work" in order to be one of them.

In the field of Jewish education, Rav Kook cooperated with the Mizrachi organization in founding a network of religious elementary and high schools through the length and breadth of the Holy Land. He headed a group of prominent rabbis in 1924 in a tour of the United States on behalf of the yeshivot in Jerusalem and Poland.

According to his own view, Rav Kook's greatest educational achievement consisted in the founding of the Yeshiva Merkazit, Merkaz HaRav—a Talmudic academy that still functions in Jerusalem today and is known as "The Center of the Rav" or the Universal Yeshiva. In the winter of 1921 at the laying of its cornerstone, the chief rabbi outlined its curriculum and philosophy. While including the usual close study of the Talmud and analysis of Jewish law in all its minutiae, the yeshiva, Rav Kook stipulated, was also to teach secular and scientific subjects. "For how can a teacher communicate and inform his people," he said, "unless he be acquainted with the ideas that set the style of the generation?" Rav Kook called for a creative approach to the study of the Talmud, an approach that would make it the basis for a renaissance in Orthodox Judaism. His dream was that great minds, in approaching Torah with fresh genius, would enrich Judaism. One of his much-quoted expressions, fervently uttered on the occasion of a visit from one of Palestine's great but nonreligious scientists, was, "May the day come when the great of the Jews will also be Jewishly great." His subsequent lectures at the Merkaz HaRav on the classic works of Jewish philosophy attracted wide attention in Jerusalem, because they served as a bridge from the long-isolated world of Orthodox thought to the great, restless battlefield of modern philosophy.

LAST YEARS

Despite the opposition of the ultra-Orthodox to Rav Kook's leniency in the interpretation of the law and his friendly attitude toward the secularists, the chief rabbi enjoyed the love and admiration of the entire Palestinian Jewish community. Rav Kook is particularly remembered for his love toward his ideological opponents, especially the young people, so clearly shown in his devotion to the *chalutzim.*

An aura of saintliness gathered about him even before his declining years, and many legends about his unique piety circulated in the streets of Jerusalem. One writer told of an evening visit to the chief rabbi. Since it was time for the religious service, the visitor asked to accompany him to the synagogue so that they might take part in public workship. The chief rabbi is reported to have replied, "I cannot go with you. I am all afire with the love of G-d. If I should now go to the synagogue, I might be completely consumed. . . ."

There were two occasions each year when the citizens of Jerusalem were enabled to glimpse their chief rabbi's religious ardor. On the first night of *Shavuot,* the doors of his house were thrown wide open while he preached from nine o'clock in the evening to dawn the following day. On the night of *Simchat Torah,* he would dance for hours with a Torah in his arms, surrounded by young *chalutzim* and *yeshiva* students.

To the last day of his life, while suffering from cancer, Rav Kook labored for the strengthening of the united community of Palestine, remarking with the last ounce of his strength, "there is nothing that justifies and permits division in Israel." On the last Friday evening before his death, he urged participation in the nineteenth World Zionist Congress, observing, "How can one not be a Zionist, seeing that the Lord G-d has chosen Zion?"

THE
WORLD
OF
RAV KOOK'S
THOUGHT

Introduction to the Conference

Rabbi Yochanan Fried

THESE WORDS ARE an attempt to express briefly the feeling—precisely that—which accompanied all those who took part in the gathering that dealt with *"Teshuvah* in Rav Kook's philosophy."

It was a feeling of appreciation and recognition for a unique personality who succeeded—perhaps better than in his lifetime—in bringing together groups and researchers, students and teachers, intellectuals and sentimental poets, men of the academic world and Bet Midrash students, men of practical affairs and creative deeds together with those who reach to the very heavens in the world of thought.

It was also a feeling of longing for a worldview embracing Torah and Law, lore and Kabbalah, *midrash* (derived interpretation) and *peshat* (plain literal sense), philosophy and religious thought. The canvas is too narrow to enumerate or describe the bounds of the concepts within this Weltanschauung. For this reason, let it suffice for me to use the woefully inadequate expression "afterword," which is not the end, for something that has not yet been plumbed to its depths.

The substance of *teshuvah* in Rav Kook's conception is expressed in various formulations. There is no doubt that its principal meaning lies in the special link between *shiva*, the "returning" of a nation to its land and of a world longing for its redemption and improvement, and *teshuvah* in the sense of a "turning back" from the crooked to the straight, from sin to correction, from the defective to the complete. These formulations require explanation and deep research in the foundations of Jewish religious thought in every generation; they need exposition and clarification with regard to method and thought processes; they demand a compelling reference to questions of the generation and of the hour and open wide the book of questions of time and place—of time, eternity, and life.

In the atmosphere of this gathering—a lofty atmosphere cleansed of all unworthy, egotistical, personal consideration—it was possible for the question of tolerance to be considered. Matters of present-day Jewish existence demand seriousness and sincerity. In this gathering, there was a desire to touch on the worlds of culture and art as the heights of divine knowledge, and all out of the soul's longing and yearning, as well as its intuitive understanding, for redemption, for its ways and its steps; in very truth, for redemption itself.

May the end be a world of blessed action, of fruitful creation, of the sovereignty of Israel and the holiness of the life of man, of light and wisdom and the glory of man.

May our world be pleasant to every seeker, and may the Divine Presence rest over all.

May our portion be among those who pray that our coming in and our going out from the sanctuary be in peace.

Opening Remarks
at the Conference

President Chaim Herzog

A YEAR AFTER the demise of Rav Kook, of blessed memory, my father was elected to the Office of Chief Rabbi of *Eretz Yisrael.* The eulogy ceremony at the funeral of my grandfather, the late Rav Joel Herzog, at which my father followed immediately after Rav Kook, was thus very symbolic. It expressed the proximity of Chief Rabbinates that was to come about between these two distinguished rabbis.

However, there was not merely a succession here of office, but a close similarity of direction; the way of greatness in Torah together with nobility of soul; an approach that sought to clear a path to the heart of the broad community—religious and nonreligious—by constantly revealing the light stored up in the Torah of Israel and by disseminating all that is beautiful and enlightened in Judaism, according to the verse "Its ways are ways of pleasantness, and all its paths are peace."

Rav Avraham Yitzchak HaCohen Kook was attacked in his day by groups of extremists on account of the great tolerance and the open and broad-vistaed personal relationship that he demonstrated toward Jews who held views opposed to his own, both from a nationalist and a religious point of view. It worries me that there are today, among products of the school he founded, some who take up extremist atti-

tudes and show a zealousness and a lack of tolerance in complete
opposition to the way and the heritage of HaReAYaH.

To this day, Rav Kook represents for the wider community, and not
only in the eyes of the religious who keep the mitzvot, a distinctive
example of a rabbi who causes people to feel an identification and a
sympathy with Judaism and brings to bear an influence for tolerance
and understanding among all sections of the people.

The principal source from which Rav Kook was nurtured was the
world of the Kabbalah, with its substance and its symbols, and there
is no concept in the tapestry of his thoughts that is not anchored in
this world. His uniqueness lies in the fact that despite his being deeply
rooted in the world of Kabbalah, he had a fine command of modern
processes of thought as well as a wide knowledge in the fields of general
learning. With tolerance and open-mindedness, he tried to grapple
with the question: how was it possible that those who brought about
Israel's resurgence in its land were not in fact G-d-fearing men? In
response to this problem, he noted that the Zionist movement arose
in a period of a general weakening in the state of religion throughout
the world. Despite this, he believed that the basis of holiness in the
process of the return to Zion was hidden in the deeds of the pioneers
and the builders; that what is hidden is bound in time to be revealed;
and that everyone will come to acknowledge that the people of Israel
can live a complete, holy life only in the Land of Israel. He emphasized
the natural morality that is in man, and he held that the fear of heaven
must not thrust aside this natural morality. Rav Kook refused to see a
conflict between the sacred and the secular, and he maintained that the
secular is an essential foundation for the sacred. According to him, the
view that holiness is complete spirituality is a *galut* outlook that developed only when the people of Israel was divorced from its land; but in
returning to it, the nation has to return to a normal existence that
embodies both secular and sacred foundations.

We are currently in the week of the portion "Judges and officers
shalt thou make for thyself in all thy gates . . . and they shall judge the
people with righteous judgment"; and next to this we read, "that thou
mayest live and inherit the land." On this, Rashi comments, "The
appointment of fit judges is sufficient merit to keep Israel alive and to
settle them in their land." Against this background, it is appropriate
to quote the words of Rav Kook on the supremacy of law and justice

in Israel. Thus, he says, "The essence of the Jewish people, its existence and its very being, its aspiration and its political status—all is dependent, built and perfected on the basis of the love of the divine law of the holiness of the commandments and ordinances. (The people) knows and recognizes with an instinctive, profound, and clear recognition, to the point of joyful self-sacrifice, that all her standing, her eternity, her character and glory—all of it is dependent upon and linked with the holiness of the love of divine legislation." And he adds, "We have to endeavor to magnify the fountain that issues from the Torah source . . . and all the multitude of great ideas that can be joined together through the greatness of their righteous character. In this way, the law arises not as a skeleton of bones, with no power of life visible to the eye of the observer, but as a hewn image,[1] as the glory of man . . . Then all the majesty and splendor of the law will again be revealed."

As we come today to mark the completion of a jubilee of years since the death of our distinguished teacher, we are in duty bound to recognize and exalt the wonderful nature of his way as a beacon and an example. The Jewish people cries out for spiritual leadership that will not be divorced from the reality of our world, that will be involved—with tolerance and broad-mindedness—with all levels of society, that will always carry the mark of consideration and compassion, of the love of Israel and the love of man; a leadership that will be at peace with all the people of Israel—not withdrawn and not estranged, but looking for the side of merit in every man in Israel. This was the way of HaReAYaH Kook, may the memory of the righteous be for a blessing. Such was his legacy, from which to our sorrow, we have strayed. The time has come to turn back to the right way, to the middle road, to the golden mean. The events marking the fiftieth year of the death of Rav Kook could be a fitting opportunity for this.

May the merit of HaReAYaH rise up for us, that there be fulfilled for Israel the word of the prophet in the Haftorah of this Sabbath: "How beautiful upon the mountains are the feet of the messenger of good tidings, that announceth peace, the harbinger of good tidings, that announceth salvation, that saith unto Zion: Thy G-d reigneth!"

1. Cf. Psalm 144:12.

The Way of
Rav Kook

Yitzchak Navon
Minister of Education and Culture

WE ARE HONORING the memory of Rav Avraham Yitzchak HaCohen Kook upon the completion of fifty years since his passing, with a deep nostalgia for his wonderful personality.

Rav Kook was one of the elect few who stood up for the Jewish people in its difficult hours. The national renaissance might have run into severe crises and could have stirred up hostile attitudes between the Zionist leadership and religious Jewry, if not for the contribution of the religious Zionist leaders and especially the decisive contribution of Rav Kook. In his thought, in his halachic approach, and in his numerous deeds, he became in himself a bridge between the different sections of the nation.

His philosophy surges with a mighty love, a love for everyone, and for everyone in Israel in particular, for all the world and for the body of Israel at its center; but he entreated for a special love for those who were renewing settlement in *Eretz Yisrael*, despite the fact that most of them were remote from him in the religious sense. His teaching in *Orot HaKodesh*, Vol. III, p. 324, is renowned: "From the day of our destruction . . . because of a causeless hatred, let us rebuild ourselves . . . by a causeless love."

But his mighty abundance of love was directed principally toward the people of the new settlement, as he says there, further on: "In this generation we have to seize hold of the quality of peace and increase love and brotherhood in Israel . . . for I am obliged to stand in the breach against all who speak ill of those who come to settle the Land of Israel . . ."

To my regret, the need for those who clutch hold of peace in our midst has not grown less, for those who hold on to strife have grown many and strong, and many are the issues of tension and hatred in Israeli society; and the issue that is most dangerous for our future is the one that arises against a religious background.

We have great need today of a personality after his likeness who might rise up and demand courageously that everyone speak well of his neighbors, that we should all look for what unites rather than what divides, for that precisely is the way to hasten the redemption.

Much tolerance is required in our time also—the relations between the Jewish nation and the other national minorities who live with us. Rav Kook excelled in this too, with a religious approach that called for a positive relationship. In his own words in *Igrot HaReAYaH*, Vol. I, p. 99: "In no way whatsoever has any nation in the world a right to circumscribe the rights of its society unless it be for a universal exalted purpose. Therefore the advocates of Israel who pleaded, "Have we not all one Father?" were right; for all nations that are hedged round by decent civilized behavior between man and man are already considered as resident aliens in regard to all man's obligations . . ."

There is an obligation upon us to meditate in his teaching, to study Rav Kook's great worldview, and to educate accordingly for an increase of brotherhood and love among Jews, and for respecting the rights of the resident aliens who live in our midst.

The Essence of
Rav Kook's Teachings

Dr. Norman Lamm

I AM HONORED to stand before you in a dual role: as an individual, influenced by Rav Kook, who has adopted his approach on most of the subjects touched upon in his writings; and as representative of Yeshiva University, the only Diaspora institution that is both an advanced yeshiva and a higher academic institute. Yeshiva University has educated generations of students, numbered in the thousands, in Rav Kook's spirit, and its mission largely mirrors principles of his thought.

Hence it is a pleasant double obligation to thank and to praise the initiators of this conference and the organizers, the lecturers and the audience, and last but not least, our host, the president of the State of Israel, Mr. Chaim Herzog. Much appreciation is due them for the energy and effort with which they labored to erect a living monument to Rav Kook's memory in the fiftieth year after his death. May their strength increase.

It is clear from the prepared agenda that we will have the opportunity to renew interest in Rav Kook's teaching, which has been more admired than understood, and to correct the deficiencies that have marred the study of his work over the past half-century. For time has not left it untouched, and Rav Kook's original teaching has passed through various vicissitudes in the hands of interpreters. The time has come to purify it, refine it, cleanse it, and "restore the crown to its rightful place."

I do not know if there is a historical law that determines the evolution of changes and transformations in the doctrine of a rabbi and teacher, when it passes into the possession of his disciples and their disciples. But it seems to me that the fate of Rav Kook's teaching in the generations that followed him is not much different from what happened to the teaching of Maimonides. In his lifetime, Maimonides was very popular and very much loved by the people, very popular even though signs of sharp opposition to him and to his views were already evident. After his death, there was a division with respect to his teaching: Some continued his theoretical and philosophical way, and forgot that he was also the author of the *Mishneh Torah* and the *Sefer HaMitzvot* and the Commentary on the Mishnah and the responsa; others erected mountains of inquiries and conundrums and resolutions, as a marvelous elaboration of Maimonides' titanic halachic work, while ignoring the *Guide* and the fact that he was the leading spokesman of Jewish philosophy and Jewish thought throughout our history.

What happened to our master Moses b. Maimon happened to our master Avraham Yitzchak. Rav Kook was a beloved and popular leader, who also had opponents and adversaries until this very day (as we say in the prayers, "He makes what is new—engages in battles"). His fate has been like Maimonides': The wholeness of his teaching and lifework have been marred.

Ask the man in the street, who knows of Rav Kook only by word of mouth, what he innovated, what he taught the people, what he contributed to the life of the state, and you will be surprised to discover the figure of a chief rabbi with a poetic sense, who was not only forgiving and beneficent, but also given to concession with respect to the principles of religion, prone to compromise in every problematic area that he discussed, lacking strong views of his own, who confronted the crises of the day with a paternal repetition: "Permitted, permitted, permitted!" So that there is hardly anything that separates him from a secularist or a Reform Jew. On the other hand (and I take license to exaggerate here too for the sake of clarity), you can find people who support his approach and claim to be his authoritative interpreters, whose words give rise to a completely different portrait: the progenitor of a militant national movement, a thinker who valued conquest much more than peace, the creator of a Weltanschauung in which the Land of Israel not only occupies a central place but the *only* place, without attending to the value he attached to peace, love of mankind, knowledge, humanity, the matrix of the sacred and profane, belief and denial, halacha and aggadah.

It is unfortunate that this fate befell a great man in Israel, the cornerstone of whose theory was the perfected harmony of all being, "the world of unification": the indication that beyond the dissonance and divisions that appear to govern the world, there exists overarchingly a complex, interlocking unity, composed of many ideas, even those that contradict each other—a totality of ideas in which each idea, preserving a spark of holiness, has value in itself. This is a sublime and sophisticated conception, bridging the gaps between all realms, a conception that looks upon the universe in the speculum of unity and harmony that seeks to encompass all, a conception that is the furnace of Jewish faith, and wholly devoted to peace—not a peace of concession and indifference, but a critical peace whose source is complete, purified, confident faith in the Creator of the world and the G-d of Israel. Whoever says that Rav Kook was open to all opinions without discrimination and without painstaking evaluation is distorting his image and introducing anarchy and confusion into his teaching; just as he who is so bold as to state that one, and only one, value, towers above all—namely, the nationalistic value—also is guilty of counterfeiting his teaching.

Therefore we, the House of Israel, "here and there," are happy for the opportunity given us to reconstruct Rav Kook's teaching in its completeness and to present a new generation with the picture of Rav Kook as he truly was—a personality in which truth and peace were manifest together, a personality of broad horizons totally lacking in narrowness of vision, neither a militant extremist nor a man of concessions without ideals.

Out of this conference, I am confident that Rav Kook's image will emerge in its full greatness, clarity, and genius.

"May my portion be with you!"

Rav Kook:
A Portrait

Rabbi Moshe Zvi Neriah

IT IS PLEASANT and fitting for Rav Kook's name and memory that these days of study should center round the subject of *teshuvah*. [1] In my student years in his yeshiva, the Merkaz HaRav Yeshiva, I was privileged to see him in the mornings of the month of Elul, after the morning service, striding up and down in the main room of his house, studying his own book, the *Orot HaTeshuvah*. His words had been written not only for others but also for himself; and in the days set apart for *teshuvah*, he devoted himself to its cleansing and elevating content.

HaReAYaH was the poet of *teshuvah*, the poet of the light that is in *teshuvah*, the joy of its salvation. In contrast to the other books of moral reproof, which concentrate mainly on the dark side of the nature of man and cast a chill feeling, the book *Orot HaTeshuvah* sets us in a suffusion of light—"Make me to hear joy and gladness, that the bones which thou hast crushed may rejoice" (Psalm 51:10). Man is illumined by the light of the Lord, all creation returns to its source, to its Maker (see *Orot HaTeshuvah*, Chap. 4b). *Teshuvah* is entirely a renewal, a source of new life. And even in the period of the rebellious, in the years

1. *Translator's Note: Teshuvah:* "Repentance, penitence, atonement, return." From the Hebrew root meaning "to return" or "to turn back."

of the Second Aliyah, Rav Kook wrote, "All the new things of life, and all the forces that overturn the world order in order to improve it; they are all paths of *teshuvah,* and *teshuvah* must always stand at the top rung of the ladder of human perfection" (*Zeronim, Orot,* p. 127).

There was someone who wrote, "The letters of *ReAYaH* are a photograph of the Rav!" In the variety of the letters, his many-sided personality is indeed revealed; yet the truth is that this is only a partial picture. This is a photograph of "the ladder set up on earth," a broad sample of his conduct as a rabbi, as a spiritual shepherd, as a leader, and, in a certain degree, as a thinker. But in order to recognize, "And the top of it reached to heaven," the flight of his ideas, the breadth of his world of thought, we need the volumes of *Orot HaKodesh.* In the three volumes, edited by one who was true to his spirit, the rabbi, the Nazirite, David HaCohen, of blessed memory, we meet the peak of his spiritual world. *Orot HaKodesh* is the soul of *Igrot HaReAYaH.*

And still the picture is not complete. For we have before us his books of halacha, *Etz Hadar* and *Shabbat HaAretz,* and four volumes of his responsa in which he appears as a paragon of wisdom, replying to his inquirers from all corners of the earth and rendering decisions on all the subjects of Torah.

Yet all HaReAYaH's books are autobiographical. They are the story of his life. For he and his thoughts are one; what he wrote was what he was.

The Baal Shem Tov said, *Kavvanah* [2] has the meaning of being like balanced scales. The level of one's deeds must be as the level of one's thoughts; not that the thoughts rise to the firmaments and the deeds remain somewhere down below. Whoever came to be in company of Rav Kook was aware and felt that he lived in some higher world, that he lived in a world of spirituality out of which—and by its direction— he acted in the world of action. In fact, he had the marvelous power to raise his "doing" to the heights of spirituality: "Thought must be expanded, in depth and in height, in its diffusion and its magnitude. We fly from spirituality to the world of action, and we turn and rise again from action to spirituality" (*Orot HaKodesh* Vol. I, Chap. 63).

---

2. *Translator's Note:* Literally, "intention" or "direction." From the root meaning "to set right," "to direct," hence "to direct the heart." Hence also, "to pray with fervor."

The secret of the link between the two worlds HaReAYaH explains to us in the first chapter of *Orot HaKodesh:* "The functional wisdom of holiness." In the view of HaReAYaH, in all secular wisdoms, in the world of science, it is possible for there to be a distinction between thought and deed; but this is not the case with sacred wisdom, for "this is exalted above all wisdom; it overturns the desire and the natural character of its students, in order to bring them near to the elevation with which it itself contends." And Rav Kook goes on to explain the reason for it: "For all sacred matters emanate from the source of life itself, from the foundation of life that is the essence of everything. . . . Therefore they can transform the thinker among them to a new creature, to set him up in the condition of a new being."

That is, that which is holy has the power of creation—"for with Thee is the foundation of life" (Psalm 36:10).

This first chapter of *Orot HaKodesh* is the principal key to the personality or image of HaReAYaH. And when we speak of aspects of his personality, we learn from this chapter that every sacred thought of his is an additional line in his image, every deed that is impregnated with spirituality is another feature in the portrait of his personality; and the more one delves into the array of his books and the more one understands the chain of his deeds, the more his wonderful personality appears in the fullness of its splendor. This is the only way to assess the exemplary image of HaReAYaH.

Concerning the Chanukah candles, we say, "These candles are holy and we are not permitted to make use of them, but only to look at them." But for the lights of HaReAYaH's books and his life, we might say, "These lights are holy and we are commanded to make use of them and not only to gaze upon them."

Introduction to the
Thought of Rav Kook

Professor Shalom Rosenberg

1. PREFACE TO THE INTRODUCTION

ONE OF THE obligations imposed on our generation, according to Rav Kook, is the duty to pay attention to Introductions. The significance of the Introduction for our purpose is twofold. We are concerned not with a general review of the subject, but with the search for a way that may make it possible for everyone to enter into it. The Introduction is the lost key: "In our generation we have to concern ourselves with Introductions, with clarifying the keys for every exalted issue" (*Orot HaKodesh*, Vol. III, p. 19). The system of Rav Kook is in the nature of an Introduction to the world of Judaism. This work of ours is in the nature of an Introduction to the Introduction.

We wish to put forward here for the reader a number of principles in the system of HaReAYaH that, in our view, are relevant for the reader of our generation who is not equipped with a philosophical background. Because of this, a number of notes are necessary. Unavoidably, the selection covered by this review will be subjective. It will not do justice to a system of which one principle lays down that seeing only a part is the source of all mistakes and doubts. The partiality of our selection flows from the very fact of having to choose subjects, but also from the fact that it is written from a particular point of view that does not have to be generally accepted. Without doubt, a great work cannot be thoroughly analyzed except through an examination of all its parts.

As far as possible, we shall refrain from dealing here with problems that belong in the field of historical-philological research, and we shall limit ourselves to clarifying the attitude of HaReAYaH on the subjects referred to. It might indeed have been possible to set out HaReAYaH's standpoint as a part of the history of philosophy, seeing that he emphasizes again and again, many times, that in every philosophical system, including every religious system, some spark of truth is revealed, without which it would not be able to stand at all. This spark exists even if those who espouse the philosophical standpoint are not aware of its true significance or even if they err in its understanding. There is one constant principle that guides Rav Kook's general approach to the history of philosophy: "There is nothing that does not have its place" (*Orot HaKodesh*, Vol. II, p. 482). The meaning of this argument is that every philosophical system is correct in revealing one aspect of existence, but errs when it turns it into a foundation for explaining all of existence, ignoring thereby the complementary aspects. The complete understanding of the place of the various approaches is one of the goals of man's development. Its ultimate purpose is redemption: "Messiah will spread the Torah of Moses by revealing throughout the world the vision of how the nations and groups suck the sap of their spiritual lives from the one single basic source" (*Arpelei Tohar*, p. 62).

The need for comparative method obliges us to relate to another problem, the problem of Rav Kook's spiritual biography. As may be easily verified, sometimes we come across a clear reference to a thinker in connection with his period. A critical assessment of such a relationship is a subject in itself. But in this review I must stress that while we have before us a clear relationship to a particular philosophy, it seems to me that we may confidently assume that this relationship arose after HaReAYaH had built up and crystallized the principles of his own stand in the subject. In an as yet unpublished research study, I endeavor to prove that certain directions in modern thought were developed in parallel—in different language and with other conclusions—with Chasidic commentary on Kabbalah. Rav Kook's conception is a climactic movement in this "Chasidic" symphony. At various stages of HaReAYaH's intellectual development, his Weltanschauung stood in conflict with general philosophical standpoints. This conflict was not a genetic reason for the appearance of the system, but it provided an excellent opportunity for its presentation and also for its understanding in more profound levels.

Here too the Introduction suffers from a deficiency. I deliberately ignored the biographical background, and consequently also the problem of the development of Rav Kook's beliefs. In any event, until HaReAYaH's still-hidden manuscript writings are published, the picture will remain partial and fragmented.

Another possible method would be an attempt to characterize HaReAYaH's thought and to put it into existing categories. It is clear to me that this kind of classification is not fruitful, and would only testify, as the testimony of a hundred witnesses, that a living system is being turned into an object for postmortem operation.

Accordingly, I shall not enter into the subject of the thought compartmentalization of Rav Kook's outlook; nor will I attempt to determine its relationship to the various systems whether of Jewish or of non-Jewish thinkers. We shall try to present here the system in its entirety and, as far as possible, on its own. Nevertheless, I shall not refrain from drawing attention sometimes either to parallel or to contrasting points when these may assist us in understanding a particular subject. I shall attempt to review briefly some of the basic principles of HaReAYaH's system so that these may serve as an antechamber, albeit richly furnished, to the hall of the lights.

Our point of departure is that one must deal with Rav Kook's thesis with philosophical seriousness. Among the obstacles that undoubtedly rise before the inquirer, we must count particularly the poetic language and style that many a time create the impression that we have before us a poetic outpouring and not a serious coherent philosophic arrangement. Against this mistaken impression, one has to do battle. Behind the poetic style, we behold the growth, the struggle, and the crystallization of ideas that form a complete tapestry of thoughts.

HaReAYaH struggled with the limitations of Hebrew philosophic terminology. Still, these limitations really testify to the flowering of the new consciousness that made the old frameworks anachronistic. Modern thought, according to HaReAYaH, necessitates the breaking down of the present linguistic frameworks and the finding of new vessels of expression.

The higher the observation point from which thought flows, the more it is obliged to face up to the difficulties in finding its linguistic expression. There exists a sort of inertia in material words that prevents them from giving full and free expression to ideas. This is the situation of which Rav Kook is conscious when he writes:

And if dumbness strikes us when we are speaking, if the concepts we are trying to express are sunk in our silence because we have not the power to release the speech or liberate the word, we shall not be frightened on that account, or retreat from our set desire (*Orot HaKodesh*, Vol. I, p. 6).

The writer's purpose is to give liberty and freedom to the words so that they may be able to express the thoughts. The task of the thinker is to bring tidings of peace, and on the basis of this message the verse will be fulfilled: "He createth the fruit of the lips. Peace, peace to him that is far off and to him that is near, saith the Lord; I will heal him." The texts before us are indeed the product of that "created fruit of the lips," an attempt to form and forge terminology, language, and style so as to convey the content that bursts out and reveals itself. The new fruit is intended to give freedom and liberty to the imprisoned secret content.

Concerning Rav Kook's thought, we can read his own words: "Poetic thinking has to be merged with intellectual thinking. There is no end to the manifold nuances of these minglings, and depending on the right direction of the mix, and its adjustment according to the state of mind at the time of the spiritual revelation, and according to the state of the world at that time, the refined creations that are brought into being interchange according to their composition; and these are the heavenly powers of the wonders of the All-knowing that are revealed in the big world of the soul of man in the splendor of its life" (*Maamrei Ha-ReAYaH*, Vol. I, p. 67).

In any event, in this Introduction I want to venture to propose an introduction to Rav Kook's method, an introduction to the mighty attempt to arrive at the perfection of that which embraces all: the harmony of matter and spirit; "the strength of life with the holiness of the soul"; the synthesis of knowledge and faith; "the capacity for understanding with the depth of faith"; and the dialogue between human activity and Divine Providence in history: "Man's ability to manage his affairs in his world, together with his longing for salvation" (*Igrot HaReAYaH* 740, Vol. III, p. 3).

2. WITHOUT FEAR

This study will be divided into three major parts and their subsections. The first section (3–5) will be centered in what may be called the philosophic principle of the theory. The second part (6–11), ideological in content, will be more general and will touch on wider aspects of HaReAYaH's teaching. The third (12–14) will be practical and will touch on examples of the practical applications of his theory, especially in the field of education. The reader may wish to leave out the first part and concentrate on the two latter sections. In any event, here an attempt will be made to open a gate to HaReAYaH's theoretical teaching—from a certain point of view.

Before opening with a presentation of the principles of the system, I think it would be proper to deal with a number of general observations concerning the importance of the study of Jewish thought, the "extra soul" (unnecessary for many) of Judaism.

The literary work of HaReAYaH embraces all fields of Judaism. Rav Kook often dealt especially with the centrality of the theoretical field: "The best of our scholars, and anyone who has the talent and ability . . . has now a heavy responsibility to set the most important note of learning and study in the heights of divine wisdom, which includes the entire range of aggadah, Kabbalah, Chasidism, philosophy, research, moral teaching, all with their varied and many-branched aspects" (*Ikve HaTzon*, p. 143).

For a long period of time, this field has been neglected; the modern Jew has to renew it. This is a part—basic and central—of the mitzvah of Torah study that is imposed upon him: "Torah scholars are in duty bound . . . to teach and spread the knowledge that the study of thought is not something passing and of secondary value, nor is it a matter of concession or prohibition; how much less a loss of time and learning" (*Ikve HaTzon*, p. 144).

Fundamentally, the modern Jew's dilemma is similar to that portrayed in the introduction to Maimonides' *Guide*. Man is steeped in deep anguish. On the one hand, his thoughts and feelings are narrow as a result of atrophy and inertia in his theoretical thought. On the other hand, when man—or the nation—desires to develop, "it seems to him as though his world has been darkened," as if this flowering implies a cutting adrift from Jewish tradition, so that "if the light of knowledge, the light of pure intelligence, should penetrate, it has the feeling as though its spiritual world is shaking beneath its feet" (p. 128), and as though "all his moral life has of necessity to be sucked from simple images, from a logic based on blindness and lack of knowledge" (p. 127).

This attitude is influenced by the spiritual conflicts in which the modern Jew is caught up. HaReAYaH teaches us to stand up against the challenges of the modern era without fear. The great danger is that the fear of sin may be "interchanged with fear of thought, and once man begins to be afraid to think, he will become immersed in the slush of ignorance that takes away the light of his soul" (*Orot HaKodesh*, Vol. III, p. 26).

Indeed, there really is no place for this fear of the conflict; not only in its subjective aspect, but also from another point of view. The spiritual world is not like the material world. "The nature of a spiritual object is such that wherever it comes up against an obstacle in its path from some other opposing spiritual manifestation . . . if it will clear a new path ahead under the influence, and with the help, of the opposing manifestation, then the opposing force will itself give it strength until they will stand together on a higher and brighter spot" (*Maamrei HaReAYaH*, Vol. I, p. 19). A clash of views does not have to be resolved by evading the encounter. The result of such an evasion would be that "even though you would remain with its picture [i.e., of the spiritual object] and you would stand firm with your opinion, you would still not escape some feeling of having been hurt and of weakness." A brave encounter brings us to an understanding of Judaism on a higher level. After all, it may become clear that the clash was not with something real at all, but with a mere fancy; "and when the spiritual object has used up the strength of its opponent, if it will then find that it is right to demolish it, it will be able to do this easily." We must overcome real obstacles; but often it is just the imagined obstacles that trouble us.

A central place in the teaching of HaReAYaH is reserved for the idea, or more exactly, the reality, of *teshuvah*. This is a many-sided phenomenon, but "one of its sides, in particular, will be the sorrow for the insult that is suffered by the great spirit stored up in everything that our forefathers bequeathed to us" (*Orot HaTeshuvah,* Chaps. 4 and 9). It is the insult that we brought about by limiting the treasure "whose strength and honor have no limit," and through our not having toiled to draw up whatever is in that "great spirit"; for if we had paid attention to it, we should have "found everything in it, everything that is desirable and glorious." The spiritual evolution of the last generations, the "heretical darkness," caused us to be separated from this source, to become estranged from the spirit of Judaism and to "stray in strange fields." *Teshuvah* will be our return to the sources of Judaism "to draw and drink to the full from that source of heavenly life," not in order to shut ourselves up in a sort of spiritual ghetto, but so as to feel that every human vista is open before us as we go forth from this source of life.

Rav Kook dreams of authentic Jewish thought that will grow "as Israel, more and more, comes to see its original strength not in borrowed garments but in its own source."[1] Albeit it is important to stress that this authenticity does not find expression in an intellectual solipsism. As against the revelation of self, there is the human creativeness, which should not be disregarded, for "whatever issues from the consciousness of mankind in general is not borrowed or foreign; it all belongs to us as it does to the whole of the world." Jewish thought does not come in place of general human thought. It includes it, and it in fact begins at the place where general thought ends.

The well-known Roman aphorism has fixed an agenda: "I am a man, and nothing human is foreign to me." S. D. Luzzatto, of the cream of the wisdom of Israel, said, "I am a Jew, and nothing Jewish is foreign to me." HaReAYaH actually taught a different way: "I am a Jew, and nothing human is foreign to me." Precisely out of Judaism will grow "the salvation of all worlds . . . the good heavenly light through which to revive society and the individual" (*Orot HaTeshuvah,* Chaps. 4 and 9).

---

1. *Translator's Note:* As a river is replenished not from rains but from its own rock—i.e., its own headwaters. The reference is to the Babylonian Talmud, *Shabbat* 65b.

3. THE EPISTEMOLOGICAL MODEL OF KABBALAH

The renaissance of Jewish thought is indeed a part of the rejuvenation and renewal of the Jewish people and perhaps the very heart of this process. The renaissance of world thought is bound up with a renewed understanding of Kabbalistic teaching. The modern world has opened the gates of science, "and the openings of the gates of *Maasei Bereshit* (the knowledge of the physical world lead to the opening of the gates of *Maasei Merkavah* the metaphysical world)." It is impossible not to pay heed to the theory of mysticism "just as it is impossible to explain even simple faith to people of moderate intelligence except by opening up the canvas of the heavenly secrets that stand at the pinnacle of the universe" (*Orot HaKodesh,* Vol. I, p. 7). Philosophy stretches only over a certain portion of existence; beyond that there is a "secrecy that by its nature penetrates all the depths of all thoughts . . . It recognizes the unity throughout all existence" (Ibid. p. 9).

The theory of mysticism is in fact the basic grammar of the world. "Basic" because it serves as a key to the understanding of various fields. However, it is "basic" not only in linguistic terms but also as that which gives us the pointer to the understanding of the essence of the universe.

Many explanations have been given to the concept of mysticism. Most or all have a grain of truth. We shall devote ourselves in what follows to one explanation that seems to me to be central to the understanding of HaReAYaH's system.

The point of departure proposed here is cognitive and epistemological. The most basic assumption of the system maintains that it does not lie within our regular power of knowledge and cognition, either sensible or intellectual, to know the true character of the universe: "It is not possible to know spiritual being in itself by any inquiring or research. Knowledge, intellectual inquiry, philosophy, these merely mark the outward signs of life" (*Maamrei HaReAYaH,* Vol. I p. 1). Apparently, we have before us the classic distinction between a corporeal world and a spiritual world. However, if this is the way we would explain the significance of the matter, we should be mistaken. It is not only the spiritual universe that belongs to the hidden; the universe that seems to us corporeal is also a hidden universe. Spiritual existence is true being in itself, "but so long as man is steeped in his senses and within finiteness, he will not recognize and will not know spiritual being. Only weak shadows will be seen through them."

Overcoming Dualism

HaReAYaH sets up before us various levels of cognitive awareness. We can picture to ourselves a hypothetical man passing through these stages while changing his understanding of the universe at every stage. Generally, it may be said that each change will find expression in that the various aspects that we usually see as separate from each other, or even in opposition to one another, will be seen by him, stage by stage, as united. Thus, the differences will disappear—with all their various phenomena.

These levels of recognition are found in Talmudic and Kabbalistic sources. HaReAYaH shows us how they actually constitute a complete, ordered arrangement. Man and all humanity must progress in this pattern. All history is really the story of man's ascent like a constant march toward a greater unity:

And the great honor is sure to come, the gates will be opened . . . the worlds will be united, the revealed and the hidden will be blended together, body and soul will be united, the lights and the vessels will be joined . . . (*Orot HaKodesh,* Vol. I, p. 32).

The low levels of awareness are known to everyone. They are the senses, the imagination, feeling, and intellect. Through his senses, man grasps physical reality. However, even this awareness is not a passive perception. The conditions of the senses are arranged by our own powers. The "vessels" in Kabbalistic nomenclature, i.e., the categories with which we act upon the world, are the product of the imagination, feeling, and intellect.

Yet these three forces are not passive, nor are they of secondary importance. In order to explain it more clearly, let us apply this argument to the function of the intellect. The intellect opens up for us hidden worlds—for instance, the world of mathematics—which are closed to the senses and other powers. With due respect to the intellect, HaReAYaH teaches that we should not belittle the other forces, like the imagination or feeling, which are also doors opening on to hidden worlds. Rationalism has put before us sharp alternatives: intellect versus imagination; intellect versus feeling. Imagination, if it is purified, feeling, if it is cleansed—these also, according to Rav Kook, become means for attaining the truth and for grasping reality.

Intellect has a decisive importance. It opens up science before us; although this is the science of the world created with our help, not of true existence. We should limit somewhat the absolute awesomeness that we ascribe to the intellect. As against this, maybe creative imagination is not so arbitrary as it seemed to us in our first analysis.

The sharp distinction between imagination and intellect, and the axiological distinction between them, were at the center of Maimonides' philosophy. Unbridled imagination does not, according to him, distinguish between the possible and the impossible. The final and authoritative verdict must be in the hands of the intellect, which poses the question in the framework of some scientific approach by which it arrives at its judgment. Whoever reads the words of Maimonides in those decisive paragraphs cannot but be amazed at the way in which his examples of the imaginatively impossible have been transformed into everyday realities in the twentieth century.

In the annals of geometry, we know of an attempt to prove an axiom of Euclides by constructing an alternative geometry that was supposed to produce a contradiction. In the event, this attempt served as the beginning of the construction of non-Euclidean geometries. The failure of the failure taught us that paths that seem to lead nowhere can bring us to views and worlds that we never previously thought of. And conversely, that which we at first envisioned as imaginary turns out to be concrete reality.

These four above-mentioned stages of normal life attain, in their climax, to the level of the *Ruach HaKodesh,* the Holy Spirit that finds expression in man's activity in its various forms: the Holy Spirit of deed, of feeling, of imagination, and of intellect. Above them is the Supreme Holy Spirit, "that is the real Holy Spirit by which all the others together are illuminated" (*Orot HaKodesh,* Vol. I, p. 268). This is the first level at which we become detached from the everyday world.

"Everyone who comes into the world merits it through his deeds" in the abundance of the Holy Spirit. However, the Holy Spirit from which were poured out the sources of Judaism was unique. The different kinds of Holy Spirit are like the different kinds of direction in thought. The highest kinds are "the secret part of the Holy Spirit and the effulgence of the light of Torah" (*Orot HaKodesh*, Vol. I, p. 29). The Holy Spirit and prophecy—the next level—open up before us the gates of the world of Torah.

In order to understand the formulations of HaReAYaH we need the language of Kabbalah. The distinction between the Holy Spirit and prophecy is represented in the relationship between the *sefirot*[2] *Malchut* (Sovereignty) and *Tiferet* (Glory): "The spirit of prophecy is full of an ideal glory, and the spirit of law is full of practical kingly might" (*Orot HaKodesh*, Vol. I, p. 24). However, we shall not embark here on an exact analysis of the differences between these stages. We now have to emphasize another aspect of our progress in the sphere of perception.

The Holy Spirit has once more brought us up against this problem of separation between "the hidden and the revealed" (*Orot HaKodesh*, Vol. I, p. 30). And not only this, but "many times the line separating and dividing between them appears in the form of a contradiction" (Ibid. p. 31), a contradiction of which "measured logic" stands in awe. This is not the only dualism. To it should be added the duality of halacha and aggadah (Ibid. p. 25), and in general the manifold and varied aspects of the sources of Judaism. From here on, another warning is stressed in our progress, that concerning unity. The person who reaches the high levels sees the unity that exists behind the multiplicity.

There are stages in which it is possible to overcome these basic situations. The duality is not in the objects themselves, but in our understanding of them. This may be likened to a man who, by reason of some momentary situation or because of illness, loses the coordination between his two eyes, and consequently whatever he sees appears to him in two images. In his world, a duality will exist. However, the correction for this duality will lie not in moving the objects, but in curing his material visual system. His salvation will be not ontological but epistemological. The true, beautiful, correct world is really there; only for us there exists a problematic, fragmented world. These are the impressions we grasp.

2. *Translator's Note: Sefirot* (singular: *sefira*) is the name given in Kabbalistic literature to the ten gradations of forces of the divine essence through which absolute being reveals itself. G-d (sometimes referred to as the *Ein Sof* or the Infinite) manifests Himself in His *sefirot*, the ten powers or emanations of the Divine. The *sefirot* are seen as "layers in the mystery of the G-dhead" (Gershom Scholem, *Major Trends in Jewish Mysticism*, p. 207).

One who reaches the level of prophecy changes his view of reality. "Wisdom . . . looks at reality from without, whether superficially or profoundly . . . but prophecy is a living perception" (*Orot HaKodesh*, Vol. I, p. 272). That is the stage at which the dividing line between meditation and action is erased. The mind again assumes "the crown of its greatness, which will be molding and creating" (Ibid. p. 273). Except that prophecy has not overcome all duality. Duality still exists in Torah and in reality.

In the Torah, the division appears in all its sharpness in the distance between the principles and the details that issue from the principles. Let us take a trivial example; namely, the distinction between major general ideological principles and the practical everyday duties. This stands out clearly in matters of halacha, but beyond it also. It finds sharp expression in the opposition between divine awareness and scientific appreciation, between the broad horizons of philosophy and narrow empirical facts.

Thus far, we have been speaking of the dualism in Torah and in theory. But the real physical world recognizes a much more fundamental dualism, that which divides between "man's inwardness"— his private world of thought—and "universality as a whole" (*Orot HaKodesh*, Vol. I, p. 23), the outer world, the cosmos that fills the space before us.

The world is perceived as though on the other side of nontransparent glass: "an unclear looking glass." But there is a level that sees it as through a clear looking glass. That is the level of knowledge and awareness in which the distinctions between principles and details lose their significance. Only at that level could the prophetic ideals be translated into practical commandments. Here is the explanation of the special quality of the prophecy of Moses our teacher. The general outlines find immediate expression also in the details that are taken from them. "The Torah issues out of the pouring out of divine truth in which there is no distinction between man's inwardness and all universalism and its source" (*Orot HaKodesh*, Vol. I, p. 23).

But not all dualism is wiped out in that level. Beyond that clear looking glass, there is the heavenly brightness of Adam, the first man. At that level of knowing-awareness, the distinction between corporeality and spirituality loses its significance. Of this level, it has been said, "I said, you are gods" (*Orot HaKodesh*, Vol. I, p. 279). Here we arrive at the last epistemological stage before perfection *(tikkun)*. That stage is closed to us, yet in some small degree it touches us.

The most important result of its revelations is the breaking down of the artificial walls that divide between the worlds, between body and soul, between this world and the next: "the supreme intellectual understanding . . . frees the physical and spiritual senses to join up with reality as it is" (*Orot HaKodesh*, Vol. I, p. 7). As a result of this, "bodily life becomes expanded, purified, holy and refined . . ."; everything functions as though "a new light" illumines existence and enables us to see it with an absolutely different vision. Then, as we shall see later on, we should even be able to understand death: "by a good light, with such a look, for that darkness that the moderate wisdom of the living calls death, the world waits" (Ibid. p. 8).

The final position is the light of life after the perfection *(tikkun)*, or heavenly lights (*Orot HaKodesh*, Vol. I, p. 10). On this level of cognitive awareness, we reach the end of the way. The final duality is that between existence and its Divine Source. This distinction is wiped out after the *tikkun*.

Philosophical Parallels

Till now we have seen how the emphasis is placed on the existence of various stages of cognitive awareness. There is a basic proximity here to certain tendencies that have developed in modern philosophic thought. HaReAYaH was aware of this proximity, but also to some existing differences.

The correspondence between HaReAYaH and Rav S. Alexandrov can help us to understand this point. Rav Alexandrov writes (spring 5666) about the spreading heresy and about some sages in the West who are endeavoring to bridge the gap between Judaism and the new beliefs.

Although a great philosopher (not long deceased) named Adolph Frank of Paris rose up for Israel and fought against the heretical denial of everything, and likewise, in our own time a redeemer was found for Judaism in the person of the German philosopher Hermann Cohen who struggles to make the theory of Karl Marx fit in with the existence of the Deity—yet their words are strange and quite unknown to most people and to the best of our nation who would surely rejoice over them as on great wealth. Similarly, from their words we still have to sift the wheat from the chaff and the work is very very great and burdensome; and meanwhile most of the Jewish people are going to a place from which they will not return, and for this we certainly weep.

The image of Hermann Cohen has been brought up here. And in order to understand what follows, it should be remembered that Cohen was a neo-Kantian, one of the great fighters who urged leaving the Hegelian tradition, with the slogan "the return to Kant." And indeed in a later letter, Rav Alexandrov mentions Kant again. And following on this, HaReAYaH refers plainly to the teaching of the great philosopher (*Igrot HaReAYaH,* Vol. I, pp. 47–48, of Kislev 5667).

Even the return to Kant does not embrace even the smallest part of Israel's strength. It is true, as we have always known, from of old, and we did not need Kant to reveal this secret to us, that all human cognitive perceptions are subjective and relative. This is the *sefira* of *Malchut* in the sense of a vessel that contains nothing of its own but is a place or point of gathering like a "synagogue," or like the "moon," which only receives illumination from without; and all our deeds, our feelings, our prayers, our meditations—all are dependent on *this:* "in *this* do I trust."

If, from this short sentence, we dare to reconstruct the idea as a whole, we shall be able to suggest a possible explanation for the entire thesis. That which is above the *sefira* of "Kingdom" is parallel to the object itself. The *sefira* of "Kingdom" is to be understood in the sense of the idea of the material object that exists outside it. In this connection, there is an exact parallel between the Kabbalistic formula "that which contains nothing of its own" and the view of Kant according to which our perceptual structure is formal and empty of content. Hence we are placed in a phenomenal world without being able to break out of it. This is the world of the *sefira Malchut*—the world of the "this" ("in this do I trust"); and all our deeds and feelings and prayers and meditations—all are dependent on "this" *(zot).*

Here is the key to the understanding of the symbolism of the theory of the Names. The relationship between the phenomenon and the noumenon is like the relationship between the Holy Names. In the Tetragrammaton, "according to the order (of the letters) and in all the ways in which they may be joined together" are included "the lights of the inner soul of all that exists, and they include the past, the present and the future beyond the order of times and their forms" (*Orot HaKodesh*, Vol. III, p. 23). As against this, in the name "Elo-Kim" there is the symbol of Providential guidance, that is, nature "which is poured into the very essence of being" (Ibid.), the world as we perceive it.

Instead of "the return to Kant" of the Neo-Kantians, HaReAYaH posits a different return:

We shall return not to Kant, but to the Red Sea, to Sinai and Jerusalem, to Abraham, for instance, to David, to Rabbi Akiva and to Rabbi Shimon bar Yochai, and to all our loved ones who are our life and the joy of our heart forever. Clear the way of the Lord, make straight in the desert a path for our G-d. A road and a way will be there, and it will be called the Way of Holiness—and the redeemed shall march.

The search after thought that will slake the thirst of modern man who has reached a high level of development—brings us to the first *teshuvah*, not "the return to Kant" but to the fountains of Jewish mysticism.

4. VICTORY OVER EVIL

In order to explain and understand the true structure of the world, we can use several models. The real world is sometimes described as being behind everything, as being in the future, as existing above the world of events or, conversely, in the depths.

There are various models before us, the common denominator among them being that existence, in all of them, is what it is by reason of the vessels by which we perceive it. As we progress in our perception, so also does the world improve. Indeed, it may be said that this is the way we should understand the concept of redemption. It is first of all an "epistemological redemption"; the world changes with the change in our perception.

One of the central expressions of this change—as we have seen—is the fact that the more we are elevated, the more we perceive things on a level of constantly expanding inclusiveness. Human error is the result of partial perception.

To explain this fact, HaReAYaH uses the example of light and shadow. We can illustrate his approach with the following example. Let us imagine for ourselves a forest that we want to illumine with a lamp in our possession. If we lift up the lamp, the light will be spread over a wider area, although it will become weaker. But if, on the other hand, we lower the lamp, we shall get an ever-stronger light, although, to our distress, the shadows that the light will cast nearby will grow bigger and bigger. The lowering of the lamp is the symbol of our partial perception. And the first result of this partiality is the creation of particular disciplines; "just as bodies cast a shadow . . . All the spiritual shadows impede the shining brightness of individual parts; but the shadows are the product of the imagination . . . or emotional wonderment" (*Orot HaKodesh*, Vol. I, p. 16). The shadows that are formed symbolize the fact that scientific growth causes errors in various fields. In fact, we shall find the solution in the quest of true, universal science: sacred wisdom. The solution is found in the constant vanquishing of the point of vision of the particular and our ascent to the universal.

The striving after constant progress is an immediate result of the universal, inclusive idea: "The concept of the spiritual unity of all of existence leads to the concept of permanent ascent . . . Seeing that all of existence is one unity, with all its great battles and clashes, there is nothing that blocks it and prevents it from its ongoing ascent . . . Therefore it is always in a state of ascending, up and up" (*Maamrei HaReAYaH*, Vol. I, p. 16). However, in order to understand the full significance of the development, let us again make use of the first illustration.

It is our limited perception that is responsible for the phenomenon of evil. Maimonides posited evil as a privation, a lack. And this was seemingly the optimistic point of view that Maimonides set against the pessimistic and Gnostic standpoints that he negated.

HaReAYaH refers to the same stance, and says things that at face value seem strange, but there is a very profound truth in them: "The existence of universal evil, whether general or individual, whether moral or practical, in whatever guise it exists, when we examine it as a whole or in its detail, we find it as an order, an organic inherent structure. And it is impossible to attribute it to chance" (*Orot HaKodesh*, Vol. II, p. 479).

Paradoxically, when we reflect on evil, whether general evil or individual evil, whether moral evil, which is the evil that a man does, or natural evil, which is the evil that a man suffers, we detect order and organic structure. Rav Kook wants thereby to stress that "the other side," or evil, is not simply a matter of chance. It appears like something tangible, ordered; even, I might say, ordered to perfection, having quite the same structure as has the good. The rationalistic philosophic outlook has revealed in the world some sort of good structure, but by its side and in a kind of chance manner, the evil appears. But this is not the true picture. According to HaReAYaH, we must understand that evil stands before us with a full structure, full of strength. Seemingly, this is a bad situation. But here we learn of the paradoxical aspect of the words of Rav Kook. The truth is, as HaReAYaH explains to us, that we can never get rid of evil as Maimonides portrays it. This is a privation that will not be abolished even in the envisioned end of days. And Rav Kook, like many philosophical and Kabbalistic thinkers who were not satisfied with the seemingly optimistic view of Maimonides, dreamed of a world that will be really all good, a world in which we shall overcome even the cosmic evil that is, as it were, planted in it. A world in which "the wolf will live with the lamb" will not be merely an allegory on political relations between states, but it will be a world in which nature will really be changed.

And Rav Kook says to us, if we perceive evil only as an absence (of good), as a matter of chance, we thereby make it into something that we must live with always. As against this, in the eyes of HaReAYaH, evil has a real existence of its own. But it is an existence that can disappear and that the perfection of the world will abolish. Rav Kook's basic thesis, with which he sums up Kabbalistic and Chasidic thought, is that in reality there is a duality: Perfection—that is, the Holy One, blessed be He—but also the process of perfectibility, that which desires and strives to become perfected.

Paradoxically, if we recall the saying of Rav Abahu, it must be clear to Maimonides that G-d chose the best of the possible worlds. But for the thinking that we now are trying to examine, He did not choose the best of the possible worlds but He chose deliberately the world that is not completely good, that is still not within the bounds of perfection or wholeness, so that men should turn it into a more perfect world. Thus, in the cosmos there is a certain note of wholeness without which existence is not perfect, for this is a world that has perfectibility. It has, so it may be said, the possibility to perfect itself, and it is our duty to complete it, for we can perfect it.

The perfection of the world thus becomes a task imposed on man, a duty that is still laid upon us. The world is indeed not the best of possible worlds, but it is a good world, because there is some sort of final perfection that we can approach nearer and nearer, and at that point death will be made to vanish forever.

Rav Kook describes evil as a tree. But like all the trees in Kabbalah, we have before us a tree turned upside down, with its roots above and its stem below. For really we have to reflect on a reality that is upside down. Therefore we have before us a tree whose roots are in heaven, and whose stem and branches are on earth.

Evil is a tree; and as with every tree, the distinction between roots and stem and branches is applicable to it. What we perceive in it is the stem, for the root itself is hidden from us. And here we see the paradox that although the evil is bad, in its root it is good, its roots are in what is good. We have before us therefore a reality that seems in our eyes evil, and in truth it is so; but it is so because of the manner of our perception of it. We perceive the bad because we perceive only the stem and the branches of the tree. But at its root this tree is good, it is nurtured from what is good; only we cannot perceive the real thing because it is covered, because it is beneath the surface. One has to remember that what in our language is "beneath the earth" means, in the symbolic language of the Kabbalah, the heavens, or what is above the heavens, i.e., the area that we cannot perceive.

Finally, we have in front of us an idealistic approach describing a situation that is really an illusion. But this, it should be remembered, is a partial illusion. It is an illusion in the stem, but not in the roots. For a part of the reality remains hidden; the things we perceive are not the right things. We do indeed perceive the evil, and this is recognized in the particular way we perceive reality, but in truth we could say that the reality has hidden itself; that there is something like a curtain in front of us, and the reality, in the way it appears to us, is not the true reality.

We could have made use of philosophic categories to describe these two strata of reality. HaReAYaH uses a word much accepted in Hasidic thought, one that is also rooted in medieval Jewish thought, namely the word *imagination (dimyon)*. Indeed, we perceive reality by means of the imagination, except that the imagination appears here in a meaning different from the current meaning. It is not as if the evil is imagined, but with our means of perception, with our epistemological apparatus, we perceive the reality, and this apparatus of ours is nothing but imagination. Understandably, it is very difficult to get away from this imagination, and Rav Kook says clearly that to get away from the imagination is really the same process as getting out of prison. Just as one is shut in a prison house and a prisoner cannot release himself from prison, so are we unable to get away from that reality. Despite this, we should know that this is not the real world, and that there is a possibility for us to leave that prison, that imaginary lockup.

The Theatrical Model

This approach has roots in the Hasidic position in relation to the problem of good and evil. We find traces of it in the writings of one of the most profound thinkers of the modern period. I refer to Rav Moshe Hayyim Luzzatto. In his *Daat Tevunot*, RaMHaL[3] describes the human predicament. I think we can clarify his thesis using the theater as a model. Actually, we are spectators in a drama that is being unfolded before our eyes. There is a kind of play taking place in our presence, but this is a play that turns out to have been constructed as if to deceive us. We are the deceived in this play. The play itself is not a true story that is enacted. This fact finds expression in that when we relate to reality, we can fall into error. For instance, we can assume— heaven forbid!—that there is no law and no Judge. RaMHaL himself emphasizes two specially blatant and important errors with regard to our problem. One is the dualism, the Gnosticism, by which existence is explained, in our eyes, as a struggle between two forces, between the force for good and the force for evil. The second is that which will be given special importance below, that is, the fate of the Jewish people.

The history of the Jewish people and its fate seems to prove the opposite of what we want to advocate. The tragic history of the Jewish people apparently constitutes a proof that the Torah is untrue, and this was precisely what Christianity argued when it used the Jewish people

3. Acronym for Rav Moshe Hayyim Luzzatto

as evidence for its position, and the Jewish fate, namely the Exile, as proof of the fact that Jesus was the Messiah, and that the Jews, through refusing to accept him, were made exiles, scattered and despised in the four corners of the earth.

History and nature seem to point to the existence of two forces. But this is so only to give expression to a situation that has been created in a theatrical manner in order to produce an unreal illusion; that is, to confront us with the great trial of faith. This trial is intended to test whether I shall be able to stand firm, whether I shall be able to believe and to understand the great principle of Judaism, namely the doctrine of unity, the unity of G-d. And this despite the fact that seemingly two parties appear in the world: good and evil. The question is, will we succeed in clinging to this belief and understand the meaning of the tree?

The branches of evil, which parked at the foundation from the striving after the perfection of the good, are in truth only an imagined reality, and their appearance shines even to themselves only so long as the light of goodness reveals itself—reveals itself in all its splendor even out of the depths of evil. But after this wicked revelation . . . it becomes clear that it is not an existent being at all (*Orot HaKodesh*, Vol. II, p. 475).

The conception of HaReAYaH is thus the absolute opposite of the Gnostic concept. It stresses the unity that is hidden behind the outward phenomena. The climax of this approach finds expression with reference to death. Redemption means the opening of the eyes, and when we sober up from the illusion, we shall understand that death simply does not exist. Death is a mistake, an error in our perception: "For this good light, for such a hope, for that darkness that the wisdom of life's experiences calls death, the world waits" (*Orot HaKodesh*, Vol. I, p. 8).

Death is nothing but an error. Now this is a paradoxical sentence that says in effect that we judge by means of the things that we perceive. That is, we are judging according to human comprehension and by human means of perception. However, seeing that these means of perception do not describe the true reality, just because they are human means of perception, therefore really death does not exist. And if at a certain stage we shall reach a true understanding of existence, we shall then understand that there is no death, and we shall also understand that there is no evil.

Life and Dream

If we would be left in this stage, we would be left within the bounds of certain Chasidic or Kabbalistic streams of thought. Only Ha-ReAYaH has an additional important principle that has significance for our generation. I refer to the argument that says that the process in which we are, so to speak, roused from the error is a process of historic significance.

Let us illustrate this in a simple way. There is a motif that appears often in Chasidism, a kind of commentary on Psalm 126, *Shir HaMaalot* ("A Song of Ascents"), that says that when the Holy One, blessed be He, will turn back the captivity of Zion, "we shall be like unto them that dream." The dominant feeling here is that we are really living in a dream, but one that is different from the dreams we dream at night, for the reference here is to a dream in installments; a dream that we know we shall go on dreaming again tomorrow when we awaken from the interruption that is sleep and its dreams. According to this perception, we are actually in a dream, albeit a dream that has laws of its own, but it does not cease being a dream. In Chasidic thought, there stands out the idea that avers that really the *galut* (exile) is only a dream out of which we are awakened by redemption. This is not simply an allegory. It is an argument that maintains that reality is not according to the way it is perceived, and while it appears before us in a very realistic form, it is not really like that. Just as the dream that I dream is not real, although it may even bring me into a distressful situation or to severe suffering that I cannot bear, it will still be a dream.

Now, redemption is the awakening from that dream. We can wake up, and when we look back, we shall become aware that everything that occurred was nothing but a dream, and that the reality is different. This approach, which I present here in an extreme form, can illustrate the different types of thought with which we are concerned.

Only this was not exactly the theory of HaReAYaH. Rav Kook drew from this approach, but he developed a view that differed from it in some way. This was because he believed in evolution that takes place in historic processes. In his outlook, the awakening out of the dream takes place in history and is observed in the fact that evil is gradually overcome and disappears, while the good expands its area of control. The awakening will therefore come to expression in the perfection of the world, in the fact that society and the world will become better every day, and good will prevail.

Rav Kook believed in progress and development. Such a view of the world is certainly optimistic, and it depends not only on an analysis of history itself, but on the assumption that the processes of history resemble the processes that occur in the cosmos. HaReAYaH knew the theory of evolution and accepted it in principle, although not from the same reasons that convinced the Darwinians. One has to see existence as a process of development marching toward the good, toward perfection. Our world, according to HaReAYaH's perception, is an imperfect world, but it has within it the principle of self-perfection. And this process of improvement leads the cosmos to evolution, brings life to fulfillment, and society to progress—a progress that is evolution in history.

Redemption, therefore, means the progress and victory of the good, and we can describe it in a sort of rising curve, albeit—and this is an important point—containing spiral loops. Sometimes we come to realize that instead of a graph with a rising line, we are faced with descents and even a falling. But these will be only temporary fallings that are part of the loop, while the positive advance toward the good continues. Assume that we would be living in the period of the Reign of Terror in France following the Revolution. What would we behold before us? We would be witness to the overthrow, if not the absolute overthrow, of the ideals in whose behalf the French Revolution had been brought about. But all this would be only a part of the temporary spiral drop. This was a fall, as was the golden calf after the giving of the Torah—a downfall that is sometimes a necessary part of the upward progress.

But if today we look back, it is clear to us that despite all the terror and the suffering, the progress was palpable, and the French Revolution was part of this advance. In like measure, it is possible that other things that we witness today and that relate to other terror-filled revolutions, gulags, and concentration camps—maybe these also constitute part of a process that in the long run will be revealed as good. For downfalls take place and obstacles lie in wait in every process of redemption, but we have to believe with a perfect faith in the victory of the good and in the positive direction of evolution. There is something compulsive about it.

Redemption and Evolution

Redemption is an infinite process: "There is no end to the ascents, and there is no wisdom or understanding of which we can say 'enough!' and which will not join itself to an even higher illumination than itself" (*Orot HaKodesh,* Vol. I, p. 9). Every *sefira* in fact describes for us a given epistemological situation, as for instance the *sefira Keter* (the "divine dimension of the Crown") which is "clear light, polished light," a thick darkness as against the highest of all heights. Every epistemological situation marks a particular perception of existence, and naturally, of a particular world.

The Holy One, blessed be He, is absolute Perfection. Our world is a world of improvement. Perfection is not complete without there being the possibility of improvement. All the world is in a permanent process of improvement.

Here is the place to understand the view of HaReAYaH on the theory of evolution. We shall concern ourselves further on with its scientific meanings. But its philosophic implications have their place here.

Against the pessimism in the theory of Schopenhauer, for example, HaReAYaH puts forward an optimistic view that is related in principle to positive progress but that is still not free of anxiety. The basis for this optimism is found in the theory of evolution:

Evolution, which proceeds in an ascending path, is that which provides the foundation of optimism in the world, for how is it possible to give up hope when we see that everything is being developed and elevated? (*Orot HaKodesh,* Vol. II, p. 655).

In this positive aspect of evolution and progress, modern theory, in Rav Kook's teaching, is mixed with philosophic and Kabbalistic motifs from classical Jewish thought.

The modern theory of evolution is linked with the medieval theory of emanation. Only here we must note a fundamental difference. The modern theory of evolution as it is presented for instance in the work of Herbert Spencer, moves from the primitive lower levels to the advanced higher levels, from the simple to the complex. In the Neoplatonic theory, and in medieval thought, there is a similar transition from the simple to the complex, but here the value connotation of these concepts is changed. This is an evolution from the higher dimension to the lower, from good to evil.

HaReAYaH joins both processes together, and argues that one cannot understand the one except on the basis of the other. They are two phases of one process: emanation and evolution. This relationship becomes necessary when we inquire not about the actual process of evolution but about its meaning, and in determining its reasons. One has to distinguish between these two questions, because in our agreeing to the fact of the existence of the evolutionary process there is no obligation whatever to explain its motivations. This distinction stands out particularly when we differentiate between two different components of the concept of evolution: evolution in the meaning of a continuous process, a gradual changing, without leaps, as against an evolution that is progress in the sense of advancing in a particular direction. It moves from a less "positive" to a more "positive" state when there is a relationship between this prevailing "positive" advance and the progress of the time. Does the ongoing change ensure also the direction of the change? What is the principle by which one passes from evolution to progress? Can one divorce the second meaning from the first? This is undoubtedly a crucial problem.

Nevertheless, the theory of evolution undoubtedly derives its influence precisely from its second meaning. Consequently, evolution has assumed a kind of mystical meaning of an effective force that explains its results from within itself.

The recognition that we have before us a position that has no rational explanation stands out all the more when we leave the heights of principle and pass on to deal with specific sciences. Thus, by contrast to the teaching of Herbert Spencer, who sees evolution as a sort of cosmic principle that does not require further explanation, we are witness, in biology, to the development of theories that explain the progress. Particularly well known are the teachings of Lamarck, and of course of Darwin. So, for instance, in attempting to answer the question we have posed, Darwin's theory assumes an evolutionary mechanism that is based on various principles but that replaces the teleological cause by chance.

Against this concept of progress, which is perceived as an accidental process, Rav Kook poses his difficulties. In answering this question, HaReAYaH links together the classical concept of emanation with the new concept of evolution—progress. Evolution is nothing other than a return to the original state—wherein is the source of the world.

Rav David HaCohen, the Nazirite, a disciple of HaReAYaH, clarified this point by means of the example of vessels that are entwined, or linked together. Let us imagine vessels linked together, that is, a vessel in the shape of a U connected to an adjacent source.

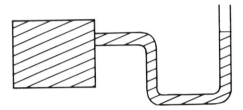

Water enters the adjacent arm; consequently the water rises to the same level in the second arm. This ascent may be difficult, but it happens through a compelling insistence. The source, the same source of light to which we are tied, is perfection; it is the Holy One, blessed be He. The universe at source is nurtured from the Holy One, blessed be He, and its evolution therefore is toward the good. The victory must be a fact, despite all the retreats and despite all the falls. A similar process takes place in human history; the good must prevail, and it will indeed prevail, despite the stumblings and despite the fact that we always live with the feeling that we are in the midst of one of these stumblings and crises, and we see no way out ahead of us.

As we see it, the rise of the water in the second arm seems to us like progress and development. However, the progress is only an external expression of a more internal fact—the water rises because it is returning to its source. The water is "returning in *teshuvah.*" The active force in the entire cosmos is the power of *teshuvah.*

Progress is nothing other than an expression for a turning back—in a reverse direction—of the original emanation. The holiness that is at the source of the universe expresses itself in the positive direction of the cosmic evolution, and this is *teshuvah,* which finds its expression in cosmology and in biology, but also in the social world. *Teshuvah* is thus not a process or an event limited to an individual person. It has significance also for the community, for society, and even for the entire cosmos. Not only that, but its prime significance is precisely that which is connected with the cosmos, while the usual understanding (of *te-shuvah*) is cut out of that first meaning. In other words, the individual's *teshuvah,* in its usually accepted sense, is but a personal incident within the *teshuvah* of all the cosmos.

The change from the usual meaning of *teshuvah* to its cosmic significance is achieved by making use of one of the basic motifs in this concept: the changing of evil to good. According to the Kabbalistic idea, this change exists in the *sefira Binah* ("divine dimension of Understanding") one of whose names is in fact *"teshuvah."*

Changing evil to good means that at a certain stage evil reveals itself in its true sense, which is a kind of hidden goodness. However, it is possible to understand this *teshuvah* not as a static condition but as a historic process. This changing of evil to good is the goal of all cosmic history, and accordingly the evolutionary force in human history is the same as the effective force in all nature. And what happened to the fluid in the linked vessels happens also to the cosmos: It tends to rise so as to get to its source. In this way, the two sides are joined: perfection and improvement.

By means of *teshuvah* everything returns to the Divine . . . and is rejoined with the reality of Divine Perfection (*Orot HaTeshuvah,* Vol. IV, p. 2).

We have before us therefore an exalted world. The link with that exalted world is *teshuvah:*

The private and the general streams of *teshuvah* are overflowing, their appearance is like waves of flame on the ball of the sun . . . There is not sufficient strength to absorb the great multitude of colors of this huge sun that shines for all worlds, the sun of *teshuvah* . . . They come from the source of life itself, one of whose limited manifestations is time itself *(Orot HaTeshuvah).*

The source of life is beyond time. Time itself is only one of its "limited manifestations." The source of life is the world of perfection. It overflows onto us, and this overflowing emanation is *teshuvah.*

Here the new concept in HaReAYaH's theory is explained. *Te-shuvah* is not only a human or a national phenomenon. *Teshuvah* is truly a universal, cosmic phenomenon. Its most prominent expression is evolution: "The universe must perforce come to a perfect *teshuvah*. The world is not something that stands still in one position, but it is constantly evolving . . . The spirit of *teshuvah* hovers over the world and gives it its essential character and the driving force for its evolution" (*Orot HaTeshuvah*, Vol. V, pp. 3–4).

5. THE MEANING OF MONOTHEISM

In a very general way, it might be said that the epistemological foundation of HaReAYaH's theory is a kind of distinction between an object and its phenomena. The object as it really is is what is hinted at in the Chasidic-Kabbalistic saying "There is no place void of Him."

For true reality and everything's complete existence is only when everything comes from the Divine Phenomenon, as a branching off of life and being from the source of life, like a weak shadow as compared with the pure and mighty being at the Divine Source (*Orot HaKodesh*, Vol. I, p. 2).

This description can be understood in two different ways. In the accepted way, the world consists of different layers, each reflecting the layer above it so that the last stratum becomes a "weak shadow" of the first. However, it can also be understood differently. When we examine the various strata, we do not pass into different worlds, but we uncover what lies hidden in our world beneath the seeming reality that we grasp. The process is thus not an ascent to a spiritual world, but the perception of the spiritual content of the world that appears before us; it is not "to ascend" to upper worlds, but to lay bare the worlds that are hidden in the here and now before us, beneath their outer garments. The ultimate goal of the laying bare is "to know everything from the point of view of the source of everything." The particular sciences remain in the phenomenal world; the science that reaches up to the real world is the wisdom of holiness.

In another place, HaReAYaH uses a slightly different epistemological model in order to explain his theory. The distinction between the object as it really is and the way it appears is expressed in *Ikve HaTzon* as a distinction between substance and attribute. "At the beginning of its development, it seems to man that he is grasping the substance of things, but later on, man acquires his complete understanding that everything that exists in the world is grasped by him only from the angle of its outward forms and their relationship to him" (*Ikve HaTzon*, p. 146). Substance becomes relationship, and relationship changes to substance. At the end of the process, the paradox occurs. The substance that is nearest and clearest, the "self," changes to relationship: "Only then will it become clear that the substantive being of man himself will be seen by him as a related attribute, and the divine relationship to him will be seen to be the substance of life and true existence."

Now we can consider one of the bases of HaReAYaH's theory—his true understanding of monotheism.

Franz Rosenzweig describes in strong terms the true significance of Nietzsche's outlook.

Atheism like that of Nietzsche has never yet been seen in the annals of philosophy . . . which does not negate the existence of G-d, but precisely in terms of the theological use of the word, "denies" [*kofer*] Him . . . "If there were G-d, how could I bear not being G-d . . . ?" . . . The first of the philosophers who really was human was also the first who saw G-d face to face—even if only to reject Him . . . The living G-d appears to living man. His self, which is full of rebellion, looks on divine freedom with an angry hatred . . . and because he is compelled to see this freedom as limitlessness, it drives him to atheism; for if this were not so, how would he be able to bear not being G-d? (*Star of Redemption*, Jerusalem 5730, p. 60).

I think there is a reaction to these views of Nietzsche in a passage in *Orot HaKodesh* in which Rav Kook speaks of a strange feeling:

There is an evil inclination concealed in the depths of the soul, a jealousy that rots away the bones, that brings weakness and darkness to every idea of light. The jealousy is strange, many do not recognize it because there are several factors that prevent language from giving it expression, but it is there, slumbering in the hidden recesses of the human soul, and sometimes it emerges in various forms, outside its real form, as is the way of all expression of jealousy, which dress up in strange garments and always assume a strange name. This strange jealousy is the being jealous of G-d (Vol. II, p. 397).

HaReAYaH's rejoinder to Nietzsche refers to "two paths" that point to the fact that the problem is only imaginary. Nietzsche's rebellion arises out of the "monotheistic view" that "sometimes brings sadness and weakness to man when he pictures himself as manipulated and limited and puny, and far removed from Divine Perfection that shines with the light of its glorious strength" (*Orot HaKodesh,* Vol. II, p. 399). Against this one must put forward "the monotheistic outlook that tends to the panentheistic explanation, cleansed of its impurities," according to which "there exists nothing whatever but the Deity." This is the concept of modern Chasidism. The solution is found then in the understanding of "the universal all-embracing unity," which recognizes only the Deity, and knows also that no particular manifestation in the world is identical with the G-d idea, but that "He is everything, and the source of everything, as well as what is high above it" (Vol. II, p. 395). This is a panentheistic definition ("cleansed of its impurities"), which means that G-d is not to be identified with any individual manifestation, not even with collective manifold manifestations, although every individual manifestation, including man, is connected with G-d. This differentiation between man and G-d "is not really true of itself, only it is our blindness that brings it about that all we recognize is the small particular, while as for us ourselves, our own individual existence, with its faults, is also blindness" (Ibid.).

HaReAYaH's reference to this matter is formed also indirectly in *Zeronim* (*Orot,* p. 125), where he says that man rebels "against submission to the Deity." However, this submission is "something natural in all creatures," and the rebellion is founded in error. It is actually the result of an anthropomorphic perception of G-d in human terms. On the face of it, anthropomorphism means the making of a graven image and a likeness. But it is not so. "Usage and childish imagination" clings sometimes even to the cleverest thinker. Anthropomorphism sneaks into every philosophic theory, and "this is a spark of the blemish of the making of a graven image or likeness of which we should always be very wary."

As HaReAYaH has written in *Orot HaKodesh,* man's rebellion against G-d is rooted in an incorrect anthropological and theological understanding. Jewish monotheism must be complemented by panentheism. Consequently, the revolt against the submission is absurd: "self-surrender to the Universal, and all the more so to the source of the Universal's Being, in whom one senses the supremacy of the infinity concerning universality—this is not sorrow and crushing contrition, but pleasure and uprightness, rulership and inner strength adorned with all beauty" (*Orot*, p. 125).

Thus, the theory of mysticism changes not only our cognitive perceptions, but also our existential situation. Among the various aspects of the discussion in *Zeronim*, there is a predominant emphasis on there being two kinds of self-surrender, compared to basic Kabbalistic concepts: "a lower fear" and a "supernal fear." The "lower fear" is the product of the theological thinking "without knowledge and without Torah," "a dim divine awareness" without the prior study of the theory of mysticism. This attitude speaks of fear of the Holy One, blessed be He, understood as "a powerful Force from Whom one cannot escape and to Whom one is compelled to be enslaved." This is the fear of small-minded persons, "which stupefies the heart and prevents man's refinement of soul from prevailing and uproots the divine spark in his soul." As against this, the "heavenly fear" is the result of knowledge of G-d that builds its sanctuary "on the flames of the ruins that atheism destroys" (*Orot*, p. 126). HaReAYaH describes the process pictorially: "the diminution of the soul before its Maker" causes "all the strength and splendor of the phenomenon of existence to go on rising and becoming more universal and mighty" (*Orot*, p. 125). Paradoxically, the diminution of man causes the enlargement of the world, and the enlargement of the world fills man with "satisfaction and life in the degree in which the individual recognizes the magnitude of the society and the beauty of its source." In the language of HaReAYaH, "this natural diminution makes a mighty greatness to flower." Against the jealousy of G-d, a feeling born in the wake of the simple monotheism, stands the heart's delight, which is the result of being convinced "that all of being is divine, and there is nothing at all other than G-d," and the substance of this spiritual pleasure is proof of the Torah that gave it birth (*Orot HaKodesh*, Vol. II, p. 396).

"The blindness of the eyes," which appears here as the source of the being jealous of G-d, takes us back to the seer "whose eye was closed" to Bilam. Bilam is mentioned in the context of the distinction between the "true prophetic spirit" *(Aspaklaria Meira)*[4] of Moses and the heav-

---

4. *Translator's Note:* Literally, "clear looking glass." This is a *terminus technicum* denoting the prophecy of Moses, the greatest of the prophets, of whom it is said that

enly brightness *(Zihara Ilaah)* of Adam. The *Aspaklaria Meira* is one
of the stages of divine revelation. This is a stage in which there is still
a dualism: "From the standpoint of the *Aspaklaria HaMeira*, the corporeality remains partly in place, and its lower half is called man."
However, "from the standpoint of the *Zihara Ilaah* of Adam, the first
man, the entire bodily aspect is uplifted, in the sense of Psalm 82: "I
said, you are gods" *(Orot HaKodesh,* Vol. I, p. 279). In the epistemological state of *Zihara Ilaah,* man attains a perception of total monism
in which all contradictions are solved. But in this brightness, "the
wicked Bilam's eye was blinded." The wicked Bilam, in my view, hints
at the philosophy of Schopenhauer or Nietzsche. The wicked Bilam
preached a "change of values." He put before his disciples a new
morality of an evil eye, a haughty mind, and a proud spirit. His being
steeped in the power of what is ugly caused his eye to be blinded
precisely in his meeting with the *Zihara Ilaah.* The *Zihara Ilaah* is the
true view of reality. When we reach it, we sense that all boundaries
become blurred. Nietzsche's call to put man in the place of G-d is
correct: "Is it not right that we should ourselves become gods so that
we should be fit for this greatness?" Yet it is witness to the fact that
he saw, and was blinded by what he saw. Likening ourself to G-d is
indeed a sacred goal. It is an expression of the absolute freedom of the
most elevated man, but it is also an expression of the holiness in him.
The centrality of the individuality in Nietzsche's philosophy distanced
him completely from an understanding of morality. "The morality of
slaves" that Nietzsche treated with contempt is an expression of the
unity of all reality.

The discussion is summarized by HaReAYaH in his reply to Alexandrov *(Igrot HaReAYaH,* Vol. I, p. 48):

"But one who is of idolatrous stock, whose fathers were able to turn their
minds away from the G-d of gods"—he will also be able to turn his mind away
from that which is perforce higher than everything; although by our values also
He is as if nonexistent, since He has no intellectual or metaphysical form. We
know, however, that no other way is possible, but everything is only from Him.

he spoke with G-d "face to face." The other prophets received their divine communica-
tions in a less clear manner, through an "unclear looking glass" *(Aspaklaria Lo Meira).*

We do not speak of, nor do we even contemplate, the Source of all sources, but from the very fact that we do not deny Him, everything goes on living and existing forever.

This idea is the pride of Israel to eternity, although, after all, even this is not revealed except through the *Shechinah* [Divine Presence]. What of it! I [*Ani*] and Nothingness [*Ayin*] are composed of the same letters.[5]

This is not the monotheism that rejects practical talents, friendship, and beauty. Monotheism has been thought up in the minds of Gentiles, and has been given an imprecise meaning as an Infinity that is a comprehensible concept and is therefore self-contradictory—and thus leads to nothing. This is not the source of the Name of the G-d of Israel. The Source of everything is the Infinity that cannot be comprehended; He is the Omnipresent Lord of the world, Who can be grasped and spoken of only through the nuances of multifarious colors, through His many deeds and abundant peace, His profusion of love and might. Only Israel . . . can say this—not the barren and desolate monotheism of Islam, or the Buddhist negation [of this world]; but only the highest form of living, which brings joy to all and gives life to everything, and is revealed through the objective revelation in the hearts of all who seek Him and comprehend Him: "Each one will show with his finger: Lo, this is our G-d; we have waited for Him and He will deliver us; this is the Lord for Whom we have waited; we shall be glad and rejoice in His salvation." "Happy is the nation that is in such case; happy the nation whose G-d is the Lord."

The solution to the problem of the jealousy of G-d: "That which brings reflection and peace of mind—this is the basis of the happiness that is in freedom"; Man, the last to be created, is divorced from his Infinite Source; He will get happiness and this from his returning to the good, while in a condition of his own freedom. Happiness is the end result of the process of his being "joined with the King" [i.e., when he is rejoined with the Source]. Man's consciousness of himself as a separate individual is an illusion. His return to the Source freely is *teshuvah*.

5. *Translator's Note:* In Hebrew the two words have the same letters, but in different order אין,אני. 'Ein' is sometimes used as part of the phrase *"Ein Sof,"* meaning "without end," i.e., infinity. Hebrew letters are each thought to have special significance; hence two words composed of the same letters must have a spiritual connection.

6. THE FOUR IDEALS

The Influence of Judaism

Rav Kook's enterprise is not exhausted in the construction of a system of true thought. It extends to the comprehension of opposing views. This derives from the principle adopted by Rav Kook according to which every position contains a spark of truth. We must uncover this spark, to redeem it, to restore it to its source. To be sure, there are other situations: "There are such ideas that necessarily, by the nature of man, cause, with their dissemination, harmful consequences."

In such cases, we must struggle in order that "one not be harmed by their extending branches" (*Orot HaKodesh,* Vol. I, p. 14). For this reason, we must respect the value of conflict. The conclusion is that man grows and develops, and with him develop his ideas as well. "The rejected ideas that return and are received—in them we find the dew of life, staunch and very holy" (Ibid.).

We shall examine several examples that are explicitly or implicitly raised by Rav Kook's approach. Christianity is an outstanding one. It would seem that Christianity is a continuation of the Bible that is oblivious to the world of the Oral Law. But this would be a very mistaken view. This common outlook does not understand the significance of Jewish history in the First and Second Temple periods.

The biblical period, the youth of the nation, was characterized by the intensity of the feeling of love of G-d. "Shechinah was present in Israel, the totality of the nation sensed and felt the divine love with all its delights" (*Eder HaYekar,* p. 29), and manifested itself in all the particulars of life, in the sense of "In all your ways know Him." This love was so strong that "it was possible, however, to change and to substitute for the holy, pure feeling, which flows from the treasury of life and the source of truth, a defiled feeling that resembles it in its external form, the love of other gods." But it was impossible to extinguish this love by negation and denial.

Historians are in the habit of reading history developmentally. Though such a reading has a great deal of truth, it also contains a "surplus of fantasy" (*Eder HaYekar,* p. 55) and at times distorts the general picture. Following Rav Kook's words, one can compare the situation to that of human biography. One can interpret the evolution of a man, or a couple, by reference to various events, but one cannot deny the presence of one basic datum: The force of love is weakened with age. The biblical period was marked by the bursting power of love, like "romantic love . . . traversing its ways" (Ibid.) at times. It suffused the nation in its totality "at intervals" and "elect individuals" . . . until the cessation of prophecy. The Second Temple, after the end of the prophetic era, lacked Shechinah and the Holy Spirit (*Eder HaYekar*, p. 31).

Christianity is a consequence of this reality; it expresses the world of the Second Temple: "When, as a result of the sunset . . . in that terrible obscurity there could emerge at the end of the Second Temple, a system of monotheism infiltrated with paganism" (*Ikve HaTzon*, p. 153). One could say something astonishing: There was here a historical accident. "Had the religious influence of Israel entered the world at a time when the nation was living with its animated inner nature, then the religious tendency of those nations would not have received . . . that dark and melancholy form that desiccates life and contracts the soul" (*Eder HaYekar*, p. 31). The circumstances were that G-d assisted those who sought to hasten the eschaton, to make *Knesset Yisrael* willy-nilly a "student unready to instruct who instructs, of whom the verse says, 'For many corpses it has brought low' " (Ibid.). The nations drew from the fountain when "it was already muddied and fouled by the feet of forest boars" (Ibid. p. 32).

In the wake of Christianity came the fragmentation of religious experience. The biblical spirit embraced all life. Christianity limited it and thus abandoned this world. This is, paradoxically, the necessary consequence of Spinoza's system as well. Spinoza substituted for the living G-d the infinite substance with its infinite modes: "he thought to obliterate the idealism of calling upon the Name of G-d by the numbing call to substance" (*Ikve HaTzon*, p. 134). For Spinoza's system, "there is neither boldness nor humility, neither holiness nor joy, neither purity nor a life of desire for true action" (Ibid.). The key for man is to walk in the ways of G-d; Spinoza's system is, in the final analysis, agnostic precisely in this area. If we accept it, then we have "no substantial knowledge for man not only in the nature of G-d but in any concept." We have no "knowledge of G-d on earth."

The practical conclusion of Spinoza's system is separation of religion from politics, i.e., the abandonment of political life to the play of forces and interests. By contrast, Judaism demands that "the ideal aspect

... be the force moving the cultural wheel in all its many aspects" (*Ikve HaTzon*, p. 135). Spinozist determinism is radically opposed to Judaism. It could unfold in his system because, paradoxically, Judaism influenced him when already dressed in Christian garb.

Divine Providence was good to us in removing Spinoza from our midst. "G-d's Hand was then with the heads of the Amsterdam congregation to expel" Spinoza (*Ikve HaTzon*, p. 134). If Spinoza had written in Hebrew and laced his prose with the language of Torah, it could have had a destructive impact on the nation. Despite the enormous, at times polar, distance between Rav Kook and Hermann Cohen, they would agree that Spinoza's system is "pagan in source and foundation" (*Ikve HaTzon*, p. 134). Pantheism and idolatry are close to one another. Nonetheless, Spinozist monism also contains "the thought of divine unity." This idea "took root so strongly in his soul" that only it could engender "such a dark, terrible shadow by the great light." The Spinozist shadow still shows signs of the thought of unity, and that is the kernel in the "thick peeled" pomegranate, the spark of holiness in his system.

The modern world was conquered by materialism: "Human idealism gradually declined, until it was compelled to turn to materialism" (*Ikve HaTzon*, p. 135). Paradoxically, what drives us away from Christianity brings us closer to modern materialism. Modern atheism is a rebellion against that antinatural religious spirit expressed in Christianity. The influence of the Christian peoples has caused "the maladies of weak-spiritedness and negation [to enter] the bounds of Israel by the stumbling and hasty among us, who found it correct to imitate the sick views of the nations in whom they mingle" (*Eder HaYekar*, p. 32). Thus, the unnatural penetration of atheism among the Jewish people.

Atheism in Israel is in effect suicide: "Such a nation that, when the Name of G-d is removed from it, has nothing ... Now there come those of stubborn heart, and precisely at a time of trouble and oppression ... bestow upon it the attentive spirit of stinking denial" (*Eder HaYekar*, p. 51). The arguments of atheism are absurd. They could bring man to agnosticism ("dubious denial") but no more; however, the atheism that we encounter is a belief "without rationality ... in the words of the inferior heretical philosophers among the Gentiles." Their words, arguments, and proofs are nothing but "imaginary catapults" (*Eder HaYekar*, p. 52). But that is the problem: Imaginary weapons can cause real harm. They "frighten the soft-hearted" and imaginary stones "cast within the dark camp, destroy the wall of the house of Israel with their wicked worthlessness."

Judaism must fight materialism and return to true idealism "to uproot the grove of negating idealism and freedom" (*Ikve HaTzon*, p. 135). Of all approaches, it is evolution that is closest to it, the approach that speaks of "graduation from the deep abyss of *tohu vabohu* to the level of the supreme elevation of supreme and lofty creation" (*Ikve HaTzon*, p. 153). We have already noted Rav Kook's attitude to evolution, and will return to it below.

Rav Kook thought that the future would bring the decline of Christianity. Through Christianity, to be sure, it seems that Jewish ideas were received by the world. However, it is only after the decline of Christianity that a new Jewish influence will become possible, "the influence of genuine culture for Israel in the world" (*Ikve HaTzon*, p. 138). However, in order to realize this goal, we must mend our own world, ethically and nationally. That is the goal of the national renaissance.

Failure to understand this task is the great sin of Jewish reformers. Religious reform identified the spirit of Israel with the ordinary religious feeling, whence its failure: "Those who thought they could explain the divine concept in Israel by the essence of the ordinary religious feeling found no desire in the practical fulfillment of Torah and mitzvot in action." Reform thus did not find a place in its system for observance of the commandments, "and from this root emerged afterward sustained hatred and vigorous contempt for the national purpose of Israel."

Judaism is thus not only a tribal framework, or a group with a common history, fate, or customs; it is rather an entity with universal significance. If one requires an additional proof of the place of Judaism in world history, that is paradoxically found in anti-Semitism. Anti-Semitism is "the terrible hatred" that derives "from religious sources and from atheistic sources" (*Ikve HaTzon*, p. 135). It is linked to Christianity but precedes it. Even when the influence of Christianity disappears, it will not. Perhaps the contrary will be the case; anti-Semitism will grow with "the forgetting of the divine ideals" (*Ikve HaTzon*, p. 134), and will return us to a confrontation between Judea and Rome "because of the great opposition in the very nature of all life" between them. A return to that confrontation we indeed witnessed during World War II.

However, the interpretation of anti-Semitism brings us to deeper layers. Anti-Semitism is the expression of a profound confrontation with what Judaism represents, the demand to guide all life in the light of the divine ideals, without spiritually ghettoizing them: "Hatred of Israel in its psychological source derives from a negation of the Israelite aspiration to life, in the national and general sense" (*Ikve HaTzon,* p. 133).

One might think there is a different matrix of causes and explanations of anti-Semitism. Ask a Jew-hater about his own comprehension of his hatred, and he will surely give you a very different answer. But though he may not reason it out, his instinct does. The opposition acts, albeit unconsciously, "for it becomes felt and affects him even without understanding and knowledge" (Ibid.).

Judaism indeed has not completed its cosmic role. In reality, it has not even begun. It has yet to bestow upon the world its true fountain, "and that is the soul of Zionism." Political Zionism is a "body without animation." The human task of Judaism is its soul, which it must animate, and build our people as a kingdom of priests and a holy nation. Our practical task in the future will be manifested in the ideals that Rav Kook sets before us.

The Faces of the Complete Chariot
Science measures the significance of certain claims according to its own criteria. Often this immanent standard does not correspond to their human relevance. There are great and important scientific discoveries that have nothing to do with the existential situation of man: "Even when men were in error—according to our current sense—and held the old system . . . the poets sang, the philosophers thought and life went its way. To the contrary, there are scientific matters that are not so important according to a superficial overview, but nonetheless touch upon man, his inner life, until he is linked with them in all his powers and without them his life is not life" (*Maamrei HaReAYaH,* Vol. I, p. 10).

Many ideas that circulate and clash with one another call out to man. Multiplicity is one of their defining characteristics. This multiplicity leads us to four principles that explain all human struggle: "Four eternal aspirations: a) the divine spirit; b) the ethical spirit; c) the social spirit; d) the religious spirit or the spirit of faith. These are the powers that act constantly consciously or unconsciously on all human societies, be they primitive or progressive" (*Maamrei HaReAYaH,* Vol. I, p. 102).

These four themes contain the source of all human ideals. We must find the balance among them: Perfection cannot be found "without the complete influence of these four spirits in their fullness." The connection among them is not simply mechanical: "The chemical reaction is wonderfully typical of the life of the spirit." The common situation, however, is tragic, in which there is a fading of the face to the point where the image is effaced. The goal is again to attain a state of "harmonic equilibrium that restores the majesty of life to its basis." The four spirits are indeed the four faces of the *Merkavah,* the prophetic and mystical chariot that symbolizes the throne of the Lord.

Elsewhere Rav Kook speaks of the synthesis among these four components:

We must always conduct our unique entity, the Israelite nationality in its divine form, "And they shall be called a holy people the redeemed of G-d" through which are unified the ethical, social, national and religious powers (*Igrot HaReAYaH,* Vol. I, p. 2).

The four forces are represented in the four competing social movements: liberalism, socialism, nationalism, and religion. These modern movements express the deep meaning of Judaism; they are not a foreign implant. They have different features that we must discover. But these factors are not complete in their isolation, and they present danger if they do not attain synthesis in religion. Only religion can save us "from that moral decline that mere nationalism can sweep with itself." On the other hand, "the national aspect . . . embraces in itself most of the nonrational commandments *(shimiyot)"* (*Igrot HaReAYaH,* Vol. I, p. 52). It does not matter where we begin, for in any case we will reach the totality of the four ideals.

In the following sections, we shall attempt to clarify these ideals in greater detail.

7. ETHICS

The ethical spirit is absolute, it is the "consequence . . . of the divine demand that sparkles in the general soul of humanity and is sometimes revealed as a grand vision in which the source is bracketed" (*Maamrei HaReAYaH*, Vol. I, p. 21). The moral aspiration of man, stamped with the seal of the Divine Spirit: "The turmoil of atheism so long as it is concerned with ethical tendencies, is literally a seeking after G-d" (*Maamrei HaReAYaH*, Vol. I, p. 41). At times these tendencies are more G-d-seeking than "seeking that comes with feelings of the heart without practical benefit to the order of life." No doubt this search is unconscious: "nonetheless human beings are to be pitied as long as they do not know that all their concerns in the expansion of ethics and the search for the good are the seeking of G-d." As in many other processes, here too there must be a transition to consciousness: "Life passes from the instinctive state to the conscious state" (*Maamrei HaReAYaH*, Vol. I, p. 29).

This discussion links up with one of the most tragic problems in modern Jewish existence and thought—the connection between the economic and social doctrines of Marxism and materialistic philosophy. This connection, between economic-social plans and metaphysical doctrines is, without a doubt, the result of what might be called a historical accident, the outcome of the state of scientific and philosophical development in the previous century. However, this accident became fateful for Marxism, and undermined any possible harmony between religion and socialism. Modern Jewish social thought had to unfold in the light of this.

As we shall see, Rav Kook held that confrontation with Marxism is only one aspect of the problem. A more general observation will offer us a more correct perspective, but this requires that we confront Judaism with another system.

Human society is the primary arena of man's ethical activity, hence it is one of the areas in which man's religious destiny—Torah—is realized. This claim will be understood properly, if we grasp it in the light of the alternative presented by classical Christianity.

"Heresy" *(minut)*, i.e., Christianity, is described by Rav Kook as it is manifest in the classic doctrine of the kingdom of heaven that is not

of this world: ". . . anarchy of the material world in all its values
. . . the abandonment of the body with its uncircumcised, defiled
element and abandonment of life and society, the realm and government in their filthy debasement . . . abandonment of the world and its
natural powers, which fell together with the sin of man in their debasement" (*Orot*, p. 22). Christianity rebelled against pagan moral abandon
but replaced it with the abandonment of a world that is hopeless of
redemption, whose foreskin cannot be circumcised, whose reality is an
irremediable distortion. Thus, there emerges a barrier between ". . .
heaven and earth, body and soul, belief and practice, image and actions,
personality and society, this world and the other world" (*Orot*, p. 23).
Abandonment of the world means erecting barriers in the face of
religious obligation, a contraction "preventing the light of holiness
from expanding in the space of being."

This stance leaves the world in its travail. Moreover, at times it offers
ideological justification for the dominion of wickedness in this world,
while contracting ethical values to the realm of the individual. Thus
is engendered a covert or overt covenant, by assent or coercion, between wickedness, which rules the world at its pleasure, and the church,
which teaches that salvation is not of this world and that therefore one
cannot anticipate its mending and redemption: "But how pitiful is this
world, in which wickedness and darkness raise their heads and lay claim
to their choice desires. What storehouses of evil are included under this
horrible, terrible lie with feet of swine that spread before every passerby
to say, See that I am pure." (Ibid.). Swine paws (a "kosher" component
in an impure phenomenon) are a symbol for the creation of an ideology
that legitimates corrupt government in the names of religious and
ethical values.

So far, we have examined one aspect of Rav Kook's critique of
the position that separates religion from society in order to abandon the
world and the society in the hands of corruption and oppression. The
second facet of his critique is an immanent religious one:

The abandonment of the practical world that comes about because of the
eruption to the spiritual world without the order and mending of the holy, just
as it prevents the light of holiness from spreading into the expanse of being,
so too it lowers its values and darkens its appearance in its supreme heights,

abased and debased "an enemy has denounced G-d and a worthless people profaned Your Name" (Psalm 74:18). "The desire of the humble" (Ibid. 10:17) is redemption of G-d (*Orot,* p. 3).

Contraction of the realm in which religion is applicable is accompanied by a shrinking of man's "image of G-d," i.e., a theological contraction. According to this, there is an inherent connection between the role of the churches in feudal society or in the modern period as allies of the nobility or of absolutist kings, and classical Christian theology. One cannot comprehend the "debasement of the image of G-d" without a broader theological context. The Christian image of G-d presents an incarnate, suffering G-d, who redeems man and the world through his suffering. But this incarnation is nothing but the "debasement of the image of G-d," which turns Him "who has no limit and bound, beginning or end to His sublimity" into one wretched "abased and debased." This theological conception appears to Rav Kook "profanation," not least because of the ethical conclusion it implies. According to the prophetic vision, redemption does not take place with G-d identifying Himself with the suffering wretch, but when He hears the "desire of the humble": "G-d, You have heard the desire of the humble; You will prepare their heart, attend Your ear. To judge orphan and oppressed, that man of the earth no longer oppress" (Psalm 10:17–18). Not the debasement of G-d, but the descent of Providence and dominion, being and creation—in other words, the rule of moral order in the world, engendering "loftiness of observation and boundless elevation."

According to Rav Kook, the fundamental difference between Judaism and Christianity is expressed in the attitude to justice (*Orot,* pp. 20–21). One should not seek the unique in Judaism in the national ethic, for that is not different in its content from human ethics. It should be sought in a "small periscope containing the substance of the Torah": "In all your ways know Him." This demand "that is actualized for elect individuals, is in truth the heritage of all." That is, the unique quality of the Torah of Israel is rooted in its being a teaching for all, not just for the individual. The positive values of reality, what Rav Kook calls holiness, are not exclusive to Israel: "there are drops of the holy in every people and tongue." What is unique in Israel is the Torah's demand and the feeling of the nation that from that holiness "all the values of life . . . grow"; "therefore Law is the Holy of Holies in Israel."

By contrast, Christianity has made theological knowledge an individual ideal, thus bringing disaster on humanity:

Heresy abandoned Law, pitched its tent in the quality of mercy and imagined grace, taking the foundation of the world and destroying it. With the uprooting of the element of justice from its divine content, its place is taken over by the most vulgar evil, filth comes to penetrate the private law of the individual personality and penetrates with a great expansion into the souls of the nations, thus establishing the hatred of nations and the evil valley of bloodshed's defilement, without moving the yoke from the neck of man (*Orot*, p. 21).

Indeed, redemption will find expression in the restoration of justice: "Indeed the eyes of all must be raised to the light of the world, the light of G-d, to be revealed by the Messiah of the G-d of Jacob who will judge the universe justly and nations righteously" (*Orot*, p. 12).

The confrontation between Judaism and Christianity presents us with different conceptions of religion; that between Judaism and socialism, with different conceptions of ethics. This difference is one of approach, in spite of the practical agreement that occasionally exists. From this perspective, our discussion is part of the relationship between religious ethics and ethics that has its source derived in man.

In order to explain his position on this matter, Rav Kook employs Kabbalistic symbols:

Two things are luminous in Israel, pure ethics in all its aspirations for the totality of the world, for man, for all life and for all being, and the knowledge that all derives from calling upon the Name of G-d and all the lights that emanate from Him, which come into the idea, until there emerges the Name that is written and read, and that emanates through the genesis of denominations and feelings that are all signs of a supernal reality, rich in being. Ethics without its source is an inner, central light, without something to encompass it, an original environment. It is destined to deteriorate, and its value while it abides is also small. The appearance of the soul in connection with the divine, when ethics and its values are not properly illuminated, is an encompassing content without a center (*Orot HaKodesh*, Vol. III, pp. 15–16; *Orot*, p. 140).

In this section, the distinction between divine ethics and human ethics is formulated by means of the Kabbalistic distinction between the encompassing light and the inner light. The context of the symbol is of course the doctrine of *tzimtzum*. Entities existing in a space that was engendered by *tzimtzum* rest between these two aspects of the light. We are aware of the source of the encompassing light, which comes from the encompassing Infinite. We are not aware of the source of the inner light, though it too derives from the Infinite. The inner light, that is "pure ethics," is found in the heart of every man in his aspiration to benefit humanity, life, and even all being. By contrast, the encompassing light is "the knowledge that all derives from calling upon the Name of G-d and all the lights that emanate from Him." Ethics is one of the manifestations of the holy. Indeed, ethics has a religious source; however, it is not a historical or literary source, but a metaphysical one.

The problems of human ethics come to expression in the relations between these two lights. Lack of unity between them engenders the tension between autonomous ethics "without its source, an inner central light without something to encompass it," and heteronomous religious ethics, "an encompassing content without a center." The former is "destined to dwindle." On the other hand, the lack of inner light is manifest in the absence of a center, a defect in the internalization of ethics, and then "ethics and its value are not properly illuminated," among other reasons because of the potential contradiction between the commandments and man's natural inclinations, a problem that we shall return to later.

According to this symbolic understanding, the distinction between the encompassing light and the inner light is close to the distinction between the transcendent and the immanent. For every idea and ideal (i.e., the encompassing light), there corresponds an inclination in the human heart (i.e., the inner light). Natural ethics is not the only example of such a correspondence; an additional instance in Rav Kook's writings pertains to the status of the Torah. Despite its source as revelation, the Torah is not an external necessity imposed upon the people. The principle of revelation implies that the Torah has a transcendent source. But the idea of the election of Israel guarantees that there is a correlation between the transcendent source and the spirit of the nation, the immanent source of man.

This distinction is also described in *Ikve HaTzon,* albeit in a slightly different form: There, Rav Kook explains that "so long as the supreme ethics of society is not nourished by the supernal intellect, in its most lofty and sublime aspect, the intellectual and ethical beacons must be eclipsed and diminished . . . For ethics, even social, national and human, can only be perfect and eternal when it derives from the highest science . . . And it is required for it the clear knowledge of G-d in its ideal form . . . and since it has not the fountain of the Infinite, immediately it dwindles and dries out" (*Ikve HaTzon*, p. 103).

This parallel between the religious and humanistic formulations of the ideal also helps us understand the phenomenon of socialism. Liberalism and socialism are movements expressing the ethical aspirations of modern man in his struggle against "evil and darkness." In Letter 44, one of the most important documents for an understanding of Rav Kook's thought in the first decade of the century, there is a detailed discussion of the relationship of Judaism to these two movements. Behind Rav Kook's discussion is the accepted assumption that a synthesis between Judaism and liberalism is possible, along the lines attained by Western European Judaism, but that no such synthesis is possible with Marxism, which negates religion totally, in the name of militant atheism.

Indeed, Rav Shmuel Alexandrov, commenting on Rav Kook's statements in *Ikve HaTzon*, wrote (*Maamrei Bikkoret*, p. 23):

It is quite true that eternal justice is the essence of Judaism, and all the various kinds of liberalism that stem from love and feeling have their blessed source in ancient Judaism, and together with this to be the most radical liberal according to the new fashion, but in no manner can we be faithful to the foundations of the doctrine of Karl Marx in the spirit of Judaism, insofar as this teaching is distant from any spirit and feeling, and in general it is not sufficient for us to find the ethical boon of Judaism but we must also find in Judaism a force that repels historical materialism and uproots it, and until that time we have nothing to rejoice about . . . For the time being the victory is beyond us except for the spark of hope we can observe that this time will come and not be delayed.

According to Alexandrov, Liberalism is close to Judaism because it views ethics as a central value. Not so socialism, "for they wish to uproot every good quality whose source is the feeling of love and general justice, saying that justice too is only the product of materialistic necessity that was needed and arose in history only for a time, but in the social [i.e., socialistic, in his language] future there is no justice and no love but common labor for all human beings in the general mechanism, so that each one benefits only from the toil of his hands and that is the pride of the socialist world . . ." (*Maamrei Bikkoret*, p. 22). Rav Kook responds to this, though he approves of socialism in itself:

We do not sorrow if some quality of social justice can be constructed without mention of any spark of the Divine, because we know that the very aspiration for justice, in whatever form it has, is itself the most illuminating divine influence . . ." (*Igrot HaReAYaH*, Vol. I, p. 45).

The unholy alliance between socialism and materialism is indeed the result of an accident that has a historical explanation, but not a systematic one. This link is the product of a historical situation, but is not a necessary one. There is no necessary transition from historical materialism to philosophical materialism that determines a theory that does not apply to historical reality but to the structure and essence of the cosmos.

The moral visions pertaining to the "spreading expanse" of all humanity, to man as man, also come "with the assurance of the particular treasure of life of Israel," a treasure in which we find "all the kernels of growth for felicity and life." We neither need nor can we "deaden anything," i.e., negate those positive universal values, although in a certain situation they are mixed with elements that contradict Jewish existence and the principles of Judaism. Jewish thought "turns everything to light, darkness to luminosity, bitterness to sweetness." Not the elimination of socialism, but its transformation, is the task facing Jewish thought.

And the good in historical materialism will stand at our right hand, when we clarify with assurance that it cannot possibly exist as a permanent system, old or novel, with all its branches and boughs, but rather requires pruning and weeding, purification and refinement, and part of it will be a boon to the world, befitting the light of Israel, its boldness and eternity (Ibid.).

Socialism as it appears before us, wrapped in historical materialism, is undoubtedly "the product of a human idea of a transient historical moment," as Rav Kook argues explicitly with regard to liberalism. Hence its form is malleable. This is not merely a matter of possibility. It will become necessary to assure its continued existence. Socialism requires "pruning and weeding, purification and refinement," and no doubt the purification involves disengagement from the connection to atheism, which contradicts by its very nature the essence of socialism.

Thus Rav Kook responds to Rav Alexandrov in Kislev 5667 (Ibid.):

We do not sorrow if some quality of social justice can be constructed without mention of any spark of the Divine . . . And if humanity wishes to establish a state of equilibrium in life and rest for the heart without any spiritual influence at all, we find in it, even if you are unwilling to recognize the nature of the consensual justice, if it is only successful, the grandest spiritual influence. "And he will say, I am not a prophet, I am a tiller of the soil, for man has trained me from my youth" (Zachariah). And if man wishes to build the general cosmological structure without any participation of spiritual influence, but through calculations of materialistic necessity, we remain serene of heart observing this child's construction, which builds the shell of life when it does not know to build life itself, and we draw closer and embrace therefore the connection to life and inner holiness. "I am the Lord your G-d who brought you out of the land of Egypt," not "who created the world" and from the supreme recognition and sublime certainty of the grand, ordered and clean-cut life itself, "And I am the Lord your G-d from the land of Egypt, and gods other than Me you shall not know, and salvation is not other than Mine, I have known you in the desert in the land of aridity."

Contradictions

The study of Rav Kook's social ethics presents us with problems that twentieth-century thought later formulated in its full acuteness:

The ethical contents contradict each other, each one builds its world in a broad radical way and is not concerned at all about the picture of the world and the demands of the other ethical contents (*Orot HaKodesh*, Vol. I, p. 12).

In order to enable a systematic discussion of these problems, we will attempt to deal with the problems in relation to four foci in which one can see, in my opinion, the fundamental contradictions that moral action must overcome. The latter ones Rav Kook notes explicitly. But I believe we ought to discuss them in the context of all the contradictions we shall attempt to describe.

The Serpent

The first basic contradiction is undoubtedly the tragic impossibility of realizing ethics completely. This world is not an Eden of harmony, and its fundamental emblem is the serpent: "And enmity I will set between you and the women and between your seed and hers, he will bruise your head and you will bruise his heel" (Genesis 3:15). It is impossible to exist without uncompromising conflict. The only possible alternatives are "he will bruise your head" and "you will bruise his heel." There are objective impossibilities and subjective impossibilities. When the rabbis state that prophecy descends only upon the wise, the heroic, and the rich, they were recognizing that ethical activity is possible only when certain conditions have been fulfilled; for example: the possibility of determining the ways for realization and emancipation from neediness and fear.

Sin Lies at the Door

The second contradiction is expressed in the fact that moral action encounters the opposition of wills and desires within us. The serpent is not only an external threat, it is within us as a temptation to evil: "And its desire is for you, but you can rule over it" (Genesis 4:7), as Rashi interprets: "the desire of sin is the evil inclination, always yearning and desiring to make you stumble . . ." This contradiction is the hinge upon which the classical ethical literature turns, which is based upon the gap between intellectual assent to the ideal and our feelings and deeds that are opposed to it.

Fruit Tree Producing Fruit

The third contradiction is that of means and goal. Rav Kook formulates this contradiction by referring to the rabbinic statement about the earth's sin; his discussion, however, points not to a contradiction, but rather to a lack of correspondence.

The rabbinic comment is well known. The discrepancy between G-d's command to the earth, "Let the earth bring forth . . . fruit trees producing fruit" (Genesis 1:11) and its execution, "And the earth brought forth . . . trees producing fruit" (Ibid. 1:12), is the backdrop for the notion of the sin of the earth:

From the beginning of creation it was fitting that the taste of the tree be the same as the taste of its fruit. Every means strengthening any high general spiritual tendency ought to have been felt by the soul's intuition at the same height and pleasantness that the tendency itself is felt when we imagine it. But the nature of the earth, the oscillation of life, and spiritual fatigue, when it is closed in the confines of corporeality, caused it, that only the taste of the fruit, of the final tendency, the primary ideal, is felt in its pleasantness and majesty, but the trees that bear the fruit, with all their necessity for the growing of the fruit, became dense and material and lost their taste. And that is the sin of the earth. (*Orot,* Chaps. 6–7)

In his writings, Rav Kook interprets this aggadic statement in three different ways. The first—in Letter 91—links the curse of the earth to its sin. The earth did not give its full blessing; it reined itself in. And that is precisely the consolation. The world was not granted to man in its full potential, because of the danger that he would misuse it. This letter resonates with earlier themes. Thus, Rav Samson Rafael Hirsch (*Nineteen Letters,* No. 5) writes of the punishment imposed upon man: "He made difficult for man the way of pleasure, not to satiate his animal desires, in order to humble his arrogance and restore his heart to himself and to his Heavenly Father, so that he may know that there is a limit to his power and that his role and greatness must be different and higher than the things that are to be given him or taken from him." Rav Kook's interpretation comes very close to that of Netziv's commentary. "Cursed is the earth for you" is interpreted by Rashi in terms of a "parable to one who goes to bad culture and people curse the breasts from which he sucked." Netziv cites an additional interpretation: "for you—means 'for your benefit'; since the love of G-d is removed from you, it is good that the earth be cursed and you will come to 'in sadness you shall eat of it' . . . for the benefit of man." These notions of Rashi and Netziv become intertwined in Rav Kook's words in Letter 91. This first theme is supplemented with two others. The second theme turns the sin of the earth into a cosmic occurrence, a symbol of the penetration of matter into the world. A third theme is that the sin of the earth is a lack of correspondence between goals and means, and that is the third contradiction that we have raised.

It is right, in my opinion, to distinguish sharply between the first contradiction and the third. In the first, the contradiction is engendered between the ethical value and some other goal, desirable or even necessary. The paradigm of the serpent exemplifies a case in which survival itself depends on immoral action: i.e., murder. In the third, the contradiction comes about because a particular moral action requires as a necessary condition resort to immoral actions. This is the distinction between the problem of "saving life overriding the Torah" and that of "a commandment fulfilled through sin." One can, of course, ignore the first problem by regarding the goal before us as a moral value, and thus eliminate the distinction between the two types of contradiction. In my view, however, it is important to preserve the distinction between them. These are different cases, and both differ from the situation engendered by the fourth contradiction.

The Conjugation of Faces

The fourth contradiction is that between values themselves. The classic problem of traditional ethical literature is the tension between duty and the difficulties in its fulfillment, that is the first category of contradiction. But that is the problem; the decoding of one's duty is not at all a simple matter. In any given situation, one can realize different values, which bring us at times to contradictory conclusions. This means that one cannot appraise the realization of the ideal without resort to a moral dialectic.

The unity of ethical principles is represented in various ways in Kabbalistic symbolism. The immediate expression is the symbol of the *sefira Yesod*, which synthesizes opposing values: "And only from the supreme cosmic fountain, from the source of the Righteous of the world, from the source of the head of the Righteous . . . the unification of all ethical demands, which convene in the heart of every creature, and which include all social groups and unify all the worlds" (*Orot HaKodesh*, Vol. I, p. 12). Thus, there is a parallel between the partial nature of knowledge and the partial nature of ethics. The "peace" represented by the *sefira* of *yesod* is the harmony between the different parts. Rav Kook discusses the dialectic between different ideas in a letter of 5667 to R. E. Neuwirth:

I will tell his honor a most important principle, that the most enlightening outlook in matters of belief and faith, as in all lofty matters, is to emerge from the narrow sphere in which are found opposing views, which conflict with each other and nullify each other, and to reach the lofty peak from which one can observe all ideas in their root, how all of them rise up to one place . . ." (*Igrot HaReAYaH,* Vol. I, p. 84).

Different views may flow from "differences of conditions in the way of life" or "the state of souls . . . that divides them." These are different possibilities that manifest different tinges of the truth, sometimes in mutual contradiction. But this dialectic has its source in the world of the ideals themselves. Rav Kook expressed this dialectic by means of Kabbalistic symbols, the emergence of the lights from primeval man, which is a "metaphysical concept in accordance with the Divine Reason as it is grasped by general thought." We shall presently attempt to reconstruct Rav Kook's reading of this symbolism, as a claim about the existence of three different stages in the development of ideas.

The first stage is that of ideas appearing in an isolated, atomic form: "the world of *nikkudin* [points]." The second stage is the construction of faces *(partzufim),* structures made of the atomic ideas. Only the third stage, however, makes possible equilibrium, when the faces come to conjugation. The faces symbolize, to be sure, structures of ideals, but they stand in contradiction to each other and can reach balance only through the conjugation. The conjugation of faces is a Kabbalistic parallel to the Hegelian dialectic.

Ethics and History
The fourth contradiction, on the one hand, and the first three contradictions, on the other hand, confront us with two meanings of the dialectic: the dialectic between ideas and the historical dialectic of the appearance of ideas and their realization.

There is a fundamental distinction between these two dialectics. The dialectic of ideas is basically positive. The historical dialectic imitates the tension of ideas, but an additional component has entered, which is a consequence of the existence of sin.

The very existence of a historical process is anchored in the dynamic quality of the world. Ideas are not realized outside of time, but rather in an unfolding process. This process of development with elevation is the first law of reality. [Man's] exposition forces him to move beyond the bounds of nature to the essence of creation. The world whose source is in the One aspires to return there, as water "aspires" to attain a certain height in linked test tubes. This aspiration is expressed in the principle of development, which thus becomes identical with the idea of repentance.

Historical development is part of cosmic development and is subsumed under similar laws. So far they are parallel, except that historical development is tied to human action, and this can lead to disturbances in this process, disturbances that manifest themselves in the dialectical nature of development.

Part of the dialectical phenomenon is explained by the very evolutionary process. The transition from stage to stage is often accompanied by spiritual crises. Thus, for example, the human spirit sometimes attains a more advanced stage than its ideas, which did not evolve at the same pace. This gap manifests itself in crisis, like that of the great souls who cannot find satisfaction in the present spiritual reality and do not yet see the coming epoch. An additional explanation of dialectical phenomena is rooted in the existence of sin. The evolutionary process continues despite sin, but takes on a dialectical character. As a result of sin, an opposing movement appears, which highlights its mending, but sometimes this involves shortchanging other positive values. Only a synthesis of opposing movements brings redemption through conflict and pain.

There are many possible examples of the analysis of moral problems in the face of these contradictions. A paradigmatic instance is, in my opinion, Rav Kook's position on vegetarianism. We have here an ideal that cannot be realized in our age, because of the contradictions it contains, but will be realized in the future, with historical progress: "The totality of laws face primarily the future." Eating meat is an example of man's dominion over nature, and the commandments connected with eating constitute a protest against this domination: "No, the destiny of the kid is not necessarily to feed your sharp teeth, sharpened and polished by your debasement and gobbling in the eating of meat, and meat hence was not destined as a condiment to fulfill your base desire" (*Afikim BaNegev, HaPeles*, 5663, pp. 714–16).

If eating meat and shearing wool symbolize the tyranny of man in nature, then slavery is a symbol of man's tyranny in society. No doubt the ideal society is one without slavery, but the vision of this fulfillment in the present is an illusion; this, because it is only apparently that slavery describes a past legal state. There is no difference in principle between the status of slaves and that of the proletariat. The tragedy of slavery is that it is a "natural law," though, against Aristotle, the concept of natural law does not engender rights, but only determines needs. This does not mean a natural state of slavery on the lines of classic status determined a man's status, but rather that as the result of a given social situation, there is a social stratum that in fact functions as a slave class. Thus, Rav Kook writes:

That there is a natural necessity in the human condition that some of them are slaves, and if they will not be slaves by law, they will be slaves by the inherent necessity of concern for their existence, if so it is not the spirit of emancipation within the human race, except to the degree that there is less need for the labor of slaves in general, which is progressively evolving through the development of industry, through which man dominates decisively the forces of nature (*Igrot HaReAYaH,* Vol. I, p. 94).

Indeed, slavery exists in modern society too, not "legal slavery" but "natural slavery." The proletariat is composed of workers enslaved to "those who have acquired much property, who exploit them by dint of the law at the wages of poor workers for their labor." Such workers are "slaves of nature as a result of social necessity." The emancipation of slaves is not necessarily the consequence of moral progress, but is sometimes the outcome of technical development. There is a parallel to the Marxist conception of the influence of the development of technology on social ethics. Paradoxically, it is precisely the fact that slaves are no longer the property of their masters that has led to a worsening of their material situation, and made them more vulnerable:

Now we require moral arousal to care for the lives of workers, materially and morally, and the rich man whose heart is closed jeers at all moral justice; it fits his convenience that a tunnel lack light and air, although through this the lives of ten of thousands of people are shortened, and they become mortally ill, so long as he does not find himself tens of thousands of shekels out of pocket in order to establish the tunnel in a better condition, and if sometimes a mine caves in, and the workers are buried alive, he does not think of it, for he will find other wage slaves.

Law must take into consideration current social and economic data, which cause a particular phenomenon to be a natural necessity, as it

were. That is the profound meaning of the rabbinic aphorism "I created the evil inclination; I created the Torah as its antidote." The
Torah, which is indeed eternal, manifests itself as an antidote to the
evil inclination of an age: "So long as natural slavery must be habitual
in human society, I created the evil inclination; I created the Torah as
its antidote, legal slavery will temper it and restore it for the better"
(*Igrot HaReAYaH*, Vol. I, p. 95). The realization of ethics is, thus, a
function of the historical situation.

And the matter of war, it is completely impossible, when all the neighbors
were literally nocturnal wolves, that only Israel not fight . . . only with hope
to bring humanity to what it needs to be, but not to force the hour (*Igrot
HaReAYaH*, Vol. I, p. 100).

The contradiction that exists between ethical imperatives and reality
is only the result of sin:

Were it not for the sin of the calf, the nations dwelling in the land of Israel
would have made peace with Israel . . . and no system of war would have been
conducted . . . Only sin caused the matter to be deferred for thousands of years
. . . And the sin of the calf will be totally effaced . . . and the world will be
mended in the path of peace and feelings of love (*Orot*, p. 14).

The implications of this position are far-reaching:

We abandoned world politics out of a coercion that contained an inner will,
until the felicitous time arrives, when it will be possible to conduct a commonwealth without wickedness and barbarism.

Thus, exile is not the outcome of disaster and punishment alone.
Exile is a "coercion," but it contains an inner goal: the abandonment
of the historical arena in an era in which politics was possible only
through cruelty and barbarity. The hidden hand that governs history
ordained exile because our souls were repelled by the terrible sins of
conducting a kingdom in evil times:

[Jacob said to Esau]: "Let my master pass before his servant." It is not proper
for Jacob to deal with statecraft, when it must be full of blood, when it

demands a talent for wickedness. We adopted this foundation only according to the necessity of establishing a nation; once the stock took root we yielded sovereignty and were dispersed among the Gentiles, we were sown in the depths of the earth until the time of the turtle arrives and the voice of the dove is heard in our land.

"The time of the turtle [*zamir*]," the time of redemption, is not only a determined date that is approaching, but also indicates a new period of cutting off [*zemir*] oppression.

During World War I, it was possible to believe that a new period was approaching: "The grass is poised at the pores of the earth" (*Orot,* p. 14). The renewed problem of religious thought in our days in this area is rooted in the fact that this state was not realized, reality still confronts us with the problems of life in a world of contradiction. Life according to the vision of peace is still "forcing the hour."

8. THE NATIONAL IDEA

One of the central elements of Chasidut was the comprehension of "strange thoughts" and man's attitude to them. Rav Kook continued in the path of Chasidut, but what it held true with respect to the individual now became true for the community as a whole. At a Zionist meeting (Marcheshvan 5677) Rav Kook spoke of "elevating national thought and its restoration to its original quarry, for then its enterprise will be established in the land of the living, for it will draw the marrow of life with great intensity and grandeur from its source of life, the soul of authentic *Knesset Yisrael* in the light of the Eternal" (*Igrot Ha-ReAYaH,* Vol. III, p. 63).

Rav Kook taught that the idea of seeking closeness with the saintly receives in our age a new direction, a cleaving unto *Knesset Yisrael:* "One must always be connected with the essence of divine goodness that is bound up with the soul of *Knesset Yisrael* as a whole (*Orot,* Chap. 13, p. 3; *Orot Yisrael* Chap. 3, pp. 3 and 143).

Rav Kook was sensitive to the historic gravity of names and terms. I doubt that I will be mistaken if I say that he did not consider the term *Zionism* particularly successful. This position was expressed sharply by Rav Joseph Rosen (the *Tzofnat Paaneach*) who argued that *Jerusalem* has a positive connotation, but *Zion* has a negative connotation.

It seems to me that a similar notion was the basis of Rav Kook's judgment when he considered the founding of a new Zionist organization, Banner of Jerusalem. Indeed, Rav Kook had qualms about many negative phenomena connected with the Zionist movement, though he undoubtedly supported its primary enterprise, the renewal of the Jewish people.

At the center of the Zionist renaissance is not a political revolution but a human revolution. That is the first condition. The generation must know itself and its qualities (*Ikve HaTzon,* p. 107). Melancholy descriptions of the people's state are correct, but the great danger that threatens the individual and the community together is the internalization of the external situation. It happens that a generation—this is also true for a person—"tosses in its bondage in terrible torment and the oppression of Sheol." Beyond the pain is the abasement—"the terrible trouble, spiritual and material at once, alas, has darkened our world, has withdrawn the glow of glory from our lives." But beyond abasement lurks the last danger, that we may internalize the external pressure and see ourselves as debased and sinful. That is the first condition, to understand that "it is not a base generation, not a sinful generation either," this suffering generation. The general hostility of enemies, and the sympathy of those "who say that it is appropriate to pity us" have both "debased our spirit so much that we too are unable to look upon ourselves but with the eye of anger, of suspicion and abasement as if we, only we, are the wicked and the sinners, the fools, and the most unenlightened of every people on the face of the earth. Alas and alack!"

Something fundamental has changed in the modern world, and characterizes the generation. This has to do not with individuals but with the "totality of the generation." The primary difference is first of all sociological. Before us are not the actions of the individual but those of the many. The emphasis passes from the individual to the community. The obligation to struggle against contraction of the individual is pertinent to the community as well. Renewal must lead to the liberation of all powers and to their harmonious development for a sacred purpose. This is possible only in the Land of Israel. Exile is the valley of the shadow of death "and there, in the valley of the shadow of death, it is impossible to walk spaciously, it is impossible to aspire to full life . . . Therefore [Israel] must limp on his hip" (*Ikve HaTzon,* p. 114). Jacob's lameness symbol-

izes the contraction of the people's life in the Exile, from which we must
be redeemed: "But this is not the Torah of life that is needed for the
generation that is the harbinger of Messiah." Nationality is common to
us and to the Gentiles. But we must find our own way. The outstanding
example is the attitude to potency and force:

Potency is good for Israel as it is for every people, but it is our special trait
not to forget the foundation of our potency . . . We must be guided to the
same order and style of the most successful elements of our history, to the best
kings and the superior heroes (*Eder HaYekar,* p. 56).

The Jewish people rejected potency "that is all material, soaked in
blood, which at last brings the entire nation to debasement and gross
bestiality that ends with annihilation and passing from the world"
(Ibid.). This is the outstanding instance of imitation without criticism
and discrimination. We must grasp "that we have no perfect model in
the world; therefore it is impossible for us to produce a historical
process of perfect imitation" (Ibid.). We must learn from the nations
"only to the degree of a weak analogy," and what must guide is always
the authentic character of the source of Israel. Rav Kook's national
thought taught us the essence of the vision, a sense of the future "even
though it has as of yet nothing in actuality" (*Ikve HaTzon,* p. 115).

Nationalism and Messianism
The national spirit that "determines the social realm" reaches its climax in the idea of redemption.

"And G-d saw all that He had made—and it was very good." These
words end the Biblical account of Creation. However, the cosmic
harmony is immediately disturbed by sin. The world that is "all good"
became a world in which "good and evil" serve together, and in which
the shadows often outnumber the lights. The world is no longer Eden.
But with the appearance of evil in the universe comes the birth of
repentance: return to Eden, redemption, and the end of days.

When man comes to inquire about the essence of the idea of redemption and to investigate its content, he will immediately find himself confronting its varied opulence of themes. Can these themes be
systematized in any way? If we put the history of the idea in abeyance,

we may propose an attempt at systematization, by means of which we can seek to take hold of the threads controlling the entire skein.

Redemption means triumph over evil. Where is evil, if not through-out the paths of reality? The suffering of Job serves as a model of the individual's problem. Exile symbolizes national evil and suffering. War represents the evil in mankind, the sin of nations.

The thematic matrix of the vision of redemption corresponds to the division of evil. Personal evil is mended in the idea of immortality: This world is not the place of reward for observance of the commandments, but "tomorrow" is. National evil is mended in the Messianic idea; international evil, in the eschatological vision, when "nation shall not bear sword against nation, and they will not study war anymore."

Thus—a final utopian vision: a mending of the world as a whole, victory even over death, the world to come with its return to lost Eden, wolf and lamb dwelling together an emblem of peace among nations. But all this also points to the fact that the impersonal cosmos also contains violence, and the final vision of the prophets means victory over this violence as well.

These four "phrases of redemption" can be divided into two well-defined dimensions. Messianism and eschatology are historical visions. Immortality and resurrection pass beyond history, to a different world.

It is impossible to understand the idea of redemption without being aware of these four motifs. The classical sources of Judaism do not contain a systematic blueprint arranging all the themes. Each thinker attempted to construct such a framework, and created his own system-atic blueprint. In any event, Judaism was unable (and unwilling) to give up these four themes and two dimensions. The idea of a Jewish state is anchored in the awareness of this two-dimensionality.

The unique character of Judaism is expressed in values, but also in the fact that these are not grasped as the task of the individual alone, but as that of the entire community. The subject of religion is collec-tive; hence collective existence, and in its wake, independence, are important components of Judaism. The Jewish call, according to Rav Kook, is a protest against paganism. However, the call is not made by the individual but by the community:

At the beginning of this people's journey, who knew to call out in the name of the clear and pure divine idea at the time of the titanic rule of idolatry in its barbaric defilement, was revealed the aspiration to establish a great human community that would "keep the way of G-d to do justice and law" (*Orot*, p. 104).

The creation of this collective personality is part of the general Jewish aspiration:

To fulfill this aspiration it is needed precisely that this community possess a political and social state and a national seat of rule, in the height of human culture, "a wise and insightful people and great nation." And the absolute divine idea governs there and animates the people and the land with its living light. For the sake of knowledge, that not only individuals—outstanding wise men, the pious, ascetics and holy men—live in the light of the divine idea, but also entire peoples, mended and consummate with all the benefits of culture and political permanence. Entire peoples, containing all the various human strata, from the lofty artistic intelligentsia, elitist, enlightened and holy, to the broad social, political, economic classes, to the proletariat in all its segments, even the lowest and most vulgar (Ibid.).

The "religious idea" contracts the Jewish ideal to the sphere of the individual, the family, and the synagogue. By contrast, the "divine idea" extends this realm and includes in it the problems of society, the people, and humanity as a whole.

Viewing collective existence, as a people, as a central component of Jewish being, highlights the need for commitment to a set of values rather than to an isolated value.

In what should redemption manifest itself: in the cosmopolitan, in which each national being is destined to be effaced, or on the contrary, in the struggle for Jewish national renewal? Besides these two positions, there is always a third possibility—individualism. From a historical point of view, one might say that against Theodor Herzl and the idea of national redemption stood as possible alternatives Karl Marx's vision of human redemption, and Sigmund Freud, who offered to redeem the individual through consciousness of personal events. This problem is expressed in *Orot Yisrael:*

In Messiah son of Joseph is the character of Israel's nationality as revealed in itself. To be sure, the final goal is not self-limitation in national uniqueness alone, but rather the aspiration to unify all inhabitants of the world into one family, that they all may call upon the Name of G-d. And even though this too requires a special center, the entire intention is not the center alone, but its effect on the great totality. And when the world needs to pass from the matter of nationality to the totality, there must be also a kind of deconstruction toward the things that were implanted by narrow nationality, which has the faults of excessive self-love. Therefore Messiah son of Joseph is destined to be killed, and the true and permanent kingdom will be Messiah son of David's. And when the degree of yearning for the general good reaches the abrogation of the value of national uniqueness, it is one step away and evil will be exterminated from the lives of individuals as well. Thus the elimination of the evil inclination and the killing of Messiah son of Joseph are close to one another in their significance. Therefore the rabbis disagreed in *Sukka* Chap. 5 about the verse "and they shall gaze upon whom they had pierced," whether it refers to Messiah the son of Joseph who was killed or the evil inclination that was killed (*Orot*, p. 160).

The basis of this section is the classic theme of the two Messiahs: Messiah son of Joseph and Messiah son of David. The first, Messiah son of Joseph, will be killed according to the Talmud (*Sukka* 52a), interpreting Zachariah 12:10–11: "And I will pour upon the house of David and upon the inhabitants of Jerusalem the spirit of grace and supplications, and they shall gaze upon whom they had pierced, and they shall mourn for him as for an only son, and bitterly as the bitterness for a firstborn. On that day there shall be a great mourning in Jerusalem as the mourning of Hadadrimmon in the valley of Megiddo."

These difficult verses receive two alternative Talmudic interpretations: Rav Dosa and the rabbis. One said it was Messiah son of Joseph who was killed; the other said it was the evil inclination that was killed.

What is the content of the great elegy in the Messianic days? One sage states that the elegy refers to Messiah the son of Joseph who was killed. According to the other, the evil inclination will be slaughtered at the end of days, and will be mourned at that mass funeral. Rav Kook bases himself on this discussion. Messiah the son of Joseph symbolizes the renewal of Jewish nationality. Messiah the son of David represents the eschaton that will arrive after the period of national uniqueness. These are two ideals—two eras in the Messianic vision. The first will come to an end, while the second abides forever, "a true and permanent kingdom." There is a transition between the periods: "when the world needs to pass from the matter of nationality to the totality"—the transition to the cosmopolitan eschaton constitutes an overcoming of the previous period: "a kind of deconstruction toward the things that were implanted by narrow nationality." Then Jewish uniqueness will attain its loftiest expression.

When is this time to be anticipated? Rav Kook formulates his response by referring to the aforementioned dispute. The different sages, in effect, said the same thing. Messiah the son of Joseph will die when the evil inclination is slaughtered, "when the degree of yearning for the general good" waxes boundlessly in humanity; then it "reaches the abrogation of the value of national uniqueness." But our world is not that world without the evil inclination, in which "evil is exterminated" from the nations, and perhaps from the lives of individuals. The real world, the world of good and evil, places us before the first ideal of Messiah the son of Joseph. We are unwilling to compromise on the second ideal, but we can attain it only by means of the former.

But here we face an additional confrontation: that between national ideal and personal ideal. Rav Kook addressed this aspect of the problem when he avowed that the "ordinary" state is not "the highest felicity for man." In his view, the state cannot substitute for the individual's quest for felicity and truth:

The state is not man's highest felicity. This can be said of an ordinary state, which has no greater value than a huge insurance corporation, where the multitude of ideas that are the living crown of humanity float above it and do not touch it. That is not the case with a state that is founded on the ideal, and imprinted in its being with the supreme ideal content that is truly the supreme felicity for the individual. Such a state is truly the highest on the ladder of felicity, and such a state is our state, the State of Israel, the foundation of G-d's throne in the world, whose only aim is that G-d be one and His Name one, which is indeed the highest felicity (*Orot*, p. 160).

This is what Rav Kook regards as needed: to bring the individual to a recognition of the national task, which is the responsibility of society and the individuals who compose it. Some formulate the national task, which the prophetic vision places on the people, as the demand to be a "light unto the nations." So Rav Kook held that the aspiration for national existence is the mending of the world:

That is the aspiration, that comes from the force of a clear, intense recognition and the general, lofty moral imperative, to bring humanity out from under a terrible burden of spiritual and material troubles, and to bring it to a life of freedom, full of grandeur and refinement, in the light of the divine idea, and to bring happiness thus to man as a whole.

The mending of the world is too great a task for a generation as poor as ours. Nevertheless, one should not despair of this task. But one should not confuse the final task with tasks that are nearer at hand. The existence of a national task is a condition of collective existence, but paradoxically this existence will also contribute to the felicity of the individual:

True, this lofty felicity requires a very long commentary to raise up its light in days of darkness, but not, for that reason, will it cease to be the greatest felicity (Ibid.).

The Election of Israel

It is well known that Rav Kook's national outlook was crucially influenced by the approach of Rav Yehuda Halevi. The conceptual network pertaining to the status of the Jewish people in Halevi's system includes as its principal components the divine faculty *(inyan HaElohi)*, the unique quality of Israel, and the parable of the heart and the limbs illustrating the relation between Israel and the nations, the husks and the brain, the seed that decomposes and brings forth fruit. Elucidation of this entire network requires the analysis of each concept in itself and its sources. Here, however, we do not wish to treat them in isolation, but as elements in that organic system that Halevi constructed of them. Hence their clarification is a function of our comprehension of the entire system.

The metaphor of heart and limbs confronts us with the dialectic of election and the relation of Israel and the Gentiles. The Jewish people is the heart. But the Hebrew for *heart* has two meanings. Sometimes it is contrasted to the limbs; at times to the husks. The two contrasts reflect two conflicting conceptions. If heart is contrasted to husks, then Israel is the elect of the human race, the entire world was created only to serve it, or to facilitate its existence. According to the other conception, however, it is Israel that serves the world, and its election is the creation of a vessel that the world needs. The metaphor of heart and limbs (*Kuzari* 2:36) emphasizes the centrality of the Jewish people in the cosmic plan. But as it stresses this centrality, so, paradoxically, it also calls attention to the organic nature of its perspective on the world; for all the nations are limbs. Moreover, it is meaningless to speak of a heart without referring to the body as a whole and all the limbs, regardless of the role that the heart plays. The general role of Israel comes to expression at different levels. On the first plane, the existence of Israel is what makes possible the adherence of the divine faculty to it:

So too the divine faculty is like the superiority of the soul over the heart, therefore it says, "Only you have I known of all the families of the earth, therefore I will take you to account," and these are the maladies. But the health is what the rabbis said: "He forgives the sins of His people Israel, passes away the first first," for He does not allow our sins to remain upon us and cause our perdition . . . And let it not be remote in your eyes that it should say with respect to this, "Indeed our sins he has borne," and we are in trouble and the world is at rest, and the troubles that find us are cause for the correction of our ways and purging of the dross from our midst, and for our sake and our mending the divine faculty adheres to the world (Ibid. p. 44).

In the following, we shall consider the other pair of concepts, unique quality *(segulla)* and divine faculty, which seems to be central to understanding Rav Kook's position. *Segulla* represents systematically the immanent element, while the divine faculty represents the transcendent element. Election can be viewed as dependent on *segulla* or on the divine faculty. In the tension between these elements is rooted the second dialectic at the basis of the idea of election.

It is surprising that precisely in the idea of Jewish uniqueness the thought of the nineteenth century found itself close to Halevi's teaching. If we set aside the complex variations, we can distinguish two themes that ground and articulate the idea of *segulla:* the biological, racial theme and the concept of "national spirit."

The view of the Jewish nation as an entity founded on racial links was a common one in nineteenth-century Jewish thought. This can be explained, in my opinion, primarily as a result of the search for a criterion that would make it possible to define the essence of the Jewish people. Other criteria, such as territory and language, did not make such a definition possible, hence the resort to the criterion of origin, which did yield, in this case, a positive answer. The paradigm of an extended family could well describe Jewish existence.

Side by side with the idea of common origin, we find in the nineteenth century various forms of the concept of "national spirit," which derived from two main sources: the philosophy of Hegel and the German historical school of jurisprudence. The "spirit of the nation" made it possible to speak of a collective motive, inward and invisible, of a collective entity that exists beyond the aggregate of individual persons before us.

There is a certain similarity between these two directions. But we ought to note what separates them. The concept of race employs natural categories, whereas the concept of "national spirit" is connected, though not necessarily, to historical elements. The concept of "national spirit" therefore served as an appropriate key for the elucidation of the nation's spiritual and cultural creativity. This explanation of Jewish spiritual creation, however, entangled religious thought in a new antinomy, which came to conspicuous expression in the question of revelation. If the Torah and religious values are the product of the national spirit, then "revelation" is nothing but the revelation to the people of the contents of its own spirit. Revelation becomes immanent, and the concept of "Torah from heaven" loses its meaning. The unique quality of Israel—*segulla*—thus takes the place of the divine faculty.

In opposition to the classic view of revelation irrupting from the outside, there now rises a different view, whose outstanding representative was Achad Haam. He was not, however, the only proponent of such a view. Various Reform thinkers like Geiger and Kahler were influenced by ethnic psychology, which was developed into a scientific doctrine *(Volkerpsychologie)* by Moritz Lazarus. As Jacob Petuchowski rightly comments, the classic Reform outlook found a support precisely in the teaching of Halevi.

This dilemma, between immanent and transcendent doctrines of revelation, is clearly expressed in Rav Kook's thought, when he addresses indirectly the problem of heteronomy. Rav Kook was not satisfied with the heteronomous position. His primary criticism of this position is not philosophical but ethical. Heteronomous religion and ethics mean the imposition of norms coming from outside, which are opposed to man's natural inclinations. Thus, putting the Torah on a heteronomous foundation means the positing of transcendence, the acceptance of "Torah from heaven," but at the price of constant tension and conflict, existential trauma with the most severe psychological and sociological implications. Thus, the problem of religion would be not theological but anthropological. The big question that must be asked, according to Rav Kook, is not that of "knowledge of G-d"—i.e., the question of theology—but rather:

Knowledge of G-d in the earth—that is, of the ethical effect that theological studies have had, in their opinion negatively, upon the human race and a burden upon his ethical and natural development . . . (*Eder HaYekar*, p. 37).

The solution to this problem is the idea of election. The essence of election is rooted in the fact that there is a correlation between revelation and the spirit of the people. Election is manifested in the link that exists between the spirit of the nation and revelation, "that all the good and all the truth is already implanted in *Knesset Yisrael* inwardly, that is our eternity and the everlasting life planted in us of the Torah of truth . . ." (*Igrot HaReAYaH*, Vol. I, p. 45). The realization of this correspondence is not assured beforehand, hence it does not exist among many peoples:

And it is not far from the truth, with respect to most nations, that their dim, attenuated knowledge of G-d is not worthy to the basis of their being and existence, and is not for them an abiding nature and national subject (*Eder HaYekar*, p. 37).

Testimony to this lack of correspondence can be found in the rebellion of a part of Western culture against the so-called "Judeo-Christian" heritage. The election of Israel means, according to this, that Israel does not regard ethics as an external imposition but as an expression of its deepest aspirations.

Many peoples accepted the Bible and its values, but sometimes this was a superficial acceptance. Great men strove "to make of idolatrous peoples adherents of Jewish ethics sanctifying themselves with the feeling of divine sanctity . . ." while this feeling was merely "garb and husk" (*Igrot HaReA YaH*, Vol. I, p. 45). The German neo-pagan revolution was a tragic expression of this fact.

The correlation between these planes does not distinguish Israel racially; it characterizes man in general. In this context, election is no more than primacy, for this harmony is the stuff of the eschaton. On that day, it will belong to mankind as a whole. Moreover, it is not true that in the life of Israel the harmony is realized without difficulties, for at times it appears that there is a contradiction between the demands of ethics and religion and the natural inclinations of man. Rav Kook's response is that these contradictions indeed seem to exist, but they are the consequence of defects that "did not come about through the influence of the Torah" and any problematic situation "depends on some flawed understanding of the Torah on our part, or some accidental cause." Ethics and religion are not just a revealed teaching, they are also an integral component of man's self-realization. The contradictions are destined to diminish "from generation to generation, and things become straight on their own with serenity and sanctity" (*Eder HaYekar*, p. 37).

Rav Kook expresses this synthesis by means of Kabbalistic symbolism, interpreting the formula "for the sake of the unification of the Holy One, blessed be He, and His Shechinah":

Complete conjugation of *Knesset Yisrael* with the Holy One, blessed be He—meaning the equation of the will that is revealed in the nation as a whole, in the foundation of its soul, with the revelation of the divine tendency at the foundation of being as a whole . . . And for the supreme level of *Knesset Yisrael* there is no separation between the inclination that is revealed by the influence of the divine life in being as a whole and what is grasped by the nation as a whole, and for the sake of this we aspire with all our deeds to the unification of the Holy One, blessed be He, and His Shechinah (*Orot*, 141).

Knesset Yisrael, symbolizing the *sefira* of *Malchut-Shechina*, represents of course Jewish being. However, according to Kabbalistic tradition *Knesset Yisrael* is the essence of all being, and in this world this essence flows upon the Israelite nation literally (Ibid. p. 138).

Tiferet (also referred to as *HaKadosh Baruch Hu,* "Holy One, blessed be He") symbolizes revelation, not only as the revelation of Torah, but in the broader sense, as "the influence of divine life in being as a whole." This is the transcendent element that makes itself manifest in being as a whole, but it can still stand in contradiction to the "will that is revealed in the nation as a whole, in the foundation of its soul." The equation of these two wills is the essence of the aspiration "with all our deeds to the unification of the Holy One, blessed be He, and His Shechinah." The unique quality of Israel is expressed in the "spirit of the nation," which is linked by an umbilical cord, as it were, with the "spirit of G-d." The immanent is bound up with the transcendent:

The spirit of the nation that is awakened now, which many of its supporters say they have no need of the spirit of G-d, if they could truly establish such a national spirit in Israel, they could represent the nation in a state of defilement and destruction, but what they will they know not themselves . . . So that even he who says that he has no need of the spirit of G-d, as he says that he desires the spirit of Israel, then the Divine Spirit is present in the heart of his point of aspiration even against his will. The private individual can detach himself from the source of life, not so the nation *Knesset Yisrael* as a whole. Therefore all the possessions of the nation . . . all of them are suffused by the divine spirit: her land, her language, her history, her customs.

And if there is found at some time such an awakening of spirit, that all these speak in the name of the spirit of the nation alone, and make an effort to deny the spirit of G-d from all these possessions and from their revealed source, which is the spirit of the nation, what should the saints of the generation then do? . . . They must labor greatly to reveal the light and the holy in the spirit of the nation, the light of G-d in all this, until all those who uphold those thoughts of the general spirit and all its possessions will discover themselves standing rooted and living in the life of G-d, shining with the sanctity and potency of heaven (*Orot,* p. 63).

The election of Israel implies a correlation between the transcendent and the immanent. It is the adherence of the people "in all the depths of its soul to the living G-d, in a deep natural demand from the profundity of its being" (*Maamrei HaReAYaH,* Vol. I, p. 74). This resonance, between what is revealed from heaven above and what wells up from the depth of the soul, is the banner essence of the election of Israel: "Not the potency of the horse or the thighs of man, not with army or with force, not with riches or majesty do the individual or people triumph, but with the element of the source of true life, which is found only in the divine faith, clear and natural from the depth of the nature of the soul" (Ibid.).

This link is not present only in the totality, it extends to individuals as well. That is the meaning of the eternal covenant between G-d and Israel: "This His covenant stands forever." It is not the result of an individual decision, of conscious assent, it is rather the expression of an existing state "in the nature of the intrinsic soul of the nation as a whole and the children of this nation" (Ibid.). This is the *segulla* of Israel.

Secularism

One last remark is required on the nature of secularism. One can only grasp secularism as a dialectical phenomenon. Dialectic means that progress does not always follow a straight line. At times it is motivated by the impulse of an inner conflict that causes it to pursue an indirect course. When there is a deficiency in "fear of heaven," there appears an opposing tendency. The decadence of faithful Jewry in the late nineteenth and twentieth centuries led to the "quality of opposition, spread by books, newspapers and influences, and there the destruction is very great, until one cannot abide their stench, and nonetheless is taken from there an essence of boldness and strength, and potency of will, and possesses the quality to fortify the intensity of life . . . and of the two forces together a world will be built and a people will be built" (*Orot HaKodesh*, Vol. III, p. 34). Hence the first commandment for any group is humility: "It is a bad sign for a party if it thinks that only with it is the source of life, of all wisdom and all righteousness, and that everything outside of it is vanity and waste of spirit" (*Igrot HaReAYaH*, Vol. I, p. 17).

An optimistic view of reality is not apologetic. In one of his most popular essays (published 5692), Rav Kook compares the Zionist renaissance to the digging of wells (*Maamrei HaReAYaH*, Vol. I, p. 72). There are those who despair at the first obstacles and withdraw, tired in body and weak of spirit. But those who continue the backbreaking work are fated to an even graver disappointment. They reach the water level, "and a flow of water has burst forth . . . but the water is turbid, mixed with mud and sand, and will not succeed to slake the thirst of man or beast." Here is another source of despair, but the source of despair is shortsightedness: "Only because we have not yet come to the desirable depth, to the place where the fresh, soul-restoring water flows . . . do we see as yet only turbid waters."

Not yet a utopian vision of the future. We have here a sober estimate of the present, which discerns its two sides: "Now it seems that the days have come when no man can deny that the well of renaissance has begun to flow with water . . . and there is a sprout of righteousness for the House of Israel and all humanity, but again the proclamation of the despairing calls out in public: The waters of the well of renaissance are turbid, they sweep with them debris and mud." Rav Kook's answer is extremely simple—we have not dug deep enough; "let us dig deeper the well of renaissance in matter and spirit . . . and the well of Israel's living, pure waters will gush, and a fountain from the house of G-d will go out and irrigate the river of Shittim soon in our times. Amen."

There is an element of tragedy in the tension and breach between the various aspects of our identity. As we shall see, this breach is a source of power and weakness at the same time.

Rav Kook commented on the breach between our national and religious identities, employing the biblical-Midrashic-Kabbalistic account of the creation of woman, as the result of the primordial hermaphrodite man's partition or severing into a man and a woman (*Orot*, p. 142). The separation of *Knesset Yisrael* from its adherence to the Holy One, blessed be He, is impossible. It has a "natural necessity" and "continues to appear in all generations." But "days are coming when a deep sleep falls upon man, and the visages are severed from one another, until complete separation becomes possible." Adam, who was originally two-visaged, was cut in two. This surgery partakes of tragedy, but it is also a new opportunity, implying the end of a natural connection "back to back" and the possibility of a new unification resulting from "rational choice." This free choice leads to complete unification, "like the joy of a bridegroom over the bride your G-d will rejoice over you . . . The end of the severing is the content of construction, which brings about consummate unity, and the Torah returns to its students . . ." The severing initiates a new unity of love, which replaces the previous natural unity. The original natural unity of nationality and religion must arise again out of love.

Our problem today is not the same as that discussed by Rav Kook, but resembles it. Again and again we confront the problem of severing, now between our political being and our religious and national identity. The many dimensions of Jewish identity serve as the source of sharp conflicts in whatever affects the short range. These conflicts obscure the positive significance of this multidimensionality, in which are rooted the people's power and ability to overcome the numerous crises throughout the generations. This determination is valid with respect to the collective identity in the past, how much more so for the possibilities of personal identity in the present. Our strength today is precisely the haziness in our identity, which enables a connection to Judaism even to Jews whose Jewish being is hazy and partial. Precisely for that reason, and here I advance my own opinion, this haziness that has not become an ideological plan makes possible, through its blessed inconsistency of many ideologies side by side. This may make possible that final integration, unification out of love, the goal of our generation according to the vision of Rav Kook.

Here is an additional meaning to the concept of repentance. Jewish existence is beyond division into camps (*Maamrei HaReAYaH*, Vol. I, p. 76). One of the foundations of our thought is the conviction of the benefits of individuality, which determines that there is value to the distinctions and differences among human beings. However, the existence of camps "blocks the road of mending and perfection on both sides." The struggle among camps does not enable "repentance," correction within the camp itself. On the other hand, division "like an iron wall . . . between camp and camp," prevents the illumination coming from above "on Israel the entire nation." Ignoring labels is the first condition of correction: "We have no other counsel, however, but to remove the names of these Baals from our camps . . . Let us make ourselves known each to his brother by the general name of Israel, not by the name of a party or camp."

9. FAITH

We will grasp the significance of Rav Kook's approach to faith if we examine it in its appropriate context of other modern positions. Although the radical enlightenment and the materialists seemed to have dealt classical theology a fatal blow, modern thought was impelled to confront a problem of prime importance. How is it that religion—the funeral of which had already been held in the eighteenth century—has yet to disappear? The religious phenomenon became a mystery. Let us briefly note a response—one among many—that was offered for this riddle. I refer to the psychoanalytic answer. Without entering into complicated details, let me remark on one of its central ideas: that the religious phenomenon is the result of the transformation of another phenomenon. Its energy is borrowed libido, sublimated sexual energy.

The foundation of Rav Kook's thought is stamped with the assumption that we have indeed two distinct sources. True self-love exists; it is the same blind substance that Arthur Schopenhauer, the great German philosopher of the past century, described so well. His system crucially affected Friedrich Nietzsche and Sigmund Freud.

Rav Kook did not directly address the views of Freud. I can conclude nothing from his silence as to his familiarity, or lack of it, with Freud's doctrines. Rav Kook certainly knew Schopenhauer and Nietzsche. Some of his reactions to Schopenhauer are relevant to other positions as well.

The blind will, "the conserving element of being," is nothing but a manifestation of "being, established with such refinement and infinite illumination, with such consummation and general perfection, that it lacks nothing in intensity and force" (*Orot HaKodesh*, Vol. II, p. 482). This blind will is a reality within man, and within the entire universe it is "the force of blind will that is so active in the fullness of the world of sense and imagination, feelings and aspirations and human thoughts, and in all the sensed universe, as the conserving element of being" (Ibid.). This conserving element is, I believe, a kind of cosmic inertia. Rav Kook agrees in principle that this doctrine tracks a reality, but not that it describes all reality: "Schopenhauer's outlook on the matter of will is not remote in itself, its evil is only that instead of understanding it as one of the visions of reality, the adherent of that approach understands it as all reality and its cause . . ." (Ibid. p. 484).

Together with this force, which is the deepest expression of the libido, there is another force, which is the result of the aspiration to perfection. To be sure, this is true not only for religion: "Therefore, then, any work of the human spirit, its purpose and inclination is to perfect that inclination that includes all that it contains" (*Maamrei HaReAYaH*, Vol. I, p. 33).

Religious thought had to fight against reductionism—that is, against the attempt to make religion a reflection, projection, or superstructure of something taking place in an entirely different realm. The primary significance of Rav Kook's position is precisely the emphasis on the existence of an additional, independent principle, side by side with the libido principle. This principle elucidates the religious phenomenon but also all higher human creations, which often appear, in the eyes of the reductionist, to be parasitic entities concealing the primitive, egoistic animal that lurks, according to their view, in each one of us.

Below we shall note additional corollaries of Rav Kook's outlook on the religious phenomenon. Here, we must first address another aspect that links us to the metaphysical assumptions of Rav Kook's thought. From Feuerbach on, certain circles have grasped the religious phenomenon as the projection of a specific structure of the human personality. An instructive example of a confrontation of this sort is Martin Buber's critique of Carl Jung's psychological reductionism. Buber defended the personal-dialogical conception at the basis of religion. I do not think it would be mistaken to suggest that Rav Kook would have responded differently. Yes, indeed personal conceptions contain an element of necessary projection, but instead of being a projection of what is in you, they are that of the reality in which you, in some sense, are included. As we saw above, the panentheistic approach must complete our Weltanschauung.

The Nature of the Spirit of Faith

It seems not to be an error to say that the Divine Spirit is a result of the irruption of a transcendent revelation, while faith is the revealing of the immanent truth within man. Faith is "the most fundamental self-disclosure of the essence of the soul . . . and when its natural path is not corrupted, it does not require any other content to support it, rather it finds everything in itself" (*Maamrei HaReAYaH*, Vol. I, p. 70).

The faithful spirit is exhibited in the phenomena of the various religions. Even if a society attains its full ethical and social development, "pitiful are the people, the essence of whose life is void of the animating light of pure faith . . . Pitiful is the people that has no divine faith" (*Maamrei HaReAYaH*, Vol. I, p. 74). The necessity of faith is a consequence of the fact that any given situation, in any image presented by "logical reason," is only a poor contraction of the truth, a partial shadow of the "supreme image of spiritual enlightenment" (*Maamrei HaReAYaH*, Vol. I, p. 75). In this faith, man's true essence comes to expression, which is beyond what human reason can determine.

If we focus on man, bracketing meanwhile revelation, we will confront two alternative paths, emotional and rational: "The feeling of outpouring of the soul that is also the source of the religious feeling, or for philosophical, scholastic enlightenment, whose power and boldness is negation" (*Ikve HaTzon*, p. 135).

The religious feeling is universal. "Negative investigation" is elitist, it must preserve the feeling "from the shadows of illusory fantasy."

In the Jewish people, a third source is revealed—"aspiration to the divine ideals"—manifest in the life of the individual and the totality, which are expressed in a religious-historical phenomenon: adherence to G-d despite suffering" (*Ikve HaTzon*, p. 136).

In employing Kabbalistic symbolism, Rav Kook hints that fear of heaven corresponds to the *sefira* of *Malchut:* "The quality of fear of heaven has not of itself anything." Therefore it is not itself a character trait. It is possible "that it is liable to debase man and humanity to the greatest abysses, just as it is likely to raise them to the highest welkin" (*Orot HaKodesh*, Vol. III, p. 23). The most correct definition is one that sees it as a treasure: "the treasure of fear of heaven in which all is concealed." When it becomes unified "in the foundation of its source," then it is the source of all blessing. Then it is, according to Kabbalistic symbolism, "a glorious crown [*ateret tiferet*] over those sustained from the womb." *Malchut* (also called *Attara*) conjugates with *Tiferet*, and receives its positive influence from the *sefira* of *Chesed*, "for she is the daughter of the generous, the daughter of Abraham our patriarch who was called generous, her name was *Bakol* [in all, the source of all blessing]" (Ibid.).

The conclusion is that faith has good and bad aspects (*Orot HaKodesh*, Vol. III, p. 19), and man must study deeply to gain the key to it "in order to know how to put everything in its place," and to mend the difficult features. The basic source of religion is universal. It may draw upon "universal consent," but that, as we have seen, is not enough. Religion is so basic that it accompanies man from his personal and collective developmental cradle. But precisely for that reason, it may be accompanied by immature ideas. Had religion appeared at a relatively more advanced stage of development, man would relate to it through more mature categories. But no generation can be bare of religion. For that reason, we confront a problem. Faith is accompanied by "immature ideas with many obtuse and dark things mixed in" (Ibid. p. 21). This darkness is double. It is rational-intellectual but also "natural," a term that is not distant from what contemporaries would term "existential." Feeling is not enough, whence a broadened obligation of Torah study.

Fear of heaven requires study (*Orot HaKodesh,* Vol. III, p. 21). However, this is not study as when one teaches a discipline, even if we give this discipline primacy "as the simple meaning of the verse—the beginning of wisdom is the fear of G-d." It is a discipline that is part of all other disciplines, just as the teaching of language cannot be a "special subject of study," but must penetrate "every part of its literature." We have no right to contract ourselves to the teaching of the grammar and syntax of fear of heaven. Its loveliness depends on the breadth of creation that is achieved through it.

10. BETWEEN RELIGION AND SCIENCE

Our discussion of the "spirit of faith" leads to another central issue: the relation between religion and science. Religious thought struggles against atheism.

According to Rav Kook, the true struggle with atheism does not deal substantially with theology but with anthropology. Not knowledge of G-d but knowledge of G-d on earth: "There came the pioneers of atheism and said that the divine concern in not at all relevant to man, for life can follow its order in matter and spirit even when human beings divert their attention from the truths of religion" (*Maamrei HaReAYaH,* Vol. I, p. 10).

This we see overtly. For instance, every intelligent person knows that there is no concern at all for sustaining faith, neither in the general divine foundation of theoretical knowledge of G-d, nor for the sanctity of the Torah in practice, respecting any state of astronomical or geological knowledge. In general the Torah has substantive relation, in terms of its revealed aspect, only to the knowledge of G-d and ethics and their ramifications in life and action,

in the life of the individual, the nation and the world, for indeed this knowledge, which is the crown of all life, is the foundation of all and includes all.
But as to the forms of knowledge that are investigative or sensate, which are
weightless sparks by comparison to the general knowledge of the knowledge
of G-d and the sanctity of life, it makes no difference with regard to the words
of the Torah, and there is no difference, for example, between the views of
Ptolemy and Copernicus and Galileo, etc. So regarding the most novel things
that exist or that might emerge, and all the opinions that follow the paths of
investigation and inquiry from time to time. It is already very well known that
prophecy takes its parables for human instruction from what is common in the
language of human beings at that time, to incline the ear as it is able to hear
in the present. And the time and justice the wise heart knows. (*Eder HaYekar*,
p. 38).

Rav Kook's addition of the phrase *at present* modifies the original
meaning of the rabbinic dictum: "the longest of human beings." It is
accepted that this statement refers to problems that stem from the
nature of man and his epistemological limitations, with their biological
and psychological bases. Adding "at present" points to differences
deriving from the historical situation of a particular period. The Torah
speaks in every generation in the language of that generation, though
the immutability of revelation is expressed in principles that transcend
the changing features.

This is the context for the closing reference to Kohelet 8:5: The wise
man knows the time in which things were stated—i.e., the historical
conditions that serve as the background of prophecy. Rav Kook's continuation illustrates with two examples:

"And it is like Maimonides as interpreted by Rav Shem Tov in the
Guide (end of Part III, Chap. 7), and the simple meaning of J. Talmud
end of *Taanit* regarding the breakdown of dates of the ninth of Tammuz."

I have discussed the first example elsewhere; the second refers to JT
Taanit 4:5. According to the Mishnah, "Five things happened to our
ancestors on Tammuz 17 . . . and the city was breached." The Talmud
asks about Jeremiah 39:2, which states that the city was breached on
the ninth. According to Rav Tanchum b. Chanilai, "There is a breakdown of dates here." This statement is also applied to Ezekiel 26:1. The
simple meaning of this Talmudic statement implies an error in count-

ing, so that as a consequence of the troubles, they no longer knew the correct date. The prophetic books thus transmit to us an imprecise date (the right one being the seventeenth). As the *Korban HaEda* comments: "as a result of the troubles they erred in counting, and Scripture did not wish to alter what they had relied on to indicate, as it were, 'I am with him in his troubles' (Psalm 91:15)." Before us is a case of "incorrect" information in which absolute truth is subjugated to some reason pertinent to the needs of the generation or to take its problems into consideration.

Rav Kook goes on to write of the nature of scientific information:

And the truth reasoned from the depths of Torah is much more lofty and elevated than this, for human images, however they might be with respect to the form of reality, certainly also have a particular path in the development of man in his ethics and other high vocations, to each generation according to its changing images, to harmonize everything to the goal of the general good and eternal divine grace, and the inner concept, which is the pure knowledge of G-d and practical and rational ethics, this abides forever. Indeed the people are hay, hay is dry, grass withers, and the word of our G-d abides eternally (*Eder HaYekar*, p. 38).

This last statement emphasizes the eternity of revelation ("the word of our G-d") as opposed to the temporary—the beliefs of each generation as expressed in scientific theories, but also in the human images of each generation that serve as the context of revelation. Thus, we need not seek revelational authority for exegesis that we feel fits the Ptolemaic theory, and to reject, on its basis, the "new astronomy."

In one of his letters, Rav Kook utilizes Kabbalistic terminology to deepen this interpretation, namely the concept of *tzimtzum*. Creation of the finite world is the consequence of *tzimtzum*, a transition from the infinite to the finite. Rav Kook discerns *tzimtzum* not only in creation, but in revelation as well:

The Midrash states, "To reveal the power of the act of creation to flesh and blood is impossible, and therefore the text says simply, 'In the beginning G-d created.' " And most important is the knowledge derived from all this in knowing G-d and the life of true ethics. The Holy One, who measures out even the spirit upon the prophets, engaged in contraction, that these great matters will enter into precisely these images that man will be able to draw upon, with all their effort, that which is most useful and lofty for them. And the precious light and that which is of little account, which are the secrets of Torah, which in this world are dear but will be taken for granted in the world to come, only He will reveal the details of the matters (*Igrot HaReAYaH*, Vol. I, p. 91).

"The power of the acts of Creation," the true essence of Creation, cannot be fully described. Every description is partial and to some degree a distortion. The "acts of Creation" in the Torah are only a contraction, and the precious light and that of little account (*kippaon*, Zachariah 14:7) are the esoterica, priceless in this world yet of little account *(kafu)* in the future world (*Pesachim* 50a), meaning that what is concealed from you in this world will rise to the surface in the world to come (*Bemidbar R.* 19), and become revealed. The contraction of the esoteric into the exoteric, according to Rav Kook, is the resolution to the problem of the relation between the Torah and science; it presupposes the basic distinction between esoteric and exoteric. The thought of the Scriptures is not *exoteric* but *esoteric,* and its true understanding is distant from a simplistic reading of the biblical text. We find in the exoteric, by contrast, only commandments and ethics, based on a fundamental axiom—knowing G-d—which is the true exoteric content of the Genesis pericope. There is no contradiction, for the Torah, as exoteric, does not transmit information that could come into conflict, in any form, with the claims of science. The information of the esoteric, on the other hand, can perhaps be called "philosophical" but certainly not scientific. Only in the end of days, with epistemological progress, will man attain the gradual revelation of the secrets.

The Genesis Pericope

Let us illustrate these principles through a concrete discussion of the exegesis of the Genesis pericope in Rav Kook's teaching. In this discussion, there is a clear but implicit distinction between two types of problems: problems we shall call formal, and substantial problems. The former refer to all those arguments about contradictions of scientific truths whose negation does not impugn the essence of the Torah. The substantive problems seem to refer to those religious principles that are necessary conditions for the possibility of religion. Without any doubt, the latter problems are more important than the former, but require a high level of sophistication, by contrast with the other, more immediate, and more noticeable problems.

Here is an example of the application of this analysis to the Genesis pericope: The contradictions between the Torah and the results of geology can be formulated in two ways. They can be raised as a question about the traditional dating of the age of the world, as opposed to other datings on a different scale, yielded by geology and cosmology. But a question can be asked about the meaning of the concept of Creation, as opposed to Darwin's theory of the evolution of the species.

The first question receives a curt answer. In Letter 91, Rav Kook points to the existence of many statements in rabbinic literature and classical exegesis, that indicate a much longer chronology than that of the traditional calendar; though, to be sure, some of these statements are open to different interpretations, they enable one to accept in principle the claim that the world is very old.

But for a full understanding of the section, we must resort again to the distinction between esoteric and exoteric. One cannot understand the essence of Jewish doctrine without the esoteric; the exoteric contains no "scientific information," for it is only the platform for "knowledge of G-d" and observance of the commandments. This does not prevent us from counting years, for practical purposes, as things appear from the simple "exoteric" meaning of the text.

As to the counting of years from creation in relation to contemporary geological calculations, it is the prevalent position that there were many eras before the present chronology. It is well known among all the ancient Kabbalists and Midrash Rabbah, that "He constructed worlds and destroyed them" and in the *Zohar Vayikra* that there were various kinds of people other than the man mentioned in the Torah. However, one must understand well the deep phrases that require a very broad interpretation . . . For we count according to the simple meaning of the Torah verses, which affects us more than paleontological knowledge, which do not have with us great value. The Torah certainly spoke in simple terms of the acts of Creation, and spoke with hints and parables, for all know that the Genesis pericope is included under the esoterica of Torah, and if all these matters followed the simple sense, what would be hidden here? (Letter 91).

However, the problem of the age of the world is a secondary problem. Rav Kook devotes attention to the primary problem. Paleontology contradicts, it would appear, not the details, but the substance of the Genesis pericope. A full comprehension of Rav Kook's response requires the analysis of prevalent nineteenth-century paleontological theory. But though the debates on these matters have dated, Rav Kook's position is not essentially connected to them, as he demonstrates an interesting ideological alternative that can contribute to our understanding of the problem. Rav Kook faced two alternative theories, tied to the names of Cuvier and Darwin. According to Cuvier, the father of modern paleontology, the evolution of species is the consequence of creation followed by destruction whose remnants can be observed in the discoveries of paleontology. Darwin's theory, however, stresses the evolution of species without leaps and without the intervention of supernatural causes.

The understanding of Creation according to Cuvier, as comprising creation and destruction, parallels strikingly Rav Abbahu's claim that "the Holy One created worlds and destroyed them" (*Bereshit R.* 9) and the Midrash on the verse "These are the genealogies of heaven and earth when created" (Genesis 2:4) that "wherever Scripture says *and these* it adds to what precedes; wherever it says *these* it eliminates what precedes."

This understanding, which views Creation as a series of creations and destructions, was accepted by several Jewish thinkers in the nineteenth century. It was the view of Rav Gedaliah Lifshitz *(Tiferet Yisrael)* in his famous *Derush Or HaChayyim.* According to this theory, he interpreted the Genesis pericope. The opening verse refers, according to him, to the first creation, while the second verse already presupposes the existence of a destroyed cosmos: "And the earth was null and void, etc., means that it had again become ruined and desolate." Of the prehistorical era, Rav Lifshitz writes, "In my humble opinion those human beings in the ancient world who are called pre-Adamites in German, I mean human beings who lived in the world before the creation of the present Adam, they are the 974 generations mentioned in *Shabbat* 88 and *Chagiga* 14, who were created before the present world."

This outlook corresponds to Rav Lifshitz's view of geological discoveries. The fossils of prehistoric animals are so strange "that one cannot imagine that they came into being except by a world revolution that occurred once by Him, may He be blessed, who chastises the sea and

turns it in an instant . . . So too there are found in the depths of the
highest mountains of the land sea creatures, who became hardened into
stone. And a wise man, the scholar Cufier [*sic!*] is his name, wrote that
of all the 78 kinds of animals that they found beneath the earth, there
are 48 species that are not extant . . . And we have already learnt of
the bones of a gigantic animal . . . And another species of animal was
discovered, called megalosaurus . . . From all of this it is clear that what
the Kabbalists transmitted to us these several centuries, that there
existed a world at one time, and was destroyed again and established
again . . . all of this is now elucidated in our time with truth and
rightness . . ."

A similar approach is also found in Eliyahu Ben-Amozag's commentary on the Torah *Em LaMikra.* What is especially remarkable is the
significant change in the treatment of the statement "G-d created
worlds and destroyed them." Medieval Jewish philosophy wavered
between eternity of the world and *ex nihilo* creation. The construction
of worlds and their destruction is problematic to both approaches. The
common resolution is to regard these worlds as possible worlds, of
which our world is the most perfect, for He said, "This I wish, those
I do not wish." This interpretation supported the accepted rationalistic
interpretation. For Kabbalistic exegesis, on the other hand, this statement received (in addition to symbolic interpretation) its full significance, e.g., in the doctrine of Sabbatical cycles. If we ignore specific
arguments, the modern geological theories appeared to fit very well that
esoteric Jewish doctrine, so long as one followed Cuvier's position on
the existence of a succession of natural catastrophes.

Rav Kook refers to this doctrine, though he does not mention Cuvier
explicitly: "If so, then those excavations demonstrate to us that there
were eras in which creatures existed, including men. But that there was
not meanwhile a general destruction and a new creation, this nothing
proves, there are only hypotheses in the air, which we need not be
concerned with at all."

This implies that Rav Kook held that there are no decisive proofs
for the Darwinian explanation. However, Rav Kook does not see it as
his task to give a scientific answer to the question, as it were. He wishes
rather to posit the fundamental claim that the Torah is not to be
harnessed to any specific scientific theory, even one that appears better
to fit the simple meaning of the verses: "In truth we do not need all

this, for even if it became clear to us that there was an order of creation in the evolution of the species, then too there would be no contradiction . . . for the basis of everything is what we teach in the world, that all is the act of G-d, be the intermediaries many or few, myriads of myriads, they are all the acts of G-d (cf. *Guide* Part II, Chap. 48) whose world lacks nothing, and there is no end to His potency and the intensity of His wisdom and majesty, blessed be He and blessed be His Name forever. And sometimes we mention the intermediaries too by name, in order to broaden the mind, and sometimes we leap over them, saying 'And G-d created' 'And G-d established' as we would say 'Then Solomon built' rather than that Solomon commanded his ministers and the ministers those beneath them, and they commanded the architects and the architects the artisans and the artisans the simple laborers, because this is the known practice, and is also not of prime importance. So too whatever is investigated in many myriads of years by increasing the ways and means that augment our reason and intellect with the greatness of G-d they are, most of the time, abbreviated" (Letter 91).

Rav Kook offers us an alternative, without deciding. The two positions differ not only as disputing paleontological theories, which imply differences in the approach to specific texts. The dispute is deeper. Before us are two differing conceptions of Creation. According to the first approach, Creation is a historical event, a breach in the order of nature whose source is transcendent. According to the second approach, the concept of Creation is out of the bounds of science, which deals with intermediate factors. The two approaches are close to the two types of positions on the concept of Creation that crystallized in medieval Jewish thought. Rav Saadya Gaon, for example, represents one kind of position, according to which Creation can be demonstrated on the basis of the laws of nature and certain empirical data. According to Maimonides, by contrast (and Rav Kook's reference to the *Guide*, Part II, Chap. 48 is not fortuitous), Creation can neither be proved nor disproved by natural science. Creation, i.e., the relation of the world, whose existence is contingent upon the necessary existence, is a question that lies outside absolutely from the realm of scientific discussion.

Detailed study of Rav Kook's discussions indicates that it does not yield an unambiguous stance describing the facts and one authoritative exegesis of the Genesis pericope. In this matter, we face uncertainty, which our generation may not overcome. This uncertainty opens before us various possibilities, all of which are legitimate in the framework of Jewish thought.

What was Rav Kook's personal opinion regarding the alternatives? We have seen that Letter 91 seems to imply support for the position that views Creation as an irruption in the natural order. On the other hand, in *Orot HaKodesh*, Vol. II, p. 537, Rav Kook indicates that the doctrine of evolution might be more attuned to "the secrets of the world of Kabbalah than all other philosophical doctrines."

A study of his teaching, under its different aspects, confirms that this was indeed his true position. But here too one cannot simply identify his approach with that of evolution. The contention has to do not with details of data but with the philosophical interpretation of evolution. One can look upon evolution as the result of the accumulation of accidental occurrences, or it can be understood as a process of development and elevation guided by a supernatural cause: "The evolution that follows the path of elevation . . . We find in it the divine matter illuminated with absolute clarity, that only the actualized Infinite brings forth to actualize what is infinite in potential."

Evolutionism is thus a principle operating in the cosmos, but it is not the only principle. When we look upon the great richness in the world, we are forbidden to deny the perfecting power, the revolution and mutation, the power of the leap:

Our eyes see that all is boundlessly great, the rule of development is great without measure and end, and the leaping power is endlessly great . . . The same axiomatic approach asserting that there are no leaps in reality, which is similar in its slackness to all the negative judgments of the ancient philosophies regarding concrete reality . . . which turn out to be chimerical more than their positive judgments (*Ikve HaTzon*, p. 154).

The world is a great chain of beings, in which all possibilities are realized, one of which is the leap. Were there no leap, the very absence of the leap would constitute a leap—"a leap of breach and destruction without mending and building, for that is indeed impossible to exist" (*Ikve HaTzon*, p. 154).

Rav Kook's discussion of the Genesis pericope is in fact an exemplar of his treatment of the problem of religion and science in general. But in addition to specific arguments in each one of the problematic areas, two major conclusions must be set down in order to elucidate the claim that the history of conflict between religion and science must be viewed in the context of mankind's spiritual development:

A) The changing understanding of the truth is itself part of the divine revelation, a constant and progressive revelation. What is revealed has significance, just as there is significance to that which was concealed in certain generations.

But all these require time and preparation, and the narrative images, whether they follow upon the survey of creation according to reason or whether they come from the revelation of G-d's hand through His prophets, must always carry with them the power that aggrandizes life and true success, not to trap for man some disconnected knowledge with which he may toy childishly. When you understand this well, you will know that there is a lofty value to what is revealed, and also to what is hidden, and the ways of hiding are many and great, marvelous in the pathways of the supreme wisdom of the Master of all acts, Marvelous Counsel, blessed be He (Letter 91).

B) The changes in religious thought that take place as a result of the conflict also take part in the constant revelation: "And in general it is a great rule in the war of ideas, that any opinion that comes to contradict something in the Torah we must not first reject, but rather build the palace of the Torah above it, and thus we are elevated through it, and for the sake of this elevation the views are revealed, and then, when we are not oppressed by anything, we may, with heart full of confidence, make war against it as well" (Letter 134).

The formulation here is ambiguous: Constructing the "palace of Torah above it" might appear to be a purely tactical maneuver. But it is more than that. The term *elevation* surely is reminiscent of the parallel Hegelian term. To quote Rav Nachman Krochmal, "The great German philosopher who lived in our generation, in speaking of this inquiry, commented that the word *aufhebung* in his language indicates both removing a thing and elevating it to a more true and abiding reality . . ." (Simon Ravidowitz, ed., *Moreh Nevuchei HaZeman*, Chap. 7 p. 290).

If we merit it, the conflict will become an opportunity: "Precisely through them [the new discoveries] the divine light will become greater and more lofty that progressively illuminates the light of Israel, by the effervescence of the idea that they bring about" (*Ikve HaTzon*, p. 155).

11: ATHEISM AND THE IMAGE OF MAN

"All controversies of opinions in the human race, within each people and tongue specifically, and even more specifically in Israel, stand ultimately on a moral base." Rav Kook says this not only about a particular conflict. Every historical process is tied, according to this claim, to an ethical infrastructure. This position of Rav Kook should certainly be observed in the context of other treatments of the problem, against a Hegelian backdrop that reads human history as the unfolding of spirit, and the Marxist approach, which views human history as a reflection of the development of the means of production, and according to which ideas are no more than an echo of economic and social history.

Rav Kook represents a third position contrasting with these two options. Rav Kook maintains that behind conflicts of ideas one can observe social, economic, and political struggles that stand upon the "moral base," in other words, that constitute a part of the moral development of humanity.

The other feature of the tension between science and religion, pertaining to the exoteric side of the Torah, is none other than the moral significance of modern scientific discoveries.

The discoveries of astronomy and geology expanded the space-time horizon of man. This expansion implies a sense of man's humility and insignificance, which manifested itself not in humility toward the Creator and meekness, but rather in the negation of the value and values of human reality. That is the primary meaning of the creation pericope and of biblical faith:

Thus *Knesset Yisrael* needed to strive mightily with all the idolaters, to teach them, that despite the vastness of creation man is, nevertheless, not so contemptible that there is no value to his ethical conduct, for the ethical creation of man is very important, immeasurably greater than that of the largest creatures (Letter 91).

In *Orot HaKodesh,* Rav Kook again stresses the importance of this problem:

Cosmological thought also brought about a great change in the manner of spiritual life; the ideas soaked up from the petty image of the total world according to the old astronomy in a state of quiet and smallness befit that pettiness of a contracted environment. The new general spirit, which came in the wake of the scientific expansion of the sense image with respect to sensate being, must initiate, with its spread among many multitudes, a new form for the spiritual world and its entire context of thoughts, that requires much study, how to reestablish everything with perfect consummation while preserving most successfully all the fundamental truth in the old (*Orot HaKodesh*, Vol. I, p. 559).

Therefore there is a new need for a study "that will erect the spiritual content upon its illuminating foundation, so that it will continue to add radiance through the good that will be assembled by the expansion of all new cognition, after they are brought into correspondence with all the good that is stored in all the old in its pure form." This function is the task of religion.

"G-d's Providence is the basis of human ethics and its success" (Letter 91). Meaning: Pure religious faith represents the only theoretical basis for ethics and the only motive that will bring mankind to ethical life. When this element, this comprehension, "becomes elucidated well in the world with great and clear knowledge, it will become the basis of felicity: 'They shall not do evil or corrupt upon my entire holy mountain, for the earth will be full with knowledge of G-d.' " This is knowledge of G-d, the primary content of the exoteric in the Creation pericope. This primary approach enables us to look upon the entire issue of relations between science and ethics in the modern age.

All know that wisdom and talent relate to the ability to strengthen and aggrandize the intellectual or practical ability of man. Ethics, indeed, is to mend the human will, that it should desire the good. Now if human capability increases sevenfold, but his goodwill does not develop according to the guidance of perfect ethics, then the multiplication of his powers will encompass only his disaster (*Eder HaYekar*, p. 36).

Human development in the modern age is primarily manifested in human "aggrandizement of ability" and depends on steady progress in two areas: science (wisdom) and technology (capacity). The Industrial Revolution, at its various levels, new scientific tools, machines, and, as an anachronistic aside, computers, "relate to the ability to strengthen and aggrandize the intellectual or practical ability of man." But this presents only one side of reality. Human activity is judged not only by its power, but also by its direction. This additional factor, which posits the purpose of human activity, is expressed, in the text we are examining, by the contrast of "will" and "ability." Just as "ability" is founded on science, so in the essence of "will" dwells the ethical. The central problem of progress is the danger that "if human capability increases sevenfold, but his goodwill does not develop according to the guidance of perfect ethics, then the multiplication of his powers will encompass only his disaster."

This point pertains to the problem of relations between ethics and science. It is accepted and clear to us today that any attempt to create a theory unifying ethics and science, deriving moral imperatives from scientific propositions, is misguided a priori. This is not only a practical judgment, for as we have already seen, scientific progress does not imply moral evolution. From a purely conceptual viewpoint, we recognize no possibility of bridging the gap between science and ethics. There is no transition between *is* and *ought.*

Rav Kook understood this very well, and regarded this fact as one of the crucial problems of our era. We confront a fact, behind which is concealed the imperfect state of man and of the world. Though these forces appear to be parallel, "they are unified in their source," "and as man adds knowledge, he will recognize more the unity of factors that are revealed in different styles."

This unity of ethics and science is a "personal nexus" *(unio personalis)* comprehended by man, who is both scientist and ethical individual. But, Rav Kook believes, a "real nexus" is also possible. Revealing this unity is undoubtedly part of the meaning of redemption.

Human history is the road to redemption, but it is not necessarily linear. The existence of the modern world depends on the requirement that scientific progress be accompanied by the development of ethics and justice. This is the function of Torah, with its nearness to that "One" who is the source of all reality. "The perfection of man," the construction of that world of which it is said, "If the righteous willed it, they could create the world" (*Sanhedrin* 65b), will become possible only "through the complete combination of the two powers in their fullness, the ability and the will in their consummate goodness." Without this combination, they are, as it were, riches preserved for their owners' undoing.

From this perspective, one can observe the relations between religion and science. One should not look upon these relations from a purely theoretical angle, as if they were expressions of an ideological struggle between worldviews that alter with scientific development. That is the trouble, that the true implication of scientific revolutions with respect to religious truth is nugatory.

To be sure, scientific development has raised certain problems that we have noted above, but these problems ought to be no more than stages in the development of human ideas.

And were it not for the hatred engendered, for example, by the poor demeanor of Catholicism, which took pride in its belief in G-d and the sanctity of Scriptures, but comported itself badly in the hearts of many pursuers of free culture, and so too other faiths sanctifying Scriptures, but acting badly with respect to human ethics in the name of their faith, it would never occur to anyone to whittle away at faith by means of new systems, neither past, present nor future (*Eder HaYekar*, p. 38).

What turned development into conflict derives from the existence of a severe moral problem that comes to expression in social iniquity, political oppression, and economic injustice. Thus, the struggle is not an episode in the class war, but a stage in the moral development of mankind. Hence, at the "moral foundation," the "antireligious" struggle serves the religious and spiritual development of man, as a reaction to chains and cages with which medieval religion locked up life and human thought. The tragic conflict in this situation comes from the fact that this moral revolution has taken the form of an ideological war against religion.

From this analysis, it appears that the intellectual revolution that constructed the modern world contains two levels, ethical and theoretical, between which rigorous distinction is required.

Referring to the conflict in Israel and the nations, Rav Kook writes:

Both [atheism based on ethical basis and that based on scientific basis] are nourished only by superficiality of the scientific and ethical understanding. It is only with the passage of much time and expatiation that the literature of atheism could present itself as a scientific literature, for which there is no place according to its character; that is, with all its "stretching of paws" nothing but an ethical literature of corrupt fantasy. It never occurred to any of the great thinkers of the human race, even to those counted as deniers like Epicurus the Greek himself and those like him, to think that they could bring scientific contempt upon the knowledge of G-d in itself, but rather upon "the knowledge of G-d on earth," i.e., the moral influence that theological studies exert, which was in their opinion bad for the human race and an obstacle to its moral and natural development (*Eder HaYekar*, pp. 36–37).

As we have already mentioned, the "stretching of paws" is evoked by Rav Kook in other places as well, especially in discussing vegetarianism and cruelty to animals (*Hazon HaTzimhonut VeHaShalom*, p. 13). The source is known: "The pig, when he wallows, extends his paws as if to say—See that I am kosher . . ." (*Bereshit R.* 62:1). The barb of the image is that the pig, in a way, is right: his paws display the sign requisite for *kashrut*. But this moral "propaganda" comes to conceal other, more severe defects. The irony in this situation is that in every conflict, however debased its true motives, they will appear as the defenders of moral values, as the lonely guardians of purity, truth, and justice. Extending the paws indicates that in the struggles of movements against religion in the name of social justice, there usually are concealed signs of defilement and base motives. This does not exempt the religious man from taking account of those signs of purity exhibited by the pig, meaning the defects in his own life.

From a purely theoretical point of view, science can only reach agnosticism: It cannot rise "to the knowledge of G-d in itself," because the gates of inquiry into problems that diverge from the narrow empirical range are shut in its face. By contrast, the conflict represents a heavy accusation against negative phenomena that accompany the major religions. This accusation is so severe that the revolt against theology is nothing but a consequence of the fact that religion was "in their opinion, negative to the human race, an obstacle to its ethical and natural development."

In summary, the "literature of atheism," which rose up against religion in the name of science, is not "a scientific literature, for which there is no place according to its character," insofar as it is a metaphysical literature that goes beyond what scientific methodology ("the scientific vision") makes possible. It is not "with all its 'stretching of paws' nothing but an ethical literature of corrupt fantasy." These last words hint to the fact that, though one should not identify absolutely and simply with this revolt, the dispute nevertheless reflects the need for social and ethical improvement of religious society.

"Therefore the uprising of atheism, when it arises in the world in general, and then infiltrates as an unnatural sickness in Israel, could not stand, except through the protection of some ethical merits, that would have no place were it not for accidental defects and laxities among the bearers of the positive views, and these set up some basis for the denial that comes with scientific arguments."

The openness of Judaism to the modern world brought the "uprising of atheism" to Israel, as an "unnatural sickness." But with respect to this "infiltration," we must distinguish between two levels—the theoretical and the ethical. If we understand Jewish thought properly, we cannot find anything in it that is liable to precipitate substantial conflict with science. This thesis we shall discuss below. That is not the case at the ethical level. The conflict succeeded in "infiltrating" the Jewish world and to "stand . . . through the protection of some ethical merits, which would have no place were it not for accidental defects and laxities among the bearers of the positive views." Indeed, there were defects in the social structure of the Jewish people, not defects intrinsic to the Torah of Israel, but "accidental laxities" among the "bearers of positive views," and these weaknesses are responsible for the birth of the conflict. Verily, the responsibility of the religious Jew is doubled. Not only must his Torah have integrity; that obligation also rests upon him personally.

Religion and Self-Realization
In the texts before us, we sense an additional theme, an echo of those spiritual movements that rose up against religion in the name of the ideal of human liberation and what is today called "self-realization." Here is the root of an important problem augmenting that "ethical element" concealed behind the historical process or the intellectual polemic. To be sure, the classical question is still formulated, as ever, as a theoretical contradiction between scientific information and religious dogma. But the real problem that requires our full attention is

whether religion is truly "negative for the human race and an obstacle to its moral and natural development."

This problem became most important and crucial as the focus of discussion moves from the natural sciences to the social sciences. Hence the need to address the question within this context. Here too the response of the religious individual would seem to be obvious: denial of all these claims. But Rav Kook concedes something: "And this is not distant from the truth. Rav Kook's answer thus contains a presupposition that is simultaneously paradoxical and self-evident. The claims in themselves are true but not significant, because they refer to "religion," which is merely an abstraction. Indeed, there were religions that were "an obstacle to the moral and natural development" of man. "And this is not distant from the truth with respect to most of the nations, whose dim, weak knowledge of G-d is not worthy of being the foundation of their being and existence and is not for them an abiding nature and national subject."

In various instances (examples can easily be found in the history of the civilized world), there is a contradiction between the values of national culture and the values of the religion dominant in that nation. This is the case for religious values that contradict ethics, as well as values that oppose man's "natural" life.

It is the opposite of the thought of the Gentile inquirers, and in Israel those who follow them, who take the Bible according to Christian interpretation, through which the world becomes a prison. But the pure understanding of the joy and light of life, in the Torah . . . (Letter 134).

We are accustomed to regard cults that extol orgies, for example, as idolatry. But is the offering of sons to Moloch, negating the joy of life and its light, any less idolatrous? This is substantially Rav Kook's attitude: "Not like these is the portion of Jacob . . ." If so, how does the problem appear in the framework of empirical Judaism? Rav Kook claims that there may be "defects." These deficiencies must be understood, in his opinion, in the light of two principles:

1. Either "it is connected with some corrupt understanding of the Torah on our part." 2. Or "sometimes the situation made it necessary to enter some deficiency in order to be spared a greater deficiency and destruction, which would otherwise have occurred."

This situation corrects itself from generation to generation, and this correction constitutes, in itself, part of the constant revelation of Torah and halacha: "When the nation does not does undergo an increase of destruction and negation, which ruins the whole secret of material and spiritual existence, it is very easy to mend, to diminish such necessities, from generation to generation, and things straighten out of themselves in serenity and sanctity."

Rav Kook adds a third claim, which he repeats elsewhere and pertains to the issue of "natural development." One cannot speak of a "uniform nature" of man. Thus, what engenders conflict in one society may not in another society. Rav Kook here is proposing the existence of a social or national psychology characteristic of different groups. Thus is reminiscent of the spirit of the nation in Achad Haam's approach, for example. But there is an important distinction. As we have seen above, the Torah was not created by this "spirit"; it was revealed to the people because of the potential harmony between its laws and the spirit of the people. This is true, according to Rav Kook, both for the rational commandments and for those that do not apparently have any reason.

The major idea implied here is that, at all levels of reality, our obligation is never that of affirming one part while negating another part, but rather the harmonious development of all components. This applies both to thought and to practice. Man's role is to combine all types of things "and the greatest combination-refinement is that what is revealed to the eye is that it has no dross, that all is life and good" (*Orot HaKodesh*, Vol. III, Preface, p. 26). This is a mission that can be called epistemological, and that we have noted above. But at its side there is a practical mission that is not merely cognitive. We are obligated to be aware of the fact that evil is a consequence of our knowledge of the world: Knowing the quality of our knowledge and our elevation to a higher level will lead us to liberation and redemption. The classical concept of *tzeruf* refers to the "knowledge that has no dross." This applies to the cognitive and theoretical planes. At the practical level, this fact takes on a different, fundamentally dialectical, expression. We cannot divide the options facing us by means of a dualism of good and evil. We may not affirm part by rejecting part. The metaphysical principle that evil is merely a privation, and that whatever exists contains a holy spark, engenders the knowledge that "all is life and good." All values are positive, and ethics ought not to decide between them, but rather seek the harmony of values: "The values must only be estimated properly." Ethics must seek the measure and quality of complementary values. "The useful side requires that it be in the correct measure in everything, whether physical or spiritual, and the scientific side must strive to know how to value everything, and then there is no adversary or impediment" (Ibid.). Value itself must be measured: It can neither be nothing nor absolute. Obliviousness to this principle is what has led to "moral dross," to tragic problems that often had implications for faith.

Fear of heaven did not weaken the powers of the ideal religious person. To the contrary, it fortified him, and caused him "to actualize every quality hidden in his soul." It led not to spiritual lameness and fragmentation of powers, but to their elevation and sublimation. This is true in the anthropological realm too, and thus in the educational as well. One can view education as a process that leads to the development of certain capacities at the expense of others. One can regard as the desired goal "discipline," social or self-imposed, heteronomous or autonomous. But that is not the ideal. The goal is not the attenuation of the human flame, but its enlargement and direction.

Thus, indeed, we can comprehend the religious anthropological project. It may be that at the initial stage the fear of G-d touches man "only in the external aspects." It is a law imposed upon man from the outside. Man obeys but thereby generates a contradiction between the inner essence of man and the external law. At this stage, "fear of G-d . . . has not transformed the wildness and wickedness, steeped in his materialistic nature, and in the nature of the defiled soul concealed in the depths of the sediment of human life . . . Hence man becomes attenuated of life, and communality becomes impaired" (*Orot HaKodesh*, Vol. III, Preface, p. 28). But this is merely the first stage. At the second, superior stage, when fear of G-d penetrates the depths of the soul, a new harmony is initiated. Man is transformed: Conversion takes the place of repression. A revolution takes place in man, transmuting evil into good, and then, "Material potency is weakened, and ideal potency takes its place" (Ibid. p. 29).

The anthropological project applies to the concept "service of G-d" *(avodat Elokim)* as well. This phrase does not fully capture its own meaning. The language implies the idea that we are enslaved to a king who imposes upon us his yoke at his pleasure. But we must not be deceived by this language, which should be treated like the corporeal terms we apply to G-d (*Ikve HaTzon*, p. 142). Like all similar concepts, this too must grow and develop with us. True service is beyond fear, "beyond petty egoism, at the level of lofty service, clear and luminous" (*Ikve HaTzon*, p. 155).

The Torah is not "service" but a network of "lofty ideals and mighty, faithful divine counsels as to their actualization for all times" (*Ikve HaTzon*, p. 145). Our exploration of the realization of these ideals is the "service" to which we are bound.

12. THE DEVELOPMENT OF MAN

So far we have examined the different highways that man must traverse. We must now look at various stages in his development, using *Orot HaTeshuvah* as the key.

Rav Kook speaks of three orders—actually four—in repentance. These are, in effect, different stages in the development of man.

Natural Repentence: Man pursues his self-interest. Rav Kook refers to three areas of human activity, which appear before man, in some way, as normative: "the laws of nature, ethics, and the Torah" (*Orot HaTeshuvah*, Chap. 1). By the laws of nature, Rav Kook does not mean physical cover laws, but the network of norms set before man in his natural life, e.g., the principles of hygiene and health. Beyond the natural realm, there are two additional ones—the ethical and the Torah: the laws of ethics and the laws of the Torah, i.e., the commandments. These three planes contain two additional dimensions—the individual and the collective. They apply both to the individual and to society.

The common tendency of thinkers is to distinguish sharply among these areas. Rav Kook finds continuity, moreover, an inner unity, between them. Different approaches are possible in all three. To take Kant's example, for instance, man protects his life out of instinct, egoistic self-interest, but a miserable, suffering man who does not commit suicide is not preserving his life out of instinct, but sometimes against it, out of obedience to a different law.

The Natural Level: This is the level of the man who judges his acts according to their consequences, and obeys the law because of the belief that the law indeed brings man to health and happiness. This is an activity guided by caution and utilitarianism, and if we allow ourselves to use a classic term not employed by Rav Kook in this context, this is the characteristic type of *shelo lishmah* (not for its sake) behavior. The basic example of natural repentance is medicine. One could include all three categories discussed above under the rubric of "medical art."

The Spiritual Level: This is obedience to the law heard in man's inner voice, "what is called the chastisement of the reins," i.e., conscience. It is a natural rectitude that utilizes psychological suffering in order to restore man to the better and to encourage him "to return and mend the warped."

Conscience is not always a faithful guide. "It has several modes of deception." The inner voice that we hear sometimes misleads us. It is utterly silent when man's soul is corrupt; it may even become an evil servant.

The Torah Level: It is based upon the authority of the Torah and halacha.

The Rational Level: This is the ultimate level of autonomy, in which "not only physical, or psychological and spiritual, sorrow and not only the influence of tradition and revelation . . . but the clear recognition, stemming from a perfect world outlook and life . . . is already full of endless light" (Ibid.). This is the resolution we achieve after we have passed through the previous stages, and this is the repentance of love, of which the rabbis spoke.

That is, indeed, the content of love; no longer is it obedience to an external necessity that continues to be external even when it speaks with our inner voice. Love is obedience to the law we legislate, which we regard as identical with the law that comes from without.

13. ART AS PARADIGM

Discussions about art in halacha and Jewish thought often focus on prohibitions of graven images. This approach is not illegitimate, but it is an oversimplification of reality. Even if we assume that certain channels of artistic expression were shut by these prohibitions, there undoubtedly remain other directions. At the side of this approach is a second position that connects the Jewish attitude toward art to exile and the accompanying alienation. Beyond the historical question, we stand here before the fundamental problem of art's place in the construction and crystallization of the human ideal of Judaism.

To the search for an answer to such a question are attached obvious halachic components. Are not such occupations a waste of time that should be devoted to Torah? Despite the decisive importance of this question, our point of departure will be the search for the anthropological roots of art. If we translate this question into the language of the sources, we will discover that several positions have been proposed for our dilemma.

The first answer can be found in the thought of Maimonides. Elucidating his doctrine of prophecy, Maimonides sets down his fundamental psychology. This doctrine distinguishes between two basic aspects of the soul: intellect and imagination. In contrast with the intellect, the image of G-d in man, the imagination is, according to Maimonides, a lower function. It is needed for certain operations; even in the learning process there is a decisive place for imagination, which abstracts various components from the sense impressions and creates the images that will give birth to abstract concepts. The imagination is indeed viewed as the ancilla of intellect and as a channel of intellectual experiences that could not find expression in any different form. But what is the status of autonomous imagination, which is to be regarded as the source of art? Maimonides' position on the operations of imagination can be summarized by means of an excerpt, in which he refers to them as incorrect images and illusory opinions: "All this is being swayed by imagination, which is in truth also evil inclination, for any deficiency in speech or traits is the operation of imagination or is influenced by its action" (*Guide,* Part II, Chap. 12). Imagination is thus the evil inclination, in contrast with intellect, which gives man truth and good: "And this is the verse, 'In Your light we shall see light,' that is the same thing, for in the emanation of intellect coming from You we shall be enlightened and made right and attain the intellect" (Ibid.).

This, in my opinion, is a faithful summary of Maimonides' view. The operations of the intellect are so positive that they precipitate a broadening of the definition of Torah study: "Those matters called *pardes* [including philosophy] come under *Gemara*" (Laws of Torah Study 1:12).

Gemara includes science and philosophy, to the degree that at the highest level a man might, while preserving in his memory the Written Torah, devote his time "to *Gemara* alone, according to the breadth of his heart and the steadiness of his mind" (Ibid.). We are given the portrait of a man who realizes the contemplative ideal while being "an artisan busy with his work" (Ibid.), meaning that he is living an active life in human society. For this ideal, I am afraid, there is no room for art in its wider significance. I have no doubt that in application of the principles stressed in the cited excerpts, we will have to view art not only as a species of time-wasting but also a negative phenomenon, stemming from imagination, which is the evil inclination, the source of every intellectual and moral defect. Art, thus, is dangerous, insofar as it is a kind of continual revolt of "obscure" forces against the rational order determined by the intellect. This is one side of the issue.

However, we must remember that art has another side, based on its effect on man, especially the masses. This feature contains the potential positive influence of art. Thus, the true criterion for judging these creations is pragmatic: "Know that the poems composed in any language are only to be tested by their subject matter, and should be treated like speech as we have already classified." Maimonides refers to his classification of speech: speech that is completely harmful; speech that is both harmful and useful; speech that is neither harmful nor useful; speech that is all useful. According to this classification, many works of art will enter, if not the first category, at least the third, which the rabbis defined as idle conversation, "and the pious strive mightily to avoid these matters."

This is one possible approach and is implied by Maimonides' anthropological principles. But one can derive from his system a different approach. Imagination may become a vessel receiving the afflux of the intellect, capable of absorbing and reworking it. This possibility leads us to distinguish between three types of men represented by the "sects"

(*Guide,* Part II, Chap. 37). The first is the sect of the wise when the influence descends upon the intellect alone. The third sect is that of "governors of cities, lawgivers and magicians, fortune-tellers, dreamers of true dreams, and those who perform wonders by strange crafts and secret arts." These receive inspiration of the imagination alone. In between is the second sect, that of the prophets who receive the afflux "upon both powers together, I mean the rational and the imaginative . . . to the extent of their perfection in creation." Though Maimonides deals here with a different range of operations that he attributes to the imagination, a reality connected with practical reason and its action in the world, there is no doubt that the same analysis would apply to the operations of the imagination itself.

This approach makes possible a new evaluation of the operation of imagination and its works. An example of it is found in the writings of Rav Zadok HaCohen of Lublin: Imaginings and thoughts that are idle and trivial in the mind and heart of each person are literally like dreams that are dreamed through the imaginative faculty.

It would seem that such imaginings and thoughts are negative, and as the products of the imagination, they are lower than the products of the intellect. But this is not true. The imaginative faculty in Israel has been mended:

Therefore the idle imaginings of Israel, since they flow from the *Chochma, Binah, Daat* in him, they have a concrete and true solution upon the place that they flow from, save that they are garbed in idle words. This is the "chapter of folly" mentioned in *Zohar* (III, 47b), from which one can gain understanding of matters of wisdom and this is like the interpretation of a dream, for the imaginative faculty is also one of the powers that G-d founded in the mind and the major element of prophecy is from it as I have heard (*Tzidkat HaTzaddik* No. 203).

A third evaluation of the essence and character of art can be derived, in my opinion, from a novel approach to the nature of intellect and imagination represented by Rav Nachman of Braslav. According to Rav Nachman, prophecy not only employed the imaginative faculty, it also mended and refined it:

Through the spread of prophecy the aspect of the imaginative faculty was refined and mended, as (Hosea 12) "in the hand of the prophets I shall cause imagination." For the principal mending and elucidation of the imagination occurs when it is in the hands of the prophets. And when the imagination is mended, thus the true faith of holiness is mended and deceiving beliefs are annulled, for the principal faith depends on the imaginative faculty (*Likkute Moharan* 8:6).

The imaginative faculty is not only a means utilized by the intellect: It is independent and reveals to us a reality opaque to intellect. But there we face a harsh alternative. On the one hand, it may be "that the imagination muddles and confuses man with deceitful beliefs . . . of folly and falsehood that are the filth of the serpent." On the other hand, faith, in its entirety, depends on the imaginative faculty: "And Your faith at night—that is the aspect of faith that is dependent on the imaginative faculty that is under the aspect of night, like the nocturnal dream that comes through the imagination."

Here, art confronts us in its full strength, power, and menace. It can express the filth of the serpent, but it can reveal to us a world opaque to intellect. This thesis Rav Nachman demonstrates in his tales, which sought to give appropriate expression to the truths of Kabbalah and Chasidism.

Rav Kook's position is bound up with the previous ones. It is interesting to note that he saw the greatness of the Land of Israel not in the fact that wisdom attains there its highest level, but rather in the fact that imagination there is mended. This explains why only the Land of Israel sustains prophecy. This approach is at the root of a vision of birth of a new Jewish art:

Imagination, in the Land of Israel, is clear and bright, clean and pure and capable of the appearance of divine truth, of dressing the high and lofty object of the ideal tendency in the supreme holiness, ready for the explication of prophecy and its lights, for the gleaming of the Holy Spirit and its shining. The imagination, in the land of the Gentiles, is obscure, mingled with darkness, with the shadows of defilement and filth, it cannot soar to the heights of holiness and cannot be the basis of the afflux of divine luminosity that rises above all baseness of the worlds and their boundaries. Because intellect and imagination are intertwined, act and are affected one on the other and one by the other . . . The air of the land of Israel makes wise (*Orot*, pp. 10–11).

The purified imagination will bestow its power also on the renewal of wisdom in the Land of Israel. So far we have elements that are relatively close to the previously discussed views. However, a new theme is here added. According to Rav Kook, art has an important role in human history. In his preface to the Song of Songs, he writes that man must actualize all the spiritual concepts imprinted upon the depths of the human soul, and that as long as even one line hidden in the depths of the soul is missing, has not been actualized, the work of art is obligated to educe it (*Olat ReAYaH,* Vol. II, pp. 3–4).

For the medieval rationalistic approaches, art—as the work of the imagination—stands in contradiction to the intellect that takes man beyond it. For Maimonides, the imagination is an instrument, a channel, through which revelation passes from what is beyond it, from the intellect. For Rav Nachman, the channel becomes the main source of this revelation, through which man grasps the secrets of Creation that are impenetrable to the dull chisel of intellectual activity. Rav Kook in effect returns to the first conception. Art reveals what is concealed in the depths of the soul. But this revelation is not to be regarded as the action of the evil inclination. To be sure, there are manifestations "whose burial is their elimination, for whom was ordained the shovel upon our side to dig and to cover"—i.e., self-censorship is necessary. "Woe unto him who uses his shovel for the opposite result, to increase its stench."

However, this is a partial aspect of reality. One is not to divide the capacities of the soul, its mechanisms and works, into good and bad. This value judgment does not correspond to psychological discriminations, but severs them. Each one of the faculties of the soul may express good or evil. "The tremors of the soul resulting from feelings of natural love, which takes a large part in reality, in ethics and in life, are worthy of interpretation by literature in all the manners whereby it actualizes what is concealed." However, such creation must preserve itself "from a tendency to intoxication that inheres in these feelings, that transforms them from natural purity to hideous defilement." From the viewpoint of art, that literature that ignores natural love is flawed, just as it is flawed when it fails to express the "high and lofty tremors . . . that flow from the love of the Master of all things." Indeed, the flaw is not something intrinsic to the work of art but something in the personality of the artist, who introduces it in his work and defiles it. Precisely "worthy men of holiness" must renew Jewish art.

What is true for art is true for other forces acting on society. We cannot be sure what Rav Kook's attitude would have been toward the electronic media that have come to influence the lives of the masses. Rav Kook wrote—at the dawn of the century—about one of the decisive factors of that time, of literature. We can be radically critical of literature, but we cannot deny its influence, "and since literature affects it so much, it is evident that the thought content of it has the effect, even though much triviality is in it too . . . Nevertheless, if it had no basis of thought, it would be impossible for it to persist and captivate so many hearts for systematic destruction and consumption" (*Ikve HaTzon*, p. 110).

The conclusion here too is that human perfection cannot be achieved through psychological lameness: "For a man cannot conquer any of the powers of his soul that they be bound and imprisoned, that they shall do nothing, unless he subjugate them with the ropes of man and by the cords of love to the good and the righteous . . . Then he will emerge from slavery and become free" (*Ikve HaTzon*, p. 112).

Maimonides' famous distinction between the "naturally righteous" and "he who conquers his inclination" (Introduction to *Avot*, Chap. 6) receives here an anthropological reading. The conflict of inclinations is the initial stage, beyond which man attains "a different . . . fear." The conclusion is that indeed "all the natural inclinations stand ready in their expansion, to fulfill the divine vocation, the good and the enlightened . . . Therefore, there is no banished power, there is no downtrodden thought—rather, all is luminous, all is alive, all is ready to serve with the serving angels (*Ikve HaTzon*, p. 113).

14. RAV KOOK'S PEDAGOGICAL POEM

The opening chapters of *Orot HaKodesh* include a complete educational plan scattered among the various sections, not always consecutively. I cannot surmise if we have here a unified work affected by editing, or whether Rav Kook used stray opportunities to write the various sections. However, it is clear to me that we have an orderly, complete system, confronting the various pedagogical problems of renascent Jewish education. Let me summarize this system, the pedagogical poem of Rav Kook, as a paradigm of the practical implications of his teaching.

One might regard education as a practical discipline. The anthropological vantage point—the image of man toward which one educates, the right and duty to educate, the problem of values, are examples of areas in which philosophical and pedagogical issues overlap. The sections before us touch upon more technical matters: curriculum, frameworks of teaching, educational tools. But here too technique overlaps with philosophy. Pedagogy in fact derives its foundations from epistemology, but it is linked to other disciplines in the study of scientific method, logic, and methodology. One should stress the importance of educational philosophy:

> It is permissible to seek aid from the good practitioners of the pedagogic art and from their attempts to make easier the burden of study . . . and there would be no criticism of this . . . when it is liberated from the intermingled elements of destruction . . . when the most important is there, when there is preservation and action, Bible, Mishnah, and Talmud (*Eder HaYekar*, p. 59).

One of the main pedagogical principles is that we must, in the interim, set up a special curriculum. It is geared to the human being who has not attained his full development. This involves making peace with an imperfect, concrete reality, somewhat like a "world as yet unredeemed." But such characterization is insufficient. Our age is an "interim time" (*Orot HaKodesh,* Vol. I, p. 51). The ultimate solution is not yet possible for man despite the fact that he feels "the general thirst" for it. The concrete historical situation in which we act bears crucial significance.

After this remark, we may illustrate some of Rav Kook's educational principles. Two stand out in particular, one cognitive, one axiological.

Kabbalah, in Rav Kook's thought, is the basic grammar, the fundamental logic, of the universe. Despite the vast distance between the different levels of reality (the cosmological, the sociological, the ethical, for example), they all have a similar structure, which finds its expression in Kabbalistic symbolism.

The *sefirotic* framework symbolizes cognitive progress. Man stands before the particulars of the world, represented by the *sefirot* of construction *(Chesed* through *Malchut).* Beyond these lies *Binah*—the breadth of the river, according to accepted symbolism—and this is the creation of the "general values" beyond the particulars (*Orot HaKodesh*, Vol. I, p. 53). A prevalent image of *Binah* in Kabbalah is the dove hovering over its nest and young. This is the fundamental operation of insight "extracting the actual from the potential, life and the hidden light in each and every particular through penetrating insight" (Ibid.).

Binah (insight) works on external data: "It is the inference of one thing from another; there is always need for something to come, to be sowed in order to enter the circle, until life shines, the life of insight." Beyond lies *Chochma* (wisdom), "which is original and does not need to take its creations from subjects outside itself" but is rather built "from its own midst" (Ibid. p. 57).

Another important educational process is called "internalization." At the first stage, values are imposed upon us by external authority. In advanced stages, this authority becomes internal. This process is truly crucial in education, but as we shall see, the schematic description we offered above is incorrect. Human development is symbolized by the transition, in Kabbalah, from the small side *(katnut)* to the great side *(gadlut)*:

Then comes the period of greatness to man, which demands of him that his actions not be the rote commandments of men, but that each action and each habit, each service and each commandment, every feeling and every idea, every Torah and every prayer, shall be illuminated in the hidden light, the general light, that is hidden in the supreme soul, before the appearance of their operation (Ibid. pp. 53–54).

"Greatness" is achieved not through internalization, but by uncovering the hidden light within man. Actions disclose the hidden light; they do not create it.

In the distinction between wisdom and insight is located the difference between the wisdom of the sacred, which is the product of revelation, and human rational creativity. The interaction between these two domains explains two tendencies in Jewish theoretical literature (Ibid. p. 68). I do not think it would be an error if we illustrate Rav Kook's words with two concrete examples: 1. "Theoretical service:" Rav Moshe Hayyim Luzzatto sought to give the Lurianic Kabbalah a logical form, to make it a rational system "although not all the depth and not all the height . . . can enter the framework of logical analysis," just as, in the language of Kabbalah, not all the lights can enter the vessels. "In any event, as much as can enter those vessels . . . is supernal good" (Ibid.). 2. A second example is the transformation of philosophical system into Kabbalah, like the utilization of Maimonides' *Guide* by the Kabbalists: "the second service, is to introduce the logical order of the heart . . . into the world of supreme freedom."

The Wisdom of the Sacred and Secular Studies

One of the general distinctions appropriate to many different areas of reality is that between information and energy. I have no doubt that the kernal of the Musar movement founded by Rav Yisrael Salanter is the awareness of the gap between moral consciousness and its active fulfillment. The answer to theoretical questions about concrete behavior becomes secondary to the central problem of practical conduct. The Socratic paradox, how is it possible that a man knows what is good and nevertheless does evil, now becomes the primary question of education. The solution is the creation of a specific discipline of Musar, or, to put it differently, the theory and technique of religious-ethical conduct. The link between information and energy is indirect, it is accomplished through a mediator, namely a moral education that is first of all emotional and practical.

In an essay eulogizing Rav Yisrael Salanter, Rav Kook writes of two foci of his teaching. The first: "He observed how deep is the sickness of inattention to self-criticism." This is no more than a return to the old principle of *cheshbon hanefesh* (the accounting of the soul), but with the added consideration of the generation's needs, demonstrating that "the matter must be imprinted in the human soul as a psychological acquisition, and for the sake of that acquisition, there must come a great constancy of repetition in ethical studies and a deep, passionate enthusiasm of the soul."

The second focus is the highlighting of the importance of ethics in addition to fear of Heaven (*Kedosh Yisrael* in *Maamrei HaReAYaH,* Jerusalem 5740, pp. 120–22). Rav Kook argues that in our time individual ethics must be supplemented by an additional emphasis: "What the generation needs now, especially, to know is . . . that together with the teaching of Musar, profoundly and with fire, he lifted his heart to feature publicly social justice, the special severity of the commandments and obligations between man and man, without which there is no basis for fear of heaven and purity of character."

Rav Kook subscribed to these principles. But the very resort to the study of a technique that would turn information into energy was not accepted by him. Thus, we read in the preface to *Orot HaKodesh:*

The wisdom of the sacred is higher than any wisdom in that it transforms the will and the character of the soul of its students to bring them near to that loftiness that it itself partakes of. This is not the case with all mundane wisdoms, even though they describe elevated matters that are beautiful and noble, that have not that active quality, to attract the intrinsic essence of he who thinks of them to their status, and indeed they have no relation at all to the other powers and self of man, save for his cognitive power alone.

There are two dimensions in human activity, specifically in ethical activity: informative (describing various matters), which may pertain to "beautiful and noble" content, and energy ("the active quality"). The sciences act on man's "cognitive power," but "have no relation at all to the other powers and self of man." Verily, knowledge does not change man; information does not automatically create energy. But according to Rav Kook, this is a partial truth, and it is correct with respect to all the particular sciences. It is not true when one rises to the "wisdom of the sacred"; hence, instead of adding a technical layer to the study of Torah, the solution is to broaden the study, to turn ordinary Torah study into wisdom of the sacred. Then the problem will disappear. The particular sciences, like the secular studies, are descriptive, they reproduce reality. The science of the holy is, by contrast, productive: "and all the secular sciences . . . do not innovate or engender what is new by themselves, rather they describe and present to intellectual contemplation what is in reality, therefore they also are unable to make him who thinks them into a new creature, to uproot him from his bad traits, and to set him in a situation of new reality . . ."

The wisdom of the sacred, by contrast, is "productive" as well: "active," it influences reality.

Disciplines and Integration

Specialization is a social phenomenon, but it expresses a deeper phenomenon of general epistemological significance. Two philosophical doctrines dispute the nature of truth and the definition of the criteria of truth: the correspondence theory and the coherence theory. Totality comes to expression in the struggle against specialization. That specialization exists is a fact. Moreover, the great "masters of one discipline, who are generally more famous in the world, because the masses grasp the glow of a particular discipline on the increase much more than they grasp the greatness of general spiritual wealth" (*Orot HaKodesh,* Vol. I, p. 50).

The classic instance of expertise that is "wisdom organized in a spirit limited by its discipline" (Ibid. p. 50) is the scientific system manifest in *Wissenschaft des Judentums,* and perhaps, one might add, in its academic legacy. There are chairs in different sciences whereby each "contracts itself in the horizons specific to it":

The pain is especially great when the masters of the disciplines, who have never tasted the pain of gaining wisdom, and are satisfied and happy with their portion, great and lofty in their own eyes with the plenitude of perfection without lack in their eyes. And they extend to us dry crumbs of such things as are fundamentally full of freshness and the vision of all. They extend to us, for example, historical lectures according to external acts and facts, and tear with main force the discipline that they are qualified in, from the great web of the great existence in its glorious grandeur (Ibid. p. 49).

Our attitude toward scientific investigation must indeed be dialectical:

We must overcome the desolation of our spirit, and learn from those searchers what they bring up in their traps. But we must then renew the face of things in their living, total originality.

The scientific study of Judaism has been enriched in the last several generations, but "their great wealth, knowledge and diligent criticism" leads paradoxically to a poverty of spirit "a lack of life and dwindling of spiritual majesty" (Ibid. p. 50).

A most fundamental example of the aspiration to totality is the integration, the "spiritual digestion" of disciplines.

First is the integration of halacha and aggadah: "We are called to pave such highways in the ways of study that through them halacha and aggadah will become intrinsically combined" (*Orot HaKodesh*, Vol. I, p. 25). This is not to be an artificial synthesis, but the revelation of "a unity implicit in them from time immemorial" (Ibid. p. 26). The educational integration is achieved by the unification of halacha and aggadah, the Oral Torah and the Written Torah and all the disciplines:

One of the great troubles of man's spiritual world is that each discipline of science and of feeling prevents the appearance of the other discipline. Thus most people remain defective and monochrome, and their deficiencies continue to increase (Ibid. p. 22).

However, the outstanding expression of the approach to Torah in Rav Kook's teaching is his refusal to regard the Torah as a discipline. The Torah is all-inclusive, hence:

When the Torah is made a specific discipline in life, then all the disciplines in the wisdom of the world are requisite in order to complete the inclusive, complete personality. But when one rises to the height of knowing the Torah as the bearer of all knowledge, all content, all being, including all, then all the disciplines branch out of it, and with the satisfaction of good all is satiated (Ibid. p. 51).

The ultimate ideal is thus that reality for which all, the sacred and the profane disciplines, are parts of the Torah. However:

Just as it is in true reality that there cannot possibly be a spiritual creation in the world that stands on its own, but rather is saturated with everything. But the denseness of the heart engenders that it is impossible to look upon these components penetrated by all spiritual being, that are found in any content. But with man's elevation his eyes shall be opened to see properly, then will the eyes of the blind be opened . . . (Ibid.).

One might say that the status of secular subjects, "natural enlightenment" in Rav Kook's term (Ibid. p. 64), is in effect that of "strange thoughts" in Chasidism. While pre-Chasidic ethics held that one must wage unconditional war against strange thoughts, and bring about their disappearance, Chasidism taught that the solution is not the abrogation of such thoughts but rather their sublimation to their origin. Whatever exists contains something holy, for otherwise it could not exist.

Thus we know that there is no idle thought in the world at all, you have nothing that has no place, for they all emerge from the place of wisdom. And if there are thoughts of vice or emptiness, that vice and emptiness is only in the external style, but when one penetrates to their inwardness, one finds in them foundations of life, for wisdom is the source of life (Ibid. p. 17).

This is the meaning of the aphorism "Who is wise, he who learns from every man, without any reservation whatsoever." The emphasis is on *every* man. Every human creation has a share of holiness.

The attitude between secular studies and the sacred disciplines is parallel to that between body and soul (Ibid. p. 65). This relationship is no doubt problematic; indeed, "it is preferred by the righteous to break their bones for the glory of G-d" (*Zohar,* II: 198; I:180). Sometimes it is preferable to the righteous to break the power of corporeality in order to prevent its influence, "which contradicts spiritual expansion." However, the problem lies not in the body but "the intellectual nexus with corporeality," in other words, the way corporeality is reflected in the soul. To apply the parable: The evil is not secular studies but the ideology that grows up around them. Just as health is a necessary condition of the soul's activity, "with the increase of the power of revealed enlightenment, so will hidden knowledge increase, and the sharpness of its insight, the depth of its idea" (Ibid.).

It is not science that is dangerous, but the false metaphysics that is parasitic on it:

The major caution is required regarding the overt influence of metaphysics that is also a spiritual influence. The influence of an entity belonging to the same types *(min bemino)* may be destructive, until the power of the holy is constructed and established in its full sense (Ibid.).

Just as evil is not in the body but in the reflection of the body in the soul, so the menace is not science but the ideology growing up around science, i.e., materialistic philosophy. However, the end of the section implies that the danger of this metaphysics is temporary, until the power of the holy is constructed and established. To borrow a famous idiom, the curriculum Rav Kook proposes is something like "a healthy science-of-the-holy in healthy sciences."

And all those revealed ideals toward which the better side of the profane, the superior portion of human wisdom and ethics, aspires are necessarily known as branches of light, "overflow of the brain," "edges of the hair of head and beard" [in Kabbalistic nomenclature], of those supernal portraits, which are revealed at the basis of the life of the Eternal through the light of Israel (*Igrot HaReAYaH*, Vol. III, p. 22).

The synthesis of the strengthening of Torah and the broadening of world wisdom is necessary (*Ikve HaTzon*, p. 129). So Rav Kook writes to his son:

With respect to preparation for university I have several times told you to follow the inclination of your pure spirit. I hope, with G-d's grace, that all your turnings are to the right and all your actions for the sake of heaven . . . The profane in its multitude of branches, studies, knowledge and thoughts, is not, in the final analysis, other than a method assisting to the ideal revelation of the Holy that we joyously draw from the fountains of His salvation, from the source of G-d's Torah that lives in our midst; fortunate is the people that it is so with him (*Igrot HaReAYaH*, Vol. III, p. 40).

The attitude to secular studies is one detail in a broader discussion, our relation to the non-Jewish world that surrounds us. To be sure, we must observe the world and learn from it. However, we must distinguish between comparison and imitation. In comparison, man attempts to set up a kind of analogy, weighing the relevant conditions; in imitation, man accepts principles from the outside uncritically, without discrimination. Tragedy results from the error that fails to distinguish between a comparison "that is good and fitting and useful when objects and concepts are resolved in their place, according to the new situation about which it reasons, and imitation, which is a brute recognition that proclaims how do these nations work and I will do so too" (*Eder HaYekar*, p. 53). Rav Kook illuminates this distinction with a halachic analogy: One distinguishes between fountain water, or for that matter natural water, and water that is drawn, that is brought "to the camp of Israel as they are without profound study, without resolute thought that sifts and purifies matters until they become worthy to confer benefit when they enter the Hebrew world" (Ibid.).

Imitation is the source of disaster. In the context of a particular society, no cultural phenomenon is isolated. When some lack takes root "in some nation, it has necessary oppressions . . . and natural defenses against it; therefore it does not injure so much although it prevents development and delays the coming of good into the world" (*Eder HaYekar*, p. 58). When a foreign nation imitates it, however, "the lacks cause it sevenfold pain," for the foreign nation has not "all those defenses found in the nature from which those imitations were copied." This is why assimilation of individuals, groups, or even the nation and the state is destructive. It is not enough to proclaim Jewish nationalism, for the nationalists sometimes "translate assimilation into Hebrew . . . a strange creature, unworthy even of assimilation" (*Eder HaYekar*, p. 59).

Curricula and the Order of Study

One of the major principles of education is study in the area to which one is attracted. This is true first of all with respect to ability: "Whoever has a specific capacity must bring it to its perfection as much as possible" (*Musar Avicha*, p. 83). Here lies the great pedagogic secret, assuring the link between study and joy. The natural animal knows instinctively to choose his food: "Spiritual nourishment also exhibits this rule: Man must always study Torah where his heart desires, as it says, 'For in G-d's Torah is his desire' " (*Ikve HaTzon*, p. 118). But this is on condition that the Torah scroll be "unrolled before in all its breadth, in all its many and varied disciplines." The inner joy that accompanies our spiritual occupations is the condition for the presence of Shechinah: "Boldness and joy in His place" (I Chronicles 16:27). Joy is a divine attribute, it may be revealed in the realm of worship and activity; but all this comes later. The first requisite is the revelation of joy at the student's bench: "The period that enables delight and joy to enter the circle of activity . . . is the period of study" (*Ikve HaTzon*, p. 117). Joy is the true measure of Torah study for its own sake, and "only the study of Torah for its sake and the rapture of its love brings about all the good consequences that arise from the light of Torah."

Here one should add a note on the place of *pilpul*. Historically one can ascribe two purposes to *pilpul* (*Eder HaYekar*, p. 45):

1) Limited *pilpul* aiming at practical halachic decision; 2) free *pilpul*, in which man discovers realities "in which to roam without restriction and limitation" (Ibid.). This is a realm that has become a kind of "aesthetic wisdom . . . as a part of belles lettres corresponding to the spirits who have arrived with their intellect and knowledge to that level of delighting over its beauty and majesty" (Ibid.).

This very demand for an unbounded domain is authentic, but it is the result of a deviation: "In fact this desire was destined for the abstract spiritual wisdom and the delicate, beautiful feelings, occupation with which and imagination of which itself is the lofty goal, such as theology and psychology and the like." *Pilpul* has its place between these goals. The tragedy of exile comes to expression here too, "for occupation with these fresh matters [i.e., theology and psychology, etc.] . . . decreased," and was replaced by *pilpul*. The resolution here must be found in the search for balance. The demand to remedy this imbalance is "that thirst [caused] by a strange disease in the past generation: not a hunger for bread nor thirst for water but to hear the word of G-d" (*Eder HaYekar*, p. 45).

Paradoxically, every man may contribute his share in the practical realm, not so "by contrast, in creating beauty," i.e., in *pilpul* "the true genius consummates the sublime with his activity, and succeeds in increasing good taste," so the lack of original genius transforms beauty into an impoverishment and lack of grace" (*Eder HaYekar*, p. 46). *Pilpul* befits "only possessors of genius indeed, of whom there are few in the world."

We can also look upon technical pedagogical details from the perspective of our sources. Let us take recess between classes as an example. Can this modern "discovery" enter our educational structure? Yes, and the practice has important sources and a deep logic:

At times, because of the flood of cognition, one feels fatigue, which comes about because one leaves no room for contemplation between each spiritual revelation, to digest the phenomenon well . . . For spaces are found in the Torah as well, to leave room for contemplation between each section [this is the case when a man learns from G-d], a fortiori to persons learning from persons. The same rule applies to every rational study, which results from the revelation of the soul in its phenomena. The break enables life, measure, character, desire, and relation to the environment to become oriented to that good and that loftiness in the appearance of the supernal (*Orot HaKodesh*, Vol. I, p. 75).

The far-reaching conclusion is that which introduces into the curriculum even matters that might be considered folly:

Among all the things that are called dear folly is one . . . Those who do not take consideration of the dearness of the point of folly, in the place of its necessary being, drive their lives and those of others from the world . . . until they again demonstrate . . . that more dear than any wisdom and glory is that petty folly (Ibid. pp. 76–77).

The exemplar of this pedagogic approach is that of Rav Hamnuna, who "introduced words of folly before words of wisdom" (*Zohar*, III:47).

The Final Goal

Let us not fear freedom. No idea stemming from "inquiry, search and criticism, when these are alone" threatens us (*Eder HaYekar*, p. 52). "Only the evil heart, the whoring heart . . . engenders all riot and defect in Israel and in man" (Ibid).

The ultimate conclusion is thus one that "strives for complete human integration between Torah and wisdom, and augments them with such conduct that brings about health and joy, and a normal state of body and soul" (*Ikve HaTzon*, p. 129).

We remarked on the place of the principle of totality in Rav Kook's system. We seem to have here a position influenced by Hegelianism and modern idealism. It should be stressed, however, that in this area too Rav Kook's doctrine is the development of Kabbalistic and Chasidic ideas: "The wisdom of truth teaches us cosmic unity, the aspect of equanimity that is to be found in the being as a whole" (*Arpelei Tohar*, p. 67). The meaning of this can be grasped by looking at an interesting parallel in *Sefat Emet* (section *Bereshit*) by Rav Yehuda Arye Leib Alter of Gur:

"And G-d saw all that He had done and it was very good." This means, as the verse says, "all G-d's actions are for Him." For the rule

is always tied to the power of the agent, although in particulars there
are things that oppose holiness, but in general it says "all He created
for His Glory" . . . And that is the statement of the Midrash, "And
it was completed [*vayechullu*]" that the creation was an instrument
[*keli*] through totalization [*hitkallelut*], and the meaning of *vayechullu*
from "my soul was consumed [*kaleta*]" for it is annihilation, for anything is annihilated to the point of life that they have from G-d
. . . and when all creation is consumed in the totality that is called
Knesset Yisrael, that is His Name is one and it is an instrument to His
Substance, may He be blessed.

The conclusion of Rav Kook's system, as we see, corresponds to this.
Man must find his way to his origin in the totality. He has before him
two alternatives. The first is to sink more and more into individualism,
that is, "the diversion of the individual will, in its submersion in the
pettiness and particularity of the partial captivity in which he is
bound," and therefore to detach himself from his source of life, thus
to bring about "annihilation, weakness of power, and darkness over
the most inner essence of his self, that is his will, that is his honor." The
second possibility is the opposite, to link up to his source, for "in the
sanctification of the will the branch resembles its great root, sucks from
it and connects to it, and is filled with the lights of the emanation of
life" (*Orot HaKodesh*, Vol. III, p. 39). Hence, "we are called to rise
above the narrow enchanted circle of petty accounts," and thus "we
connect the disengagements of life to the great curtain of life" (Ibid.
p. 40). Individual life appears to be disengaged from life, detached from
the totality, and must deliberately become part of the complete canvas
connected to the Creator. Totality is real, not merely abstract. Cleaving
unto G-d is the connection to the true totality: "Cleaving . . . unto what
is all and the source of all and more all than the all" (*Igrot HaReAYaH*,
Vol. III, p. 741). The nexus between the individual and being as a
whole is the origin of every individual. "This recognition is the foundation of ethics, even social ethics . . . and the foundation of humility,
even practical humility." Humility, according to this, expresses our
knowledge of our true nature, an essence that is the source of novelty,
the dynamic and nourishing power in man:

The thought about the unity of reality as a whole leads to the thought of the
unity of souls in a simple way and immediately it effects, through this genesis,

its best influence, the ideal of peace and general love, from which grow all good personal and social traits (*Arpelei Tohar,* p. 56).

We have mentioned Rav Shmuel Alexandrov, the admirer of Rav Kook's writings. He regarded *Ikve HaTzon* as a masterpiece of modern Hebrew literature, "the essence of the Judaism of the *Kuzari* and the softness and feeling of the Kabbalists and the Habad masters," written in "an unsurpassable popular style" (*Maamrei Bikkoret,* p. 26). But he saw Rav Kook as an isolated instance, "one swallow will not bring the spring," whereas "the majority of the great [rabbis] . . . not only will not inform the public of a solution . . . to the great spiritual questions but, to the contrary, wage war against such resolvers . . ." The war indeed took place, but the swallow did bring the harbinger of spring.

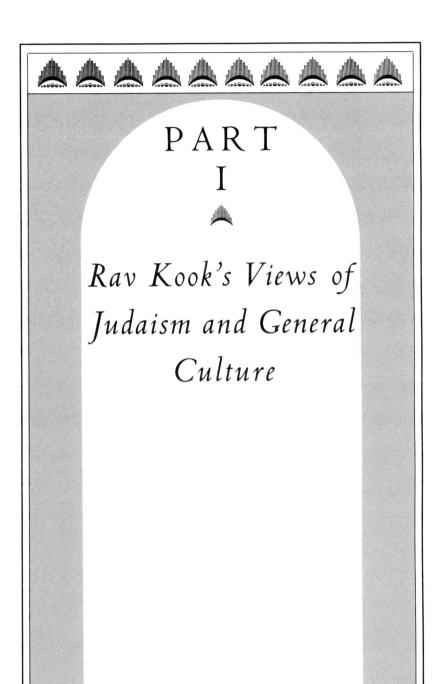

PART
I

Rav Kook's Views of Judaism and General Culture

The Uniqueness of
Rav Kook

Professor Ephraim E. Urbach

TWO APPROACHES ARE found in assessing the great sages of Israel in past generations. One approach sees all of them as beloved, pure, mighty, and holy. The other sets out to differentiate, to divide, to characterize them, and to mark them off one from the other; to define wherein lie the greatness and strength of this one and of that one. For the one is not the same as the other. This work is not at all easy or simple; for it is necessarily linked not only with piling up words of unlimited praise, but also with the characterization of that which is unique and that which is set apart. What makes this attempt easier is the fact that the distinguished sages are not many.

Our early teachers felt this, and each in his own way stressed this fact. Disciples characterized Rashi as "one whose linguistic style is not like any other linguistic style," for it is "more perfected than the language of all men." This was sufficient to establish him as unique within the entire camp of commentators that arose in Israel.

There were also numerous attempts to distinguish the personality of Maimonides, and Rav Kook is not absent from them. It seems to me that in his words Rav Kook affirmed not only Maimonides' distinctiveness but also his own special place in the rabbinic world and that of the great Torah personalities of his generation. HaReAYaH devoted a special article to this matter in which he came out against Zev Javetz's assessment of Maimonides in his book *Toldot Yisrael* (2:13), and here are his words: "All the words of honor and fitting admiration that the rabbinic author, of blessed memory, adduces for Maimonides, deserve to be placed in the most honorable place in our literature; but we cannot agree with him in the ridicule he poured on Maimonides' central scientific work, namely, his *Guide*. In our generations . . . the *Guide* also has to be included among the holy books that are the 'possessions of Torah' . . . and it is our duty today . . . to delve deeply into all of them and to extract their qualities together with the qualities of Torah . . ."

It would seem that Rav Kook was referring to the words of Javetz, of whom he was not an admirer, and in one place he did not refrain from expressing reservations with regard to words of exaggerated praise that certain circles heaped upon him. His reservations give him an opportunity to emphasize his view unequivocally that religious thought deserves the same position as halachic thought. "Just as in regard to the halachic laws of the Torah," argues Rav Kook, "there are various approaches and differences of opinion, and we are accustomed to follow the rule, Let your ear be like a funnel so that you will hear both the words of those who declare [the thing] pure as well as those who say impure, those who declare unfit as well as those who declare fit . . . although in matters of practical halacha there is a decision in favor of one of the views; so does this attitude apply also in matters of beliefs and opinions. Far be it from us to treat them frivolously and to decide with regard to any of their opinions that they are heretical and to be banished from the boundaries of Israel." HaReAYaH rejects absolutely the argument of Javetz that Maimonides clutched the strings of Aristotelian philosophy and Arabic wisdom. These difficulties of those who argued against Maimonides when the book appeared are not worthy to be made, in his phrase, "delicacies in our faithful literature." And this is not only because Maimonides did not follow blindly after Aristotle and his Arabic commentators, but he inquired and examined and purified the matters. Only when it became clear to him that they contained nothing that contradicted the fundamentals of the Torah, and his own view inclined to them—then he did not conceal the truth and declared that they were in fact his views; and he deemed it proper to explain words of the Written and the Oral Torah in accordance with them. In showing that there is no contradiction between cultural ideas of contemporary science and the fundamentals of Torah, he established the basis of pure faith in the hearts of many, and thereby saved the life of Torah and tradition for many generations. Rav Kook also brings a proof of this act of deliverance for generations which Maimonides himself was unable to envision. In the *Guide of the Perplexed*, Part III, Chap. 13, Maimonides taught that the view that the goal of Creation was only for the sake of man is not a fundamental principle of the Torah, but there is a superior purpose for all being, known only to its Creator. After the theory of Copernicus was accepted that the earth is to be seen only as a small speck in infinite space, all those who thought that the basic principle of faith was rooted in the idea of man as the center of all existence found themselves in absolute heresy. And this, writes HaReAYaH, is why we should glory in the outlook of our teacher (Maimonides), which saved faith.

It seems to me that the matters to which we have alluded testify, from the point of view of both their content and their style, that Rav Kook was unique in the rabbinic world, and that he was describing not only the path of Maimonides but also his own path and position. Against the argument that Maimonides introduced "a new face within the boundary of Israel," concepts such as "the hylic intellect" and "disembodied intellects," he retorts, "I do not know what place there is for this superzealousness. Are then all the ways of human intellect forbidden to Israel? And where then is 'the beauty of Japhet in the tents of Shem'? And where is the plain association with the overall divine image that the Holy One, blessed be He, put into man—as a result of which we honor everyone, among all men, who is wise and of upright heart, and we accept truth from everyone who utters it? Whoever says something of wisdom in our faithful literature, even if he is from the nations of the world, is called wise" (*Megillah* 16a). These ideas, and others like them, appear in HaReAYaH writings even in unexpected places. In his book *Eder HaYekar*, thoughts and impressions on the life of his father-in-law, *HaAderet*, Rav Eliyahu David Rabinovitz-Tomin (Jerusalem 5666), he comes out against "teaching that is divorced from all reflection and thought in those parts of the Torah that touch the feeling heart and the thinking mind." He attributes it to the spiritual decline of our generation. For in the generation into which his father-in-law was born, that is the year 5602 or 5603, the spiritual movement in the camp of Israel grew strong. On the one hand, Chasidism strove to uplift and enlarge the "feelings of holiness that slumbered in the heart of nature." And on the other side, the movement of the *Mitnaggdim* (literally, "opponents"—i.e., of the Chasidim) was concerned "that the practical, realistic basis should not disintegrate through an overemphasis on feeling . . . which might go beyond its proper bounds." These two forces worked together for the rejection of the negative influence that burst forth in the Berlin movement, i.e., the Haskalah movement. And here came an assessment no less surprising, namely, that in fact "this [Haskalah] also would have found itself a proper place in the nation as a platform for general humanity" joined with the love of G-d and the love of His Torah and mitzvot, and then it would not have encountered any obstacles in its path. But once it adopted an all-righteous stance and exalted itself to seize control of the nation, it brought about a narrowing of the opposition, in practice, between Chasidut and the Mitnaggdim. The former strengthened the understanding of halacha and its development within its essential spirit, and the latter tried to instill all the strength of holiness into its love of Torah. This dialectic explanation of the process of religious history in recent generations is out of context so far as the life of his father-in-law, *HaAderet,* is concerned; and this paradox is even more forcibly apparent when we read the autobiography of *HaRav Aderet* himself. (Mosad HaRav Kook performed a great service in publishing it under the title *Seder Eliyahu* together with his rules of conduct, Jerusalem 5744). How far removed was *HaAderet,* and all his thought and speach, from the world of ideas and concepts and visions of his son-in-law! The difference stands out prominently despite Ha-ReAYaH's structured literary effort not to sever entirely the thread connecting his essay with the subject of the biography. Thus, for instance, he says of his father-in-law that "he was wonderful at constructing wide-ranging *pilpul* discussions that excited pleasurable feelings by the sparkle of their sharpness and the richness of their marvelous and overawing wide-ranging knowledge" (p. 45). But this sentence is set in a general appreciation of *"pilpul* and its development." At first the Torah scholars were not pleased with him. Only slowly did he conquer the Talmudic world, and even those who were drawn to him did not understand his character. He merited the privilege of a citizen of Israel when brilliant scholars ascribed a standing to him befitting his proper stature in halachic learning as opposed to other demanding areas of the Torah. For him, *pilpul* was an aesthetic expression, and the general principle in works of beauty is that just as the true genius perfects that which is most exalted among his works, and labors to increase the good taste, so does he who is lacking in original brilliance turn beauty into something poor and graceless. Therefore *pilpul* is fitting only for those who truly possess the powers of a genius, and these are few in the world.

The fact of writing a biography brings HaReAYaH to incorporate a complete essay on historical research. Rav Kook is convinced of the necessity of research. According to him, research and criticism in themselves "will never lead to evil, not in the universal faith that all men of upright heart and all great thinkers, in all the human race, have in common." Thus, one can learn from historic philosophy in general that the distant past is not to be judged by our present standards. But one should not forget that we have an obligation not to behave simply according to apelike imaginings and imitations. "Examples are good for us if we learn from the customs of the world as a whole." But we have to differentiate between example and copying lest these words refer to Achad Haam's distinction between imitation and assimilation. Rav Kook speaks out sharply against those who would like to attribute to Israel new ideas that are strange to Israel and its spirit and, all the more so, things that have been a shame and a disgrace among the best and greatest thinkers of every nation and tongue; and he directs his criticism against a section of modern Hebrew literature and the degraded position in which it stands. HaReAYaH's studies are devoted to the needs of the hour and the renascent life. He writes, "In a time like this, a time for the awakening of the need for physical strength as a defense against the weakness and exaggerated unsureness that has been with us from of old and, in our generation, has fallen to the lowest degree, . . . how great is the responsibility to be on guard against its extreme forms, and certainly against the striving for physical strength on the part of Israel that should be filtered, purified and preserved from all negative ways that may be bound up with her. We have to discern and know well that we never excelled in physical strength against all the nations, nor have we ever until now risen up and stood upright by means of human physical strength. It is true that we have become too much weakened in bodily weakness, and this also helped to cause a spiritual weakness, and we must now strengthen our neglected and slumbering force. But, precisely at this same moment, we must not forget that we have an obligation not to act out our deeds through comparisons and imitation" (pp. 52–53).

It is characteristic of HaReAYaH that with all the emphasis on distinctiveness in his perception of Israel, *Eretz Yisrael,* and the process of redemption, he does not neglect a reference to the array of universal humanity. And this principle holds good also, as we have hinted above, for his direction in Torah study. Let me bring another illustration. At the beginning of the second volume of *Otzar HaGeonim* on Tractate *Shabbat,* which appeared in the year 5690, the editor, Dr. B. M. Levin, printed a letter of Rav Kook. It opens with the words, "Uncovering treasures from ancient collections that have been hidden from the eyes of generations has become in our time one of the greatest foundations of knowledge. Large societies, representatives of nations and kingdoms, compete with each other for primacy in this great field of work, the uncovering of ancient relics." Rav Kook bestowed many crowns and great hopes on the discovery of the Geniza documents of the Geonic period and their arrangement and editing in which Dr. B. M. Levin was engaged. "This gigantic work, by which Israel will be blessed for generations, will bring light on its wings into the House of Israel to illumine the paths of Torah and the sacred wisdom of Israel."

Absolutely different was the attitude of the "Chazon Ish" to the treasure trove of the Geonim. I shall not rely on the oral testimony of one of his close associates, but on Letter 32 in the collection of his letters. He says there, "I saw hardly any help in arriving at the truth through the versions being sought in the Geniza documents. Their only use is to subvert justice and turn truth aside, and it would be best to hide them away, for the loss is greater than the truth." And this difference is not to be wondered at, for in the eyes of Rav Kook the *Otzar HaGeonim* of Dr. Levin is not only a contribution to the study of Talmud and halacha, but it is to be considered as belonging "among all the major works being undertaken for the building of the nation and the flowering of the horn of the Lord's salvation."

In stressing HaReAYaH's uniqueness among the men of his generation and his time, we must not blind ourselves to articles, speeches, and letters that contradict not the lines of his character to which we have given prominence, but the ideas and perceptions that are frequently emphasized. We are accustomed to note Rav Kook's quality of tolerance toward the pioneer builders of the Land, the *chalutzim,* and his restraint from sharp controversy. We quote his words: "Therefore pure tzaddikim (righteous men) do not complain of wickedness, but rather they increase righteousness; they do not complain of heresy but rather increase faith; they do not complain of ignorance, but increase wisdom" (*Arpelei Tohar,* p. 28). "It is not my way to go searching out the sins of Israel . . ." (*Igrot HaReAYaH,* Vol. II, pp. 30–32). The love of Israel and the task of public defense was, in his eyes, an important subject in the Torah. But against all these there are the words he wrote to the writer Alexander Ziskind Rabinovitz, who had invited him to write a eulogy for the young fallen members of the *Shomer,* who were killed at Sejera on Pesach 5669. He sets forth freely and openly the problems he feels concerning the sort of eulogy he can give them without infringing the laws of mourning regarding those who had gone away from the ways of the community and cast off the yoke of Torah and mitzvot. Finally, he includes them in the category of "the Martyrs of Lod" of whom it was said, "No creature can stand in their orbit." Side by side with his appreciation and openness toward general science, there are not wanting expressions of reservation with regard to European culture, which, at least from the point of view of morality and purity of character, was bankrupt. To one of his pupils, he writes, "I beg of you, my friend, throw away at once all the works of vain fancy woven by the lifeless diggings and scratchings that we have absorbed from the nations who have defiled our pure oils by the hands of Esau" (*Igrot,* Vol. II, p. 119). And in another place: "This error of thinking the world to be perfected while it is still full of impurities that need to be refined . . . has cost us dearly" (Ibid. p. 174). Rav Kook presented Judaism as the inner essence of humanity, but he did so out of an awareness that truth must embrace everything, and he therefore also found in Judaism signs of a moral liberal anarchy, and even an individual physical anarchy; but he believed that both would be purified when they would reach the bounds of purity. In a fountain of words of confession, HaReAYaH wrote, "Whoever said of me that my soul is torn spoke truth. It is not possible for us to imagine with our intellect a man whose soul is not torn . . . It is the task of man to unite the conflicts in his soul, but this is only an ideal toward which we strive . . . We can come near to it with our strivings . . ." Indeed, whatever he produced is evidence of this constant endeavor of his; but one really should examine and clarify his conflicts and anxieties in order to understand their surrounding causes and circumstances.

There is no need to add anything concerning Rav Kook's special place, with which I commenced my remarks. But with all his feeling and consciousness of this distinctiveness, he saw himself as a link in the chain of Kabbalah and tradition. In a note, full of admiration, on the *gaon* and *admor* Rav Avraham of Sochotchow, author of the *Avni Nezer,* Rav Kook explained a contradiction between the statement that Rav Eliezer b. Hyrcanos never taught anything that he had not heard from his teacher (*Sukkah* 27b) and the tradition conveyed in *Avot d'R. Natan* (Chap. 1) that "Rav Eliezer expounded things that no ear had ever heard." This implies that Rav Eliezer taught things of his own. HaReAYaH says that there is no contradiction. It was Rav Yochanan b. Zakkai who taught also these things; but Rav Eliezer was the only one who listened so carefully that his ear heard what others did not hear. I think we may say of Rav Kook that his ear heard what no others heard in the sources of Torah and wisdom and life.

Rav Kook's Relation
to European Thought

Professor Eliezer Goldman

I

IN ORDER TO grasp the full influence of modern European thought on Rav Kook, it is necessary to study his early essays of the decade in the century. In these essays, the influence is overt, while in the later writings the same ideas appear behind a veil of Kabbalistic terminology. This reflects Rav Kook's conception of the way Judaism accommodates outside ideas. In his essay "Thoughts" in the collection *Ikve HaTzon* (published 5666), he offers a tripartite classification of outside ideas: a) Ideas whose scope and clarity are so great that they are absolutely universal "and do not descend to occupy with them a unique social character. The great of the generations from time immemorial were accustomed to accept lovingly what was said, of this type, by the pious and sages of every nation"; b) Ideas specific to Israel "from the perspective of their content and inner quality, and he who mingles with these matters external plants is confusing and harming"; and c) Matters that in their content are "so universal that it makes no difference in which language or tongue and by the member of which nation they are uttered, but nevertheless depend upon feelings of the heart and close practical effects so that they are altered as a result of their style according to the content of each nation." Here, "we are required not to mingle our unique pure style with a foreign style . . . And sometimes there are found valiant men, wise of heart, who know how to filter and purify the inner content, which is substantially the same, to present it well in the unique pure Israelite style."[1] This was indeed Rav Kook's practice in his later writings in dealing with ideas whose outside source is quite evident in the earlier writings.

II

An obvious sign of the European climate of influence in this era is the adoption of evolutionary ideas and the faith in progress that character-ized European thought in the nineteenth century. In two essays—*Teudat Yisrael uLeummiyuto* and *Afikim BaNegev,* which appeared early in the century before he settled in Palestine, Rav Kook developed a conception of the Jewish people's national vocation and the telos of the Torah that is associated with the idea of progress, and bears a distinct religious character.[2]

"I will be what I will be"—The Name, the vocation of your mission, that is called by the Name of its Transmitter, whose actions are His Names, you know not as something that may have a past, but ever as future "I will be," because it flows from the source of light, from the well of living water of G-d's perfection to His creatures. It is something that becomes illuminated, be-comes elevated, becomes developed (*Afikim BaNegev,* p. 24).

Here the vocation of the Jewish people is identified with G-d's activity in the world. Its realization is a principal component of divine govern-ance in the world, which is nothing but "G-d's perfection to His creatures," the elevation of Creation. This elevation is an ongoing process, hence it is always directed to the future. It is never fully fulfilled. Rav Kook regards it as an infinite process. Hence the vocation of the Jewish people is an eternal occupation. It distinguishes the Jewish people, but is universal in its goal, the nurturing of humanity and its elevation.

1. *Eder HaYekar VeIkve HaTzon* (Jerusalem: Mosad HaRav Kook, 5727), pp. 122–23.
2. *Teudat Yisrael uLeummiyuto* (*HaPeles* 5661); *Afikim BaNegev* (*HaPeles* 5663–4).

A brief passage on the Sabbath elucidates the character of the vocation in a concentrated form:

Sabbath! . . . Commemoration of Genesis. The commemoration that indicates that it is a vocation and intention of felicity and perfection for which the world was created, and that one G-d created all that exists. Understandably it is a high and lofty vocation, which we know as the arrangement of the life of the entire human race according to the ways of love and brotherhood. And in order to bring about this lofty purpose, the one nation was elected for its ability to adopt an order of all life according to the Will of G-d, in such a manner that its spirit strives for a life of love and grace that would serve as a model for the whole world (*Teudat Yisrael uLeummiyuto,* p. 158).

The construction of all life in accordance with the Will of G-d is, to be sure, the organizing of national and social life according to the Torah, but all this for the sake of promoting the goal of founding human life on the principle of unity, a unity that is made manifest in love and brotherhood. "That all the entire human race shall live the life of one integrated family, that each one recognize and know that he ought to be assiduous in promoting the benefit of his neighbor, and that it is his duty to love and respect his fellow without distinction of race and nationality" (Ibid. p. 82). This purpose is to be achieved by deliberate human activity. Nonetheless, this development "must, of necessity appear eventually in the world as an aspect of the conditions of development of the Creation" (Ibid.). The elevation of mankind should be seen as a stage in the divine plan for all creation. It "accompanies the vocation of nature in its generality, whose law is to consummate all existents and bring them to the height of perfection" (Ibid. p. 47).

If we examine the components of this schema, we will find all of them in Moses Hess's *Rome and Jerusalem:* The idea of elevating reality at all its levels, in which the elevation of humanity is but the current stage of the general plan; the identification of the process of progress with divine activity in the world; the depiction of the divine unity as the paradigm for the ideal of humanity; and conduct its communal life according to the model of family life; the vocation of the Jewish people in promoting this goal by exemplifying the possibility of constructing a national life in all its ramifications on the basis of the unity ideal. Even such details as reference to the Jewish people as the people of the future, the Sabbath as a symbol of "perfected" creation, the exegesis of the Name "I will be," turn up in Hess. We know that Rav Kook read *Rome and Jerusalem,* and that the book appeared in Hebrew translation about two years before Rav Kook published *Teudat Yisrael uLeummiyuto.* [3] Thus, we know that a collection of ideas central to Rav Kook's thought is anchored in nineteenth-century European thought. We can even identify the channel through which he received these ideas.

III

Doubtlessly there were certain aspects of the thought of Moses Hess that Rav Kook could not accept. Chief among them is the pantheism that completely rejects all divine transcendence. Hess identified the Divinity with the process of perfection of reality. Rav Kook too tended to view the movement to perfection of reality at its different levels as a kind of divine immanence, but an immanence whose source is in the divine transcendence. For this purpose, he found it convenient to deploy the Kabbalistic schema of the Blessed Infinite *(Ein Sof),* which thought cannot grasp, and the Emanation *(Atzilut),* which alone is known to man and to which worship is directed. However, at least at this stage in the evolution of his thought, the *Atzilut* of which he writes is not the world of Kabbalistic *sefirot* but the immanent goal of created reality. Rav Kook writes about the "divine ideals" to the realization of which all creation aspires, and the fulfillment of which, in human life, is the conscious desire unique to Israel. By way of analogy to Plato's notion of time as the moving image of eternity, one can view *Atzilut,* as Rav Kook treats it in this period, as the manifestation of the unity of the transcendent G-d in the evolutionary tendency implanted by Him in creation.

The earliest work in which Rav Kook expounds this position is his essay *Daat Elokim* in the collection *Ikve HaTzon* (published 5666).

3. Moses Hess, *Romi VeYerushalayim: Sheelat HaLeom HaAcharona,* letters and notes, Hebrew trans. David Tzemach (Warsaw: Tushiya, 5659).

This essay, which was directed primarily to Torah students, he establishes his stance on the basis of epistemological claims, reflecting familiarity with modern philosophy.

Rav Kook opens with the statement that any conception, be it sensuous or intellectual, has a double aspect. One aspect is "the thing itself"; the other is subjective "deriving from the attributes originating in the subject that is concerned with those matters" (*Ikve HaTzon,* p. 130). A naive conception of the nature of knowledge would lead us to think that we know the object itself. But epistemological sophistication shows that we know the object only as it appears to us, not as it is in itself. "Every existent in the world is available to him only from the perspective of its relation to him" (Ibid. p. 146). In this respect, there is no difference between sensual and intellectual apprehension. "Thus [thought] frees itself of the astonishment and confusion brought about by an alien object. For it is not really an alien thing; rather it is dealing with parts of its own being" (Ibid. p. 130). Were it otherwise, knowledge would be impossible, for in a meeting with an absolutely alien object—as the object is in itself—thought would be unable to get a hold on it. Thought can grasp the object of knowledge only because it is itself reflected in this object.

From Rav Kook's letters, it is apparent that he regarded this as a Kantian view; e.g., *Igrot HaReAYaH,* Vol. I, p. 47. To be sure, he claims that this view is already found in Kabbalah. But a reading of *Daat Elokim,* the first place where Rav Kook proposes this idea, indicates that he is building on modern epistemology. This conclusion follows, both from the formulation and from the emphasis that he is speaking not only of theological knowledge but all forms of knowledge: "For beyond clear and self-conscious knowledge, man has no knowledge of anything in itself; neither of the nature of G-d nor of any concept (*Ikve HaTzon,* p. 134). "Self-conscious knowledge" means knowledge that knows its character, does not deceive itself into thinking that it knows its object in itself, and understands that it fails to apprehend the thing in itself.

When we speak of religious knowledge, we have at our disposal only the truths imprinted upon our souls. "We do not know G-d in the world and through the world but from within our inner souls, and thus appointed we proceed to acquire the broad knowledge of the world"

(*Igrot HaReAYaH,* Vol. I, p. 45). We do not infer the existence of G-d from the attributes of reality outside ourselves, and certainly do not know His attributes in this manner.

According to all this, both the knowledge of G-d and His true worship are inconceivable via relationship to His Substance—i.e., to divine transcendence. The knowledge of G-d is knowledge of the divine ideals; genuine worship grows out of the aspiration to realize these ideals.

IV

The question arises as to the sources from which Rav Kook drew his philosophical knowledge. A comparison of terms and formulations indicates that an important source was Fabius Mieses's *History of Modern Philosophy [Korot HaPhilosophia HaChadasha]*, published in Leipzig, 5647. From this book, Rav Kook could have learned the principal doctrines of Kant. However, it appears that he was especially influenced by the chapters on Solomon Maimon and Schelling. We have seen that, according to Rav Kook, that which is completely external to thought causes it astonishment and confusion "brought about by an alien object," and that the knowledge of an ordinary object is possible only because it is not truly alien, but rather "a part of the being" of thought. He repeats the idea that the thing in itself is strange and alien to thought, and the clearest knowledge is that which comes from the depths of the soul. Such views, in precisely that formulation, are attributed by Mieses to Maimon or appear in sections of Maimon that he translates.

Rav Kook emphasizes that G-d in His Being is inaccesible to man, not only epistemologically but religiously as well. The attempt to worship Him as He is in Himself breaks down because in this aspect the divine has no relation to human reality. Such piety is possible at most as an enclave of human activity. It does not find a place in the broad expanse of human life. Such worship is "bondage and service to a sublime being; in itself, such worship has no ideal implications. This is a worship whose source is fear and trembling, not the reverence of glory and splendor. It is a religion of melancholy and despondency" (*Ikve HaTzon,* p. 147).

The fault is in the attempt to relate to G-d as substance. "Substance is, by its nature alien and strange to it . . . [the soul] and when one sees that it encompasses all its life, all its feelings and being, so that there is hardly place for its own feeling of selfhood, then one shuns it" (Ibid. p. 132).

Such a critique of religiosity oriented to the Divine Substance can be found in Fichte, as translated by Mieses:

The G-d of those heretics [his philosophical opponents] called the Deists and who are accustomed to a naive respect for substance make their concept of G-d a low and contemptible one . . . All definitions and concept of the infinite are only negations of the concept and definitions applicable to the finite and limited abstracted from them by thought. . . . Thus the positive concept of the substance of G-d in His essence fails to be caught, and the true, unique, infinite being is lost.[4]

The identification of the "worship of substance" or "glorification of substance" is common to both accounts, despite the important differences between their critiques of the religiosity that derives from the attempt to relate to G-d Himself in His worship. But there is some similarity in their positive conceptions as well. Again let us cite Fichte as presented by Mieses:

Belief in a moral world order is the best confirmed assumption in the depths of our souls . . . This ideal of moral world order is the most refined and necessary belief for the knowledge of the supreme being called G-d (Ibid. p. 129).

This conception is not far from Rav Kook's idea about the divine ideals as the aspect of G-d to which worship should be directed, and his conception of the divine activity as the drive toward the realization of these ideals. This is a dynamic moral order.

4. Fabius Meises, *Korot HaPhilosophia HaChadasha* (Leipzig 5647), p. 128.

V

An examination of Mieses's book also uncovers the influence on Rav Kook of his description of Schelling's system. That there was such an influence I have attempted to demonstrate in detail elsewhere. Here I will only note several themes in Rav Kook's writings that can be found in Schelling, especially as presented by Mieses.

1. The idea of the unity of opposites, which plays such an important role in Rav Kook's thought, is usually traced to the influence of Hegel, which he is presumed to have assimilated in one way or another. Indeed, there are places where Rav Kook presents this concept in a manner reminiscent of Hegel's approach. Most of his discussions, however, are closer to the polar unity in the early system of Schelling. An example from Mieses's chapter on Schelling:

Absolute Substance includes in itself all the qualities and attributes, both positive and negative; the opposites of infinite and finite, subject and object, life and nothingness, thought and extension, spirit and nature, for all these oppositions as apprehended by our naive reason, are found and are distinguished in it, in such a manner that they are annulled in the truth of its unity and overcome in pure identity.

All oppositions in general are not essential in their truth and do not exist in themselves, but subsist in it, and it embraces them together (Ibid. p. 142).

Of course, the theologies of Rav Kook and Schelling are radically different. One could argue that in those places where there is a similarity, Rav Kook might have found the idea in Kabbalistic literature. But the conception of the unity of oppositions is similar. Both view contradiction as the consequence of a partial and limited perspective; both regard oppositions as overcome in the divine unity. Rav Kook's special innovation is his dynamic sense of created reality, aspiring to become like unto the Divine Unity, to reach "closeness to G-d," if we borrow the title of one of his most clearly formulated.

2. In *Orot HaKodesh*, we find a sequence of sections devoted to the idea of the world soul, which is the source of life of all creation. It is described, on the one hand, as an architect during Creation, and, on the other hand, as immanent in the already created world. "In the realization of Creation, the light of this power that deals with the repelling of its actions is demeaned and obscured. Through generations

and epochs the world soul is gradually refined and united with the source of its being, the soul of the universe" (*Orot HaKodesh,* Vol. II, p. 350). "With all its greatness and puissance it is oriented toward the quality of that which is limited, and manifests measure and the contradiction" (Ibid. p. 352).

This sequence includes a chapter dealing with the question "How do the ordinary ideals that illuminate the limited horizons emerge from the lofty ideals that stand at the heights of the world beyond any limit, meter and measure?" He responds that "its very unlimitedness in itself includes the finite content. Precisely that which is destined to be finite in its self-determination as well is included in the glow of the unlimited" (Ibid. p. 353).[5]

Rav Kook's problem arises from the finite nature of all ideals to which human beings actually strive in any historical period, as contrasted with the aspirations of the soul that are beyond all limits and definition, and toward which the finite ideals tend to aspire in their cosmic-historical progression. The finite ideals derive from the unlimitedness of the Source of all. The problem is how the finite emerges from the unlimited. The answer is that, somehow or other, the content of the finite is included in the unlimited.

The world in all its parts is animated by the world soul, hence there is nothing completely inert. There is life in all and continuity between the inanimate and the animate: "The souls of inanimate, vegetable, animal and rational in their plurality are connected one with the other and in the particularity of their natures they become distinguished each from one another" (Ibid. p. 415).

The idea of a world soul is ancient. It appears in Plato and is of special significance in the philosophy of Plotinus. But it seems that the formulation, the problem, and the combination of themes resembles particularly what is found in Schelling, again as cited by Mieses (p. 144):

One animate soul, unique in its decisiveness, flows and operates in the entire world, the Divine Spirit of general animation hovers over the phenomena of generated being, and the universe that comes with it is part and parcel of the

---

5. Cf. *Ikve HaTzon,* p. 113, on the finite ideals and the yearning for "what is above every telos, superior to all measure."

absolute, infinite Substance, which is identical in all yet particularized in all the forms and the distinctive levels in the order of nature.

The problem of the finite deriving from the unlimited is presented in the same manner, and is similarly resolved (Ibid. p. 146):

All that emanates and flows from His Substance cannot emerge into being without this quality of infinity, I mean that it must of necessity be in the radical state of this infinite!—But in this way it is impossible to arrive at finite being . . . Now because it is impossible that there be anything limiting and defining the infinite movement and activity of the Absolute Infinite outside of itself, therefore it is necessary to imagine and assume in thought and knowledge, that the quality and nature of the Infinite itself contains, in a hidden and sublime manner, the power that limits and holds back the Infinite's effluence.

In Rav Kook's language, "its very unlimitedness in itself includes the finite content." The citation from Mieses also affords us an interpretation of Rav Kook's strange phrase "the power that deals with the repelling of its actions." Apparently, he means the power that limits and withholds.

Here there is no doubt that the style and formulations of Mieses, with their abundant associations to the concepts of Kabbalah, facilitated the assimilation of the ideas. In any event, the relation between Rav Kook's discussion of the world soul and the universal anima and what we have seen in the corresponding chapter of Meises appears to be beyond any doubt.

The Use of Kabbalistic Concepts in Rav Kook's Teaching

Professor Yehuda Ashkenazi

THE SUBJECT BEFORE us is broad and complex, both in terms of its pervasiveness in Rav Kook's writings and the many areas that concerned him, and in terms of the unique linguistic, stylistic character of his holy words and the various strata hidden in his books. I wish to concentrate on a brief analysis of one section in *Orot HaKodesh,* called "the secret of the straight line *(yosher)* and the circles *(iggulim),* "[1] which clearly belongs to the subject of our discussion. I will try to clarify two matters: 1) One cannot understand the straightforward statements of Rav Kook properly without considering their exact Kabbalistic source, while comprehending the specific meaning of the ideas for him, and 2) The novel significance that Rav Kook discovers in the clear-cut Kabbalistic content of those concepts, which are read by the mystics in their own holy manner, is connected to general philosophical questions, with the intention of elucidating them according to the view of the Torah and the faith of Israel.

In order to understand Rav Kook's approach to the use of Kabbalistic concepts, one must first note that there is an essential difference be-

1. *Orot HaKodesh,* Vol. III, pp. 24–25.

tween the basic presuppositions of philosophical thinking and those of Kabbalistic thinking. Philosophical thought defines itself from the outset as purely human thought. It negates any "revelation," in the genuine sense of the word, that is the revealing of a divine message to man. By contrast, the Kabbalists accept as an unassailable fact the existence of a historical period of divine revelation through the medium of prophecy.

The Kabbalist, however, like the philosopher, finds himself in the world after the end of the prophetic epoch. This would seem to give a theoretical advantage to the method of philosophical inquiry, as an agreed-upon point of departure for thought, over the approach of Kabbalah. Indeed, this assumption prevails in wide religious circles, which believe in prophecy as a principle of religious faith without penetrating the theological significance of this fact, meaning the revelation of the Divine Will, in words and actions, as the Bible testifies. Thus, we find ourselves, from the end of the First Temple on, in a cultural era in which the same thinker can relate—in a seemingly paradoxical manner—both to a human philosophical perspective and to the perspective of the Torah sage, who interprets prophetic statements as prophecy. Inasmuch as we generally draw upon both the concepts of the biblical world and the world of philosophy, one can find serious thinkers of stature who deal equally with the content of thoughts deriving from human subjective philosophical analysis and to the content of beliefs coming to us from the words of prophecy. The student is not always able to distinguish the two sources.

This was not Rav Kook's approach. In principle, he has reservations about any mingling between the two worlds. At the same time, he does not negate the legitimacy of philosophical problems as questions,[2] deriving, as they do, from the fact that our cultural world is a postrevelational one.[3]

---

2. Rashi's commentary to the Talmud is illuminating on this issue. On *Shabbat* 116a he interprets *philosopha* as *min*, i.e., heretic. On *Avoda Zara* 54b, he interprets the same word as *chachmei ummot haolam* (Gentile sages). There is no contradiction. He who denies biblical revelation is called a heretic, especially when the reference is to a Jewish philosopher. However, a Gentile philosopher who denies the false prophecy of idolatry (cf. Jeremiah 15:19): "and they shall say but falsehood inherited our ancestors, emptiness with nothing of use" is a sage.

3. The topic of the cessation of prophecy, its causes and meaning, is a separate matter beyond the scope of this paper.

In this respect, Rav Kook differs radically from those who adopt an apologetic approach along ethical, religious, emotional lines, who make the sacred work easy on themselves. To the contrary, he penetrates to the essence of things in their full philosophical significance, exhibiting, in his particular way of employing Kabbalistic concepts, the view of the Torah on the matter. It may very well be the case that Rav Kook is elucidating for us, as a faithful witness, the intention of the Kabbalists in disseminating their wisdom beyond the four walls of their schools, which would have been worthy of serving as a hiding place for their teaching until the era of renewed prophecy, as befits the glory of the king's daughter inward, in the secrecy of the righteous congregation.

THE SECRET OF THE STRAIGHT LINE AND THE CIRCLES

The straight is that which is most primary in being, the circles are secondary to it, meaning that the freedom of life, the absolute freedom from the aspect of the source of being, the freedom that is in the divine concept, that the creation of being comes from its ethical side, this is all . . .

. . . Among the circles themselves, within the necessary laws of being, within the steady iron laws, that do not vary in their operations on nation and man together, which do their good to all the wicked, and sear with their burning aspect the good and righteous as well, in their inner midst only the straight acts, they go in the traits of the straight and for its sake . . .

In this section, Rav Kook addresses one of the most serious problems of general metaphysics, the tension between the concept of ethical choice on the one hand and the regularity of nature on the other hand. Natural regularity is known and defined as totally determined. It is revealed as an absolutely impersonal reality, given over to a blind determinism. This presupposition is accepted by all scientific epistemologists. This reality in our world is called "the *sefirot* of the circles" in Kabbalistic sources. However, it is impossible not to discern in our world an opposing feature, the personal aspect, the "I" that is revealed in the self-consciousness of a man who lives according to spiritual and ethical values. In Kabbalistic terminology, this dimension of reality is called *"sefirot* of the straight line."

The contradiction between the two opposing dimensions of the same world, which is irreducible by human reason, is one of the major obstacles facing the philosophical search for an understanding of the world. For the predicate of the problem is its very subject. On the one hand, man's self-consciousness makes him part of the world of the straight as an ego inclined to aspire to free ethical choice, while on the other hand he belongs to the nature of the external world, insofar as his body conforms to natural law, which enables him to exist in the world. From a rational, philosophical perspective, there is, thus, room for an obvious contradiction—insofar as deterministic regularity in the world, if it exists, as indeed it does, eliminates the theoretical possibility that there exists any exception, including man. Moreover, what makes things infinitely more difficult for the philosopher from an existential point of view is that he, in the act of discovering the regularity of nature, at the same time discovers himself as an exception. This may very well be the source of philosophical pessimism, which prefers agnosticism to the danger of the philosopher regarding himself as different, as an exception in the world.

Philosophers generally tend to the assumption that ultimate necessary truth is the impersonal law of determinism. Even when, in ancient times, philosophers accepted the possibility of supreme pagan deities, they assumed that these powers are subservient themselves to a natural framework over them. This is precisely what led them from the outset of their deterministic thinking to the denial of the pagan gods. In any event, this is the presupposition behind scientific deterministic thinking in contemporary culture. To be sure, many philosophers assent to the existence of an ontological basis for man's free will; for if not so, it would remain no more than wishful thinking. However, this should be explained as the private belief of the philosopher as a human being rather than as a philosopher. In practice, philosophical reflection in itself tends to regard the issue of free will as problematic and requiring explanation. And here each one chooses his subjective approach.

Now this problem, containing the tension between freedom of will and the regularity of nature, which cannot be solved properly by philosophical thought (for if lawful regularity comes first, there is no theoretical possibility for the creation of ethical will out of it), is investigated by the Kabbalah on the basis of the principle of absolute monism, stemming from Hebrew monotheism, which sets down will as the first reality, before the "sphere that moves but is not moved." Here the question is reversed: How can one explain, based upon common reason, without presuppositions, the coming into being of those worlds that obey necessary, blind regularity?

The masters of Kabbalah, primarily Rav Yitzchak Luria and his school, present the unfolding of the world as follows: First the reality of our external world (i.e., nature) is emanated by the light of *Ein Sof,* through an emanation of innumerable stages, under the aspect of the "*sefirot* of the circles." A new development bursts forth at the second stage, the emanation of the *sefirot* of the straight line (i.e., the human image). Here, one may ask, How can one root, which contains in itself both the dimension of being under the aspect of the circles and the dimension of being under the aspect of the straight, manifest two modes of existence that are opposed to one another in our world, though they stem from the same root, according to the Kabbalistic reading of the verse "The Lord is G-d" (I Kings 18:39)? The questioner might say, What we have here is merely a verbal solution, in which the problem is presented as an original assumption—one presupposes at the root of things the same tension that requires resolution in reality! The key, therefore, is an understanding of the notion of contraction *(tzimtzum);* in order to show its pertinence to our discussion we must distinguish three definitions in their terminology:

1. *Tzimtzum* as causing the place of the worlds to come into being;
2. The nature of *tzimtzum* acting in the light of the *sefirot* of the circles;
3. The nature of *tzimtzum* in the light of the *sefirot* of the straight.
   a) There was a need to solve a basic question: If the *Ein sof* is defined as an absolute reality preceding everything, it is clear that, theoretically, there is no room for anything else, be it the world of nature or the soul of man who dwells in it. Hence, in order to "emanate that which is emanated and to create the creatures . . ." a vacuum was created in the midst of primeval being, as an absolute ethical act, which is the making of place for the existence of the other.
   b) In the *tzimtzum* that engenders the *sefirot* of the circles, the primeval light is emptied of the "ego" in being, and exhibits the "impersonal" aspect that is concealed in it as the "backside" of

the will, and constitutes the basis of the development of the law of the worlds through the infinite stages of evacuation down to our world.

c) According to the principle "the final act in first thought," the expansion of the light of the straight line again bursts forth through the world of circles, and constitutes the root of the being of the human soul. To be sure, this *tzimtzum* is a diminution of light, also through infinite stages, not an evacuation like the *tzimtzum* of the light of the circles, which is designated the primeval *tzimtzum.* [4]

This image of the unfolding of things adequately explains that the engendering of the primeval space did not occur through an arbitrary mechanical necessity, but from the potency *(gevura)* of the Divine Will. As the Mishnah states (Avot 4:1): "Who is *gibbor?* He who reins in his inclination." And we ascribe, in the daily prayer, *gevura* to G-d. At first glance, what is this *gevura* attributed to the Creator! It should be understood precisely with respect to *tzimtzum* as we explained: the reining in of the expansiveness of primeval being engenders a place for the other, and that is the absolute ethical act. This sheds light on Rav Kook's words:

"The straight is that which is most primary in being, the circles are secondary to it, meaning . . . the absolute freedom from the aspect of the source of being . . . that the creation of being comes from its ethical side, this is all . . ."

On this foundation, Rav Kook goes on to develop the validity of his faith in the ultimate victory of the forces of absolute ethics, "freedom in the divine concept," redemption over "the necessary laws of being . . . which do their good to all the wicked, and sear with their burning aspect the good and righteous as well." Here again we have an illustration of our thesis: It is impossible to understand his simple statements utilizing only philosophical categories, unless one studies the Kabbalistic concepts behind them. For rational philosophical thought, there is

4. See the parallel in *Sefer HaBahir,* Chap. 1: "Rav Berechia said, What is the meaning of the verse 'And the earth was null and void *(tohu vabohu),*' implying that it was already existent, and what is *tohu*—that it confounds *(ma'the)* people, and what is *bohu?* Rather it was *tohu* and reverted to *bohu,* and what is *bohu,* something that has reality as it says *bohu=bo hu* (it is in it) . . ."

here only a desire of the heart without ontological foundation, which leaves us in the realm of religious faith, certainly an exalted, noble, and courageous faith, but one without rational conviction. For if so far the lights of the straight light have not overcome the law of the circles, there is no reason, other than faith, to expect their triumph in the future. Whence did Rav Kook draw this absolute optimism, expressed in the following words: "Among the circles themselves, within the necessary laws of being, within the steady iron laws . . . in their inner midst only the straight acts, they go in the traits of the straight and for its sake . . ."

Another key to the issue is the Kabbalistic concept of *reshimu* (imprint). The primeval *tzimtzum* that caused the forming of the space in which the *sefirot* of the circles expanded, was indeed absolute. But it was not for naught that the Kabbalists indicated that the withdrawal of the Infinite Light left behind an imprint of the light, in each stage of withdrawal. The imprint is called *reshimu*, whose nature is, of course, that of the light of the straight line that penetrated through the *sefirot* of the circles. Hence it appears that the connection between the lights of the straight line and the *reshimu* concealed in the *sefirot* of the circles themselves is what operates in maintaining the world as a unity. And this is an ontological basis for Rav Kook's view about the positive process of development of world-mending.

A KIND OF SUMMARY

In such subjects, which touch upon matters of the greatest importance, all is clearly up for discussion and debate, each individual following the spirit of the root of his thinking; I certainly do not wish to impose my opinion. However, basing myself on what little I have had the merit of learning from my mentor and teacher Rav Zvi Yehuda Kook zt'l, I am inclined to remark that it was his view that the uniqueness of Rav Kook zt'l's teaching was not the search for a synthesis between the world of Kabbalah and that of philosophy, nor was it a systematic philosophical interpretation of Kabbalistic terms. It was rather the clarification and elucidation of the "revelational" content of the Kabbalistic concepts in relation to the philosophical problem present in general contemporary culture as it stands.

Aspects of
Rav Kook's Practical Approach
to Society and Culture

Dr. Nachum Arieli

THE CENTRAL CONCEPT of Rav Kook's teaching, one coined by him, is "the inclusive unity" *(haachdut hakolelet)*. This term is fundamental to his thought, and elucidates both his doctrines and the background both of his ideas and his remarkable attitude to the secular world. This attitude, which finds expression in a kinship and a coming close to secular society, can be interpreted as a reaching out to straying brethren, in order to bring them nearer to the Torah of Israel from which they had fallen away. Rav Kook appears in the social arena of the 1920s in a central, public executive role. To be active at that time has special significance. It was a time of renaissance and renewal for the Jewish people. Herzlian Zionism begins to take on a practical character, and the return of the people to their land emerges from the realm of vision into that of realization. The realizers, however, in their great majority, are irreligious persons. They cling, to be sure, with all their heart to the idea of return to the Promised Land. But aside from the love for the Land of Israel embedded in their hearts, which for Rav Kook is a religious love, aside from the commandment of settling the land, the renewal in this age of renaissance is classically secular. Rav Kook, meanwhile, befriends the secularists, does not shun them, visits them and receives them as welcome guests in his home.

Yet beyond the educational side and the desire to influence the secular community for his known religious purpose, Rav Kook's actions can be viewed as an additional layer in the general framework of his thought. His attitude here is an integral part of his doctrine. Thus, the question about befriending the secular world should be seen as far more than a matter of sociological-religious motives. The stance of friendship may indeed arouse debate against this background: Is it really the correct way? For too great an intimacy with the secular community by a supreme religious authority is liable to be interpreted as the yielding of consent to their behavior. Insofar, however, as Rav Kook's attitude to the world of Jewish secularism is an essential part of his philosophy, he is compelled to treat this stance positively, indeed to cultivate it. Thus, Nathan Rotenstreich puts the situation: For Rav Kook, "It is no longer possible to look upon the national existence of Israel according to the usual criteria and it is no longer possible to judge Israel by the accepted standards. The national existence of Israel is an entity *in itself* [emphasis in the original], different in kind from other national units."[1]

What makes Jewish national existence by its very nature a national entity answering to different criteria than those of any other nation? Is it at all possible to speak of one or another ethnic group as free of sociophysical laws?

Rav Yehuda Halevi's doctrine of the five levels of reality is well known. According to this teaching, the Jewish people is assigned to the fifth level, unrecognized to us via the physical experience of the general world: "Indeed so, this level, if it exists, is divine-angelic, and is not subsumed under the law of the intellectual, the spirited or the natural, but rather under the law of the divine matter."[2] One may assume that this doctrine influenced the thinking of Rav Kook. But it seems that this influence alone does not exhaust the matter. We must return to the central motif of his work, i.e., "the inclusive unity." According to this motif, the people Israel is not a fifth level of reality, but something entirely different.

1. *HaMachashava HaYehudit BaEt HaChadasha* (Tel Aviv 1966), p. 274
2. *Kuzari* 1:42, based on Y. Even-Shmuel translation (5733).

II

Reality, as it appears to us, is a congeries. But the multiplicity of things grasped by the senses does not reflect the truth behind the things. The Pre-Socratics spoke of one principle that is, in fact, the ultimate basis of reality. All things are the crystallization of the one material element. This was surely a bold move that opened, in effect, the road to scientific thought. Thus, the history of science begins in the sixth century B.C.E., and marks the transition from mythos to logos.

The Pre-Socratic thesis, however, is primarily physical-material. Hylistic matter is realized in an endless number of forms. Empirical reality is of one material quality; the differences between things are merely quantitative. Therefore they do not attribute a spiritual dimension to things. Such a dimension appears obscurely in the Pythagoreans and Anaxagoras, who speaks of intellect *(nous)* as responsible for becoming. The spiritual element as such appears explicitly in Plato.

Rav Kook was familiar with ancient thinkers, and one may assume that their ideas and their scientific ideal stood before his eyes when he coined the term "inclusive unity." He is referring, however, to something different. Before coining the term "inclusive unity," he addressed the "totality of being" *(kelalut hahavaya)*. Being appears as an organic unity, and the man who knows himself knows at the very same time the negation of his individual being. The individual has subjective meaning so long as he has not yet come to know himself. Once he knows himself, he knows that he is nothing but a part of the whole, and he lives as part of the general life.[3]

The world, "being" in Rav Kook's language, is an organic entity that is grasped as one totality. But in order to know the cosmos as such, one must first know the individual. Only through this knowledge is one to reach the totality of being. It is somewhat like the Platonic process of cognition. As long as the single entity is grasped as an individual, the knowledge of the entity is incomplete, for it is lacking the nexus connecting it to the totality. Rav Kook says:

"There is not an isolated, atomistic, severed soul in all of being, but rather all is connected, intertwined, interwoven" (*Orot HaKodesh*, Vol. II, p. 351). And much more explicitly: ". . . Man may arrive at

---

3. This formulation corresponds to Spinoza's doctrine about degrees of knowledge. See his *Ethics,* II:40, n. 2.

such a degree that he discovers within himself the centrality of all being within him, and then he feels in his spirit all that is felt, all that is done, all that scintillates and all that moves throughout the fullness of being in all the particulars of its stages" (Ibid. Vol. III, pp. 357–58).[4]

With this thesis, Rav Kook returns us to the cosmological conception that points to a regular, all-pervading cosmic law. Man, in this sense, is no exception. Plato saw man as a "small model" faithfully reflecting the "big model." That is, cosmic order is reflected in the social order and in the structure of the physiological organism.[5] This doctrine had enormous influence on medieval thought, which identified man as microcosm. In the mystical literature, the Torah of Moses is the first model of the existing world, according to which G-d created the universe.[6] The second model is depicted as the "glory" *(kavod)*. Rav Shimon b. Tzemach Duran describes the Tabernacle as a copy of the "paradigmatic Torah."[7] The last model is man the microcosm.

Indeed, Rav Kook bestows upon the totality of being a spiritual significance. The world breathes the soul of being in general and steeps itself in the fragrance of all-pervasive holiness. Here we find an element of all-infusing holiness, akin to the Stoic pneuma or the Platonic world soul. From this perspective, the doctrine is not physiocosmic but psychocosmic. The soul of the individual derives from the soul of the world, breathes the spirituality of all being, and unites with it. The

4. It seems to me that this thesis contradicts Maimonides' view on the question of foreknowledge, and that man's knowledge as opposed to G-d's is taken out of itself through a gradual knowledge of the object by which the object becomes gradually known. See *Guide*, Part III Chaps. 20–21; MT *Hil. Teshuvah*, Chap. 5, halacha 5, and Raavad's note *ad loc.*—he apparently failed to get to the bottom of Maimonides' epistemology. See also *Orot HaKodesh*, Vol. I, p. 216.
5. *Republic* 367a.
6. This mythos first appears in the Tannaitic literature and was later transmitted by Rav Hoshaya Rabbah, third-century Palestinian Amora. *Sifre Dvarim* 10:48, *Bereshit Rabbah* 1:1. On preexistence, see E. E. Urbach, *Chazal*, p. 255.
7. *Magen Avot*, Livorno 5545, 18b. Duran states that the Tabernacle is a model of the superior world (20a). See Aptowitzer, *Bet HaMikdash shel Maala al pi HaAggadah* (*Tarbiz* 2); Heineman, *Philons griechische und judische Bildung* (Breslau 1933), pp. 43–81. The doctrine of the four models of the structure of the world has much significance. The Tabernacle and its vessels served for Second Temple literature and later aggadic literature and church fathers as allegorical symbols referring to cosmic forces. For Philo and Josephus, who took the sanctuary and its cult literally as well, they offer symbolism of cosmic and supracosmic beings, and bear pneumatic value in addition. In the *Zohar*, following aggadic literature, the erection of the Tabernacle is a parallel to the Creation of Genesis.

physical laws that penetrate the world, as Rav Kook puts it, are spiritual laws, laws of holiness. Holiness overflows everywhere with life—"The mysteriousness penetrates *the particulars and particulars of particulars* [emphasis in original], there is no line or point over which it passes in silence, no jot or tittle on which it will not contrive a multitude of wonders . . . There is no haughtiness before G-d, or abasement, no smallness or greatness, for all is lofty and elevated from the aspect of the original life of the Light of the Eternal, which sweeps all . . ." (*Orot HaKodesh,* Vol. I, pp. 105–6).

What is revealed to us is physical material reality, but in truth empirical reality is saturated with spirituality, pure animation, which irrupts into being and unifies the separated. Material reality is divested of its materiality and receives a spiritual ideal (in the Platonic sense) and is emanated (in the Neoplatonic sense. For how is it possible to give a spiritual meaning to the material world? Not for nothing did the Pre-Socratics base everything on matter, for the reduction of matter to spirit cannot be logically grasped. Even unto the rise of modern philosophy in the seventeenth century (Descartes' "mariner and his ship"), the connection between body and soul remained difficult.

If the materiality of the world is conceived as a mere external layer, a valueless rind as it were, then sense experience fails to grasp true being, which is by its very essence spiritual. Against the classical materialistic conception, subsuming everything under sense experience, the spiritual component abides as the ultimate explanation of the universe. This explanation is the content of the knowledge that recognizes spirituality as the operative fact in the universe. This is the spiritual element that infuses all, unifies all and gives reality a unified spiritual meaning. In Rav Kook's language, "We view being in its spirituality, the inner life, how it operates, how it gradually becomes the soul revealed in the animate and in the sapient, how it abides in its hiddenness . . . And all is alive, all is perfect, all is fresh and all shines, when all is known in one unity, when the luminous shines and infiltrates its light, to know and to make known, how from the Source of all, lives all" (*Orot HaKodesh,* Vol. II, p. 385).

Rav Kook criticizes rationalistic philosophy that "swallows the minute, specific points and lines within the *general enlightenment,* and thus conveniently becomes elevated to the *general expanse* [emphasis in original]. But failure awaits it insofar as it was not well established by penetration to the precise particulars. This appearance is perceived as the consequence of rationalism both in the profane and in the holy" (*Ibid.* Vol. I, p. 105). That is to say, in his opinion this conception, which is usually regarded as supporting mysticism, does not necessarily belong to the realm of the mystical. To be sure, rational contemplation is likely to bare the spiritual roots of all, yet this must be accompanied by a measuring of each individual detail with constant precision.

III

From here it is a short distance to the thesis of "inclusive unity." If the material world has incorporated the spiritual element, then its materiality is merely an external shell. In other words, the dynamic universe, infinitely flowing and revealed each time in different forms, is no longer the material world known to us from everyday experience. It is, in substance, spirit, or something like a Leibnizian monad, whose character unfolds and is revealed to us. In this framework, the problematic dualism of spirit and matter is broken; it is no longer necessary to explain the insurmountable difficulties connected with the mutual effects of two entities that influence one another without sharing a common ground. We regard this nexus as an empirical fact indicative of a mechanical phenomenon of life devoid of the spirit of life that is responsible for the flow of phenomena. Malebranche formulates the doctrine thus: "Animals have no intellect or consciousness in the usual sense of the term. They eat without appetite, cry out without pain, grow without knowing of it. They do not lust, they do not fear, they do not know, and if they act in a manner that appears intelligent, the reason for this is only that G-d, for their self-preservation, made their bodies such that, in a purely *mechanical manner* and without any sense of fear, they withdraw from whatever is liable to destroy them."[8] Only man, according to Descartes, is composed of two substances, soul and body, where their unity is certain but incomprehensible, i.e., the manner in which the nexus is executed remains obscure.[9]

Now Rav Kook, to begin with, ascribes the concept of soul, or spirit,

8. Malebranche, *Recherche de la vérité, livre sixième: De la méthode, 2e partie, chap.* 7. I have used the Hebrew translation in S. H. Bergmann, *Toledot HaPhilosophia HaChadasha*, Vol. I (5730), p. 155. See also his discussion of Descartes.
9. See Descartes, *Méditations* VI.

to all beings in the universe: "The souls of the inanimate, vegetable, animal, man, are in their totality connected one to the other, and in their specific characteristics they are differentiated from one another" (*Orot HaKodesh*, Vol. II, p. 429). There is nothing inadequate about this. On the other hand, even for an organic-mechanistic concept of the universe, "we see the organic quality of material and spiritual reality. With confidence we can observe the interrelatedness of all, and by that token the activity where everything is affected by everything else, and everything affects everything else. There is no corporeal or spiritual atom that does not affect, that is not affected by fully and in the fullness of all" (Ibid. p. 367). In other words, the mechanism of the universe is not necessarily blind, reflexive, instinctive. It is a psychological, spiritual activity. But at the same time there is a mutual influence that creates the organism of the universe and makes it one world. Dynamic spirituality unifies all. And what is this spiritual element if not the all-penetrating Deity? For "True being is divine being . . . and this being of the return of all unto the Deity is the supreme perfection of being, and there is no power to grasp its value . . . The idea that all being is only the affair of Deity and there is nothing completely devoid of G-d greatly pleasures the heart" (Ibid. p. 400).

Divinity, then, penetrates everything. Because of it, all is encompassed in an inclusive unity. The universe breathes a divine pneuma that alone truly is. Whatever is devoid or opaque to this breath does not truly exist. Such words, which are repeated constantly in Rav Kook's writings, arouse pantheistic associations. Nonetheless, this idea of Rav Kook differs from the view that identifies Deity with nature or even with the laws of nature immanent to nature. First of all, for Rav Kook material existence is not illusory. Not that pantheism views the universe as illusory, but that Rav Kook does not identify Deity with the empirical world known to us. Material reality has its own existence, but as for Alfarabi, Avicenna, and Maimonides, it is not true reality; its existence is dependent on the spiritual being that penetrates material being, and that spiritual being is the Divine.

The theosophic concept of Rav Kook does not present G-d as transcendent but as immanent. It is an immanent conception in the full sense of the word. Rav Kook speaks of the magical intensity affected by the various combinations of the Divine Name: "Full of power is the letter, performing wonders, when it follows its path, when it connects with its source, when all the plentitude of life in the treasure of thought of the Eternal spills into it. These are the *wonders of the Names,* the mighty of life, the decisive of powers, the flashes of being, that the supreme nothing fulgurates in its great hosts. One cannot reveal the hiddenness of Your Name" (*Orot HaKodesh,* Vol. I, p. 117).[10]

Rav Kook expatiates at length on the specific intentions of the Names and their powers, which deepens his immanentist orientation, but also arouses the problem of divine corporeality. Does this approach not treat G-d too much like a body? Rav Kook is not oblivious to the problem, but he negates it from the start: "He who studies Kabbalah must remove from his heart the fear instilled in the heart as a result of logical inquiry, that he may be offending against divine belief, that he may be corporealizing; these are nothing but empty delusions" (*Orot HaKodesh,* Vol. I, p. 416).[11] In this spirit, Rav Kook states, "It is a foolish fear that they are afraid of the corporeal parables in the esoterica of Torah" (Ibid. Vol. I, p. 100).

Rav Kook, then, is not apprehensive of anthropomorphic tendencies, inasmuch as he has excluded from the outset any material element. His immanentism is classically Hegelian, stressing the infinite dynamic of the spirit: "All know that the Holy Spirit strives to illuminate the world with supreme divine light, and it finds its way in the contemplation of the life of the great Divine Being, which is known in spiritual actions much more than in corporeal actions . . . But the spiritual actions necessarily emerge from the hand of a reality full of supreme perfection. Precisely this perfect supreme knowledge in its wealth of detail reveals the triumph of the supreme unity and its superior sources, which illuminate with such sublime purity, to the point where the expression 'unity' is also deficient and inadequate to it, and it says *before one what do you count"* (Ibid. Vol. II, p. 416).

10. Cf. Maimonides *Guide,* Part I, Chap. 62: ". . . When wicked foolish men found these matters, deceit widened in them and the statement that they may gather what letters they would and say that it is a 'Name' that can do and act, when it is written or pronounced in this manner."
11. Cf. *Guide,* Part I, Chap. 35: "But insofar as it is necessary . . . that it spread among the multitude . . . so it must be transmitted to them . . . that G-d is not a body . . ." MT *Hil. Teshuvah,* Chap. 3, halacha 7; "Five are called *minim* . . . and he who says there is one Master but He is a body and has depiction . . ." See Raavad's criticism *ad loc.* Maimonides' view on corporeality expresses the prevalent conception of rationalist medieval thinkers.

Inclusive unity is thus not only a matter of the unity of the cosmic in its fourfold forms of reality, but also the dependence of each existent on the one divine spiritual foundation, which is its condition and upon which everything depends. In other words, matter is no longer the partner of spirit. One cannot speak of the mutual interaction of matter and spirit; there is no equality of effect, surely no equality of value. Matter is expelled not only from the supreme spiritual world, but from the empirical world as well; there is in fact no appropriate expression that can present or represent matter. There is no reason to fear anthropomorphic manifestations in relation to the spiritual Deity, insofar as the corporeal world has no existence worthy of serious notice. Any reduction of spirit to matter must fail, since true being is the being of spirit, and this being expresses the *inclusive unity* as ultimate being in the full sense of the term. Hence the inclusive unity is the end point of scientific knowledge: "The difference between G-d and the world depends only on knowledge and comprehension and the way of life. The more knowledge is raised, the closer man and the world come to the greatness of the Divine, and with the supreme elevation of man and his full awareness he finds that everything is included in G-d" (Ibid. p. 412). The life breath of the universe is the one all-pervasive G-d, as the Neoplatonists put it, the world soul. There is no identification of the material substance with the spiritual substance; rather the dependence of the former on the latter is so absolute that it is utterly impossible to grasp the corporeal substance in any kind of autonomous form. Thus, this conception expresses immanentism, not so much because it identifies matter and spirit (since such identity does not exist) but because of the severe, absolute dependence of each entity on the Divine Spirit. One may compare it to the dependence of the fire on the fuel: There is no possibility for the fire to exist independently of the fuel even for an instant. Therefore the multiplicity found in matter and corporeal substance characterized by the concept of plurality is nothing but a relative, untrue concept. For the multicolored world of matter is unified in the spiritual substance, which is one by its very nature.

IV

Rav Kook clearly formulates the concept of divine immanence: "Cleaving unto G-d, which is the *life of all,* does not budge from any existent in truth" (*Orot HaKodesh,* Vol. III, p. 58). Meaning, of course, that this cleaving affects all "being," spiritual and material, the superior world and the world of experience. In his opinion, this fact is not given to philosophical perception. He says, "Philosophy does not extend beyond a specific segment of the spiritual world, by nature it is detached from what is outside its limits and precisely thus it is separated in its inwardness, an essential separation. The appropriation of knowledge, how all opinions, emotions and tendencies, all of them from the smallest to the greatest, are connected one with the other, and how they affect one another, and how separate worlds are coordinated, this it has no power to conceive. Therefore it will always remain an aristocratic logic, particular to individuals among men" (Ibid. Vol. I, p. 9).

In other words, the *inclusive unity* that expresses the immanence of G-d determines, in effect, three things: 1) Matter has no autonomous meaning and cannot be discussed in a spiritual context. 2) Spiritual unity embraces a plurality of material and spiritual forms. 3) The spiritual, garbing matter and the creatures of the higher world, creates at the same time the organism of all being. This organism is only partially grasped by philosophical thought.[12] But this thought, according to Rav Kook, does not exhaust the entire truth—"When *organic comprehension* in all its greatness increases, and makes all being into a *Shiur Koma magnum,* the great relation between the whole world and its particulars, events and occurrences, its ways and all its values and the supreme worlds, abiding and sublime, is immediately clarified" (*Orot HaKodesh,* Vol. II, p. 368).[13]

Now it is against this background that the question of evil in the world arises: if indeed no existent has independent meaning but is rather directly contingent on the Divine Spirit from which it draws. What kind of evil is it that is contained in the panorama of inclusive unity? Take it either way: If immanentism includes evil, then evil

12. Cf. *Guide,* Part I, Chap. 72: "Know that what exists in its totality is one entity, not other than this . . . ."
13. See further Ibid. pp. 374, 378, 386, 419, 431.

cannot be evil, as it contains something of the Divine Spirit; if evil is outside, it is merely a meaningless illusion.[14]

Rav Kook does not recoil from the conclusion that is necessarily implied by the doctrine of inclusive unity: *"There is not in reality evil,* for it is all good. And G-d saw all that He had done and it was very good . . . In the totality of the world, the practical and the spiritual, no evil exists except in its isolated value; in the gathering of all, all is in reality good . . . There is no good confronted be evil, but there are levels of reality, there is good confronted by a superior good, life and the life of life . . . And of its shining light it is revealed that the image of evil that we describe in the limited reality is only a temporary image, according to the limits of our cognition, and in truth all blackness is merely diminished whiteness, and all wickedness is shrunken righteousness" (*Orot HaKodesh,* Vol. II, pp. 469–75).

There is here, then, a negation of evil as a substance: "Evil for itself is something that cannot possibly exist in the world" (*Orot HaKodesh,* Vol. III, p. 328). And evil, not for itself, is covered by the divine light and therefore cannot be evil. Thus, it is a relative perspective detached from total reality.

Rav Kook also denies moral evil that derives from interpersonal relations: "The moral evil in the world also, were it not for the good aspired, to raise all to the full goodness . . . were it not for the hidden felicity, then the eye would see that moral evil too is nothing but diminished good, and all wickedness nothing but meager righteousness . . ."

Clearly, Rav Kook has before his eyes Maimonides' treatment of evil, and it appears that he negates it completely. According to Maimonides,

---

14. In medieval thought, evil was grasped as the absence of the good. But this thesis does not deny evil as an experienced fact in the here and now. Evil is possible when good is absent, just as darkness, the absence of light, is not illusory just because it does not require a positive creation. See Maimonides, *Guide,* Part III, Chap. 12. Maimonides describes the various forms of evil as experienced facts confirmed by anyone who has encountered evil. There is no attempt to deny it or to introduce existential or axiological relativism. This is said not only regarding inescapable physical evils, "the kind of evil that happens to man because of the nature of generation and corruption . . ." Maimonides attempts nonetheless to play down this kind of evil. He states, "And behold it was very good, that the existence of this base matter as it is, of a composition that is necessarily susceptible to death and all evils, this too is good for perpetuating being and continuing existence when one comes after the other has been removed . . ." (Ibid. Part III, Chap. 10).

natural evil, as manifested in death and in the corruption of matter, belongs to the natural order and to the essential nature of matter. Nature in general cannot take into consideration particular facts, and since the regularity of nature is possible in this manner, then death serves in its own way the general interest of nature. Moral evil, for Maimonides, is the product of man. Rav Kook does not share this view, neither with respect to cosmic evil nor even regarding moral evil. But this can be understood without recourse to philosophical cognition. He states, "Esoteric wisdom explains the reality of the spirit in all its values, describes being in all its character, good and evil in all their fullness. Through the clear looking glass of the holy we observe that the depth of the good engenders the depth of the evil, in order that the good become more profound through the evil, and exist in its fullness and most complete goodness" (*Orot HaKodesh*, Vol. II, p. 491). Evil lets itself be conquered by the good. This surrender is the good in evil. Moreover, "Total and absolute evil, which has no spark of good, rejoices in its destruction and perdition and annihilation, that is the greatest perfection of its development" (Ibid. p. 509). If that is the case, there is no place for sadness. For "the good is the absolute, the abiding, and evil is merely imaginary. If so a clarity of mind and strengthening of spirit are sufficient to transform all into good, and there is no place for mortifications and melancholy, and joy and uplifting of the soul must fill everything" (*Arpelei Tohar*, p. 48). Rav Kook never tires of proclaiming the nihility of evil. Again and again he exclaims, "Evil is nothing but a deceptive imagination and a misguided illusion, because it is not in reality" (*Orot HaKodesh*, Vol. III, p. 178). It is a hiding of the face of the good that leaves the impression that evil has an independent dominion. There is no such ontological realm, and evil is nothing but a methodological thesis by which to clarify, through an artificial hypothesis, the various levels of good. It is one of the signs of evil, that it cannot be discussed without reference to the good. Hence "there is no evil existence, neither in the material world, nor in the ideal formal world, except to that degree that the good is clipped and encapsulated and does not stretch out its rays of light to all the nothingness, but when the good is freed from its chains, there is no evil thing in reality" (Ibid. p. 183). The good is the explanation of reality, that is the ontological meaning of everything in the cosmic framework. The withdrawal of the explanatory principle is a kind of alienation within

this framework. However, in the ontological framework a real alienation cannot occur, therefore it must be a relative, subjective detachment from an outside perspective that fails to see the flow of being and
the unifying texture of things. For things are to be measured acccord-
ing to their most far-reaching consequences as well, for it is these that
determine their dimensions. When there is an alienation, it is a rending
of the texture and narrowing of perspective.

Against this background, Rav Kook views the entire issue of evil.
That is, from a total perspective there is no place for pessimism, for
each occurrence is only one segment of the general arrangement. It is
only a question of definition, but from an ontological perspective, evil
does not exist. Rav Kook explicitly addresses the Aristotelian view
(including Maimonides) and finds the approach of "esoteric wisdom"
more convincing than that of rationalistic pessimism, "which views
general evil and its many particulars as the content of accidental affairs,
in which the only persistent element is the natural necessity of matter"
(*Orot HaKodesh*, Vol. II, p. 497). In truth, there is no natural necessity
but rather the organic interaction of entities in reality. Over against this
general perspective stands the individual perception that is the source
of pessimism, because it relates to evil as an experiential fact in itself.

These two perspectives are found in Spinoza. Relativity derives from
the individual perspective, in which time also appears in its internal
division. In this individual perspective, the particular empirical fact
penetrates the sensibility and creates the experience of evil. Rav Kook
launches a sharp attack on Schopenhauer, who continues the pessimism
of the medieval al-Ghazali. He wars against the conception of "blind
will" ruling the world—"The substance of this misguided science, when
its images wax, is itself the greatest cause of the darkening of the world,
through the expansion of this brutal and vulgar will, in all its branches
and hosts, its impure spirit was thus poured into the substance of human
civilization, and became an agent in its culture, its images of life, its art,
poetry and all its imagined glory" (*Orot HaKodesh*, Vol. II, p. 499).

Such an attack is found in Maimonides against the pessimism of
al-Ghazali's claim that there is a preponderance of evil over good in the
world.[15] Maimonides demonstrates that this is not so, for it is not

15. *Guide,* Part III, Chap. 12: "It often occurs to the masses that the evils in the world
are greater than the good . . . And al-Ghazali has a famous book that he called the

delimited by experience alone. Maimonides' attack focuses on the quantitative aspect alone. He concedes that evil exists in a portion of physical life, but insists that within the boundaries of being that include the supralunar world of the separate intellects, evil is engulfed by good. By contrast, the debate between Rav Kook and the pessimists takes place on the qualitative plane. He denies the existence of evil completely, locating it only on the psychological plane of individual perception. This is not to relegate evil to the level of illusion or delusion; evil has a practical reality and causes real suffering. But this evil is limited to the individual perception, when man becomes detached from the general perspective, that which embraces reality, and becomes submerged in the particulars, in their appearance in themselves. Only then does the experience of evil ensue.

In this context of a general perspective in which all is integrated, even "death is an illusion, its defilement is its falseness, what people call death is only the strengthening of life and its intensification, and through an abysmal submersion in pettiness, in which the inclinations of man's heart have submerged him, he imagines this strengthening of life in a morose and dark manner that he calls death" (*Orot HaKodesh*, Vol. II, p. 392). In other words, the vision of overcoming death is in no way eschatological; it is rather an overcoming that occurs whenever one's persepctive is removed from the particularity of experienced reality to the totality. It is an experiential event of the human spirit: "The spirit of man waxes, he surveys matter and spirit under one great survey, death completely loses its value and is annihilated from reality, through clear recognition and confident knowledge. Life will spread over everything. Spiritual nature and material nature, nature and the soul of nature, nature and the supernatural, all will become one assembly" (*Arpelei Tohar*, p. 71).

This, then, is the immanentist doctrine of Rav Kook, which leaves nothing outside spiritual reality, for insofar as the divine light is absolute good, whatever is infused by that light is grasped as good. This teaching recalls the pantheism of Spinoza.[16] The universality of G-d

---

book of divinity, in which he included much of his raving and folly, among them his fantasy that evil in existence is greater than the good."

16. Rav Kook criticizes the philosophy of Spinoza. He justifies his excommunication at the hands of the Amsterdam Jewish community: "The hand of G-d was on the heads of the Amsterdam congregation to exclude from the group he who wished oblivion on

prevents particularization, negates the independence of the particulars. Only Divine Substance exists, and everything else exists in Him; in this realm one cannot speak of evil or about death. Evil for Spinoza appears only as opinion or as imagination, a perception of the sense. What characterizes such knowledge is the narrow perspective, concentrating on the particulars. Opinion isolates the particulars but does not view them under the aspect of eternity. Thus arise such confused notions as good, evil, beautiful, ugly—a subjective judgment guided by particular emotions.[17] Spinoza states, "The more objects the mind understands by the second and third kinds of knowledge [reason and intuition], the less it suffers from those emotions which are evil, and the less it fears death."[18] In other words, different realms of knowledge are distinguished by their respective kinds of knowing. The clearer the knowledge—and what makes the knowledge clearer is the emancipation from particularity—the reality of things, their truth and eternity, their modes and states of existence, gain the correct perspective. According to this view, evil exists only as a confused awareness of things, in which their connection to their pure spiritual source is obscured.

v

The systematic structure of Rav Kook's immanent-theological doctrine reaches a special expression in relation to man. What is man? This anthropological question has many dimensions, each one of which seems to iluminate the question from a different perspective. Thus, the

---

the idealism of calling upon the name of G-d, by replacing it with the shocking call to self that bears with it neither boldness nor humility, neither sanctity nor joy, neither purity nor a life of desire for true action . . . that is in truth merely a call that to a strange god, and a great facilitation to an eventual vacuity of thought" (*Eder HaYekar*, pp. 130–41). See Zvi Yaron, *Mishnato shel HaRav Kook* (Jerusalem 5734), pp. 58–60: "Nevertheless Rav Kook notes that Spinoza had a 'considerable power' and that it is no wonder that this power appeared in a Jewish man for whom 'the thought of Divine Unity had taken such strong root in his soul.' In the philosophy of Spinoza is hidden a great light that it received in a 'broken, twisted manner' and with great labor it is possible to extract from this thick-skinned pomegranate too, some essential content that is worthy of enduring after scouring, cleansing and purification."

17. *Ethics*, II, Proposition 28.

18. Ibid. V, Proposition 38. See S. H. Bergmann, *Toledot HaPhilosophia HaChadasha*, Vol. I, pp. 286–91.

epistemological approach is unlike the ethical, and neither resemble the discussion of man as standing before G-d. Is man an integral part of nature, of the world, of the totality of creatures? Is he one more creature, or one who confronts the world, struggles with it, rebels against it, paves his own road, and determines his path as he sees fit? Aristotle attributes to man the naturalistic qualities of all beings, save that he has the capacity for knowledge and his happiness depends on that capacity, his function and achievments. Leibniz sees man as a windowless monad among the other monads or souls that populate the universe. Descartes stresses the dualism of body and soul. Spinoza sees him as a mode of the substance, so that man, in effect, expresses two aspects of the Divine Substance.

For Rav Kook, however, man is neither this nor that. He is all of these together. Man is manifest in the special role to which he is destined in the doctrine of inclusive unity. To be sure, man is integrated in the total organism of reality. Like every other part, he is reflected in the organic framework of reality. Nonetheless, Rav Kook expects more than this from man: "Man in his superior spirituality is the greatest power of agency in all reality" (*Arpelei Tohar*, p. 26). How is this "power of agency" expressed? It appears that Rav Kook diverts the center of gravity from the theoretical realm to the ethical. For the question what is man is particularly grave in the realm of ethics. For if man is a being who exists for himself, then he is liberated from collective responsibility and from relating to the world. This is because there no collective activity in which he takes part; hence it is impossible to obligate him regarding that which takes place outside his inner, self-enclosed world. He is responsible only to himself. He need not account for his actions to anyone else, for nobody else really exists. In this context, society is a mere aggregate of entities who maintain a purely external partnership, based on agreement or contract. On this plane, there need be no altruistic relationship or any responsibility beyond the obligations of legal contracts. The individual appears in his closed solitude, and for him the world is a collection of individuals like him. The relations of neighbors add up to external relations that, by their very nature, demand nothing beyond this. Man's alienation from the world around him necessarily implies a rigorous solipsism, which manifests itself in the lack of awareness of the outside world and in the absence of responsibility toward it. Man's isolation implies a separateness that lays claim to ultimate reality. Thus, in the final analysis, the rejection of moral responsibility toward the other is not only the negation of ethics, but also the rejection of ontological plurality. The monistic idealism of Schopenhauer views plurality as a subjective image. Thus, epistemology is necessarily affected by ethical negation. For separateness that claims ultimate reality also negates knowledge of that which lies beyond the "separateness." Clearly, in this context one cannot speak of interpersonal or intersubjective relations with respect to man.

Such thoughts are absurd from Rav Kook's point of view, both epistemologically and in terms of collective moral responsibility Rav Kook maintains that man is indeed a creature who is, from an anatomical point of view, one of the weakest living beings, an infinitesimal grain in the mighty world of celestial beings and infinite space. Yet his greatness is not in his body, but rather in the fact that his spirit is not encapsulated in a rigid shell, that it bursts into the outer world, knows it, and gives it meaning. The expression "world-embracing spirit" is interpreted literally: Spirit is suffused with consciousness of the universe. As a result of this irruption into the outside world, Rav Kook can view man as the center of creation. The world picture of modern cosmology does not eliminate the centrality of man: "In vain the short-sighted think that after the introduction of the cosmic picture the centrality of the human spirit has been abrogated . . . But also in the deep mysterious idea that finds an important place in religious life, and has enormously expanded in recent generations, there too nothing has been harmed, but rather the vision has been amplified. Moral responsibility increases with such interaction of being and this also lends extra energy to the spirit of man in his development" (Orot HaKodesh, Vol. II, p. 447).[19]

There is no scientific development that does not bear the stamp of the human spirit. Without man, there is no meaning or significance to the universe, which apart from its size lacks life and self-consciousness. The human spirit, aware of cosmic causality, also knows how to direct the evolution of the world, and thus to become its center. This idea does not make Rav Kook a partner of the Kantian conception that denies the operation of objective causal laws, and that man recognizes

19. See Y. Haddari, Perakim BeMishnato HaIyyunit shel HaRav Kook (5721), p. 7ff.

this lawfulness that stands outside him. According to Kant, causality is one of the categories of pure reason, similar to intuitions like space and time. Rav Kook conceives of the universe as it is, i.e., as the organic universe that exists in itself and that is known to us as such. However, in it and in its spirit is reflected objective being: "Man can reach such a quality that he discovers within himself the centrality of all being within him. And then he feels with his spirit all that is felt, all that is made . . . and all that moves with all the fullness of being at all of its levels" (*Musar HaKodesh*, p. 357). In man the universe is reflected as in a mirror. This is a microcosmic reflection of true being in itself.

Viewing man as the center of creation is not new in Jewish thought. This was a methodological thesis from Saadya on. Saadya emphasizes that the centrality of man is rooted in the fact that he possesses a spiritual soul. He states, "I observed and said, how is it possible that the goal of all that is in the world is man, for behold we see his body small and frail . . . Though his body be small, his spirit is broader than heaven and earth, for his knowledge encompasses whatever is in them."[20] Thus, there is no contradiction between man having a feeble body, dwarfed by the titanic dimensions of nature, and the fact that he is the center of creation. For his all-encompassing spirit is not bound at all to the tenement of clay in which it is housed. Hence the all-embracing moral responsibility of man in the systematic thought of the middle ages.

In Rav Kook's teaching, however, this point is sharpened, both in the light of modern scientific developments and in the light of man's unique status according to the doctrine of inclusive unity. Rav Kook states, "The nature of the world and each particular creature, human history and each individual man and his deeds, must be appraised under one scrutiny, as one content with different sections" (*Orot HaTeshuvah*, Vol. IV, p. 4).[21] And because it is all "one content" wherever you touch it, you are touching the same thing. The stress for Rav Kook is not on the cognitive dimension, and the greatness of man is not

---

20. *Emunot VeDeot* (Kaffih, ed., p. 152). Cf. Pascal (*Pensées*, No. 347): "Man is but a reed, the most feeble thing in nature; but he is a thinking reed . . . But, if the universe were to crush him, man would still be more noble than that which killed him, because he knows that he dies and the advantage which the universe has over him; the universe knows nothing of this."
21. 5726 edition, p. 30.

measured by the degree of knowledge. It is rather the Divine Spirit with which man is imbued. Hence it is a new stress that underlines the revoking of matter and its lack of significance. In what respect is man, indeed, a frail creature? His body? What significance has his body? The body is merely a tenement of clay, an external shell, like unto an afterbirth, what value has it? From his inception, man is founded on his spirit, and from this perspective the entire world is open before him.

The doctrine of cosmic organism receives a unique character with respect to the human spirit. But for that very reason, that is the greatness and centrality of man, his responsibility for his actions is enormous. Man performs an action here and now, yet insofar as the content of the cosmos is all one, it is all scrutinized together. The forms are differentiated, but their essence is one. Thus man holds in the palm of his hand, as it were, the totality.

Inclusive unity displays, thus, a new illumination: there is one, and only one, content woven into the texture of the many generations. That content becomes manifest in a most rigorous way through the immanentist conception. The Kabbalists maintain—and Rav Kook keeps this statement before his eyes—that "man gives power to the heavenly hosts." Man holds, as it were, the infinite threads that pull together the one content. Thus, his status in the inclusive unity is unique. The final and perfect expression of the inclusive-unity doctrine is found in man whose private actions, as it were, hidden from others' eyes, make ugly the entire world.

VI

So far we have discussed the collective responsibility of man and his unique power in the inclusive unity. But we have yet to state explicitly how that moral responsibility works itself out in the details that stress by their very nature the ontological, objective dimension. What exactly is brought about by individual actions? Are there indeed individual acts in the organic world—and if there are, what is their precise cosmic meaning? Rav Kook speaks of "one scrutiny," meaning that the particular in effect is eliminated, and you cannot speak of a particular act unless, at the same time, you survey with it the totality. If one must ever diverge from the particular, then the particular is nothing. Nonetheless, we treat of the particular act: in vain?

Obviously, even if we relate to man as a solitary creature completely detached from his environment, even then we cannot regard his actions and take into account whether they injure others in any way. One cannot be oblivious to the empirical fact that people are affected by the actions of others. But Rav Kook is not concerned with juridical questions relating to tort law, or sociological effects that are consequences of normative social contracts. In any society, whatever its arrangements, there is a concern with transgression. Even in a solipsistic world, it is discussed under two aspects: 1. As corruption of the individual organism. If the corruption is final, then the creature is eliminated, but individual perdition does not necessarily lead to the destruction of others. 2. If the corruption affects another, the transgression is grasped as an immoral act, on the assumption that one form of morality is the social contract, which regulates decent life for a society or congeries of individuals. Nothing is said here about the nature of those individuals, whoever they may be: Insofar as they are commanded or obliged to live together, there must be a norm of commonality. To be sure, there may be no congress between them: They may be windowless monads. Yet though we may have difficulty explaining how one is affected by the other, we cannot deny the fact of harm done. Thus, there is a place for morality that determines external rules of conduct. Of course, these laws have nothing in common with the organic laws of nature. They are merely conventional. At this level, one cannot speak in terms of organism. This is a level at which the unintentional sinner, for example, has his own law. If a man is unaware of his actions and did not intend to do evil, there is no point to punishing him from an ethical standpoint, unless this case too is anchored in the law and comes under societal convention.

Here the doctrine of inclusive unity moves into an absolutely different dimension. It addresses straightforwardly the unintentional act as well. Modern psychology and philosophy deal with aspects of unintentional acts, not only from a juridic-social perspective. Sophocles' drama *Oedipus the King* merited philosophical treatment in Aristotle's *Nicomachean Ethics*. The prevalent reading is that Sophocles intends to testify to cosmic determinism: Fate cannot be avoided; all must take place according to the preordained determination of fate; it is not in the hands of man to guide his realization. But among the other interpretations the play is judged from the viewpoint of unintentional sin.

Sin is grasped as an objective reality that takes place beyond the closed sphere of the transgressor. Sin is not only an ethical concept pertaining to the sinner alone or his immediate environment (if it was affected by this act). Sin, on this conception, is something that pertains to the totality of the world. When man sins, something happens to the world, something moves, the pile of nuts has altered its configuration by the slight movement of one individual nut.[22]

This conception is identical with that of Kabbalah and Christian mysticism regarding the sin of Adam. Adam's fall, which is verily the deterioration of one man, is at the same time the fall of the universe from its superior status, not only in the sense that a particular sin leads to an additional sin by another, through negative environmental impact (like the pile of nuts), but in the sense that the particular sin is the sin of the world.[23] Oedipus, according to Greek philosophy, does not sin from an ethical point of view. After all, he did all he could to avoid grave sins, such as parricide and incest. He does not undermine ethical norms, but does all in his power to strengthen them. But Oedipus killed his father and married his mother. That is a fact. That is a disturbance of ontological order. The acts of Oedipus are free of ethical opprobrium, but he must confront reality, and that is not the same reality that existed beforehand. The presence of that act is not engendered necessarily by acquiescence; it is an ontological fact. As long as the act is not redressed, order will not be reestablished. And it is impossible to redress the act unless Oedipus bears its punishment. This is part of the cosmic order according to Plato. The punishment of Oedipus has no ethical character, for it is not a criminal who is punished; it is rather a mending of the world. Jesus, who bears the suffering of the world, heals an objective deficiency in it. The act of Oedipus is grasped as the physical undermining of the world even if it was done unknowingly; only suffering can restore the balance. Plato ties man to a global framework guided by the celestial spheres. Man chooses his fate before birth; his state in the world is determined on the basis of his state before birth.

---

22. The Kabbalists claim that *chet* (sin) has the same numerical value (17, omitting the final, silent *alef*) as *egoz* (nut). Therefore one should abstain from eating nuts on Rosh Hashanah, the Day of Judgment. See S. Y. Agnon, *Yamim Noraim* (Jerusalem and Tel Aviv 5733), p. 71.

23. Chasidism speaks of the inclusive soul of Adam, which was woven of all human souls till the end of time. All future souls were thus present in that sin. See M. Buber, *Or HaGanuz* (Jerusalem and Tel Aviv 5737), p. 226.

This is the outstanding indication of man's connection to two worlds, both before birth and after death, when he receives the recompense destined him on the basis of his actions.

With Rav Kook, there is nothing essentially new regarding the idea of individual sin as a cosmic disturbance. Instead, he broadens the framework, as he is obliged to do, given his doctrine of inclusive unity. On the one hand, the sinner undermines all creation, but insofar as all is nourished by the divine light, the sinner severs his connection to the divine light. He falls into an abyss of isolation, and this is the source of the pain that accompanies the sinner: "Every sin torments the heart, because it contradicts the unity between the individual personality and all being . . . The basis of the sorrow is not of the substance of the sin itself but from the foundation of the sin and the content of the soul's passage, which has become the opposite of the order of being, which shines with the direct divine light upon all that exists that is organized harmoniously and under superior guidance" (*Orot HaTeshuva*, Vol. VIII, p. 3). The sinner excluded himself from the community, but this exclusion is simultaneously the detachment of the thread of life. All this with respect to the sinner as an individual; but just as he is part of the community, suffused by the totality, the totality of the world also passes through him. This is a two-sided affair, for all the threads of the world pass through the spirit of man. Therefore, "any ethical truncation, in idea or action, in trait or temperament, leads to many lacerations that bring about many internal torments to all the orders of the soul, for the basis of these spiritual torments is the jarring force of the withdrawal of the light of life belonging to the general order of all being from the channels of life of the sinning soul" (Ibid. Vol. VIII, p. 7). Here, Rav Kook stresses principally the psychological split in man as a result of his alienation from the channels of life. But between the lines one can hear the tremor of reflection. The sinner disturbs the cosmic order, but the undermining of order causes a secondary disturbance of his soul. Now the sinner does not suffer directly from the sin, but rather from the fact that he is living in a disharmonious world. There is thus a second "withdrawal of the light of life" as a consequence of the rending of "the general order of all being."

VII

Rav Kook's doctrine of inclusive unity receives its primary confirmation in the idea of repentance. Here is his principal contribution that exemplifies his teaching. Repentance is a problem that has, it would appear, no rational solution. For what does it mean that a man repents? The act that was done is done, it cannot be erased; what can it mean to atone for a sin? Can the murderer resurrect his victim, and if not, what means his repentance? If he expresses regret, beats his breast, resolves not to return to his folly again, does this have the slightest effect on the sinful act that is now part of his past? How can a present act of repentance that does not affect the original act of sin relate to the past action?[24]

These questions give repentance, from the outset, a special status beyond the limits of reason. This status pertains to the realm of divine grace bestowed upon the contrite. G-d reaches out to the sinner mired in his transgression. This is the central idea of the monotheistic religions; the idea of grace plays an especially important role in Christian thought.

Plato finds this concept irrelevant to the problem of sin. He scorns the popular idea that sacrifices alone can atone for sin. Punishment is recognized as the only possible way to mend the soul of the violator. At times there is no appropriate compensation in this world, because of a lack of proportion between crime and punishment; in which case, according to Plato, man receives his punishment in a future world. Particularly grievous sins have no expiation at all. Men who have performed such acts remain forever in Hades, the underworld. Plato does not recognize the idea of repentance; presumably it is a classically Jewish conception, connected to G-d's general graciousness.

Now Rav Kook takes the problem of repentance out of its religious-ethical context and deals with it as a matter given to philosophical psychosomatic inquiry. Repentance is a philosophical term, for him, that is yet to be properly investigated. At the same time, his immersion in the subject also inspires him to lyrical heights. He expounds the vision of a radiant future in which the entire universe is mended, when man lays upon his brow the crown of repentance. But this vision is not

24. See M. C. Luzzatto, *Mesillat Yesharim,* Chap. 4 (Jerusalem 5709), p. 32.

without the grounds of philosophical inquiry; repentance is a specific aspect of the inclusive unity system in which it finds its ultimate place.

The idea of repentance is based on a systematic conception of world-unfolding. This idea can already be found in Herder. For Herder, though his discussion is not without irony,[25] the world is developing toward the good. However, Rav Kook gives this idea a different flavor. He sets down a fundamental thesis: "The world must attain perfect repentance. The world does not remain in one state, it unfolds, and the genuine, perfect unfolding must bring it to complete health, material and spiritual, which brings the light of the penitent life with it" (*Orot HaTeshuvah*, Vol. 5, p. 3).[26]

Is this naive optimism? Upon what indeed is this thesis based? Is this merely a poetic vision, an eschatological ideal? What guarantees that the world will reach complete health? Does the twentieth century confirm this? And how do we know that it is at all possible to attain a better world? It is important to note that Rav Kook is aware of all these problems. He finds the strongest assurance of development toward the good in the fact that "man was very happy, and only an incident of sin made remote his path. It is self-evident that an incidental stumbling must be corrected, and man will return to his estate forever" (*Igrot HaReAYaH*, Vol. I, p. 74). In other words, the world was in a sound state, or in the language of Maharal of Prague (who influenced Rav Kook), sin is a deviation from the natural order; therefore the development of the world is toward a return to the natural order. The norm set for the world from its inception remains imprinted on it, and it attracts or guides evolution toward a reversion to it, even to a necessary reversion. Development, according to this conception, is not linear but circular. The healthy state of Adam in the Garden of Eden is the point of light to which man must return. Man deviated from it but will revert to it. Here is where the Fall occurred: The Fall

25. On Herder, see S. H. Bergmann, *Toledot HaPhilosophia HaChadasha* (Jerusalem 1973).
26. Rav Kook comments directly on modern evolutionary theory. He writes, "The doctrine of development, which is now conquering the world, coheres with the cosmic esoterica of the Kabbalah, more than any philosophical doctrine . . ." (*Orot HaKodesh*, Vol. II, p. 555ff). S. H. Bergmann compared modern evolutionary theory with that of Rav Kook. See his *Anashim uDerachim* (Jerusalem 5727), p. 350. See also Zvi Yaron, *Mishnato shel HaRav Kook* (Jerusalem 5734) p. 96ff; Y. Haddari, *Perakim BeMishnato HaIyyunit shel HaRav Kook* (Jerusalem 5721), p. 22ff.

indicates, on the one hand, a distancing from the source, but at the same time, as the Fall continues, there are signs of an approach from the other side. Since development is circular, one moves away from the point of light only to encounter it from the other side.

And surely without the point of light there is no guarantee for the development of the world. Rav Kook's optimism is accompanied by the fear that the development or return will stand still, swerve, or even retreat. But this fear is not dominant, since the felicity of the Garden of Eden is a nature imprinted upon man; it will guide evolution until we finally reach the original point of light.

At this point, one can discern Rav Kook's originality. His teaching cannot be identified with doctrines like those of Hegel or Herder, which insist upon the necessary progress of the universe, albeit they apparently had some influence on his thought. Modern evolutionary theory removes from man, in effect, his mastery over the evolutionary process. The cunning of reason is such that the world will evolve in spite of man, if necessary. In any event, man is liberated from responsibility for cosmic occurrences. If to be sure man's actions are accompanied by a sense or feeling of free choice, this too accords with the law of the cunning of reason motivating man, giving him the sense as if he wills because he has so chosen. Universal reason exploits man to fulfill its own needs.

For Rav Kook, this is not so. The term that expresses the development of the world toward the world that is all good is *repentance.* Just as he denies the blind will of Schopenhauer with the incidental evil it precipitates, so too he does not accept blind evolution, even if it is a beneficial evolution. What is done in the world is done by man, by his choice and through him. But since once in the history of the world man was rooted in happiness, a happiness that was natural to him and belonged to the cosmic order, this fact guarantees above all the possibility of attaining that happiness again. The highway to felicity, though it be overgrown with ragweed, nevertheless remains. It illuminates for man the road to felicity. Man, insofar as he is capable of free choice, may refuse, deviate again, retreat. But in the final analysis, how can one refuse happiness?

Rav Kook thus uproots repentance from man's particularity. Repentance is the organ of natural reality, suffused with cosmic lawfulness. This lawfulness is connected to all the motives of development, in medicine, technology, and all the forward-marching natural sciences. Nonetheless, this development is not detached from man and his activities, but depends upon them. This dependence increases man's ethical responsibility immeasurably. The sciences promote the return of the world to the original point of light, but it is man who steers the wagon of science with the beneficial intent of returning the world to its pristine state. Man, through repentance, motivates the wheels of progress, and by lack of repentance halts them. While for Hegel man is merely the tool of reason's cunning, for Rav Kook reason is the tool of man, through which his eyes are opened so that he can progress toward the point of light. For Rav Kook ties to the idea of repentance the doctrine of universal development, which is basically a religious idea, marking a knowing ethical deviation and a knowing return from sin. For Rav Kook, it is all one question: When man returns from his sin in accordance with the religious halacha of repentance, the world is mended. Nature and man turn from their evil ways, and cannot be separated; the same principle applies to both and conditions both.

Rav Kook's doctrine of repentance has an additional aspect, perhaps the crucial one with reference to the idea of inclusive unity. We noted that the flow of evolution is not linear but circular. The cyclical idea presupposes that nothing is canceled out. Everything flows constantly, but the flowing is that of the one totality, perfect in itself and given, in his phrase, to one scrutiny. The flowing is unified within the universe with all the entities of the world. Totality flows within itself, and outside of itself is a consolidated, unified block in its significance. History is frozen in its unity without the differentiation of past, present, and future. The division of time is internally subjective, when one is within the flow, but beyond it the unitary totality contains simultaneously all occurrences: "The nature of the world and each particular creature, human history and each individual man and his deeds, must be appraised under one scrutiny" (*Orot HaTeshuva*, p. 30). Man, by his sins, estranges himself from the totality, like a link detaching itself from the chain. Through repentance, man reconnects the link to the totality: "Every thought of repentance binds the entire past to the future, and the future is elevated through the elevated will of repentance out of love" (Ibid. p. 43). Here, then, is the solution to the problem of repentance, i.e., how it mends past actions. The past was never erased; it was detached and must be reintegrated.

Rav Kook does not recoil from the conclusion implied by his teaching. The world exists in its total unity. The point of origin of this world is man's experience in the Garden of Eden. That is the eternal hour of life, and the flowing world approaches that living hour. Rav Kook is no Parmenidean, despite his conception of the totality as a rigorous unity, because the totality flows, changes. Nor does the flowing make him Heraclitean, since for Heraclitus flowing negates identity and reversion; it is a linear flow, whereas Rav Kook's is circular. Man does enter the same stream twice; he returns to it. When the evolutionary circle is closed, we shall find ourselves in eternal life. Rav Kook calls death a deceit; a temporary oblivion. Death is a fiction. In truth, death is only the great return of man to the inclusive unity. Man returns to his G-d. This does not necessarily refer to the Neoplatonic conception of immortality of the soul, i.e., the return and merging of the soul in the encompassing light. Rav Kook says nothing of the abrogation of individuality or the loss of self-identity. Rather, he speaks of taking hold of the true reality of a world united and uniting itself with its Creator. Man is called upon to tear the veil from his eyes. The Jewish people, Rav Kook maintains, is called upon to roll the disgrace of death out of the world and to reveal eternal resurrection. Bergman regards this philosophical element in Rav Kook as the pinnacle of his thought.

VIII

In the context of Rav Kook's inclusive-unity idea, there is special significance to the Jewish people as a distinctly defined entity. Rotenstreich explains, "It is therefore impossible to define the essence of *Knesset Yisrael* by usual standards, for the ordinary standards can define social entities that are only social entities. The usual standards, which are drawn from the terminological and conceptual stores of sociology, have no validity for a reality that diverges beyond the limits of humanity."[27] What, then, is this distinctiveness, which makes the Jewish entity different from any other social group? This difference is the key to Rav Kook's positive attitude to the nonreligious part of the people, which is not necessarily a pedagogical tactic but an integrated implication of his general theory.

27. *HaMachashava HaYehudit BaEt HaChadasha*, p. 275.

We spoke above of four "models" of the universe in the medieval tradition. For Rav Kook, the model is imitated by the Jewish people. The Jewish people is not a society in the usual social-physical sense, but rather reflects the totality of being: "All these objects and whatever is above them, without separation or split, are set in the soul of all, in the form of *Knesset Yisrael,* in the image of the portrait of Jacob" (*Orot HaKodesh,* Vol. II, p. 299). In greater detail, he states, "*Knesset Yisrael* is the essence of all being, and in this world this essence suffuses the people of Israel literally, materially and spiritually, in its genesis and faith, and Israelite history is the ideal essence of general history; you have no movement in the world among all the nations the like of which you will not find in Israel" (*Orot, Orot Yisrael,* p. 138).

This thesis has large-scale ramifications for epistemology, insofar as reality as a whole—being at its various levels, spiritual and material, both of which are aspects of the spiritual—this reality is organically, inseparably integrated. A partial knowledge of reality is not a genuine knowledge, since it is contingent upon other organic components.[28] If knowledge of the totality is lacking, how can partial knowledge be attained?

Rav Kook states, "We have the capacity in our individual and general selfhood, in the form of our genesis, in the nature of our flesh, the temper of our land, the souls of our great ancestors, to know the truth" (*Orot HaKodesh,* Vol. I, p. 90).[29] Rav Kook sees an essential distinction between Israel and the nations based on an intellectual distinction:

28. A uniform world picture was accepted by Christian scholastics. Albertus Magnus (*De Animalibus,* Book II) states that "nature does not make [animal] kinds separate without making something intermediate between them; for nature does not pass from extreme to extreme *nisi per medium.* " Aquinas notes "the wonderful linkage of beings that nature reveals to our view. The lowest member of the higher genus is always found to border upon *(contingere)* the highest member of the lower genus." A. O. Lovejoy, in *The Great Chain of Being* (Harvard 1936, pp. 79–80), notes that we have here a hackneyed example borrowed from Aristotle. He also cites Nicholas Cusanus, who states, "All things, however different, are linked together. There is in the general of things such a connection between the higher and the lower that they meet at a common point; such an order obtains among species that the highest species of one genus coincides with the lowest of the next higher genus, in order that the universe may be one, perfect, continuous." See also F. Copleston, *A History of Philosophy,* pp. 326–29.
29. This conception has affinities to the thought of Rav Yehuda Halevi, who regards the people of Israel as a fifth level of creation. Rationalists like Maimonides et al. see no epistemological distinction between Israel and the Gentiles.

"The substantial difference between Israel and the nations, in the root of their souls, is that human reason in general, which is no more than a descriptive reason . . . but the divine paragon of creative reason, that is the marvel of Israel's excellence, which distinguishes it from all the nations with such superiority, that no difference of kind can be compared to it" (*Orot HaKodesh*, Vol. III pp. 67–68).

Naturally, Rav Kook does not adduce proof for this rather chauvinistic concept. It sounds like a vision borne on the wings of fantasy. But such distinctions are found in the nonrationalistic tradition from Rav Yehuda Halevi to Maharal of Prague. Avraham bar Chiyya speaks of three souls in man: rational, animal, and vegetative. In Israel, unlike the Gentiles, the rational soul is not mingled with the others. Duran distinguishes between theoretical reason and practical reason; the former, in his opinion, is found only among Jews. In any event, according to Rav Kook, the knowledge of truth is found in Israel because its creative reason comprehends the totality of being, the organism in its completeness. This is, of course, not discursive-dialectical knowledge, but rather confrontation with truth deriving from an inner intuition of the all that knows all, the perfect knowing the perfect. In other words, the knower and the known are one.

If so, then the Jewish people reflect faithfully the nature of being. This reflection is not abstract. It does not mean that the idea of Israel is an idea containing the totality of reality, but rather that the concrete Jewish people in all its members are microscopic limbs of reality. This is the context of the nation's uniqueness, and especially the unique status of its constituents. Rav Kook says, "The relation of *Knesset Yisrael* to its constituents is different from the relations of any national collective to its individuals. All the national collectives give their members only the external aspect of their nature, but the nature itself each one draws from the total soul . . . Not so Israel . . . if one considers detaching oneself from the nation, he must detach his soul from its source of life, and therefore the requirement of each Jew for the community is great indeed" (*Orot Yisrael*, Vol. I, p. 144).

Cleaving unto G-d (in the sense of the German *Einfuhlung*) in Israel is at one and the same time a merging "into the light of the G-dhead that is revealed in all being." Any other society is an accidental combination of people, not founded on an inner essential nexus; hence it is a membership in a formal world of citizenship that engenders normative obligations only. By the same token, secession is the abrogation of that membership. For the Jewish nation, however, "Only it has inner powers, only it is not based on merely economic partnership. All other entities outside of Israel are to be defined as "society (*hevra* according to the definition of Gordon), in other words aggregates founded on common economic interests."[30] Rav Kook says this explicitly: "The Land of Israel is not something external, an external possession of the nation, merely a means toward the goal of general organization and maintenance of its material, or even spiritual, existence. The Land of Israel is a substantial entity vitally connected to the soul of the nation, embraced by inner distinctiveness with its reality" (*Orot, Eretz Yisrael,* p. 9).

Jewish existence is a complete entity closed in itself. In its content it is the reflection or essence of all being. This fact engenders its supranormative character. Every Jew belongs, on the one hand, to the general organism of being, but on the other hand he is now an integral part of the Jewish entity. The individual cannot secede from the entity, nor can it do without him, just as the body cannot give up one of its limbs and no limb can exist independent of the body.

The doctrine of inclusive unity of Rav Kook informs us of two principles: 1. Being is nourished by, and draws its life from, the Divine Spirit. The world is an organism because of the "immanent theism" according to which everything aims to contribute to the Divine Spirit, and from which its existence or the possibility of its existence derives. Matter is without ultimate significance, therefore it cannot be self-subsistent. Every withdrawal from the divine infusion amounts to self-annihilation. "Immanent theism" stresses, thus, the Divine Spirit found in every immanent being, on the one hand, and on the other hand, that only this Spirit exists, and whatever exists does so only within it. 2. The Jewish people constitutes a complete entity, a copy of the universal prototype. Therefore there can be no change in the mode of life of this people, because each individual characterizes one feature of all being. Just as the totality of being is a complete organism, so the Jewish people is a complete organism with the identical content.

Thus, the attitude of Rav Kook toward the nonreligious Jew is a consequence of his fundamental theology. It is an attitude implied by

30. Rotenstreich, p. 277.

his general outlook, which precipitates the integrity of the Jewish people. That nothing can deviate from this line is not a matter of pedagogic tactics that can be altered or given up. Rav Kook appears against this backdrop with a message of social unity that is identical with the message of his unique theology.

Art

Rabbi A. Yehoshua Zuckerman

"IF WE WISH to revive Israel's literature, we must proceed in this holy way, coming from holiness to literature" (*Orot*, p. 82).

HaReAYaH, of blessed memory, did much for the revival of Israel's literature. Literature should be seen as one expression of art, and Rav Kook uses it in defining art in general. In the Introduction to his commentary to Song of Songs, he says, "Literature, its design and its tapestry gives material expression to all the spiritual concepts implanted in the depths of the human soul; and as long as even one single line hidden in the depth of the soul has not been given outward expression, art, craftsmanship, or literature has a duty to bring it out. It is understood that it is good and lovely to develop only those treasures that, in being opened up, add fragrance to the air of existence. 'The whole world was filled with fragrance from every word that went forth at Sinai from the mouth of the Holy One, blessed be He.' (*Shabbat* 88b)" (*Olat ReAYaH*, Vol. II, p. 3).

From these two quotations, it appears that the function of literature—or more generally, of art as a whole—is to bring to realization that which is hidden, to make tangible that which is abstract, to activate that which is concealed in the soul, to reveal the sacred in its spontaneous manifestations.

In order to understand this, let us explain the root of the word *omonut* (art) (from which comes also the word *emet* (truth), that is the acknowledgment of reality as it is, as will be understood later)—*AMN alef mem nun*—in its various forms: *aman* (artist), *neeman* (faithful), *omonut* (art), *emunah* (faith, or faithfulness). The common denominator linking these words is that they indicate the bringing out into the open of an inner content. Thus one can understand why Rav Kook connects art with holiness. (It is this connection that determines the relationship between the people of Israel and art; as will be explained at the end of this article.) An artist is a person qualified and capable of expressing his own inner world in material creative form. One whose talents enable him, in the work of his hands, to be faithful to his feelings, his thoughts, his imagination and his will—such a person is called an artist. In HaReAYaH's own words, "He actualizes the lines of his soul."

For Rav Kook, art is related closely to holiness because, like all creation, its purpose is to reveal the Infinite, blessed be He, in the finite world and within material bounds. He deals with this at length in Chapter 16 of *Orot HaTechiyah* (*Orot,* pp. 67–69), where he commences as follows: "It is plain that a righteous man performs all his deeds with holiness, and all his material actions lead to the perfection and completion of the world, and this is 'love of work,' which, apart from its own worth, was given in a covenant, as was the Torah (*Bereshit R.* 74:12). Consequently, there is no doubt that the perfection of the entire world and the diffusion of the light of holiness are really to be found in all workmanship; in every action that delivers any part of existence from the rule of chaos there is something great and of general significance."

The same applies also with reference to the word *emunah*. It is generally thought that *emunah* is an idea, the acceptance in the heart of man of the concept of the existence of the Creator, or even feelings of holiness and the stirrings of love toward the Holy One, blessed be He. But this is not what Rav Kook teaches in his lessons on the *Kuzari* (*Maamrei HaReAYaH,* Vol. II, p. 489): "The content of *emunah* is not an idea but something completely existential that is found in all parts of creation, even in the inanimate; and this is the secret of the world's existence." HaReAYaH describes the Creator, blessed be He, as the "Artist" who reveals the innermost worlds in the midst of the

material world "in image and likeness"; with the faithfulness of One
who is marvelous in counsel, He restores souls unto the dead. And with
regard to the prayer that speaks of the Creator's great faithfulness: "I
give thanks before Thee, O King, living and everlasting G-d, for Thy
having mercifully restored my soul to me; great is *Thy faithfulness,*"
Rav Kook explains this faithfulness as the function of the One Who
faithfully actualizes all His inner desires and brings them to realization
in the lower worlds. Here are his words: "Divine faithfulness is that
which legislates the duties of all the forms of G-d's creations, ordering
them to perform their service with complete strength, enthusiasm,
stability and eternity, and with all the reality and force of existence and
triumph with which the mighty force of the light of divine faith
illuminates them . . . (*Olat ReAYaH,* Vol. I, p. 3). G-d is, if we may
say it, the artist who does what is necessary to bring harmony—with
perfect unity—between spirit and matter, and to transfer into the one
what is in the other without blurring the special form of each world
and without betraying the original inner, hidden intention. The Infinite, blessed be He, is revealed with wondrous faithfulness in the
physical universe, and His Will is done in the netherworld just as it is
in the abstract upper world. "I was its artisan . . ." says the Torah: "I
was the instrument of the Holy One's craftmanship, blessed be He. It
is the custom of the world that when a king of flesh and blood builds
a palace he does not build it out of his own thinking, but according to
the plan of a craftsman; nor does the craftsman build it out of *his* own
fancy, but he has plans and books that tell him how to make rooms and
closets. So also the Holy One, blessed be He, looked into the Torah
and created the world" (*Bereshit R.* 1:1).

The quality of faith is inherent in the work of the artist as it reveals
itself in his creations. Just as the Almighty has faith, so we too have
to have faith and to actualize the divine that exists in our souls. It is
possible to do this by means of the practical commandments that fulfill
the Will of the Creator as it influences the 248 limbs of our bodies
(*Makkot* 23b). "All Thy commandments are faithful" (Psalms 119:
86). Faith is an experience ("And the righteous shall live by his faith"
(Hab. 2:4)) that is elevated above the power of the soul—intelligence
and feeling—for it is the soul itself. The same applies to the artist. He
offers all his inner strength; the secret of his life-strength is poured out.
Therefore (Rav Kook adds), "likewise with the inanimate." Moreover

faith is not an idea, a metaphysical philosophy, originating in man and reaching up to the heights above. Faith is that which appears to us and descends upon the soul's inclination even prior to the stirrings of intellect and feeling." And HaReAYaH continues, "Faith's strength is a general strength and not a private one, an enveloping light that flows from the source of the entire creative experience and spreads everywhere; and all the learning, the sciences and the general research work are but instruments and means that help to implant faith deep within the heart of man" (*Maamrei HaReAYaH*, Vol. II, p. 489). Furthermore, "the power of faith is the image of the Divine that sheds light out of the innermost recesses of the Holy One's creatures, blessed be He, and it is the very essence of the soul. . . . When the power of faith is developed, the soul is in a normal, natural, healthy condition, and man then finds himself in a spiritual paradise that quenches his thirsty soul longing for the word of the Lord . . . and therefore the power of faith that is so treasured in the world is the foundation of the world's existence . . ." (Ibid. p. 487).

G-d is the believing Artist and we are His art, the work of His hands by which He is glorified. Man, the man of faith, is capable of living according to the actualized principles of the Eternal. He recognizes that the Eternal fills everything. The narrow horizons of our material world do not confine Him, for everything is divine art and poetry. Our prophets were able to liken the image with its maker; for the enlargement of the Lord is in everything. If we could put the Infinite and the sacred into words, we would all become writers with the power of speech of the prophets, disciples of Bezalel, who was capable of joining together the divine letters from which heaven and earth were created.

"Our wondrous tzaddikim, for whom this world held no importance from the point of view of its boundaries, its lowness and its limitations—they were in fact the ones who esteemed and respected it, because they saw in it a heavenly universe, brightness and purity from the source of life; its beauty and goodness ascending with great gradations. With them the feeling of pleasantness and beauty in the world grows with the greatness of a heavenly holiness and refinement, so that they come to live a full life with the refreshing sap of all the aesthetic pleasures that adorn life to a very high degree" (*Orot HaKodesh*, Vol. III, Chap. 44, p. 306).

There is nothing here of the crude divisiveness found in Christian idolatry, or in others who preceeded it, where a distinction is made between matter and spirit, between society and the kingdom of heaven, between bachelorhood and the married estate, etc.; on the contrary, everything is a wonderful unity. Indeed, the more rooted elevated concepts are, the more their influence spreads to the lowliest earthly places. And here is one aspect of the definition of beauty: an overflowing of pleasure from seeing. A body will be called beautiful when it attracts to itself, and then envelops and spreads upon its environment the essence of the splendor that is poured on to itself. The word *beauty* primarily means enlargement and expansiveness. "May G-d enlarge Japheth" (Genesis 9:27), on which Rashi comments, "The Targum renders the verb by *Yafti*, meaning, 'May He extend.'" Likewise, "When the Lord thy G-d shall extend thy border" (Deuteronomy 12:20), which the Targum renders, "When [the Lord] shall extend *(Yafti)* thy boundary." Now there is no diffusion greater than the revelation of the Infinite. And when the Infinite is revealed in the body, which then immediately radiates the incomparable light and reveals the Infinite, blessed be He, through its actions and thoughts, there can be nothing more beautiful. Thus also the *Gemara* in *Zebachim* (54b) explains that the Temple is called "the adornment of the world." The lodgement of the Divine Mighty Presence in this great and holy house and its construction according to measurements fitting for a temple are the guarantees of the building's beauty; and it was from there that the singing of the Levites burst forth at the hour of their service. This is because "the foundation of beauty is the direction and the relationship between the parts" (*Olat ReAYaH*, Vol. I, p. 333), and it is the radiation that emanates from the source of the overall unity that enables the parts of the body that reveal it to relate to each other in peaceful harmony. Therefore, "regarding our wonderful tzaddikim . . . their spiritual senses, even in relation to normal aesthetic content, recognizing the beauty in art, in song, in order, in the state and in morality, and in every value, are doubled in a magnificent degree so that they become the sources of beauty and order in life" (*Orot HaKodesh*, Vol. III, p. 306).

The beauty that accompanies this craftsman's art is nothing but the manifestation of heavenly holiness. In the verse of Proverbs, "false is favor and vain is beauty"; this is true when these attributes stand by themselves as simply physical values or the pursuit of sensual pleasure, but "the woman that feareth the Lord" can be praised for her beauty as well as for the thread of graciousness that is drawn over her head. "In the magnitude of holiness there is room for all the esthetic pleasures that adorn life in a very high degree."

We have referred (very briefly) to the conception of unity that joins the sacred to all its many manifestations—all creation and all creatures—spirit to matter, the abstract to the concrete, so that it is possible truthfully to find the upper world in the lower world. Now we must go further and explain what is the role assigned by Rav Kook, of blessed memory, to the people of Israel in all this "artistic" process. There is no room here to assess at length the special qualities of the people of Israel; but it may be said that just as every nation has a certain mission that it has to fulfill, and it has also the talents to do this, so also the people of Israel has its role and the qualities enabling it to fulfill its purpose. On the verse "The people believed" (Exodus 4:31) our sages add (*Shabbat* 97a): "The Holy One, blessed be He, said to him: "Israel is believers and descendants of believers." Similarly, also with our teacher Yehuda Halevi (in his book The *Kuzari*, 2:36). He likens the people of Israel among the nations to the heart in a human body in which each limb contributes its share to the wholeness of the body in a peaceful harmony; and the heart, through its centrality and its own function, cooperates with all the parts of the body. In the words of Rav Kook, "The body of Israel is the essence of all existence, and in this world this essence overflows into the very nation of Israel, both in its physical and its spiritual being, in its history and its faith" (*Orot*, p. 138, para. 1). And further: "The inner beauty of the body of Israel, through which she draws to herself the heart of all her children, is the divine grace that is poured over her; for in her wholeness, which envelops all, she attains from the Divine a supreme, refined purity, such that no other nation or individual is able to achieve" (*Orot Yisrael*, Chap. 2, para. 6).

Yet HaReAYaH does not regard lightly every outward pleasant accomplishment of the nations of the world. In his speech at a Chanukah gathering, he referred to the *Gemara* (*Bava Kama* 83a): "Greek language is one thing and Greek wisdom another," and remarked, "The meaning is that one must distinguish between content and style. Greek wisdom, as a Weltanschuung, seriously hurts that which is holy, profanes it, makes it impure. But the Greek tongue, the language from the point of view of its power of expression, its power of description—that is quite another matter. Here there is no conflict of substance, no system of beliefs and views; here there is only an external perfection that, in itself, does not affect inner matter (and language can cover everything that does not concern beliefs, including practical science). Our sages expounded the verse 'May G-d enlarge Japheth so that he may dwell in the tents of Shem' to mean the beauty of Japheth (i.e., the Greek language) will reside in the tents of Shem" (*Megillah* 9b. Talk quoted in *Moadei HaReAYaH* by Rav Neriah, p. 183.)

And even with regard to Greek wisdom, about which the Talmud (*Bava Kama* 82b) decreed, "Cursed be the man who would teach his son Grecian wisdom," Rav Kook saw here a prohibition concerning only the education of children, as can be inferred from the language of the decree. And this accords with the *Gemara Menachot* (99b), where we read that Rav Ishmael noted to his nephew ben Dama that he should not occupy himself with Grecian wisdom because it would lead to dereliction of Torah study, as it is said, "This book of the Torah shall not depart from thy mouth, and thou shalt meditate therein day and night," and not because of a prohibition of the study of that wisdom per se. (In fact, so far as the study of Torah is concerned, or desisting from it, limits have been set; but this is not the place for these details. Ibid.)

In general terms, HaReAYaH distinguishes between Grecian wisdom—the influence of opinions, and Greek language—influence through style. "The Holy One, blessed be He, dealt charitably with his world by not putting all the talents in one place, not in any one man or in any one nation, not in any one country, not in one generation or in one world; but the talents are scattered . . . The store of the special treasure of the world is laid up in Israel. But in order, in a general sense, to unite the world with them, certain talents have to be absent from Israel so that they may be completed by the rest of the world and the princes of the nations. That is to say, the inwardness of life is complete in Israel without need of help from any strange force in the world . . . but the externals of life may sometimes need completion from without: 'The beauty of Japheth will live in the tents of Shem' (*Megillah* 9b); 'Ye shall eat the wealth of the nations, and in their splendor shall ye glory' (Isaiah 61:6). But because of the abundance of the inwardness of its life, the Assembly of Israel only exercises an outward influence (on others) but receives nothing (from others). 'The Lord alone doth lead him, and there is no strange god with Him' (Deuteronomy 32:12)" (*Orot,* p. 152, para. 2).

And since art is a matter of "faith"—the presence of inwardness in the framework of externals—and Israel is the nation of the prophets, consequently Israel constitutes the living force that fructifies every form of art in the most complete form. Only the holy nation can be the nation whose Temple is the beauty of the world and is destined to become a house of prayer for all nations.

"And the world is brightened with its beauty and elevated with its glory through the influence of the splendor of their souls (i.e., of the most wonderful 'tzaddikim' or righteous men); and all artists and scientists are elevated, ornamented and blessed by the influence of their work. For they themselves dwell in the realm of the *sefira* of divine glory *(Tiferet),* which includes in one unit all the splendor of heaven and earth, and the glory goes on being diffused upon every creature and upon all their deeds, upon all the feelings and leanings of their hearts; and the light of a king in his beauty is increasingly imprinted upon them" (*Orot HaKodesh,* Vol. III, p. 306).

Aesthetics

Dr. Yehuda Gelman

A RECURRENT MOTIF in Rav Kook's writings concerns an opposition and tension between the quest for order, balance, and restraint, on the one hand, and the quest for spontaneous self-expression and spiritual freedom on the other hand, and the reconciliation of that tension. Rav Kook lived this opposition and yearned for resolution in his own soul. This subject finds expression in different spheres of his work, including ethics and aesthetics. I wish to address the area of aesthetics as representative of his interest in the opposition between the two principles.

Rav Kook's interest in this subject has parallels in late nineteenth-century European philosophy. His aesthetic attitudes are fully understood only in this context. Many thinkers of this period discussed the idea of a contradiction between these two quests. The most impressive formulation of the problem, however, is that of the German philosopher Friedrich Nietzsche. Although Rav Kook does not mention Nietzsche in his writings, he was familiar with nineteenth-century philosophy. In my opinion, his attitudes to aesthetics were crucially influenced by Nietzsche. Rav Kook specifically confronted this confrontation. Thus, I shall present the general subject as treated in Nietzsche's oeuvre, particularly his aesthetics.[1] Having clarified the context in which Rav Kook wrote, we can turn to his own aesthetic doctrine.

For Nietzsche, there are two vectors of aesthetic creation, which draw their power from two more general opposing tendencies. Nietzsche speaks of Apollonian and Dionysiac creativity, named after the Greek gods Apollo and Dionysus.[2] In Nietzsche's eyes, these two gods represent the deep cleavage between two elements of life. Who are Apollo and Dionysus?

Apollo proclaims at his birth, "I will transmit to mankind the unchanging will of Zeus." This he accomplishes through messages transmitted by oracles. The priests who speak in his name receive the word in a calm, quiet religious experience. The Delphic Oracle says in Apollo's name, "Know thyself"—a call to intellectual insight and rational analysis of the individual's existence. With the passage of time, Apollo becomes the god of rhythm, harmony, restraint, and law. As such, he is the god of ethics, social order, and the order of human creation. The emblem of Apollo is his bow, which, according to Heraclitus, symbolizes the unity integrating opposition.

Dionysus is the polar opposite of Apollo. He was born of Zeus and a human mother, and then begotten again by Zeus himself! At first he was not one of the gods; he introduced himself into the pantheon. As an infant, Dionysus was dismembered and reunited. Everything about him is marvelous. He appears suddenly and disappears the same way. He performs the most impressive wonders—extracting water from a rock, growing a vineyard overnight, and the like. Dionysus is the god of wine, and represents the constant renewal of life in nature. The Dionysiac cult is all ecstasy and orgiastic uproar. The frenzied dance, the wild and forceful head movements, the spontaneous music and song, are all features of the Dionysiac cult. The cult has a religious significance, for in orgiastic mania man is liberated from human inhibitions, and the individual loses his self-consciousness to the point where

1. Nietzsche dealt with aesthetics in many of his writings, but particularly in *The Birth of Tragedy, Thus Spake Zarathustra,* and *Twilight of the Idols.* I have here summarized his general views.

2. On Apollo and Dionysos see Guthrie, *The Greeks and their Gods;* Walter Otto, *Dionysos: Myth and Cult;* E. R. Dodds, *The Greeks and the Irrational;* Mircea Eliade, *A History of Religious Ideas,* Vol. I.

he becomes *entheos* (full of gods). Dionysus frees man from conventional moral prohibitions and hedges—i.e., from the Apollonian state. In a word, Dionysus represents spontaneity and departure from the limits of self-consciousness. Dionysus is the redeemer.

Nietzsche sees the Apollonian and Dionysiac elements as the root of artistic creation. Apollonian art is expressed in the molding of form and its definition, in highlighting the individual. It is a descriptive, representational art. The principal Apollonian arts are sculpture, painting, and programmatic music. This art is dreamlike, for it deals primarily in images. But unlike the dream, it is orderly, measured, balanced, and free of untamed feelings. Apollonian art is the actualization of a preexisting idea; its success is tested by the degree of resemblance between the original idea and its execution.

Dionysiac art is inebriated without wine. The Dionysiac artist abandons the limits of the individual to merge with the unity of being. Like the Dionysiac orgy, which abrogates the private consciousness of the participants, it erases individuality and self-awareness. It does not imitate an existing idea but is rather spontaneous and immediate, liberating the artist from aesthetic subjugation. It is found primarily in poetry, dance, and music. It does not deal with phenomena or images, but, to use Nietzsche's phrase, "with the realm that precedes phenomena and goes beyond them."

The contradiction between these two polar aesthetic forces is resolved, according to Nietzsche, in Greek tragedy, where the two forces act together. The Greek chorus, which abrogates personality and erases the individual, exists side by side with the personal protagonists of the scenes: the Dionysiac and the Apollonian.

As noted above, this is the context in which Rav Kook wrote on aesthetics. To be sure, I do not believe that Rav Kook thought specifically in terms of "Apollo" and "Dionysus." But I submit that the Nietzschean notions were before his mind, and serve as the background to his reworking and transformation of profane ideas into sacred ideas. In order to understand properly Rav Kook's discussions and to evaluate his approach to aesthetics, one must grasp the Nietzschean background. It is also necessary to understand the complementary relationship of the two forces in Rav Kook that contrasts with their relationship according to Nietzsche.

In my opinion, Rav Kook recognized three levels of artistic creation. The lowest corresponds to the Apollonian. At this level, art arranges the constituents of an external beauty according to definite principles and relations. Such creation Rav Kook calls *tiferet* or "external *tiferet.*"

The structure of the world in its totality, in the arrangement of its constituents and the wonderful value of their relation one to the other . . . This *tiferet* state is founded on firm laws, the laws of beauty and value (*Olat ReAYaH,* Vol. I, p. 230).

The foundation of the appropriate is fit and relation between the constituents . . . between external constituents that appear to the eye . . . since the human soul is founded on the values of which it is worthy, it is already worthy of performing many actions of external *tiferet* (Ibid. p. 233).

At this level, beauty is merely an "external good"[3] dealing only with the realm of images and phenomena, but does not penetrate to the inner realm that precedes the phenomena and transcends them.

Of this level of creativity, Rav Kook wrote to the Bezalel Association upon its establishment in 5668 (*Igrot HaReAYaH,* Vol. I, pp. 203–6). The Bezalel Association would deal primarily with representational art and crafts, both of which are Apollonian in nature. In his letter, Rav Kook calls upon them to avoid "intoxication and exaggeration" and "the wild sense of beauty." He states that "beauty itself is liable to be turned, in the hands of the vulgar mob, to a kind of oleaginous cake and intoxicating beverage." In his opinion, it is the function of halacha to set a measure and limit on beauty, lest it break out of its Apollonian bounds and deteriorate into Dionysiac wildness. The limitation is indeed "refined and soft, delicate and beautiful . . . hedged by roses," yet "even what is hedged by roses should not be breached." External beauty must be guarded against degeneration into Dionysiac madness, restrained by halacha—the ally of Apollo.

There is a second, higher, level of aesthetic creation. Like the first level, it answers to laws; unlike the first, however, it deals with that which lies beyond the phenomena, with inner spiritual existence. This aesthetic level is attained by poetry and music. Rav Kook resorts to the metaphors of music and poetry when he wishes to describe inner life,

3. *Ein Ayya,* cited in *Maamrei HaReAYaH,* Vol. I, p. 214.

a use that testifies to their pertinence to the realm beyond phenomena. Thus, for example, he describes the saint:

The divine song plays always according to harmonic rules in the inwardness of his soul, and the relation of the part to the whole, and to the source of the whole, flashes and is revealed in manifold different appearances (*Arpelei Tohar*, p. 38).[4]

And:

Sometimes the thirst for the original divine enlightenment increases . . . and sometimes the thirst for imagination and image increases, and sometimes the thirst for feeling increases, and sometimes the thirst for learning increases, and sometimes all these thirsts together increase and rise intermingled in the chambers of the heart, blended in various combinations, and a complete harmony of sacred melody comes into being from them (*Orot HaKodesh* III, 213). All the senses of the true saint are given to the divine connection of all the worlds . . . All of them without remainder are accords of the sacred music, through which the life of the Deity, as it permeates through all the worlds, vents its voice, a robust voice (Ibid. p. 259).

These two aesthetic levels are given different names. The first, lower one, is beauty (or the beautiful, *yafeh*); the second, higher one, is called holiness (or the sacred, *kadosh*). External beauty is not called *kadosh* by Rav Kook. Occasionally, with respect to tefillin for example, he calls inner beauty *pe'er* and connects it to the inwardness and essence of the soul:

Tefillin are the robustness of Israel, our grandeur [*pe'er*] wrapped about our heads . . . The primary splendor and grandeur [of the soul] is buried and concealed in the depths of the *pe'er* hidden in the mystery of its spiritual essence . . . (*Olat ReAYaH*, Vol. I, p. 22).

The *pe'er* of this divine naturalness . . . stands out in its sacred splendor through the commandment of tefillin, the glory of our majesty and the featured prominence of our own sanctity, which is hidden in the depths of our being (Ibid. p. 23).[5]

4. Published by Rav Z. Y. Kook Institute
5. See also Rav Kook's treatise *Chavash Pe'er*.

Thus, the second level generates the sphere of *pe'er*, of inward, hidden holiness far removed from the phenomena. It too is subsumed under firm laws.

In Kabbalistic terms, Rav Kook may have recognized two aspects of the *sefira Tiferet*, one external and one internal. There may be an essential distinction between then apart from externality and internality. In *Chavash Pe'er*[6] he distinguishes two types of combination *(tzeruf)*. In one of them, each constituent preserves its identity, and the constituents, combined, become a new entity. Each constituent contributes to the complete unity. For example, if two men lift an object that each one of them could not lift by himself, each one contributes half the effort, thus creating the possibility of the object being lifted. Such is descriptive art, which is constructed through the correct arrangement of constituents. The other kind of combination is total. The resulting unity is a new entity, transcending the nature of the constituents. Rav Kook offers the example of two millstones: The action of the millstones is not the sum total of the action of each stone, but rather a new action that could not have occurred when they were separate. This is the *pe'er* of internal beauty. The second aspect is superior, and is found in the interrelationship between the sanctity of tefillin and the sanctity of the Jewish people. One may conclude that external *tiferet* is a combination of constituents of the first type, whereas internal *tiferet* is a total unity.

Alternatively, one might view external *tiferet* not as an aspect of the *sefira Tiferet*, but rather as a reflection of *tiferet* within the *sefira* of *Malchut;* internal *tiferet* would be identified with *Tiferet* proper. As noted, *kadosh* can refer to internal *tiferet* in Rav Kook's language. *Kadosh*, in Kabbalah, usually refers to the *sefira* of *Tiferet* (or to Chochma) and not to that of *Malchut*. Balance and measure exist, under certain conditions, within *Malchut* as well, as a result of the action of *Tiferet* upon it. This effected *tiferet* majesty may be denominated "external *tiferet*."

The second level, i.e., inward *tiferet*, penetrates to the inner nature of the artist; as Schopenhauer put it, "Music sees the heart alone." Nonetheless, it is subject to the limitations of the first level, insofar as it is based on rules and harmony. Beyond this, Rav Kook expresses a

6. *Derush* 6, pp. 31–32.

higher level of artistic creation, above both beauty and the sacred. The third aesthetic level is above all laws, all harmony, all restraint. It partakes of Dionysiac spontaneity and a free creative flow; it partakes of that Dionysiac enlargement of the ego into an ego that merges with the expanses of being. Rav Kook lived and created in the most significant sense at this third level. He wrote of this level of existence in his poem "Expanses":

> Expanses, expanses,
> The expanses of G-d my soul craves.
> Don't shut me in any cage . . .
> My soul roams the breadths of heaven,
> It cannot be contained by the walls of the heart
> Or the walls of action,
> Ethics, logic, custom—
> Above all these it roams and it flies . . .
> Exalted above delight,
> All pleasantness and beauty . . .[7]

Elevation above all logic and beauty precipitates new heights of aesthetic creation. Hence Rav Kook's description of his poetic style:

My thoughts are broader than the sea, I cannot express them in the language of prose, against my better interest I am compelled to be a poet, but a free poet. I cannot be bound to the chains of meter and rhyme, I flee simple prose, because of the heaviness in it, because of its restriction, and I cannot place myself under other restrictions, greater and perhaps more oppressive than the oppression of prose from which I flee.[8]

Bialik characterized Rav Kook's creativity as one that flows from the immediate selfhood of the creator, not the result of contrivance:

I know that whatever is printed of his, this is as the rabbi wrote the first time, and to write that way the first time—only R. Kook can![9]

7. A. M. Haberman, *Shirat HaRav* (Sinai 5705), p. 13.
8. Y. Hadari and Z. Yaron, *Perakim BeMishnato Halyyunit shel HaRav Kook* Part II, pp. 55–56.
9. M. Z. Neriah *HaReAYaH Rishona VeHemshechah* (Moreshet 5733).

At this level of creativity, there are no laws; the artistic substance flows freely from the artist. Picasso has testified that he did not know which colors he would employ in a particular painting until he actually reached for them; the author Henry Miller once said, "I know nothing in advance. Often I put down things which I do not understand myself, secure in the knowledge that later they will become clear and meaningful to me."[10] Though Schopenhauer stressed the "idea" before the artist's mind, he nonetheless knew of the artist who works under an immediate, spontaneous impulse not planned in advance. Schopenhauer compares this artist to a beaver that constructs its dam without prior benefit of engineering training. (The image of the beaver is reminiscent of Rav Kook's comparison between the untrained hive-building bee and the Jewish people at Sinai, who proclaimed "we shall do" before "we shall hear"—instinctive acceptance of the Torah preceding the hearing, the study.[11] The beaver must conform to principles of building, unlike the third level of aesthetic creation.

The two lower levels pertain to the intellect, while the third does not, apparently, conform to the intellect. This level is valuable in and of itself:

Even when the intellect does not agree with the representations of the imagination, they nonetheless retain their value in themselves, for imagination too is a complete world (*Orot HaKodesh*, Vol. I, p. 233).

Thus, there is a contradiction in Rav Kook's words between two aesthetic forces. On the one hand, he requires adamantly that art be contained within well-defined limits. On the other hand, he desired to attain a freedom of expression that knows neither laws nor barriers, a spontaneity flowing immediately from the creative impulse.

As noted, Nietzsche identified a reconciliation to this tension between the two elements in Greek tragedy, which includes both the Apollonian and the Dionysiac. For Rav Kook, by contrast, the two elements are resolved in a reconciliation that leads to a unity of synthesis, which is an entirely new entity. This is a kind of internal *tiferet* at a higher level, which crowns the entire aesthetic creation.

10. Henry Miller, "Reflections on Writing" in *Wisdom of the Heart* (1941).
11. *Naaseh VeNishma* (*Netiva* 5692, 5 Sivan), in *Maamrei HaReAYaH* (Jerusalem 5740), Vol. I, pp. 171–72.

Here are two passages that contain expressions of the supreme reconciliation. The first refers to the cosmic dimension of the reconciliation; the second to reconciliation in the realm of the aesthetic.

The first passage is taken from Rav Kook's comment on the benediction "Whose force and power fill the world":

The character of the order and the general beauty that man discovers when he observes reality as a whole that points to order . . . gives pleasure to the soul aroused by their vision . . . Sometimes specific natural visions . . . disturb the soul from its elevation, so that it gathers in its heart darkness and disturbed images, disordered to the eyes of flesh. But man must take heed, for . . . all these disturbances of lack of order . . . that derive from sights that appear strange to him, they derive only from the small compass of human eyesight . . . How splendid is the value [of all creatures] in the totality of what exists, and from this we shall perceive that even in the depths of our own cognition they are full of splendor and order (*Olat ReAYaH*, Vol. I, pp. 383–84).

The second passage deals with the supreme unity between "imagination" and "intellect":

Grant greatness to the strength of life of our supreme imagination, which soars above all the dry confines and limitations pertaining to the conditions of poor, dry existence. With the power of the imagination, moist and full of the marrow of life, we soar very high indeed, and it unites with the supreme intellect, to which the name intellect is inappropriate because of its greatness and the vigor of its illumination (*Orot HaKodesh*, Vol. I, p. 223).[12]

That is, that the contradiction between order and disorder in creation exists only in the eye of the beholder. Order and disorder appear to be opposing principles in their very essence. The truth is otherwise. Both order and disorder are resolved in the higher unity in which both are at one within a superior "order," which contains both of them at peace.

12. Later in the passage cited above from *Orot HaKodesh*, Vol. I, p. 233, Rav Kook writes, "It is only its [the imagination's] augmented blessing *(tosefet beracha)* that unites with the intellect, and together they unite in their supreme Source, which is exalted in Its measure above both intellect and imagination.

This reconciliation is that between the higher *(illaa)* repentance and the lower *(tataa)* repentance:

> The higher repentance is repentance for himself, and the lower is for the world . . . But it must be recognized that we are always called upon to grasp these two repentances together . . . For although in their external form they seem to contradict each other, in their inner meaning they are two inseparable lovers (*Orot HaTeshuvah,* p. 153).[13]

The concept of reconciliation here is influenced by Rav Kook's understanding of the Kabbalistic "shattering of the vessels." This can be seen in the section of *Orot* entitled "Souls of *Tohu,*" a section that is replete with Nietzschean echoes. *Tohu* (the nullity of Genesis 1:2) refers to the *tohu* emanated by the *Ein Sof,* which forms an unstable constellation of "vessels" and "lights." The instability occurs because the lights are too great and each vessel seeks to receive as much of the light as possible. The lights descend and are withdrawn from those vessels too "small" to contain them.

Had the vessels moderated their longing for light and attained a common structure, they would have succeeded in containing the immense light radiating from above. Each individual vessel, however, had its own yearning for light, its own lust for "sovereignty," and as a result the entire constellation of vessels was toppled, causing the shattering of the vessels. The world of mending *(tikkun)* is in the process of forming from the broken vessels by an involved plan interrelating the Kabbalistic spheres through connecting "lines" and mutual penetration of the vessels, a "totalization" as it were. In the *tikkun,* each vessel moderates its own longing for the sake of the general mending of the vessels. The souls of *tohu* are found in the world of mending, though their root is in the superior world of *tohu.* They are unable to restrain themselves in order to be integrated into the spirituality of *tikkun.* They continue to wreak havoc, and by preventing the mending, they cause chaos in the world of *tikkun.* The following passage deals with the clash between the wild, undisciplined lust of those *tohu* souls and the souls of *tikkun,* obedient to the laws of ethics and the order of *tikkun.* To the "weak," the situation is hopeless. There is no possibility

13. Rav Filber's edition.

of reconciliation with the souls of *tohu.* The saintly individual, however, recognizes the positive nature of this phenomenon, from which a higher unity is to grow.

The souls of *tohu* are higher than the souls of *tikkun.* They are very great, they seek much from reality, more than their vessels can suffer . . . Whatever is limited, measured and arranged, they cannot bear . . . They chose destruction and are destroyers . . . but the essence of courage in their will is a point-of-holiness. For when it is absorbed into the souls, which are controlled in their paths, it gives them the boldness of life. They are most revealed at some eschatological moment . . . when the law above laws has not yet been born . . . And the weak ones in the constructed world, the controlled and courteous, are alarmed by their bearing . . . But the heroic ones know that this manifestation of power is one of the phenomena that are needed to perfect the world . . . Though at first this power manifests itself in the form of *tohu,* in the end it will be taken from the hands of the wicked and given in the hands of saints" (*Orot,* pp. 122–23).

Indeed, for Rav Kook the shattering of the vessels is not an uncontrollable cosmic catastrophe, sabotaging the emanation of the *Ein Sof* in the world; rather it is an intentional event, introducing forces of *tohu* into the forces of *tikkun,* as a process of new creation that would have been impossible without the forces of *tohu.*[14] The wild element and the orderly element together build a superior world. The weak cannot bring about this synthesis; this task was placed upon the saint, who engenders the supreme unity between the measured, controlled forces and the bursting, undisciplined forces.[15]

    The reconciliation between the Apollonian and Dionysiac elements in aesthetics is part of the reconciliation between the force of *tikkun*

14. *Orot HaKodesh,* Vol. II, p. 527 presents the shattering of the vessels as an intended occurrence: The Infinite gives according to Its power, the finite cannot accommodate it and breaks, yet in this manner the yearning to grow toward the Infinite is implanted in the finite. This yearning could not have existed without the shattering.

15. In *Orot HaKodesh,* Vol. I, p. 189 Rav Kook describes the intended goal of the supreme synthesis that arises from the shattering of the vessels: "That separation, the life that is satiated by tumult and contradiction, leads to death and annihilation, to wickedness and falsehood. The essence of tumult is removed, as is the hum of movement, the lift of renewal, and arrives at a sublime, elevated world, in which the quality of *nekuddim* [of the *tohu* world] is illuminated by the rectitude of the *berudim* [of the *tikkun* world], the orderly lines, in the aspiration to the supreme *akeda* [the world before *tohu*] that stands at the apex [See Genesis 31]."

and the force of *tohu*. For Rav Kook, the opposition Apollo/Dionysus is parallel to that between *tikkun/tohu*. The problem in its philosophical formulation is resolved in a Kabbalistic formulation.

In aesthetic creation, Rav Kook discovered the resolution precisely in the realm of visual art, the descriptive character of which would imply, at first blush, that it is rooted in the Apollonian realm. In the supreme reconciliation, visual art too can unite Apollonian lawfulness with the great Dionysiac ambition. In the course of a conversation with the Jewish sculptor Melnikoff, Rav Kook spoke of the halachic attitude to sculpture, and related:

"When I lived in London, I would visit the National Gallery, and the paintings that I loved the most were those of Rembrandt. In my opinion Rembrandt was a saint.

When I first saw Rembrandt's paintings, they reminded me of the rabbinic statement about the creation of light. When G-d created the light, it was so strong and luminous that it was possible to see from one end of the world to the other. And G-d feared that the wicked would make use of it. What did He do? He secreted it for the righteous in the world to come. But from time to time there are great men whom G-d blesses with a vision of that hidden light. I believe that Rembrandt was one of them, and the light in his paintings is that light which G-d created on Genesis day.[16]

Thus, in visual art exists the supreme reconciliation, the place of the hidden light, the resolution beyond all contradiction of opposites, for contradiction is fundamentally not contradiction, for all is one.[17]

16. *The Jewish Chronicle of London,* September 9, 1935.
17. I have not succeeded in discovering any written remarks of Rav Kook on architecture as an aesthetic art. For Hegel, architecture is ranked below plastic art, which is itself ranked below poetry and music. On architecture in Jewish thought, see Moshe Bar-Ner, "Jewish Thought as a Source of Inspiration for Modern Architecture" (*Niv HaMidrashia* 5745/6, Vols. 18–19).

Nationalism, Humanity, and *Knesset Yisrael*

Rabbi Yoel Ben-Nun

MANY QUILLS HAVE been broken, much ink has been spilled, on the definition of the nation in general and particularly with respect to the Jewish people, without reaching a clear conclusion. Many of these questions remain almost completely obscure.[1]

For us, the central question is the riddle of Jewish existence over two millennia in the absence of most of the classic components of normal national definition: no land beneath one's feet, no state, no common language for all Jews and no common culture, dispersed throughout the world with many loyalties and significant differences between communities even in religious consciousness, way of life, understanding of the common past, and the dream of redemption. What all Jews clearly held in common seemed pale in contrast with the differences. There are two common solutions: The first depends on a dual internal factor—the

---

1. For various approaches to the subject, see Professor Jacob Katz, *Leummiyut Yehudit* (Jerusalem 5739), Part I, with a rich bibliography in the notes to p. 15ff.; Professor S. Ettinger, "The Uniqueness of the Jewish National Movement" in *Ideologia uMediniyut Zionit* (Shazar Center, Jerusalem 5738); Professor B. Akzin in his article on *Leummiyut* for the *Encyclopedia Hebraica* and *State and Nation* (1964). Particularly important for our purpose is the essay by Rav Mordechai Breuer, "People and State in the Teaching of Rav Isaac Breuer: On the Debate between Rav I. Breuer and Rav Kook" in *HaKinnus HaShnati LeMachashevet HaYahadut* (Jerusalem 5725).

Torah and national distinctiveness; the second on an external factor—
the hatred displayed by the Gentiles.

So powerful were these explanations that mighty efforts were made
over the past two centuries to put them to the test: both to divest the
Jewish people of their obligation to the Torah, primarily to the commandments, and to solve the problem of anti-Semitism by assimilation,
emigration from Europe, or (very differently) by Zionism. These explanations, however, are in my opinion, additional parts of the question.
That the Jewish phenomenon is complex and multifaceted is well
known. It involves the riddle of a most unusual existence. The Torah
too, despite all its partial similarities to phenomena of the ancient and
modern worlds, remains exceptional. Neither irrational inner and outer
intimations of uniqueness, nor an unusual history of environmental
enmity, *explain* the phenomenon; to the contrary, they *amplify* it.
Various aspects of the Jewish phenomenon "explain" each other in
various ways, whose primary importance is immanent: the role of the
Torah in Jewish identity, the role of Jewish nationality, Zionism, the
Land, etc. But as a general explanation, all these contribute to the intensification of the problem. So too the movement of millions of Jews
from Eastern Europe to North America and the formation of communities there, Zionism and the building of the land and its society, the
endless conflicts about the scope of commitment to Torah, and above
all the destruction of millions of Jews in a manner unprecedented in
its brutality—all these did not succeed, and apparently will not, in
"normalizing" the phenomenon, i.e., in extracting from it the unex-
plained and inconceivable element. To the contrary, all these phenomena together rendered the problem perhaps insoluble. For the hatred
of the Jew and his achievements has no precedent or parallel. Attempts
at assimilation and, on the other hand, the establishment of the State
of Israel, did not alter the Jewish anomaly but rather increased it. The
question then remains, despite all attempts to muddle or to solve it, and
it includes clusters of secondary questions: 1. Is it possible to explain
the general concept of nationality with respect to the Jewish people in
Jewish theological terms beyond the simple distinction of Jews from
Gentiles? Is it possible to explain Jewish existence in general terms
where the Gentiles are part of the terminology? 2. Can anti-Semitism
be explained in general terms that will also explain its difference from

other forms of xenophobia?[2] 3. Can Zionism and its motivations be exhausted by the language of national liberation and emancipation used to interpret other nations when other nations are liberated on their territory whereas the ingathering of exiles to Israel is an unusual event, unique to the Jewish people? 4. Are the Jews a people in the national sense common to the world? If so, how to explain the difference—the House of Israel is not like all the nations—and if not, why do Jews need Zionism, i.e., a land and a state and national rights in the family of nations? Is there not a necessary contradiction between Judaism and Zionism? 5. If the Jewish people are chosen, does this imply an essential difference between Jew and non-Jew? Is this not a fundamental discrimination? 6. Can one champion a fundamental distinction between Israel and the nations without degenerating into vulgar, inhuman nationalism, for whose spokesmen even the basic commandments obligating Noahides become an intolerable burden? 7. Finally, what is the status of the nonreligious Jew, who *as a matter of principle* does not observe the Torah but who binds his life and future with that of the Jewish people, and aspires to preserve with all his strength his Jewish identity? What is the status of the Jew who defines himself as a secularist *(chiloni)*—is he nefariously wicked or a legitimate phenomenon? What solution can be found for this schism, if it is indeed soluble?

All these questions merited a fundamental, profound treatment in Rav Kook's writings, and in particular in *Orot.* The sections are, to be sure, not arranged systematically, they are not written in scientific language, they hardly ever contain precise formulations of problems and responses. They seem to contain blatant contradictions.[3] Nevertheless, they constitute, in my opinion, a complete, consistent system, with determined, defined terms that treat all our questions in one totality.

2. For broad surveys of ancient "anti-Semitism" in contrast with modern anti-Semitism, its roots, variants, consequences, and attempts to explain it, see the collection *Yehudim VeYahadut BeEinei HaOlam HaHellenisti* (Shazar Center, Jerusalem 5734); S. Ettinger, *HaAnti-Shemiyut BaEt HaChadasha;* J. Katz, *Anti-Semitism: From Prejudice to Destruction,* and the articles on Anti-Semitism in *Encyclopedia Hebraica.* The ancient point of departure was religious difference; the phenomenon, however, intensified and took on a new form in the era of nationalism. With the founding of the State of Israel, it has developed a new face. The various theories only sharpen the question; they seem to address appearances but not essence.
3. E.g., between *Orot HaTechiya,* Chap. 10, p. 64 and *Orot Yisrael,* p. 144, on one side, and *Mahalach HaIdeot BeYisrael,* Chap. 1, p. 102. See *infra.*

Rav Kook, in his own illuminating way, attained an encompassing solution of these questions, and with that same set of concepts, based on a specific interpretation of Kabbalah, he elucidated both general human nationality and the unique status of the Jewish people, both the relation of nations and their members and that of the Jewish people to its members, be they Torah-observant or alienated from observance. The same conceptual framework also proposes a theoretical solution to the phenomenon of anti-Semitism and to the place and function of Zionism as a solution to the problems of the Jewish people. By attempting to demonstrate this, we shall be contributing to the fulfillment of the great mission that Rav Kook himself required of his readers.

In one section of *Orot* (p. 155), he writes, "The form of Israel must be refined, whether the general humanity of human nature has the same character that it has among all the nations, upon which is constructed the unique Israelite form, or that it is all unique from head to toe. This clarification requires the employment of different sources, revealed, rational, historical, esoteric, phenomenological, poetic, and at times political and economic." Rav Kook invited here a wide investigation in all areas in the light of the thesis he wishes to test, which he presents succinctly in the continuation. It is a fundamental question, the gist of a solution, and instructions for further study. What is lacking—and remains lacking—is the further investigation itself. This study is a very limited attempt to fill in what is missing. It is, perhaps, the beginning of an effort by others.

The three mystical terms for soul (*nefesh-ruach-neshamah, naran* for short) are well known to Kabbalists and in modern Hassidut. They are generally applied to the individual. They resemble somewhat the three Platonic souls, despite the vast difference between philosophical contemplation and its concepts and esoteric meditation.[4] With respect to the Gentiles as well, the mystics used the language of *naran,* but distinguish drastically between Jews and non-Jews. The nations have *nefesh* and perhaps certain aspects of *ruach,* but *neshamah* is found only in Israel.[5] Among the proof texts is Isaiah 42:5–6: "Who gives

4. See the summaries in Rav David HaCohen (the "Nazirite") *Kol HaNevua,* pp. 37–71, 166–80, and 264–67.
5. Rav Chayyim Vital (*Etz Chayyim, Heichal 7 Shaar 8,* Chap. 2) writes that the Gentiles have only *nefesh,* like the sea monsters of Genesis 1, where the male was

neshama to the people upon it and *ruach* to those who walk in it
... And I created you and assigned you to be a covenant-people, a light
unto the nations." We confront here a sharp, explicit line of the
mystical literature, which, like the *Kuzari*, establishes a complete separation between Israel and the nations, between Jews and non-Jews, to
the point where they are defined as different species, even different
genera: "insofar as we are the choice of the human race" (*Kuzari* 1:27).

Rav Kook would seem to have followed faithfully the *Kuzari*, the
mystics, Maharal, and Rav Moshe Hayyim Luzzatto, and even goes
beyond them: "The difference between the Jewish soul, its self, its
inner desires, aspiration, qualities and position, and that of all nations,
at all their levels, is greater and deeper than the difference between the
human soul and that of the animal; between the latter there is merely
a quantitative distinction, between the former an essential qualitative
distinction pertains" (*Orot*, p. 156). But if that is the case, then how
can Rav Kook also write that the commandment to love one's neighbor
may include non-Jews who are righteous and faithful (*Maamrei Ha-
ReA YaH*, p. 252), how can he decide straightforwardly in accordance
with the view of Meiri that Gentiles who accept practical moral discipline are to be treated no differently from Jews with respect to their
lost property or error in trading (Meiri to *Bava Kama* 113; *Igrot Ha-
ReA YaH*, Vol. I, p. 99), and how can he rule straightforwardly like Rav
Meir that a non-Jew who is concerned with the study of Torah is like
unto a high priest (*Bava Kama* 38; *Igrot HaReA YaH*, Vol. I, p. 71)?
Moreover, he writes:

The love of people requires much nurturing, to extend it appropriately against
the superficiality that appears at first blush through incomplete apprentice-
ship, from the perspective of the Torah and ethical custom, as if there is

---

castrated (*Bava Batra* 74b); *ruach* and *neshamah* are reserved for Israel. However, Rav
Moshe Hayyim Luzzatto (*Derech HaShem*, Part 2, Chap. 4) writes that humanity has
neshamah like those of Jews, although their level is significantly lower and these are
the Noahide commandments. Like all Kabbalists, he distinguishes between Adam
before the Fall and afterward. Humanity as we know it with its different peoples is not
the product of Creation but of the sin of the Tower of Babel, which engendered human
collectives with all their belligerence; see Ibn Ezra to Genesis 11:6: "With the variation
of religious customs is introduced envy and hatred, so too the variation of language.
Therefore I interpreted on this basis that with the creation of world man was born;
the nations were born in the sin of Babel." See *infra* n. 18.

opposition or at least equanimity toward this love, which must be fulfilled always with all the chambers of the heart. The highest position in the love of people must be taken by the love of man, and it must extend to all men, despite all differences of opinion, religion and faith, despite all distinctions of race and climate. It is right to penetrate the mind of the various peoples and collectives, to learn as much as possible their character and qualities, in order to know how to establish human love on foundations that are close to realization. For only upon a soul rich in the love of people and the love of men can the love of the nation descend in its lofty nobility and spiritual and practical greatness. The narrow-mindedness that leads one to see whatever is outside the bounds of the unique people, even the bounds of Israel, only as ugly and defiled, is a terrible darkness that causes general destruction to the entire edifice of spiritual good, the light of which every refined soul hopes for.

The love of people must be alive in the heart and in the soul, the love of every man specifically, and the love of all nations, the desire for their elevation and spiritual and material welfare; hatred must be directed only toward wickedness and filth in the world. It is totally impossible to attain the lofty-spiritedness of "Praise G-d, call upon His Name, proclaim among the nations His wonders," without an inner love, from the depths of heart and soul, to benefit all nations, to improve their estate, to ameliorate their lives. This quality enables the spirit of the messianic king to relate to Israel. Wherever we find intimations of hatred, we know clearly that the reference is only to wickedness, which forcefully fetters the associations of many peoples, both in the present and especially in past times when the obscenity of the world was even more rife. But we must know that the point of life, light and holiness never moved from the divine image bestowed upon man in general, and bestowed upon every people and tongue, each according to its significance, and that this holy kernel will elevate all. Because of this point of life we wish for the total elevation that will affect the world, the light of justice and righteousness, which merges with the *Hod* and *Tiferet,* with the *Gevura* and the *Netzach,* the perfection of all that is created, and man and all his limbs first. This is the inner *neshamah* that reposes at the intellectual depth of *Knesset Yisrael,* which, with the spirit of G-d upon us we progressively arouse into practical and spiritual life (*Musar Avicha,* pp. 96 and 98).

Any simplistic attempt to locate Rav Kook on a particular side of the debate on Jewish-Gentile relations misses the truth.[6] However, the

6. E.g., Professor M. Greenberg's attempt to set the mystics in the tradition of the *Kuzari,* and including Rav Kook, with those tending toward general human culture

tension in content and approach among Rav Kook's statements is quite remarkable.

In fact, Rav Kook interpreted the esoteric dicta such as those of the *Kuzari* in an original way: The uniqueness of *Knesset Yisrael* is precisely in its general soul; the radical gap between Israel and the Gentiles is that between *Knesset Yisrael* and national collectives. When, in the spirit of contemporary individualism, one transfers the discussion to the individual level, distortion is the likely result. The value of the individual Jew is measured according to his degree of connection to *Knesset Yisrael,* while the value of the individual Gentile is determined by his degree of connection to universal man, in the best case, and to Gentile nationality in the worst case. All this is expressed systematically by Rav Kook in the light of his original interpretation of *naran* as it applies to Gentiles; for Rav Kook differs from Chasidism in that he is concerned with the constitution of the nation.[7] What are *naran* of a collective entity?

1. *Nefesh*[8] is in each man that which animates the body in the psychosomatic sense, manifesting itself in the digestive and circulatory systems, in the respiratory and nervous systems, in the reproductive system. Among peoples and publics, it is economic power and social status, the intense energies that accompany them, motivate them, and sustain them, and of course the will to dominate and the patriotic tendency. Economic-social energy can be likened to the systems circulating blood, oxygen, and nourishment through the collective organism, while domination reminds us of the nervous system. A bankrupt social economy is like a collective blocked artery; governmental malfunction is like a neurological deficit. The emotions aroused in the group when the nation is under attack are some of the varied psychosomatic phenomena of the collective organism.

2. *Ruach* activates the individual personality in the psychological sense. It expresses itself in sensations and reactions, instincts, feelings, and dreams. Its instruments are the respiratory and neurological systems (in a different sense than that of *nefesh*), the senses, and primarily

---

following Maimonides and Meiri, and his own effort to decide in favor of the latter (*Al HaMikra veal HaYahadut* (Tel Aviv 1989), p. 55ff.

7. Following *Orot HaKodesh*, Vol. I, p. 21.

8. Of course, these concepts derive from Kabbalah, and do not necessarily overlap with modern psychological and sociological terminology.

the power of speech. Among peoples and publics, it is the spirit of culture[9] that makes manifest the sensations and reactions, instincts, feelings, ideas, and dreams that grow from a group or from the land, in various styles. Paralysis or eclipse of the cultural creativity of a people or a group is like a stroke or injury to an organ of perception in the body. According to the intensity of the creativity that is blocked, so is the degree of injury to the collective organism as a whole.

3. *Neshamah* in man is the intellectual illumination in all its forms, the "extra dimension" of man, who reasons and deliberates. It is expressed in the superior will that thinks and governs the brain and the systems that serve it,[10] and of course the power of speech that externalizes thought. In human and national groups, it represents faith and ethics, religion and enlightenment, awareness of the sacred, the search for and dialogue with G-d, the aspiration to the good and to benefit others, charity and justice, the aspiration to elevation and study, inquiry and thought, philosophy and ideology—all these are revelations of *neshamah,* the divine part supernal, in man and in humanity. Paralysis, even a partial one, impairs the very essence of man, be it the individual or the race, so severely that even proper functioning of the *nefesh* and *ruach* systems cannot overcome the breakdown at the highest point. Thus, one would expect the defect of *neshamah* to affect *ruach* and *nefesh* as well—that is, culture, economics, and society. For, in the final analysis, the creative power itself (as distinct from its products) and the intelligent, ethical control that operates in economy and society, derive

9. The difference between Israel and the Gentiles, which is primarily located in the general *neshamah,* according to Rav Kook, affects the spirit of culture as well. The Israelite spirit is inward and connects to the *neshamah,* while the cultural spirit of the Gentiles is external, with the implied differences between Jewish and Gentile culture. In any case, each nation or group of nations has a language, speech, and culture, through which is expressed the spirit of the nation. So too the Jewish people. Thus, different peoples speaking the same language and sharing the same culture differ only in their *nefesh.* Thus, we can resolve the disputes discussed *supra.*

10. I have said nothing about the location of *naran* in the human body, though I have intimated the ideas accepted by the mystics, because the liver and heart are no longer considered to be the bearers of essential functions in the human personality; only the brain is thought of in that way. It seems to me that Rav Kook does not make much of this either. Nonetheless, I must note that it is within brain physiology that we have come to recognize different levels, or lobes (frontal, occipital, parietal, temporal) whose functions can be differentiated with barely a change in the general concepts we are employing. In any event, the frontal lobe is specific to man, with his autonomy and capacity for responsible choice.

from the human *neshamah*. Thus, *neshamah* is, in effect, everything.

Having explicated Rav Kook's original interpretation of the concepts *naran* for groups and peoples, we must raise the question that concerned the greatest thinkers—nationalism versus humanism. Each human individual, regardless of distinctions, regardless of his environment, possesses *naran*. His potential is the personal manifestation of the *imago Dei* in man qua man (including the phenomena of sin and repentance). Adam is the father of all humanity, the progenitor of each individual. However, does the group, the nation, or any other congeries of human beings carry full human potential?

According to the definitions set down above, each consolidated group or nation has *nefesh* and often *ruach* too: i.e., an economy, society, government, and unique cultural creativity. Are, however, ethics and religion, faith and sanctity, justice and charity, inquiry and thought, unique to the group or are they universal? If there is a group law or ethic or a national faith or science, what value have they?[11] If it is only a matter of a collective cultural style of universal values, then we have a virtuous society or nation. Sanctity and ethics, justice and science, are universally grounded in the divine unity of the world and man; only their style varies between peoples and groups. Cultural styles indeed distinguish peoples and groups in the realm of the spirit (though it is the nature of the spirit to overcome barriers), but absolutely not in the realm of the *neshamah*, for that is surely universal, like the divinely bestowed *neshamah* of Adam. There is, therefore, no French ethics or Greek science, German justice or Japanese faith, although each nation defines itself and takes pride in its culture and in the human achievements of its members, and each nation imparts a unique cultural style to universal values. If, however, there emerges in a people or any group a special group ethics or group faith such as German justice or national deity as in the pagan world, that is an idolatrous degradation—to measure the supreme divine unity not in the language of *imago Dei* but in the stooped image of the bestial collective.[12]

---

11. See *Orot*, p. 107, on Rav Kook's attitude to the national religion common in the ancient world.

12. The prophetic literature often presents kingdoms in the image of beasts: Numbers 23–24; Daniel 8: 11. See Rashi to Genesis 15:10 and Ezekiel 1:4–5 for the difference between the revelation of G-d's kingship to the Gentiles and to Israel—the image of man represents the patriarch Jacob. See Maimonides, *Hil. Melachim* Chap. 12, halacha 1. A broad exposition of the meaning of this phenomenon can be found in *Orot*

Loyalty and commitment to members of the group together with profound hatred to all others—that is the morality of the gang; there is no difference between gangsters and a nation if right is no more than might, the good is only what is good for it and its interests, and the patron gods are Kemosh or Marduk or Baal and their numerous consorts and offspring. This is the pagan world, disastrously awakened in the twentieth century, the world of monsters—racist, imperialist, Bolshevist—which fill the world with abominations more than ever in the past. Its most horrible exhibition was the Nazi abomination.[13] Of this Rav Kook states:

Just as spiritual filth can accumulate within an individual soul, to divert it from its good quality, to convert it to a base quality, to debase it to the nadir of life, so too it can accumulate in the general soul of an entire nation, to make it a base, wicked, contemptible, soiled nation, so that it would deserve to pass from the world in order not to prevent the universal beauty, the beauty of the world, from expanding.

Divine purity, when it is well illuminated, refines the heart. The unique *neshamah* of the individual becomes luminous, holy and heroic through the divine light that shines upon it its radiant beams with power and fullness, and it becomes defiled and darkened to the degree that the divine light is distant from it or vitiated within it. So too the *neshamah* of the entire nation; when it is suffused with the living flow of the divine phenomenon, it is healthy, strong and pure, and when the Shechinah withdraws from its midst, it immediately begins to wilt and its defilement is revealed in its midst. The national *ruach* can be affected by defilement just like that of the individual, can take in baseness and wickedness, which, given its great power, is much greater for evil than the wicked aspirations of wicked individuals. Therefore purity re-

---

HaTechiya, Chap. 2 (*Orot,* pp. 49–50). Rav Kook grants importance to the collective animal power, but only when science and ethics refine and sweeten the natural forces. 13. Wicked kingdoms and wickedness in general are described in prophecy and biblical poetry as serpents, crocodiles, and leviathans, beginning with the serpent of Genesis 3 through Job 40–41. See Ibn Ezra to Job 40:15 and also Deuteronomy. 32:24, Isaiah 27:1; 51:9, Ezekiel 29:3. Psalms 74 and 89 do not speak of creation through battle with the monsters (as in Near Eastern myth) but of governance and the destruction of wickedness in the world. This may be the meaning of Rav Chayyim Vital's comment (see n. 5 *supra*), that the nations have only *nefesh* (he mentions only the crocodiles of Genesis 1). Perhaps he referred to the wicked empires that spread through the world and conquered it, from Babel until now, and that are destined for the righteous in the world to come, when a small human child can rule over all the animals, and this is the messianic era, see Maimonides *Hil. Melachim,* Chap. 12.

quires *ruach*, purity in the pure source of the divine fount. When actions are good, when character is refined, the nation dreams of supernal sanctity, its intelligence shines with the divine light, and when actions are debased and character murky, then national aspirations too become low and ugly, hence weak, for there is no true power *(gevura)* save the higher power, the power of G-d (*Orot*, p. 63).

The Gentiles, in their aggregations, represent only a collective *nefesh* and collective *ruach*, i.e., economy and society, political power, at times a particular style of culture. But the depth of *ruach*, and more so the *neshamah*, do not take part in these aggregates but merely affect it—in the best case—keeping the collective from being evil. *Neshamah* remains above crystallized national forms, or any other form; from it derive all universal elements and values whose national character, even when it exists, is clearly ancillary to the living, inner meaning, in its full universal scope. If—G-d forbid—the collective overpowers ethics, faith, science, or law, the *neshamah* vanishes, and the barbaric, idolatrous waves well up. If a great nation becomes a criminal gang with a pagan religion and mafia morality, then it is a disaster for all humanity, and a great and terrible war will break out, as we know all too well.[14]

Precisely the individuals, and primarily the select individuals in the world, express the best of humanity and not the group, they reveal the general *neshamah* of man, more than any national rivalry:

All national collectives give their members only the exterior aspect of their nature, but this essence each man draws from the universal soul, from the Divine Soul, without the mediation of the group, because the [national] group has no divine entity, meaning an inherent divine tendency diffused in its midst (*Orot*, p. 144).

But such a world is pitiful, cruel and desperate, for the few individuals surely exhibit in their lives the soul of man and his potential, but the groups, whether national or other, dominate the world and conduct their wars and contests, so that even the civilized nations display primarily their group mentality and much less the sublime spirit and the general soul. The world becomes an arena of conflict, from which the

14. See Rav Kook's outburst against Europe and its civilization, confronting World War I (*Orot*, pp. 15–16)

neshamah vanishes, and *ruchot* and *nefashot* distant and estranged from their general-human source engender titanic abominations that obscure the good deriving from the world of the individuals. It is wishful thinking that some good, righteous people, dispersed in every place, are sufficient for the world to turn into a better place. For this purpose, it is an absolute necessity that there be in the world one nation that knows its *neshamah,* in the full measure of all reality, whose ethics and justice are sufficient to nourish all beings, a nation whose G-d is the G-d of the cosmos, one G-d who is the source of all reality and all men His creatures.[15] A nation with this awareness can save humanity from the violence of wicked idolatry, and such a people is *Knesset Yisrael,* which was elected not only for its own sake and not in order to separate from the world, but for its salvation. "I will make you a great nation," says G-d to Abraham, in order to fulfill, "And all the families of the earth will be blessed through you" (Genesis 12:2–3). In essential contrast with the nations of the world and the families of the earth, the Jewish people is not a powerful social economy or merely a creative cultural spirit, but a general *neshamah* elected from humanity to accept G-d's Torah for the sake of humanity, and is not just one people among others, but all humanity in microcosm. That is the precise meaning of the famous verse, "A people that dwells alone and is not counted [*yithashav,* i.e., *cheshbon,* calculation] among the nations" (Numbers 23:9)—it is not counted as one of the nations because it is equivalent to all of them.[16] The seventy offspring of Jacob who descended to Egypt correspond to the seventy offspring of Noah (Genesis 10): "When the Most High divided to the nations their inheritance, when He separated men, He set the bounds of peoples according to the number [70!] of the children of Israel. For G-d's portion is His people;

15. See *Orot,* p. 104, explaining the distinction between individuals living in the light of the divine ideal and entire peoples, whence the need for the election of Israel.
16. The common interpretation that Israel cares nothing for the opinions of the Gentiles and wishes to be detached from the world is not based on the Torah, but on a modern etymological midrash of a modern verb form (*hitashev,* to ascribe importance), and on Sabra insouciance. The enormous prohibition of desecrating G-d's Name and the Commandment to sanctify His Name take place before the eyes of the Gentiles, and the rabbis taught that it is better to uproot a section of the Torah to avoid desecrating G-d's Name in the world (*Yevamot* 79); they also teach that there is nothing that G-d more wishes than that the Gentiles should say, Blessed is the G-d of the Jews (*Yer. Bava Metzia* 2:5); cf. Rambam *Hil. Melachim* Chap. 6, halacha 5, on the fulfillment of agreements to which the Jewish people has consented.

Jacob the lot of His inheritance" (Deuteronomy 32:8–9). Therefore Isaiah's famous universal-Israelite prophecy speaks of all the peoples going up to G-d's mountain, to the house of Jacob's G-d, to learn Torah and justice from Zion, for the cessation of war. In 19:25, we read, "Blessed is My people Egypt and My handiwork Assyria and My inheritance Israel." This is the true, undistorted vision of Rav Yehuda Halevi in the *Kuzari*, who did not conceive of Israel's uniqueness as that of a separate organism but as the heart among the members of the body; the heart outside the body is not norm but pathology. The organism is humanity and not the Jewish people in isolation; an organism that wishes to live does not conduct a war among the members. So much falsehood has been said about the so-called racial mysticism of Halevi, whose ethical and universal perspective is so much broader than his critics' that it is necessary to quote verbatim:

Israel among the nations is like the heart among the members (*Kuzari* 2:36).

And those souls, their origin is in Adam . . . from whom the election, which is the heart of the fruit, continued generation after generation, era after era, while the multitude of people in the world except for the select individuals, are like the shells, leaves, twigs and the like (Ibid. 4:15).

It is clear that Halevi's organism is all humanity, and not Jewish people alone. There is no heart apart from the members or detached from them; hence Halevi, precisely because of his particularism, is an extreme universalist. In the living creature, there is no place for questions about spiritual or practical-democratic equality, because within each organism there is indeed no equality but rather unity and cooperation.[17]

Rav Kook drew his definitions from the treasure chest of the nation,[18] but gave them a modern exposition. Thus, he interpreted Halevi

17. At times it appears that egalitarianism engenders intense competition for the realization of equal opportunity, in which there is a built-in advantage to the educated, cultured, wealthy aristocracy. By contrast, the multitudes generally cry out for sharing and unity and are quite suspicious of democratic egalitarian concepts. This leads one to suspect that the "nobility" advocates democratic equality because of its advantage in the race. In any event, he who would interpret corporate concepts based on a vision of society, the nation, and humanity as organisms, in terms of exclusively atomistic views, does both the former approaches and right thinking an injustice.
18. See *Shaarei Ora*, Chap. 5 (Warsaw ed., pp. 96–105), which states that the seventy

and the mystics on the meaning and role of *Knesset Yisrael* and the distinction between Israel and the nations (note the precise use of the *naran* terminology):

The Essence of Knesset Yisrael *and the* Character of Its Life

Knesset Yisrael is the essence of all being, and in this world this essence is infused in the Israelite nation literally, in its materiality and spirituality, in its genesis and faith, and Israelite history is the ideal essence of general history, and there is no movement that you will find in the world that you will not find the like of in Israel. Its faith is a sifted essence and the source that inspires good and idealism upon all faiths, and then the power that discriminates among all concepts of faith, until it brings them to the level of a clear language to call all in the Name of G-d, and your G-d, the G-d of Israel, will be called the G-d of all the earth.

Knesset Yisrael is the highest spiritual manifestation in human existence. Just as one ought not to marvel that the brain and heart display such forms of life that there is nothing like them in the entire body, so one should not marvel about the display of life of marvels, miracles, prophecy, the Holy Spirit at Its highest level, eternal hope, triumph over every obstacle, which are exhibited in the highest form, which astonishes every reflective heart and thinking mind. *Knesset Yisrael* manifests G-d's seed in the world, G-d's hand in being, in the construction of the nations. It surely has an important relation to that which is most lofty and revered, sacred and sublime, in whatever is, in all its circumference, physical and spiritual. It is impossible to think otherwise (*Orot*, p. 138).

We—that is, *Knesset Yisrael*—wish to live precisely for the ethical goal of being as a whole. Insofar as we know within us that the concentration of life is for us the general ethical direction, because of this we are confident that in our lives we assist its completion. If at any time the ethical direction of being were lost to us, then we should have lost absolutely the aspiration of life and hence general life would be null and destroyed without mending. But the ethical direction will not be lost completely, and even one spark remaining completely hidden in the depths of the *neshamah* will restore all to life (*Orot*, p. 139).

---

nations together constitute the form of man, and that they encompass Israel by equal measure, according to their dimensions. Their division is that of Babel, which undermined the world and precipitated the selection of Israel for the sake of G-d.

Nefesh *and* Ruach *Among the Nations—*
the Neshamah *of* Knesset Yisrael

The quality of *nefesh* of *Knesset Yisrael* is different in principle from that of the *nefesh* of any people and tongue. In every people and tongue the inner point of collective will to life is based on the economic content in all its forms, on the element of inner care that permeates man to fortify his state of physical existence and the supreme *ruach* that animates and illuminates this point is the *ruach* of order and beauty, which is the desire for the delight of the senses according to the quest of the human heart, and when these exist in any group according to one style, this uniformity makes for the national content. In Israel, however, the divine quality rests in the depths of the nature of the nation's *neshamah.* [19] The thirst for knowledge and the sense of G-d, in its highest, purest purpose, is the point where life is felt, and the refinements that flow from the perfection of this image in all the expanses and depths of life are the aesthetic directions. The inner awareness, knowing that in the fulfillment of the highest desire all is fulfilled, that there is nothing of all the directions of life and the refinements of life, the order of life and its content, that is not included in this eternal point—this awareness is a matter unique to Israel, resting in the nature of the nation, revealed in the inner awareness even of the multitudes, and becomes lucid and clear to the most elect in every generation. The divine concern, within every value of life in the deep nature of the *neshamah,* corresponding to the marrow animating national history, which is revealed in the capacity for prophetic creation in the elect of its sons, which leads to the level of an eternal people, whose uniqueness of *neshamah* will be recognized by all humanity, being the Israelite substance whose attributes are exhibited in all the various movements, and the spirit of Messiah acting to complete this character until the absolute eschaton (*Orot,* p. 64).

The Neshamah *of the Individual*
and the Peoples

The most perfect and sweet comprehension of the knowledge of G-d is consciousness of the divine relation to the general world and to each and every particular in it, material and spiritual, the relation of the *neshamah,* the spiritual aspect that animates and fills with the light of existence and flourishing, to the body, to that which is required by life for light and flourishing. This

---

19. Rav Kook is very precise in determining that the difference in the quality of the *nefesh* of *Knesset Yisrael* derives from the divine tendency resting in the deep nature of the nation's *neshamah,* i.e., a stature that runs through the three components of *naran.* The fullest discussion is in *Orot, Zeronim,* Chap. 7—"The *Neshamah* of Nationality and its Body," pp. 132–35.

relation, when it is fulfilled heart and soul,[20] suffuses them with love more than fear, and the pleasantness of meditation and serenity more than the bitterness of quaking. The cultivated consciousness of the most correct enlightenment is engaged in consummating very well this sweet awareness.

In the life of the individual it is easier to attain this level, by the improvement of practical and intellectual ethics and by elevating the light of consciousness in general. Where human character relates sympathetically to the lofty, to the absolute good, in thought and in life, immediately the *nishmati* awareness of G-d takes secure hold of him, is assimilated in all his thoughts and fuses with all his senses and feelings to refine them. The collective organ, which has a special psychology,[21] if it too tends at its deepest level to the supreme ethical sympathy, and the love of the noble good is well imprinted upon its very nature, according to its choice or in any event the inheritance of parents,[22] then it can infiltrate well in the midst of the nation through the *nishmati* awareness, and the pleasantness of divine love together with a sweet, well-formed reverence-fear suffuse the nation as a whole and straighten all its ways.

But to the degree that the organic psychology is distant from the inner affection to the absolute good, so too the *nishmati* relation cannot penetrate into the divine relationship, and the link to G-d must then be an alien link, and G-d will be to it a strange and alien G-d. A strange god acquires peculiar attributes and caricatures, which distort life much more than they can straighten it. As of now culture has not yet attained that level, to provide a divine sympathy for the absolute good in the depth of the *neshamah* of organic collectives,[23] hence we see in them yet signs of wickedness and oppression and the ethical essence becomes attenuated and abandoned by the general heart

20. Meaning that the *neshamah* illuminates and the body is suffused with *ruach* and *nefesh*, thus bringing to perfection *naran*.

21. See N. Turov, *HaPsychologia shel HaTzibbur* (Tel Aviv 5714), pp. 111–204).

22. Clearly, Rav Kook, despite his use of general or conditional language, is referring to *Knesset Yisrael*. Terms like *Shechinah* or *inheritance of parents* demonstrate this indubitably. By contrast, when he speaks of the national *ruach*, then he may refer to Gentiles as well, save for the fact that *ruach* requires purification through the Divine Source above it, which is not part of nationality. Consider this carefully.

23. One might have thought that culture can still "as of now" bring collective organs to a divine sympathy toward the absolute good in the depths of their *neshamah*, and our definitions, according to which the *neshamah* is beyond these groups, would be rendered only temporarily valid. But in *Orot*, p. 156—a section quoted *infra*—Rav Kook clarifies what is behind the statement that "as for now culture has not yet attained that level," for in section 11 Rav Kook anticipates a future unification of all humanity, i.e., the abrogation of the Babel division and mending of the sin that led to it. This is "the depth of the *neshamah* of the collective organs" in the present passage, meaning the collective organs consolidated, the general humanity of the seventy nations *together*.

of the groups. But humanity has a heritage of refuge in *Knesset Yisrael,* for the divine sympathy is found in its inner circle. Feeling attests and intelligence elucidates that the one, unique eternal G-d is the absolute good, life, light, all, sublime over all and sublime over all sublimity, better than all good, good to all and His mercies upon all His creatures, animating all and preserving all, growing salvation for all, and this general sympathy penetrates in this nation not only to the particulars, but precisely to the totality. If it happens that it forgets its *neshamah,* the source of its life, comes prophecy to recall it and the exiles to straighten its crookedness until at last the sympathy to the absolute good triumphs within it (*Orot,* pp. 144–45).

After the primary explication of *Knesset Yisrael* and its role in the world, for the sake of humanity, we must pass on to the relation between the communal and the individual among the nations and in Israel, and this relation will lead us further, to the place of the commandments and their observance in Rav Kook's view, as the special system of nourishment that ties individuals to the *neshamah* of *Knesset Yisrael:*

The relation of *Knesset Yisrael* to its members is different from the relations of any other national group to its members. All national collectives give their members only the external aspect of their nature, but this essence each man draws from the universal *neshamah,* from the divine *neshamah,* without the mediation of the group, because the [national] group has no divine entity, meaning an inherent divine tendency diffused in its midst. Not so in Israel, the *neshamah* of the individuals derives from the source of the Eternal living in the general treasure, and the totality gives *neshamah* to the individuals. If he wishes to detach himself from the nation, he must detach his *neshamah* from its place of life; therefore the affinity of each individual Jew to the totality is great, and he always commits his life[24] in order not to be torn from the totality, because the *neshamah* and its inner mending require this of him. To be sure, the channels of *nishmati* recognition and its self-preservation are done

24. Sacrifice of life is that famous stubbornness of Jews to remain Jews, and to be identified as Jews, even under great pressure and heavy costs. Often this commitment appears, unconscious of the meaning of being Jewish, of the historical Jewish people, and, of course, oblivious to the *neshamah* of *Knesset Yisrael.* Nonetheless, it is a historical-empirical fact that Jews give up their lives for their identity immeasurably more than any other group. This can be explained in the light of the special relation of the Jewish *nefesh* to its source the collective Jewish *neshamah.* Exactly this stubborn self-sacrifice, unconscious of deeper meanings, brings closer to rational reflection the organic-*nishmati* explanation of Rav Kook.

in *Knesset Yisrael* by the commandments, the word of G-d; this is the great divider realized in the way of life design in His plan . . .

And the mysterious secrets of the superior world . . . are made with the commandments . . . and infiltrate lofty paths in the life of eternity, in the relation of the nation possessing great spiritual gravity and the world as a whole, and the holy is elevated and the human form is filled with light, and the worlds—eternal joy from the light of Torah and the candle of commandment.

The true relation of each individual in Israel to *Knesset Yisrael,* in the full spiritual sense, encompassing all life, ethical, spiritual and natural,[25] requires constant nourishment beyond what is needed by the member of any natural nation with respect to his connection to his nation. Natural inclinations do not require as much strengthening as ethical inclinations, which require constant nurture and care in study and deed, and therefore the nations, the foundation of whose national being is more directed toward the fulfillment of their natural inclinations, so long as they exist, impart their connection to all their members without the necessity of special nourishment. In Israel the integument is very strong toward the aspects of ethics and idealism, which are common to the entire nation; and insofar as the spiritual tendencies require in each individual constant nurture, that they not become debased or effaced, how much more the relation of the individual to the totality requires encouragement and frequent nourishment. The choice nourishment is the study of Torah in all its aspects, which includes the study of the historical in all its entirety, and observance of the commandments with deep faith illuminated by the light of knowledge and clear awareness (*Orot,* pp. 144–45).

Because the idea of the *neshamah* of *Knesset Yisrael* is the absolutely ethical, therefore any ethical deficiency detaches the individual, according to his value, from his connection to the *neshamah* of the nation. This is the way it is both with respect to a general moral deficiency or a special moral deficiency that is considered a deficiency and a sin only according to the special character of Israel. For it is obvious that the color of ethics must, in certain details, be affected specifically by the character of the nation.[26] In a nation that is so

25. Ideal ethics is here the *neshamah.* Spiritual life is, of course, that of *ruach,* and natural refers to *nefesh,* in complete correspondence to our reading of *naran* in Israel, among the Gentiles and for humanity.
26. The distinctions between nations refer, of course, to details and form, not to the primary ethical essence, that is the national spirit rather than the depth of the *neshamah.* Later on he speaks again of Israel, even though the language is general. In Israel, the ethics of the general *neshamah* appears with an enormous multiplicity of detail, even in areas where there is a common denominator with the ethics of Gentiles,

distinguished from all peoples, those things that are unique in its ethics are many, and all, when honored, affect for the good the state of the nation, and, when degraded, cause destruction and weakening of the connection (*Orot*, p. 144).

But lest one think that it is the commandments alone that define the difference between Jew and Gentile, Rav Kook returns to the *neshamah*:

One might think that the difference between Israel and the nations stands out in the performance of the commandments, for the idea can encompass man as a whole.[27] But this would be a mistaken overview. For if indeed the spirit and the idea encompassed all, there would be no need for the practical distinction, and it would not be useful or subsist. But the content of the matter is that the *nefesh* element, upon which the idea is built, over which idea the entire texture of practical law extends, that element is the *neshamah* substance, which characterizes Israel as a special entity, unique in the world, and from this distinction flow all the practical distinctions. Even when the latter are impaired, they cannot affect the supreme element, the entity of *nefesh*, from which all the distinctions arise. Forever will remain a distinction between

---

as in the seven Noahide commandments. For example the stringencies set down by the Torah regarding bloodshed, especially in the Land of Israel, beyond the general "Thou shalt not murder." Only in the Land of Israel did the Torah prescribe cities of refuge (Deut. 19:2—"in your Land, that G-d gives you to inherit."), required the burial of the hanged criminal, both because of *imago Dei* ("the curse of G-d is hanged") and for a particular Israelite reason—"thou shalt not defile thy land that G-d gives you as inheritance" (Deut. 21:23), prescribed the ritual of the beheaded calf for a corpse whose killer cannot be identified "on the land that G-d has given you to inherit" (Deut. 21:1). See also Maimonides *Hil. Rotszeach* beginning of Chaps. 8 and 9: the cities of refuge and the beheaded calf apply only in the Land of Israel; note that Joshua 10:27 applies the commandment of burial to the kings of Canaan. Those who strive for the sanctity of the Land of Israel should give thought to the fact that the Land requires a higher standard of concern for human life than universal standards. Jewish sensitivity to the value of human life is not the imitation of Western humanism, but an authentic Jewish trait. The best of the nations followed us in this. Viewing the Land of Israel as an antithesis of ethics and meticulous care for the image of G-d in man is a tragic distortion, deriving from a chain of serious errors, and not without a large measure of desecration of G-d's Name.

27. The preparation for the divine idea is the content of the general human spirit and is "found in all human hearts upon all their divisions, families and nations" (*Orot*, p. 102). The element of *nefesh* is expressed the practical-juridic law, but the supreme element is the substance of *neshamah*, which characterizes Israel as a nation, as explained *supra*. The distinctiveness of the Jewish *nefesh* derives, therefore, from the nation's *neshamah*.

Israel and the peoples, in order to give foundation through separation to the profane content and the sacred content of the world in its proper impression (*Orot*, p. 155).

Therefore Rav Kook can serenely sum up his view and state that there is contradiction between ethical universalism, which requires that we relate to every human being according to his full human potential, that is, no less than the image of G-d bestowed upon him at creation, and the radical distinction between Israel and the nations, not only in special duties (as Amos 3:2 puts it, "Only you have I known of all the families of the earth, therefore I will hold you to account for all your sins") but precisely with respect to the specific quality of *Knesset Yisrael,* and hence to its members, as a distinct potentiality. Thus, Rav Kook does not detect a fundamental dispute between Rav Shimon b. Yochai's statement, "You are called men but the Gentiles are not" (*Yevamot* 61), and that of his teacher Rav Akiva, "Beloved is man who was created in His image" (*Avot* 3:14) or his colleague Rav Meir, who equated a Gentile concerned with the Torah to a high priest (*Sanhedrin* 59, *Bava Kama* 38). Hence he sees no contradiction between the view of Maimonides, who opens prophecy and priesthood to the entire world (end of *Hil. Shemitta* inter alia), and Halevi, who limits prophecy to Israel in its Land, for all these distinctions and disputes touch only on the ramifications of the basic idea. Rav Kook's basic position[28] is that with respect to individual human beings, so long as they are connected to the sanctity of man, halacha and belief conform to Maimonides and Meiri; with respect to the quality of the nation as a whole, the determination follows Halevi and Maharal and the mystics. Thus, we have a synthetic decision that sublates the dispute to its point of origin, as is typical of Rav Kook, and overcomes the partial views with its comprehensiveness. He does not accept an insoluble moral dichotomy between "trends in Judaism" where psychological, sociological, and ideological factors have led most Yeshiva students and their teachers to adopt, in literal simplicity, the paths of Halevi, Maharal, and the mystics, while

28. Halachic determination precipitates a decisive factor that complements one or another of the original sides of the debate. While many present Halevi versus Maimonides as a dispute requiring a sharp decision, Rav Kook deploys his authority on the side of Maimonides with respect to individuals, while in the realm of nations confronting *Knesset Yisrael* he sides with Halevi. At the spiritual level there is no decision here, but rather a synthesis rising above the dispute and its roots.

most academicians, professors, and students committed to Judaism follow Maimonides and Meiri and dismiss the others as mystics.[29] Rav Kook was above such distinctions, and built a system that has room for both sides, without practical or spiritual dispute. His simplest, clearest formulation of this difficult issue is found in his letters:

I have already written in my letters that from the perspective of select in-dividuals we know no distinction between peoples and languages and "an alien who studies Torah is like a high priest." Our early sages have already said, "Let us receive our colleague the philosopher." But our extolling of *Knesset Yisrael* in general is due to the divine quality that is found in the *neshamah* of the nation as a whole, which is hence revealed to each individual in a special form. This is an explicit verse: "And we shall be distinguished, etc." It is our absolute freedom to raise our heads openly with the pride of the love of *Knesset Yisrael,* carved upon our inner *neshamot,* and we ought not to deny this pure love, neither because of any scientific logic nor for cosmopolitan piety. When we drink from our well, the well of Israel, we will have all, both piety and intellect, and with the broad-mindedness of inner opulence we can observe the human square, take honor in our part of the general treasure and our special part in which strangers have no share—Praise G-d all nations, for His loving-kindness has overwhelmed us (*Igrot HaReAYaH,* Vol. I, pp. 70–71).

Lest we think that Rav Kook is engaged in some sort of tepid compromise, he offers a criterion for his distinctions, with respect to the love due the image of G-d, to know if it is pure or not:

Breadth of heart, which sometimes wishes to bring the entire world, all humanity, under the special affection exhibited to Israel, requires examination. When the recognition of the specific holiness characteristic of Israel exists authentically, and from its brightness affection and love, with a generous eye, expands to every nation and man together—that is the trait of our patriarch Abraham, the father of a multitude of nations ("And all the families of the earth shall be blessed in you, and in your seed"). But it happens that the basis of the expansion of this affection is an obscurity of feeling and eclipse of the holy light of the knowledge of the supreme quality of Israel, and then it is

29. E.g., the pamphlet *Am LeBadad Yishkon* by Rav M. Tzuriel, privately circulated in the yeshivot, and directed against Yochanan Ben-Yaakov's anthology *Chaviv Adam SheNivra BeTzelem* (pub. Bnai Akiva), and opposing both Professor Greenberg's essay (*supra* n. 6). All these opposites are entangled in their intense dispute, and fail to recognize Rav Kook's unifying approach, even when they quote from him.

poisonous, and its operation is full of terrible destructiveness, from which one must remove oneself as from a goring ox (*Orot,* p. 169).

All this implies clearly that nationality is a limited value, that it endangers man's soul and all his achievements and attainments, and that individuals are more important.[30] The trend to an international world, one governed not by the unity of peoples but by the love of people, is a positive trend, destined to succeed. That worldwide movement of culture and art that negates nationality in favor of human love, the message of the New Left in America, Europe, and the rest of the world, which attracted youth (generally in its superficial anarchy), truly contains a spiritual kernel of great light, though it appears in polluted garb. From the human point of view, Rav Kook said some very radical things[31]:

Humanity ought to become unified as one family, and then all quarrels and bad traits that come from the separations of peoples and their borders would cease. But the world requires essential refinement whereby humanity is consummated by the wealth of special characteristics of each nation. This lack shall be completed by *Knesset Yisrael,* whose quality is like that of a great spiritual treasury including every capacity and every superior spiritual inclina-

30. One of the sharpest formulations on this matter is that of our mentor Rav Zvi Yehuda Kook, *LiNetivot Yisrael,* Vol. I, pp. 11–15, e.g., "The whole principle of nationalism, as is current in our marketplace, is something novel and strange among us, as if from the outside it has come to us. The impulse of external life has aroused among us the general rubric of 'the people as a whole.' This nationalism is for us, in the final analysis, a kind of homonym. We have no outright chauvinistic nationalism as do the other nations. Our nationality is always cosmopolitan, always universally human and universally cosmic . . ."
31. Here we see Rav Kook's tendency to unify extremes while getting at the depth in each approach. On the one hand, he is a great spokesman of national renaissance; on the other hand, he champions a cosmopolitanism almost as radical as that of the Jewish socialists. The spiritual encounter of these polar approaches is made possible by understanding the Jewish people at the special level of the *neshamah* of Israel, which contains the universal dimension. This is a kind of Torah parallel to one tendency of socialist Zionism, which also sought to merge nationalism with universalism. See Ehud Luz, *Makbilim Nifgashim* (Tel Aviv 1985), Chap. 7, pp. 243–68 and especially the approach of Nachman Syrkin. Of course, Rav Kook differs in drawing upon sacred sources. Whether such an encounter between spokesmen for different movements can take place today, with the retreat of socialism and renewed interest in Judaism, the future will determine. It is interesting to consider why such an encounter has not yet occurred.

tion. With the complete fulfillment of *Knesset Yisrael* will be preserved in the world, especially through its connection to the world as a whole, all the good that comes from the division of nations. There will no longer be a need for concrete division, and all the peoples will become one entity, and over them as a holy treasury, the kingdom of priests and sacred people, unique among the peoples, as G-d has spoken (*Orot*, p. 156).

Moreover, denial or doubt about the validity of absolute ethics appears to Rav Kook to be a consequence of the expansion of European nationalism. Humanity as a whole would never separate itself from the source of its soul, from the absolute good. But European nationalism debased the stature of humanity, toward the herd bestiality of the collective; fascism becomes an inevitable outcome:

Europe rightly despaired of a G-d it had never known. Individual persons oriented themselves to the supreme good, but not an entire nation. How to yearn for the encompassing good no nation and tongue can comprehend, much more so they are unable to seal thus the foundation of their existence. Therefore when in our time nationalism became stronger and penetrated the systems of philosophy, the latter was forced to put a big question mark next to the content of absolute ethics,[32] which in truth came to Europe only on loan from Judaism, and like any transplant is not yet accepted in spirit. For us, if we are what we are, and do not make an effort to dress up in strangers' garb, the question of ethics will not be a piercing one. We feel in ourselves, all of us, the nation as a whole, that the absolute good, the good to all, that is worthy of longing, on that basis ought one found a commonwealth and conduct politics, and we see in our flesh that the absolute good is the eternal divine good in all reality, and we aspire to follow it always in the national and human sense. Therefore the divine love and the cleaving unto G-d is for us something substantive that cannot be erased or altered.

32. What Machiavelli achieved with the political philosophy of the state against the sovereignty and influence of the church was accomplished by the relativists leading up to Nietzsche against German idealism, which was still affected a bit by Judaism via Christianity, at least in the area of ethics. The culmination of this development of immoral nationalism was a series of massive disasters for Europe and its culture. See also Rav Kook's description (*Orot*, pp. 15–16) of Europe during World War I. The appropriateness of his severe description becomes much greater with World War II and its aftermath.

Knesset Yisrael differs in its essence:

The national tendency in Israel is a field blessed by G-d, for though the plants are not yet complete, because of the great desolation of Exile, it is worthy, by spiritual and practical work, that all the good plants in the world should grow in it in order to extract from its overflowing great and superior *neshamot* that illuminate the entire world with its honor. And there is a corresponding national tendency among the nations, which is ruin and wilderness, in no way is it worthy to grow plants, and the evil plants like the vine of Sodom, the poison of dragons and bitter clusters—their absence would be better than their existence, as we find everything in them total privation and absolute ruin, and those "nations shall surely be ruined."[33] Only the influence of holiness, intertwined with the Israelite national tendency, refreshes these human tendencies in general and restores them for the better, until they too become elevated to be worthy, by virtue of their frequent connection and relation to Israel, for spiritual growth. "The wilderness and the solitary place shall be glad for them; and the desert shall rejoice, and blossom as the rose." All this will come about by the complete redemption of Israel, may it come soon" (*Orot*, p. 65).

Therefore Europe, by and large, viewed the Jewish people as a foreign body, neither digestible nor ejectable, that affects all Europe with ethical and cultural ideas of a universal tendency. This Europe found hard to tolerate.[34] A Frenchman or Pole, Englishman or Italian,

33. The ruin of the nations, according to Rav Kook, need not be the destruction of individual human beings, but the destruction of Gentile nationalism in those places where the collective is brutal and feral. The degree of harm to people is proportional to the brutality of the specific nationalism and its opponents, who annihilate each other in their wars, and drag to perdition millions dominated by them. Only elite individuals are unaffected by this. To be sure, the influence of Israelite sanctity can illuminate, albeit indirectly, with knowledge and ethics, the national tendencies of the entire world.

34. The reason for the varied forms of anti-Semitism are many and complex (see *supra* n. 2). Yet it is impossible to ignore the consistent voice of modern anti-Semitism in Western Europe, which declared war on "Jewish ethics and its weaknesses," as it perceived these, whether in Christian, liberal, and especially socialist garb, the latter overtly advocated by so many young Jews. To be sure, ancient anti-Semitism developed on a social-religious base rather than a racial one, and thus differs fundamentally from the modern; nonetheless, one can demonstrate that it too saw the Torah of Israel and its adherents as a danger and threat. See Josephus, *Contra Apion;* Philo, *Contra Flaccus,* the Mission to Gaeus; Tacitus, *History,* Book 5. Comprehensive overviews in Y. Heinemann, "Judaism in the Eyes of the Ancient World" (*Zion* 4, 5699, pp. 269–93), D. Flusser, "The Blood Libel Against the Jews" (*Y. Levi Festschrift,* 5709,

who emigrates from his land would experience a crisis of *nefesh* (the economic-social aspect) and *ruach* (culture), i.e., world and social standing, and the language of speech and creation. It is difficult but doable, for man, just as he is one species biologically, is also one in the general human categories of righteousness and justice, faith and ethics and religion, and science and inquiry. With time he discovers that the concerns of human beings are the same in every place, humanity is beyond the barriers separating peoples and cultures. This enables man to rediscover his place in a new society, especially in those dominated by the world religions whose source (not fortuitously!) is the Torah of Israel. But the Jews—for them emigration is not assimilation. Emigration is suffered only when necessary. But assimilation is a trauma, for the Jews had always preserved with enormous stubbornness their identity and membership in their community.[35] Rav Kook explains this in the special connection of the Jew to the *neshamah* of *Knesset Yisrael:*

If one considers detaching oneself from the nation, he must detach his soul from its source of life, and therefore the requirement of each Jew for the community is great indeed, and he will always sacrifice his life to avoid being torn from the nation, because the *neshamah* and its self-mending demands this of him (*Orot,* p. 144).

In other words, the assimilation of a Jew, though not impossible, is an all-inclusive crisis of identity. His adaptation is more difficult than that of other people, for in addition to the economic, social, linguistic, and cultural crises, there is an apostasy in the religious, ethical, and even rational dimensions. Even after several generations of attempted

---

pp. 104–24); see also A. S. Hirschberg, "The Great Conversion Movement of the Second Commonwealth" (*HaTekufa* 12:129–98; 13:189–210); M. Stern, "Sympathy for Jews in the Circles of Roman Senators" (*Zion* 29:155–67).

35. Precisely Jews who were relatively detached from their people and well integrated in their foreign environment often stood out in the awareness of their neighbors by virtue of "Jewish values" and "Jewish ethics" much more than ghetto Jews. This helps explain why anti-Semitism was particularly intense at the height of Jewish involvement in the surrounding culture. Even today, Jews who are far from their people and religion are highly visible in the areas of social and political ethics, in struggles for universal principles, in science and education. Likewise in the United States and in Israel, where the environment is radically different from that of Europe; hence the difference in reactions as well.

assimilation, the Gentile society identifies him as a Jew if only by his obsession with justice and morality and universal principles. No doubt there is a certain danger in the attempt to understand anti-Semitism, lest, perish the thought, it tempts one to justify it. Thus, we shall say that, according to Rav Kook, anti-Semitism is not only an abomination in terms of right and ethics, law and justice, but also a terrible ungratefulness, a severe damage to the anti-Semitic peoples themselves. This damage is not only the loss of the benefits perpetually conferred by Jewish intellect, resourcefulness, and commitment to their countries, but principally the loss of the profound ethical moment of culture that was Jewishly inspired.[36] The unbreakable connection between the nations and Israel was transformed, in Europe, from a living tie, to a teratological bond of anti-Semitism.

The same is true of entire peoples. When a people is exiled from its land and enters the economic, social, and cultural frameworks of other peoples, it loses its own governmental and economic-social cast (its *nefesh*), and its cultural language *(ruach),* and becomes fragmented into myriads of individuals who will serve as "raw material" for a new national or multinational organism that will derive its content from humanity and mold for itself new forms for that content. This is the essence of the historical-national process. Nations are born, develop, age, and die.[37] But Israel awakes and remains alive in exile, because of its special *neshamah,* which makes possible the resurrection of the dry bones[38]:

The divine creation that is revealed in the world, its power fills the universe, appears upon all creatures, aspires to the highest perfection. Because of this He wears out His handiwork, makes creatures and brings their perfect forms into actuality, and the form becomes girded with *gevura,* and intensifies to

36. This seems to be one point of resemblance between Rav Kook's way of thought and that of Dr. Herzl, who viewed anti-Semitism as the severe disease of the nations suffering from it. Hence, the solution to the problem through the political-historical redemption of Israel is in the interest of all civilized peoples. If only they understood this, they would support the renaissance of Israel.

37. Rav Kook uses Hegelian language like that of Rav Nachman Krochmal (see *Orot,* pp. 102–4 and 159) but the terminology of *naran* is unique to Rav Kook, who "adapts" some of Krochmal's ideas to the concepts of Kabbalah and Chasidut, creating, in the process, a fundamental difference.

38. See *Orot,* p. 108: "that the divine idea, as a result of its superiority and the intensity of the light of life in it, is able to restore the spirit of life even to dry bones."

create a loftier, more majestic, more delicate and uplifted creation, and this effaces the realization of the imperfect form, and makes its way toward the appearance of more perfect life, more mended reality. In the national life that is exhibited in the world, in which the historical *neshamah* is revealed, this divine light is a consuming fire to all the nations that are ephemeral and transient, their form is effaced to create a more perfect national form. Only in Israel the national trait attains its place of repose, and the *Shechinah* rests in Zion, and the fire of G-d that takes hold of it animates it and perpetuates it, gives it light and warmth, not burning and annihilating—"And you who cleave unto the Lord your G-d all live today." We have in our hands a panacea for the entire world in the national sense. This is the matter that is agreed upon in history, that a nation must die and pass from the world, for almost all the ancient peoples have passed and disappeared from the world, and if any people has survived from olden times it did not suffer from dispersion, neither did it develop properly to have an impact on the world. But to be a living, acting nation, steadfast and solid enough to overcome several crises, this has not been seen in the world outside of Israel, through the Name of G-d that is tied to them and the panacea of the living Torah in their midst, and this panacea is destined to emerge from us to the entire world, and nations will rejoice and chant for You will judge peoples righteously and guide nations upon earth. Selah (*Orot*, p. 157).

The diminished features of Jewish existence in the exiled community are possible, however anomalous, because the Jews, despite their integration in the economy (and even in society under certain circumstances) and in the linguistic culture of the host country, are unique in their general *neshamah*, i.e., in religion and ethics, faith and commandments. Often they stand out in their commitment and loyalty to the universal ideas common to that country, in their government and jurisprudence and science, a phenomenon most noticeable among those Jews who are most integrated or assimilated. Thus, the anomaly of exile has become the hallmark of the Jews, like the land and state and other distinguishing marks of all others. Thus, the Jews became enamored of their exile, which disease led to its own prolongation, beyond any logical reason.[39] To be sure, this disease too contains a profound point of inner truth. One of the boldest assertions of Rav Kook is the idea that exile was necessary in a certain sense, because of

39. See introduction to Rav Jacob Emden's *Siddur Bet Yaakov, Sullam Bet El,* pp. 13–14 (Lemberg ed., 5664).

the strong impact on the Jewish people when it became corrupted during its first period on the Land and the inner necessity to become purified and to await the time when it will become possible to establish a commonwealth on the foundations of the divine good:

We could not have withstood the general currents of the world, which have nothing, at the bottom, other than vulgar self-love, and when we associated with the neighboring nations we incorporated their foreign spirit, which could not unite with ours and became our nemesis. Now we have been purified in the furnace of penury, millennia have passed in which we have had, from the viewpoint of the nation, no involvement with material matters, we were a nation floating in the air and dreamed only of the kingdom of heaven, of the absolute divine good. This strange situation was a good cure for us: Our natural aspiration for the general divine good became internalized in us (*Orot,* p.32).

We abandoned world politics under a duress that contained an inner consent, until the arrival of a felicitous time when it would become possible to conduct a commonwealth without wickedness and barbarism; the time for which we hope. Of course, in order to realize it, we must rouse ourselves with all our powers, to use all means that time provides: All is guided by the hand of G-d, Creator of all worlds. But the delay is a necessary delay, our *nefesh* was revolted by the terrible sins of the government of an evil kingdom in an evil time. And the time has arrived, it is very near, the world will become fragrant and we can already ready ourselves, for it will already be possible for us to conduct our state on the foundations of the good, wisdom, righteousness and clear divine illumination: "Jacob sent Esau the porphyry": "Let my master pass before his servant." It is not proper for Jacob to deal with statecraft, when it must be full of blood, when it demands a talent for wickedness. We adopted this foundation only according to the necessity of establishing a nation; once the stock took root, we yielded sovereignty and were dispersed among the Gentiles, we were sown in the depths of the earth until the time of the turtle arrives and the voice of the dove is heard in our land.

Here we must address the Zionist question: If Zionism is the attempt to restore Israel to the life of all other peoples, i.e., a nation with a land, economy, society, language, and culture of its own, and if the cultural depth resonates to the link to the *neshamah* so that the *neshamah* of *Knesset Yisrael* will reappear in its full stature of *naran* in the public sense—then this is literally redemption, which is vital not only to the *nefesh* and *ruach* of Israel but to the whole world, which is dependent on the revival of Israel. Therefore—if only they would understand this—the whole world would support Israel.

The inherent color of *Knesset Yisrael* is revealed, its powers develop, its wisdom returns to it, the potency, righteousness and inner purity, the nation is built up, mended for redemption, eternal redemption, it blossoms with the glow of its majesty. From the multitude of waves of reverence that pass over it, from all the nations, from all dispersions, it introduces great wealth and a sweeping perspective and adds the pure aspects from the outside to its own possessions. The zeal of the people intensifies, its knowledge of its force increases. It knows already that it has a land, that it has a language, a literature, that it has an army—it began to know in this world war. Above all, it knows that it has a special light of life, which crowns it and crowns the entire world through it, and through all this together it knows its firmness that it has strength in the true G-d (*Orot*, p. 15).

But now we are again called to realize it in life—that is the matter of renewal. If many parts of the ramifications of our vision are diminished when they meet reality, at the beginning of our road, that is not bad. Reality has not the rapid wings of vision. The renewal accumulates all our eternal ideals and secretes them in small deeds, in the effort bequeathed to generations, to the land, to the place where our rights and qualities await us, in an attitude of respect toward our entire treasury of the past and an uplifted spirit toward the elevation of the nation in the future, which is being raised through our will and labor. The historical fondness for the people and the land must live off the faith and beliefs of the past. To be sure, as the aspiration of our spirit is raised, so increases in us the light of the past; certainly it will not decrease or cease. Never will the knowledge of G-d in our midst revert to a kind of mechanical, blind-deaf nature, bound by sterile beliefs that have nothing to fructify and nothing to animate, but rather "they will go from success to success, G-d will make Himself seen in Zion." If the personal attitude, of each individual in all the ways of life . . . to the general national spirit, which aspires only to the total divine good . . . has not yet developed—it will become developed through the swelling of our people's spirit, and when it thus reaches that degree that its voice is heard in the political world, as it is heard in the ethical and theological worlds, then its power and force shall be revealed (*Orot*, pp. 52–53).

Until the era of future redemption we inspired the world only to the learning of duties, ethics and justice that derives from genuine knowledge of G-d. Duties the world does not wish to accept, and if it does accept, there remains in the heart resentment toward the principal arouser to awareness of the duty, which does not permit the barbaric *nefesh* to stretch out according to all its desires, but when the era arrives for the eternal light to be revealed, it will be known to the world that the way of life of true delight is what we have inspired in the world, the felicity of life that gives it its value, without which it is deprived of all value. Delight and felicity are something equal to all, at least the desire for them, and the source that bestows felicity and delight is respected and loved; therefore "ten men of all the languages of the nations shall take hold of the hem of a Jewish man" (*Orot,* pp. 157–58).

Such a Zionism, in working toward a Jewish state, is not aiming at an ordinary state from which the concepts of the *neshamah* are excluded, but a Jewish state that will manifest in the world the true uniqueness of Israel, as a paradigm of justice and righteousness and law to all peoples according to the Torah of Israel and the vision of the prophets of Israel.[40] Such a state would be to the world of politics what Israel was destined to proclaim to all the peoples:

The state is not man's highest felicity. This can be said of an ordinary state, which has no greater value than a huge corporation, where the multitude of ideas that are the living crown of humanity float above it and do not touch it. That is not the case with a state that is founded on the ideal, and imprinted in its being with the supreme ideal content that is truly the supreme felicity for the individual. Such a state is truly the highest on the ladder of felicity, and such a state is our state, the State of Israel, the foundation of G-d's throne in the world, whose only aim is that G-d be one and His Name one, which is indeed the highest felicity. True, this sublime felicity requires a long interpretation to elevate its light in days of darkness, but it does not cease for this reason to be the greatest felicity (*Orot,* p. 160).

However, if Zionism entered the world only to "normalize" the Jewish people, to solve the problem of anti-Semitism through collective assimilation, by abjuration of Judaism, transforming the Jewish people

40. Such uniqueness was willingly accepted by Dr. Herzl and his heirs, and in the social-political realm it is characteristic of David Ben-Gurion and many others. "The vision of the prophets of Israel" is inscribed in the declaration of independence, and in the mouths and hearts of its architects. At many political crossroads, this voice is heard again, that the State of Israel is obligated to maintain higher ethical standards than other peoples. Even those who disagree with specific conclusions cannot deny this public tendency.

into one of body, *nefesh* and *ruach*, i.e., land and sovereignty, econ-omy-society-culture, to subjugate Judaism to "culture" in the manner of radical Zionism[41]—this is impossible and cannot happen, according to Rav Kook. The Jewish people is linked essentially to the *neshamah* of *Knesset Yisrael* and cannot break the connection, even if it wished to, and surely most Jews will not wish to. Thus, a Zionism of normality that "has no connection to religion"[42] and cares only for a terrestrial country like all others and for the solution of the problems of physical, economic-social and cultural existence, like all peoples—such Zionism is problematic and dangerous because it threatens to detach the natural unity of *Knesset Yisrael.* Rav Kook states confidently that it is not only prohibited, but also impossible to sever the natural unity of *Knesset Yisrael* or to alter it. Here he differs radically from the Charedim:

It is a great mistake on the part of those who do not feel the unique unity in Israel, and wish in their imagination to equate this divine element that is unique to the Israelite character, to the content of all peoples and nations among all the families of the earth, whence comes the desire to divide the national element and the religious element into two, with both components thus inheriting falsehood. For all elements of thought, feeling and idealism that we find in the Israelite nation are one indivisible entity, and all together make its special form. However, as mistaken as are those who strain to separate the inseparable, even more mistaken are those who think that it is possible for those who strain to accomplish the division and separation to succeed, which

41. E.g., M. Berdichevsky in his great polemic against Achad Haam, *Nemoshot* (War-saw 5660), pp. 18–23, 82–96; Y. H. Brenner, *BaChayyim uBaSifrut* (Collected Writ-ings Vol. II, p. 61). Eliezer Ben-Yehuda, *Yisrael LeArtso veLiLeshono,* p. 9; and see Y. Klausner in *Eliezer Ben-Yehuda, Kovets LeZichro,* pp. 11–12. It is no wonder that the crucial cultural impact was that of Berdichevsky, who was captivated by Nietzsche (see *supra* n. 32). The development of radical Zionism is surveyed in Ehud Luz, *Makbilim Nifgashim,* Chaps. 6–7 (pp. 214–68). In our day, A. B. Yehoshua has raised this banner again ("In favor of Normality"). It is interesting to note that most spokes-men of the Israeli left advocate greater morality, and not necessarily greater normality, and distance themselves from the cult of national force that grew out of Berdichevsky's radicalism.

42. See Rav Kook's letter against the editor of *HaHashkafa* (E. Ben-Yehuda!) for his dismissal of our past—to the point of dropping from the tree (*Igrot HaReAYaH,* Vol. I, p. 18). See *HaTzon HaGeulla,* pp. 186–97, for his vehement struggle against the shameful pagan, seemingly neutral determination that "Zionism has nothing to do with religion." Dr. Herzl's attempt to neutralize the questions of religion and culture in the context of Zionist Congress politics was rejected by Rav Kook no less fervently than the radical negation of Ben-Yehuda. For a different evaluation of Herzl's policy, see Luz, op. cit. Chap. 5, pp. 187–207 and 314–16.

is why they wage war against those who uphold one component of the Israelite entity with burning anger, with their vain separation, without considering how this struggle should be conducted. If it were indeed possible to separate the spiritual contents of *Knesset Yisrael,* except that the matter is prevented because of some Torah law, then the struggle must be directed against those who uphold a certain separate component, to engulf and annihilate their features from beneath the heavens of the nation. But since the impossibility of separation is an absolute impossibility, we are confident that dividers who uphold the isolated components are mistaken only in their imagination, not in their actual being, for truly this individual component, as it is founded in the life of the nation in general, then everything is already contained in it, and the struggle must be specifically to reveal to them their error and to clarify to them that all their efforts to shake the supreme Israelite unity will not succeed. And the adaptation of the paragons of Israelite thought and will, with all the depth of its nature, must only be to criticize the partial vision from all its sides, and to demonstrate in himself all the signs of his integrity and totality in all subjects, including those ideas that spiritual persons have wished to ignore and uproot from their *nefesh.* By clarifying this true matter, all the upholders of separation will eventually recognize that they have sufficiently wasted their strength in vain, and instead of upholding an imagined separate component, in which all the aspirations and general content of the nation in all its values are to be included in an obscure and faded form, and thus deny the souls upholding it their spiritual satiation, they narrow their spiritual space and guide it along obstacle-filled paths—it will be easier for them to recognize truly the real truth and to take hold of all the living sacred content of the perfect light of Israel in all its revealed appearances. Thus they will save their souls from trouble and darkness, and shall look upon and flow toward G-d and His goodness, and will no longer need to torment themselves with fragments of obscure and faded ideas that, on the one hand they will never be able to get rid of, and on the other hand can never find in them clarity and illumination of the spirit, for they are contents whose goodness and the marrow of whose enthusiastic, intense life will only be exhibited upon the broad and perfect vista where all Israelite life in its total and complete essence appears in its full strength (*Orot,* pp. 45–46).

There is a covenant bestowed upon *Knesset Yisrael* as a whole that it shall not be defiled completely. Defilement can affect it, cause it defects, but not cut it off completely from the source of divine life. The *ruach* of the nation that is aroused now, which many of its supporters claim does not need the *ruach* of G-d, if they could truly establish such a national *ruach* in Israel, they could represent the nation in a state of defilement and destruction, but what they will they know not themselves.[43] So connected is the *ruach* of Israel with the *ruach* of G-d that even he who says that he has no need for the spirit of G-d, since he says that he desires the spirit of Israel, then the divine *ruach* is present in the heart of his point of aspiration even against his will. The individual can detach himself from the source of life; not so the nation *Knesset Yisrael* as a whole. Therefore all the possessions of the nation that are beloved to it from the aspect of the national *ruach,* all of them are suffused by the divine *ruach:* her land, language, history, customs. And if there is found at some time such an awakening of *ruach,* that all these speak in the name of the *ruach* of the nation alone, and make an effort to deny the *ruach* of G-d from all these possessions and from their revealed source, which is the *ruach* of the nation, what should the saints of the generation then do? To rebel against the *ruach* of the nation, even in words, and to reject its possessions, this is impossible: The *ruach* of G-d and the *ruach* of Israel are one,[44] except that need to labor greatly to reveal the light and the holy in the *ruach* of the nation, the light of G-d in all this, until all those who uphold those thoughts of the general *ruach* and all its possessions will discover themselves standing rooted and living in the life of G-d, shining with the sanctity and potency of heaven (*Orot,* pp. 63–64).

However, the very thought of separation is already like a thought of idolatry, of a division within G-d, because *Knesset Yisrael* is G-d's estate in the world, and the thought of idolatry destroys a great deal even if it does not come, and never will come, to action. This destruction is caused both by the pious who fear G-d and by the secularist scoffers. At either extreme, both are ready for such a separation; in the

43. This sentence is one of the sources for the common claim that Rav Kook and his disciples know better than the secularists what they want and what they think, and thus negate their primary right to define themselves. See a penetrating discussion of this question in E. Schweid *HaYahadut VeHaTarbut HaChilonit,* pp. 111–42. A careful study of this section indicates that Rav Kook does not refer to the consciousness of the individual, but to the general meaning of the *ruach* of Israel. "What they will they know not themselves" necessarily means that they intend to resurrect the historical Jewish people, which necessarily includes the link to the spirit of G-d, hence there is willy-nilly an objective contradiction between the national-Israelite consciousness and the individual secularist consciousness. With the passage of time, according to Rav Kook, a clarification is inevitable between those who give up their national consciousness and those who give up their secularist consciousness; it seems that such a process is operating in our own time.

44. "Israel, the Torah and the Holy One Blessed be He are one." *Zohar Vayikra* 73:93. See also *Berachot* 6a ("G-d's tefillin" and those of Israel); *Sukka* 45b; *Vayikra Rabbah* 2, *Tanchuma KiTissa* 18, *Tazria* 5; *Sifre Ekev* 47, *Haazinu* 312; *Tanna DeBei Eliyahu Rabbah* 19:21 ("Israel and the Torah").

middle are heard feeble voices favoring a compromise "for the sake of peace." In one of his most vehement sections, Rav Kook cries out:

The conflict of opinions regarding the direction of the community, whether in this period, when the number of insurgents has increased who raise up the flag of anarchy, it is proper to divide the nation, that the fit ones who raise up the banner of the Name of G-d should have no relation with the iniquitous who have cast off the yoke, or whether the power of general peace overcomes all—this entire dispute has come about because of the general debasement, in that the purification is yet to be completed in the fundamental character of the nation, from the aspect of its external soul, and it is becoming purified. Both these sects are like the two harlots who came to Solomon: The one who ought to be rejected argues "Cut," and in its rancor highlights the truth of the resentment of the heart that it feels, whose content is only "Neither mine nor thine—cut!" while the merciful mother, the true mother, says, "Give her the living child, do not put it to death," and the Holy Spirit cries out, "Give her the living child, she is his mother!" There is no end to the physical and spiritual evils in dividing the nation to components, although complete separation as is considered by those who would dissect brutally is impossible and will not occur. This is literally a thought of general idolatry, which we are assured will not be fulfilled: "that you say, We will be as the nations, as the families of the lands, to serve wood and stone. As I live, says G-d, surely with a mighty hand, and with a stretched-out arm, and with fury poured out, will I rule over you!" And like any thought of idolatry it is destructive and distressing—even when it has not come and will not come to action. The basis of the saintliness of the saints in each generation is supported by the wicked too, for with all their wickedness they cleave in the desire of their hearts unto the totality of the nation, of them it states, "And you people are all righteous," and the externality of their wickedness makes it possible to embrace the power of the saintly "like wine in its barrel," and the imagined division undermines the entire element of sanctity, like the acts of Amalek who attacked the stragglers, ejected from the cloud, "He put forth his hands against such as be at peace with him; he broke his covenant" (*Orot,* pp. 73–74).

How, then, does Rav Kook confront the phenomenon of widespread secularism? Not by denial or diminution in a spirit of defensive acquiescence—Rav Kook was the last man to acquiesce to evil, in all of Jerusalem there was no true zealot, militant and patient, like him.[45]

45. See *Orot, Zeronim,* Chap. 6, pp. 130–31.

Rav Kook also does not adopt simplistically the doctrine of the good spark in the depth of every Jewish soul,[46] and does not argue to the secularist that he is other than he thinks and acts. This is one of the major errors in understanding Rav Kook; many have embraced it without comprehension and burdened him with their own ideas, which are quite distant from his. Rav Kook recognized with great pain the secularism of the radical Zionists, who considered the Jewish *neshamah* à la Rav Kook to be the product of exile,[47] while Rav Kook states that it is essential and natural to Israel, and that exile came about to save the people from the burden of sins in their Land, in ancient times. Rav Kook had no illusions about the wickedness of the scoffers as it was, hence he reacts so sharply to Eliezer Ben-Yehuda, who took pride in having turned his back on our past (*Igrot HaReAYaH*, Vol. I, p. 18), and used harsh language in writing of the guards who fell in Galilee, in the unwillingness to give up one jot or tittle of mitzvot in exchange for Zionist nationality, as do many of the compromisers *(Al Bamotenu Chalalim)*. At the same time, he recognized the intense bond by which they tied themselves, knowingly, to the Jewish people. All this, because the Jewish people is *not* in any way what they consider it—a normal people like all others, whose return to history will cure it not only of exile but also, as it were, of the Jewish *neshamah*. Therefore, their stubborn clinging in the desires of their heart to the totality of the nation ties them to the *neshamah* of *Knesset Yisrael* in opposition to their individual-secular consciousness. Not to desire the people of Israel and its *ruach* in any case, that is also impossible according to Rav Kook!

In other words, the secular consciousness and sense of Jewish identity of the alienated are objectively opposed to one another, and essentially so. This contradiction is solved by the secularists by interpreting the Jewish people as an ordinary people, with body, *nefesh, ruach,* like

---

46. Baal Shem Tov, *Leshon Hasidim,* section *Kedushat Yisrael,* pp. 250–51; R.S.Z. of Liadi *Tanya* Chaps. 18–19; *Tzemach Tzedek, Derech Mitzvotecha, Mitzvat Ahavat Yisrael,* pp. 55–58; R. Tzadok HaCohen of Lublin *Yisrael Kedoshim,* p. 86. In some of these sources, it can be demonstrated that Hasidut too discovered the good in the wicked only in his link to the totality of Israel, and as a result of the general holiness of the Jewish people. This connection is much stronger in the Land of Israel, as is implied by *Zohar Vayikra* 93, on the verse "Who is like Your people Israel one nation on earth" (II Samuel 7:23)—"with the land they are called one nation, but not in themselves."

47. See *supra* nn. 41–42.

all peoples. But this is an erroneous solution, which contradicts not only the unique essence of Israel but the Jewish history to which the Zionists so wished to return, as well.[48] The secular solution, which "heals the breach of my people with facility," is obviously incorrect, and therefore cannot endure, according to Rav Kook. In order to sustain the Jewish people in its Land and in its state, under all pressures, a Jewish-Zionist consciousness beyond secularism is required; therefore, the necessity of existence and the effect of the people as a whole in the Land of Israel will bring secularism to bankruptcy and the secularists to a crossroads— to accept what derives from the *neshamah* of *Knesset Yisrael* as the total identity of the unique Jewish people in its unique land, or, G-d forbid, to abandon everything and to disappear as isolated individuals, assimilated Jews, throughout the world, in any place where, for a time, the illusion of integration blooms.[49] Rav Kook does not argue with the radical secularist about his self-awareness but about the definition of the essence of the historic Jewish people. Rav Kook disputes only the secular definition of the Jewish people. Self-definition can be adopted by the individual, but we have no reason to accept the definition of the essence of the Jewish people from the secularists. (And there is no personal insult in the fact that we do not accept such a definition from them.)

Rav Kook's remedy for the problem is a nonsuperficial unity of political camps and educational-ideological trends (*Orot*, pp. 71–72), and even more so of people themselves, who will influence each other through mutual recognition of the good in each group. Rav Kook does not recoil from defining the dissident *chalutzim* as possessors of a mended *nefesh*, and the Charedim as possessors of *ruach* as we have come to know these concepts. But only the superior saints, "masters of *neshamah*," can unite them all, for Haredi spiritual piety in its

48. Most spokesmen of secular Zionism, especially its practical leaders from Herzl to Ben-Gurion, recognized the uniqueness of the nation and of Jewish history in terms of morality and spirituality, or in terms of a "light unto the nations." In this they differ from the radical secularists.

49. In the American Diaspora, Jewish integration in political, economic, and cultural life again appears, this time more radically and more successfully than ever in Europe. It has new ideologists (e.g., George Steiner, Noam Chomsky, and the Breira group) who set it up as a more spiritual counterweight to Zionism. Nonetheless, it appears to me to be a severe long-range delusion like that of Hellenistic-Roman Alexandria, the Spanish "golden age," or Hungary, Austria, and Germany before the extermination.

essence is not unique to Israel as a nation of destiny; it is found in various forms also among unique individuals in the world. However, the total unity of the Israelite national community (*tzibbur,* for which read *tzaddikim-benonim-reshaim,* saints-mediocre-wicked[50]), upon which the Name of G-d is called precisely in its Israelite nationality—that is the uniqueness of Israel. Thus, Rav Kook views the crisis of secularism and its inevitable solution (note the exact employment of the *naran* concepts):

The *nefesh* of the wicked of Israel during the time of Messianic portent *(ikveta DeMeshicha),* those who associate lovingly with the concerns of the Jewish totality, to the Land of Israel and the renaissance of the nation, is more mended than the *nefesh* of Jews with perfect faith who lack this advantage of feeling themselves for the benefit of the totality and the building up of the nation and the Land.[51] But the *ruach* is far more mended among the G-d-fearers who observe Torah and mitzvot, even though the sense of self and the awakening of the power to act on the concerns of the Jewish totality are not yet as vigorous among them as they are among those whose hearts are clouded by the twisted *ruach* in their midst, to the point of associating with strange views and actions that defile the body and prevent the light of *ruach* from being corrected, so that the *nefesh* also suffers from their defects. The restoration that will come through the light of Messiah, which will be greatly helped by the diffusion of the study of the esoterica of the Torah and the revelation of the lights of divine wisdom, in all its forms that are proper to be revealed, is that all Israel will become one bundle, and the *nefesh* of the reverent Torah observers will be mended by the perfection of the *nefesh* of the sinners who are good with respect to the concerns of the totality and the physical and spiritual hope that is grasped by human knowledge and feeling, while the *ruach* of these sinners will be mended by the influence of the G-d-fearers, keepers

50. See H.Y.D. Azulai, *Kikkar LaAden* (Livorno 5561), 196b: "Do not separate from the *tzibbur,* for its letters spell *tzaddikim-benonim-reshaim,* and you should associate with them for the sake of all Israel." Rav Zvi Yehuda Kook, of blessed memory, used to cite this idea in the name of HatAri zt'l. However, this unity is called *tzibbur* only in this hierarchy, with the saintly ahead. When the wicked lead, it is "the ass of your enemy oppressed *(robets)* under its burden," which one cannot abandon and is obligated to assist as the verse concludes (Exodus 23:5). These words of Rav Zvi Yehuda are quoted in *HaTorah HaGoelet,* Chap. 1.
51. Rav Kook's opponents cited this sentence in their placards without its context. See M. Friedman, *Chevra VaDaat,* thus deliberately distorting its meaning and precipitating a long schism between Rav Kook's disciples and the Haredim. The schism arose, at least in part, from a chain of errors and defamations that might have been corrected.

of the Torah and great of faith, whence will come to both a great light, and a phenomenon of complete repentance will come to the world, and then Israel will be ready for redemption. And the superior saints, masters of the *neshamah,* will be the unifying channels, through whom the flow of light of the *nefesh* will pass from "left to right" and the flow of *ruach* from "right to left," and the joy will be very great . . . "Your priests will wear justice and your pious shall sing." This will be by power of the light of Messiah who is David himself who "erected a whole-offering of repentance . . . For the sake of Your servant David do not return the face of Your anointed."

We have a tradition that a spiritual rebellion will occur in the Land of Israel and among Israel, in the era when the beginning of the revival of the nation arrives. The physical serenity that comes to part of the nation, who imagine that they have achieved their entire goal, will diminish the *neshamah,* and the days will come of which you will say, I have no desire for them.[52] The aspiration toward elevated and sacred ideals will cease, hence *ruach* too will sink, until the storm arrives and overturns, and it will then become obvious that the strength of Israel is the eternally holy, the light of G-d and His Torah, the lust for spiritual light, which is the complete potency that triumphs over all the world and their powers. The need for this rebellion is the inclination to materiality that must firmly come about in the totality of the nation after so many periods of time have passed in which the nation as a whole was stripped of the need and the possibility of material concerns. This inclination, when it is engendered, will rage and beget turmoil, and these are the harbingers of Messiah that will intoxicate the world with their pains.

As one cannot have wine without lees, one cannot have a world without the wicked. And as the lees stabilize the wine and preserve it, so the vulgar will of the wicked causes existence and stability to the flow of life as a whole, of all the mediocre and the saintly. When the lees diminish and the wine remains without them, it is liable to decompose and go sour. Exile dwindled the force of life in the nation, and our lees were very diminished, to the point where there is a danger to the continued life of the nation because of the lack of a thick sense of life, anchored in the animal and the land and its material decline.[53] Existence in exile is a fragmented existence, and this

52. It seems to me that these words fit our age even more broadly than would have appeared in the time of Rav Kook. The idea itself is based on G-d's words to Moses about what will happen after his death, when the people settle down and get fat (Deut. 31:20 and 32:15).

53. See *Orot HaKodesh,* Vol. II, pp. 360–65, on the earthly inclination that combines with the "saintly man" in Noah. Nonetheless there is an encumbering weight to this inclination of "Noah the man of the earth," as displayed in the story of his

dwindled existence that is more cessation than being could have continued for some time even without lees if necessary, but not forever.[54] The power is already gone, and independent existence claims its role, and the return of Israel to its Land for the sake of its self-existence is a necessary event, and the fulfillment of it precipitates the lees: the bearers of wickedness and brazenness of the premessianic period whose very mention causes all hearts to tremble. These are the murky aspects by which transparent, joyous existence comes into being, and the end of the process is that the lees sink to the bottom of the barrel, the powers of evil are submerged in the depths of life, and then they lose their painful, shuddering content. But in their continued creation, when they are together with the wine, with the life of the nation and its awakening *ruach,* they muddy it and hearts clamor at the sight of the ferment, and the heart rests and finds calmness only with the vision of the future,[55] which is in the process of making its way, according to marvels of Omniscience, "Who can make pure of the impure? Only One" (*Orot,* pp. 84–85).

---

intoxication. The corrective to this inclination comes with the patriarchs. This matter of embracing the will and the powers of life is explained there in terms of the association of the elite with the multitude. In the section from *Orot,* the phenomenon is interpreted at the level of the revival of Israel as a nation.

54. Rav Kook states here as in many other places—e.g., *Orot,* p. 116, *Igrot Ha-ReAYaH,* Vol. II, No. 378, p. 37—that the era of redemption has arrived. Thus, he wished to solve the problem that so troubled the strictly Orthodox community, i.e., the question of the "Three Oaths" that the Jewish people swore, including "not to scale the walls" (*Ketubbot* 112). The verse cited includes also the resolution that the oath ends, "If you awake and if you arouse the love until it desires" (Song of Songs 2:7; 3:5; 8:4). According to Rav Kook, one cannot doubt the awakening of desire for redemption in all sections of the nation. See Rav Yehoshua of Kutna (*Yeshuot Malko,* Chap. 56) cited in the preface to Rav Zvi Yehuda Kook, *LiNetivot Yisrael,* who also pointed to this sign.

55. The absolute inner assurance in the vision of contemporary redemption, as it is reflected here and in other places, is more typical of Rav Kook than of other thinkers in this area, and is the consequence of his intense vision, particularly after the outbreak of World War I (*Orot, HaMilchama,* p. 13). I do not believe that this implies absolute determinism with respect to the future, to the point where human action no longer has significance. Despite the phrases quoted by Dr. A. Ravitzki from Rav Zvi Yehuda and his disciples, one gets a picture of deep visionary anticipation of G-d's acts in the world, as they have been revealed in *facts,* the ingathering of exiles and cultivation of the land (*Hatsafuy VeHaReshut Netuna,* in *Yisrael Likrat HaMea Ha-21,* Van Leer Institute, Jerusalem 5744, pp. 146–64). According to this conception, there may be no necessary dependence of redemption on the sin of any individual, but it is impossible that it be independent of the community as a whole. And if the redemption itself is not dependent on deeds, certainly the mode of redemption and its complexity is. See *Orot,* pp. 165–66, para. 13, on the dependence of the national renaissance upon the revival of each individual soul, even if one is oblivious and unconcerned with this, and even if the process is complex.

Radical secularism in its positive aspect is recognized here as an extreme phenomenon of negation of exile.[56] If Jewish exile is identified with Jewish *ruach* nourished by the *neshamah* and detached from the body and the *nefesh*, then the *chalutzim* represent a mended Israelite *nefesh* struggling to revive the Israelite body—the people and the land. Rav Kook elucidates secularism and even the wickedness in it and notes its positive features: the desire to resurrect Israel simply as farmers and soldiers. On the other hand, he is not oblivious to the evil in the individual consciousness confronting the awareness of belonging and identity with the Jewish people.

If so, what must be done, or can be done, in this situation? Rav Kook is aware of the difficult problems of divisiveness that stem from multiple national characters, and proposes the way and the foundation for the required unity in the nature of the national *neshamah:*

The many different characters that are divided among many peoples are included in Israel together: "He set the borders of peoples according to the number of the children of Israel." Hence they are more liable to divisions and inner disputes, hence they can be forever a people that dwells alone without mingling with the nations, since there is no lack of all the various inclinations and capacities, "a metropolis containing all, its priests, its prophets, its ministers, its kings, as it says—From him a cornerstone, from him a peg, etc." The Torah as a whole, which includes, with the intense essence of its quality, and its equitable way of life, the entire totality and all its members, is the shield against the schisms. Of all the variations of opinions and types, in many spiritual and material matters, there appears through it the general good, which unites them all in the total fulfillment of the Torah, except for the totally wicked who uproot the House of Israel and cast off the yoke with high hand, as Beruria said to the heretic: Rejoice barren women who did not bear children to Gehinnom like you; for the multiplicity of forces is appropriate to the nation when they are united in the root of their existence in the Torah.[57]

More than any people and tongue, we cannot tolerate contradiction and spiritual lack of unity. Peace and unity in their ideal form are an eternal quality

56. See *Orot,* p. 118: ". . . and *Knesset Yisrael* began to sense inwardly its righteousness and integrity and to look upon exile with chagrin and contempt . . ."
57. The source of the nation is the special quality of its *neshamah.* But precisely from this source flow different, clashing traits that the Torah unites, preventing the destruction of conflict. The actual exhibition of the *neshamah's* unity is thus dependent on the Torah of Israel.

in us. Therefore our entire dispersion is only temporary, and we are destined to be united and to be one nation on the earth (*Orot*, p. 169).

When life flowers with the appropriate displays of creation and reason, it is impossible that opinions be set according to one stamp and one style. The order of traits is one that always moves from below up, from a limited fullness of life to a fullness of life in a greater degree, from a weak glow to an intense, radiant glow.[58]

However, all this is when they have, with free creativity and reason, the fundamental basis of the only *ruach* of the nation, of the aspiration to the divine good that is set in the nature of its *neshamah* (*Orot*, p. 52).

Here we reach the heart of the problem that troubled Rav Kook as the rabbi of the Land of Israel. The Zionist movement with its secular orientation did not aim only for the settlement of the land and the renewal of the people. Important segments of it aspired openly to rebel against the national *neshamah*, and regarded everything connected with it as nothing but exile. The high-handed desecration of Torah and mitzvot by the *chalutzim*[59] meant that they wished to redefine not only themselves but the nation. Rav Kook was absolutely confident that this was impossible and mobilized all his powers to explain it. In any event, however, the very attempt surely presented troubles and problems. The Zionist movement proclaimed that it had "nothing to do with religion," and Rav Kook angrily took exception, never ceasing to protest.[60] He refused to accept the explanations of the Mizrachi, which preferred that the Zionist movement stay out of matters of religion and culture, in order that it not adopt unacceptable decisions.[61] In Rav Kook's eyes, however, this meant setting up a national leadership dealing with matters of the body, *nefesh*, and *ruach* as among all the nations, while the Jewish *neshamah* remains caged in the synagogues

58. Rav Kook requires the freedom of creativity in many texts: *Orot HaKodesh*, Vol. I, pp. 165–66; *Olat ReAYaH*, Vol. II (Introduction to the Song of Songs) p. 3; *Igrot HaReAYaH*, Vol. I, No. 158 (letter to Bezalel), pp. 203–6. But this is also fundamentally limited by Torah-halacha, which stems from the national *neshamah*.
59. Rav Kook's distress and shudder in the face of this phenomenon are apparent in many letters. See, for example, *Hatzon HaGeulla*, pp. 231–43; *Maamrei HaReAYaH*, pp. 89–93; *Igrot HaReAYaH*, Vol. I, No. 18, pp. 16–18.
60. See *supra* n. 42.
61. Rav I. J. Reines, *Shaarei Ora VeSimchah*, pp. 16–24, *Or Hadash al Zion*, *Shaar* 3, Chap. 3, p. 14, and see G.. Bat-Yehuda *Ish HaMeorot*, Chaps. 16–18. For a description from a different angle, see E. Luz op. cit., Chap. 9, pp. 299–316.

to which Dr. Herzl would consign the rabbis.[62] Precisely this division, which Rav Reines favored in order not to become entangled with the redemption promised by the prophets, was rejected by Rav Kook, who saw in the epoch and the movement the first revelations of that redemption. For the same reason, but out of contradictory outlooks, these two titans chose opposing sides of the issue.[63] Then, when it was clear that this definition of Zionism could not be changed fundamentally, Rav Kook faced the difficult question—can one save the Israelite unity of *naran* in practical life? In other words, can one fully link Zionism to historic Judaism through the cooperation of different people and movements, even if they are not bound together, in order to renew Israel as a people that constitutes a complete human self, and as a human self that is a complete people?[64]

62. *The Jewish State,* Theocracy. However, when he described his plan for mass immigration, legal and orderly, he spoke in a slightly different spirit: "The rabbis will be the first to understand us, the first to show enthusiasm for our concern, and from the pulpit they will stimulate the others . . . We recognize our historical fellowship only in the faith of our fathers (Ibid., "Shepherds of the Congregation").
63. Most of the Lovers of Zion in the camp spoke of redemption: e.g., Rav Kalischer *(Derishat Zion),* Rav Alkalai *(Shelom Yerushalayim, Raglei Mevasser,* etc. in *Kitve HaRav Alkalai,* Mosad HaRav Kook, Jerusalem 5735), Rav Gutmacher (afterword to Rav Kalischer's volume) and Rav Mohaliver. Rav Kook, of course, continued in their path, also following the Netziv of Volozhin, where he had studied. Rav Reines took a different position, according to his understanding of the needs of his generation, whether because he considered the physical danger to be urgent or because he hoped to conciliate the Orthodox to the political Zionism of Herzl, and regarded neutrality in matters of religion and culture as the only way to bring them together. One should remember that Rav Reines spoke before World War I, when the Zionist movement was organized for action "according to the laws of nature," according to politics and international law and the Ottoman laws that governed the Land of Israel. World War I reshuffled the deck, and also pushed Rav Kook to a more unequivocal certainty regarding the redemptive process, which had commenced in the "overt eschaton" of cultivating the desolate places. Most of his writings on this subject come from this period of the war in London, and afterward in Palestine. Rav Reines was no longer alive, and it is impossible to know how he would have reacted to this bouleversement, and to the salvation of Israel in its midst. Hence one must qualify to a great extent the determination that there was here an unambiguous dispute.
64. This idea I heard from my mentor Rav Zvi Yehuda zt'l: The redemptive Torah of "man-people" and "national man" interprets the well-known statement of Rav Shimon b. Yochai, "You are called man *(adam)* and the Gentiles are not" *(Yevamot* 61) refers to the national, not the individual, Gentile. It is interesting that Rav Shimon said this with respect to the defilement of a tent by a corpse, which expresses the link between those who are underneath the same roof. Thus, it is a novel Jewish concept that defilement can be transmitted in this manner, whereas among the Gentiles it is transmitted only through touch and carrying, like other forms of defilement. See *supra* nn. 5 and 13. I note the parallel, in almost the same language, though with different

And if not—is it conceivable that national religious or human contents will operate within the Jewish people in the ways and methods common to the rest of humanity and other nations, and that above all this the Israelite *neshamah* will find its scope of action and influence? Such a situation is liable to create a strange combination of national renaissance of the sort common in the world in an age of national awakening, together with the parallel continuation of and influence of the Exile and its institutions. The Zionist movement, on one side; the "Torah world"—yeshivot and Chasidic courts, on the other side: the situation that we have come to know for the past several generations. If, G-d forbid, no link is formed between them—can Zionism carry on the great work of national renewal as a stage in complete redemption, meaning full unity of the people-humanity? This question oppressed Rav Kook both theoretically and practically, i.e., communal practice and educational practice.

In Rav Kook's answer, we can find three directions or emphases: theoretical, philosophical, and historiosophical. He presents the question in a style that is unusual for him, and does not exempt himself from the requisite clarification. In a rare formulation—which we quoted at the beginning of this essay—Rav Kook says:

The form of Israel must be refined, whether the general humanity of human nature has the same character that it has among all the nations, upon which

---

emphasis, in A. D. Gordon: "This is the basis of our idea, the idea of our renaissance and redemption, this is the foundation of the idea of people-man. Without people-man there is no human-man, there is no individual-man, and who like us, the children of Israel, should be aware of this?"; "Our renaissance requires a spirit from on high, from the four corners, a giant idea takes possession of man and fills all his being, the power of a religious idea overturns man's world and renews the human spirit" (Dr. J. Schechter *Mishnato shel A. D. Gordon*, Dvir, Tel Aviv 5717, p. 124). Similarly, "In order to resurrect the Jew, one must begin from the foundation: from the man, but the Jew cannot be a complete human being without being a complete Jew. The assimilationist is wrong when he thinks that to the degree that he is less of a Jew he becomes more of a man. To the contrary, to the degree that he becomes less of a Jew he becomes less of a man, for there is not in the world a human being in general, there are only Russians, Englishmen, Germans and so forth. To the extent that the Jew destroys in himself the natural Jewish element, he becomes an unnatural Russian, an unnatural Englishman, etc." (Ibid., p. 103). To be sure, the point of origin for Gordon is the individual, and that is his goal and ideal. Rav Zvi Yehuda, by contrast, starts out from the nationality of *Knesset Yisrael*, which is his goal and purpose. Nonetheless, it seems to me that there is a connection and overlap between the sides of this great idea.

is constructed the unique Israelite form, or that it is all unique from head to toe. This clarification requires the employment of different sources, revealed, rational, historical, esoteric, phenomenological, poetic and at times political and economic. It appears that it was first arranged that the form of man be perfected in general, and as a supplement and bonus the spirit, majestic in its sacred splendor, of the special nation, would be revealed. But matters deteriorated and the spirit of man was so debased in general that the profane could not become the foundation for the sacred without corrupting it, and the exile in Egypt became necessary as the iron furnace, which refined the human side of Israel, until it became a new creation, and its profane form was completely dimmed. A nation was born at one time by virtue of the human kernel into a form that, from head to toe, was totally Israelite, Jacob and Israel (*Orot*, pp. 155–56).

The question exists, then, and needs to be clarified. Rav Kook's answer implies that there is some profane-communal root that could have grown, in a rather complicated way, from the stage of the patriarchs and the tribes preceding the Exodus and Sinai. From the traditions of the patriarchs in Genesis, there could have developed national phenomena without legitimation in the Torah of Moses.[65] Rav Kook refers to this phenomenon elsewhere with respect to ancient times—the period of judges and kings, in which such factors operated as well (e.g., *LeMahalach HaIdeot BeYisrael* end of Chapter 2, beginning of Chapter 3, *Orot*, p. 105). There is strong evidence for this phenomenon both in the Bible and in contemporary reality.[66] The bondage in Egypt and the Exodus utterly effaced this profane form in its unity with the sacred, but did not annihilate it completely, and there may be historical circumstances in which it will return—perhaps until

65. The outstanding example is the *matseva* (pillar), which was commended in the days of the patriarchs (Genesis 28:18–22; 31:45; 35:14) and rejected outright in Deut. 16:22 (see Sifre and Rashi ad loc.). Indeed, in the age of the judges and the first Temple, pillars abounded in spite of the prohibition and the chastisement of the prophets, e.g., Hosea 10:1. Hosea directly attacks the popular beliefs of his time, attributed to Jacob, to legitimize the cult of the calf in Bethel. Against this popular "exegesis," he places the absolute prophetic authority of the Exodus. Note Hosea 12–13:6. This issue is manifested in many other examples, such as marriage with sisters, marriage practices, inheritance, incest, punishment, even prayer and sacrifice.

66. Beliefs, commandments, and traditions connected to the Jewish family, from circumcision to hospitality and other traits of our father Abraham, and of course the promise of the land, are closer to the consciousness of our generation as a whole than the halachic totality deriving from the Torah and Sinai.

the unifying *neshamah* of Moses appears again in the world (See *Orot,* p. 121).

In the communal arena, Rav Kook engaged alone in an effort that was virtually impossible for one person, whatever his stature. With no organizational backing, he undertook two public projects intended to unify the body, *nefesh,* and *ruach* of the nation from the depth of its *neshamah:* the Banner of Jerusalem movement and the Chief Rabbinate. This is not the place to analyze these two enterprises, the first of which failed in Rav Kook's lifetime, while the second—the Chief Rabbinate—enjoyed enormous success in his time.[67] What is important is not only the fact that we have here a conscious effort to solve the great spiritual problem by practical-organizational means, by setting up a Jerusalem movement parallel to and above the Zionist movement. Despite the difficulty connected with organizational separation, Rav Kook hoped that the Banner of Jerusalem would supply what was lacking in the Zionist movement, and that the two movements would act cooperatively. Perhaps the failure came about because the religious Zionists wished to act entirely within the Zionist movement and devoted all their energies to it; were it not for this, Zionism might have become completely secular in its practical character and institutional composition. The Haredim of Aguddat Yisrael organized outside, but in bitter, profound rivalry rather than love and respect. Thus Rav Kook remained between the camps.[68] Indeed, the Israelite *neshamah* continues to illuminate the *ruach* in its exiled form outside and far from the Zionist renewal, and the gap has progressively widened until it greatly threatens both sides.[69] To be sure, a covenant was bestowed upon *Knesset Yisrael*—but no covenant ensures against great difficulties. By

67. On the Chief Rabbinate in the time of Rav Kook, see Dr. A. Morgenstern *HaRabbanut HaRashit LeEretz Yisrael* (Shorashim Press) and G. Bat-Yehuda, "The Establishment of the Chief Rabbinate and the Mizrachi" (*HaTzionut HaDatit,* Vol. I, p. 409. Note especially the speeches of Rav Kook on the eve of the electoral assembly and at the opening of the organizing conference of the Chief Rabbinate.

68. On Banner of Jerusalem, see the letters and proclamations appended to *Hazon HaGeulla,* p. 281ff; *Maamrei HaReAYaH,* Vol. II, pp. 333–40. See also *Igrot Ha-ReAYaH,* Vol. IV (index), for the fizzling out of the affair, while correspondingly the idea of a central yeshiva, which was part of the platform of the Banner of Jerusalem, becomes more important. See *Hatzon HaGeulla,* pp. 296–97 and 293.

69. The remnants of the Diaspora, primarily in the United States, and the Israeli *Yishuv* are both rather weak demographically and culturally-spiritually. In both places, a progressive polarization divides different groups and threatens the unity of the nation.

contrast, the Chief Rabbinate, even after its decline, which came after Rav Kook's death, became an important dam preventing complete separation of camps and content. To be sure the Rabbinate has failed to explain the importance of the matter to the broad public, the majority of which is oblivious of it, and has a low image of the Rabbinate. Nevertheless, the Rabbinate has served to prevent division on the part of extreme secularists and religionists, both of whom attack it sharply for that reason.

In the third area, the educational, Rav Kook displays the greatest command—here there is no compromise of the full unity of *naran,* as is evident from the sections quoted from *Orot* and especially the struggle for the unity of the indivisible nation (*Orot,* pp. 45–46). Any thought of separation comes under the rubric of idolatry (pp. 73–74). This educational completeness was expressed in the plan for the central world yeshiva. A good summary is the following poetic section:

One cannot define the essence of *Knesset Yisrael* within specific limits and limited attributes. It includes everything, and all is founded on its soul yearning for G-d, on its sense of the sweetness and supernal pleasantness in all the depths of its *neshamah,* in all its array of delight. And the desire for the Deity with genuine enthusiasm is revealed in all its features, is revealed in Torah and mitzvot, is revealed in ethics and virtue, is revealed in spiritual elevation, in inner poetry, in the sanctity of life, in unknowable thirst, "My soul is consumed—for a living G-d," is revealed in constant commitment of life, in bearing the yoke of exile with love, only not to abandon the order of life, practical and spiritual, through which the divine light adheres to it. This thunder-potency brings to it in the end of days absolute salvation. He who dispersed Israel shall gather it and watch it like a shepherd his flock (*Orot,* p. 138).

Thus, Rav Kook commenced the great enterprise of establishing the central world yeshiva, as the capstone of the entire "yeshiva world," and its planned curriculum was intended to cultivate the unifying Torah leadership of the Jewish people.[70] This is not the place to

70. On the plan for the central Yeshiva see *Maamrei HaReAYaH,* Vol. I, pp. 62–65. On the transition from Banner of Jerusalem as a public movement to the erection of the yeshiva as part of the public plan, see *Maamrei HaReAYaH,* Vol. II, pp. 344–49. Though there is a great distance between the plan for the yeshiva and its realization, especially after Rav Kook's death, one cannot deny that the yeshiva, in all its mutations,

analyze in detail this immense project, but one may say that the yeshiva indeed reared an entire generation of such leaders, a generation that fulfilled its role with the establishment of the state and in its early years. With all the crises that visited the yeshiva from Rav Kook's death on, it renewed itself during the years of statehood, integrating and guiding the leadership of religious-national youth, and has enjoyed historical success, especially in the past twenty years. One might even suggest that the Banner of Jerusalem has been reestablished by dint of the yeshiva and its periphery.

Confronting the doctrine of *Orot,* we stand as pupils and ask, Is the State of Israel, as it is now, the first fulfillment of Rav Kook's great vision? Is it a polity of the complete man in his full stature? Does it at all wish to be such? Some young people and serious thinkers believe that they know with certainty Rav Kook's answer to this question, and there are two simplistic and opposing responses in their mouths.

To me, it seems that political and practical Zionism have never abdicated the proclaimed desire to be a light unto the nations by establishing a state that would constitute a model society, administered by the light of the prophets of Israel, a state of ingathering of exiles. This demand, despite all the shadows and disillusions of everyday public life, not only has not weakened, but to the contrary has intensified. In broad circles, and surprisingly precisely among those very distant from the life of Torah, the ethical demand has been raised that befits a people that is human, and a state with a human face. Of course, this demand takes on all sorts of peculiar exaggerations, but this should not obscure the great light it contains.

On the other hand, it is true that Zionism and the state have never assented to a normative relationship to the Torah of Israel, neither halachically nor in any other sense, with the exception of specific limited areas like personal status and family law, and these too are in dispute. It is also true that the normative relation of the state to Torah is the subject of the most difficult public and political conflict. (The very conflict and its stubborn character demonstrate, in my opinion, the degree of connection between all Israel and the Torah of Israel,

---

reared an entire generation of Torah-Zionist leaders, which brought the extremes closer. Today, we can see the fruits of the second generation.

to the point where all wish to participate in the debate on its validity in the state.)

It is true that the spiritual link of Zionism and the state is to the prophetic vision more than to Torah; from the standpoint of *Orot,* this is an essential defect.[71] Nonetheless, the State of Israel has become so deeply intertwined with the *neshamah* of *Knesset Yisrael* that I have no doubt as to the justification of its inner existence as the historical totality of Israel, if only because almost everything built in the state and by its power is arranged and organized for the sake of gathering in the exiles, settling the Land of Israel, sustaining Jewish sovereignty in Israel, assuring our ability to survive, to create a Jewish culture, to maintain a just society and institutions of Torah and knowledge in the Land of Israel, to a greater extent than had ever been the case. Only pessimists and defamers can obscure this with their set complaints against this or another political personality, his plans and actions. Without ignoring any defect or shadow and beyond all disputes, the basic light of all that is accepted, in spite of everything, by the Jewish people in its Land, rises up: the willingness to commit life for the State of Israel as the state of the Jewish people, and to carry on high this banner—upon which the Name of G-d is assuredly inscribed—among the nations.

Precisely according to the doctrine of *Orot,* the creation of secularists need not become secularism. The secularist leadership determines its quality in an individual way, but its adherence to the Jewish people and the spirit of Israel in general transforms its political creation into a holy phenomenon, by dint of the totality of Israel, beyond the particular situation of the responsible parties. Therefore it is precisely this teaching that enables us to see the great general light and to continue our progress to general redemption, without harming or impairing the contemporary State of Israel, but restoring and elevating it with the effort to mend the world in general, as "our state the State of Israel" "the foundation of G-d's throne in the world, in accordance with the vision of the thinker of the lights.[72]

71. See *Orot,* pp. 20–21; 26; 120–21.
72. *Orot,* p. 160, para. 7.

Rav Reines and Rav Kook:
Two Approaches to Zionism

Dr. Michael Zvi Nehorai

1.

THE FOLLOWING REMARKS will be devoted to an examination of Rav Kook's attitude to religious Zionism as shaped in the spirit of Rav Reines, the founder of Mizrachi. Actually, it is usually accepted and agreed that Rav Kook and Rav Reines should both be seen as the spiritual fathers of historic religious Zionism. However, an examination of the writings, the actions, and the way of thinking of their disciples shows that these two personalities are divided, to the point of opposition, in the basic questions touching the character and function of Zionism in general, and of religious Zionism in particular.

Already at the beginning of our century, religious Judaism found itself in a state of confusion in the face of the changes taking place in Jewish society, with the spread of secularism, and the revival of the national Zionist spirit that came in its wake. On the one hand, the setting up of the Zionist movement had about it something of the realization of the messianic hopes stored up in the heart of the nation, hopes directly connected with the dream of the return to the Land of Israel. Yet on the other hand, it had been traditionally accepted in Israel that the redemption would come by heavenly means as the result of a religious awakening and a turning back in *teshuvah*.

And here was Zionism seeking to go up by force and redeem the Land by natural means! This was a sort of defiance of the Lord's decree, and it could cause the spilling of Jewish blood.[1] This tension between the two manifestations of the phenomenon gave rise to three reactions in religious Judaism, and these developed in time to three streams: 1) the Haredi (ultra-orthodox) anti-Zionist Judaism; 2) the religious Zionism founded by Rav Reines; and 3) the redemptive Zionism founded by Rav Kook. For our purposes, we shall deal with the last two.

The heart of the controversy between Rav Reines and Rav Kook is centered in the question, What is the connection, if any, between Zionism and the promised redemption? This connection, or its absence, led to a situation pregnant with consequences for the way the Zionist undertaking was developed and shaped. Rav Reines took up a firm stand that the Zionist idea "carries no note whatever of the idea of redemption, nor does it in any way touch anything that relates to it. In all the actions and endeavors of the Zionists, there is no hint of the future redemption, and their entire aim is simply to improve the Jewish condition and raise the people's dignity and standing, and bring them to a happy life . . ."[2] In Rav Reines's view, therefore, there was no connection between Zionism and redemption. Not only that, but he also sought to prevent the formation of any such connection.

In seeking to explain Herzl's success in spreading his proposal, as compared with the attempts of those who preceded him, he says the following:

How well we see that a statesman who never isolated himself in deserts and forests, or hallowed himself by immersing his flesh, who is not adorned with tallit and tefillin, who does not meditate on G-d's Torah, who has not afflicted his soul by fasting, and has not rolled in the snow or lain with worms . . . yet he succeeded in making a great impression, and attracted to himself a large part of our people who place faith in his words and promises. Is not this something marvelous? Should we not pay attention to this?

And yet really it may be seen as something very simple. All those who appeared as saviors in former times, and brought tidings of salvation and comfort for

1. On the relationships between religious Jewry and Zionism, see A. Luz, *Parallels Meet* (Tel Aviv: Am Oved, 5745), p. 187ff. Also, A. Ravitsky, "Pre-Determination and Free Will," in *Israel Approaches the 21st Century (Yisrael Likrat HaMeah Ha-21)* (Jerusalem: Mosad Van Leer, 5744).
2. Y. Y. Reines, *Shaarei Orah VeSimchah* (Vilna 5659), pp. 12–13.

Israel—they had in mind a spiritual salvation . . . But here this man came to us to foretell a simple salvation, without reference to the general redemption. He only showed that there is a way to improve the situation of the Jewish people and raise its standing and dignity by endeavoring to find a place of shelter and refuge . . . And all this he demonstrated with words built on the knowledge of statesmanship as foundation . . . and therefore his words found paths in the heart of the people. And seeing that the faith that the people placed in the words of the material savior is itself only material, and has nothing spiritual in it—therefore so long as the project remains material and political one can have confidence in it . . . but if they cross the boundary that was set up for them and enter into fields that are not theirs, they will weaken the strength of the people's faith in them, and the whole matter will be almost a physical loss, and far from a spiritual reward, and they will succeed in neither the one nor the other . . . Heaven forbid to think such a thing! . . .[3]

We see clearly that Rav Reines's decision concerning the nonmessianic nature of Zionism was not merely a matter of outward appearance, nor was it used simply as a debating tactic against his opponents from Haredi Jewry. For his words were written about a generation after the publication of the teachings of Rav Yehuda Chai Alkaly and Rav Zvi Kalischer. In his book *Minchat Yehuda*, Rav Alkaly had called for Jews to organize themselves for settling *Eretz Yisrael;* it was steeped entirely in an atmosphere of messianism, in a yearning for *teshuvah,* for redemption and "the end of days." Similarly, Rav Kalischer, in his book *Derishat Zion*, speaks of the beginning of the settlement of the Holy Land as the beginning of the flowering of the promised salvation. Their words, it is true, were spoken against the background of an absolutely different reality from that in which the Zionist movement operated, both from the standpoint of the historic situation and also from the point of view of the audience to which it addressed itself. Despite this, had Rav Reines wanted to, he could have used them to give redemptive legitimation to the Zionist movement. Except that, as we have noted, Rav Reines did not think it would be beneficial to Zionism to draw religious Jewry to it by dwelling on messianic yearnings. The use of such motifs might have decided the way of the national revival undertaking at its very commencement, for he could not have stood against

3. Y. Y. Reines, *Or Chadash al Zion* (Vilna 5662), p. 278.

the powerful pressure of the demands inherent in the ultimate redemption ideal. Rav Reines was interested in the success of the Zionist undertaking; he was not concerned about the realization of the
messianic vision. In this, Rav Reines differed both from those who
preceded him, the forerunners of the Zionist movement, and also
from Rav Kook, who followed him. It may be said, therefore, that
Rav Kook was the spiritual successor to rabbis Kalischer and Alkaly.
Like them, he also was steeped in the vision of redemption. Basing
himself on supports from Scripture, he called for bringing to fruition
in the here and now what was already decreed by Providence in the
past. In opposition to this, Rav Reines held that it was wrong to
impose on the Zionist project demands outside its natural needs. At
this stage, the concern was only for the duty to work for the improvement of the physical-material living conditions of the Jewish people.

Thus, Rav Reines agreed absolutely with the other great rabbinic
authorities who saw both a prohibition and a danger in the attempt to
operate from a redemptive euphoria. Here are some of his words in this
connection:

The belief in redemption is one of the principles and fundamentals of the
faith, and without the *belief* in redemption, the redemption itself will not
come about . . . And it is well known that *teshuvah* is one of the principal
conditions essential for redemption . . . for among the principal conditions is
the abolition of human corruption, such as wars and cause less hatred; and we
see before our eyes that corruption is growing, and the disunity between hearts
grows stronger from day to day.[4]

. . . For if now we should attempt to do as our fathers did, should we then
shout and cry out triumphally, "Let us overcome our enemies!"? This would
bring us no benefit, for such actions are forbidden to us, for the Holy One,
blessed be He, foreswore us against forcing the end . . . (*Shaarei Ora VeSimchah*, p. 240).

Ramban [Nachmanides] did not intend to say that conquest [of *Eretz Yisrael*]
by war is a positive command, for the people of Israel stand under oath
through all the days of the exile to keep far from a planned rebellion and
trespass, heaven forbid [against G-d's word] . . . Therefore let us put all doubt

4. Y. Y. Reines, *Sefer HaArachim* (New York 5686) p. 75.

aside: What he meant was that we would be taken [out of Exile] by the agreement of the nations (Ibid. p. 36).

Yet with this, Rav Reines does not maintain as they (i.e., the other rabbinic authorities) do that there is a permission, and even something of a positive command, to participate in solving relevant national problems. In history one must act not out of a dependence on redemption, but with the purpose of "making endeavors on behalf of the material position of the nation and for raising its dignity and honor":

Nevertheless there is no doubt that not only are we permitted, but an obligation rests on us, to attempt to improve our situation . . . The transfer that the Zionist movement intends is by no means a total one, for at best we may hope to transfer to Zion a large part of our people. And why should we not occupy ourselves with this? . . . The hope of redemption will not close off the way of searching and endeavoring; the battle for existence by legitimate means is permitted by the Torah, and it is a mitzvah and even an obligation to fulfill it . . . (Ibid. p. 231)

As against Rav Reines's perception of the concept of "Zionism," in Rav Kook's eyes it stands as a chapter in the march of redemption, directed by Divine Providence toward its ideal realization. If Rav Reines sought to persuade the faithful of Israel to join the Zionist movement by freeing it of all connection with the idea of redemption, Rav Kook turned toward that same audience with an opposite proposal. In his words, Zionism is directed essentially and specially to the redemption of the spirit and the Torah:

It happened already in the days of Ezra . . . through the blossoming of this salvation . . . we were privileged to see the public proclamation of the Oral Law and the expansion of the decrees of the sages and the spread of Torah in Israel . . . So shall it be in our days, with the help of the Lord, as a result of our strengthening of the growing *Yishuv* (i.e., the settlement in the Land of Israel) with G-d's help . . . the light of redemption and salvation will flourish. And eventually all the rebels and sinners will return in complete *teshuvah* out of love and rejoicing (*Igrot HaReAYaH,* Vol. I, p. 348).

The difference in their respective attitudes to Haredi Jewry, which stood outside the Zionist camp, is characteristic and significant. Rav

Reines pours his wrath upon them; Rav Kook, his love. Here are the words of Rav Reines:

Therefore when I remember the deeds of these people and how they tried to besmirch this holy idea and to delegitimize it so as to turn the heart of the people away from it; and when I consider that if not for their efforts the *Yishuv* might have grown to twice or three times its present size . . . when I consider all these things, I cannot at all forgive them . . ."[5]

Against this, Rav Kook says:

But it is simply not possible that the largest, most understanding and sincere part of Israel, who are the majority of the Jewish kosher[6] world, should remain standing at a distance. For this reason we are raising the *Degel Yerushalayim*[7] before all the Jewish kosher world, so that all the kosher ones of Israel should be organized beneath it . . . according to the really true spirit of the kosher Jew who is, and will always be, the kingdom of priests and the holy nation of all the world . . . We are certainly called to turn back to its ancient cradle, there to renew our ancient holy life. It is the kosher Jewish power alone that carries and preserves the sacred oath which we swore.

We kosher Jews must know and believe deeply that it is the holy Divine Hand that is now leading us with our exalted idealistic aims openly displayed. We have to make the whole world recognize the great solution contained in the marvelous world events that point directly and openly to the goal of bringing near our redemption and our salvation, from which alone the redemption and salvation of all mankind will certainly come forth" (*Maamrei HaReAYaH*, Vol. II, pp. 333–35; 340–48).

Rav Kook prefaces these words by saying that he is not dealing with the question whether those who kept withdrawn from the wider religious Zionist movement were right or not, although it is clearly noticeable that full understanding is accorded to them. The Mizrachi Zionism seemed to him like someone planted in the midst of a secular

5. Y. Y. Reines, *Shnei HaMeOrot* (Pietrokov 5673), p. 48.
6. *Translator's Note:* Kosher: fit; legitimate. HaReAYaH uses the term here, no doubt, in its halachic sense as related, for example, to a Jew whose testimony is acceptable (see, e.g., Maimonides, *Choshen Mishpat, Hilchot Edut,* Chaps. 12, 34).
7. *Degel Yerushalayim* literally, "Banner of Jerusalem"; the name given by Rav Kook to the movement which he founded.

framework—like one who, despite his importance, is still only the element of lesser importance, or at best a receiving vessel for the really important spiritual qualities. Naturally, according to his world perception, it was not possible for Rav Kook to come to terms with a movement whose aims went only so far as the provision of the nation's material needs. Therefore, his approach is to the "kosher Jews," as he calls them; they are the bearers of the vision of Zionism of redemption, as he puts it in the foundation proposal of the movement *Degel Yerushalayim*:

We need a holy movement, to lift our national revival from its secular lowness . . . So long as we allow our regeneration movement to rest only on its secular foundation, we endanger all its standing . . .

And he expresses his view of the Mizrachi with greater clarity in the letter "The Sacred Call":

. . . We do not denigrate the Mizrachi propaganda . . . which is put out for the sake of heaven and for the strengthening of religion and Jewry. Likewise it is plain and clear that we do not denigrate the foundation of Agudat Yisrael, which is striving to join together all the Haredi forces and solve living problems in the Land and the Diaspora according to the Torah . . .[8]

8. Here let us question the relationship between the religious Zionist movement and Rav Kook as expressed in practice, in theory, and action. (1) The Mizrachi Conference resolved (Iyar 5679) to accept Rav Nissenbaum's position permitting the election of women, in opposition to the view of Rav Kook (see *Maamrei HaReA YaH*, Jerusalem 5740, Vol. I, pp. 189–194). Concerning this decision, Rav Kook wrote that "it is against the law of Moses and Judaism." Reacting to Rav Kook's words, Rav Binyamin (Yehoshua Radler Feldman), one of the leaders of Mizrachi in *Eretz Yisrael* and one of the founders of the newspaper *HaTzofe*, declared, "Is this right, without taking account of the Mizrachi rabbis who dwell among their people? The few rabbis whom we have in *Eretz Yisrael* who are connected at once with Torah and life? Is it right . . . to push aside the Mizrachi, the one organization standing on a religious and national basis, and to give oneself into the hands of a group of *batlanim* of the type of Mendel Porush and his friends . . . ? From now on, in general community matters, we Mizrachi members will not take account of those rabbis who do not stand openly on a national religious basis . . ." And for the attitude to Rav Kook of the *chalutzim* of the Second Aliyah, see Yossi Avneri, "Rav Kook and the Men of the Second Aliyah," in: *Bishvilei HaTechiyah, Studies in Religious Zionism* (Bar Ilan University Press, 5743), p. 59ff. (2) In reply to religious farmers, Rav Ben Zion Meir Chai Uzziel permitted milking on the Sabbath inter alia also because of "settling the Land of Israel." Rav Kook came out strongly against the permissive rabbis, and took a firm stand that the milking was to be permitted only by a non-Jew. "It is altogether impossible

2.

In the light of what has here been advanced, it has to be said that Rav Kook's attitude to Zionism in general, and to religious Zionism in particular, is extracted from his overall metaphysical and historical world picture. Indeed, in his world perception, isolated and transient historic situations have no meaning except when seen in this way; and these can be viewed as links in the general process of redemption.[9]

As opposed to him, Rav Reines was set in the cycle of the given historic reality. From this point of view, he was completely at one with Herzl's way of thinking, albeit he felt bound to respond to the demands of the time also from the halachic standpoint.

We previously mentioned Rav Reines's words, "the battle for existence by legitimate means is permitted by the Torah, and it is a mitzvah, and even a duty, to fulfill it." This legal opinion made it possible for religious Zionism to exist and to be involved, overtly and actively, in one union with those who did not observe the Torah and its commandments. This ruling of his pertained also to the command of the settlement of the Land of Israel that he was compelled, by the

---

that some non-Jews should not be found in a Jewish settlement . . ." (This was his view also in regard to the *shemittah* [seventh year]). Rav Weinberg of Switzerland also supported the permission given by Rav Uzziel: "For the sake of the livelihood of Jewish families who have no other place of livelihood." The members of the Kibbutz Rodges (1933) turned to Rav Kook and asked for sanction for milking on the Sabbath "because the farmer cannot yield concerning the milking . . ." and, further, because milking by non-Jews incurs difficulties since in many places there are no non-Jews, and also because of the fear of disease and of spying for the purpose of attack or stealing or injury. And this in addition to the principle of Hebrew labor. For all these reasons even the most religiously punctilious of the farmers used to do the milking on the Sabbath themselves. In his reply, Rav Kook wrote, "they should not buy a single cow if they do not first have a non-Jew available to do its milking on the Sabbath . . ." To this ruling, Rav Gedalia Unna reacted, saying, "the conduct of the rabbis authorized to give rulings in the Land of Israel—including Rav Kook whom I greatly admire—does not reflect the needs of the time . . . I think that Rav Kook does not altogether understand the seriousness of the matter despite his scholarship . . . and that he is not quite able to cope with the situation . . ." For this entire matter, see *in extenso* H. Y. Peles, "The Problems of Milking on the Sabbath in the Religious Settlements of Eretz Yisrael," in *Barkai*, Vol. 2, published by the World Mizrachi Movement, Autumn 5745.

9. On Rav Kook's cosmic perception, see N. Rotenstreich, *HaMachshava HaYehudit BeEt HaChadasha* (Tel Aviv: Am Oved, 5706), pp. 275–76. Also Yosef Ben Shlomo, *Shelemut VeHishtalmut BeTorat HaElohut shel HaRav Kook*, in *Iyyun*, Vol. 33, pamphlets 1–2, Tebet-Nisan 5744.

realities of the situation, to confine within the category of laws between man and man. The uniqueness of the laws between man and man, as distinct from those between man and G-d, is characterized by two points: a) their observance is subject to the relevant requirements for benefitting the Jewish people; that is, the law is designed to benefit Israel, rather than Israel having to serve as a means for the observance of the Law for the sake of heaven; b) they have been ordained to be kept and fulfilled even without requiring a religious motivation:

... This is not the case with the laws of the intellect, between man and man, where Haredi and irreligious Jews meet in practice, the difference between them being only in thought and sentiment. For the G-d-fearing keep them because of the mitzvah, and the irreligious because of sentiment. And despite this, no one cavils at the mitzvah of charity and acts of loving-kindness, for sometimes the irreligious also involve themselves and take part in it ... Why then should the Zionist idea be seen differently, as though something bad, for it, too, is, after all, the product of the sentiment of the nation's honor, and in this the irreligious also participate?"[10]

The Jewish people is steeped in troubles and persecutions. It will be like keeping the mitzvah of doing acts of benevolence if a Jewish organization arises that will assist the needy to move to a place of refuge, and even Uganda ... and certainly to the Land of Israel if this can be attained legally. Accordingly, just as the setting up of charitable and benevolent institutions is in the category of mitzvah, even though the motivation for their establishment comes from social pressures, and not specifically from religious motivations, so does this apply also in relation to the mitzvah of participating in the Zionist project of settling the Land of Israel. In the present stage, the mitzvah will be the product of the need of the times, until the time of the heavenly redemption, when it will stand in the fullness of its ideal scope.

This is the attitude that characterized the vision of the religious Zionism of the school of Rav Reines. This vision developed, in the course of the years, into a creative, constructive movement. This was centered in the shaping of the world of the here and now, in the spirit

10. See *supra* n. 5, and loc. cit. p. 40.

of modern social and humanist ideas worked out and hallowed in religious frameworks of those who keep the Torah and command-ments.[11]

All this as against the Zionism of redemption in whose eyes wordly reality is only hylic matter that it is a duty to shape according to models drawn from the tradition of mysticism. It is therefore understandable that, by its very nature, it was impossible for it to recognize and take note of the objective limitations of the given reality. This reality will fly away as smoke, and the word of the Lord shall stand forever. This attitude to the limitations of reality may be seen from the following words of Rav Kook:

There are some righteous people (tzaddikim) who, if they are given complete freedom, would like to destroy everything . . . so that everything should be made anew in a better form . . . because they are unable to accustom them-selves to the lowliness of the limited creation; and all this is because of the deep strength of the holy flame that is in them, so that they cannot tolerate anything except absolute divine perfection (*Arpelei Tohar*, pp. 21–22).

11. "Among the thinkers of religious Zionism we shall find the aim of interweaving the religious tension with the social-Zionist longings for redemption. The basic pur-poseful program of the nation's revival is what justifies the movement and gives it value and content; all the rest is commentary. The existence and importance of all the other things depend on what they do for the revival and on the need it has of them. This includes even the building of the Land, for the Land is for the Jewish people, not the people for the Land. And if indeed national religious Jewry marks its work of building the Land as "the mitzvah (positive command) of settling the Land of Israel," this also has its reason and basis in the idea of the revival of the nation" (Shmuel Chayyim Landau, "Clarifying Our Way," in *Torah VaAvodah*, Kfar Etzion 5743). Rav Isaiah Shapira also expresses himself in this spirit: "This seeking to bring proof from the halacha for the value of labor would be proper it we would say that self-labor is taught by the halacha. But no one of us has said this. If there were such a paragraph plainly in the *Shulchan Aruch* there would be no place for debate" (Ibid. "Thou shalt do what is right and what is good"). Rav Kook, who held that "the heart of man is not logical and it was not the spirit of flesh that conceived all this great vision," would surely not agree with these formulations. (Rav Kook, *Matter and Spirit in the Redemption of Israel*, Zionist Organization, Jerusalem 5733, p. 28). In the religious Zionist school, there was room for expressions such as, "Our prophets stood on guard in matters of right and justice no less, and perhaps more, than in matters of nationalism and reli-gion . . ." (S. Borochoni, *Anthology of Articles of Torah VeAvodah*, Jerusalem 1931, p. 52). And in the redemptive Zionist school, they accuse religious Zionism ". . . for not having seen the political-social-national problems of the Jewish people as spiritual questions that drew their strength from sacred sources . . ." (J. Zulden, "Tefisat HaRav Reines Nidcheket Mipnei Tefisat HaRav Kook," *Nekudah*, No. 88, Tamuz 5745-1985).

Clearly, with such an attitude, it would have been impossible for the Mizrachi to exist. In fact, the formulation that facilitated the integration of Rav Reines's movement within the Zionist Organization was that "Zionism has nothing to do with religion." This formula, which was considered a great achievement from the point of view of religious Zionism, was angrily reviled by Rav Kook, who portrayed it as an abomination that should be cut off and torn out by its roots. It is appropriate to say something by way of clarification of this fundamental matter that directly concerns the subject under discussion in this article.

Beginning with the period of the Haskalah (Enlightenment) the gap widened between the old generation and the young intelligentsia, which increasingly moved away from Judaism. The Maskilim in the Zionist movement therefore demanded urgently that Zionism must deal also with matters of culture and education in the spirit of the Haskalah, whether in order to attract the youth to itself, or to prevent its assimilation. In practice they wanted to direct the Zionist movement toward cutting it asunder entirely from religious tradition, which they saw as hindering modern social development. The religious Zionists, headed by Rav Reines, naturally opposed these aims. They even had the support of Herzl, who kept proclaiming that Zionism would do nothing against religion. Herzl's position was the only possible compromise that could save the wholeness of the Zionist movement. From the point of view of the religious Zionists, this could certainly be seen as an important achievement. It was this that avoided the withdrawal of the religious Zionists and also of the Maskilim. Thus, the Zionist rabbis did all they could to preserve this achievement. They stood guard to prevent this subject from being raised for discussion at Congress, knowing that the proposal of the Maskilim might win a majority of the members' votes. At one of the congresses, Rav Reines even burst into tears and excitedly demanded that the subject be withdrawn from the agenda.[12]

Yet the question of "culture" kept coming up again and again, and the position of the rabbis grew weaker because of the paucity of the religious members. Rav Reines was therefore put into a position of having to choose either to withdraw from the Zionist movement or to

12. See A. Luz, *Makbilim Nifgashim*, (Tel Aviv: Am Oved, 5745), p. 319.

agree to a compromise proposal by which Congress would recognize the legitimate existence of two streams in Zionist education. According to this proposal, each party would attend to the education of its own children in its own spirit.

We have already said that Rav Reines was blessed with the talent of recognizing reality. Nothing was left to him therefore but to yield a little on the principle that Zionism had nothing to do with religion, and to accept the proposal that was in fact the foundation stone for the Mizrachi education. The considerations that preceded his decision he conveyed in the following words:

I will not conceal that there were times when the idea of withdrawal was aroused within me, that is, leaving the organization, and especially at the time of the last Congress in 5671 when it was decided to introduce culture into this movement. For many years I fought against this, so that it should not be introduced; I fought and prevailed. Yet on this occasion it was decided by a majority vote to introduce it . . . and then I saw that not only would withdrawal bring no religious benefit, but it would even lead to religious damage . . . And there is hope that the Mizrachi will yet be able to put some matters right . . . for the withdrawal might harm more than it would mend . . .[13]

Rav Kook came out very sharply against the Mizrachi—i.e., Rav Reines—not only because of his readiness for the said compromise, but also because of his very agreement with the formula that Zionism "has nothing to do with religion." The formula, which was an achievement from the point of view of the Mizrachi, could twist and uproot the whole Zionist mission, which, as Rav Kook saw it, was designed only to prepare the machinery for bringing into being the Law of the Torah as in days of old, and to turn Israel back to *teshuvah*.

Here are a few passages from the letter devoted to this subject:

This ordinance [that Zionism has nothing to do with religion] really makes nonsense of all the Mizrachi propaganda. For Mizrachi takes its stand on the platform of Torah . . . and all we faithful ones of Israel know well that the success of Zionism, and its growing strength, today and in the future, are dependent only on the entire nation's loyal connection with our living Torah; while in forsaking the Torah there is no hope and no expectation, and every

13. See *Shnei HaMeOrot*, supra n.5, p. 19.

flower must fade, and every root will be as dust . . ." (*Igrot HaReAYaH,* Vol. II, p. 134).

In his view, Zionism as a movement has to be concerned "that the soul of the nation should blossom," and the life of the national soul is dependent on the existence of the Torah as a whole: Shabbat, kashrut, purity of family life, etc. . . . Zionism must demand these things forcibly, and Mizrachi ought to be the one appointed "to overturn the pagan ordinance that Zionism has nothing to do with religion, for it is an abomination for Israel." Mizrachi should express its inner character in working "to cut down this idolatrous tree and tear out its roots, which bear gall and wormwood." Furthermore, Rav Kook stresses that only if Mizrachi will get away from this "darkness that has descended over it" is there a chance that those who stand opposed to Zionism will come and gather under its banner. Here we hear a note that has already been heard above, expressing understanding for the faithful ones of Israel who were opposed to the Zionist undertaking in the given situation.

It is quite clear that had Rav Reines adopted Rav Kook's path, it would have led to his withdrawal from the Zionist Organization, and the religious Zionist movement would not have come into being. It may therefore be said that although Rav Kook gave the title "Zionist" to his redemptive visionary movement *Degel Yerushalayim,* it had nothing in common with Rav Reines's religious Zionism except only the common name.

PART
II

Teshuvah
in the Philosophy of
Rav Kook

A Note on the
History of *Teshuvah*
Among Ashkenaz Chasidim

Professor Joseph Dan

1.

Teshuvah, AND THE way it is perceived, is one of the most dynamic ideas of the Middle Ages and the modern era. The word itself, together with its biblical and Talmudic-Midrashic connections, and its meaning in the writings of prominent Jewish thinkers from the twelfth to the twentieth centuries, are many and varied. When we come to discuss some aspects of the perception of *teshuvah* at the beginning of the development of the idea in medieval Jewish thought, we should take into account that eight hundred years of rich dynamic development separate between the early perception of *teshuvah*, which we shall discuss, and the theory of *teshuvah* that is at the center of Rav Kook's philosophy. The sole justification for this discussion is that, in the history of ideas, the commencement is always hidden within the end, and the root always influences the fruit. Even though the modern perception of *teshuvah* is far removed from that which was created by the early thinkers who devoted books to it in Hebrew, still the one is the continuation of the other, and the one is the result of the other; and the recognition of the roots of things always deepens our understanding of the essence of their being.

The beginning of systematic thought concerning the quality and significance of *teshuvah* in our literature of the Middle Ages is in the writings of the Jewish philosophers who wrote in Arabic, chiefly Rav Saadya Gaon and Rabbenu Bachaye Ibn Pakuda. Rav Saadya deals with this matter in his *Emunot VeDeot.* In this work, he laid down the two principal bases that characterized the perception of *teshuvah* for many hundreds of years. The one is that *teshuvah,* from its very source, is a spiritual process that takes place in the heart of man. Its root is in the contemplation and the obligations that a man takes upon himself before his G-d and before himself. Rav Saadya's parameters of *teshuvah* do not include action; they are entirely a crystallization of man's decision to turn in *teshuvah,* to turn back from his evil way and not to sin anymore: a decision that he assumes within his heart and communicates to his G-d.

The second trait laid down by Rav Saadya Gaon is that *teshuvah* is the concern of the individual in Israel, a matter solely for himself. It has to do only with the man who sins. *Teshuvah* is tied with a strong link to sin and to the sinner, and it is the consequence of the individual's decision to change his ways. In the framework of the perception based upon Rav Saadya's teaching, there is no meaning to *teshuvah* that is not for sin—to *teshuvah* as a way of life, to *teshuvah* as a perfection of the world, to *teshuvah* as a preparation for redemption, to *teshuvah* for the sins of others and of former generations, and so on—ideas that characterize modern thought in the field of *teshuvah,* especially from the sixteenth century on. At source, *teshuvah* is the ointment that the religion of Israel prescribes for the sinner's wound. It has no place except as a cure for sin. A long period of development was necessary for Rav Saadya's approach to be put aside, for the idea of *teshuvah* to assume a mystic dimension, and for its broader significance to become a central value in Jewish thought and morality.

Rav Bachaye Ibn Pakuda developed and expanded Rav Saadya Gaon's theory. The fact of the inclusion of a chapter on *teshuvah* in his book *Chovot HaLevavot (Duties of the Hearts)* is evidence of the firm acceptance of Rav Saadya's principles. "Duties of the hearts," as Rav Bachaye describes them, are spiritual mitzvot that a man experiences in his heart, and they are the links between his spirituality and the spiritual world of the Divine. By their nature, the duties of the hearts do not include any kind of action. Those mitzvot that do include action the author counts as "duties of the limbs," and even Torah study and prayer are not "duties of the hearts," since limbs and senses take part in their performance. Against this, *teshuvah*, just like trust in G-d, and the fear and love of Him, is a purely spiritual value that is executed by man's soul alone. All the more is this so when it refers to an individual person. The national and universal bases are almost entirely absent from Rav Bachaye's teaching; and his perception of *teshuvah*, like his understanding of the other "duties of the hearts" is absolutely individual. *Teshuvah* is the concern of the one who has sinned, who now wishes to turn back from his sin and to renew the spiritual link between him and his G-d.

The theories of Rav Saadya and Rav Bachaye in the tenth and eleventh centuries concerning *teshuvah* form a sort of "prehistory" to the Hebrew *teshuvah* literature of the Middle Ages. The beginning of the Hebrew literature of *teshuvah* is in the twelfth century when Rav Avraham bar Chiyya wrote his book *Higyon HaNefesh (The Logic of the Soul)* and when Maimonides wrote his *Hilchot Teshuvah* as part of his *Sefer HaMadda (Book of Knowledge)*. These two works served as the infrastructure for the Hebrew *teshuvah* literature, which was limited by the principles of Jewish philosophy. And the foundations laid down by the philosophers who wrote in Arabic formed a basis for those who came after them and wrote in Hebrew. Only in the first half of the thirteenth century did a Hebrew *teshuvah* literature begin to develop that was not based on foundations of philosophy, and the first of whose authors were, by all appearances, from the Kabbalistic circle of Gerona—at the head of them being Rav Jonah Gerondi, the author of *Shaarei Teshuvah (Gates of Teshuvah)*. It should be mentioned that these thinkers, who were fiercely opposed to Jewish philosophy—they too accepted many of the principles of the teaching of *teshuvah* that had preceded them. In their eyes, *teshuvah* was tied directly to a particular sin, and they also stressed the spiritual character of the process of *teshuvah*.

From here it can be seen that we can point clearly to three stages in the development of the theory of *teshuvah* in Jewish thought and in the moralist literature in Spain and Provence. The first stage is the general works written in Arabic. These embodied detailed discussions on the teaching of *teshuvah* on the basis of the developing Jewish philosophy. The second stage we see in the beginning of the Hebrew *teshuvah* literature in the writings of Jewish philosophers who began to write in Hebrew in the twelfth century; and the third stage is the development, side by side, of philosophic *teshuvah* literature in Hebrew and *teshuvah* literature whose authors were opposed to philosophy but nevertheless accepted some of the principles laid down by rationalist thinkers who preceded them in this field.

Parallel with these stages of development another *teshuvah* teaching and *teshuvah* literature was being fashioned, that of the Ashkenaz (German) Chasidim, which is the subject of our further discussion.

2.

The theory of *teshuvah* of the Ashkenaz Chasidim is known to us chiefly from the *Sefer Chasidim* and from the sections devoted to matters of morals in the writings of Rabbi Elazar of Worms, the pupil of Rav Judah the Chasid. Three generations of sages participated in the creation of the texts in our hands: the first was Rav Shmuel ben Kalonymos, that is, Rav Shmuel HeChasid, whose composition *Sefer HaTeshuvah* was incorporated apparently at the opening of *Sefer Chasidim* in the version of the Parma MS printed by Wistinetski and Freimann (*Mekitzei Nirdamim*, Frankfurt 5684). This version of *Sefer Chasidim* opens with an essay on matters of fear (of heaven), and this is followed by an essay dealing with *teshuvah*. As far as can be seen, Rav Shmuel HeChasid was the author of these pieces.

The second generation of contributors was Rav Judah HeChasid, the principal author of *Sefer Chasidim* and the son of Rav Shmuel. In the body of *Sefer Chasidim*, there are detailed discussions on matters of *teshuvah*. Apparently, these reflect the perception of Rav Judah He-Chasid in this matter. Fragments of Rav Judah's teaching are woven also into the writings of his pupil, Rav Elazar of Worms, who represents the third generation in the Ashkenaz Chasidic movement. He devoted a detailed discussion to the subject of *teshuvah* in the frame of his *Hilchot Teshuvah* and set it at the beginning of his great halachic work *Sefer HaRokeach.* The discussion is also found in a special, separate pamphlet.

These three generations spread over a period beginning in the middle of the twelfth century and ending near to the year 1230, when Rav Elazar of Worms died (Rav Judah HeChasid died in 1217). The compositions of these three thinkers reflect a unity of opinions and a common tradition, even though there are significant differences, especially between Rav Judah HeChasid and Rav Elazar of Worms. As we shall attempt to show below, there also existed, it seems, a layer of "prehistory" in the teaching of Ashkenazic Chasidic *teshuvah*, apart from these three generations.

The *teshuvah* perception of the Ashkenaz Chasidic movement is frequently described as a teaching of self-torment, opposed in its spirit to the spiritual perception of the sages of Southern Europe. Indeed, it is a fact that in our medieval literature from before the sixteenth century, we don't find any open and clear statements approving self-torture except only in the discussions of the Ashkenaz Chasidim on matters of *teshuvah*. While the Ashkenaz Chasidim are occupied with day-to-day matters of moral behavior, their approach emphasizes a separation and a distancing of oneself from this-worldly pleasures. Yet we do not find teachings connected with real, deliberate self-afflictions. Against this, these things are found clearly in the field of *teshuvah*. Withal, it seems that there is some exaggeration in some of the descriptions of the self-torture of these Chasidim. Later, we shall attempt to place the theory of the Ashkenaz-Chasidic torture in the area of *teshuvah* in a proper intellectual and historic perspective.

Rav Saadya Gaon's teaching with regard to *teshuvah* was known to the Ashkenaz Chasidim, albeit not firsthand and not through Rav Judah Ibn Tibon's translation of *Emunot VeDeot*, but thanks to the early paraphrastic translation of this book that was in their hands. A fragment of this translation, and specifically the passage dealing with paths of *teshuvah*, was included in *Sefer Chasidim* in the Parma MS version. Yet the fact that they knew the Gaon's teaching did not obligate them to accept it as it was; and in the writings of the three thinkers mentioned above, we find a completely different picture of the four paths of *teshuvah*. The consistency and uniformity with which the material is presented testify that it refers to one of the most common and most formed foundations among all the Ashkenaz Chasidim of the school of the Kalonymos family. Not only this, but in the *Sefer Chasidim* we find not a few examples of teachings and stories in which these paths of *teshuvah* find concrete expression. It is clear, therefore, that we are not speaking here of a theoretical crystallization alone of a perception of *teshuvah*, but of the practical application of law that the teachers of the movement taught and that their followers practiced.

The four paths of *teshuvah* of the Ashkenaz Chasidim are well known. Let us review them briefly. They are called: *"teshuvat havaah"* (i.e., *bringing* himself into a certain situation); *"teshuvat hagader"* (literally, the "fence" *teshuvah*); *"teshuvat HaKatuv"* (i.e., the *teshuvah* of Scripture); and *"teshuvat hamishkal"* (*teshuvah* of "balance"). It is clear enough that no one is expected to conduct himself according to all the four ways, since the four are made up of two pairs, and in each pair man has to choose one of the two. It follows that in order to turn in *teshuvah* the sinner has to act either according to *teshuvah* of *havaah* or of *hagader;* or in accordance with *teshuvah* of *mishkal* or of *HaKatuv*—all depending on the circumstance and the situation.

Similarly, it is clear that really none of the four ways deals with *teshuvah* in the meaning in which it is understood in the Jewish philosophic literature in Spain. The first two—*Teshuvat havaah* and *Teshuvat hagader*—deal with the ways in which a man should behave after he has turned in *teshuvah;* how he should conduct himself in his everyday life, and how he should demonstrate that he has repented with a perfect *teshuvah.* The two latter, *teshuvah* of *mishkal* and *teshuvah* of *HaKatuv,* have to do with the punishment of the sinner, a punishment that the one who repents takes on himself in order to wipe out the transgressions that have clung to him, so as to be pure in his *teshuvah.* The process of *teshuvah* itself, the thoughts and speech of him who makes atonement—these are not included in these four ways. Rav Elazar of Worms, in his *Hilchot Teshuvah,* includes a number of paragraphs dealing with *teshuvah* itself, and he even suggests, by way of example, "the *teshuvah* of one who returns with all his heart," and he details the repenting sinner's way of thinking, and his confessions before G-d. In the writings of Rav Judah HeChasid and Rav Shmuel HeChasid, these principles are found only little. It follows that the Ashkenaz-Chasidic ways of *teshuvah* emphasize aspects of the *teshuvah* process in its broad meaning, aspects that were less emphasized by the philosophers in Islamic lands.

Teshuvah of *havaah* is concerned with the ability to resist temptation on the part of the one who "returns" in *teshuvah.* If, after his *teshuvah,* he finds himself in the same situation as that in which he sinned at first, in the sense of "the same place and with the same woman," and this time he prevails over his temptation and does not sin, he has now clearly proved that his *teshuvah* is complete and that he is weaned of his sin. Contrary to this, *teshuvah* of *hagader* constitutes an opposite way: the obligation of the one who "returns" in *teshuvah* to distance himself far from everything near to or reminiscent of the abyss in which he had sinned, and to keep himself away from every temptation that might bring him to repeat his sin. If he had sinned with a woman, he must remove himself absolutely from seeing women; he should not go into the market, should not look at women's clothes, etc. That is to say, that man must build fence upon fence, and add boundary to boundary, so as to keep himself from every possibility of coming near to the subject of the sin he had committed and run the risk of repeating it. It is understood that no man can grasp both *teshuvah* of *havaah* and *teshuvah* of *hagader* at the same time. In order to put himself into the test of temptation in terms of *teshuvah* of *havaah*, he has to break down all fences and boundaries. Not only must he approach the subject of his sin, but he must put himself into exactly the same situation as that in which he had sinned—and restrain himself. Against this, the one who follows the rule of the "fence *teshuvah*" in practice will not be able to reach a real trial of temptation since he distances himself from every situation that might attract him to it. Thus, we face two alternative ways: the bold, dangerous way of *teshuvah* of *havaah*, which incorporates a severe and serious trial in a matter in which he has already stumbled previously; and a cautious, careful way, the "fence *teshuvah*," which prevents him from being tempted near to the sin and the danger of repeating it.

The danger in the way of *teshuvah* of *havaah* is great for the *baal teshuvah* (the one who "returns"). He may not be able to withstand the temptation, and may repeat his sin; and this time he will be considered as an entirely deliberate sinner, since he has knowingly and deliberately "brought himself" to the sin situation by design despite his having already stumbled in it. His sin is therefore much heavier than it was the first time. But this danger is not less great for the moralist-teacher who writes these words. For, if sinners will pay heed to him and put themselves into temptation as a result of his teaching, and will repeat their sin by design, the responsibility will fall on the one who directed them to act in this way—that is, on the author of the *Sefer Chasidim* or the *Hilchot Teshuvah*. It is no wonder that the Ashkenaz Chasidim, in their reviews, played down the *teshuvah* of *havaah;* and

Rav Elazar even adds that "it does not apply." Loyalty to the tradition of the generations compelled him to include this way among the other paths of *teshuvah*, but the caution of the moralist-teacher obliges him not to direct people to this way, because of the great danger connected with it. As distinct from this, the "fence *teshuvah*" was expatiated on in detail. There is no doubt that, at least in the appeal to the public in writing, the teachers of Ashkenaz Chasidim preferred it over the *teshuvah* of *havaah*. They recommended the cautious and careful way, and preferred it over the daring and dangerous way connected with such great risk.

It should be emphasized that with regard to these two ways, the "fence *teshuvah*" and the *teshuvah* of *havaah*, there is no place for the claim of "self-torment" as against "spirituality." There is no foundation in these ways for self-punishment; they represent ways of life chosen by spiritual considerations. Not in this area shall we find the basic difference between Ashkenaz Chasidism and those who taught the rabbinic philosophic *teshuvah* in Spain.

3.

The second set of ways, *teshuvah* of *HaKatuv* and *teshuvat hamishkal*, is the one that expresses the idea that there is no sinner who is not punished. These two ways represent different theories in which the sinner takes upon himself a punishment that wipes out his sin and completes his return in *teshuvah*. In *teshuvah* of *mishkal* ("balance"), which is the most important new concept of Ashkenaz Chasidism in the field of *teshuvah* teaching, the sinner is obliged to accept sufferings that balance out the pleasure that he had enjoyed from the sin. The religious and mystical perception of the Ashkenaz Chasidim saw pleasure in every sin by the fact of its being sin; and contrary to this, every act of mitzvah and morality was linked, for them, with sacrifice and sufferings. He who succumbed to his inclination and chose the way of pleasures, the way of sin, had to balance them out by taking upon himself torments equal to the pleasure that he had enjoyed from the sin. (The question as to *whether* he had had enjoyment from the sin does not arise at all; the *fact* of the sin means a succumbing to man's corporeality, and this is linked with bodily and sensual pleasure). The purpose of *teshuvah* of *HaKatuv* (Scripture) is to ease the choice of the sufferings with which the sinner is to be tormented: If it is a matter of a Torah sin, for which the Torah has decreed the punishment, then the sinner must accept sufferings according to what is written *(Katuv)*, or similar to what is written, and thus he will fulfill willingly the punishment laid down in Scripture.

In this perception, the ways of the Ashkenaz Chasidim parted from those of the teachers of philosophic morality in Spain. Maimonides, for instance, does not recognize the idea that sin causes pleasure. On the contrary, in his view sin is opposed to man's nature, and therefore no pleasure whatever can be wrapped up with it. In the view of most of the scholars of Spain, the nature of the heart of man is good from his youth. Sin is a perversion, the removal of which causes man benefit and enjoyment. Against this, the Ashkenaz Chasidim saw the tendency to sin as actually the human nature of man. For them, in order to walk in the ways of G-d, man has to subdue his body and his inclination, in the sense of "sanctifying the Name," and choose the way of Torah and mitzvot—which is opposed to his human inclinations.

Both in *teshuvah* of *HaKatuv* and of *mishkal,* the idea of torments is included. Yet it is a fact that in the details in our possession from the writings of the Ashkenaz Chasidim concerning specific punishments for particular sins, almost all the directions deal with the fasts that man takes upon himself. Only with regard to most serious sins, such as murder and adultery (of which it is difficult to believe that they were frequent and widespread in German Jewry of the twelfth century and the beginning of the thirteenth century, a Jewry suffering under the yoke of the constant evil decrees of the Crusades), do we find a punishment like exile from a man's own place. As a general rule, Rav Judah HeChasid and Rav Elazar count the number of fasts (from morning to evening) that a man had to accept for each sin, and they number tens and even hundreds. It is difficult to classify this kind of fast: Is it "abstinence" or "torment"? A fast from morning to evening is surely the borderline between these two, and this is the principal practical way that the moralist-teachers of the Ashkenaz-Chasidic movement recommend.

In the above-mentioned writings of Rav Shmuel HeChasid, Rav Judah HeChasid, and Rav Elazar of Worms, there is one passage that is repeated almost word for word in their discussions. It describes torment of an entirely different kind: sitting naked, on hives of worms or bees, in summer, or breaking the ice of the river and bathing in it in winter. These are found in a context close to *teshuvah* of *HaKatuv*, and by all appearances they are connected with this way of *teshuvah*. It is very probable that the intention was that man should take upon himself torments "such as death imposed by the *Bet Din*" in a case in which he committed particularly serious sins. From the context, it seems that the intention was generally for the punishment of one who had sinned in adultery.

It was this passage that clothed the *teshuvah* teaching of the Ashkenaz Chasidim with the imagined garment of an extreme and picturesque theory of self-torment quoted by everyone who wishes to attribute this aspect to the teaching of the Chasidim. Yet it is surprising that the passage recurs unaltered in the writings of these three generations, as a kind of agreed text, by rote, without explanation or application, with no clear understanding of the conditions necessitating it and without it being really woven into the life of religion and morality set out by the teachers of Ashkenaz Chasidism. I suggest that this passage should not be seen as a substantive and organic part of the practical teaching of *teshuvah* of the Chasidic philosophers. In my view, this is a remnant of an early tradition that reached them in a framework honored by them, and they incorporated it in their own words out of respect for all tradition—and Ashkenaz Chasidim were outstanding in their conservatism and their loyalty to earlier traditions. It simply expresses their main perception in the field of *teshuvah*, and is certainly not to be seen as directives and rules that they propose to their contemporary reader. This is a plucked remnant, evidence of there having been before them an early tapestry of thought concerning *teshuvah* that had fallen away, but this relic remained and was restored in its own textual form in their writings on *teshuvah*.

The first scholars to give detailed investigation to Ashkenaz Chasidism and its teaching in our generations, Yitzchak Baer and Gershom Scholem, both suggested seeing the Ashkenaz-Chasidic *teshuvah* teaching as a whole and the self-torment in particular (that is, the above-mentioned passage), as the fruit of Christian influence that had penetrated the world of the Ashkenaz Chasidim. Hence they too recognized the strangeness of these things within the Ashkenaz-Chasidic context and sought to explain it as the fruit of an external influence. In the past fifty years, several attempts were made to identify a Latin,

Christian source for this perception of *teshuvah* (the principal attempt was that of Professor Ivan Marcus). These attempts yielded no fruit. To this day, we cannot point to the source from which the Ashkenaz Chasidim drew (if they drew) their perceptions concerning *teshuvah* and self-torment. Absence is no proof, and there is no way of showing that the Ashkenaz Chasidim were not influenced by Christianity. Maybe a source will be found in the future to prove it. But we are obliged to affirm that till now no proof has been found that there *is* such a source, or that the Ashkenaz-Chasidic theory of torments is the fruit of Christian penitential influence in the center of Europe in the Middle Ages.

If it was not Christian influence, we are bound to assume that these things represent a pattern of behavior and thought that developed in German Jewry before Rav Shmuel HeChasid and was lost to us, and only a remnant of it was incorporated in the writings of the Ashkenaz Chasidim. It may be, however, that there is a "prehistory" to the Ashkenaz-Chasidic *teshuvah* teaching, an earlier layer of thinking and conduct in this field, of which the sources describing it in detail, although committed to writing, have been lost to us. If this is indeed the case, the teaching of the Ashkenaz Chasidism will be found to be a sort of second layer in the history of *teshuvah* teaching of German Jewry, a layer that apparently displaced most of the theory of the previous layer and left only a tiny relic of the way of thought of someone who thought and behaved in this way before the middle of the twelfth century.

The possibility that this was indeed the development of the theory of *teshuvah* in Ashkenaz Jewry points to a further plank in this process. If the passage describing the torments linked with *teshuvah* of *HaKatuv* represents an earlier layer of thought about which the teachers of Ashkenaz Chasidism had reservations, we should be able to point to a clearly spritualizing aim (relatively, at any rate) in the perception of *teshuvah* in this movement. If Rav Shmuel HeChasid and Rav Judah HeChasid rejected the extreme self-mortification customary before them, and exchanged it for a more cautious approach of abstinence, they thereby expressed an aim of strengthening the spiritual foundation of *teshuvah* and limiting the physical part of its performance. If this is the case, one may see in the theory of *teshuvah* of Rav Elazar of Worms a further step in this direction. By way of illustration, Rav

Elazar rejected the perception that confession in *teshuvah* had to be made before a scholar or a rabbi, and argued that confession is an inner, personal process between man and his G-d. It was he who also added prayer texts and expressions of regret in describing the process of *teshuvah.* Thus we learn that in spite of the great difference between the Spanish and the German scholars in this matter, the historic process that took place in the twelfth and thirteenth centuries tended to bring them nearer to each other.

Whether this assessment is exact or not, we still have to affirm that in relation to the theories of *teshuvah* that developed in the Jewish people, especially from the beginning of the sixteenth century, the Spanish and German scholars are found to share a common position. For all of them, *teshuvah* is the cure for sin, for the particular sin of an individual; and it takes place mainly in a spiritual process of a turning back of the soul of the sinner to his G-d. The German scholars saw no possibility of completing the course of the *teshuvah* without some physical cleansing of the bodily sin that man has committed—a view that was not accepted by the South European scholars. Yet despite the two schools, the revolution in the perception of *teshuvah* that led to national and cosmic dimensions being attributed to it, a revolution whose principal proclaimer in our generations was HaReAYaH Kook, was still hidden in the far dim future.

The Concept of *Teshuvah*
in the Teachings of
Maimonides and Rav Kook

Professor Itamar Gruenwald

1.

THE METHOD WE shall follow in setting out the material in the present article will be directed toward clarifying the typological lines that characterize the idea of *teshuvah* as it appears in the teachings of Maimonides and Rav Kook. As we shall see, the idea of *teshuvah* as it emerges in the thought of these two personalities can direct us to a certain typological presentation of the idea of *teshuvah* as a whole. The concern with typology enables us to focus attention on the theological distinctiveness of the matters to be discussed here, without undue commitment at this stage of the discussion in regard to the determination of the historical factors that served to shape the idea of *teshuvah* for our two personalities. At the same time, the typological discussion compels us to say a few words about the nature of the *teshuvah* concept as it appears in Scripture and in the rabbinic literature of our ancient sages. For despite the fact that it is not done in the majority of cases, there is no way of presenting a particular idea in the history of Jewish thought without first presenting, even if only by chapter headings, the precursors of the idea in biblical literature and among our sages.

In Scripture, the *teshuvah* idea occupies a relatively limited place. Indeed, the name *"teshuvah"* is found in the Bible, but there it does not have the spiritual significance that we understand by it today.[1] At the same time, the verb *shuv* ("return"), which is found many times in the Bible, often has a meaning close to that which we attribute to it when it relates to matters of sin and atonement. In fact, the verb *shuv* occurs in Scripture in the sense of moving toward or from G-d: On the one hand, we find the expression "to turn back from following the Lord,"[2] and on the other hand there is "to turn unto the Lord."[3] In Scripture, *teshuvah* has no well-defined, independent ritual and theological position. It may be said of it in general terms that it marks the condition demanded of the individual and the community for the renewal by G-d of the covenantal link with those who, by their wicked deeds, caused it to be severed.[4] In brief, we have a good illustration of the idea of *teshuvah* in Scripture in the words of the prophet: "Turn unto Me and I will return unto you" (Malachi 3:7) and in Lamentations (5:21): "Cause us, O Lord, to return unto Thee, and we will return." Scripture stresses particularly the deeds of expiation demanded of man so that he should merit G-d's forgiveness. Yet, in these expiatory deeds, which are mainly sacrifices, *teshuvah* is not mentioned as an act of institutional value, and its place is taken by the confession *(viduy)* that accompanies the offerings.[5]

In the literature of the sages, *teshuvah* has a different position: "Death and Yom Kippur effect atonement if there is *teshuvah*. Teshuvah effects atonement for lesser transgressions against both positive and negative commands; while for graver transgressions it suspends punishment until Yom Kippur comes and effects atonement. If a man says, 'I will sin and repent, and will sin again and repent,' he will be given no chance to repent [literally, to do *teshuvah*]" *(Mishnah Yoma* 8:8–9). Not only is *teshuvah* accorded here an independent position similar to Yom Kippur, but from a halachic standpoint, and therefore also from an institutional point of view, the transgressions for which

1. See, for instance, I Samuel, 7:17: "And his return was to Rama, for there was his home."
2. So, for instance, Numbers 14:43.
3. See I Kings 8:48. A preliminary classification of the verb *shuv* ("return") in Scripture is found in Avraham bar Chiyya, "The Logic of the Sad Soul," *Bereshit*, "the third column."
4. See Deut. 30:1ff. Although the word *covenant* is not mentioned there clearly, it is yet found in the previous verses.
5. See under *viduy* ("confession") in the *Biblical Encyclopedia*, Vol. II, p. 873ff.

teshuvah makes atonement are laid down. Likewise the circumstances in which *teshuvah* is of no effect are also fixed. *Teshuvah* and atonement are concepts that, in the literature of the sages, complement one another, and there is no doubt that thenceforth the concept of *teshuvah* has theological significance of central importance in Judaism. This is not the place to discuss in detail the change of outlook that took place in the concept *teshuvah,* nor its position in Judaism, in the transition from the Bible to rabbinic literature, but by way of a hint it may be said that the offshoots of the change are recognizable in postbiblical Jewish literature, as, for example, in the *Book of Ben Sira* and in the scrolls of the Sect of the Judean Desert.[6]

In this framework, we cannot consider the full variety of meanings that may be found in the concept of *teshuvah* as they appear in rabbinic literature. However, this much we have to declare—and this declaration has considerable importance for the subject matter of our present discussion—that there is an interesting development in the definition of the content of the *teshuvah* concept in its various changes from Scripture on. What seems like a narrow idea in its theological significance, in Scripture, is revealed as a central idea in rabbinic literature and in later Jewish literature. In every stage of Jewish thought, an attempt is made to reach a new depth in the concept, be it in the realm of halacha and established custom, or in that of thought and morality. To sum up, one can distinguish today between different types of the *teshuvah* idea seen historically, and it is to the one that emerges from the thought of Maimonides and of Rav Kook that we shall direct ourselves in what follows.

However, before we proceed to deal with the words of Maimonides and Rav Kook, we should emphasize one aspect of the *teshuvah* idea that is found already in the Bible and that goes on developing from there in the various literary sources. In Deuteronomy we read, "And it shall be that when all these things shall come upon thee, the blessing and the curse which I have set before thee, and thou shalt put them to mind [literally, "to thy heart"] among all the nations whither the Lord thy G-d hath driven thee, and thou shalt return unto the Lord thy G-d and hearken to His voice . . . then the Lord thy G-d will turn thy captivity and will have compassion upon thee, and He will return

6. See, for instance, *Ben Sira* v:7.

and gather thee up from all the nations whither the Lord thy G-d hath scattered thee" (30:1–3). In other words, in these verses we find the idea of *teshuvah* linked with the idea of the ingathering of the exiles. Similarly, we shall find also in the words of the sages the well-known dispute concerning making the redemption conditional upon the act of *teshuvah:* "Rav Eliezer said: If Israel will turn in *teshuvah*, they will be redeemed; if not, they will not be redeemed. Said Rav Joshua to him: If they do not repent, will they not be redeemed?—Yes, they will. For the Holy One, blessed be He, will appoint a king over them whose decrees will be as cruel as Haman's, so that Israel will repent, and thus He will make them return to the right path."[7] The connection between *teshuvah* and redemption is a subject to which both Maimonides and Rav Kook devote special attention, and we shall return to this matter in its proper place later on.

2.

The distinctiveness of Maimonides' words concerning *teshuvah* is given emphatic expression by their position. Maimonides puts his "Laws of *Teshuvah*" at the end of *Sefer HaMadda (Book of Knowledge)*, as though he wants thereby to stress the philosophic character of the concept of *teshuvah*. Nevertheless, as we are dealing here with *Hilchot Teshuvah (Laws of Teshuvah)*, it seems that Maimonides wishes to indicate that the idea of *teshuvah* has halachic (legal) force even in its philosophic aspect. As a rule, we know that the laws of *teshuvah* are linked with the laws related to the days between Rosh Hashanah and Yom Kippur; whereas, in placing them outside this framework, Maimonides is seeking to emphasize the general, universal nature of *teshuvah*. In Maimonides' *Hilchot Teshuvah*, there are indeed some things about the importance of *teshuvah* as related to Yom Kippur, and on the direction of this *teshuvah;* yet the principal teachings of Maimonides concerning *teshuvah* present it as a spiritual-moral process comparable in fact to the way of life of someone capable of attaining the height of intellectual life, that is, to the way of life of the

7. See *B. Sanhedrin* 97b–98a. For the answer of the sages, see E. E. Urbach, *The Sages: Concepts and Beliefs* (tr. from the Hebrew), Jerusalem 1975, chap. XV, Section V. See also recently, M. Behr, *Al Maasei Kapparah shel Baale Teshuvah Besifrut Chazal*, in *Zion*) 46 (5741), 159–81.

sage-philosopher. In Maimonides' theory, *teshuvah* is a central and vital value in the life of man, with no connection at all to a particular period in the year's seasons. Hence the principal aspect of *teshuvah* is not to atone for daily sins, but specifically to assist man to turn away from mistaken conceptions and from a way of life that Maimonides sees as the path of heresy and error. Among the varied subjects to which Maimonides refers in *Hilchot Teshuvah*, there stand out the issues of repentance and redemption and the good that is stored up for the righteous in the world to come. In my view, there is no doubt that these are the main essence of his *Hilchot Teshuvah*.

According to Maimonides' outlook, the main basis of *teshuvah* is determined by its ultimate goal: It brings man to the life of the world to come. The "world to come," for Maimonides, marks the peak of man's spiritual achievements. Whoever merits the world to come attains the level of the "angels." And in Maimonides' perception, they are simply "separated intellects," that is, intellectual entities that exist independently of material or bodily existence.[8] The true conception of the Creator is not attainable other than in this condition of the existence of the intellect in independence of the body. There is room for assuming that in a certain place Maimonides even gives a hint that the perfect philosopher may reach up to the level of "the world to come" while yet during his life on earth.[9] According to Maimonides, "wherever the term *nefesh* (soul) is used in this connection [i.e., that of the world to come]," it does not mean the soul that needs a body, but the vital form of the soul that is the intellect that has comprehended the Creator according to its capability and has understood the separate (disembodied) intellects and other (heavenly) elements "and this is the

8. The definition of "the world to come" as the subject of similarity to the intelligence that functions by cleaving to it is found in Maimonides' Introduction to his commentary on chapter *Chelek* in *Mishnah Sanhedrin*. With reference to the angels as separate (or disembodied) intelligences, see *Guide to the Perplexed* Part II, Chap. 6.

9. Next to the setting out of the Thirteen Articles (principles), Maimonides says, "And if he has done it, his human aspect is perfected and he is separated from the animals. And seeing that he has become a complete man, it is for the honor of man that nothing should hinder his soul from intellectual existence, and this is the 'world to come' as we have explained." Parallel to this, Maimonides holds the view that in the messianic days, "whoever will be there in those days will attain a great perfection and will merit the life of the world to come." It is possible to explain these words as though they also are intended to say that in the days of the Messiah many will attain this level of the life of the world to come that only very few people indeed can attain in the life of this world.

"form" [i.e., of the soul] that we have explained in Chapter IV of *Hilchot Yesodei HaTorah,* and which is called *nefesh* in this regard" (*Hilchot Teshuvah,* Chap. 8, halacha 3). As is known, the form of awareness of the Creator, of which Maimonides speaks here, is the cognitive position in which the recognizing object, and the subject that is recognized, as well as the means of awareness, are united into one entity, like the comprehension of the separated intellects and the functioning intellect. This cognition is made possible only through an attachment, or a cleaving, to the functional intellect.

The meaning of the process of which Maimonides is speaking is clear: The special potential of *teshuvah* is in the fact that it marks out for man the path of ascent that cuts him off from the material and bodily life of this world and leads him to the absolute and eternal life of the world to come. From this point of view, the essence of *teshuvah* for Maimonides is to be seen as a process of progression, not of return; and the progression is toward a cleaving to G-d (*Hilchot Teshuvah,* Chap. 7, halacha 6–7). In its simple and daily aspects, *teshuvah* will help man free himself from his feelings of guilt, feelings that stem from failure or from a transgression against his neighbor or against the Divine Presence. Yet it is in the power of *teshuvah* to assist man to attain greater achievements than these, and especially in the spiritual field; attainments that can lift man up to the highest levels of human existence. In this way, Maimonides bestows on *teshuvah* a complex of tasks that cuts it away from the relatively narrow limits of routine ritual. *Teshuvah* at its best is not tied to this or that deed or action. It is what gives man the consciousness of the need to cut himself away from the path of evil and change to the path of the good: "It is proper for us to turn in repentance and forsake our evil" (*Hilchot Teshuvah,* Chap. 5, halacha 2). The essence of the idea of *teshuvah* for Maimonides is therefore "Do not say that there is no atonement save for transgressions in which some act is involved, such as immorality, robbery, and theft; but just as man has to repent of these, so also must he search out any bad beliefs he may have, and repent of anger and enmity and jealousy and mocking; of pursuing after wealth and honor and all manner of foods, and so on; from all of them one has to turn in *teshuvah*" (*Hilchot Teshuvah,* Chap. 7, halacha 3). The *teshuvah* to which Maimonides refers is total *teshuvah,* and its advantage is portrayed thus: "Great is *teshuvah* for it brings man close to the Shechinah . . . If you turn back in *teshuvah,* cleave unto Me . . . How wonderful is the advantage of *teshuvah:* Last evening this man was separated from the Lord G-d of Israel . . . and today he cleaves to the Shechinah" (Ibid., Chap. 7, halacha 6–7). The closeness of the Shechinah and the clinging to it are, in Maimonides' perception, the stage of the world to come, and "in the world to come there is no body or human form, but only the soul of the righteous without bodily form, like the ministering angels"; there and then "they will know and comprehend the truth of the Holy One, blessed be He, something they cannot know so long as they are within the dark and lowly body" (Ibid., Chap. 8, halacha 2). In a word, one can discern in Maimonides a process of intellectualization of the idea of *teshuvah.* [10]

Maimonides does indeed speak there of *teshuvah* as bringing redemption in its historic dimension (Ibid. Chap. 7, halacha 2), but his discussion is centered principally in the *teshuvah* that leads the individual to cleave to the Shechinah.[11] Maimonides cannot close his eyes to the historic processes, but as a philosopher he does not attribute to history a substantive value of its own. He is chiefly interested in qualitative processes that have the power to lead man to the peak of actualization of his spiritual qualities. From this standpoint, history has only an instrumental value. Within it occur the events that can advance or retard man in the attainment of his spiritual goal. In this way also, the correct dimension is determined for the messianic days, and according to Maimonides' conception, as he has expressed it in several places, these are the days in which it will be made possible for all Israel to reach achievements that, in this world, only very special, exceptional individuals are able to attain.

With Maimonides, the idea of *teshuvah* strives for selectivity. There are some things that interest him more than others, and there are people who presumably are not fit to take a part in the progressive and exalted processes of *teshuvah.* This demands special emphasis when we move across to speak of the *teshuvah* idea as it is discussed in the writings of Rav Kook. This selectivity is not found with Rav Kook. According to Rav Kook's conception, all parts of existence ideally take part in all the processes of *teshuvah.* Out of Rav Kook's universal

10. Compare *Guide for the Perplexed,* Part I: Chaps. 40 and 41.
11. *Hilchot Teshuvah,* Chap. 7, halacha 6–7.

approach, a positivistic-universalist approach comes to expression, that is, an attempt to attribute a positive function even to those aspects of existence that are generally thought to be its negative factors; and from this flows the conception that there is no one and nothing that, as a matter of principle, cannot take a part in *teshuvah*. From this standpoint, Rav Kook does not accord secondary importance to history; rather, he sees in it a qualitative process for the realization of the divine program as it is revealed to man in its dialectic complexity.

3.

Before we proceed to consider Rav Kook's actual teachings on the subject of *teshuvah*, let us first direct attention to two matters connected with the general context in which Rav Kook's words on the subject are to be understood. The first matter touches the general character of Rav Kook's thought, and the second relates to the distinctiveness and the place of Rav Kook's teachings on the subject of *teshuvah* within the general framework of his thought.

With regard to the first matter, touching the general character of Rav Kook's thought, it needs to be observed that different scholars assess his thought in different ways. Some see in Rav Kook a Kabbalist or a mystic; others see him as a philosopher and thinker; yet others describe him as a poet; and there was even someone who saw in him a man of tidings in the broad sense of this concept.[12] Indeed, the central problem facing the student of Rav Kook's thought lies, in my view, in the fact that it is very difficult to find the common denominator characterizing the man's general thinking. Binyamin Ish Shalom proposed an acceptable solution when he declared that "the various approaches to Rav Kook's work establish, at least, that we have before us a multidimensional phenomenon that, if we wish to understand it, it must not be given a narrow definition, nor should one affix a particular label to it for the sole purpose of identification."[13] In my estimation, these words of Ish Shalom constitute a correct starting point for a study of Rav Kook's thought—which contains, perhaps more than in any

12. In this connection, see the summary of opinions in B. Ish Shalom, "Rav Kook's Thought between Rationalism and Mysticism." Dissertation for the degree of Doctor of Philosophy (Jerusalem 1983), p. 1ff.
13. Ibid. p. 2.

other instance in the history of Jewish thought, subjective personal foundations. As Ish Shalom also sees it, the actual difficulty of defining the man's character and his thought lies not so much in them as in us. We are accustomed to limit our definitions to single-dimensional forms, the molds of which are fixed from the outset and are not given to change.

Rav Kook is neither a mystic nor a philosopher; he is not a halachist or an aggadist; he is not a poet, nor is he a man of tidings. Yet it may be said of him that he embodies an amazing mixture of all these qualities, but even their combination is not sufficient to exhaust his personality. Let me admit without shame: For many years, I was unable to find my way to the man and to his thought, and I also found colleagues who concurred in my perplexity. I was unable to see in Rav Kook a professional philosopher, or even a mystic in the full meaning of the word. Kabbalah did indeed serve as a background for him, not as a systematic framework for conveying his thought, but mainly as a general ideological and conceptual presentation. Now that I have been given another opportunity to deal with the man and with his thought, it has become clear to me that the problem was not in Rav Kook's words but in thought habits that accustom one to affix a label, and in the feeling that in the absence of a label the student will be lost. In my estimation, one would see in Rav Kook an interesting example of *Homo religiosus,* that is, a personality searching for religious forms of expression for the enormous tension in which his soul is steeped.[14] This tension issues from various matters connected with philosophic-metaphysical problems, with historical processes, with problems of morality and society, as well as with complex psychological problems. This is a tension caused by the dualism that exists in the world and that divides between matters belonging in the area of the divine and matters that seem outwardly to be found outside this area. The philosophical, moral, and psychological problems referred to are in fact the dialectic pattern

---

14. The characterization that follows differs in some essential respects from what Ish Shalom puts forward, *Ibid.* p. 131ff. Ish Shalom suggests defining man's quality, according to Rav Kook's perception, as *Homo religiosus* (cf. *Homo sapiens*). Our usage here of the concept *Homo religiosus* is functional more than qualitative. We see in *Homo religiosus* one whose conceptualization is full of paths of religious thought. His entire perception of the world is in religious terms, and when necessary he will argue that even secular or nonreligious thought concepts and systems are fundamentally of religious significance.

into which are woven the conceptual motifs with which religious man seeks to express his position and his relationship to G-d. For the religious man, the presence of G-d is a certainty that seeks to be actualized in a complex conceptual world. Some find this conceptualization in the ritual motifs of religion, and some wander further and look for additional motifs through which this conceptualization is made possible. It seems to me that Rav Kook's rich personality is a major example of a limitless search for varied conceptual motifs that complement each other and through which he is able to express the religious tension within him. In these conceptual motifs, we shall find not only the key to Rav Kook's spiritual tension but also the possibilities and the methods by which this soul tension finds its release. The measure of Rav Kook's success in bringing a harmony and balance to these motifs is what establishes his greatness as a religious thinker.

The feeling of alienation and fragmentation that stems from the dualism that separates the divine world from the world outside it is a basic feeling that accompanies us through all of Rav Kook's writings. Beside this feeling of alienation and fragmentation stands the tremendous urge to do away with the duality, not only on the personal plane but also on the historic plane and the cosmic plane. This is the framework within which one should grasp the meaning of the idea of *teshuvah* in Rav Kook's thought. After a detailed analysis, accompanied by spiritual pain and suffering from which it is hard to turn aside, and by means of which the complexity of the dualism becomes clear, Rav Kook attempts to lay down the possible ways of doing away with this dualism. This annulment means a return to the sphere of the Divine. In other words, the annulling of the duality is the essence of the idea of *teshuvah* as it is put forward in Rav Kook's teaching. As, according to Rav Kook's perception, all of existence is intended to take part in the processes of the return to the Divine, various ways and means are required for the realization of this goal. Hence the seeming eclecticism of the systems and methods followed in Rav Kook's thought is not accidental, nor the result of an inability to think through a logical theory to its end, but a deliberate system stemming from the problematic issues that Rav Kook tries to present and for which he also tries to propose a solution. Rav Kook joins philosophy with Kabbalah and psychology with halacha so as to bind together in one band all the methods and all the systems by the light of which the problem can be illuminated from every side, and by the help of which the believer may bring the processes of *teshuvah* and redemption within his reach. It is, however, difficult in my estimation to establish with certainty whether Rav Kook's words necessitate a word-by-word explanation of the processes of which he speaks or whether one may leave them a certain measure of metaphorical or symbolic freedom. In any event, the spiritual kaleidoscope created in Rav Kook's teaching is not the expression of a confused and mixed-up soul, but, on the contrary, of a rich soul that is attempting to cope, very courageously, with basic problems that call for illumination from different sides, without for a moment losing hold of the central backbone that is the religious meaning of the problems and their solutions.

The second thing we wish to make clear here as background for a study of Rav Kook's teachings of *teshuvah* is that the things Rav Kook says plainly and clearly about *teshuvah* are relatively few. Apart from the teachings collected together in the book *Orot HaTeshuvah,* of which only a small part come from Rav Kook's own pen as they stand, there are in Rav Kook's writings numerous expressions on the subject of *teshuvah,* but only in very few of them shall we find the term *"teshuvah."* This is surprising, for it could be said of *teshuvah* that it is the main pivot on which his philosophy turns. If the concept of *teshuvah* is absent from his writings, and is replaced by other concepts, this is done apparently in order to prevent the ideas connected with the term from becoming banal through overuse of the concept, for habitual linguistic use might have reduced its significance. There is no doubt that Rav Kook struggles with the words he uses. His language testifies to the fact that he is not drawn after attractive phraseology. On the contrary, his leaning on rich terminology taken from different disciplines is witness to a creative force that tries to weave new conceptual patterns by plaiting together threads that others spin separately. I have no intention of denigrating any scholar who attempts to find order and system in Rav Kook's way of using concepts. But the way Rav Kook gives meaning to his spiritual problems and the solutions he seeks is basically a synthetic method that grafts things together, and not an analytic method that keeps them apart. Consequently, it seems to me that the best way to clarify the conceptual world in Rav Kook's thought is not through attempts to identify the sources of this world but by a discussion that clarifies the system of conceptual links in his philosophy.

4.

In my judgment, the essence of Rav Kook's importance as religious thinker is in the inner awareness that finds expression in most of his writings and that deals with the subject of the ideal perfection of existence and the constant struggle of the religious man who experiences the separation from G-d and the never-ceasing striving to return to the bosom of the Divine. The essence of Rav Kook's thought is found in the perception that sees the fullness of existence as a Divine Presence that in theory—although not in practice—cannot be divided. The separation between G-d and the world is not real, but the result of a mistake in the systems of being. The striving of cosmic existence, with man at its center, is to return to its Divine Source. It seems to me that this duality that perceives the world as cut off from the Divine Being, even if only temporarily, is what prevents us from seeing Rav Kook as a pantheist in the classic meaning of the word.[15] The identification of G-d with the world is only partial: More than it is to be found in reality, it is the longing of the heart of the religious man of Rav Kook's type. Rav Kook longs for G-d to enter into him, particularly when he studies the Torah's secrets, and he also longs for his soul to ascend to G-d. Nevertheless, since his words never go beyond the realm of longing, it seems to me that the division between G-d and the world is carefully preserved; hence it is difficult to see him as a mystic or a pure pantheist.

As we have in our possession two summaries of Rav Kook's theory of *teshuvah*, let it suffice us here to present its main feature.[16] The beginning of the process necessitating *teshuvah* and correction is, "The worlds have fallen, with the fall of the Will, man has fallen into the abyss of sin" (*Orot HaKodesh*, Vol. III, p. 81). There is a connection between the fall of man, the microcosm, and the fall of the worlds, the macrocosm. From this fall, we must ascend: "It is demanded of us to

15. In this matter, I am not in agreement with N. Rotenstreich, *HaMachshava HaYehudit BaEt HaChadasha*, (Tel Aviv 1966), Vol. II, p. 263ff. See also Y. Ben Shlomo's article, "Shlemut VeHishtalmut BeTorat HaElohut shel HaRav Kook," in *Bein Iyun Lemaaseh—Mechkarim Lichvod Natan Rotenstreich Bimlot Lo Shivim Shanah* (Jerusalem 1983), p. 289ff.

16. See H. Lifshitz, "HaTeshuvah Meshachreret Miyirat Hammavet," *Proceedings of the Sixth World Congress of Jewish Studies*, Vol. III (Jerusalem 5737), p. 241ff., Ish Shalom, *Ibid.* p. 124ff.

lift ourselves up" (Ibid. Vol. II, p. 587). Man's ascent has an influence and an effect on the elevation of the worlds: "We want to lift up everything, the whole world, all creatures, the entire soul; and we need to elevate and purify the root of everything" (Ibid. Vol. II, p. 173). There is a mutual sympathy between man and the universe in which he lives; hence also man's responsibility to join the perfection of the worlds and the creatures living in them with the perfection of his own self. This is in fact the process of *teshuvah:* "And this quality of raising up small things to greatness never ceases; and this is the perfect *teshuvah* through which completely righteous men come to ascend on the steps of *baale teshuvah* . . ." (Ibid. Vol. III, p. 262). This process of causing things to be elevated is identical with the process of the perfection of the worlds, that is, the improvement of creation and bringing it to a condition of perfection that will prepare it and make it fit to be received again into the bosom of the Divine: "The supreme form of cognition, reserved for the highest thinkers, is concerned with the essence of sweeping the evil away and perfecting the entire world" (Ibid. p. 181).

On the personal level, the Fall is "the sin of the first man [Adam] who was alienated from his own self . . . He forsook his own ego . . . and the 'I' goes on being forgotten; and since there is no 'I,' there is no 'He,' and all the more so there is no 'Thou' " (Ibid. p. 140). In these words, Rav Kook conveys a radical idea: Sin and the Fall are in fact man's denial of his self. The loss of self keeps man from the possibility of forming a contact by dialogue not only with his fellow man but also with G-d, whether this contact is formed on the level of the "He" or whether it is formed in the realm of the "Thou." We are faced with the breaking of the conceptual circle formed in the school of Rav Yitzchak Luria *(HaAri),* and an entry into dialogical fields of thought that draw inspiration both from the Hasidic world of thought and from the philosophic world of Kierkegaard and Buber. A man who has lost himself must search for himself and for his soul: "The greater the man the more he has to search for himself . . . the more he must abound in solitariness, in elevation of mind, in depth of thought . . . until his soul will at last be revealed to him . . ." (Ibid. Vol. II, p. 270). This process is also identical with "the preservation of the soul's self, which, in its abstract spiritual form, is found in the soul's own very essence" (*Olat ReAYaH,* Vol. I, p. 2). Only after the perfection of the self of the soul comes ". . . the general perfection of the entire world" (*Orot HaKodesh*, Vol. III, p. 148). This general perfection of the world is connected also with the historic process of "Israel's return to its spiritual fortress" (Ibid. Vol. I, p. 155). Or, put in other words, "The inwardness of the worlds is perfected by the spiritual affluence, the central foundation of which is the light of Israel" (Ibid. Vol. III, p. 181). Thus, we have perfection in three concentric circles: the personal circle, which is psychological and is ruled by mystical and philosophical motifs; the national circle of the people of Israel dominated by historic processes; and the cosmic circle, in which forces of nature operate. The perfection of these three circles necessitates a joint interwoven action of the spiritual and soul forces that are at man's disposal. And these are the methods and the means through which this goal may be realized: "Inner depth of study in the secrets of Torah" (Ibid. p. 116); "practical cognitive awareness, and all social, aesthetic and artistic culture" (Ibid. p. 181); "Torah and the fear of G-d, wisdom and prayer, cognition and worship, when they come together—these improve the world both inwardly and externally" (Ibid. p. 88). To sum up, "Man must indeed always occupy himself with Torah and holiness, with mitzvot and good attributes, with wisdom and elevation of thought . . . so that through his good deeds and his sacred work, he will always know and recognize the elevation that elevates all the heavenly hosts and all the earthly hosts; all the living in their various groups; all bodies and all souls" (Ibid. p. 257).

Finally, a word on the method by which the processes of *teshuvah* are formed: "The supreme *teshuvah* comes from an inner drive that issues from a heavenly external propulsion; and the entire world, material and spiritual, is perceived in its unifying form" (*Arpelei Tohar*, p. 36). The awakening for doing *teshuvah* comes from above, from a heavenly external drive that influences the internal drive that awakens man to the act of *teshuvah*. Naturally, here we are speaking of *teshuvah* of an entirely different nature from the *teshuvah* known to us in man's usual religious life, especially in the days between Rosh Hashanah and Yom Kippur. In this type of *teshuvah*, man is dependent not on his conscience, which awakens by itself, or on the fact that the halacha obligates him to render an account of his deeds to himself; he rather depends on a fountain of heavenly help that rouses him out of the intellectual slumber in which he lies even while performing the acts of *teshuvah* to which he is accustomed. In this special process, the righteous man also has a position of decisive importance: "There is a kind of righteous man who can guarantee that the whole world will be perfected and all Israel will return in a complete *teshuvah*" (*Orot HaKodesh*, Vol. I, p. 119). In a further stage of development of the idea, we find Rav Kook identifying this tzaddik with the messianic phenomenon: "And such righteous men must be found on the heels of the coming of the Messiah" (Ibid. p. 120). In fact, says Rav Kook, the ideal image of such a tzaddik is the Messiah: "The light of Messiah lights up the whole world and changes all of existence by the brightness of Torah . . . and the nature of its light is the appearance of the Torah in the light of all the world, the manifestation of the holy in the light of all the secular, of the purified spirituality in the midst of all the materialism, of the soul inside all the flesh; the raising of the value of all life, the shining of the light of the Holy of Holies through all the levels of existence, into all the movements of being" (Ibid. p. 151). It is worth noting that the position of the Messiah in the process of *teshuvah* as detailed here has nothing whatever to do with national-political messianism. All that interests Rav Kook is the basic process formulated here in an idealistic-philosophic mode.

If we may summarize this section in one sentence, we may say that Rav Kook's theory of *teshuvah* is woven into the pattern of ideas that have been developed in Jewish thought and that have sought to pour the idea of *teshuvah* into molds broader and deeper by far than those laid down when the idea was placed in its halachic-ritualistic framework. From a comparative and relative point of view, one gets the impression that the act of maintaining of the idea of *teshuvah* in its halachic and ritualistic framework is as child's play against the spiritual demands made of man who seeks to realize *teshuvah* for himself in its spiritual-philosophic and mystical molds. While the preservation of *teshuvah* on its halachic plane is generally not a factor for substantial change in man's position or in his stand in the presence of his G-d, this change *is* meant to come from his actualization of the *teshuvah* idea in its radical spiritual aspects, as Rav Kook, and Maimonides before him, sought to realize them. Only in this way does man leave his existential solitariness and succeed in removing himself from the world that is estranged from G-d into the world of the divine. In short, both with Maimonides and with Rav Kook, the *teshuvah* idea undergoes a spiritual radicalization.

5.

If we review what we said about Maimonides' concept of *teshuvah* and connect it with what we said about Rav Kook, I think it will be possible to find a structural similarity in their thinking on the subject of *teshuvah*. Both in Maimonides' theory of *teshuvah* and in that of Rav Kook there is a radicalization of the concept of perfection connected with *teshuvah* as opposed to what we hear in Scripture and from the sages. This radicalization is spiritual in essence and is connected with the idea that with the help of acts of *teshuvah* and processes of perfection, which involve the whole of personality as a way of life that strives for a cleaving to G-d, a man can attain to a position of being cut away from his material being and of returning to the divine reality. We could have been satisfied with this conclusion and thus bring our discussion of this matter to a close. Yet it seems to me that there is one aspect of this structural appraisal that requires further and deeper consideration.

This idea of returning to the Divine Source as the supreme expression of cleaving to G-d, which is the root of the *teshuvah* idea with Maimonides and with Rav Kook, is frequently found among the Gnostics at the beginning of the Christian era. In the writings of the Gnostics, whether known to us through the church fathers who debated with them, or whether known to us from the Gnostic library revealed at Nag-Hamadi in Upper Egypt, the thought recurs that the great achievement of man's spiritual soul is in its return to its divine origin. As a matter of fact, it has recently been shown that the whole distinctiveness of Gnostic thought is in the longing, or in the belief, that eventually everything will return to its divine origin.[17] Clearly, while we look to the writings of the Gnostics to illustrate a structural matter, we do not intend to suggest Gnostic influence on the writings of Maimonides or of Rav Kook. We know indeed that Gershom Scho-

17. See H. M. Schenke, "The Problem of Gnosis," *The Second Century II,* Vol. III (1983), p. 73ff.

lem, in his researches, has uncovered certain Gnostic influences on Kabbalistic literature and its thought,[18] and there are several scholars today who even speak of a Gnostic stream in Kabbalah. But we have no interest in the unraveling of these or other influences on the two personalities who are the center of our present study, more especially as the subject of direct Gnostic influences on Jewish mystic literature is not without problems.[19] Our interest in what is hidden in the understanding of the writings of Maimonides and Rav Kook stems from the desire to classify the ideas of these two personalities concerning *teshuvah* from a phenomenological point of view. Such a classification seems important to us if we wish to inquire into the uniqueness of the thought of the personalities whose teachings we are discussing. The basic structure of their thought concerning *teshuvah* is what interests us here, and it is this that draws us to the structure of the Gnostic way of thinking. In parentheses, it may be said here that if it would be possible to show that there are certain structural aspects in Gnostic literature that appear also in the writings of religious thinkers who are not a priori suspect of Gnostic heresy, it would be possible to change our understanding of the entire Gnostic phenomenon decisively. Under the influence of the church fathers, we are accustomed to seeing and emphasizing the heretical nature of the Gnostics. But for the scholar whose central interest is the phenomenology of religion, it would seem justifiable to demand that he consider the structural character of the Gnostic documents per se, and not as it is perceived from the Christian point of view. Here, we may find ourselves surprised if we discover that the basic religious drives expressed among the Gnostics are not heretical a priori, and we are likely to find similar ideas also among thinkers who are not suspected of being Gnostics.

The two ends of Rav Kook's thought on *teshuvah* are found in the being roused to the act of *teshuvah*, which comes from above, and in the perfection that causes everything to return to the bosom of the Divine. From the standpoint of the possible sources in these two matters, according to Rav Kook, we can point to Kabbalistic literature,

18. See G. Scholem, *Reshit HaKabbalah* (Jerusalem and Tel Aviv 1929), p. 26ff. See also the following note.
19. On the problem of the links between mysticism of *Merkavah* and Gnosticism, see I. Gruenwald, "Jewish Merkavah Mysticism and Gnosticism," in *Studies in Jewish Mysticism*, ed J. Dan and F. Talmage (Cambridge, MA, 1982), p. 41ff.

while not referring at this moment to the question of its direct and
exact sources.[20] However, from a structural point of view the process
may be elucidated by the fact that the first complete formulation of
that idea is found in Gnostic writings. Thus we find in the *"Evangelium
Veritatis,"* which some attribute to Valentinus, one of the first Gnostics in Rome, the idea of the "call" that comes to man from heaven
and rouses him from "his sleep" to the act of repentance: "Therefore,
if anyone has knowledge, its source is from the upper worlds. If they
call him, he hears, he answers and he returns [a pun on the Hebrew
verb *shuv*] to Him Who called him and he ascends to Him."[21] It is
quite likely that the idea of man's return to himself is also found in
"Evangelium Veritatis": "Anyone who is supposed to have this kind
of knowledge knows whence he came and whither he goes. He knows
it like one who was drunk and now has sobered up from his drunken-
ness, has returned to himself and corrected whatever relates to him."[22]
Finally, the notion of all things returning to their Divine Source in the
pleroma (*apokatastasis,* in Greek), is found in a few Gnostic writings.[23]
According to their perception, the source of all things is in the divine
pleroma, that is, in all those places to which and within which the
supreme Divine Presence spreads without mingling with the material
foundations in the world. It is unnecessary to emphasize explicitly that
even in the Gnostic passages to which we have referred here, there are
things that are absolutely foreign to Rav Kook's teaching. Especially
foreign to Rav Kook's teaching is the context in which the mentioned
Gnostic theory is set, a context that maintains that the material world
and the creator of the material world are evil and hostile to the G-d
of goodness. Similarly foreign to Rav Kook is the messianic approach,
found both in Christianity and in the Gnostic writings, according to
which the function of redeemer belongs to a messianic personality who
by his very appearance freed mankind from its dependence on the
Torah. Notwithstanding these ideas, we must not forget that in Rav

20. As far as can be seen, Rav Kook was influenced in these matters by the thought
patterns of Lurianic Kabbalah. A summary of Luria's theory may be found in Tishbi's
"Tales in Praise of the ARI" (Philadelphia 1970); G. Scholem, *Sabbatai Sevi* (Prince-
ton 1973).
21. The official mark of the loc. cit. in the writings of the Gnostics discovered at
Nag-Hamadi is: *Codex Gnosticus* (CG) 1, 3, 22, 4–7.
22. *Codex Gnosticus* 1, 3, 22, 13–20.
23. *Codex Gnosticus* 1, 5, 133, 7; 1, 5, 123, 20; 1, 4, 44, 30–32.

Kook's theory of *teshuvah* a task of central importance is assigned to the righteous Messiah.

However these things are viewed, in my estimation there is no doubt that, from a structural point of view, one can see Rav Kook's theory of *teshuvah,* and certainly also that of Maimonides, as belonging in a field of thought whose first illustration is found in the Gnostic writings, and probably also in Plato.[24] In other words, we have before us a Gnostic type of thought, and this assertion will guide the consideration of the question whether Rav Kook was a mystic or not, and if so, what kind of mystic was he? Binyamin Ish Shalom dealt with this question lately in his doctoral thesis, and he tends to see Rav Kook as a mystic, although he does so cautiously and with reservation. Still, anyone who examines Rav Kook's words with precision will recognize that they display a high degree of awareness of the mystical dimension. Rav Kook knows how to distinguish between rational knowledge, which comes to man from intellectual considerations, and the knowledge that a man gets from the glittering of the soul in superintellectual lights. However, it is very difficult to decide with certainty whether Rav Kook himself actually had a mystical experience or whether perhaps his mystical inclination found complete expression simply in a mystical yearning and in a longing for a mystical experience. In referring to these things, Rav Kook speaks often about "the pining of the soul," about the fact that "the soul thirsts for G-d;" about "a high and broad spiritual panting;" of his "desire . . . that the divine pleasantness may spread through me entirely"; and of the fact that he is "full of pains, and hoping for salvation and light, for a high exaltation, for the appearance of knowledge and light, and the flowing of the dew of life."[25] All is ready for a mystical experience, for the separation of the soul from the body and its unification with the heavenly light, or at least for seeing the heavenly light face to face; but seemingly all this does not reach to a mystical experience. It seems to me that it is no accident that one finds in Rav Kook's writings no report of an ecstatic experience in which the soul would be described as leaving the body, ascending to the upper worlds, seeing and experiencing G-d, and eventually return-

24. On the connection between these things and philosophic traditions stemming from Plato, see my above-mentioned article, n. 39, p. 51.
25. All the quotations are collected in the work referred to by Ish Shalom, p. 81ff.

ing to the body. Such an experience, marvelous as it would be, would not in the final analysis answer Rav Kook's real hopes, which are connected with the soul's return to the divine world. Whatever man can attain in his earthly life is in the nature of transient illuminations. This is in itself also an achievement; but the great and real attainment can only be reached after the final departure of the soul from the body, that is, after the death of the body. We find similar ideas in Maimonides also, when, as we have already noted above, he argues that man's highest level of intellectual achievement is attainable only when the soul is separated from the body. Only very rare, exceptional people are likely to get to a condition of "the future world" *(olam haba)* while they are alive.

In other words, when we speak of the soul's ascent, two basic structures are observable: The one stresses the ascent of the soul as an ecstatic experience in the life of man—and this is the mystical structure; and the second emphasizes the ascent of the soul after death, and its return to its divine origin—and this is the Gnostic structure. It is possible to find mystical ascents of the soul within the Gnostic circles too, but even if they are capable of real actualization, they are still only anticipatory of the principal experience, which will come only after death. As against this, the entire subject of the soul's return to its Divine Source is almost not stressed at all where the ascent of the soul according to the mystical structure is being discussed. Moreover, while in the mystical structure a complicated and difficult technique of self-preparation is present at the center of man's activity, despite the occurrence sometimes of spontaneous experiences—in the second structure, the Gnostic, there is a high degree of self-awareness at the center, which emanates from the awakening from above. If, then, it is possible to focus—even if only schematically—on the difference between these two structures, we find the technique in the mystical one, while in the Gnostic one we find the knowledge. This structural typology may assist us with the correct placement and assessment of thought patterns with whose characterization scholars have difficulty. Furthermore, it seems to me that in the two structures to which we refer, there is a clear basic assumption: The divine world is beyond man and his usual comprehension. Whether we look to an ecstatic experience or whether we have to wait until after death, the world of the divine is perceived decisively as a transcendental world; hence it is very difficult to speak of a pantheistic perception with Rav Kook, at least not in the usual sense of the word.

One final word in conclusion: The potential ascent of the soul after death in fact nullifies the sting of death. If death is perceived as equivalent to evil, then the vitiation of its pain is equivalent to the vitiation of evil, and naturally the theodicy problem is done away with—i.e., the need to justify G-d's actions in the light of the existence of evil and death as a realistic presence against goodness and life. Both in Maimonides' system and also in Rav Kook's perception, man has to try to attain to a level in which death will be, for him, a sort of great opportunity to return to the bosom of the Divine; and from here the way is open, with Rav Kook, for the perfection of the world and for vitiating the dualism that undermines the foundations of its existence.

To sum up: We have presented the main features relative to the teaching of *teshuvah* as it appears with Maimonides and with Rav Kook. From a comparison, brief as it was, to the *teshuvah* teaching in Scripture and in the words of the sages, it appears that the teachings of Maimonides and Rav Kook on the subject of *teshuvah* are inter-linked with the pattern of ideas required to bestow upon *teshuvah* certain spiritual dimensions—philosophical and others—beyond the ritual and ceremonial dimensions found in Scripture and with our sages. With Maimonides and with Rav Kook, there is a prevailing desire to give *teshuvah* also a redemptive dimension, whether it is a redemption of the soul from the material world, or whether it is a more general redemption in which, especially for Rav Kook, historic and national processes are interwoven. From a structural point of view, we attempted to present the *teshuvah* teaching of these two personalities in a Gnostic framework as opposed to a more mystical structure. It is not our desire to affix a new label either to Maimonides or to Rav Kook. We rejected the tendency to characterize Rav Kook's thought in its entirety within the framework of one all-embracing label. All that we have sought to do is to present the character of these two personalities' theory of *teshuvah* in a structural framework designed to clarify its special position. The emphasis we put on the Gnostic structural pattern was meant to distinguish it from the mystical structure. The one sees the soul's ascent as an ultimate return to the sphere of the Divine Presence; the other sees it as an experience limited in time during which the soul is able to have a godly experience that sometimes, though by no means always, is a kind of anticipation of what is in store for the soul after the death of the body. From a certain point of view, one may see the Gnostic structure as a radicalization of the mystical structure. Or alternatively, the mystical-structure pattern acts as a restraining factor on the Gnostic structure.

Status of
Baale Teshuvah

Dr. Shimon Shokek

THE QUESTION OF the religious standing and status of the penitent *(baal teshuvah)* as compared with those of the righteous man *(tzaddik)*, preoccupied the prominent scholars of Jewish moralist literature of the Middle Ages. It marks one of the principal points of controversy among the scholars of the *teshuvah* literature, even when the debate is referred to in their writings not directly, but only by implication. The question is bound up with the basis of the psycho-anthropological and religio-educational perception of the writers with whose works I shall deal below,[1] and it points to the central hinge on which turn the philo-sophic-rabbinic perceptions of *teshuvah* on the one hand, and the Kabbalistic-mystical philosophic perceptions on the other. That is, this question marks a dividing line between the *teshuvah* literature belonging to the rabbinic-philosophic group and that which looked for support in mystical foundations.

The roots of the problem are to be found already in the Talmudic source that presents the well-known debate in Tractate *Berachot* (34b)

1. Further on I shall deal with the question of the penitent's status by examining the works of Rav Saadya Gaon, Rabbenu Bachaye Ibn Pakuda, Avraham bar Chiyya, Maimonides, *Sefer HaYashar,* and the Book of the *Zohar.*

concerning the teaching "In the place where penitents stand, even the wholly righteous cannot stand." Rav Abahu there differs from the opinion of Rav Yochanan as stated by Rav Chiyya bar Abba. The controversy is rooted in the understanding of the verse (*Isaiah* 57:19): "Peace, peace, to him that was far and to him that is near." In Rav Abahu's opinion, the penitent stands on a higher level than the righteous man, for the verse opens with the *baal teshuvah*, who is hinted at, in his view, in the word "far," and ends with the *tzaddik*, referred to in the word "near." However, the concluding part of this Talmudic passage hints at a possibility of siding with Rav Yochanan; that is, that the one who was "far" is really the *tzaddik*, since he is far removed from transgression and consequently he is on a higher plane than the *baal teshuvah*. This controversy is not decided by the *Gemara*, and the two views remain unresolved beside each other, the one opposite the other.[2]

The discussion on *teshuvah* and penitents in medieval Jewish thought opens in the book *Beliefs and Opinions* by Rav Saadya. Men are there classified into "ten categories: righteous, wicked, obedient, disobedient, perfect and imperfect, sinner, corrupt, heretic, and the penitent" (*Emunot VeDeot*, Treatise V, p. 173).[3]

From Saadya's discussion of these "ten categories," which he defines as "gradations into which men are divided according to their merits and demerits" (Ibid.), it is clear that the quality of the righteous man (the *tzaddik*) is higher than that of the penitent. Nevertheless, the question of the penitent's status as compared with that of the *tzaddik* is not clearly decided in his teaching. The *tzaddik* is defined as "he whose good deeds predominate" (Ibid.), while the penitent is "he who carries

2. The view concerning the possibility of the righteous man's superiority over the penitent is formulated by Rav Chiyya bar Abba in the sentence "All the prophets prophesied only for the penitent; but as for the perfect righteous man, 'the eye hath not seen a G-d beside Thee' (*Isaiah* 64:3)." See also *Sanhedrin* 99b. In the Talmud and the Midrashim, the main emphasis was transferred to the repentance of the individual, while the original sense of *teshuvah* in the adjurations of the prophets was directed to Israel's return to G-d. For this subject, see C. G. Montefiore, "Rabbinic Conception of Repentance," *JQR*, XVI (1904), pp. 209–57; also G. F. Moore, *Judaism in the First Centuries of the Christian Era* (1927), pp. 460–534. On *teshuvah* in Scripture and its evaluation by the rabbinic sages, the nature of *teshuvah* and the broadening of its limits by the *Amoraim*, see E. E. Urbach, "The Sages: Concepts and Beliefs" (tr. from the Hebrew), *Magnes* (Jerusalem 1975), Chap. XV, Section V. See also, A. J. Heschel, *Torah Min Hashamayim BeAspaklaria shel HaDorot* (New York and London 5722), Vol. I, *Teshuvah VeKapparah*, pp. 143–47.
3. Rav Kapach edition.

out the terms of repentance" (Ibid. p. 182). But the question Which one is greater than the other? is not dealt with at all in Rav Saadya's teaching.

The question was formulated for the first time in the first Hebrew moralist work to have a special section dealing with the subject of *teshuvah* ("repentance"), the work *Chovot HaLevavot* by Rabbenu Bachaye Ibn Pakuda. Rav Bachaye asks, "Is the penitent equal to the righteous?" And his answer is, "There is one kind of penitent who, after his repentance, is equal to a righteous man who has never sinned; another may be superior to such a righteous man; and there is a third penitent to whom, notwithstanding his repentance, the righteous man is superior."[4]

Bachaye's division is in accordance with the sin that the man has committed. If he is guilty of a sin of omission of a positive command that does not carry the punishment of extirpation and later repents, then he is equal to the righteous man who has not sinned. If he committed a minor sin concerning a positive command that does not carry the punishment of extirpation and he repents, then he is superior to the righteous man. But if he sins against a positive command that does carry the punishment of extirpation and death by the hand of heaven and then he repents, he does not rise to the level of the righteous man.

In the work *Higyon HaNefesh HaAtzuvah* by Rav Avraham bar Chiyya of Barcelona, the first of the medieval Jewish philosophers who wrote in Hebrew, Bar Chiyya deals at length with the question of the status of the penitent as compared with that of the righteous man. He classified men according to five gradations:

1. A completely righteous man who is of humble bearing and has only a good inclination. He is the highest of them all and is completely separate from the penitents.
2. A completely righteous man who is of a subdued heart and conquers his inclination. He is higher than all the penitents.
3. A completely righteous man, who commits a transgression once and repents, and does not repeat the sin.

---

4. *Chovot HaLevavot*, "The Gate of *Teshuvah*," beginning of Chap. 8 (in the Rav Kapach edition), p. 320.

4. An intermediate person—that is, one who repents of his sin but repeats it, or who does not repent fully.

5. A wicked man who walks in his evil way all his life and never repents. He is the lowest of them all.

From this five-runged ladder, it seems that there is no doubt, in Avraham bar Chiyya's view, that the righteous man is on a higher level than the penitent. Here is how he puts it: ". . . It has been made clear to us that those who walk the upright path and those who depart from it should be divided into five groups: first, two completely righteous men. The one is 'of humble spirit,' that is, his soul and his good nature rule his evil inclination from the day of his birth to the day of his death; to him the term 'repentance' does not apply at all, since he is too holy for it. The other is known as 'of subdued heart.' This one directs his inclination away from lust, from his heart that lusts for the things of this world, and forcibly conquers his inclination, reducing its strength, right from his childhood through his old age. To him the term 'penitent' does apply, since he needed at first to subdue his inclination; but he is the most excellent and praiseworthy of all penitents.

"After these two completely pious men come three more who are not completely righteous and are not called righteous *(tzaddikim)*. With regard to two of them their penitence depends on them. The one repents of his sin after having committed it, regrets it, and never repeats it to the end of his days. The other repents of his sin but repeats it; or he does not make a complete repentance. As for the third one, he is completely wicked; he goes his evil way without ever repenting of it all his life. And just as the first completely righteous man is holy beyond even being called a penitent *(baal teshuvah)*, so is *teshuvah* itself holy beyond being applied to this completely wicked man. Thus the penitents *(baale teshuvah)* are three different types of people: one is completely righteous, the second is intermediate, and the third is wicked."[5]

Avraham bar Chiyya's decisive view that the status of the righteous man is higher than that of the penitent is put forward again in the teaching of Maimonides, albeit in a more complex and multifaceted

5. *Higyon HaNefesh HaAtzuvah,* in the Geoffrey Wigoder edition, (Jerusalem: Mosad Bialik, 5732), p. 92. Also Ibid. pp. 60–66.

manner. Maimonides approaches the elucidation of the problem from two different starting points. In his legal code, he writes, "Our sages have said, In a place where penitents stand, the completely righteous cannot stand. That is, their standing is greater than that of those who have never sinned at all, since they subdue their [evil] inclination more than do the others."[6]

Here, Maimonides is making an analysis of the degrees of physical and spiritual effort required of the *tzaddik* on the one hand and the *baal teshuvah* on the other. The superiority of the penitent over the righteous man is determined only from the point of view of the obstacles and practical difficulties that stand in his way, these being certainly immeasurably greater than the obstacles and difficulties in the way of the *tzaddik*. Underlying his teaching there is surely also an educational aim, the purpose of which is to attract the penitents and to encourage them to turn away from their wickedness. However, when Maimonides sets out to deal with this problem in his moralist-philosophic work, in his Introduction to the Tractate *Avot*, he puts forward a question, Who is to be preferred, one who has never sinned, whose soul is pure and clean without any tendency to sin or any thoughts of transgression, or he whose soul surges with evil inclinations over which he prevails, who keeps away from sin despite his urges? His decisive answer is that the completely righteous man is to be preferred, without any doubt, over him who "conquers the inclination" (it being clear that the penitent is in the category of "he who subdues his inclination"). For, in Maimonides' view, it is the purity of the soul and its cleanliness of all bases of wickedness that are the supreme religious value. As he puts it, "There is no doubt that the soul [of him 'who subdues the inclination'—S.S.] that hankers after some evil deed is faulty, while the soul of the *tzaddik* or the wholly pious person, will not lust after any evil deeds and will not regret keeping away from them."[7]

Maimonides explains those teachings of our sages in which we find that the subduer of the inclination is higher than the righteous by saying that they refer to some of the ritual commandments the reason

6. *Sefer HaMadda, Hilchot Teshuvah,* Chap. 7, halacha 4. Following Maimonides, this is also the position of *Sefer Hasidim.* See Margolioth edition (Jerusalem: Mosad HaRav Kook, 5717), Sec. 60.
7. Introductions to the Mishnah Commentary, *Shemonah Perakim,* in the Rabinovitch edition (Jerusalem: Mosad HaRav Kook, 5721), Chap. VI, pp. 193–194.

for which is not clear to us, like *shaatnes* and the laws of kashrut. So far as those are concerned, a man is permitted to have some inclinations and urges to sin. If he repents of these with a full-hearted repentance that cleanses his soul and makes it purer than it was formerly, then he has attained a status even higher than that of the perfect *tzaddik*. But this answer of Maimonides to the problem is forced, and it certainly does not alter the fact that he absolutely prefers original purity to a prevailing over the evil that is in man's soul.

The question of the penitent's status received greater emphasis in *Sefer HaYashar*, attributed to Rabbenu Tam, than in any other Hebrew moralist literary work of the Middle Ages. The anonymous author of this work devoted a special section to a consideration of *teshuvah*[8]; yet, beyond his concern with the actual nature of *teshuvah*, he deals with the question of the status of the penitent as compared with that of the *tzaddik*. At the very beginning of the section, the author explains that complete repentance does indeed cleanse the evildoer of all his sins and delivers him from punishment by the Creator, "yet—in his words—he has no merits, and he cannot aspire to the rung of the pure righteous men who never in all their days committed a transgression" (*Sefer HaYashar*, p. 98). Metaphorically, he explains that one cannot imagine that two servants of the king, one faithful and the other rebellious, should merit the same equal status before the king, even though the rebellious servant surrenders himself to his king and admits his sin and asks the king's pardon, and the king even forgives him: "Like Shimei the son of Gera when he came and abased himself before David the king, peace upon him; it is obvious that although the king pardoned him, his standing in his eyes would not be as that of his faithful servant" (Ibid).[9]

The basis for the view that the penitent is on a lower rung as

8. *The Tenth Gate*, pp. 98–102. My subsequent quotations from *Sefer HaYashar* are from the Eshkol edition (Jerusalem 5738), based on the first printed editions of *Sefer HaYashar* (Constantinople 1520 and Venice 1544). For a study of *teshuvah* in the *Sefer HaYashar*, see *in extenso* chapter vii of my doctoral dissertation, entitled "*Sefer HaYashar* in the Context of the Hebrew Moralist Literature of the 13th Century," written under the supervision of Professor Yosef Dan, to whom I express thanks.
9. Moses and David also sinned, and therefore they can be included among the penitent. However, the author "ignores" their sins and portrays them as righteous *(tzaddikim)*. There would seem to be a contradiction in his statement, but this will be explained later.

compared with the *tzaddik* comes in what follows, with the author basing himself on the words of the sages in Tractate *Berachot* (34b), which he explains in an opposite sense to that of the original intent in the Talmud: "What our teachers, of blessed memory, said (*Berachot* 34b), 'Where the penitent stands, perfect righteous men cannot stand,' they spoke the truth. For it is known of the righteous and the intermediate[10] that each has a rung of his own with the Creator, blessed be He, the one higher than the other, and that is why our teachers, of blessed memory, said that the righteous do not stand on the rung of the penitent, for it is not their proper place and they do not belong in the sect of the penitents, but in another place" (*Sefer HaYashar,* pp. 98–99).

Thus, the conclusion from his words is that every man has a religious rung with the Holy One, blessed be He; the penitents in their place, and the righteous on their rung. But the penitents, as against the righteous ones, are only "intermediate," that is, of lesser stature than the religious rung of the righteous.

Also, when the author of *Sefer HaYashar* clarifies the help that G-d gives to the righteous and the penitent, while he justifies the preferential help given to the latter, he uses a string of arguments that lowers the stature of the penitents. In his view, G-d helps the penitent so as to show the wicked his love for the *baale teshuvah;* and there are times when He performs miracles for the penitent, the like of which He does not do for the righteous. However, it is "not because the penitents are on an equal rung with the righteous, but because the penitents, if the Creator will not accept them and will not show them His love, will return to their evil deeds" (Ibid. p. 99).[11]

10. In the distinction he draws between "righteous" and "intermediate" (and later also with "wicked"), the author has in mind, apparently, the distinction made in Tractate *Rosh Hashanah* (16b): "On Rosh Hashanah three books are opened, one book of the completely righteous, another of the wholly wicked, and another of the intermediate. The completely righteous are immediately written and sealed for life; the wholly wicked are written and sealed for death; the intermediate are suspended from Rosh Hashanah until Yom Kippur: if they merit it—they are inscribed for life, if they do not merit it—for death." This teaching is the opening of Nahmanides' *Shaar HaGemul;* and see his comment thereto, as well as on "Three categories for the Day of Judgment" in the Chavel edition, pp. 264–67. And see also Maimonides, *Sefer HaMadda, Hilchot Teshuvah,* Chap. 3, halacha 3.
11. On G-d's help to the penitent (based on the teaching of the sages in *Tosefta, Shabbat* 104a, "One who comes to be purified is helped; one who comes to be defiled, the way is opened to him") see: Maimonides, *Hilchot Teshuvah,* Chap. 5, halacha 5;

He illustrates this assertion with a parable. It is like a king who prefers fulfilling the request of his servant who flatters him rather than of his faithful servant. For the "faithful servant" knows his Creator and will not be angry at His laws even if his request will not be fulfilled; while the "sycophantic servant" may think ill of the king, and he may go and say to his friends, "One cannot serve such a king as this; I upset him in a small matter and he refused to grant my request; how can one trust him?" (Ibid. p. 79).

Thus, we find that the preferential help that the penitent is privileged to receive from the Creator also points directly to his lesser intellectual and religious standing.

The author of *Sefer HaYashar*'s uncomfortable feeling with his own assertion that the penitent is on a lesser level than the righteous is recognizable in the continuation of the tenth section (literally, "Tenth Gate") of his work. To what he has said so far he now adds the following sentence: "Another, correct, explanation is that there are penitents whose heart is as true as that of the righteous, and these are called *tzaddikim,* for they were upright at first but they erred, or, transgression chanced their way and temptation overcame them; but afterward they returned to their former condition and to their uprightness, and their righteousness and service [of G-d] was doubled because of the sin they had committed. These people are more to be honored

---

the book *HaEmunah VeHaBitachon,* p. 376, *Shaar HaGemul,* p. 273 (the two last in the Chavel edition). Saadya Gaon explains in his *Emunot VeDeot* (Treatise V, Chap. iii) that G-d extends the life of heretics (as He did for Manasseh) so that they may turn from their wickedness. And Rabbenu Bachaye Ibn Pakuda describes the character of *teshuvah* as G-d's help to the penitent out of compassion and as an act of kindness affording man an opportunity to correct his error and return to the line of discipline (See the beginning of the Seventh Gate in *Chovot HaLevavot*). In the view of Rav Avraham bar Hiyya, repentance is a two-way act. Therefore it is said with reference to the penitent who turns from his transgressions (*Hosea* 14:2 "Return, O Israel, unto the Lord your G-d") and also concerning G-d, blessed be He (*Malachi* 3:10, "Return unto Me and I shall return unto you"). Rav Jonah Gerondi writes in *Shaarei Teshuvah* (i:4): "For the Lord will assist the penitent when they cannot manage themselves"; and Rav Yehiel of Rome writes in *Maalot HaMidot:* ". . . Not only this, but the Holy One, blessed be He, hath sworn that He will receive the penitent . . . Thus said the Holy One, blessed be He, to Israel, You are ashamed to do *teshuvah,* [therefore] I shall return first, as it is said (*Jeremiah* 30:18) "Behold I will turn . . ." (Ibid. *Maalat HaTeshuvah* Eshkol edition, p. 224, Jerusalem 5738).

On G-d's assistance to the wicked and to the penitent according to the *Zohar,* see *Mishnat HaZohar,* Vol. II (Jerusalem: Mosad Bialik, 5735), pp. 671–72.

than the righteous, for their righteousness is double that of the *tzaddik* who has never sinned; and in respect of these it may be said—Where the penitents stand, perfect *tzaddikim* cannot stand" (Ibid. pp. 99–100).[12]

In these words, the rung of the penitents is set above that of the righteous. However, this explanation does not apply to the repentance of the righteous who all their lives were upright until they stumbled into transgression just once—and repented. Therefore this explanation should not be seen as a withdrawal from the main assertion of the author, namely, that the penitent who was formerly wicked is of lower moral stature than the righteous. Moreover, further on, the author lays down a sort of ideological parallel between the four basic elements from which the world and man were created, and the four elements comprising *teshuvah*.[13] "Know," he writes, "that the world was created from four elements, man's pillars on which everything depends, namely fire and water and air and earth.[14] And just as these elements unite and mix, so is *teshuvah* (repentance) the pillar of the world on which everything depends, and it also is made up of four things: The sinner must put away his sinful deed completely; he must have regret for what he did; he must undertake before his Maker not to repeat the sin that

12. This commentary is parallel to the third of the five human levels listed by Rav Avraham bar Chiyya (see above). In this commentary, the author has in mind Moses and David, to whom he refers as righteous, but he refrains from mentioning it. The idea that the honored penitent is he who has stumbled and transgressed once, but repented of it and returned, is found in the Talmud with the additional note that the *baal teshuvah* "whose *teshuvah* reaches up to the Throne of Glory—he is the one who, having been tested, has emerged clean in the same circumstance, in the same place and at the same time" (*Yoma* 86b). And see *Shaarei Teshuvah* of Rav Jonah Gerondi, Vol. I, p. 49; and on *teshuvah* of *havaah*, of the Ashkenaz Hasidut, connected with this matter, see the book by Yosef Dan, *Sifrut HaMusar VeHaDerush*, Keter edition (Jerusalem 1975), pp. 130–33.

13. Rav Avraham Saba writes in his work *Tzror HaMor*, "And see, the conditions of repentance are many . . . and many authors have spoken of them . . . but of all of them only the words of *Sefer HaYashar* seem right to me . . . I do not remember the words exactly—for my sins I do not have the book, all my books having been left in Portugal, but as far as I recall, he says that there are four conditions of *teshuvah*, based on the four elements" (Venice edition, 1567), p. 153, line 3.

14. The creation of the world and of man through the unification of the four elements is known as an Aristotelian concept, but it is found already in the theory of Empedocles. See Pepita Haezrahi, *Al HaYesh HaMushlam* (Jerusalem: Academon, 5724), pp. 51–53. See also Marcus Manilus, *Astronomica*, Vol. II, pp. 115–16, Vol. IV, pp. 905–7.

he committed; and he must make verbal confession of what he did, with his lips.[15] The most important of these four is the forsaking of the sin,[16] just like fire that ascends to heaven and is separated from its [earthly] place never to return. Second, he should have remorse for what he did and mourn for his sins and always think of them, like the air that is continuously going round the world. Third, he should testify[17] in the presence of his Creator (as his witness) that he will not return and repeat his sins, like the water that comes down to earth never to be gathered up again. And fourth, he should confess his sin with a subdued soul, and humble himself, and surrender himself like the earth that he treads down with the sole of his foot. And let him know that whoever does these four things will be rewarded with four good things: first, a good name in the world; second, deliverance from punishment by the Creator; third, his goodness will be carried over to his children after him; and fourth, he will find his reward in the world to come and will have the merit of seeing the face of the Creator, may He be blessed" (Ibid. pp. 101–2).

At first sight, these words seem to embody a pattern of thought giving *teshuvah* a strong position by exaggerating its importance to the point of likening it to the four elements through whose unification the world came into being, and which, in the words of the author, are "man's pillars." Accordingly, the penitent's standing is elevated and exalted with the standing of *teshuvah*. But anyone who studies some other passages in *Sefer HaYashar* cannot but come to the paradoxical conclusion that it is precisely the likening of the four categories of

15. The author does not use the linguistic combination "categories of *teshuvah*" that was normal among students of morality in the Middle Ages since Saadya Gaon set it down in his work *Beliefs and Opinions;* but "Four elements" of which teshuvah is composed. On *Gidrei Teshuvah* (categories of teshuvah) in other sources, see *Emunot Ve-Deot,* the Fifth Gate, Chapter V; *Chovoth HaLevavot,* the *Gate of Teshuvah,* Chapter IV (this is where "confession" first appears); Maimonides' *Hilchot Teshuvah,* Chap. 2, halacha 2; *Sefer HaRokeach* of Rav Elazar of Germiza, *Hilchot Teshuvah,* para. 1; *Sefer Hasidim,* Margoliot edition, Section 42; *Shaarei Teshuvah* of Rav Jonah, Vol. I, p. 19.

16. Saadya also stressed the category of *teshuvah* above the others: "I have no fears, so far as the majority of our people are concerned, in regard to their being remiss in their fulfillment of any of the conditions [categories] of repentance except for this fourth category—I mean that of lapsing back into sin" (Ibid.).

17. Concerning "he will testify," "he should testify," cf. Maimonides, *Hilchot Teshuvah,* Chap. 2, halacha 2, and see how Maimonides uses, in this connection, the word *Od* (more, again, etc. . . .) in the verse in *Hosea* (14:4) with reference to testimony.

teshuvah to the four elements, "the pillars of man," that establishes and deepens the author's point of view concerning the lesser value of the penitent and of repentance itself. For, in the context of the anthropological perception in the fifth section of this work, the ingredients of man's body, consisting of fire, water, air, and earth, are set out as inferior in relation to the ingredients of his soul. This (the soul) is more refined and, in the author's view, is made up of four divine forces: "The body consists of four elements, fire and water, air and earth, and these combine and stand together so long as there is life in the body . . . But . . . the soul is noble and is constituted from heavenly forces; for the Creator, may He be blessed, constituted it from four elements—from the power of His existence and life and wisdom and unity; and it is from all these four that the soul is composed . . ." (*Sefer HaYashar,* the Fifth Gate, pp. 54–55). Thus, even if repentance is symbolically parallel to the four elements that are the "pillars of man," these are only its four lowest pillars. They represent man's lower dimensions—the body, as distinct from the soul. And even though the four elements are essential for the existence of the world and of man, they still do not express either the world's spiritual value or the divine-soul aspect of man.

The discussion, up to this point, of the question of the penitent's position expresses a clear purpose that is plainly set out in the principal works of Hebrew moralist literature from the *Sefer HaEmunot VeHaDeot* until the *Sefer HaYashar.* According to them, it can be determined that the superiority of the perfect righteous man above the penitent was never in doubt among the Jewish teachers who fashioned the rabbinic-philosophical moralist literature. The question is, why is it necessary to determine from the outset that the problem of the penitent's position vis-à-vis that of the *tzaddik* was central to the studies in medieval *teshuvah* literature; and was this question really put forward by the moralist scholars in the Middle Ages as a problem demanding clarification?

Above all, it should be emphasized that the question of the penitent's position did in fact present a problem to the medieval Jewish moralist sages. And even though Rabbenu Bachaye, Bar Chiyya, Maimonides, and the author of *Sefer HaYashar* do not specifically mention an opponent, yet behind their statements one can detect that they are taking up a position in this matter polemically, and the question itself was anyhow known already in Talmudic literature as a controversial problem. This is particularly noticeable from the literary style of the author of *Sefer HaYashar*. It seems that his words were written as a reaction to other positions and in an atmosphere of polemic surrounding the question of the level and the position of the penitents. The seriousness of the problem under discussion was greatly increased by the penitent's position being primarily a didactic touchstone for the author of moralist literature. In other words, on the one hand, the Jewish moralist sage wants to attract the wicked and put them back on the straight path, but, on the other hand, he finds difficulty in presenting his views. For the portrayal of the penitent on a lower level than the *tzaddik* has something unattractive about it that might result in leaving the sinner in his wickedness. This tension is seen in the words both of Maimonides and of the author of *Sefer HaYashar,* as has been hinted at above. Moreover, if we study two of the most classic Hebrew works for our purpose, the book *Gates of Repentance* by Rav Jonah Gerondi, and the book *Maalot HaMidot* of Rav Yechiel ben Rav Yekutiel of Rome, an astonishing literary and thoughtful phenomenon stands out. These two authors hardly touch on the question of the penitent's station, even by way of hint.[18] The book *Shaarei Teshuvah (Gates of Repentance)* is one of a handful of basic works dealing with the subject of *teshuvah* encompassed from every aspect; and the book *Maalot HaMidot* sets aside a special section for a discussion of this subject, in the part entitled The Merit of Teshuvah. Nevertheless, neither of these two works includes the teaching of the Talmudic sages referred to from the Tractate *Berachot:* "Where penitents stand, perfect righteous men cannot stand." The work of Rav Yechiel of Rome presents an outstanding example of an ontological work of morality, filled to overflowing with Scriptural verses and teachings of the sages.

---

18. In Rav Jonah Gerondi's other work, *Yesod HaTeshuvah* (Jerusalem: Eshkol, 5738), p. 92, printed together with *Shaarei Teshuvah* and other works, he says, "And they said, Greater is the level of the penitent than that of the completely righteous, and this is what the sages meant in saying, In the place where the penitents stand, the wholly righteous cannot stand." Here we have a hint of Rav Jonah's view of the superiority of the penitent to the *tzaddik.* However, Rav Jonah does not discuss all this in connection with the penitent's standing, but he merely quotes the saying of the sages in *Berachot* (34b) verbatim. We know of no answer to the question—was *Yesod HaTeshuvah* a part of Rav Jonah's magnum opus *Shaarei Tzedek,* which, according to the sources, included within it also *Shaarei Teshuvah.*

For this reason, the noninclusion in the book of the above-mentioned teaching of the sages is especially noticeable. This is true also of the book *Shaarei Teshuvah,* which really represents a different literary genre from that of *Maalot HaMidot,* but is still an embracing work for matters of *teshuvah,* comprising 158 pages with numerous teachings of the sages scattered throughout. The absence of this teaching of the sages from these two central works of the thirteenth century testifies to the profundity of the problem of the penitent's station, and there is no doubt, in my opinion, that this indicates that Rav Jonah and Rav Yechiel deliberately refrained from quoting it in their works out of a conscious intention to avoid the controversy.

The major change in regard to the station of the penitent began with the works of the Kabbalists of Gerona and was sharpened more and more until it was entrenched in the Kabbalistic work that appeared at the end of the thirteenth century: the *Zohar.* In opposition to what was said in the *teshuvah* literature of the rabbinic-philosophic group preceding the *Zohar,* which taught that the purity of the soul of the tzaddik represents the supreme religious value and therefore the tzaddik is always superior to the penitent, the early Kabbalists put forward, as the chief motif of *teshuvah,* the sages' idea that repentance preceded the world's creation.[19] This motif points to a sharp opposition to the basic point of departure of the scholars of the moralist literature discussed above. For, in the theory of the first Kabbalists, it gave rise to a new perception according to which repentance is to be seen as a sort of restorative religious foundation that restores the defiled existence to its original perfect condition. In their theory, the act of repentance is not perceived merely as a psychological, educational, and religious process by means of which the wicked man repents of his sins and returns to the straight path, but it becomes a supreme, religious alternative value put forward in the theory of the philosopher scholars of morality. The principal innovation in what the first Kabbalists say about the motif under discussion is in their presenting original repentance as the third *sefira* (divine dimension), the *sefira* of understanding *(Binah)* from which, in the words of Rav Azriel of Gerona, there has

---

19. "Great is *teshuvah,* for it preceded the world's creation" (*Midrash Tehillim,* Buber, Psalm 90, 196a); "The Holy One, blessed be He, designed the world and did not rest until He had created repentance" (*Pirke d'Rav Eliezer,* Chap. III).

been set aside "a light of repentance that illumines the thought of the penitent."[20]

In his aggadic commentaries, Rav Azriel writes, "Repentance has been created so that they should return from their sin, and so that their spirit should return to their body, and they should live a life that has no death after it. Repentance maintains everything, and was created before the world was brought into being, and the world could not have arisen except through it" (*Perush HaAggadot*, p. 98). And elsewhere he adds, "And since [the world preceding this one] was created by justice, it was not able to exist—it was wiped out, and a universe was made that was ready to receive the ways of the Torah, and to behave in the ways of *teshuvah* that were created, primarily, for bringing about the existence of those ways of Torah" (*Ibid.* p. 102).[21]

The author of the Book of the *Zohar* established the mystical and Kabbalistic basis of the quality of *teshuvah* more deeply than did the first Kabbalists. He elevated the penitent from his lowliness and from the defilement in which he had been immersed to the point of giving him an exaggerated importance, for he has a short approach to G-d. Therefore the level of his elevation is higher even than that of the *tzaddik:* "Happy are the penitents, for behold, in one hour, in one day, in one minute, they are near to the Holy One, blessed be He—something that does not happen even to the completely righteous men who draw close to the Holy One, blessed be He, in the course of several years . . . We have learned: In the place where the penitents stand, the completely righteous are not permitted to stand, because they (the penitent) are nearer to the King than all of them, and they draw others unto themselves with great willingness of heart, and with great force, to get them to approach the King" (*Zohar,* Part I, 129a–130a).[22]

---

20. *Perush HaAggadot l'R. Azriel MiGironah,* Tishby edition (Jerusalem: Academon, 5738), p. 96. The term *"teshuvah"* served as a fixed term for the *sefira* of *Binah,* though unconnected with man's penitence; and the meaning of the term is explained in Kabbalistic philosophy mainly on the basis of the relationship between the *sefira* of *Binah* and the other *sefirot* (see Tishby, *Mishnat HaZohar,* Ibid. p. 738, n. 3).

21. See also Ibid. pp. 2–3, concerning "the *teshuvah* that preceded" the world; also pp. 96, 99, and 116 concerning "The light of *teshuvah* and the light of the Messiah and the light of the souls have been and will be . . ." See also: *Perush HaTefillot l'R. Azriel,* Oxford MS 1938, 224B, 236A: *Perush HaAggadot* of Rav Ezra, Vatican MS 294, 37a: the book *HaEmunah VeHaBitachon* of Rav Yaacov b. Sheshet Girondi, Chap. XVIII.

22. Cf. *Mishnat HaZohar,* The Status of the Penitent, p. 759.

The high elevation of the penitent, according to the *Zohar,* not only lifts the penitent above the completely righteous, but also gives the penitent a greater ability to activate the heavenly powers and draw on them abundantly.

In another treatise, the quality of repentance is compared to the Shechinah ("G-d's Divine Presence"), and therefore it is lower than the quality of piety (the *sefirah* of *Malchut* as opposed to the *sefira* of *Yesod*).[23] However, the penitent, i.e., *baal teshuvah* (with the accent on the first word of this linguistic combination) is himself elevated even above the perfect *tzaddik,* since he climbs up as far as the mother, or arch, *sefira,* namely the *sefira* of *Binah* (the "intelligence" of G-d.): "And as soon as the penitent clings to the tree of life [*Tiferet*— "Beauty" or "Compassion" of G-d] he is called *baal teshuvah,* since even the *Knesset Yisrael* [Shechinah] is called *teshuvah;* and he is called the *baal teshuvah* [literally, "husband" of the Shechinah]. And the early Kabbalists said the term means really "husband of *teshuvah*" [held by *Binah*—S. S.], and therefore even perfect righteous *tzaddikim* [*sefira* of *Yesod*—S. S.] cannot stand in the place where the *baale teshuvah* stand" (*Zohar,* Part III, 16b).

Thus, the Kabbalistic basis that the *Zohar* laid down for the theory of repentance puts forward a new intellectual alternative perception of the essence of *teshuvah.* Within this context, the penitent's station is lifted higher and higher above the standing of the perfect *tzaddik.* However, the author of the *Zohar* is not satisfied with that, and his chief innovation appears in his portrayal of the act of repentance as something working not only for the pardoning of the sins but also for the good of all Israel, by easing their hardship in exile and hastening the redemption: "Whoever performs *teshuvah* causes G-d to return [*Malchut*] to the sixth place [of the *sefirot,* i.e., *Tiferet*], and redemption depends on this; and that is why everything depends on *teshuvah,* for our early sages said (*Sanhedrin* 97b): all the predestined dates (for redemption) have passed, and the matter now depends only on repentance" (Ibid. 122a, *Raya Mehemna*).

23. Gershom Scholem, in his book *Major Trends in Jewish Mysticism* (p. 213), defines the two *sefirot* mentioned here as follows:
Malchut, the "Kingdom" of G-d, usually described in the *Zohar* as the *Knesset Yisrael,* the mystical archetype of Israel's community, or as the Shechinah. *Yesod,* the "basis" or "foundation" of all active forces in G-d.

Hence the penitent is not perceived merely as one who has turned back from sinning to the straight path, but as one who performs an outstanding metacosmic and eschatological deed.

The question of the penitent's position as compared with that of the tzaddik not only indicates the controversy over the religious status of the one against the other. This is the key point for the understanding of the chronological and ideological borderline between the moralist literature of the rabbinic-philosophic group that preceded the *Zohar*, and the repentance literature that sought to lean on Kabbalistic foundations in forming a different value perception of the act of repentance beginning with the *Zohar*. This is not the place to discuss the history of the repentance concept, beginning with the Book of the *Zohar* at the end of the thirteenth century and from there on, for space is too short. However it is right to emphasize one or two examples indicating a change of direction that occurred in the perception of *teshuvah* since the Book of the *Zohar*.

In the mystic-moralist work of the Maharal of Prague in the sixteenth century, the character of repentance is defined as a return to the order of the world in an outstandingly eschatological sense: "The principal meaning"—writes the Maharal—"is that repentance is a returning to G-d with all the heart and all the soul, and this is the order of the world; for this world harks back to G-d. It has no independent existence of its own, only it returns to G-d from Whom it draws its existence, and all things return to Him" (*Netivot Olam, Netiv HaTeshuvah*, Chap. II, p. 154).[24]

The emphasis, then, in these words of the Maharal is on *teshuvah* as a cosmic act according to which the act of repentance leads not only to the purification and cleansing of man's sins but to the overall perfection of creation and the redemption, in his words, of "the world order."

A few decades before these lines were written in Maharal's *Netivot Olam*, it was the Lurianic Kabbalistic literature (which apparently was not known to the Maharal) that had wanted to establish the intellectual roots of Kabbalistic literature, from the time of the *Zohar*, in a new garb. Rav Yitzchak Luria (known as *HaAri*) and his Kabbalistic circle in Safed claimed that it is the blemish that was fastened onto man following the first sin that is the point of departure for man's mission

---

24. *Yahadut* edition, Bnai Brak 5740.

on Earth. His entire purpose is to redeem the sparks imprisoned in the defiled *kelipot* (husks, or "bark" of the cosmic tree[25]) so as to hasten the redemption. The essence of man's repentance is in the work of "perfection." And not for nothing was the restoration of the worlds to their proper place left, according to *HaAri*'s teaching, to the time of the prayers for the Sabbath; and, in Lurianic Kabbalah, this was also the secret reason for the prohibition of going away beyond the Sabbath limits. For the Sabbath symbolizes the return to within the limits of holiness. From here man looks for his perfection in his prayer, "to restore the worlds to their true high place as at the beginning, and not to let them come down outside the Sabbath limit . . ."[26] But here already a new chapter opens.

25. See G. Scholem, *Major Trends,* p. 239.
26. Cf. Tishby, *Tales in Praise of the ARI* (Philadelphia 1970), re: man's purpose. The divine level of the holiness of the Sabbath according to the *Zohar* is in three *sefirot:* *Binah, Yesod* or *Tiferet,* and *Malchut* (*Zohar* Part I, 47b). The Sabbath symbolized in the *sefira Binah* is "The heavenly Sabbath" (Ibid.), and the Sabbath prayer as a whole is intended for the *sefira* of *Binah.* See *Mishnat HaZohar,* p. 492, and nn. 100–2.

Repentance in the Thought of Rav Yisrael Salanter and the Musar Movement

Dr. Mordechai Pachter

I

IT IS A distinction of Rav Yisrael Salanter's ethical teaching that it does not deal with the substance of ethics but rather with the conditions of its fulfillment and realization. Moral education, rather than the virtues and values of ethics, are the theoretical focus of the founder of the Musar movement. Therefore, his primary concern is the totality of factors and means—first and foremost, psychological factors and means—that are likely to facilitate improvement of character, and the practical attainment of ethical and religious values.[1]

This fact explains the two-sidedness of repentance in Rav Yisrael Salanter's teaching. On the one hand, repentance resembles the vast majority of ethical-religious virtues and values. That is, repentance, like them, belongs to the subject matter of ethics, and thus is not a topic of theoretical study for Rav Yisrael. Hence we shall search his writings in vain for a discussion of the nature and meaning of repentance. On the other hand, Rav Yisrael does not set it aside completely, as he does, for

---

1. See the introduction to my edition of *Kitve Rav Yisrael Salanter* (Jerusalem: Mosad Bialik, 5733) [hereafter *KRIS*], pp. 38–39. Cf. Etkes, *Rav Yisrael Salanter VeReshitah shel Tenuat HaMusar,* Jerusalem 5742), [hereafter Etkes], pp. 104–6; my review of the book *Rav Yisrael Salanter Behaara Chadasha* (*Tarbiz* 53), p. 641.

example, the love of G-d of the Commandment to cleave unto Him. In this respect, repentance resembles fear of G-d, especially fear of punishment, for which Rav Yisrael carves out a special niche in his thought.

For this reason, the following comment of Rav Yitzchak Blazer about fear of punishment as it contrasts with reverence-fear and love in his master's teaching can shed light on repentance as well:

> My master . . . of saintly memory, in his ethical path did not conduct himself with the great and marvelous, and did not lift up his words on elevated aspects of the ways to reverential fear and love of G-d. Rather he held to his saintly path, the way of holiness, in his many moral teachings, only through fear of punishment, for that is primary knowledge and the first step toward His worship, may His Name be blessed, to turn away from evil and to do good [cf. Psalm 34:15].[2]

Rav Blazer stresses here the minimalistic feature of punishment-fear. However, one should not ignore another feature that led Rav Yisrael to attribute great importance to this fear. I mean his conception of punishment-fear as the basis and the point of origin for moral education. Rav Yisrael esteemed punishment-fear because he recognized in it a powerful psychological potential, capable of deeply influencing man's moral formation.[3]

The characteristics that Rav Yisrael Salanter discerned in punishment-fear he found in repentance as well. Repentance too appeared to him as a fundamental medium for the ethical education of man. It is not accidental that repentance serves as the framework for most of Rav Yisrael's letters, just as it is not accidental that these letters were generally written during the annual season of penitence. Insofar as Rav Yisrael sought to exercise an educational influence on his correspondents, he chose to write them during the month of Elul or the ten days of penitence, thus utilizing the actual seasonal background as the relevant context for his reproof.

A typical example of this approach of Rav Yisrael Salanter is found in Letter 6 of *Or Yisrael,* the writings compiled by Rav Yitzchak Blazer.[4] This letter includes several basic themes of Rav Yisrael's sys-

---

2. *Shaarei Or, Sefer Or Yisrael* (Vilna 5660), 17b.
3. See *KRIS,* pp. 59–60; Cf. Etkes, pp. 110–111.
4. On these letters, see *KRIS,* pp. 66–67, 199.

tem. We do not know the year it was written,[5] but it was undoubtedly written during the ten days of penitence, which provide the circumstantial background for its writing and make repentance its thematic backdrop. Thus the second sentence inducts us into the atmosphere of the penitential season preceding Yom Kippur: "The *Mesillat Yesharim* is not before me now, so I will only write what has been said and repeated many times, that Yom Kippur, apart from the magnitude of its own commandments (a positive commandment with the potential penalty of *karet,* being cut off, etc.), is beneficial to man to save him from many severe troubles" (*KRIS,* p. 213). This sentence in effect determines the thematic setting of the letter, which after several paragraphs becomes explicit again: "And these ten days of penitence are days of activity to see how to improve our ways for the next year, may it come in peace" (Ibid. p. 215). In greater detail:

Also during the ten days of penitence it is in a man's power to become a different man, to be righteous in the next year, may it come in peace . . . Particularly in the ten days of penitence the primary element is to observe and scrutinize his ways and guard at least a small part of it according to his state and his fear, and by this he will be saved from the most severe part of that transgression as noted above (Ibid. p. 216).

This statement opens, in effect, the principal section of the letter, in which Rav Yisrael clarifies several central themes in his teaching. Of these one would stress in particular the issue of transparent and opaque powers in the soul,[6] the idea of lighter and graver mitzvot and transgressions connected to the problem of reward and punishment[7] and the combination of ethical study with the general ideal and framework of Torah study.[8] The elucidation of these problems concludes with a summary that relates these matters to repentance:

Thus the atonement of sin on Yom Kippur that depends on repentance, i.e., abandonment of the sin, is very grave[9] . . . and he will be considered a penitent *(baal teshuvah)* on the Yom Kippur that comes upon us for good at least in

5. See my comments on this letter in article cited *supra* n. 1, pp. 633, 648.
6. Ibid. pp. 216–17 and my discussion 39–40.
7. Ibid. pp. 220–21 and my discussion 58–59.
8. Ibid. pp. 216, 218–220 and my discussion 45–47; in greater detail Etkes, pp. 111–15.
9. I omit here an important section that will be quoted in full *infra* p. 329.

resolving to abandon the sin, i.e., the aspect of lightness. And for such, he who wishes to be pure G-d will help him to rise from level to level to fulfill Torah and mitsvot in the aspect of gravity as well, for the benefit of man—that is the ego, in his eternal world (*KRIS*, pp. 221–222).

With these words, Rav Yisrael ends his letter: As it begins with the matter of Yom Kippur and repentance, so it ends with that matter.

This general overview of the structure of the letter demonstrates that the problem of repentance serves not only as its framework but also as a central organizing motif. The circumstantial and structural aspects, however, merely reflect something more essential, which is expressed in the above quotation from Rav Yisrael Salanter. Note that of all his comments on repentance, Rav Yisrael sees fit to emphasize in particular the abandonment of sin. Of the three well-known building blocks of repentance—regret, abandonment of sin, and resolution for the future—he mentions only the latter two. But he underlines the second element, for his definition of repentance identifies it with abandonment of sin alone ("the atonement of sin on Yom Kippur, which depends on repentance, i.e., abandonment of the sin"). Even when he refers to resolution, he stresses this aspect ("at least in resolving to abandon the sin"). This recurs many times in the letters, for example, Letter 7:

Yom Kippur is a great boon, a day of forgiveness and atonement; there were no festive days for Israel like Yom Kippur (end of *Taanit* 26b). We have nothing better than it, if we would prepare properly to mend our ways, for Yom Kippur atones with repentance, i.e., abandonment of the sin. Nonetheless, even a bit is very good, priceless in the affairs of the world, to see at least that there be some resolution for the future on Yom Kippur (Ibid. p. 225).

Here Rav Yisrael speaks of an unspecified resolution for the future, but the end of the letter implies that he is referring to abandonment of the sin:

Whence the hope to reach some level regarding this transgression on Yom Kippur as a complete penitent, to resolve upon the abandonment of the sin, in the aspect of lightness before him, a genuine resolve, priceless in the greatness of its degree to benefit him in this world and the next (Ibid. p. 227).

Rav Yisrael Salanter emphasized the abandonment of sin as the main principle of repentance, as he formulates it explicitly in Letter 8: "How venerable are these matters during the ten days of penitence, to seek some degree of abandoning the sin, which is the leading element, the cornerstone" (Ibid. p. 230). Abandoning sin is in his opinion "the leading element, the cornerstone," because it is the beginning of a process of upheaval in man, which is indeed the basis of ethical education:

Let a man not be disheartened when he studies Musar and is not roused, and detects no imprint in his heart to change his way. Let him know faithfully that if the impression is not revealed to eyes of flesh, yet the eye of intellect sees. With the passage of time, and propagation of study, the hidden imprints are amassed, he turns into a different person; his lust is restrained so that it cannot burst out and sometimes is annulled (Ibid. p. 234).

Man's becoming a different personality is a long process, sometimes a hidden one, but it begins with the awakening of man to reformation that is repentance. In this manner, repentance is a point of departure for moral training and thus is similar, as we have noted, to the fear of punishment.

The resemblance to fear of punishment becomes even clearer when we attend to the nature of man's awakening to repentance. In his essay *Berurei HaMiddot*, Rav Yisrael Salanter addresses this problem[10]:

What is the principle that makes man capable of repentance? It is the feeling that he is a living being aware of his deficiency, and then there is hope that he will awaken to repentance. But if that feeling is absent, whence will repentance be born? To be sure this is only when the feeling is completely extinguished from his soul, until he does not respond to reproof or arousal by another, for then he is not under the category of repentant at all, since no one else has the power to awaken him from his senseless slumber (Ibid. p. 155).

Prompting to repentance is thus a distinctively emotional matter. It should be stressed that Rav Yisrael is speaking here about the arousal of the soul. In other words, we are dealing with the primary psychological means that should be exercised, in his view, in the study of Musar,

10. This is, incidentally, the only place in his essays where repentance is discussed.

because it has a lasting effect on the opaque powers in the human soul.[11] Inasmuch as awakening to repentance is primarily a matter of arousal, it has the psychological intensity that matches the psychological intensity that Rav Yisrael ascribed to fear of punishment. However, arousal to repentance is also like punishment-fear with respect to its emotional quality: "What is his remedy? It is the renewal of the feeling that arouses care and anguish so that he enters the category of repentant and shall live" (Ibid. p. 156). Care and anguish are the principal emotions that characterize arousal to repentance; they are clearly the primary components of punishment-fear.

Moreover, when fear of punishment itself takes on the form of dread, it becomes a central component of repentance. Rav Yisrael comments on dread with respect to the month of Elul, the month of repentance:

Once it was as I have known—every man was seized with shuddering from the voice announcing the month of Elul. This dread bore fruit to bring him closer to His worship, may His Name be blessed, each according to his degree (Ibid. p. 238).

This dread is apprehension of judgment and its outcome, i.e., punishment. Indeed, it is identical with fear of punishment, and Rav Yisrael often does not distinguish between them:

How must the heart of man tremble who loves himself and his family who depend upon him (though eyes of flesh see that some people seek the just without preparations and arousal to fear and Musar) to improve his ways, and at least to break his spirit with a broken heart, which is the basic element to protect him with respect to the great danger that hovers (Ibid. p. 234).

It should also be stressed that this passage deals with a dread concerning the most elementary matters pertaining to the individual and his family, and derives from self-love and domestic love. It belongs, therefore, to the most fundamental realm of affect, thus constituting, in the view of Rav Yisrael Salanter, a primary motivation in the process of repentance.

Here we encounter an additional common ground between punish-

---

11. See the full discussion of this, *KRIS,* pp. 43–46.

ment-fear and repentance, i.e., the minimalistic vantage point. We have seen this aspect of punishment-fear in the words of Rav Yitzchak Blazer cited above. Indeed, punishment-fear, insofar as it is the lowest rung on the ladder of religious values, represents the typical minimalism of Rav Yisrael Salanter's approach. To be sure, if we examine Rav Yisrael Salanter's statements on repentance, we shall recognize the aptness of Rav Yitzchak Blazer's formulation here as well. That is, even with regard to repentance, Rav Yisrael did not "conduct himself with the great and marvelous." Not only are the general metaphysical and theological meanings of repentance absolutely outside his range of concerns, but even the immanent dimensions of the subject, such as the different levels of repentance or the typology of repentance, did not engage him. He himself testifies, in one of his letters, to this effect. In that letter, he comments on his correspondent's question about "commensurate repentance" *(teshuvat hamishkal):* "About commensurate repentance I know nothing, [it is] damaging to health in this weak generation, and might, G-d forbid, lead to decrease in study of Torah, which is the main thing."[12] Clearly, he refrains from stating an opinion about one type of repentance and is satisfied to express his misgivings about possible deleterious consequences, because to say more would be "conducting oneself with great and marvelous things." This suspicion is consistent, of course, with the basic approach of minimalism.

In accordance with this approach, he focuses on the primary stages of the repentance process exclusively, and even then he stresses only the minimalistic features. Thus, we have seen that in the arousal to repentance, he highlighted only the elementary dread. With abandonment of sin, he raised the banner of abstention from sin, at least the lighter aspect ("he will be considered a penitent on the Yom Kippur that comes upon us for good at least in resolving to abandon the sin, i.e., the aspect of lightness." "Whence the hope to reach some level regarding this transgression on Yom Kippur as a complete penitent, to resolve upon the abandonment of the sin, in the aspect of lightness before him."). Together with these two concepts, which are basically passive in character, Rav Yisrael posits an additional stage of active character, that is the study of Musar in the house of

12. *Igrot uMichtavim,* ed. Rabbi Wilman (Brooklyn 5730), pp. 68–69.

Musar. It is instructive that this too is presented in a minimalistic light:

Let man not be negligent in preparing for Yom Kippur in the aspect of lightness, i.e., to involve himself during the ten days of penitence with matters of repentance at least according to the aspect of lightness: to go to the house of Musar at night when he is free of his business, to study Musar with enthusiasm almost every night, from which will be born some dim *(dunkele)* sense to receive the study of Musar heart and soul at least on the holy Sabbath [ancillary to the study of Talmud, as noted above]. And to run several times a week, at least a few minutes, in order not to eliminate the dim impression by the passage of time, as mentioned above, and to accustom himself to scrutinize his ways, to feel and to distinguish between the light and the heavy, so that at the very least Musar will help him to keep Torah and mitzvot according to the aspect of lightness (*KRIS*, p. 221).

The principal act of repentance is thus attendance at the house of Musar and the enthusiastic study of Musar. This act, which Rav Yisrael Salanter placed at the center of his educational program of ethical-religious reform of the generation and that became the hallmark of Musar movement activity, was grasped by him also as the core of repentance, at least in its initial stages and as a minimal demand. However, as noted, whatever goes beyond these initial stages and these minimum demands of the man awakening to repentance is already outside Rav Yisrael Salanter's scope of concern.

Despite this, one cannot remain oblivious to the fact that it is precisely the study of Musar as the main repentance-oriented activity that gives repentance the character of an ongoing process not limited to the month of Elul and the ten days of penitence. The fact that Rav Yisrael focused on this period of the year derived from his wish to concentrate on the beginning of the repentance process. However, it is clear that he regarded the month of Elul and the ten days of penitence as a paradigm for the entire year, and repentance as a framework for the continuing process of ethical and religious improvement over the year—nay, over the human being's lifetime. Thus, the crucial difference between repentance and the fear of punishment comes to the fore. To be sure, punishment-fear too must accompany man through life, but fundamentally it is only one, albeit important, psychological motive. By contrast, repentance is a totality in which the fear of punishment also finds its place, as we have seen. When repentance is presented as a Musar study in the house of Musar, it becomes the general framework of man's ethical training. From this perspective, it is possible to view the Musar movement, founded by Rav Yisrael Salanter to bring about religious-ethical renewal, as a repentance movement in the broad sense of the term. Indeed, many of the practices of this movement gave it the character of a repentance movement.[13] Nonetheless, it is important to note that, with regard to repentance, Rav Yisrael did not originally intend only a movement. He viewed repentance as universally relevant. Insofar as every person needs ethical education and improvement, all, of necessity, stand in need of repentance. Thus, repentance becomes, for Rav Yisrael Salanter, one of the foundations and necessary conditions of religious life.

Thus, as a principle without which religious life is impossible, repentance resembles not only fear of punishment but belief in reward and punishment. Hence what we said of the resemblance and connections between repentance and fear of punishment is also appropriate to its relation to belief in reward and punishment. In truth, belief in reward and punishment, fear of punishment, and repentance are bound indissolubly to one another in Rav Yisrael Salanter's thought. Together they afford the firm foundation of religious life. Belief in reward and punishment is a fundamental belief, on which everything, according to Rav Yisrael Salanter, rests, out of which everything branches, from which everything must begin. Fear of punishment is the religious-ethical feeling that derives from belief in reward and punishment, and that motivates appropriately ethical-religious activity. Repentance is that religious-ethical activity which includes as a matter of course both the fundamental belief in reward and punishment and the fundamental feeling of punishment-fear.

In summary, Rav Yisrael Salanter discusses repentance in a fairly narrow focus. Its metaphysical presuppositions and general theological significance concerned him not at all. For example, he never thought of raising the metaphysical problem of the possibility of repentance, while he never thought of doubting its psychological possibility. The

13. See *KRIS*, pp. 61–62.

focus of his discussion is indeed repentance as a psychological conversion. But he did not see this conversion as a sudden, onetime revolution, overturning in one fell swoop structures of soul and ways of the spirit, but rather as a continuing process, identical, in effect, with the process of ethical training. Rav Yisrael was aware of the fact that the process is not an easy one. The man who takes part in it is called to a hard, perpetual conflict with himself, and to strenuous work on himself. Therefore Rav Yisrael's counsel is not to "conduct oneself with great and marvelous things." Like any educational activity, so too ethical education is an antlike labor, whose fruits ripen slowly after a prolonged time. It can also be compared to a building, requiring firm foundations if it is to stand and then the placing of brick on top of brick, without shortcuts. The three foundations upon which the educational structure stands are belief in reward and punishment, fear of punishment, and repentance. While the first two are essentially cornerstones, repentance is both a cornerstone and the central pillar without which the building is liable to collapse.

II

Rav Yisrael Salanter's first two generations of disciples, primarily the school of Chelm in its various branches, broke out of the constricted framework allotted by their master for ethical discussion. They extended it beyond the narrow psychological range and were not averse to general metaphysical and theological studies,[14] as is evident with respect to repentance as well. This stands out most clearly in the schools of Telz and Slobodka, as formulated by Rav Yosef Yehuda Leib Bloch and Rav Natan Zevi Finkel. Their views of repentance stand, each from his own unique perspective, poles apart from those of Rav Yisrael Salanter.

While Rav Yisrael Salanter focuses completely on the human-psychological aspect of repentance, Rav Yosef Leib Bloch disregards this perspective almost completely. He deals with repentance specifically from the metaphysical point of view. His central question is the very

14. I discuss these intellectual developments at length in my forthcoming essay *Hitpattechutah HaRaayonit shel Tenuat HaMusar BiShnei Hebbeteha: Tefisat HaAdam VeHaYachas LaKabbalah.*

possibility of repentance, not because it involves a complicated, intricate psychological process, but because the phenomenon of repentance categorically departs from the laws of nature. Rav Bloch's basic assumption, upon which all his studies of repentance rely, is that repentance is a metaphysical entity that cannot be explained through the laws of nature and its concepts. In order to underscore this basic assumption, however, Rav Bloch finds it necessary to introduce the notion that repentance in its metaphysical essence does not differ, at first blush, from all created nature, inasmuch as the latter is also, in the final analysis, metaphysical in essence. As such, nature too in its generality and in its details is not fully comprehensible to us:

Thus the entire mystery of Creation is wondrous and closed to us so that we do not understand it, and every small detail of natural matters is concealed from us, its entire being, becoming and development are hidden and obscured from us . . . We only see the wondrous reality as it is. Why then should we be astonished when we see the subject of repentance and know not its essence or its mode of action.[15]

Moreover, from this point of view, repentance is not different from the other commandments:

Do we know in general regarding all the mitzvot, when a man performs them, how they work their action on the human soul to cleanse it and elevate it? Do we apprehend the power that raises the soul of man by donning tefillin or *tzitzit* and the like? Do we understand what is the slime and filth that cling to the human soul when he transgresses the commandments of G-d that are not to be done and becomes guilty? Why then should we wonder that the soul is purified by repentance from the slime of sin? Just as the soul can be sullied by sin, it can be cleansed by repentance (Ibid. p. 188).

Thus, just as creation as a whole is a phenomenon incomprehensible to the human intellect, and as the essence of the commandments and their mode of action are beyond rational attainment, so too with regard to repentance.

In truth, however, this similarity between repentance and nature or the commandments in general is only apparent, for the metaphysical

15. *Shiure Daat,* I (Cleveland 5724), pp. 187–88.

character of repentance differs absolutely from that of nature and the commandments. Though nature as a whole has a radically metaphysical essence that renders human reason unable to understand it completely, it is nonetheless a coherent pattern determined by definite laws that cover its details:

So too all matters of creation were ordered according to set laws and known arrangements, and the reality of each creature and its action was determined by the law of nature, and what was not determined by the law of nature has no place for being (Ibid. p. 189).

Likewise the mitzvot in general. Moreover, the network of commandments is intertwined within the network of natural laws so that they are correlated to one another:

They were arranged in the pattern of creation according to the set laws, and the law of nature determines the reward for each commandment and punishment for a transgression (Ibid.).

Not so with respect to repentance. This was understood, according to Rav Bloch, by the rabbis, for "Our sages o.b.m. whose power was to G-d and who knew the laws of nature and all its secrets and mysteries, according to the depth of their knowledge recognized that repentance is opposed to the order of creation and its laws" (Ibid. p. 188). This is the meaning of their assertion that repentance is one of the things created before the creation of the world, "for in the creation of the world repentance was not found at all, and it is higher than creation" (Ibid. p. 131). Thus repentance differs from the other commandments. It is not correlated to the laws of nature, because it is above and beyond the laws of nature. The action of repentance corresponds to a divine law that is higher than the laws of nature. Basing himself on Rav Moshe Cordovero's *Tomer Devora,* which states that G-d Himself mends the sins of man, Rav Bloch sums up the whole matters as follows:

It would appear that we cannot understand how repentance is more in G-d's hands than other things, for everything is in the hand of G-d! But this is as we have explained that all the matters of creation were arranged according to known orders and set laws and he arranged for each matter that which necessitates its existence and the powers appointed to influence it. But repentance is not part of the order of creation and there is no power appointed over it in the constant pattern of creation, except that when man repents, G-d brings into existence the factors of atonement, and these are the superior washing waters that purify man's soul from its filth, and therefore it is as if G-d Himself without any agent washes and cleans man of his sin (Ibid.).

We learn, then, that through repentance the penitent diverges from the network of natural law and becomes integrated into the pattern of direct relations with the Divinity. All this because repentance is a divine matter.

Rav Bloch illuminates the total divergence of repentance from all matters relating to creation and the other commandments from another angle. We have already noted that both creation and the commandments are not fully comprehended by human reason. Nevertheless, Rav Bloch sees fit to stress that they are not beyond human apprehension. He refers to two principal means for knowing creation and its mysteries: wisdom and prophecy. These are two modes of cognition through which man may attain knowledge even of the roots of creation and the mitzvot. Through wisdom man is elevated from knowledge of the terrestrial world to its superior supernatural roots; through prophecy the roots of creation are revealed to him and he derives the emanation of all created matters from above to below (Ibid. p. 192). Now repentance differs so sharply from creation and mitzvot that the two aforementioned means of cognition fail to yield its root: "For through the knowledge of created reality by these two means—wisdom and prophecy—it is impossible to discover the root of repentance, for its root is not of creation" (Ibid.). Repentance is, therefore, absolutely transcendent. Its appearance in our world signifies the direct intervention of G-d in the process of creation.

This intervention is not merely the irruption of the transcendent into the ordinary process of nature, but also a kind of anticipation of the perfected eschatological creation. The fact that repentance does not belong in any way to the lawful regularity of creation testifies, according to Rav Bloch, to the deficiency of creation. As in the present state of affairs creation is flawed, one cannot locate repentance among its laws. Repentance belongs to the perfected pattern of laws pertaining to an ideal reality that precedes creation and that will be realized in the mended world of the future:

Now this creation that was created with these limits in which no place was given to repentance is this one that was created for six thousand years, i.e., the six days of Creation; but the seventh day that is the seventh millennium, there will be a new heaven and a new earth and creation will be perfect according to His will may He be blessed . . . And it will be in a state of ultimate good . . . This future creation can be called "G-d's thought" for it only arose in His Mind to create but its governance has yet to enter our world (Ibid. pp. 193–94).

Against this background, one may naturally ask, How then can we explain the existence of repentance in our flawed world? Rav Bloch's answer to this question is clear and unambiguous. The very existence of repentance in our flawed world is a manifest expression of divine loving-kindness *(chesed)*: "Our words imply that the matter of repentance is higher than all the roots of creation and by G-d's *chesed* he ordained for us the ways of repentance when we turn to Him wholeheartedly and abandon our evil deeds" (Ibid. p. 195). Repentance is thus a manifest act of divine *chesed*. [16]

This fact underlines again the essential difference between Rav Bloch's conception of repentance and the way it was grasped by Rav Yisrael Salanter. While the latter focused exclusively on the psychological processes of repentance, i.e., repentance as a human act, the former focuses on the theological aspect. It should be noted, however, that he too cannot remain oblivious to the human aspect. And when he finally does get around to discussing this issue, we discover some closeness between his approach and that of Rav Yisrael Salanter. Precisely because he lays such emphasis on the transcendent character of repentance, he cannot avoid confronting the question about the human possibility of repentance. Willy-nilly, he states that "it is hard work for man and requires enormous valor in order to reach the level of true repentance where he can call to witness the Knower of hidden things that he will not return to folly again" (Ibid. p. 195). In truth it appears that Rav Bloch maintained that this level

16. See Ibid. p. 193: "G-d ordained that He Himself removes the sin and washes Himself the slime and filth of the sinful act."

of genuine repentance cannot be achieved in our world. Therefore he chose to indicate a lower level of repentance that can be attained in this world, insofar as it too exists within the order of nature rather than above and beyond it:

However, while man has not attained true repentance, it is still possible for him at least to arouse G-d's mercy and stay his judgment for a time, so that he will not be lost, Heaven forfend, because of his sin. And this measure is apparently not above creation but within the order of creation was devised this quality of mercy (Ibid.).

It is probable, then, that there exists a level of repentance that, like other commandments, is correlated with the order of nature. The rabbis called this kind of repentance a bribe that G-d receives, in their words, in this world but not in the next.[17] Rav Bloch here finds support for his argument:

Meaning that this is not the perfect repentance in which the soul indeed washes itself of sin and becomes purified. . . . And this repentance, together with the good deeds that they perform to sanctify His Name, may it be blessed, are the bribe that G-d receives in this world according to the order of this world and its laws (Ibid. p. 196).

He speaks here of repentance that does not alter the order of the world, arousing rather the quality of mercy and thus successfully staying the judgment.[18] This repentance answers to the criterion of minimalism, thus revealing his closeness to Rav Yisrael Salanter. The fact that man is incapable of scaling the heights of perfect repentance

17. See *Yalkut Shimoni*, Vol. II, p. 670.
18. It is not impossible that the Kabbalistic distinction between "higher repentance" and "lower repentance" serves as background to Rav Bloch's distinction between supernatural repentance and the repentance that is embedded in the order of creation. The higher repentance is inherent in the *sefira* of *Binah*, which is above the seven *sefirot* of "world construction," and thus symbolizes the world to come; while the lower is realized in the *sefira* of *Malchut*, which symbolizes the lawfulness of creation (see I. Tishby *Mishnat HaZohar*, II (Jerusalem 5721), pp. 738–39). On the general relationship of Rav Bloch's views to the conceptual universe of Kabbalah, see my essay *supra* n. 14.

need not bring him to despair. He need not begin immediately with big thoughts. He ought to begin with fundamental things:

But how will man arouse the mercy of G-d upon him when he has not returned with full repentance before Him? At the least he must demonstrate that he wishes to improve his actions and to mend his ways, and he must strive, at the least, to be more careful than he had been accustomed to conduct his business honestly, to guard his tongue, to scrutinize all his actions until little by little he may attain the level of repentance, and primarily he must demonstrate his will that the name of heaven be sanctified and magnified . . . For if man lacks the aspiration to sanctify His Name, may it be blessed, and is not aroused to magnify and to elevate it in the world, he is distant from G-d and how then can his prayer reach to arouse His mercy to have compassion for him against the quality of judgment? (Ibid. pp. 195–96).

The style is that of Rav Yisrael Salanter's minimalistic demand, though the emphasis is not where the founder of the Musar movement placed it, i.e., on such matters as fear of punishment or the study of Musar. Another aspect of the similarity between the approaches of Rav Yosef Bloch and Rav Yisrael Salanter becomes apparent here, and that is the grasp of Musar as an ongoing process. Like Rav Yisrael Salanter before him, Rav Bloch too regards repentance as an ongoing process, because he starts out from a minimalist point of departure.

However, in all that relates to the process of repentance, Rav Bloch's approach diverges from his predecessor's. As we have seen, the process for Rav Yisrael Salanter is primarily educational. It is characterized through and through by a Salanterian minimalism that renders it somewhat static in nature, for it is a process that repeats itself annually. This is not the case for Rav Bloch. His language implies clearly that the process is developmental. The metaphysical, metahistorical dimension of repentance is responsible for this character. The penitent begins, to be sure, at the minimum level, but he need not necessarily remain at that level, or to repeat it year after year. The way of repentance is a rising path from the lower stage to the hoped-for goal of perfect repentance that is above creation and beyond history. He who goes up that pathway finds open before him the possibility of scaling the supreme religious heights, that mankind and creation must aspire to attain, for these are the levels of perfect creation, of the future world. Therefore, repentance contains within it not only the entire life of man, but the whole of human history, which appears to be the history of repentance activated by divine *chesed.* [19]

The recognition of divine *chesed* is also fundamental to Rav Finkel's conception of repentance. From this perspective, he represents a position very close to that of Rav Bloch, but completely different from that of Rav Yisrael Salanter. The polar contrast with the approach of Rav Yisrael Salanter is already revealed in the point of departure for Rav Finkel's discussion of repentance:

Man must reach repentance not by acknowledging punishment and suffering that G-d brings upon him, but by recognizing the many kindnesses *(chasadim)* that G-d bestows upon His creatures. Moreover, the *chesed* of repentance itself, that G-d accepts those who return to Him after they have sinned before Him, suffices to bring man, through his awareness of this *chesed* alone, to repentance. [20]

Rav Finkel here explicitly opposes the approach of Rav Yisrael Salanter, which posits dread and fear of punishment as the principal factors in arousal to repentance. By contrast and in their place, he presents the recognition of divine *chesed.* This stance is connected, of course, with the "Sage of Slobodka's" basic conception of the movement of *chesed* inherent in creation. [21] Note well: The Slobodka concept of repentance, like that of Rav Bloch, is not limited to the four cubits of human psychology, but extends into the wide realms of metaphysics and philosophy of history. Indeed, we discover here the salient points of contact between the two approaches. Like Rav

19. One should note that Rav Bloch's conception of repentance as enfolding all history, consequently all creation, is similar to Rav Kook's idea of repentance. This is not the only area where a resemblance between the concepts of the two men can be discerned; apparently they drew on common influences. This matter requires detailed investigation beyond the scope of this study.

20. *Or HaTzafun*, Vol. II (Jerusalem 5728), p. 28.

21. See on this extensively D. Katz, *Tenuat HaMusar*, Vol. III (Tel Aviv 5716), pp. 119–207.

Bloch, so too Rav Finkel stresses that repentance is not grasped by human logic. In fact, it is opposed to logic:

According to logic there is no place for repentance, for since man is impervious to his Creator and follows his arbitrary will and corrupts his ways, is it reasonable that it shall be overlooked and that his iniquities and sins be wiped away? (*Or HaTzafun*, p. 28).

Moreover, basing himself on the same rabbinic statement, Rav Finkel, like Rav Bloch, insists that the logic of wisdom and that of prophecy together is inadequate to the concept of repentance (Ibid.). From this point, however, their ways diverge, as Rav Finkel draws a different conclusion from these assumptions than does Rav Bloch. If the latter's conclusion is that repentance absolutely transcends nature and its laws, then the former's inference is that repentance stands as the foundation of nature:

Moreover G-d has set repentance at the foundation of creation, as the rabbis say that repentance was created before the world was created (see *Pesachim* 54) ... So far does G-d's *chesed* extend Who created the world from the first on condition that His creatures who sin before Him be granted the opportunity to return to Him and to be purified before Him (Ibid. pp. 28–29).

This statement, that repentance is set at the foundation of nature and is integrated into its regular laws, is consistent with his general view that the regularity of creation is nothing but the clear expression and reflection of divine *chesed*.

Based on these assumptions, Rav Finkel reaches what might be regarded as the major theme of his concept of repentance, its definition as a species of delight. This definition is anchored in the metaphysical view that the form of all creation is holiness, and that its essence is delight. This is demonstrated by reference to the Sabbath:

For on Sabbath the form of all creation is completed ... And what is the form that was bestowed upon the Sabbath day? Holiness ... We find, therefore, that the form of creation as a whole is holiness. How does the holiness of Sabbath express itself? In delight *(oneg)* ... Thus it is revealed to us that the essence of holiness is delight and we discover that the form of all creation is delight and refinement (Ibid. p. 122).

The Sage of Slobodka now draws an inference to repentance, pre-cisely by accenting the fact that Sabbath is principally manifested in corporeal pleasures:

Thus the sanctity of Sabbath infiltrates also the corporeal pleasures until they too become holy and it is impossible to sanctify the Sabbath without them. We find that all creation, which is holy, cannot express itself but through corporeal pleasures. Hence repentance too does not come about but through corporeal pleasures, for the essence of repentance is to mend the defect by which he has impaired holiness, and if holiness is delight, then the defect in holiness is the absence of delight and cannot be mended unless through the completion of the delight, that is, by corporeal pleasures (Ibid. 123).

No doubt this is an interesting, surprising line of argument, and it seems that Rav Finkel knows it. Therefore he saw fit to support it as well as to qualify it from a certain perspective.

First of all he finds support from the acts of Ezra, who, one would expect, was to teach the people

to mourn and sorrow over the sins and to fast and mortify themselves over them. But behold we see the opposite: When Rosh Hashanah arrived, the first day of judgment of the ten penitential days, Ezra said to the people; "Do not mourn and do not cry . . . Go eat the fat and drink the sweet . . . for the day is holy to our Lord" (Nehemiah 8). Thus it is precisely through pleasure, and corporeal pleasure, such as eating the fat and drinking the sweet, that one is to attain repentance (Ibid. p. 124).

He brings support from Yom Kippur itself, whose sanctity is to be enhanced by "utilizing corporeal refinements and distinctions, such as clean raiment, and thus to become purified and distinguished and come to repentance and holiness" (Ibid.). Moreover, relying on the rabbinic statement that urges people to eat and drink on Yom Kippur Eve, he concludes:

The principal form of pleasure is delight, and by preceding the day before to take pleasure in eating and drinking, he has complemented the fast and it is considered as if he had fasted on the ninth day as well and augmented the holiness (Ibid.).

In a word, the major theme of Yom Kippur is not the fast but the delight, the delight of holiness, which is the delight of repentance.

Nonetheless, it seems that Rav Finkel himself recoils from the full implications of his words, therefore he saw fit to point to man's capacity to elevate corporeal matters to the status of holiness. In addition, he also asserted that in reality creation does not contain corporeal values, insofar as it is, from beginning to end, spiritual (Ibid. pp. 124–25). Thus, he sought to qualify his statements about corporeal pleasures and to clarify that he should not be understood superficially; when he speaks of physical pleasures in the context of holiness, he truly intends to refer to spiritual matters. Along these lines, he can summarize the entire discussion thus:

Thus we may understand that on the Sabbath day, or on other holy days or the days of awe, which are days of rest and holiness, all corporeal pleasures are raised to the spiritual, and man is elevated by them to supreme spiritual levels and achieves insight into the form of creation and the superior recognition • that is repentance (Ibid. p. 125).

Hence we learn that the delight of repentance is the spiritual delight of a superior consciousness, which is no less than knowledge of the form of creation that is itself identical with delight.

How opposed this conception is to that of the founder of the Musar movement can be demonstrated precisely from Rav Finkel's attempt to locate the common denominator uniting his approach to repentance with those akin to Rav Yisrael Salanter's. I refer to his proposed interpretation of views that contradict his, such as that of Rav Asher (Rosh) "in whose opinion repentance comes from fasting and mortification, not through delight" (Ibid. p. 126), or that of Rav Jonah of Gerona who founds repentance on anguish (Ibid.). Now, according to the Sage of Slobodka's reading of these views, the main thing in fasting and mortification for the sake of repentance is precisely the delight. Without the sense of delight in the supreme recognition of repentance, the anguish, the fasts, the mortifications, lose their meaning—nay, they even add a blemish:

This is the aspect of anguish that derives from purity of soul and spirit as mentioned by Rav Jonah of Gerona, not that he should aggrieve himself, but that he should mold for himself a different form of pleasures that derive from the soul's anguish. Whoever does not attain such a level to imitate his Creator, to make of the punishments with which he afflicts himself in order to mend his sins, delight and refinements, and he suffers from his mortifications real aggravation, not only has he no repentance but he has removed himself from it to the utmost distance, for repentance is pleasure and refinement and the absence of pleasure is sin (Ibid. p. 127).

In summary, pleasure is the inner essence of repentance. Hence it is the criterion by which all the actions and passions connected with repentance are tested. Indeed, Rav Finkel weighs by this standard the various modes of repentance and reaches the conclusion:

That the way of repentance by suffering is only for fools and Gentiles. But for Israel this is not the way to lead them to repentance, for they were given the Torah from which they can learn of the beneficent qualities of G-d and His manifold mercies, and primarily His great *chesed* in the very acceptance of repentance, as said above, and from this awareness they are to attain perfect repentance (Ibid. p. 31).

Thus, according to the Sage of Slobodka, the Torah both teaches and reflects the *chesed* movement of all existence, and whoever attains knowledge of this lawful regularity of creation will reach, of necessity, a repentance that is pleasure and refinement, not one that is rooted in fasts, mortification and anguish.

III

The two conceptions of repentance discussed in the last section, though they both crystallized within the Musar movement, are totally opposed to the concept of repentance of Rav Yisrael Salanter. They even attest to ideological developments within the movement that extended beyond the intellectual borders set down by its founder. The Musar movement, however, knew another path of development that can be viewed as a consistent continuation of the Salanterian mode of thought. I refer to the Musar approach of Rav Yosef Yosl Hurwitz, the Sage of Novaradok. This is evident in his conception of repentance as well. We are entitled to regard it not only as continuous with that of

his master Rav Yisrael Salanter, but as its extreme, inexorable elaboration, antithetical to views of the sort developed by Rav Bloch and Rav
Finkel. Moreover, precisely because he draws the ultimate inferences
from some of Rav Yisrael Salanter's theses, Rav Hurwitz's concepts
may clarify them more fully. Thus, for example, he offers an explicit
formulation of a reason for abstaining from any discussion of the
general metaphysical and theological aspects of repentance, a reason
one might assume to be Rav Yisrael Salanter's too, although the latter
never stated it overtly. Rav Yosef Hurwitz, like Rav Yisrael Salanter,
raises no doubt about the possibility of repentance, whether from the
metaphysical or psychological points of view. This question does not
come up for him at all, and the reason is simple: The laws of repentance
are stated in the Torah. He presents this reason precisely in connection
with a matter where the laws of repentance could engender difficulties
and doubts, namely the law of instantaneous repentance:

Thus one can explicitly consider the law of instantaneous repentance, and if
the law is so, presumably reality is so, for if it were impossible, the law of
repentance could never be imagined, for how could one imagine a law without
reality? The law is repentance and repentance is the law.[22]

Therefore, since the law of repentance exists in the Torah, all the
metaphysical problems connected with repentance become irrelevant.
Hence the remaining task, in addition to the proper clarification of the
laws governing repentance, is to describe, on the basis of the laws, the
psychological processes of repentance. Note that in the realm of psychology of repentance as well the question of possibility has no significance. Our work is merely descriptive. We must describe the
psychological reality of repentance as is, i.e., as it is shaped by halacha.

As noted above, these were almost certainly the considerations that
led Rav Yisrael Salanter to confine himself to the realm of psychological
processes pertinent to repentance. But it is only in the writings of Rav
Yosef Yosl Hurwitz that they come to open expression. It appears that
the Sage of Novaradok was impelled to this expression because his
description of the psychological process of repentance is quite extreme.
Like his master Rav Yisrael Salanter, he insists on the spiritual conver-

22. *Madregat HaAdam* (Jerusalem 5730), p. 151.

sion in repentance. But unlike his master, he does not view this conversion as an ongoing process, but rather as a sudden revolutionary turning:

If we consider the matter well, we observe that this is true in reality as well, that in reality a man can transform himself in one moment, and it is not that this capacity is a special quality in man, so that this capacity cannot be employed except by the most pious of the pious; rather it is necessary for every man, for if he cannot transform himself in one moment, he will not transform himself forever (*Madregat HaAdam,* p. 151).

The demand for a total spiritual revolution knows no compromise. For Rav Hurwitz, repentance and compromise are a contradiction in terms:

For he who leaps from sin to commandment without repentance, he composes in his mind the compromises, and since he has compromise in mind, how can he come to repentance? For compromise is the opposite of repentance, for what repentance uproots, compromise composes, and if he considers compromise his doctrine *(torah),* why should he repent?[23]

The penitent must pull out from the root his entire past, a complete extraction without room for compromise. Therefore the Sage of Novaradok stresses so much the suddenness of repentance, by contrast with any concept of repentance as an ongoing process. Hence he again sees fit to emphasize in this connection that this is the law of repentance, and therefore that reality must be so as well:

For in reality a man who comes to dwell beneath the wings of the Torah can emerge in a moment from darkness to great light, and were this not so, one could not imagine the law of repentance, for it is the law that in a moment he is a penitent, and if that is the law, then so too is the reality (Ibid. p. 156).

The total spiritual revolution that knows no compromise and takes place instantaneously is, according to the viewpoint of the Sage of Novaradok, perfect repentance—in other words, repentance enfolds all

23. Ibid. p. 173; cf. p. 155.

aspects of human life; in Rav Yosef Yosl's words, "the outward and the inward":

Indeed if we study all the ways of deficiency and nature, and the ways of repentance and perfection, we find that the deficiency is a double deficiency and the repentance is a double repentance, meaning: In each deficiency there is the deficient place and the deficient man, and for each repentance there is a return from the place of sin and return from the sin itself, and these are the outward and the inward (Ibid).

Thus, when the Sage of Novaradok speaks of repentance, his reference is to repentance under the outward and inward aspects at once. He describes the occurrence of repentance under both its aspects:

For some are able to go out and breach, broadly and deeply, the barrier of nature, and the separating curtain of the old habits, so that in one hour he has emerged from darkness to great light, and has become a different man both outwardly and inwardly, so that all the emotions and impressions that were woven upon his heart were effaced from reality and became as if they had never been at all, and as his heart had been fastened and bound to the transgression, so it shall be turned in one hour to be bound and fastened to G-d (Ibid., p. 157).

This description becomes forthwith a normative demand upon every man who seeks to repent:

We find that the man who genuinely wills to repent must consent to two things: the outward perfection and that is to forsake the place of the transgression, and the inward perfection, which is to right himself so that he should have no irrelevant preoccupation other than the love of truth alone. The external he can forsake immediately and this is necessary; and to the inwardness he must consent, and seek completion in all his matters, and thus complete all the matters of repentance (Ibid. pp. 161–62).

Note that while the description of repentance emphasizes the sudden aspect of repentance, the normative formulation lacks this aspect completely. Moreover, it even implies the possibility of treating repentance as an ongoing process, and in any event, as a transition from a lower stage of repentance to a higher one. But this should not be seen as a contradiction to the previous description of repentance, or even as a deviation from it. To understand this correctly, we must first attend to two phrases in the citation that call for analysis: "love of truth" and "must consent."

The delineation of the inward aspect of repentance as a repentance out of love of truth, leads naturally to Rav Yosef Yosl's distinction elsewhere between repentance out of fear, primarily fear of punishment, and repentance out of love. The former repentance is not, in his opinion, genuine repentance:

It is not so if he repented out of fear, that is fear of punishment, that he repents not because he recognizes the truth with an intellectual awareness and out of love for truth, but the punishment impels him to repent, and were the fear of the punishment to pass from him, he would not have repented the sin (Ibid. p. 164).

This implies clearly that only repentance because man "recognizes the truth with an intellectual awareness and out of love for truth" is genuine repentance. That is repentance out of love: "at the time that he repents out of love for the truth his primary desire is to uproot his thoughts from where they were" (Ibid.). We infer that the earlier depictions of repentance in fact revolve around repentance out of love, which includes the two aspects of repentance, the outer and the inner. Moreover, although he speaks here of love, Rav Hurwitz's concept of repentance carries no emotional weight. Unlike his master, Rav Yisrael Salanter, he does not speak of an element of emotional affect in repentance, but rather of the intellectual, conscious element. Not that love in this context is not the love of G-d, but the love of truth. The second phrase—"must consent"—supports this interpretation. It hints at what Rav Yosef Yosl elsewhere defines as the core of repentance, that is consent:

So too with regard to repentance, all depends on consent. For immediately he consents to a new way there is no need for more, for the consent will illuminate his way, discriminate the evil and choose for him the good, and he must only strengthen and encourage his consent and decision, and from there on the new way begins for him, and his thought and speech and actions are transformed, and all his movements, whether external or internal (Ibid. p. 165).

Thus, the total spiritual conversion, sharp and conclusive, that at once transforms a man into a completely different man, derives, according to the sage of Novaradok, from the conscious decision of man. In sum, that decision that Rav Hurwitz calls consent based on recognition and love of truth, can be regarded as the main theme of repentance.

Now, through the distinction between what he calls strong consent and what he calls consent that is not strong, we can understand more clearly the implications of Rav Hurwitz's instruction to the man who seeks to repent genuinely. It seems that the description of repentance so far corresponds fully with the description of what he calls strong consent, which I consider the most inclusive and incisive description of repentance in the teaching of Novaradok. It is worthy of full citation:

Man may consent so strongly that he acquires his world in one hour, totally, comprehensively transformed, both from the place of transgression and in the mending of character, and the consent affects him so intensely that he can stand on the right way immediately . . . For he stands so strong that he can utilize all his qualities in a timely manner, as the Torah demands of him, because he desires only the Will of G-d, and he is in the hands of the Torah like clay in the potter's hand, that whatever he must he is able to do and will never stumble in calculations, whether these be calculations that abridge the way of the Torah or calculations through which he would exceed on his own the way of the Torah: He does not need any of this, because he has no self-interest but is rather ready, like the angel, to choose whatever the Torah chooses for him, without questioning what is written in it, for whatever shall be found of the good he accepts immediately and whatever he senses to be of the evil he forsakes immediately, without any argument or discrimination, for he has perfected all the portions that man must perfect in all features, and will not deviate from them even a hair's breadth and all the gales in the world shall not budge him from his place (Ibid. p. 166).

This strong consent, which transforms man completely, so that from here on he is absolutely committed to the Torah to the point of self-abrogation before it, this is perfect repentance.

However, the Sage of Novaradok was aware that perfect repentance, while desirable, is not always prevalent, for not every man can attain so intense a consent. If he has not, this does not mean that the path of repentance is blocked to him. Such an individual

must go forth to consent only to the outward, to forsake the source of the transgression, and this is in his hand, but his inwardness he cannot complete at once . . . That is because his consent does not transform nature, to be affected by G-d's Will only, but rather there are in him many sorts of effect that wholly contradict the true way, each one of which is liable to sweep him away, and therefore he must go to the other extreme of effect, to educate his nature not to be affected by the corruption of the varieties of illusory effect (Ibid. pp. 166–67).

In these words, we hear a recognizable Salanterian note. Repentance is a process, if you will, in moral education. However, between the lines of the Sage of Novaradok, one gets the impression that he did not consider this process as *echt* repentance, but rather as a merely educative process of moral improvement, the importance of which is neither to be doubted nor to be equated with that of repentance. The theme of consent here points to resemblance, perhaps more than resemblance, to repentance, but insofar as the consent extends only to the outward, it clearly is not perfect repentance. In keeping with the extreme uncompromising approach of Rav Yosef Yosl Hurwitz, the Sage of Novaradok, incomplete repentance is not repentance.

Our survey has advanced several outlooks on repentance that found expression in the literature of the Musar movement. We noted the differences, even the inconsistencies, among them. However, we must end by stressing that differences and discrepancies are not necessarily contradictions. The different views do not contradict one another, because they illuminate the phenomenon of repentance from different angles; hence they are perfectly capable of coexistence. This is attested by various attempts at synthesis between these views in the later development of ideas within the Musar movement. The most impressive and important of these attempts, in my judgment, is the doctrine of repentance of Rav Eliyahu Dessler, as formulated in the four volumes of *Michtav MeEliyahu.* But Rav Dessler's theory is a separate matter, as is his concept of repentance.

Repentance in
Twentieth-Century
Jewish Thought

Professor Eliezer Schweid

1.

RAV AVRAHAM YITZCHAK Kook, as a Torah thinker confronting the problems of his time, allotted repentance a central place in his teaching. Repentance as a personal and national spiritual process, even as a cosmic process, is the key to the uniqueness of his ontological, historical, and psychological outlook. It is also the key to understanding his complex, daring attitude to the great problems that arose in contemporary Jewish history: assimilation and denial, secularization, political nationalism, and negation of exile in its secularist meaning, and the tragic breaches that all these engendered in our people, between religious and religious, between religious and freethinkers, and among the freethinkers themselves. Rav Kook defined all of these phenomena in terms of the concept of repentance, in the dialectic of which process he sought the solution.[1] It is certainly not an absolute innovation. It has a basis in traditional thought, especially in Lurianic Kabbalah and

---

1. The centrality of the repentance process in Rav Kook's teaching is especially noticeable in the essays collected in *Orot,* especially *LeMahalach HaIdeot BeYisrael* and *Zeronim.* But *Orot HaKodesh,* Vol. III too highlights, in effect, the theme of repentance as one that unifies the Torah way of life. However, it is summed up in *Orot HaTeshuvah.*

Chasidism. In these sources, we already find the nexus between the process of emanation and repentance, and between Jewish history and the transition from exile to redemption and repentance. Those sources already display the paradox of "descent for the sake of elevation," breaking for the sake of mending. Rav Kook applied the paradigms of Kabbalistic thought to the historical reality of his time. However, insofar as he conceived of the reality of his time not only as the fate of a people, but also as a cultural, historical consciousness of clashing segments of the people, he derived from the tradition layers of depth capable of responding to novel challenges to thought, and tried to bridge, in this manner, the unprecedented abyss.[2]

This, it seems, would have been impossible were there no basis for his approach in the thought of those who would be involved, in his opinion, on the road of repentance. Rav Kook, to be sure, was aware of the tension between conscious and unconscious in the deeds and thoughts of spiritual leaders struggling with one another. He believed that the significance of their activity went far beyond their self-knowledge in the present, while recognizing that what is hidden beyond the horizon of self-awareness must also display signs that can be persuasively interpreted. This means that he had to discover the signs and expressions of repentance in the thought of those who had distanced themselves from the way of Torah as he, a G-d-fearing thinker, understood it. Such signs and expressions indeed showed themselves to him in the work of several of the best writers and thinkers of the generation. In what follows, we shall deal with this aspect of the issue. We shall not deal with Rav Kook's thought in itself; rather, we shall examine the place and content of the idea of repentance in the religious thought of some outstanding thinkers in the first half of the twentieth century. Whether or not Rav Kook read their words and made use of them, this was the spiritual atmosphere to which he reacted.

---

2. A penetrating empathy to the experience and thinking of the younger generation, rebelling against Torah and mitzvot out of a rejection of the exile and its ways, is one of the most original characteristics of Rav Kook as a religious thinker. He succeeded in integrating with concepts drawn from tradition paradigms of modern philosophy and ideology, thus bridging the gap, dialectically, between the clashing worlds. *LeMahalach HaIdeot BeYisrael*, cited above, for example, presents a synthesis of Kabbalistic thought with Hegelian thought, à la Krochmal, and historiographic thought à la Graetz. This is a matter that still requires fundamental research; see Eliezer Goldman, "Secular Zionism, the Vocation of Israel and the Purpose of the Torah" (*Daat*, 11 (Summer 5743), 103–27).

2.

Let us state the historical fact: Repentance plays a central role in Jewish thought of the twentieth century, to the degree that it rises above the level of political ideology and expresses a complete Weltanschauung. Moreover, the idea of repentance appears not only as the subject of serious analysis, but also constitutes the framework of discussion for fundamental theological issues or, alternately, issues of Jewish ethics and culture; in the process it becomes a shaping influence on the process of thought. In other words, the centrality of the idea of repentance stands out both formally and, in the context of philosophical thought, methodologically.

Thus, we note a phenomenon that can be proposed as a typical mark of distinction between Jewish thought in the nineteenth century and that of the twentieth. This distinction should be stressed as the point of departure for our study of the historical process. Historians of modern Jewish thought assume that their research period commences with the ideological and historiosophical struggle about emancipation, beginning with the late eighteenth century.[3] In their opinion, the Emancipation inaugurates the modern era, which continues until our day. Let us not be oblivious to the correct considerations behind this conception, which has been prevalent for a generation. Nonetheless we shall argue that it is fundamentally mistaken. It ignores the revolutionary turning that took place in Jewish reality, and hence in the thought responding to it, at the end of the nineteenth century and the beginning of the twentieth. I hold that Rav Kook's thought is an outstanding witness to that revolution. For, although he received a great deal from the Jewish scholarly and historiosophical heritage of the nineteenth century,[4] his thought confronts that fateful "crossroads" described by

3. In fact, this is the result of the periodization of Jewish history as determined by early twentieth century historiography, based on an observation of the past without assessing the turning point taking place in the present. Typical is the discussion in B. Z. Dinur's well-known "The Modern Age in Jewish History," *BeMifne HaDorot* (Jerusalem 5715), pp. 19–68. Dinur criticizes his predecessors, yet argues, for nationalistic reasons, for an earlier onset of the modern age, precisely because he wants to preserve the continuity between the nineteenth century and the twentieth, i.e., to include in that continuum the national-Zionist turning. The conception that considers the Emancipation as the general turning point is well represented in Yehezkel Kaufmann *Gola VeNekhar*, Vol. II, Chap. 1 (Tel Aviv 5721). Historians of modern Jewish philosophy, like Julius Guttmann and Nathan Rotenstreich, follow the historians.
4. See *supra* n. 2.

Achad Haam in his collection of essays of that name, the crossroads between fatherland and exile, religious identity and national identity, faith and denial, as it appeared after the struggle for emancipation, on the threshold of the great revolutions and wars of the first half of our own century. We cannot go into detail in the present context. However, for purposes of our discussion, we must point to one dimension: the change of orientation among all the spiritual movements that arose in the Jewish people, from a tendency defined by escape from the ghetto to the social-cultural expanse of the European nations, to a tendency defined by the aspiration to a full Jewish life and to Jewish particularity, after the achievement of internalizing modern European culture was already assured.

In the nineteenth century, even the Orthodox "guardians of the walls" had to determine a new attitude to the external world, and that is what characterized the generations' general thought. In the twentieth century, even thinkers speaking for Orthodoxy in its varieties had to confront the many attempts to define anew a full, authentic, unique Jewish identity by creating a new connection to the continuum of Jewish history and its religious and cultural heritage. In the twentieth century, the historical pendulum of the Emancipation began to turn back, after it attained the realization of its hopes and inevitable disappointments. A new generation arose, of young Jews well integrated in the humanistic culture of their European environment but who sensed a lack in terms of belonging to a people, a sense of superficiality in terms of spiritual identity, whether as Jews or as members of Western civilization, a deficiency in creative roots.[5] This generation raised questions about faith, the way of life and uniqueness of Judaism, against the background of rootlessness and alienation. It required a reorientation in its attitude to Judaism, and such a reorientation would put the idea of repentance at the foundation of the experience that nourished its thought.

A classic formal expression of the change described above is the biographical dimension typical of twentieth-century thought. We have a propinquity, at times approaching synthesis, between philosophical

5. This reality is reflected in the personal testimony of outstanding scholars and thinkers of German Jewry at the beginning of the century, such as Rosenzweig, Buber, Scholem, Bergmann, and others. See Robert Weltsch's preface to Martin Buber *Teuda VeYeud*, Vol. I (Jerusalem 1959), pp. 7–15.

literature and poetry or narrative. In Eastern Europe, the tendency was to belles lettres. This became the major mode of expression for the *de profundis* of this generation, its confessions of faith and crises of denial, the sense of alienation and the yearning to belong. Ideology is important in Eastern European literature, but philosophical inquiry is virtually absent. Poetry and narrative accommodated thinking that confronted questions of faith and way of life, and whoever seeks to understand in depth the frame of reference of "the Generation"[6] must attend first and foremost to the poetry of H. N. Bialik, the stories of M. Y. Berdichevsky, Y. H. Brenner, U. N. Genessin, and S. Y. Agnon, because these poets and writers are, in fact, representatives of the religious thought of their time. In Western Europe, by contrast, particularly in Germany, that tradition continued that regarded philosophical and theological reflection and research in Jewish scholarship as the highest and most important literary expression in the struggle for Jewish identity[7]; these forms, however, took on a clearly literary dimension. First of all, there is the presentation of a personal life story, which describes one's path to Jewish creativity and interprets it in a confessional manner. It is generally difficult for the reader to penetrate the thickets of theoretical work without knowing the personal story behind it, because the motive for writing is also its object. Second, the style, which is a mixture of theoretical content and artistic form. Indeed the thought of these theologians lies on the border between the philosophical, universal-conceptual discipline, and poetry as an existential expression anchored in the unique personal experience.[8]

There is then a gradual transition marking the move from nineteenth-century thought to that of the twentieth, from observation focused on the historical perspective to thought focused on the biographical. Personal, individual experience, sometimes recounted by the author, sometimes combined with the testimony of his contemporaries, and often crystallized mythically, stands at the origin of discussion, and explains how the thinker came to write his work. Take, for example,

6. Rav Kook's essay of that title, *Ikve HaTzon* in *Eder HaYekar* (Jerusalem 5727), Chap. 1, pp. 107–16.
7. The literary output of the best writers of Jewish origin in Germany did not identify itself as Jewish literature. Works written in order to express Jewish identity are primarily theoretical and scholarly.
8. As outstanding examples, we may mention the poetic quality of Rosenzweig's *Star of Redemption*, the essays of Buber, and the writings of A. J. Heschel.

Rosenzweig's story about how Hermann Cohen came to write his *Religion of Reason from the Sources of Judaism*[9]; or take the story of Rosenzweig's road to his *Star of Redemption,* as recounted by his friends and in his letters[10]; or take Buber's testimony about his road to the study of Chasidism and the Bible[11]; or the story of Gershom Scholem's path to the study of Kabbalah and to Zionism.[12] Similar stories are significant for almost every leading figure. Each story is unique, and all of them together set down parallel lines describing an orientation of life and the problem of life for a generation knocking upon the gates of repentance and wondering if they are still open, and if the "gatekeeper will allow them to enter."[13] It is clear from all this that we have here a body of thought reflecting on the road from an alienation that in many respects had become like a home, to a home that was in many respects alien, and thus it is only natural that repentance, for this thought, would be both the subject and the method, both the content and the style.

3.

A theology generated by reflection on the experience of repentance sets its own priorities for questions and issues. It also formulates its questions in its own special way. The affair of theology in its classical sense is the question. What do we know, or what can we know, and based on what sources do we know, about G-d and His relation to man and to the world?[14] Those who follow the road of return first ask, Is it possible, and how is it possible, to establish anew a real relation between man and his G-d? This is because they begin with the feeling that the relationship expressed in traditional religious institutions has been sev-

9. F. Rosenzweig, "The Jewish Writings of Hermann Cohen," in *Naharayim* (Jerusalem 5721), pp. 109–54.
10. N. Glatzer, *Franz Rosenzweig, His Life and Thought* (New York 1961).
11. Martin Buber, "Translation of the Bible, Intention and Methods," in *Darko shel Mikra* (Jerusalem 5732), pp. 346–47.
12. G. Scholem, *From Berlin to Jerusalem.*
13. See Franz Kafka, *The Trial.*
14. A comparison of the systematic discussion in works like Saadya's *Emunot VeDeot,* or Maimonides' *Sefer HaMadda,* with Jewish theological works of the twentieth century illustrates this distinction. The medieval theologian does not deal with the concept of religion, but examines the issues: existence of G-d and His attributes, Creation, revelation, etc.

ered, and that they are no longer able to experience it. To be sure, this way of formulating the questions presupposes acquaintance with earlier sources, including the thought of the classical theologians. The answers offered by the great theologians of the past to the doubts and perplexities of their contemporaries are an important part of the cultural memory of the repentance theologian. But though he presupposes these recollections when he speaks of G-d and belief in G-d, he does not reexamine the validity of those responses in terms of his own experience. Instead he asks the questions anew. He may arrive at the same answers. But first he is obliged to work through two prior issues. First, what is the crisis that has distanced him from the circle of experience upon which classical theology had rested? Second, what is that spiritual reality that classical theology presupposes as something that does not even require an accounting? What is the experience that lends certitude to reliance on the sources? In other words, before it is time for the question about man's capacity to know G-d, the theologian of repentance must examine the question about his capacity to know *religion,* which includes the realm of experience of believing people, and which gives this experience its expression as a way of life. The question about the nature of religion precedes the question about the content of religious knowledge.

Having reached this conclusion, we move on to the manners of thought articulated in specific approaches. Let us begin with two important theologians, different from one another, whose work exemplifies the turn from the nineteenth century to the twentieth: Hermann Cohen and Aharon David Gordon.[15]

An exhaustive analysis of the issue in Hermann Cohen would require an account of the process by which he constructed his entire system, stage by stage, beginning with logic, through aesthetics and ethics, to the doctrine of religion. In fact, the process of system construction overlaps with the process of Cohen's increasing return to Judaism— that is, we have a road of return that becomes conscious and emphatic in the last stage: the transition from ethics to religion. For in this

---

15. As background for the discussion, see S. H. Bergmann, "On the Road to Faith and Trust," *Anashim uDerachim* (Jerusalem 5727), pp. 249–391; E. Schweid, "Foundations of the Religious Philosophy of Hermann Cohen," *Jerusalem Studies in Jewish Thought* 2:2 (5743), pp. 255–306; Schweid, *HaYahid: Olamo shel A. D. Gordon* (Tel Aviv 5730). Chap. 2, pp. 76–98.

transition, Cohen realized that the completion of his system required him to introduce a corrective, and to continue in a manner that he had not foreseen.[16] As opposed to his position when he set down the ethics (namely that ethics includes and exhausts philosophical reflection on the relation between G-d and man), it became clear to him that religion posits a realm of knowledge separate from and beyond ethics. Thus, it is likely that when he was occupied with the earlier stages of his system, Cohen was completely oblivious to an entire domain of philosophical inquiry. Something hid from him the unique character of religion, in spite of the religious training he had received in his parents' home. He needed a second testing, uncovering, and elucidating to overcome the barrier, whose source is easy to identify: i.e., the idealist-humanist philosophy of the Kantian and Hegelian schools. The caesura is located in this philosophical tradition. He must overcome it in order to stand before the explicitly formulated question about the nature of religion. Note well, Cohen does not begin with the question about what we can know of G-d, but rather with the question about the character of religion as a domain of relationship between G-d and man. Immediately, he seeks after the sources that testify to this relationship, in order to make them the subject of philosophical inquiry.[17]

At the center of Cohen's religious philosophy is the famous idea of correlation between G-d and man. Correlation is a necessary mutual relation as appropriate between distinct entities. G-d and man are distinct, but obligated to each other in their nature. Nonetheless the relation is not symmetrical. G-d is the Creator and man the creature. G-d reveals and commands; man receives revelation and is commanded. G-d judges; man is judged. From man's point of view, G-d is the absolute, transcendent ideal of reason. Man conceives of himself as necessitated by the absolute ideal essence of G-d, but in this manner his prior knowledge of G-d is no more than a knowledge of the rational nexus between them, by virtue of which man (each and every man) bears absolute value: The one G-d posits man in his uniqueness. Again

16. The turning point is indicated in the book that preceded the "Religion of Reason," i.e., *Der Begriff der Religion in System der Philosophie* (Giessen 1915).
17. This entire process is captured in the name of the book, *Religion of Reason from the Sources of Judaism*. Its justification we find in the introduction dealing with each word in the title. See the introduction to the Hebrew translation by Zvi Wisslavsky (Jerusalem 5732), pp. 37–70.

note well, Cohen discovered the substantive, distinct realm of religion when he discovered that, in the ethical realm, he could only speak of the concept of humanity and of the individual as representing the concept of humanity. The absolute value of the individual, without which ethics lacks its purpose and its highest criterion, is not included in ethics. It enters ethics from the supra-ethical sphere of the religious relation: the correlation of G-d and man.[18]

Thus, in the course of reorientation, Cohen discovered the substantive domain of religion, whence he reached the idea of correlation between G-d and man, which is the fundamental content of religion. This is the basis, and it does not yet reveal the idea of repentance as the shaping religious idea. This idea comes to the fore, however, when we attempt to exhaust the implications of the asymmetrical character of the correlation between G-d and man. G-d's relation to Himself, to the world, and to man is absolute and eternal, while man's relation to himself, to the world, and to G-d is relative and changes in time. Hence man must reestablish his relation to order in order to be worthy of the Holy Spirit, i.e., reason, which is the revelation of G-d in man, or the creation of man with that which defines him as man. Hence man's duty, deriving from his rational nature, to reestablish his relation to G-d in order to enter the domain of relationship between G-d and man is what grounds repentance as the shaping element in religion. We can observe this in every chapter of *Religion of Reason from the Sources of Judaism*. For our purposes, however, it is especially important to stress the centrality of the problem of sin and the problem of moral suffering connected to sin in Cohen's religious teaching.[19] Awareness of the absolute value of the individual is connected, for him, with the basic moral feeling: compassion, which is identification with the moral suffering of the individual for whom we are responsible. We refer to moral suffering, meaning the suffering of the "poor," which stems from the network of relations among people. For this suffering we are responsible, and it testifies to our guilt. When the poor man cries out not only because of his physical pain but also as a consequence of spiritual pain bound up with the perception of injustice, we are guilty. The suffering

18. *Religion of Reason*, Chapter 5: The Creation of Man with Reason.
19. Ibid. Chapter 8: Revelation of Man as Neighbor, and Chapter 10: The Individual as Ego.

of the poor, ever present in society, is the immediate sin that accuses us, and it impugns the core of our selfhood: i.e., our rational will, the consciousness of moral freedom that is our human dignity. In order to save our humanity, we must become purified of sin. Hence the need for atonement and the forgiveness of sins, without which our humanity is lost. But only G-d, before whom we are responsible for our neighbor, for He is the common source of our uniqueness as human beings, can atone for our sins and again visit us with His Holy Spirit.[20] According to this, it is obvious that the relation between G-d and man, which constructs the domain of ethics on the religious foundation beyond ethics, must be interpreted as repentance. Note well, the relation between man and G-d is tied to the relation between man and his neighbor, so that the most intimate presence of man before G-d is the expression of regret and act of atonement on the part of man, and the gracious, forgiving atonement on the part of G-d. Indeed, this is the pivot of Cohen's discussion of all forms of interpersonal religious relationship between G-d and man. In his view, that is the meaning of worship in the framework of the religion of reason, in terms of the direct relationship between G-d and man.[21] Therefore prayer, for Cohen, is the climax of the religious experience. What is prayer? Man's standing before G-d to be judged by Him, to express regret for his sins, to seek atonement, and beseech the renewal of the Holy Spirit within him, which is the supreme moral will. An answered prayer is one that fills our heart with a feeling of thanksgiving for the sin that has been atoned and the renewed ability to return to the world, i.e., to society, to bear the responsibility placed upon us to mend the world in the kingdom of G-d. It is obvious that in this manner repentance is connected to redemption, which is the mending of the world in the kingdom of G-d, the fulfillment of the moral imperative.[22]

From the obvious centrality of the subject of atonement in the religious thought of Hermann Cohen, moreover, comes the centrality of the Day of Atonement in his thought. These two topics constitute the heart of his book. They are located at the midpoint of the book, the center of the system, Chapters 11–12 of twenty-two. One should

20. Ibid. Chapter 11: Atonement.
21. Ibid. Chapter 16: Law.
22. Ibid. Chapter 17: Prayer.

note the unusualness, both in subject and in method. First of all, the duality: two chapters devoted to the same topic. Second, a discussion dedicated to a specific date in the calendar. Cohen did not do this regarding any other topic, nor did he devote a chapter to any other festival. The latter is only natural, for the *Religion of Reason* is a philosophical composition presenting the conceptual framework of a theory of religion, not the description of a religious way of life. Yom Kippur thus merited an extraordinary status, which underlines the absolute importance that Cohen ascribed to it. For him, one might say, Yom Kippur is the day that was elevated to become a supreme ideal. As such it is the climax, and if it is the climax, then repentance is the essence of religion.

A. D. Gordon's approach to the understanding of the essence of religion is different from Cohen's, even as Rav Yehuda Halevi's differs from Maimonides'. It is precisely the blatant difference between them that elucidates for us the important parallel in terms of the status given to repentance as the basis of the religious relation. Let us begin by stating that Gordon, like Cohen, defines religion as a *relation*[23]; the quality of the relation turns out to be a constant experience of return. If we use Gordon's own terminology, religion is the most real and inclusive relationship of man to nature as an infinite being. This definition demands precise inquiry into each of its components, which goes beyond the scope of this discussion. But we will get the gist if we examine Gordon's theory explaining the development of religion as a personal experience in the life of each individual and as a historical occurrence.[24] Gordon argues that man, like every animal, feels at birth a sense of unconscious belonging to his environment. He acts on the basis of his drives as part of the real continuum of the nature that surrounds him. The one nature indeed works about him and within him, continuously. Gradually, as the consequence of a social process, there emerges in man an awareness that specifies him as a human creature. That awareness distinguishes the "I" from the "not-I," and presents man as a separate being in the face of nature. This experience invigorates, but at the same time fills one with trepidation. By nature

23. A. D. Gordon, "Our Account with Ourselves," in *HaUmma VeHaAvoda* (Jerusalem: HaSifriyya Hatzionit, 5712), p. 351, and "Man and Nature" in *HaAdam VeHaTeva*, p. 112.
24. Gordon, *HaAdam VeHaTeva*, pp. 71–76.

man seeks to confirm his unique, separate self, but he dreads detaching himself from the flowing source of existence; for if he becomes detached, he becomes nothing. Religion emanates from this tension between the desire to confirm the separate self and the desire to sustain the preconscious experience of belonging. Let us be precise: Religion is the willed, experienced effort to repair the breach between man and nature, without abrogating the knowing "I" and without denying the self. In other words, religion is a new, postcognitive constitution of primary belonging, a reconstitution that is no longer a return to the previous situation, as such a return is not possible. It is opposed to the direction of natural evolution that has attained the human level.

Gordon recognizes four ways of overcoming the crisis of isolation: 1. "I" confirms its selfhood and imagines that it is reality, that the surrounding reality is merely a projection of its imagination. 2. An effort to overcome the caesura by external domination of nature and its submission to the fulfillment of man's needs. 3. An effort to become reunited with the universe to the point where awareness of the separate "I" disappears (mysticism). 4. A yearning to abrogate self by negation and evacuation (Nirvana).[25] Clearly, all of these attempts contain inner contradictions. It is possible to categorize the extant religions according to this schema, signifying that human beings have erected cultures around these life orientations. However, they are unable to offer man a genuine overcoming of the crisis. The right way (if you will, the true religion) is that of fortifying selfhood by work that draws upon the effluence of nature and gives it a higher form directed to the benefit of the other, the benefit of society, the benefit of nature. Thus, the separate self is strengthened, but with it are strengthened the participation and belonging of man to the universe. Gordon calls this a "life of expansion," and identifies it with the Jewish religion.[26] In any event, let us consider that we are dealing with varieties of return, and that the true variant is the mature ability to reestablish, on a higher social level and on a higher creative level, the unity that was splintered by consciousness. Thus, the splitting of self-consciousness in man is both the beginning of the sin of separation (eating from the Tree of Knowledge

25. Ibid. p. 132.
26. Ibid. pp. 88–90, and "Toward an Elucidation of the Difference between Judaism and Christianity" (Ibid. pp. 271–96).

of Good and Evil!)[27], while religion is the yearning to return to Eden. The return, however, will not succeed if you do not see it as a return to the previous point of origin; it will succeed only if we find in it the constitution of a superior social reality.[28]

4.

Hermann Cohen and A. D. Gordon thus defined religion, each in his own peculiar concepts, as a living relation exhibiting three levels of expression: emotional, cognitive-rational, practical (the creation of social life). Religious philosophy is identified with the cognitive-rational level, meaning that religious life takes place in the thought processes as well. If we comprehend religious life as a dialectical movement of repentance, this means that repentance is not only the content and subject of religious thought, but that it occurs within the process of thought itself, thus becoming the distinctive characteristic of religious thought. In this sense, one can say that repentance is identical with the methodology of religious thought. This may be observed in Cohen's *Religion of Reason* as in Gordon's "Man and Nature." We prefer, however, to illustrate this characteristic of repentance theology in the work of a third theologian, who has exercised a significant influence and has consciously contributed to methodological renewal in religious thought. I refer to Franz Rosenzweig.[29]

We do not need to recount Rosenzweig's biography up to the writing of his *Star of Redemption*. The story of his return has become an oft-repeated myth, well known to all students of Jewish philosophy in recent generations. For our purposes, it is necessary to repeat our claim about the necessary connection between biography and the philosophy that interprets reality, which thus ascribes to Rosenzweig's life methodological status: One must reject the idealistic outlook that presupposes a concept of pure rationality, which thinks itself and from itself all of reality. Against this presumptuous view one may set the empirical fact

27. *HaAdam VeHaTeva*, p. 71.
28. The climax of the national-religious stage is the "people-man" *(Am Adam)*. See the essay with that title in *HaUmma VeHaAvoda*, pp. 258–63.
29. For a fuller analysis of this subject, see my "Spiritual Reorientation as a System of Thinking" in *Israel Efrat: Meshorer VeHoge* (Tel Aviv: Katz Institute for the Study of Hebrew Literature, 5741), pp. 231–58.

that philosophy is the creation of a thinking man, a particular, unique man, who confronts reality under the aspects that he comes upon in his life as an individual, in his society, in his culture.[30] The questions that philosophy deals with ought to be the questions that the individual asks in the face of his concrete life experiences, and confronting the fear of death that awaits him. Not death as a general concept, but his death as an individual. By dint of this crucial argument, Rosenzweig became an existential philosopher, on its basis he developed his original philosophical methodology that he calls the "new thinking,"[31] as distinct from classical, idealist philosophical thinking.

The claim about the nexus between philosophy and the individual who thinks it has double significance for us. First of all, it explains the necessary connection between the story of his return to faith and to Judaism and his philosophical work. This is its status as a *personal* philosophy. Second, and most important, it points to a conscious parallel between the story of his repentance, with its turnings and crises, and the process of rejection of the idealist methodology and the formation of the "new thinking." Rosenzweig started out as an idealist; his turn to faith is inherently a recognition that idealism is founded on a wrong methodology; moreover, that this mistaken methodology is simultaneously arrogant and cowardly, i.e., its foundation is sin, the sin of the human spirit toward itself, toward the world, and toward G-d.[32] The alternative philosophy that Rosenzweig develops through his novel methodology is the corrective to sin. Most significant is what he calls, in one of his essays, "believing science."[33] It is, in his opinion, the philosophy that sustains man's humility and his courageous trust in G-d. Moreover, the methodology of the "new thinking" is essentially a process of reorientation. It begins with a critical awareness of the mistaken methodology in order to return from it to the natural, healthy outlook that restores man to himself, to his world, and to his G-d.

The point of the last sentence is well illustrated and highlighted in a short popular work that Rosenzweig wrote after publishing the *Star*,

---

30. Franz Rosenzweig, *The Star of Redemption*, Hebrew trans. Y. Amir (Jerusalem 5730), Introduction: On the Possibility of Knowing the Totality, p. 51.
31. Rosenzweig, "The New Thinking," in *Naharayim*, trans. Y. Amir (Jerusalem 5721), pp. 219–40.
32. Introduction to *The Star of Redemption*, especially pp. 45–46, but typical of Rosenzweig's view of philosophy up until Hegel throughout the book.
33. "The Unity of the Bible," in *Naharayim*, pp. 29–30.

in order to make his thought more accessible to the public: *The Sick and Healthy Understanding.* [34] We admit that Rosenzweig was dissatisfied with it and set it aside, but for us the narrative image underlying it is relevant. It is the story of a sick man, whose mental disease is idealist philosophy. He has lost his connection to reality by the habit of pure conceptual thought. Knowing himself ill, he travels to a sanatorium for a cure. There he is taught, by repeated exercises, to rely on his senses and his common sense, and to adopt toward reality a natural, spontaneous attitude that is essentially an attitude of *faith.* Of course, the attitude of faith can be rehabilitated only by liberation from idealism, thus the cure requires philosophical inquiry as well, namely a reflection on the process of natural cognition. A healthy man does not need such philosophy. He believes. But our sick contemporary requires philosophical therapy, which is a kind of intellectual parallel to psychoanalysis. The therapy requires diagnosis for the sake of a restoration to the source. If we compare this small composition to the *Star of Redemption,* then Rosenzweig's new thinking is a therapeutic thinking. In other words, the new thinking is a remedial methodology. Observe: In the *Star* too, Rosenzweig conducts the reader, step by step, from the philosophical death offered us, in his view, by idealism as an imaginary refuge from the literal death awaiting us,[35] to the true life proposed by faith.[36]

We cannot offer a detailed description of the new thinking as a remedial process, but we can indicate some central points. First of all, let us return to Rosenzweig's assertion that, at the basis of idealism, which appears to be a complete philosophy, there is a trivial and obviously groundless prejudice: that beyond the objects we encounter in direct experience, the objects that appear and then disappear one after the other, there exists an eternal "totality" that is the true substance, of which individual objects are only the phenomena. The sophisticated consciousness of the philosopher identifies the totality with itself. It seems to discover the manifold phenomena that appear to derive from *outside* consciousness—*within* consciousness. Obviously, this presupposition has no empirical basis. It is totally undermined by

34. Finally published long after the author's death in N. Glatzer's English translation: *Understanding the Sick and the Healthy.*
35. *Star,* p. 45.
36. Ibid. pp. 432–37.

experience, for the idealist philosopher is smarter than experience and goes beyond it to ground it too in the totality of mind. But this sophistication teaches us that the seemingly naive error is, at bottom, a sin of the spirit. The fear of death casts its shadow over the philosopher, and in his cowardice he seeks refuge in an arrogant fantasy: He inflates himself and identifies his consciousness with the totality that unifies G-d and world. There is, in Rosenzweig's view, no greater presumption, no greater lack of humility, no greater idolatry than this. But the source is, as we noted, the fear of confronting death face to face as a concrete fate and the desire to discover, in the face of death, the simple secret of life.

The conclusion that we must reach from the preceding analysis is that there is no unified totality.[37] From our experience, we recognize the individual entities of nature—that is, the world, G-d—whose presence is revealed by the wonder of the renewal of creation of the world and by the wonder of speech renewed in us—and ourselves, as creatures in nature yet outside of nature. G-d, world, and man are three different entities. They are different and distinct, yet interrelated.

The second point to be noted after the dissolution of the idealistic totality is the role of speech in Rosenzweig's existential philosophy. In his view, there is an identity between thought and speech. There is indeed a pre-thought beyond speech, but all actual thought is speech created in man. Speech occurs as a meeting of man and G-d, who gives the power of speech, and with the world reflected in speech.[38] According to Rosenzweig, this is an empirical observation and it shapes his philosophical methodology. In place of decoding the logical structure of consciousness, Rosenzweig demands a decoding of the dynamic modes of speech as a creative process. G-d creates the world through speech. G-d reveals Himself to man by speaking to him and in the wondrous capacity exhibited in man's ability to speak. The puzzled

37. Ibid. p. 56.
38. Rosenzweig makes the methodological transition to the philosophy of speech when he moves, stressing the continuity of his discourse, from the introduction to the first book of the *Star* to the body of the book. One can see this by reading carefully from the section on Mathematics and Signs in the Introduction (p. 60) to the Note on Method in Book I (p. 65). That he is now concerned with a reflection on the "grammar" of language becomes explicit in the section on Primary Words (p. 72). The theological significance of this transition is discussed in Part II of the *Star;* see Part II, Book I, pp. 184–85.

man, who wonders where the direct Divine Presence, available to experience, can be found, suffers, according to Rosenzweig, from a philosophical blindness that hides from him the simplest and most intimate of experiences: creative speech. The "new thinking" rehabilitates the personality from this blindness by attending to the modes of the dialogical gesture.

The third point is the status of sources, especially that of the Bible. These are creative bodies of speech giving primary, conscious form to G-d's revelation to man and man's response to G-d. Human beings require these dialogical expositions. They support a word that has been spoken, and that is repeatable now as in the past, in order to awaken their hidden power that strives for expression. This means that if the principles of philosophical thinking are inferred through reflections on the act of speech, then the philosophy of religion—the heart of that philosophy which concerns human life—is derived from reflection on the linguistic-literary exposition present in the Bible and the Prayerbook. Indeed, the philosophical climaxes of *The Star of Redemption* are exegetical inquiries, better yet *midrashim,* on selected chapters of the Bible, the prayers, and the ritual symbols of the festivals.[39]

Thus, we find a methodology of renewed adaptation of religious sources as an actual linguistic exposition, in which the full intensity of religious experience is potentially contained like a flame in a glowing coal: the return to the primacy of speech as a psychic gesture, return to the linguistic network as the potential for renewed creativity, return to religious sources as the sources of living faith. As we stated, in the thought of Rosenzweig repentance is more the inquiry itself than the topic of inquiry, hence it is precisely the reflection on method that reveals its centrality.

5.

We saw before that the theology of repentance opens with a discussion about the nature of religion. Let us be more precise and state that, from the outset, religion is conceived by this tendency of thought as the

39. Each chapter of Part II in the *Star* ends with the "grammatical analysis" of a biblical section: Genesis 1 (pp. 185–89); Song of Songs (pp. 232–35); Psalm 115 (279–80). Part III contains a decoding of symbols and ritual in Judaism and Christianity.

creation of human consciousness. For it is evidently impossible to presuppose a knowledge that is bestowed upon man by any external source above him before the awakening of consciousness. Does man have such knowledge? Is it possible for him to have such knowledge? To answer, he must thoroughly examine his immanent faculties. Thus, we have a theology that starts from man's knowledge of himself as part of the world, which can be defined as a philosophical anthropology (if we consider thinkers like Cohen and Gordon), or as individual self-knowledge, as a philosophical psychology (if we consider thinkers like Rosenzweig). The state of loneliness of man, for himself, within himself, is the point of departure. That state is also man's deepest existential problem. It is easy to observe that this discussion proves the intimate connection between the theology of repentance and the great philosophical process that began with Descartes and led to Hegelian idealism on the one hand and Marxist materialism on the other hand,[40] i.e., the philosophical process that began with the doubting of man's cognitive ability and led to certitudes estranged from the religious truth of Scriptures. This is a natural continuity, implicit in the background of the problem. Rosenzweig too began as an idealist, and the examination of his thought reveals that he carried with him, throughout his life, some of the shell of the idealist egg from which he had hatched. This means that his intellectual revolution did not take place all at once. Each stage cost enormous labor, and the stages describe a road to repentance. Indeed, in this context it is interesting to investigate not only the individual paths of those who follow the road of repentance, but also the road created by the propinquity and continuity of activity of thinkers who learned from one another, who were mutually influenced, and who sought, consciously, to take the other's activity one step farther. Such a development becomes clear when we observe the road leading from Cohen to Rosenzweig and to Rav Soloveitchik, from Rosenzweig to Buber and from Buber to A. J. Heschel. We have here a philosophy distilled into the story of a pathway, not a system. It is a pathway with turns and twists, divagations and digressions, for matters depend on the conscious, deliberate decisions of the thought-

40. This "hidden" story of the theology of repentance is surveyed by Rosenzweig in the Introduction to the *Star*, where he proposes the history of Western philosophy as the background to the book.

creating individuals. If, however, we follow the most radical pathway, we discover an intellectual bouleversement: It begins with thought seeking the presence of G-d in human reason, and ends with the uncovering of the truth that when man seeks a Divine Presence that is immanent in his reason, he is in fact hiding from G-d seeking him. This development begins before Cohen, in the remarkable composition of Samuel Hirsch *Der Religionsphilosophie der Juden,*[41] and the circle is closed with the philosophical boldness of Heschel's *G-d in Search of Man.*[42]

We have added to our list one classic thinker of the nineteenth century. Samuel Hirsch is important for our discussion because his system is fully anchored in idealism, for which G-d is an immanent ideal of human reason, yet nonetheless Hirsch already sets foot deliberately on the road leading back to the historical mythos of the Bible in which he sees the incarnation of religious truth. He is also important because, on the methodological plane, he stresses the role of philosophy of religion in enabling man to attain a depth of understanding of himself that will open him to the higher truth. Hirsch stressed that in order to again attain faith, one must begin with man in his historical context, and to press on from what is known to what lies beyond the known. Long before Hermann Cohen, Hirsch thus discovered that religion grounds ethics beyond its domain. On the other hand, when Cohen discovered the idea of correlation as the central content of religion, he was going beyond his predecessor and marking the degree to which idealism could come close to a personal, transcendent conception of G-d, for the idea of correlation implies that the religious relation is not only man's relation to G-d, but also G-d's relation to man. This is clear from what we said above about repentance and prayer in Cohen's thought. Prayer is answered speech; repentance and atonement are not completed with man's action alone. The sinner must take upon himself his sin, to confess and regret and beg pardon and forgiveness. But man cannot efface his sin as if it had never occurred. Only G-d, Creator of man, can atone, i.e., cancel the sin outright, so that the sin of a man will not be a factor that determines his fate, and to

41. Leipzig 1842. For a fuller discussion, see my *Toledot HeHagut HaYehudit BaEt HaChadasha,* Chap. 7 (Jerusalem 5738).
42. New York 1955.

renew in man the Holy Spirit, the freedom of rational will in him. Man
is purified and sanctified, but only G-d can bestow purity and sanctity.
With deliberate precision, Cohen repeats the statement of Rav Akiva:
"Fortunate are you, Israel, before whom you are purified and who
purifies you? Your heavenly Father!"[43] By this he means that becoming
purified is the role of Israel, but our heavenly Father alone purifies. This
is the completion of the traditional idea of repentance, but it remains
in the setting of idealist philosophy.

Cohen brings about his turning point without breaking out of the
idealist system, but it is not surprising that Rosenzweig viewed the idea
of correlation as a deviation from idealism and a precursor of existential
philosophy. Indeed, Rosenzweig was inspired by his teacher's idea of
correlation, and developed the concept, requiring a formal logic, as an
implication of the conceptual methodology of idealism, in order to raise
it to the linguistic level of poetry. With sharp irony, he rejects the
"mathematical" formula of the relation G-d-man, replacing it with the
poetic metaphor, rich with personal connotations.[44] He does not speak
about correlation, but about the love described in the Song of Songs,
about the covenant of Sinai between the Jewish people and G-d. He
then proposes the psychological-philosophical analysis of these metaphors. Man and G-d confront one another. Their isolation precedes
their encounter. Love erupts from them as the revelation of a hidden
self. Note well that already for Rosenzweig, G-d initiates, not only in
Creation, but in the manifestation of love that is identified with revelation. Out of the necessity of the divine nature there erupts the virile,
conquering imperative to the human soul: "Love me!" (and this is, for
Rosenzweig, the First Commandment, which is the source of all others[45]). The absolute command directed to it liberates the soul of man
from its determination in the depths of its nature and closure of its
character. It responds to the demand breaking through from the outside. Indeed, it is likely to become totally subjugated to the absolute
demand of G-d. This would have about it some of the tyranny of lovers,

---

43. *Religion of Reason*, Chap. 12, p. 258.
44. Rosenzweig's remark in "The Builders" about "the pseudo-logical theory of the
unity of G-d and the pseudo-ethics of loving one's neighbor . . ." (*Naharayim* p. 85)
is directed at Geiger, but it seems to fit the formulations of Cohen as well.
45. *Star*, Part II, Book II, pp. 208–9.

except that here G-d's love restrains itself. It emancipates man from its dominion through the commandment of loving one's neighbor (which is, according to Rosenzweig, the Second Commandment, which details the First and includes Commandments relating to life with neighbors, with family, with the community, and the people).[46] The love of G-d thus frees man from the prison of self, the prison of his sin and rebellion, and again offers him his freedom so that he may live his destined life and redeem the world. In other words, the love of G-d opens before man the road of return to G-d, to the other, to society and the world.

The same dialectic of encounter between G-d and man is found in the religious thought of Martin Buber. In Buber's teaching, the relation between man and G-d is the most inclusive form of dialogical relation.[47] The human "I" encounters the divine "Thou," and the presence together, the meeting, fulfills the being of the "I." Who initiates? In Buber's systematic work *I and Thou,* the answer is unclear, but in the scholarly-exegetical works on the Bible, which contain Buber's Jewish theology, the answer is quite clear[48]: The faith of Israel comes to existential expression in a series of unique personal and historical events in which the patriarchs, and later the nation as a whole, encounter G-d. The individual and the people are on the way. They have undergone a crisis that impelled them to leave their place and seek their land and destiny. G-d meets them on their way. He proposes His leadership, which is also a test. For G-d demands that the people believe in Him—i.e., that they follow Him, not the goal that the individuals, or the people, had chosen, but the goal that He will show them; they must trust Him, trust that in precisely this way they will find their destiny. Meaning that the search on the part of man is a preparatory stage, but it is G-d who initiates and man who is called upon to respond. So it was in the past, so it continues in the present, so it will continue in the future. As opposed to Rosenzweig, who conceived of the Jewish path in terms of the liturgical calendar, Buber stubbornly sought to breach the cycle and to grasp each present in a

46. Ibid. Book III, pp. 242–45.
47. Buber, *I and Thou,* Part III (Heb. trans. Wisslovsky (Jerusalem 1959), p. 57.
48. A perspicuous summary of the idea central to all of Buber's biblical studies is found in the introduction to the first edition of *Torat HaNeviim* (Tel Aviv 5710).

linear, historical manner, leading from the past to the messianic future.[49] In each "now," the believer is on the way and encounters G-d. The commandment of this "now" is not that of the previous "now," at each point it is necessary to choose anew, to respond or refuse. One might say precisely that every "now" confronts the believer, according to Buber, with the decision of repentance. He must overcome the nature that imprisons him, to "turn on his own pivot,"[50] in order to hear the voice speaking to him at that moment, and to turn from the present to the future.

The doctrines of Rosenzweig and Buber are the background to the sharpened formulations of A. J. Heschel. It appears that Heschel's innovation is the radicalization of two themes in his predecessors. The first is the theme of man's hiding from G-d, out of a rebelliousness that would confirm his own independent self. The second theme is G-d's relation to the creature He has made to be His partner in conversation, i.e., man. By emphasizing the first theme, Heschel meant to offer a victorious answer to the question of skeptics who are not even heretics in the traditional sense. After all the upheavals that have affected Western society and culture in the twentieth century, the exuberance of heresy has been dampened, and its place inherited by a dejected agnosticism. Many of those who do not believe confess that they wish for faith. But how can they believe if there is no opening for a convincing experience of the presence of G-d? Heschel turns upon these skeptics their pious doubting.[51] In his view, the form of the question about the presence of G-d is the refuge behind which they hide from the manifestations of His presence. G-d never hid. From time immemorial, He has called to man, "Where art thou?" It is man who sinfully hides himself, and it is this weak-spirited hiding that is his sin. Thus, modern agnosticism, according to Heschel, is no more than a strained refusal of man to stand before G-d, i.e., to hear His commandment and respond to it. When men recognize the concealed refusal and its motives, they will become convinced that G-d is very intimately

49. This idea too is repeated in almost all of Buber's Jewish writings. Let me point especially to the essay "The Holy Way," in which the title already conveys Buber's concept of the way. See *Teuda VeYeud*, Vol. I (Jerusalem 5720), pp. 89–116.
50. This phrase is taken from "Our Contemporary and the Bible," *Teuda VeYeud*, Vol. I, p. 153.
51. *G-d in Search of Man*, Chapter 15: Faith, pp. 152–58.

present to man, wherever he turns, in the universe, in the encounter with men, in the encounter with inwardness and with their cultural heritage.[52] In other words, the point of departure for repentance is the readiness to recognize the sin of refusal and to confess it. With the second theme, Heschel attempts to uncover the motivation of the concealed refusal. The skeptic waiting for faith is hoping for a crutch that will assure him of happiness and peace of mind. His very hope gives away the egoistic motive behind his refusal. He will not find his way to faith as long as he is so radically mistaken about its character. Man, to be sure, needs G-d, but that is because G-d had quested for man in order that man fulfill his mission in the world. To have faith means to stand in full readiness for one's vocation. This is what man hides from; straighaway he senses his isolation and loneliness, but so long as he is unwilling to hear the commanding voice, he will not emerge from his loneliness. Repentance is thus the first step, preceding faith, though faith is always available to man from the outset.

6.

We will end with two remarks. First of all, we cannot assert that Rav Kook read the works of the aforementioned thinkers; with respect to some of them, he most assuredly could not have done so. Both Buber and Heschel may have been influenced by Rav Kook. He certainly could not have known their primary work. However, our concern was to characterize the spiritual reality of a generation, and this was clearly and systematically expressed by those thinkers. Let us repeat in this context that the most intimate and fruitful contact for Rav Kook was with the works of "believing heretics," tormented by rebelliousness toward heaven and pangs of repentance, men like Bialik, Berdichevsky, Brenner, and Agnon. Their work, which is not philosophical, we could not discuss. We can only assert that they articulated, at the experiential level, themes that the thinkers mentioned above struggled with. The outstanding point of relation with Rav Kook is, in this respect, the doctrine of A. D. Gordon, which strikingly parallels his ideas.[53]

52. *Ibid.* Chapter 2: Ways to His Presence, pp. 24–33.
53. I have alluded to this parallel in my book *HaYachid: Olamo shel A. D. Gordon* (Tel Aviv 5730). Indeed, the matter calls for detailed investigation.

Second, the concept of repentance as it appears in Rav Kook's thought and in that of the other theologians discussed here is very far from the concept of repentance as it is interpreted by the contemporary public. The differences are many, but they all stem from one fact: Repentance in its accepted sense today is nothing but a return to the historical mold sanctified by Charedi Orthodoxy, while our thinkers of repentance intended to return to a perpetual line of innovative religious creativity. It was not a call to return to the past, but to create a continuous future that would restore unity to the faith of Israel and the way of life governed by it, along with the expansiveness of a complete culture and fullness. Repentance in its contemporary meaning is a retreat from that bold charge into the future; needless to say, it has no real answer to the questions pressing upon the contemporary Jew. It appears that in order to confront those questions one must "return with a question" *(lachazor bisheela)* to the highway of renewed religious thought, and thus return to repentance in its original significance.

Religion, Repentance, and Personal Freedom

Dr. Benjamin Ish Shalom

I.

"ALL HUMAN CULTURE may be described as the process of man's gradual emancipation." With these words, the renowned philosopher Ernst Cassirer summarizes his book *Essay on Man*.[1] Language, art, religion, and science are all, in his view, stages in this process. It seems that in principle Rav Kook would agree with this formulation, but with one significant difference. In his way of thinking, religion is not one of the ingredients of culture, and consequently is not a stage in the said process. The opposite is the case: Culture is a stage in a process whose deep motivations are to be understood only in terms taken from the field of religion. This principal difference, which will be further clarified below, is the main feature of the message that issues from Rav Kook's original work that seeks to grapple with the main philosophical challenges of his time.

From the point of view of religious thought, the challenges presented by that period were unparalleled in their scope and their severity. From various directions and on several planes, there burst forth an absolute

1. Ernst Cassirer, *Massah al Haadam* (Hebrew translation of *Essay on Man*) (Tel Aviv 5732), p. 230.

protest against the basic tenets of religion and all it seeks to convey. The idealistic philosophy that might have been thought to go hand in hand with the "true" characteristics of religion[2] began losing its attractiveness, and set up its own ideas in opposition to it: Marxism on the one hand and existentialism on the other. These two streams of thought seized hold of Hegel's philosophy just as he in fact wanted it to be accepted, "as the supreme crystallization of the classic conception of truth based on concepts of universalism and objectivity."[3] Both rebelled against him, each in its own way, out of a similar motivation: saving the private individual from being completely ignored by the idealistic philosophy.

Marx, however, in the end, returned to the same basis of universalism against which he had originally rebelled. Nevertheless, the appearance of materialism as a philosophical trend, which captured its place more and more in the public consciousness, deepened and sharpened the onslaught of the secularization process that was already in full force. Henceforth it was no longer a specific scientific discipline or philosophic theory that rose in opposition to theology, but a complete and embracing world perception that explained reality in material and mechanical terms. This was a universal outlook, in whose understanding of reality, its laws, and its activating processes, there was no room left for G-d, for the spirit of man and his freedom.[4]

On the other hand, existential philosophy, at whose fountainhead stood man, the individual, the dignity of his personality and his freedom as well as a concern for his problems of existence, also was not welcomed easily by the conservative theologians, because it rejected every dimension that was absolute and fixed in reality, and thought of all reality as a dynamic process. In its conception, reality is not any longer "essence" but "existence"; that is, it is not something of a circumscribed content, but it is open to all possibilities, to man's perpetual creativity. From here on, consequently, it is not the "concept" that is the object of philosophical scrutiny, but man. Man is the starting point and the end of every discussion, he is the yardstick of truth and goodness; and in Nietzsche's revolutionary philosophy man

2. The works of Rav Krochmal and of Hermann Cohen reflect this perception.
3. See Ron Segad, *Existentialism* (Jerusalem 5742). See there also detailed bibliography.
4. For the development of spiritualism in Europe and America as a reaction to materialism, see G. W. Butterworth, *Spiritualism and Religion* (London 1944).

even fashions his own values. It is needless to say that in this new outlook the brightness and rationality of religion have gone. It is portrayed as naked, lacking in all meaning, freezing its preserves and keeping man away from the dynamism and creativity that are his breath of life. In the thought of Nietzsche, even morality is perceived as religion's wild fruit; it should be exchanged for new norms that would reflect man's modern perception.

Within Judaism's own confines also, the doorposts moved. The national revival and the growth of the new *Yishuv* in *Eretz Yisrael* through groups of young idealists who, while they loved their people and their land, yet threw off the yoke of religion, posed a challenge and demanded attention on the theological level. In the spirit of the new philosophy, the pioneers of the settlement of *Eretz Yisrael* proved that it was possible for the Jew to take his fate in his hands and bring about his redemption without depending on help from heaven; indeed, in open revolt against the kingdom of heaven.

From Rav Kook's standpoint, it was not possible to hide oneself from the pioneer Zionist undertaking or to negate it, just as one could not evade grappling with the spirit and philosophic theories that sustained the literature of the period and kept the wheels of the social and scientific revolutions of the generation turning. Rav Kook could not but take note of the progress, the blessing, and the positive qualities stored up in these events. He valued greatly the sincerity, the search after the truth, the avoidance of sham, that found expression in the great revolt of the period, and he was party to the consciousness of freedom that characterized it.[5] It was essential to give a religious explanation for the central processes and the spiritual and social phenomena that at best regarded religion as unnecessary and as absolutely irrelevant. Against this background, Rav Kook's philosophy appears as a revolution in the field of Jewish religious thought, as a general philosophy seeking to put forward an alternative to all the existing theories through a reinterpretation of reality, of the nature of man, and of religion itself. If the main sting of Nietzsche's thought was expressed in his sharp criticism of morality, of the hypocrisy and falsehood in it, in order to build a new

5. For a wide-ranging discussion of the great significance of the consciousness of liberty in Rav Kook's writings and his perception of freedom, see Benjamin Ish Shalom, "Rav Kook's Thought Between Rationalism and Mysticism," a dissertation for the doctoral degree, Hebrew University, Jerusalem 5744 (hereafter referred to as "My Essay").

morality on its ruins, it can be said that Rav Kook seeks to battle with the religiosity of his time with regard to the hypocrisy and the falsehood that, in his view, are bound up with it, not in order to create a new religion, but so as to develop a renewed understanding of the significance of religion. In Rav Kook's view, religion is not a cultural phenomenon. The understanding of the religious phenomenon is bound up in a qualitative manner with the understanding of the nature of man, and even beyond this, with the understanding of the nature of all reality.

2.

Rav Kook holds the opinion that occupation with metaphysical questions does not serve the goals of cognitive awareness alone.[6] In his view, metaphysical contemplation is itself an expression of a basic soul-need of man.[7] Metaphysical study, which, it may be said, stands at the peak of cultural creation, and all manifestations of culture on their various levels, reflect, in Rav Kook's view, a basic psychological quality in man: a sense of unhappiness, or even of fear, because of the impermanence, the incomprehensibilities of life and reality, and the lack of perfection. In the striving after eternity, Rav Kook sees the basis of all of man's cultural creation; in his own words: "Eternity is the firm foundation for all cultural life in its full sense. The striving after the splendor of eternity conquers death and wipes away tears from all faces."[8]

6. See "My Essay," pp. 47–50.
7. In this context, the words of Albert Einstein are interesting: "There exists a longing for understanding, exactly as there exists a longing for music. Such a longing is common mainly among children, but is absent from most people later on. Without this longing, there would be no mathematics and no natural sciences." See Albert Einstein, "On the Generalized Theory of Gravitation," *Scientific American*, Vol. 182 (1950).
    Words similar to these were heard from Rav Kook with regard to the longing for the nearness of G-d, which also is found mainly among children and usually disappears later on. Further on I shall quote his words. Clifford Geertz, a contemporary researcher, also deals in his book with man's need to understand, to find an explanation, as a biological need. Here there is no reference yet to an explanation in the existential sense of Victor Frankl, but the way to the existential meaning is very short. See: Clifford Geertz, *The Interpretation of Cultures, Selected Essays*, (New York 1973), pp. 140–41. Similarly: Victor Frankl, *Man's Search for Meaning* (Tel Aviv 1970). For more on Rav Kook's position on this subject, see *Needar BaKodesh* (Jerusalem 5693), pp. 7–8; "*Orot HaTechiyah*" in *Orot*, (Jerusalem 5727), pp. 72–73.
8. *Arpelei Tohar* (Jaffa 5674), p. 36. All further references are from this edition. Reprinted in Jerusalem 5743 with some changes that were introduced into the body of the text by the editors, and see in this connection in "My Essay," p. 163 and n.

In Rav Kook's view, this striving after eternity is fundamentally a religious striving. In his opinion, religious striving is man's most natural striving, and it is recognizable already in his childhood, "while his soul has still not been sullied by the loathsomeness of "the leaven in the dough" that is part of the tumult of life."[9] He believes that religious striving is the central and dominant motivating force in the life of mankind. In his words:

We are compelled to decide that the striving after the nearness of G-d, with all its might—this alone is the central basis for all the tendencies, the longings and the strivings of the soul of all mankind; they all flow from it and return to it. So it is in general, in the soul of mankind as a whole, as a collective entity, and so also with regard to the individual—the personal life of every single individual human being.[10]

Rav Kook goes on to describe the processes of development and rationalization, to which culture is subjected, and the demand for "ordered life," as being hindered by the striving for the nearness of G-d.[11] He sees the religious striving as flowing from "an inner natural compulsion" and as the central foundation for all the strivings of the soul. It should be mentioned that this psychological phenomenon is in his view only the tip of the iceberg of that quality that characterizes all existence, and it is described by him as a law of nature that "does not change its function whether for many or for few, for great or for small" (*Kirvat Elokim*, p. 3).

It should be made clear that Rav Kook was not so sure in his view that all human beings are indeed hindered in all their works by the power of the religious striving, and anyhow not out of awareness of such striving. But HaReAYaH believed that even if many human strivings,

---

115 thereon. And in parallel: *Orot HaKodesh*, Vol. II, p. 377. And see also *Orot HaKodesh*, Vol. III, p. 222. Compare Franz Rosenzweig, *Star of Redemption* (Jerusalem 5730), p. 45: "The awareness of the universe begins with death, with the dread of death. To calm the dread of destruction, to take bitterness out of death and destruction, out of the netherworld—this is what philosophy purports to do." See there the passage in its entirety. See also: S. H. Bergmann, "Death and Beyond Death in the Teaching of Rav Kook," in *Thinkers and Believers* (Tel Aviv 5719), p. 101.
9. *Berachot* 17a—This is the term for the evil inclination.
10. "The Nearness of G-d," in *Tachkemoni*, 2 (1911), pp. 1–2. See also: *Orot*, p. 119: "It is not possible to find a basic position for the spirit except in the air of the divine."
11. "Nearness of G-d," in *Tachkemoni*, 2 (1911), pp. 6–7.

such as the striving for social justice and equality, the striving for
meaning and significance, the striving for knowledge and enlightenment, and above all, the striving for freedom—even if these may be
explained in anthropological, psychological, or sociological terms, at
base one cannot understand them except in terms of religious perception. For all the strivings are united by the totality—the striving after
perfection and the absolute—which is none other than a religious
striving. The occupation with the improvement of society, and with
political and economic action, is not sufficient in itself to satisfy man's
spiritual needs. "Not this is its rest and its goal."[12] In his opinion, "it
is impossible to live without the influence of the faith of holiness," for
"man's thinking is too narrow to explain the depth of existence" (*Arpelei Tohar*, p. 45).

In other words, Rav Kook argues that when man looks for the
meaning of existence, he will find it only in what is beyond concrete
existence:

When we are asked what is the purpose of social life, we have no answer from
within that life itself but we have to come to the striving of a larger and more
exalted life than this one . . . and for this the perfection of the world demands
a profound longing for salvation from the foundations of heavenly salvation.
And Israel's eternal hope for the light of the Messiah, for the light of the Lord
in His world—this is the foundation of the world, of all its conditions, even
of the social world with all its branches" (*Orot HaKodesh*, Vol. II, p. 561).

The messianic idea and the messianic hope are therefore vital for the
world's existence. They are the very essence itself of the religious
phenomenon. For the significance and purpose of an undertaking must
always come from beyond the actualization of the undertaking itself.[13]
Otherwise, the entire undertaking will be doomed to disintegrate and
disappear immediately after its substantiation and realization. The
existence and vital importance of the undertaking itself make it necessary that its significance be understood in terms from the field of

12. *Orot HaKodesh*, Vol. II, p. 375. Compare *Orot*, p. 119: "The place of our rest
is only in G-d."
13. Indeed, in the monistic perception of the HaReAYaH, the absolute dimension of
reality is immanent in concrete existence; but, with this, it is important to distinguish
between the various dimensions. See *Orot HaKodesh*, Vol. III, p. 141.

eternity or from the field of the absolute, that is, in religious terms. Man must know "that one cannot manage with practical observation alone; nor can the world of practical affairs of itself, even when it is ordered and arranged with every perfection and good order, be the source of life for man whose soul is exalted high above all those boundaries within which practical plans are defined. And it is essential to bind man with a permanent bond with the superior aspects of being, with spiritual heights" (*Arpelei Tohar*, p. 9).

Consequently, Rav Kook makes clear that when he himself uses psychological and other similar terms, i.e., secular terms, when he is explaining these phenomena, this is only "to let the ear hear what it can absorb." That is, he does so for a *didactic-explanatory* purpose. According to his words, the striving in man for G-d's nearness is not one of many strivings, nor is it a central or principal striving. This striving is in fact the soul's self, its being, and the foundation of its existence . . . the character of the essence of its life" (*Kirvat Elokim*, p. 3).[14] In Rav Kook's perception, man's uniqueness is not in his being endowed with understanding *(animal rationale* or *Homo sapiens)* or even in his being a maker of symbols, according to Cassirer's definition: *animal symbolicum.* In his view, man's humanity is in his religiosity, and maybe the fitting term for him is *Homo religiosus.*

From what has been said above, one may get the impression that the application of religious categories to the description and analysis of the nature of man, as well as to the motivations of human culture, blurs the issues and clouds the theoretical discussion of the religious phenomenon itself. Indeed, even though Rav Kook rejects such a distinction between religion and culture from the point of view of their character, he does not hide from the fact of their appearance as specific and separate revelations in human history. Moreover, Rav Kook even refers to the distinction, accepted in the study of religions, between natural religion, or "religious feeling," and traditional institutional religion, and he discusses the link between them:

. . . The wholeness of faith is when its body and soul are well grasped together . . . Sometimes it occurs that these two aspects hang loosely and natural faith

---

14. For the understanding of the roots of this perception against the background of Rav Kook's general metaphysical outlook, and in particular in the light of his perception of the "Will," see "My Essay" (*supra* n. 5), Chaps. 4 and 6.

and tradition are separated from each other, and then there appears a sickness of faith . . . The healthy content always proceeds in harmony, and in the same degree that spiritual faith ascends so does traditional faith ascend with it . . . And for Jews this connection and unity are what the performance of every mitzvah inwardly seeks" (*MeOrot HaEmunah*, p. 15).[15]

It is not surprising that Rav Kook demands a harmonious relationship between natural faith and the traditional religious framework, and all disharmony is perceived by him as sickness—as an unhealthy condition. It is interesting that when Rav Kook criticizes Christianity on this point, he portrays natural belief as the lesser value, while in the above passage it is perceived as "the soul" of tradition. Thus, he says:

Paganism perceived the content of natural faith, but went wrong in separating it from everything above it, and inevitably cut off all the branches. Natural faith is a basis for a suitable vessel for containing and receiving the heavenly lights that are above all order and nature, and in this way natural faith is elevated and purified and the nature of man and of all the world is elevated and purified and comes to be joined to the perfection of its ideal form (from a manuscript).[16]

In any case, the fact of the distinction that Rav Kook makes, and the attention he devotes both to natural faith and to traditional religion, shows how aware he was of the tension between them in practice. He even says this plainly. Rav Kook leaves no room for doubt that one must not forgo the keeping of the mitzvot; and even according to the rabbinic view that "in the time to come" the mitzvot will be annulled, Rav Kook lays down that "before the advent of the new world . . . of which it might be said that the mitzvot will be annulled in the time to come," there will first arise "a situation of a complete Torah-mitzvah-observance revival in the full splendor of its beauty, a *teshuvah* out of love embracing the entire nation and also influencing the whole world" (from manuscript).[17]

How will this Torah-mitzvah revival come about? It will be in the

15. Photographic edition, together with "A Special Article," without bibliographical reference.

16. Manuscript, Collection 5, p. 57a.

17. Manuscript, Collection 2, p. 55a. More on the position of the practical commandments see "My Essay," Chap. 10.

same way in which all human culture works and sets its stamp on human nature:

The mitzvot will develop human nature until they will themselves become the fixed nature of man, and just as human culture aims at making its educational properties fixed nature, so also does divine culture rise up in the striving for the renewal of human nature to a supreme divine degree that will stamp an inner desire for the Torah in its entirety; and the reward of a mitzvah is the mitzvah (from manuscript).[18]

In the framework of this discussion, we shall not refer in detail to Rav Kook's attitude to the status of the practical mitzvot. Nevertheless, there is one aspect that we wish to stress, namely the natural character of religion. Rav Kook believes that there is basically an essential identity between natural religion and the qualities and norms of institutional religion. In an ideal situation, man has no need at all of mitzvot and laws, for these exist as natural deeds and as behavioral patterns that are mandated by plain intelligence:

When intelligence illumines with the fullness of its light, there is no need for any special guidance by laws and statutes. The goodness that is brought to completion in an action follows after the light of intelligence, and all life's obstacles are straightened out by themselves. Laws and statutes exist not as laws and statutes that are commanded, but as natural movements for matters in which the illumination of the intelligence is taken for granted.

Good and evil and all their values . . . came after intelligence was deprived of its light, and feeling, wonder (admiration) and pressure of the physical senses took its place; after the original sin of eating the fruit of the Tree of Knowledge of Good and Evil (*Orot HaKodesh,* Vol. III, p. 129).[19]

The idea that the intellect compels the observance of the religious mitzvot includes inevitably the assumption that religion is rational. Indeed, Rav Kook believes that one of the causes of unbelief in the modern age is the fact that such a logical connection between the details of religion and any general principle is not clearly visible, while "the world is so sophisticated as to demand to have an understanding

18. Manuscript, Collection 4, p. 31b.
19. Compare: Maimonides, *Guide for the Perplexed* Part I, Chap. 1.

of how all the details are connected with the whole" (*Arpelei Tohar*, p. 1).[20]

Yet, despite the fact that what is wanted is an understanding of the rationalism in religion, Rav Kook maintains that this understanding cannot be attained by the intelligence, "for the intelligence has to toil to find the relationship between the principal [matter], which the heart readily accepts, and the distant branches of the private meanderings, and it constantly stumbles and grows weaker in life's paths; nor can the limited intelligence, with all its reckonings, illumine its path" (*Arpelei Tohar*, p. 17). In other words, another, superrational ability is needed to understand the rationalism in religion. "And if the world would occupy itself with the light of Torah to such a degree that the spiritual soul would grow to recognize the proper connection between the parts and the spiritual whole (in everything), then *teshuvah* and the perfection of the world would be realized" (Ibid. p. 1).

Rav Kook himself does not believe that this analysis exhausts the causes of the crisis of religion, or, naturally, the factors for healing and correcting it. In speaking of the crisis of religion or of its collapse, one should distinguish between the general, human crisis, and the crisis that faced Judaism, for, in the view of Rav Kook, the roots of the crisis in Israel (i.e., in Judaism) and among the nations are completely different.[21] Rav Kook argues against the assumption, which was generally accepted in his time among researchers in religion, that religion is merely an anachronism, a "fossil" of the past, a mode of thought that enlightened humanity has already cast away.[22] In fact, he accepts this assumption insofar as it applies to the nations of the world, since "the idolatrous part in whose trend of thought it falls, because of the strengthening of the intelligence and man's progress as a whole, and on account of the fact that this idolatrous aspect is deeply rooted in their religiosity—therefore their whole force of religion collapses" (*Needar BaKodesh*, p. 19)[23] But so far as Israel is concerned, the foundations of the Jewish religion are not interwoven with idolatrous motifs, and there is nothing to prevent them from being accepted by people even on the highest level of culture of the modern period.

20. See "My Essay," Chap. 6, p. 99.
21. *Needar BaKodesh* (Jerusalem 5693), p. 19.
22. See William James, *Varieties of Religious Experience* (Jerusalem 5729), p. 321.
23. See in the dictionary of *Even Shushan* under "Nbk."

The crisis of faith in Israel is rooted, therefore, in another cause—that is, in the demoralizing and limiting character that religiosity took on in the course of the generations. Here are the words of Rav Kook verbatim:

Fear has a shortcoming from the point of view of its exterior, in that it softens the heart too much, forces out of man his quality of heroism, so that he remains like a man without strength. Thus fear, even though it be a heavenly fear stemming at source from a pure tradition, prevents the completion of the world and the perfection of man's form. When matters come to this stage that the quality of fear is filled with much bitterness so that its influence helps to crush the heart overmuch—when its spirit sinks too much—then it is smitten with a humanity of another spirit, the spirit of licentiousness, which comes to weaken the poison of the external fear.

When these two external spirits struggle with each other, the world is filled with intoxication, and dust rises up to the throne of glory; weakness, jealousy, hypocrisy, and exceeding wickedness on one side, and boldness, strife, licentiousness and an emptiness of spirit on the other, cause many to be slain, and the tumult grows fainter and fainter until the sun of righteousness will shine and supreme divine knowledge will appear in its strength, bringing healing in its wings (from manuscript).[24]

Thus, secularism and nihilism are perceived as a reaction to a long period of the crushing of man's spirit and his natural strivings by religion. "The need for this revolt is the leaning toward materialism that is bound to have an effect on the nation as a whole in a forceful manner, after long periods of years have passed in which the need and the possibility of material concern have been entirely canceled out from the whole nation" (*Arpelei Tohar*, p. 60). And when "the holy is bound up with the profane until it causes the matter to disintegrate," argues Rav Kook, there comes a period "when the matter demands justice for itself 'and the creditor presses,' and then the profane collects its payment from the sacred with interest and usury, and its impudence becomes overpowering" (*Needar BaKodesh*, p. 4).

Indeed, the result of the wrestling of these two false spiritual movements is the absence of truth and authenticity from both equally.

24. Manuscript, early collection, p. 57.

Weakness, jealousy, hypocrisy, and wickedness take hold of the religious camp. Impudence, licentiousness, and emptiness characterize the secular camp. The neutral approach that Rav Kook takes in describing and analyzing the processes of secularization in Israel has its roots deep in the metaphysical foundations of his teaching, and we shall not expatiate on them here.[25] The fact that unbelief, like belief, is also perceived as "a life force, the leaven of the life of heavenly brightness being clothed in it" *(Arpelei Tohar,* p. 32),[26] makes it possible to see its positive aspects also, and to examine the positive role it fulfills:

In order to cleanse the individual soul and the soul of all society from that impurity of the fear of punishment, which frightens and leads to sickness—for this the basis of every negative influence has been created in the world. And the poison of the vulgar heresy that destroys the world was established at its base so as to constitute a poison antidote against these impurities of the fear of punishment in its descent lower and lower as it is cut off from the light of the Torah, from the principle of heavenly fear, from true love (from manuscript).[27]

This tolerant attitude characterized Rav Kook's relationship not only to the phenomenon of secularism. It was precisely out of a most profound religious position that Rav Kook was capable of seeing not only what was useful but also what was true in strange religions and beliefs. Thus, he says, "Because the way that joins human thought and feelings with the infinite and supreme divine light must be in variegated colors, therefore the spiritual way of living is different in every known nation and group" *(Orot HaKodesh,* Vol. III, p. 15). That is, the particular way that characterizes every national culture and every religion is only a particular manner of revelation of the divine light; hence there is truth at its base.

25. See "My Essay," Chap. 6.
26. And see also Ibid. p. 19. Also, *Orot,* p. 127.
27. Manuscript, Collection 3, p. 21. With this, Rav Kook does not hesitate to direct sharp criticism at blasphemy and blasphemers, from various points of view. In a manuscript, Collection 2, p. 34b, HaReAYaH expresses himself sharply and sees in the blasphemer "a lost soul" whose "life is no life." See further: *Arpelei Tohar,* p. 20; *Orot HaKodesh,* Vol III, *Rosh Davar,* pp. 24 and 34; *Igrot HaReAYaH,* Vol. I (Jerusalem 5722), p. 126, and *Iggeret* 20, p. 369; *Igrot HaReAYaH,* Vol. II, p. 4 para. 7; *Orot HaTeshuvah* (Or Etzion 5730), p. 40; *Orot,* pp. 79–101; *Teudat Yisrael uLeumit,* p. 62.

The question of tolerance, in the view of Rav Kook, is first and foremost a moral question.[28] Yet Rav Kook was well aware of the problematic aspects of religious tolerance from the point of view of a believing man.[29] In his view, a tolerant stance is opposed in essence to natural belief, and the stronger the belief, the greater is the measure of zealousness. "Normal theology believes," argues HaReAYaH, "that religions have to stand in opposition to each other" (*Tallelei Orot*, p. 17). Yet a religious position is not hindered by the natural religious sentiment alone. A position of faith includes the rational basis,[30] and from the point of view of religious consciousness, a tolerant approach is the outstanding expression of the understanding of the divine revelation in the richness of its colors. Here then are Rav Kook's words verbatim:

The state of belief has in it a natural content and a content of awareness and enlightenment. From the side of its natural content it is full of strength and flaming fire, and cannot tolerate anything that opposes it. Not only does it not tolerate whatever opposes its own essence, but also whatever stands in the way of its private path and its special style. Therefore particular faiths cannot dwell together in one company, or be mixed together one with the other, without some natural damage developing for all of them; and the mightier, the healthier, the greater and the more important is the belief, the more its natural strength will grow and so also will its zealousness grow, and its scrupulosity with regard to its purity. However, from the aspect of the awareness content of the belief, it is full of breadth of knowledge and is thereby adorned with much kindness and great tolerance. In its cognitive awareness it knows that the inner spirit of the divine pattern, and the heavenly perfection it strives for, is also rich in colors so as to be able to clothe itself in a large variety of garments as well as in contrasting description; and by these means it rises above every contradiction and is elevated above every opposition (from manuscript).[31]

28. *"Tallelei Orot,"* in *Tachkemoni* (5670), p. 17.
29. On tolerance and Jewish tradition, see, A. Holtman, *The Face of Judaism*, (Tel Aviv 5743), p. 217. On tolerance in the perception of Rav Kook, I have dealt at length in a separate article that is due to appear soon.
30. See Rav Otto, *The Idea of the Holy* (Oxford 1972–73), pp. 1–40. Rav Kook also distinguishes the rational basis as one of the components of the religious phenomenon, but his analysis of the components of the phenomenon is different from that of Otto. See *infra* n. 40.
31. Manuscript, Collection 5, p. 76b. On the distinction that Rav Kook makes between the emotional and the rational basis, see *infra* n. 40.

These words are not left only on a theoretical plane, as a phenomeno-logical analysis bereft of all practical meaning. On the contrary, Rav Kook deduces practical conclusions from his basic position, and he does this with great boldness:

One really has to concern oneself with this with all the wisdoms of the world and with all of life's teachings, and with all the methods of the various cultures and the teaching of the morality and religion of every nation and tongue; and with greatness of soul he will be able to purify them all" (*Arpelei Tohar*, pp. 32–33).

Despite the varieties of opinions among religions and beliefs, and despite the differences of race and climate, it is right to get a complete understanding of the views of the various nations and groups, as far as possible, to study their character and their qualities, so as to know how to establish human love on the foundations of those who are close to the action . . . And a mean, grudging outlook, which leads one to see only ugliness and uncleanness in everything beyond the confines of a particular nation, even if it is outside the scope of the Jewish people, is one of the most serious clouding factors causing a general breakdown of every good spiritual edifice for whose light every refined soul longs (from manuscript).[32]

Of course, one must emphasize that Rav Kook's pluralistic attitude does not imply an indifference to the value distinctions of religions and beliefs. Although in his view, one should see "all the spiritual sides as one organic institution," yet one should not hide from differences "between principal and secondary, high and low, severe and light holiness, or between both of these and profane" (*Tallelei Orot*, p. 17). Furthermore, Rav Kook adds:

We are lifted up above the lowliness in which the nations of the world find themselves and we have become the principal object of scrutiny among their finest scholars on account of the difference between the Semitic and the Aryan spirit. We raise the banner in the name of the Lord G-d of the World Who created all mankind in His image, in the image of G-d He created him. And all the branches go either to the right or to the left, for they really do have among them high and low, right and left. But basically everything ascends to

32. Manuscript, early collection, pp. 1–8.

one place, and in time to come everything will be exalted so as to perfect the world according to the kingdom of the Almighty, and all the children of flesh will call upon Thy Name (from manuscript).[33]

This is undoubtedly an interesting expression of Rav Kook, which rejects discrimination and distinctions in the field of the spirit that stem from differences of racial or national origin. Rav Kook's formulation in this passage is especially surprising in the light of his perception of the mystical-metaphysical quality of the people of Israel.[34] One really has to acknowledge that it is difficult to accept these two ideas together unless one accepts them both as qualified, as is indeed to be inferred from the words of Rav Kook concerning the differences of worth and the various functions of limbs in an organic body.

How are the differences between Judaism and other religions expressed? Surely, in the moral and spiritual aims, and not in the metaphysical outlooks: "The difference stems not from the aspect of the statement of the idea of metaphysical truth contained in the concept of divine unity, something that can be stated by every nation and tongue, but from the aspect of the inner divine character of the love of probity and justice, and the powerful striving for these divine ideals in all their strength" (*Ikve HaTzon,* pp. 147–48).[35]

Nevertheless, one cannot hide from the clear link between the Jewish metaphysical outlook, which Rav Kook explains as a monistic perception, and the spiritual and moral aim of Judaism, which he regards as a unifying aim. Rav Kook devotes a few chapters to a discussion of the nature of the moral spiritual aims that characterize the various religions. He distinguishes among four main strivings in the human spirit: a) the striving for the imposition of absolute evil in all sectors of life—a striving that he ascribes to idolatry; b) the striving for destruction, posited on the assumption of the absolute rule of evil in reality— this characterizes the Buddhist religion; c) the third striving, ascribed to Christianity, defined as "part despair," that is, despair of the material world and its relegation to the power of evil, and the search for salvation of the soul only; d) the fourth striving, which characterizes

33. Manuscript, Small Collection, p. 97.
34. See "My Essay," pp. 100–104; also p. 40 n. 51.
35. *Eder HaYekar VeIkve HaTzon* (Jerusalem 5723).

Judaism. This aims at "delivering all . . . the body and the soul . . . evil itself as well as the good . . . and to elevate the world and the fullness thereof in all its aspects and modes."[36]

The outstanding weakness that Rav Kook sees in idolatry and in Christianity is the imposition of a divisiveness in reality. "The pagan world," in his view, "strives to be linked with nature as it is," and sees in it "its final goal" (from manuscript).[37] Against this, Christianity has distanced itself from nature and has rejected it, and through seeing the entire sphere of natural life as opposed to religion, "it injected poison into the mythical content and put it in opposition to the strong bastion of the halacha" (from manuscript).[38] That is, the rejection of life in Christianity has brought about the rejection of the mitzvot.

Differences of aim stamp their mark on the religious consciousness of man the believer in every one of the religions, and certainly also on the nature of the worship.[39] Rav Kook believes that these differences are rooted in the different character of the basic religious experience in each one of the religions. In all religions, Rav Kook maintains, the religious service has its source in the experience of "trembling and stirring,"[40] that is, a negative experience. In opposition to this, the experience that moves the spirit of Judaism is described as "love" and as "a striving for divine ideals,"[41] that is, a positive experience.

36. *Orot HaKodesh,* Vol. II, p. 488, and Ibid. p. 486 (and in parallel: *Arpelei Tohar,* p. 68).
37. Manuscript, Collection 2, p. 15b.
38. Manuscript, Collection 5, p. 103b.
39. *Eder HaYekar VeIkve HaTzon* (pp. 147–48).
40. Ibid. It is interesting to compare Rav Kook's analysis in this matter with the perception of Rav Otto (*supra* n. 30). In an article, "A Portrait of the Personality of the Rambam," which was published in the Erev Pesach issue of the newspaper *HaAretz* of 5695, even Rav Kook determines, like Otto, that the religious phenomenon embraces two foundations: the emotional and the rational. In his view, the emotional basis expresses itself in a natural longing for the nearness of G-d, a longing that also caused negative side phenomena. The rational basis was intended to restrain the emotional basis and to purify and cleanse religious thinking. The difference between Rav Kook and Otto is in their perception of these two bases. With Otto, the emotional basis, or, in his words, *Das Numinose,* is expressed in dread and fear in the presence of G-d, the mystery *(Mysterium Tremendum),* and the rational basis creates descriptions and concepts that seek to make possible some sort of rational perception of G-d. As against this, with Rav Kook the emotional basis does not express dread and fearsomeness but, as stated, a longing and a striving, and the rational basis does not create labels and concepts, but on the contrary, rejects every description and conceptual formulation out of a striving for the purification of religious thought.
41. *Ikve HaTzon,* Ibid.

Religious consciousness whose source is in a negative experience bears the character of dependence and servitude, or in the language of Rav Kook, "The servitude of a slave,"[42] but "the enlightened service of G-d," whose foundation is in positive feeling, is a consciousness of creating and building, "and this is the service of divine ideals, to serve them, to improve them, to attempt to strengthen them, to ennoble them among the people, among mankind and in the world" (*Ikve HaTzon*, p. 145). As against the consciousness of servitude, the heritage of primitive religiosity, HaReAYaH sets up a religion of freedom[43] that is the goal of the struggle against "idolatry":

Divine ecstasy, when it descends from its place, when it serves in an area outside that of the G-d of truth . . . the divine relationship to that which is no-god, hinders the ascent of creation . . . The freedom of the world is in the radical ugliness of every idolatry, from the point of view of thought, language and deed, of sentiment, temperament and leaning; of national, mental and religious substance. And toward this the Assembly of Israel strives, and in that day the Lord Himself alone will be lifted up and He will chase away idols altogether (from manuscript).[44]

Rav Kook thus perceived Judaism as the actualization of the possibility for the freedom of the individual, for the freedom of the nation, for the freedom of the world.

3.

Consciousness of the question of freedom is one of the most characteristic features of Rav Kook's work, and it defines freedom both as an ideal of the religious-mystical way, and as a central idea in his academic thesis.

The mystical striving is perceived by Rav Kook as the most authentic revelation of man's self[45] or as the most definitive expression of free-

42. It should be noted that Shleiermacher also put forward favorably the "feeling of dependence" as a central and characteristic note of the religious phenomenon. See Rav Kook's discussion in *Ikve HaTzon*, p. 145.
43. See *Orot HaKodesh*, Vol. III, p. 75: "The limiting of vexations is one of the aims of the divine Torah."
44. Manuscript, Collection 3, p. 9.
45. For a description of the phenomenological analysis of the mystical way of Rav Kook concerning the tensions that characterized it, see "My Essay," Chap. 5.

dom: "Let a man know in his soul, when divine longings seize hold of him in his heart, then is his soul revealed within him" (from manuscript).[46] Consequently:

As the light of the soul bursts forth, he must give it its freedom immediately so that the man may expand, draw, imagine, consider and apply a critical faculty; strive and feel an intense longing for the greatest heights, for his original root, for the life of his soul, for the light of the life of all the worlds, the light of G-d the Supreme, for His goodness and splendor (*Arpelei Tohar*, p. 42).[47]

The fact that Rav Kook, throughout all his writings, chooses to describe the striving and the religious and mystical experience in terms of freedom and of man's liberty leaves no room for doubt concerning the decisive influence of the spirit of the period.[48] "To liberate man," Rav Kook says in *Orot HaKodesh*, "that is our aim" (Ibid. p. 97). This liberation is the aim of religion, and it is attained through a mystical effort: "Through his elevation, his development, by the revelation of all his inner faculties . . . For the inwardness of everything is the divine aim in existence, the aim of the hidden longing of man" (Ibid.).

In the same direction, Rav Kook sharpens his definitions to the point of complete identification of mystical thought with freedom and with the essence of the soul. He says, "The secret logic is the Israelite's

46. Manuscript, Small Collection, p. 224.
47. See Ibid. p. 13: "One should not disturb the actions of the soul and with overmuch toil, whether physical labor or spiritual toil. One should not vex the refinement of the world with hard labor."
48. See "My Essay," Chap. 1, p. 18, and also n. 101 there. Like so many of those who battled for the idea of freedom in the modern era, so also Rav Kook saw ecclesiastical tyranny and philosophic determinism as one of the factors that have to be struggled with. See *Eder HaYakar Velkve HaTzon*, pp. 153–54: "Only stupidity and personal derogation through the dimness of life of the Middle Ages, whose mark is seen also in the modern age upon anyone who permits himself to be smitten with the sickness of this darkness—this is what has caused the sentiment of freedom to be so silent, especially through the papal influence; so that philosophy, particularly rationalist philosophy, which is supposed to stem from life itself, has lost its life-force and its great strength so that it is unable, with its own strength, to plead the cause of the healthy spirit that is proclaimed by the entire stream of human life, saying, "How can this man deny the reality of divine universal freedom while both the inner and external freedom is the choicest of his ideals and the peace of his soul: 'Engraved on the Tablets: read not *charut* [engraved] but *cherut* [freedom]' " (*Avot* 6:2).

freedom, that is, the Jewish soul . . . When freedom ascends to its highest point, when the soul does not have to tolerate the yoke of any accepted opinion stemming from a non-Jewish source, then the ideas that are gathered up by this pure holiness are really the secrets of Torah (Ibid. p. 135). Similarly, he says (Ibid. p. 99), "The obscured enlightenment . . . is tied together with the self-essence."[49]

Indeed, Rav Kook speaks of two kinds of "intellectual works," the difference between them being described in terms of limitation as opposed to freedom and enlargement. The one work is the rational one that "seeks to clothe the overflowing Holy Spirit with human garments of logic and intelligence." Against this is the mystical work whose aim is to exclude "the logical thoughts of the mind . . . from the narrow and limited life in which they are in profusion, to the heavenly world of freedom" (from manuscript).[50]

Yet, it is not only that the mystical road is perceived as the expression and actualization of freedom, but freedom itself, or in the language of Rav Kook, "the freedom of opinions," is perceived as an essential condition for attaining *devekut* (spiritual ecstasy):

According to the outer, false, imagination, it seems to man that freedom of opinions and divine ecstasy are contradictory things; but when man ascends to the heights of refinement of the pure opinions he will come to see clearly that only through complete freedom of opinions can he attain to a rational purified divine ecstasy *(devekut).* And out of this free ecstasy his own cognitive awareness will be elevated and will raise up, together with itself, all his desires and the essence of his being, his attributes and his strivings (Ibid.).[51]

49. Ibid. p. 99; Similarly, *Arpelei Tohar,* p. 59.
50. Manuscript, Collection 2, p. 35.
51. See also Manuscript, Collection 1/2 p. 11: "And this manifestation [of the supreme Divine Perfection] in its breadth and its pleasures is on condition that it embraces man's free will." In our discussion of this subject, we are interested also in the existential dimension of the link between the mystical elevation and the sense of freedom, and I therefore quote Rav Kook's words in this matter:

Those who have the highest wisdom feel the supreme freedom, and they cannot be subjected to any servitude, for every servitude is of human flesh and blood. Even the acceptance of the yoke of the kingdom of heaven, which is normal among people, is also a human subjugation . . . and the striving for absolute freedom is the highest form of *teshuvah"* (*Arpelei Tohar,* p. 40).

He whose spirit is filled with the effulgence of the light of the *Ein Sof* [Infinity], all fixed ideas pressure his heart, and he finds no peace of mind in them. Therefore he has to adorn his soul

Freedom is usually perceived as a quality or condition related to the subject. Freedom can be tested in action, in social or political activity, in artistic creation, or in independent thought. In whatever way it shows itself, one may perceive freedom as a capability or autonomy. In Rav Kook's teaching, the concept of "freedom" *(cherut)* is not quite the same as the accepted perception. Indeed, HaReAYaH describes freedom as "the choice ideal," as man's "upliftment of soul" (*Ikve HaTzon*, p. 53) and as an idea "whose flag our people bears" (*Igrot HaReAYaH*, Vol. II, pp. 41–42). Yet all these descriptions do not exhaust his opinion on the subject. We shall try to show below that in the perception of Rav Kook, freedom is not a quality or condition related to the subject. Freedom is the subject itself. Or, in the language of Jean-Paul Sartre, "Seeing that man's freedom is not a quality among other qualities—clearly man himself *is* freedom."[52]

The metaphysical foundations of Rav Kook's perception[53] allow us to reach a general conclusion that one should see in freedom a process of actualization of the self. The degree of freedom is commensurate with the degree of realization of the "self." We shall see below that, in Rav Kook's opinion, one should not speak of freedom as a title related in some way to the "self," for it is completely identified with the "self." This idea is stated in the two bastions of freedom: the human and the divine. It is therefore of interest to explain the link between these two bastions.

In Jewish theological thought, this link is perceived, generally, as problematical, and philosophers come to terms with it as an inescapable or imaginary paradox. Either way, "Everything was foreseen, yet freedom of choice was given" (*Avot*, 3:19) became one of the pillars of faith.[54] Nevertheless, in a monistic-pantheistic perception the question could lose all understanding. In such an outlook, there is a tendency toward an identification of the personality of man with G-d. One is not speaking any more of *devekut* in the sense of "thou shalt walk in His

---

with the supreme free pleasure of the world of freedom" (*Orot HaKodesh*, Vol. III, p. 186. See further, *Orot HaKodesh*, Vol. I, p. 107).

Just as the inner nobility prevails within him . . . so also the spirit of freedom prevails within him . . . and he is granted freedom from all his enslavements" (*Orot HaKodesh*, Vol. III, p. 97).

52. J. P. Sartre, *Selected Writings*, Menachem Brinker, ed., Vol. I (Tel Aviv 1977), p. 6.

53. See "My Essay," Chap. 4, p. 71.

54. See Maimonides, *Sefer HaMadda, Hilchot Teshuvah*, Chap. 5.

ways—just as He is merciful, so be you also merciful, etc. . . ." or of a rational *devekut* (literally, "clinging") of the philosophers, but of the mystical understanding of *devekut* through ecstasy[55] or of the quietist sense of the crushing of the "ego."[56] Accordingly, in this perception, the meaning of the concept of "freedom" will be altogether different from the accepted meaning. And really, in Rav Kook's metaphysical position, although it can be seen as a monistic position, the concept "freedom" and its relationship to the concept of "self" stand in the shadow of the tension between the transcendental aspect and the immanental. Let us pause therefore to clarify the question of the status of the human "self" as against the divine "self," and to clarify the exact meaning of the concept of "freedom" in Rav Kook's teaching, with its implications and moral significance.

In one of his short articles,[57] Rav Kook analyzes the difference between the condition of freedom and the condition of slavery, not as a contrast between freedom and compulsion, but as the difference between a condition of complete harmony in man's inner world and a condition from which such harmony is absent. He defines freedom as "that exalted spirit" of loyalty to "the inner self," to the quality of "the image of G-d." As against this, "the spirit of slavery" implies the absence of this loyalty or the lack of harmony between the content of life and emotion, and the "independent soul" quality. There is no talk here of freedom as capability, as freedom of choice or as creativity. All these Rav Kook perceives as the expressions of freedom, not as the essence of freedom itself. In this passage, freedom is perceived as the spirit of loyalty to the self. There is still no clarification of the quality of this "self," nor shall we anticipate. Let us point only to the strong connection between the concept of "freedom" and that of the "self." This connection is recognized in a further passage that perceives freedom as a "self" attribute in a positive sense in which there is an absence of the attribute of jealousy:

Supreme freedom is connected by its illumination with supreme loving-kindness, and these gaze into the world only through the purity of the most

---

55. See Plotinus, *Anadot,* 7:9; See "My Essay," Chap. 1, n. 54.
56. See R. Schatz, *Chasidism As Mysticism* (Jerusalem 5740), especially Chapters 1, 2, and 7.
57. *HaYesod* (13 Nissan 5695), issue no. 126–27.

supreme attributes, and this purity consumes all jealousy from the heart
. . . and through not being tainted by the attribute of jealousy it is acceptable
in its "self"; nor does it move away from its inner attribute; and it is not jealous
of the external features of anyone else nor of his inner qualities; and it is
through this that its self exists (*Arpelei Tohar,* p. 41).

Man asserts his existence, and maintains his freedom, by the positive
aspect of his self. True, at certain times people use the term *freedom*
to denote a title or a quality, and so on. Yet what they mean thereby
is only the outer appearances of freedom. Thus, it becomes clear that,
in Rav Kook's view, freedom is not one revelation or another of life,
but the very essence of life itself. Except that life—in the degree of its
being or of its freedom—must find an expression in different presentations of thought, of creation, and of action. Man—by the fact of his
being a man—is free. His freedom is his humanity. This freedom has
to be expressed in original thought, for it is only original thought that
reflects personality.[58] It is true that original thought involves daring,
for it is bound up with a measure of anger, but one has to know that
it is in the nature of a condition for human existence.

One whose soul does not roam in broad places, one who does not search for
the light of truth and goodness with all his heart—he does not suffer spiritual
demolitions, but neither does he have independent buildings. He takes shelter
in the shade of the buildings of nature, like the badgers whose shelter is the
rocks. But man, he in whom is the spirit of man, his soul cannot find shelter
except in the buildings that he erects with his own spiritual toil, for he never
ceases from his industrious labor (*Orot HaKodesh,* Vol. II, p. 314).

And yet it is not original thought alone that reflects personality. In
Rav Kook's view, there are two authentic revelations of personality:
desire and thought. "Desire teaches more about the one who desires
than the deed teaches about the doer; and likewise, all thought teaches
more about the thinker than does any activity about the one who
performs it" (*Arpelei Tohar,* p. 63).[59]

58. *Orot HaKodesh,* Vol. I, p. 175.
59. *See Orot HaKodesh,* Vol. I, p. 259. The will is perceived there as the first revelation
of the spiritual entity; and the intellect and character attributes are the second and the
third manifestations. But one should not deduce anything from this, for in *Orot
HaKodesh,* Vol. I, p. 260 a distinction is made between "secular intellect" and "sacred

It is no accident that the Deity Itself also is revealed in the two aspects of desire and wisdom. This attests not to a chance imagination but to a qualitative relationship between human personality and the Deity; and this will be further explained in the course of the discussion.

Two principal channels of freedom need to be considered: freedom of choice and original thought. These two channels, just as they reflect faithfully man's personality, so do they represent, like magical forces, the relationships of the Deity and the world: "It is a matter of simple observation that the world's relationship to the Deity from its spiritual aspect, namely the forces of desire and cognitive awareness of the G-dhead, is more evident than that of the material aspect, namely the mechanically functioning forces. And just as this is evident in the world, so is it even more evident in man" (*Arpelei Tohar*, p. 46).

Rav Kook deals with the character of this tradition of the relationship between the Universal Presence and man in a detailed letter to Moshe Zeidel.[60] In this letter, Rav Kook explains the dependence of freedom on reality. The degree of substance in substantive existence (or, in his language, "full [or complete] reality") is in accordance with the degree of the revelation of its absolute essence. And the degree of revelation of essence is as the degree of freedom of choice. Hence freedom of choice determines the substance or the existence of man and the world. The link between the Deity and the world is not based on a deterministic principle as formulated by Plotinus or Spinoza, but on a principle of freedom that is part of the substance of absolute reality ("completed reality"). The absoluteness of this principle, insofar as it is absolute, makes possible and compels the existence of nonabsolute freedom ("conditional reality"); all in accordance with the understanding of the concept "absolute" or "perfect" as a concept calling for contradiction, and therefore including its opposite.[61]

Conditional reality, then, is fashioned in the image and the likeness of the absolute "complete reality," in the sense that the principle of its existence, like that of absolute substance, is identical with freedom of choice or with the concept of "freedom." This, in Rav Kook's view,

---

intellect," and the "sacred intellect" is perceived as the source of the will. The question depends on the question of the relationship between will and wisdom as metaphysical fundamentals; and with reference to this, see Chap. 4 of "My Essay."

60. *Igrot HaReAYaH*, Vol. II, pp. 41–42.

61. For an analysis of the concept "perfection," see "My Essay," Chap. 4, pp. 54–55.

is the true meaning of the concept "the image of G-d": the likeness between the G-dly and the human in the context of freedom and existence. And yet, this context in its actualization brings man out of the category of "conditional reality," for through this, "the conditional reality is led to its ascent to the heights of the absolute reality." The actualization of freedom in man is thus a process of man's spiritual rise and his move from conditional being to absolute being.[62]

In his letter, Rav Kook qualifies the formulation concerning the revelation of the self by free will, for he is not interested in being punctilious over the single-minded distinctions on the metaphysical plane. His chief interest is not in knowledge for its own sake but in the moral significance of the knowledge: "We want only to see in the vision of right and wrong a hidden law that matches the wisdom of being, and the righteousness of everlasting justice." That is, to see the phenomenon of morality as a "law of nature," as a cosmic phenomenon. Yet, not being punctilious in the formulation does not mean blurring the main dominant thread that sees freedom as a quality of being and as man's self: "Naturally, we are more inclined to the unity of the things [i.e., that free choice and self are one], and we have no need at all to ascribe essential being to something other than the free will."

On the surface, it appears that the said likeness between the two foci of freedom, the divine and the human, is a resemblance in principle and not a resemblance in the details. Yet it is not so. Rav Kook maintains that there are two kinds of choice[63]: "The hidden choice" that is the Divine Will that constitutes all of reality,[64] and "the open choice" that is only the revelation of the Divine Will and expresses itself in man's capacity to choose. Yet this distinction between open and hidden choice is not a distinction between man and being only, for this distinction is seen also within man himself. That is, the Will as a force that constitutes life, and as against this, will as an ability to choose.[65]

This perception, which sees freedom of choice as reflecting the "self," is what determines its moral significance. For this moral vision

62. We shall deal with this further on.
63. *Orot HaKodesh*, Vol. III, p. 84. See also *Arpelei Tohar*, p. 2.
64. On "the Will," see "My Essay," Chap. 4.
65. *Orot HaKodesh*, Vol. II, p. 368.

of the success of Him Who chose the good, brings "satisfaction to the sense of justice in us."[66] HaReAYaH is speaking here in esthetic terms, namely, It is a pleasant satisfaction to see the beauty in the similarity between authentic good, which is revealed in free choice in the sense of the expression of the Divine Will, and the moral good, i.e., the ethical nature of G-d, which is evident in the chooser's success.[67] Yet, the main importance of free choice is not in the satisfaction caused by the appearance of moral vision, but in the responsibility that it imposes on man: "One of the foundations of *teshuvah,* in man's thinking, is the recognition of man's responsibility for his deeds, which comes from the belief in man's freedom of choice" (*Orot HaTeshuvah,* p. 14).

In Rav Kook's view, one must not accept the anarchist goals that are the product of modern psychology and that seek to deprive man of his moral responsibility.[68] He is indeed conscious of the fact that it is difficult to wish away deterministic claims by a reliance on what may be perceived as the evidences of freedom in reality, for absolute freedom in its purity is not yet apparent in the world, but this does not mean that it is entirely absent.[69]

We have said that in Rav Kook's view there are two authentic revelations of personality: desire and thought. We broadened the discussion a little on desire as it is expressed in freedom of choice. Let us, then, go back and turn to thought. The demand for freedom of thought, "which every thinking man claims for himself,"[70] is not in the

---

66. *Igrot HaReAYaH,* Vol. I, p. 319 (the letter of M. Seidel).
67. I was aroused to the understanding of Rav Kook's words in this matter by some words of Professor Adi Zemach that I heard on the relationship between art and morality, and on moral judgment as aesthetic judgment.
68. *Orot HaKodesh,* Vol. III, p. 297.
69. See Ibid. p. 35. In Rav Kook's view, Israel is the only exception to this rule, for it has been favored with complete freedom. This freedom was acquired at the exodus from Egypt and is expressed as "divine servitude of the Lord G-d of Israel."
70. *Orot HaKodesh,* Vol I, p. 177. The longing for breadth of freedom of expression found poetic expression in Rav Kook's poem "Merchavim": "Broad spaces, broad spaces, my soul longs for the expanses of G-d. Do not shut me up in any cage, neither physical nor spiritual. My soul floats in the broad spaces of heaven; the walls of the heart cannot contain it, nor the walls of activity, morality, reason or politeness. It floats above all these, above everything whatever its name, above every pleasure, every pleasantness and beauty, above everything that is exalted and noble." (Published by A. M. Haberman in *Sinai,* Vol. 17, 5705, among a collection of poems, and quoted also in Zvi Yaron's book, *The Teaching of Rav Kook,* p. 24).

nature of luxury, but a condition of human existence.[71] We have already spoken of original thought as a form of revelation,[72] and we also dealt with Rav Kook's perception of the position of free Jewish thought as "the secrets of Torah."[73] In this matter, HaReAYaH uses definitive language and lays down clearly, "Secret logic is Israelite freedom, that is, the Jewish soul."[74] This is a three-sided triangle. Secret logic is identical with Jewish freedom, which is defined as "the Jewish soul." In that case, Jewish mysticism is not a system or a school. For, insofar as the secrets of Torah reflect the freedom of every individual, his "self"—the content of his thought, that is, the "secrets" themselves— also has particular and original content. Every man's faith is connected by a qualitative link with his personal individuality, and consequently there cannot be a unity of beliefs and opinions. Here are HaReAYaH's words themselves:

Concealed enlightment is particular in every man in a manner special to him. It is bound up with the individuality that is not repeated under any circumstances and cannot be transferred in any thought or explanation. They shall be yours only. The righteous shall live by his faith, his own precisely. And with his own illumining faith that prepares for him a separate Eden by itself, he goes forth to walk in the courtyards of the Lord, which is also the public domain, and thus his outlook is mixed with that of mankind. Let your fountains spread outward in the broad water courses (*Orot HaKodesh*, Vol. I, p. 99).

These words are said not only in regard to the content of original thought but also concerning the mode of expression, language, and style.[75] Accepted terminology, argues Rav Kook in *Orot HaKodesh*, must not limit free creativity: "Look at the lights in their inwardness. Let not names, expressions, letters, swallow your soul. They are given into your hands; you are not given into theirs" (Vol. I, p. 83). The sources that lie before the thinker are clay in the hand of the potter. The free soul is a creative soul,[76] and there is no way of limiting it in

71. See "My Essay," p. 108.
72. Ibid. Chap. 6.
73. Ibid. Chap. 4, p. 47
74. Ibid.
75. See "My Essay," Chap. 3.
76. *Orot HaKodesh*, Vol. I, p. 191.

its creativity.[77] Rav Kook sees it as important that no external influence should be mixed in one's personal spiritual creation, so that the uniqueness of the individual's road to G-d should be preserved:

Whatever enters one soul through the influence of another, although it will be helpful from some point of view, for after all it conveys some knowledge or sometimes a good and useful feeling, yet, for all that, it also injures in adding an admixture of a foreign basis to its quality; and the world cannot be perfected except by the rejection of the outside influence, when no one will teach his brother or his neighbor to know the Lord, for they will all know Him, young and old. The road that rejects the strange influences for every individual, although it seems destructive to him, is in fact the destruction that leads to the firmest and most complete building, and this is the only introduction to the life of the world to come; for the Holy One, blessed be He, makes a separate Eden on its own for every single person. Scripture does not say "your Eden" but "your Edens" (*Arpelei Tohar*, p. 43).[78]

4.

We said above that individuality is a condition for freedom, or to be exact, it is freedom and existence themselves. Acceptance of the individuality implies the absence of jealousy of everything else—both for its externals and its internal content. The consciousness of the "self" implies a satisfaction with the fact of existence. The loss of this consciousness is in the nature of the sin of suicide. This is evident from the exact meaning of the word (literally, in Hebrew, "loss of self"). For, in dissatisfaction with oneself, in jealousy, in a striving after ends that are external to the action itself, in every longing for something beyond that which exists or what is capable of being attained through some

77. Ibid. pp. 168, 173. See autobiographical expressions of this in *Igrot HaReAYaH*, Vol. I, p. 154: "I am not an educated man . . . but only blessed by G-d with original talent, but it simply must spread out with complete confidence, with no external servitude." Likewise we find the quotation in Z. Yaron's *The Teaching of Rav Kook*, p. 23: "I am compelled to be a poet, but a free poet; I shall not be able to be tied by the fetters of meter and rhyme."

78. Likewise, *Orot HaKodesh*, Vol. I, pp. 95–96. In *Orot HaKodesh*, the version is a little different: "Every tzaddik has an Eden of his own." At the same time it is important to note that Rav Kook does not reject absolutely any external influence, and he recognizes many positive aspects of such influence. See *Orot HaKodesh*, Vol. I, pp. 67 and 176.

action by itself—in all this there is an attempt to glorify the "self," to aggrandize it, to improve it. Yet, from out of itself, the very opposite of this goal is arrived at. A process takes place of the destruction of the "self." This, in Rav Kook's opinion, is the meaning of alienation:

And I am in the midst of the exile. The own inner self, whether of the individual or the community, is revealed in its innermost sense only in proportion to his holiness and purity, in proportion to the heavenly strength that is absorbed from the pure light of the splendor from above that is kindled within him. With our fathers we have sinned the sin of Adam who alienated himself from his own individuality, who took note of the opinion of the serpent and lost his self—he was not able to give a clear answer to the question "Where art thou?" because he did not know his own soul, because he had lost his true "self-ness" in the sin of worshipping a strange god. Israel sinned, it went astray after strange gods; it deserted its own quality of self; Israel rejected what was good. The Land sinned, it denied its own special self, it limited its power, it went after desires and purposes, it did not apply all its store of strength so that the taste of the tree should be as the taste of its fruit.[79] It directed its eye outward, thinking of chances and careers. It accused the moon, lost the joy of its portion; it dreamed of the external splendor of kings. And this is the way the world proceeds to sink through the loss of the self of every single person, of the individual and of society.

Learned educators come, look only on the outside and they also become oblivious of the self and add fuel to the flames; they give the thirsty sour wine to drink; they fatten the minds and the hearts with everything that is outside of them, while the self is forgotten; and seeing that there is no self, therefore there is no "he," and certainly there is no "you."

"The spirit of our life is the annointed of the Lord. His might, the majesty of His greatness, is not outside us. He is the spirit of our life; we seek the Lord our G-d and David our king, we stand in awe before the Lord and before His goodness. We seek our Self, we shall seek and we shall find ourselves. Remove all strange gods, remove every stranger and *mamzer,* and know that I am the Lord your G-d Who brought you out of the land of Egypt to be your G-d. I am the Lord" (*Orot HaKodesh,* Vol III, pp. 140–41).

In this passage, the consciousness of the ego is defined as a confirmation of the self, as finding the reason and the significance of an object

79. On the basis of the Midrash in *Bereshit Rabbah* 5 (Theodore and Albeck edition, p. 38): "Just as the fruit is eaten, so also will the tree be eaten." Compare *Orot HaKodesh,* Vol. III, p. 294.

inside that object itself and not outside of it. This definition is appropriate both to the "selfness" of the individual and to that of the community, as well as to cosmic facts like the moon and the earth. Yet it still leaves unanswered the qualitative question, namely, after all is said and done, what is the "self" about which so much is spoken? As we have said, here, in the passage we have quoted, an answer is suggested. HaReAYaH hints here at an identification of the human "self" with the divine "Self," or, an identification of the quest for the human "self" with the quest for G-d: "We shall seek the Lord our G-d and David our King . . . we shall seek our own Self."

It is absolutely clear that the terms "David our King" and "the spirit of our life (literally, "breath of our nostrils") the anointed of the Lord," denote the messianic longing, "the waiting for salvation," and they are also identified with the human "ego" and also with the Deity itself. This idea and our conclusion above that the concept of "freedom" denotes the category of the "self" fit well with another formulation of Rav Kook regarding the identification of freedom with "the longing for G-d's nearness" on the one hand and "the nature of the essence of life" on the other: "It is the freedom of the human spirit that pleads the cause of the striving for G-d's nearness in all aspects of life, for it is only this nearness that, with all the force of its perfection, is the high peak of the great ideal of freedom" (*Kirvat Elokim,* p. 2). And Rav Kook goes on to say:

Life itself, all life, the quality of life, this is it, this and nothing else—and it cannot be otherwise—nothing but the basic longing for the nearness of G-d. And this completes the distinctive definition of the life of man as that which is made up of a desire for the establishment of one's own feeling—common to all living creatures—with the feeling of striving for perfection . . . that makes it a true shadow of the absolute unconditional life of the absolute Deity. "In the image of G-d created He him" (Ibid. p. 3).[80]

Here we see a principle according to which there is an identification of freedom with existence both on the divine plane and on the cosmic and human plane. This, as we have noted, is the meaning of the

80. See *Bereshit Rabbah,* Theodore and Albeck edition (Jerusalem 5725), pp. 74, 78, 218, and 452. Also M. Jastrow, *Dictionary for the Targums, the Babylonian and Jerusalem Talmuds, and Midrashic Literature,* p. 305.

concept "the image of G-d,"[81] and it is this which is the perpetual "exodus from Egypt" according to the verses that HaReAYaH quotes in this connection: "And you shall know that I am the Lord your G-d" (Exodus 6:7), "Who *brings* you forth from the land of Egypt to be unto you for G-d, I am the Lord" (Leviticus 22:33).[82] That is, the constant process of actualizing the heavenly freedom. Nevertheless, it is not possible to have a real definition of freedom and of the nature of man's self. In a very characteristic and fundamental note, Rav Kook qualifies every possible definition and fixes the bounds of the discussion:

It is not possible for any man to know the character of the self—even his own, how much less of anyone else; not of an individual, how much less of a nation. We go round the center of the notion. We are occupied with suppositions and estimates, to come to an understanding on the basis of open deeds, which are also mainly hidden from us, and especially their complicated reasons; and on the basis of such evidence we speak of a unique character and a distinctive soul. We are forced to decide that our knowledge of this is suspended on nothingness, and the judgment is G-d's" (*Orot HaKodesh*, Vol, III, p. 119).

Man's "self" is understood as "the thing in itself"[83] and therefore it is impossible to know it. "The object itself" is one and unique: G-d. Thus we are back to his conclusion concerning the identification of the human "self" with the Divine: "Only the holy content, personal and universal, has the character of self as well as living existence of an inner-self originality. But the secular content, and certainly the evil, unclean content, has no character of self . . . and you who cleave to the Lord your G-d are alive, everyone of you this day" (Ibid. 115).

Thus, this absolute "self" is holy, and in proportion to its cleaving to the sacred, so is the force of the human "self." As a matter of fact, it is not exact to speak of a human "self," for a human ego does not exist at all. Man has a "self" in so far as he is an instrument for the revelation of the divine "Self." Yet his self is identical with the divine absolute "Self" that is revealed in man. This idea is conveyed especially

81. Compare A. Altmann, *The Face of Judaism* (Tel Aviv 5743), pp. 11–30.
82. Cf. *Olat ReAYaH*, Vol. II, p. 286 (on the Pesach Haggadah).
83. *Translator's Note:* "The thing in itself" is a technical term used by Kant. It means the real object that is in fact the ideal, and is not seen or discerned. Its opposite is "the phenomenon," i.e., that which is discernible; the object as it is seen.

with reference to the Jewish nation, which, in Rav Kook's view, has been favored with an extra degree of freedom:

One who is in the quality of *Malchut* [the *sefira*—the divine dimension of Sovereignty] has nothing whatever of his own [for this is a passive quality, serving only as a vessel for transferring godliness—trans.], and this is a quality that has in it both deficiency and advantage. Such a person is ready to absorb everything. When he turns to the good and recognizes how he really has nothing of his own, he is ready to be filled with everything that is good of all the qualities, all the aspects, and there is nothing contradictory in him. And he has such a depth of self that those things that he absorbs are his very own self since he has no defined particular self of its own. . . . And this quality is really the quality of *"Knesset Yisrael,"*[84] which is the natural "self" of the Jewish nation. The absorbed qualities constantly grow less, and they [the people] of Israel feel their smallness; they know that whatever they have absorbed is not their own self, for they are only a vessel for receiving light and overflowing blessing form the heavenly G-d; and the purpose is always a bounteous overflowing (Ibid. p. 117).[85]

Israel's freedom expresses itself therefore paradoxically in the absence of the consciousness of the "self" in the usual sense. Its freedom is rooted in this, "that they are constantly minimizing themselves and they feel their smallness—they feel that whatever is absorbed in them is not their own self." Together with this, they constitute a vessel for the "divine desire" in whose actualization their freedom takes on form. The manifestations of desire in the works of the Jewish nation are, as we have noted, the revelations of the divine desire. This humility of the limitation of the self makes way for the consciousness of a different kind of ego, namely, taking a part in the Absolute. The quality of humility and the negation of the self change, involuntarily, to an assertion of self, to a cognitive self-awareness[86]: "Man will eventually be elevated so as to become aware of his desire and confess it to himself,

84. *Translator's Note: Knesset Yisrael.* Literally, "The Assembly of Israel." A term used in Jewish mysticism to denote the heavenly image and the Divine Spirit of the entirety of the people of Israel, *Knesset Yisrael* represents the *sefira* of *Malchut.* The kingdom of heaven is revealed in the world through *Knesset Yisrael.*
85. On the identification of *Knesset Yisrael* with the *sefira* of *Malchut* (the divine dimension of kingship) see "My Essay," Chap. 3, p. 40, and n. 51.
86. See *Orot HaKodesh,* Vol. II, pp. 414–15.

until he attains to the supreme perception of the happiness in making his will as the Will of his Maker, because his will is nothing other than the Will of his Maker. And the further this cognitive awareness penetrates, the more it gives form to its being" (*Orot HaKodesh*, Vol. III, p. 46).[87]

We are not speaking here of annihilation, which is the logical conclusion of the pantheistic perception.[88] There is no demand here for "the annulment of our will before His Will," but, on the contrary, a confirmation of self is called for, an assertion and a strengthening of the human will. It is true that this perception implies an awareness that man's will is only "one spark of the great flame of the great Will that is in all being entirely, the phenomenon of the Will of the Lord of all worlds, blessed be He" (*Orot HaKodesh*, Vol. III, p. 39). Yet it is certainly not to be understood as a demand for the annulment of the self. If, as is sometimes the case, a quietistic note is heard in Rav Kook's words, this hearing is an error. The question under consideration with him is not the nullification of life but its expansion: "The supreme holiness is the holiness of silence, the holiness of being, in which a man sees himself as nullified in his private inwardness, and lives a general, universal life, the life of everyone; he feels the life of the inanimate, the vegetation and the living creatures, the life of all society, of everything that speaks, of every single man, the life of every intelligence and every recognition, of every thinking and every sentient being" (Ibid. p. 297).

It is important to emphasize that the self-annulment is in the consciousness, not in the will. "In his consciousness man is as if without existence." There is a consciousness that categories of individual as of general existence are not real, and in this way the error of seeing them as real and tangible is nullified. As against this, the Will is not nullified at all. On the contrary, the strengthening of the will is a constant undertaking:

When man feels that his will is weak, he should make a big effort to strengthen it with every kind of support, so that he should be able to execute every good

87. Similarly, Ibid. pp. 39, 40, 41, 43, and 53; *Orot HaKodesh*, Vol. II, p. 302; *Arpelei Tohar*, pp. 2, 51–52, and 65; *Eder HaYakar* and *Ikve HaTzon*, p. 146.
88. See *Orot HaKodesh*, Vol. II, pp. 395–401. See also R. Schatz, *Chasidism As Mysticism*, Chaps 1 and 2.

thing as befits his nature. It is better to devote oneself to the strengthening of the will than to occupy oneself with details of moral improvements. Of course, while devoting ourselves to strengthening the will, we must not forget to deal also with its purification and refinement, and with raising the level of desire to a stage of holiness. But the basic occupation of those who are smitten with weakness of will must be the strengthening of the self-essence of the will by various natural, moral, intellectual and Torah devices, and he should not desist from any device that may be able to help in attaining the supreme goal of strengthening the will in its entirety (Ibid. Vol III, p. 77).

Strengthening the will is not achieved through abstention and self-affliction, which suppress desire, but precisely through a full involvement in natural life.[89] Man "is not sanctified, separated and set apart," but "he is alive." Yet withal, "all his life is Holy of Holies" (*Orot HaKodesh*, Vol. II, p. 297). Even in "the sanctification of silence," natural life is not set aside from its character, from normal human thought and speech, from individual physical life and social life, from politeness and respect. It is not confused; it only rises in an ideal ascent. The quality of life is elevated, and its goal is sanctified. The desire for a superior good, general and inclusive, yet also personal and penetrating, goes on expressing itself in a living expression in practical attire" (Ibid. p. 292).

As we have said, Rav Kook saw the will as the foundation of life. He spoke of a conscious effort for the development and strengthening of the human will and the awareness of the "self," and he rejected every approach that might weaken them.[90] From a series of expressions, it becomes clear that it was precisely in religion that Rav Kook saw a tangible danger to man's freedom, and he was not deterred from warning of this danger:

The will is the foundation of life; it must be pulsating in life. Morality, Torah, every holy and heavenly light, all have to work on it to keep it on a straight path, but not to blur its force. The weakening of the power of desire by the imposition of disturbing burdens, even when, according to man's knowledge, these stem from a high and holy place, impoverishes the supreme form of man's splendor. The light of holiness reveals itself in the might and freedom

89. See "My Essay," Chap. 10.
90. See *Arpelei Tohar*, pp. 13, 60, and 61.

of the Will, in its fresh majesty. "For thou hast not called on Me, O Jacob, for thou hast wearied of Me, O Israel." And the lessening of hindrances is one of the aims of the divine Torah that sets a path for life and a straight way for all power of will from His strong fountain, from the Source of life (*Orot HaKodesh*, Vol. III, p. 75).

In Rav Kook's view, the Torah is interested in man's freedom, in "the lessening of the hindrances."[91] Nevertheless, religion, as it is perceived by men, "impoverishes the supreme form of man's splendor." Furthermore, "even the acceptance of the yoke of the kingdom of heaven, as is customary among men, is a human servitude because the kingdom of heaven itself descended from its glory and "retreated" (or withdrew itself)[92] because of the darkness with which humanity darkened its light" (*Arpelei Tohar*, p. 40). Therefore, those "who have a heavenly vision" cannot be enslaved by any servitude, not even that of the acceptance of the kingdom of heaven in its accepted sense, for "every enslavement is a servitude of human beings" (Ibid.).

Rav Kook numbers the deficiencies of the fear of heaven, which is not in harmony with the true goal of the Torah, and says that "instead of the fear of sin, it changes to fear of thought" and thereby robs man of "the light of his soul, weakens his strength and clouds his spirit" (*Orot HaKodesh* Vol. III, *Rosh Davar*, p. 26). Such fear of heaven brings upon man "boredom and idleness, and he loses his will and his essential self . . . so that inevitably man comes to have his life weakened and the community essence becomes sick, there is no courage and no determined desire for improvement, for making the life of society proper and right" (Ibid. p. 28).[93] "Fear of heaven that has no knowledge makes man timid and idle" (*Arpelei Tohar*, p. 32).[94]

Of course, a brave stand in the face of the truth, a recognition of the deficiencies of the fear of heaven, does not imply its nullification or the setting aside of the value of the fear of heaven. For, after all,

91. It is interesting to compare his approach with the perception of Maimonides who saw the Torah as freeing man from the arbitrariness of idolatrous belief. See *Guide for the Perplexed*, Part III, Chapters 26, 29, 30, 37, 46, and 47.

92. *Translator's Note:* The word used here is from the term *tzimtzum* used in Kabbalistic literature to denote the opposite of emanation, suggesting that G-d, the *Ein Sof*, Infinity, contracted, as it were, and withdrew into Himself, or limited Himself, to make room for the world.

93. Ibid. p. 30.

94. These words are not just theory. They reflect a reality that HaReAYaH knew well.

"this feeling of divine fear is everything, all life and all the good" (*Orot HaKodesh*, Vol. III, *Rosh Davar*, p. 25). Whoever recognizes this "will not forsake his treasure, and no matter what he may suffer, whether physical afflictions or spiritual afflictions, all those things in which it may seem that he cannot stand firm—against the modern freedom, against the striving after the cultural greatness of contemporary life, against bewitching beauty or against the noisy ferment of life, and sometimes even against natural morality and equity, which cannot always be beaten into the shape of the fear of G-d according to his understanding—none of these will have the power to interrupt the thread of life or the strength of acceptance that only in the fear of G-d can man have Almighty shelter" (Ibid.).[95]

The way the fear of G-d finds expression in life seems opposed to the modern concept of freedom and is not in tune with "the striving after the cultural greatness of contemporary life." Sometimes it also stands in conflict with moral values and conscience. With this, it must not be given up, for these deficiencies stem only from the "external aspects" of the fear of G-d, which, in its essence, is the force that motivates life: "It is everything, all life and all the good."

Moreover, the degree of servitude bound up with the fear of heaven, with the acceptance of the yoke of the kingdom of heaven in its pure form, bestows a deeper dimension to freedom itself. The decision of the acceptance of the yoke of the kingdom of heaven, made in freedom, is the more complete freedom, for here man has control of the freedom by reason of freedom itself. This is the depth of the meaning of responsibility that stems from the attribute of freedom: the ability to set bounds even to freedom itself. "Complete freedom is when a man is so free that, in his absolute freedom, he is able also to enslave himself in a proper place, and to be a slave in a place where servitude is the true freedom" (*Olat ReAYaH*, Vol. II, p. 261). "A free man in truth is he who rules also over the greatest of forces—which is the power of freedom itself" (Ibid. p. 289).

Yet not only is the acceptance of the yoke of heaven perceived as an expression of the ability of freedom to limit itself, but the religious striving, or in the language of Rav Kook, "the striving for the nearness

95. Cf. Ibid. p. 27: "The fear of heaven must not pressure man's natural morality, for then it would no longer be a pure fear of heaven."

of G-d," is described as "the pinnacle of the great ideal of freedom for which the best of human beings yearn and the entire human soul and the life of society in all its many shades long for. 'Unto the utmost bound of the everlasting hills [literally, the hills of the world], the world of the Jubilee—the world of freedom' (*Zohar*, II: 22, 29). Therefore all the work of man's spirit, its goal and its desire, is—to complete the desire that embraces everything in it, that always pulsates inside it and concentrates all of its being" (*Kirvat Elokim*, p. 2).[96] From this Rav Kook deduces conclusions concerning the character and task of education.

Rav Kook believes that the function of education is not to teach and form the personality of the pupil. As he sees it, the task of education is to help him lay bare and reveal his "self," that which is hidden in his soul.[97] Education's function is to uncover the similarity between the pupil's inwardness and the natural depth of general culture. From this point of view, education fills a central role in the manifestation of freedom and in strengthening the consciousness of the "self." And since freedom is perceived as "the confirmation of the self" or even as the definition of the essence of human life, the absence of consciousness of self, or in the language of HaReAYaH in *Orot HaKodesh*, Vol. III, "he knows not his name" (p. 137), is likened to the death of the personality: "We are like the fallen who lie in the grave" (Ibid.). Man's striving for freedom in fact reflects his dread of death: "The individual self is afraid of the destruction of its essence" (*Orot HaKodesh*, Vol. II, pp. 381–84).

We have before us a very interesting perception of the concept of "death," which enables us to cope with the fear that death imposes on man. Death already exists during the life of man in the form of the rejection of his freedom, a denial of his self. However, Rav Kook proposes a way whereby "we shall certainly arrive at the freedom for which we live" (Ibid.).[98] That way is "the elevation of the Will" (Ibid.)

96. Cf. Cassirer (*supra* n. 1).

97. *Kirvat Elokim*, loc. cit. Compare this idea with Plato's theory of anamnesis. See Plato, *Menon* (Tel Aviv 5735), pp. 81–86. See also R. Schatz, *Chasidism As Mysticism*, p. 171. It seems that Rav Kook was influenced in this matter by the Romantic individualistic perception in educational thought. For a detailed description of the emphasis on the individual as a basic tendency in the Romantic revolt, together with a sharp criticism, see J. Babbitt, *Rousseau and Romanticism*, (1928).

98. See also *Orot HaTeshuvah*, p. 66. On the perception of death, see S. H. Bergmann,

and the self-awareness: "The soul's making itself known in whichever manner is itself a corner of redemption" (Ibid. Vol. I, p. 197). Rav Kook calls for a deepening of reflection on existence and a strengthening of awareness of the self through which man's freedom is attained, as well as control of his fate and his condition (Ibid. pp. 83–84).

5.

The special weight that Rav Kook ascribes to the freedom of the individual and the fostering of the consciousness of the "self" on the one hand, and, on the other hand, his metaphysical-monistic theory, leads to an original individualistic outlook. In a letter written in 5668 (1908) to Rav Shmuel Alexandrov, HaReAYaH reacts to a question concerning the presence in Judaism of liberal anarchism, and he argues that the outlook of Judaism, being monistic, is also individualistic, for there is only one individuum in reality. The existence of the human individuum depends on its link with, or more exactly on its inclusion in, the group unit—that is, the nation; and, on a higher level, also on the cosmic and divine unity:

The matter continues to a state of elevation of all creation as one individual unit. In that case we have need only of anarchy—a tremendous, mighty, developed self-love. But the paths that lead to it are the paths of life that emanate from the source of the unity of the One, the Life of all worlds, namely Judaism (*Igrot HaReAYaH*, Vol. I, p. 177).

In Rav Kook's words, there is a fruitful tension between a monistic metaphysical outlook and a strong existential tendency. One might have expected that a monistic outlook would lead to a quietistic moral theory marked by an absence of the "self." If Rav Kook had wanted it, he could have found worthy trees on which to fasten.[99] Yet HaReAYaH deliberately chose to affirm the "self." Indeed, already the early Kabbalists proclaimed positively the idea of mystical-individual redemption[100]; and in Chasidism they spoke of the ending of the spiri-

---

"Death and Beyond Death in Rav Kook's Thought" in *Thinkers and Believers* (Tel Aviv 1959) pp. 101–111.

99. See R. Schatz, *Chasidism As Mysticism*, Chap. 2.

100. See G. Scholem, "The Idea of Redemption in Kabbalah" in *Devarim BeGo* (Tel Aviv 5736), pp. 159 and 199.

tual *galut* through the expansion of the "self."[101] Rav Kook also speaks
here of the idea that "the individual unity expands"; but the emphasis
on the individual did not result in a negation of an actual national
redemption: Its influence was directed toward a religious individualism
that is of course possible only in the framework of a religious community ("those who keep faith").[102]

When Rav Kook speaks of "the elevation of all creation as one
individual," he is removing the individualistic perception from its literal understanding. As we have noted, because Rav Kook's theory is
monistic, it is individualistic, since the true individuum is none other
than "the One, the Life of all worlds." Through such an interpretation
of the concept of "the individuum," it was possible to keep away from
the anarchistic meanings within an individualistic outlook and from the
existential emphasis on the understanding of the "self." Yet, this is not
the way of HaReAYaH. Rav Kook does indeed maintain that "the
paths that lead to it [to anarchy] are the paths of life that emanate from
the source of the unity of the One, the Life of all worlds, namely
Judaism." But it must not be forgotten that anarchy is not negated in
principle, but, on the contrary, it is allowable in a limited way to special
individuals in the framework of a community of "those who keep
faith."[103] Rav Kook's approach in this question is an existential approach that presents the claim to freedom of the individual person, but
recognizes the dangers that lurk in the way of a freedom that is uncir-
cumscribed by the consideration of the Jewish religious-cultural existential claim of the community of which the individual person is one
component. His position is in the nature of "the golden mean" between an extreme individualistic position and its extreme negation.
The following words of his clarify his position well:

The individual claim, which does not recognize subjection to any general
principle, which establishes anarchy in its most terrible form, itself also emanates from the highest moral and scientific inner propulsion, which does not
recognize the principle of the group that includes workers and those who are
forced to work, those who are active and others who are activated. Ideal
morality at the height of its purity does not wish to recognize a particular

101. R. Schatz, op. cit. p. 171.
102. *Orot HaKodesh*, Vol. III, p. 102. See also *Eder HaYekar* and *Ikve HaTzon*, p. 39.
103. See "My Essay," Chap. 10.

personality. Every pleasure and every sorrow is felt equally where it is found in the entire expanse of the cosmos to infinity; consequently we have here only one absolute individuality . . . Really, the two extreme ends are the borderlines of the "Orchard in which to wander" of the spirit of life and knowledge, and they can never be reached, neither at the high point at which details are negated in favor of the stream of generality, nor at the lowest point where the generality is denied in favor of the actuality of the close and exciting details (*Tallelei Orot,* pp. 14–15).

In this question also, that of the personal freedom and the fostering of the individuum, religion and morality pile up problems, in Rav Kook's view, on the positive road of general culture. Culture, "when it is found to be restrained by religion and morality, fights against them and overcomes them. But the end of the battle is the revelation in which religion and morality discover their light, to the point that this personal freedom, with its good natural demands, comes to be recognized as one of the principles of religion and morality themselves" (*Orot HaKodesh,* Vol. III, *Rosh Davar,* p. 31).

Indeed, when it becomes clear that personal freedom is one of the foundations of religion and morality themselves, Jewish morality can then be defined as "individual morality."[104] And yet it can be individualistic morality because basically it is not morality at all, or, at all events, it is not human morality. Human morality sees in an individualistic approach an undermining of the personality, for morality seeks to lay down rules for the proper behavior and ordered relationships between men, based on giving way. Against this, divine morality is set in an ideal of holiness, which implies an exertion for limitless perfection. Holiness is perfection, or the all-inclusive unity,[105] and divine morality, whose aim is improvement, or an elevation to holiness, embodies a powerful tendency for the affirmation of the ego. The stress on the consciousness of the "self" in divine morality has no adverse effect on the demands of human morality, since it is accompanied by a struggle for the expansion of the individuum that embodies a nullification of the quality of giving way, and this is characteristic of human morality.

Friedrich Nietzsche was the one who drew attention in unequivocal terms to the contradiction within human morality. He argued that

104. *Orot HaKodesh,* Vol. III, p. 66.
105. See N. Rotenstreich, *Studies in Modern Jewish Thought* (Tel Aviv 5735), p. 42.

"morality is a turning of the back on the desire for existence," and that "as much as we believe in morality, we settle the fate of existence." Because of this, in his view, morality is simply not possible: "Egocentricity is hateful to us, even after our assertion that whatever is not ego is not possible."[106] It seems clear that Rav Kook adopted Nietzsche's basic position in this matter, and the following words of his are a suggested alternative to Nietzsche's rejection of morality:

The ultimate goal of life is holiness. Holiness is a heavenly unity that has nothing of the weakness of morality. Holiness does not battle at all against the self-love that is embedded deep down in the recesses of every living being, but it puts man into such a superior situation that the more he loves himself, the more will the good in him spread out over everything, over all the surroundings, over all the world, over all being.

In the character of a community collective there is no possibility whatsoever for implanting a weakening of self-love, and there nothing in it except moral ruin (if it should chance to appear) and an inner decay that consumes everything.

Therefore it is not at all possible to demand that there should be a moral nation in the world, but only a holy nation, a nation that, the more it strengthens its self, the more it exalts its worth within and without, the more it will exalt and strengthen the light and the good in the world. Thus it will be found that the essence of the good in morality is already embraced within the holiness in a more glorious, beautiful and ornamental form (*Orot HaKodesh*, Vol. III, p. 18).

This "self-love" that Rav Kook extols is not egoism in its narrow meaning. For the striving after the expansion of the "ego" that is linked with the "self-love" is *ipso facto* the expansion of love.[107] The assertion of the "self," the consciousness of the "ego," is a condition for the affirmation of the self of everyone else round about, "and since there is no 'I,' there is also no 'he,' and most certainly there is no 'thou' " (*Orot HaKodesh*, Vol. III, p. 140).

The implication of this individualistic conception is recognized in the emphasis on the distinctiveness of every individual and in the

106. F. Nietzsche, *Desire for Power* (Tel Aviv 5739), Vol. I, pp. 14–15.
107. See *Orot HaKodesh*, Vol. II, pp. 55–68

legitimation of the personal and original ways of everyone.[108] This outlook imposes on man all the "dread of responsibility" whose implication is a striving for a merging into the general framework of the community, of Torah, of mankind and of all being,[109] despite the independent position that he has to develop. This is especially so in face of the enormous area allowed for the individual free man who determines his values himself:

The basis of happiness is the love of truth with the intellect, the love of uprightness in life, the love of beauty with feeling, the love of the good in the deed. And with all these values everyone builds for himself truth, uprightness, beauty and goodness, each one for himself according to his measure. And all of them, all these qualities of every single individual among men, all are gathered into a single unified store in which all the truth, uprightness, beauty and goodness arrange themselves. And in this way they come to the path of the knowledge of the Lord, enlightened, full of holiness and a clear fear of G-d (*Orot HaKodesh*, Vol. I, pp. 91–92).

We have already noted that freedom, for Rav Kook, is not a mere theological-philosophical question, but a test of existence. Apparently, it will not be possible to understand the astounding daring of many of his formulations without taking this fact into consideration. In the context of our discussion, let me quote here a characteristic passage, with a personal touch, which contains an outstanding expression of the experience of freedom:

I have to find my happiness within myself, not by the approval of people and not through any career no matter what it may be. The more I recognize my own self, and the more I permit myself to be original and stand on my own

108. See *Orot HaKodesh*, Vol. III, p. 221: "Every man has to know that he is called to serve according to his particular awareness and feeling, according to the root of his soul." And Ibid. p. 139: "Every single person builds a spiritual world for himself within himself. The whole purpose of listening is simply a preparation for the building by the individual of the everlasting building of his self; the central focus of the Torah is the verse of his own personal name. This is the full weight of the law, the entire depth of the enquiring, all the awesomeness of the responsibility, all the dread of the grave." And see Ibid., p. 137. Cf. "The dread of the grave" in A. Jellinek, *Bet HaMidrash*, (Jerusalem 5727), Vol. I, p. 150. Here "dread of the grave" means the torments connected with the effort to build the individual's spiritual world, that is "the confirmation of the self."

109. *Orot HaKodesh*, Vol. III, p. 120.

feet with an inner awareness composed of knowledge, cognitive awareness, emotion and poetry, the more will the light of the Lord illumine me and the more will my powers be developed to be a blessing for me and for the world (*Arpelei Tohar*, p. 22).

Not taking "the approval of people" into consideration and the striving for an independent and original position is guided by the belief that originality is a guarantee of truth, in that it is in the nature of revelation. "The righteous, with all the peace and honor with which they seek to guide the masses, will return to the Lord Who continuously reveals Himself to them through their special windows and lattices" (*Orot HaKodesh*, Vol. III, p. 122). The revelation of the individual in meditation and musing with himself is not only divine truth; it is also identified with "the Source of Torah,"[110] and this determines the individual's position and his ardent meditations as the content of words of Torah.[111]

Still, in Rav Kook's theory, these words are only one face of a system of dialectic relationships between the individual and society. To the extent that the private personality's qualitative advantage predominates,[112] as well as its progress, both from the point of view of the objects of awareness which constitute a challenge to the spiritual and intellectual endeavor,[113] and from the point of view of society's dependence on its components,[114] to that extent one may speak of society's advancement from those same points of view.[115] On the face of it, these things appear to be in serious conflict, but in practice this is a very fruitful paradox: The extent of the spiritual and thoughtful freedom that an individual can assume for himself is in accordance with the extent of the soul relationship and practical loyalty to the community, its values and devotion:

We shall be safe from all wickedness, from every falsehood, with which the imagination may insult us, if we hold fast to the Tree of Life of our ancestral

---

110. The Kabbalistic basis for this idea is rooted in the identification of *Knesset Yisrael* with the Oral Torah in the *sefira* of *Malchut* (Kingship). See "My Essay," Chap. 3, pp. 39–40, and Chap. 6, p. 100.
111. *Orot HaKodesh*, Vol. III, p. 122.
112. *Arpelei Tohar*, p. 35.
113. *Orot HaKodesh*, Vol. II, p. 447.
114. *Arpelei Tohar*, p. 36.
115. See *Orot*, pp. 144 and 59; *Orot HaKodesh*, Vol III, p. 147.

Torah, to the pleasantness of its morality, to its commandments and injunctions in all walks of life; to our faithful relationship to everyman, to family and to nation, to life and all its demands. With this we do not have to be chained with social chains that choke the free heavenly spirit and profane the sacred that comes from the upper world, from the world of freedom where liberty was granted to the seraphim, absolute freedom to all striving, complete freedom for the planting of desire and creativity. As the greatness of the freedom so will the holiness be great—so will life be exalted . . . Let everyone depict for himself in truth and honesty what his soul shows him. Let him bring forth his spiritual produce from potential to execution, without lips of guile; and from such sparks will be gathered together torches of light that will illumine all the world with their glory. From such inner pieces of truth the Great Truth will appear" (*Orot HaKodesh*, Vol. I, pp. 165–66).[116]

6.

Rav Kook's position in the matter of the affirmation of the self finds expression also in his perception of the concept of "sin" and in the idea of *teshuvah*. The pair of concepts "sin" and *teshuvah* are the theological expression of the idea of freedom.

Usually, the meaning of "sin" is the nonfulfillment of duty, the nonobservance of a norm with which is linked the basis of an offense against Him Who imposed the duty or established the norm. The meaning of *"teshuvah"* is a turning back from "sin" to the straight path, the way of keeping the duty, and thus also a return to faithfulness to Him Who imposed the duty ("Return to Me and I shall return to you"). In any case, the concepts of "sin" and *"teshuvah"* leave freedom as a given fact. From a philosophical point of view, it is freedom that makes sin possible; it is freedom that gives a deed, which is basically neutral, the significance of "sin" or of *"teshuvah."*

In Rav Kook's teaching the concepts of "sin" and *"teshuvah"* take on a meaning qualitatively different from the accepted teaching, which is entirely within the bounds of the relationship between man and G-d. In his theory, these concepts are connected with the category of the "ego"; sin is, first and foremost, sin against the "self"; and *teshuvah* is a return to the "self," to the "ego." But not only that. In this theory,

116. See G. Scholem, *Devarim BeGo* (Tel Aviv 5736), p. 565.

the concepts of "sin" and *"teshuvah"* mark cosmic processes in whose formation man is an important part. Thus, even man's actions assume a significance divergent from the well-known frame of obedience or rebellion; and man's action is a creative action in the sense that not only does he reveal and lay bare the meaning of human actions and of all existence, but also, to a certain degree, he is a partner in the determination of this significance and of its creation.

Let us, then, open with an examination of the concept of *"teshuvah."* In Rav Kook's treasury, a special book is devoted to the idea of *teshuvah—Orot HaTeshuvah,* albeit the subject is also discussed in various connections in his other books. In *Orot HaTeshuvah,* there is a definition of the concept of *teshuvah* that is general but also unequivocal: *"Teshuvah* is basically a movement to return to originality, to the heavenly Source of life and being in their perfection" (*Orot HaTeshuvah,* p. 75).[117] This general definition is true on various levels, and Rav Kook explains it in detail:

When one forgets the essential nature of one's own soul, when one ignores the quality of introspection, everything becomes confused and in doubt. The principal *teshuvah,* which immediately illumines the dark places, is that man should return to his self, to the source of his soul, and he will immediately return to G-d, to the Soul of all souls, and then he will go on and progress higher and ever higher in holiness and purity. This applies both to individual man and to an entire nation; to all mankind as well as to the perfection of all existence whose corruption comes about always through its forgetting its own self. And if you will think that it [existence] desires to return to G-d, but is not establishing itself "to gather in its dispersed"—this is a *teshuvah* of deception wherewith the name of the Lord is borne in vain.

Therefore only through the great truth of the return to the self can there be a return of man and the nation, of the world and all worlds, of all existence, to its Maker, to the Light, in the light of life. And this is the secret of the light of Messiah, the manifestation of the world's soul; when it will shine the world will turn back to the root of existence and the light of the Lord will be manifested upon it. And from the source of this great *teshuvah* man will draw the life of holiness of *teshuvah* in its true sense (Ibid. p. 111).

117. Or Etzion edition, 5730.

Man's return to his self, his faith in himself and his powers,[118] are *ipso facto* a return to G-d. We have already noted above the identification between the human and the divine "I." The act of *teshuvah* brings about this identity, and in opposition to it sin is perceived as causing a separation between things that are joined.[119] By strengthening the consciousness of the "ego," *teshuvah* becomes identified with freedom, and consequently sin—as an act of divisiveness, limiting the "ego" by obscuring its divine infinite dimension— is perceived as slavery.[120] This assertion can be formulated also in a contrary fashion, namely: All slavery is, in a certain sense, sin. Intransigent assertiveness in practical affairs and a stubborn stand on a spiritual and theoretical level will be considered as sin in that they reject man's freedom:

Obstinacy in standing always by one opinion and focusing on it with ropes of sinfulness that have become customary, whether in deeds or in opinions, is a sickness that results from being immersed in hard servitude that does not allow the light of freedom of *teshuvah* to shine with all its force; for *teshuvah* longs for real original freedom, which is divine freedom completely devoid of enslavement (*Orot HaTeshuvah*, p. 36).

We spoke above about the identification of freedom with existence. Now we may add that with Rav Kook *teshuvah* is perceived as "a renewal of life" (*Arpelei Tohar*, p. 73); and the freedom of choice linked with it is possible so long as "there burns a spark of life" (*Orot HaKodesh*, Vol. II, p. 492). Just as freedom contains within it victory over death, so also in *teshuvah*: "The more profound the *teshuvah*, the less becomes the fear of death until it vanishes entirely" (*Orot HaTeshuvah*, p. 66). *Teshuvah* is "the complete self-essence of the soul" (Ibid. p. 54), "And in accordance with the abundance of *teshuvah*, so is the measure of its freedom" (Ibid. p. 74).

Nevertheless, just as the concepts of "freedom" and "coercion" are different aspects of one reality, so are *teshuvah* and sin connected one

118. *Orot HaKodesh*, Vol. I, p. 173.
119. *Orot HaTeshuvah*, pp. 72–73.
120. Ibid. p. 26.

with the other. Just as *teshuvah* is part of the essence of reality, so also is sin an expression of this essence:

Teshuvah preceded the world and it is therefore the foundation of the world. It is the perfection of life as it constantly reveals itself in accordance with its independent nature. And since nature itself has no freedom of choice, therefore sin is forced to come this way, "and there is no man righteous upon earth who does good and does not sin" (Eccles. 7:20). And the vitiation of the natural essence of life so that man should be a nonsinner is itself the biggest sin; "he [the priest] shall make atonement for him for that he sinned by reason of the dead" (Numbers 6:11; and see *Nedarim* 10). Therefore *teshuvah* cures the corruption and returns the world and life to its source precisely through revealing the heavenly foundation of their self-essence, the world of freedom; and because of this we call the name of the Lord 'the living G-d [or the G-d of Life]' " (*Orot HaTeshuvah*, p. 37).[121]

In another place, we noted that in Rav Kook's view one cannot squeeze the many-sidedness and the infinity of reality into a narrow definition, and one must recognize its multidimensional nature, as it appears to the human intellect, as a paradox.[122] Through the power of this paradox one may understand HaReAYaH's argument concerning the ability of the human will to shape not only the future, but also the past. The idea of "deliberate premeditated sins that are changed to deeds of merits" is explained by the fact that the evil deeds do not require "creation anew" in order to change their character, but all that is required is "the revelation of their real source" (*Orot HaTeshuvah*, p. 70); that is, the revelation of the aspect of merit that they have at their source. Since there is no severance in reality and there is a continuity of life that determines the connection of all deeds to the essence of life, to their source—therefore "one has the power to impress a new character also on deeds that are past" (Ibid. p. 41).[123] The

121. See further *Orot HaKodesh*, Vol. III, p. 11.
122. See "My Essay," Chaps. 2 and 4.
123. Cf. *Orot HaKodesh*, Vol. II, pp. 527 and 377. Compare Rav Kook's words with the perception of the Polish logician Jan Lukasiewicz, who argues that it is proper that we should not have behaved in the past differently from the way we behave in the future. One cannot say of facts whose effects have quite disappeared that they really occurred, but only that they were in the realm of possibility. In his view, it is good that this is so, for there are in the life of everyone moments of suffering or of guilt that we should be happy to obliterate not only from the memory but also from very

ability that is revealed in freedom to change the past implies an acceptance of the basic unity among the various aspects of reality, which
makes it possible to expose the aspect of the positive merit in the evil
deed. In any event, the ability to turn back in *teshuvah* is perceived as
the dominant actualization of freedom, which is nothing other than
civilization in its process of formation.

---

existence. See Jan Lukasiewicz, "On Determinism," in *Polish Logic,* ed. Storrs McCall
(Oxford 1967), pp. 38–39. Jan Lukasiewicz in his scholarly work sought to undermine
logical certainty and philosophic determinism. Already in 1917 he worked out a
three-valued system of logic in which the "law of the absent third" is invalidated, and
philosophers accepted this until now; that is—a sentence is either true or false, and
there is no third option. According to the logic developed by Lukasiewicz, a matter
can be settled as being correct, false, or uncertain. The new logic had logical rules and
processes of its own. On the scientific and philosophic revolt against determinism at
the beginnings of the twentieth century, see the book by Las Foiv, *Einstein and the
Men of His Generation* (Tel Aviv, 5739), pp. 174–96.

PART
III

Rav Kook's Contribution to the Revitalization of Jewish Thought

The Significance of Rav Kook's Teaching for Our Generation

Rav Yehuda Amital

"It is forbidden for the fear of heaven to push aside man's natural morality, for then it would no longer be pure fear of heaven. There is a sign showing that the fear of heaven is pure, when the natural morality, planted in man's honest nature, ascends through it (the fear of heaven) to higher levels than it would attain without it. But if the fear of heaven is made to appear as though even without its influence, life would tend to function well, and would still have everything functioning for the benefit of the individual and society, while with its influence that power would be less—such fear of heaven is invalid" (*Orot HaKodesh,* Vol. III, p. 27).

1.

FIFTY YEARS HAVE passed since our teacher, HaReAYaH, left us. However, if we ask ourselves how many years have passed since his words were formulated and most of his teachings written, we get to the number seventy or almost eighty years. And since then vast changes have come about in the Jewish world and in the world as a whole.

There were two events, of which it may be said that no one foresaw them in his lifetime, that had a profound influence on what is taking place in our generation: the Holocaust and the Israel-Arab conflict. Likewise, it is doubtful whether HaReAYaH foresaw the phenomenon of waves of immigration of ordinary, simple Jews from East and West, and the mass discarding of the yoke that followed in its wake, without any ideological or intellectual motivations. As to the world as a whole— without referring to the enormous technological changes affecting all walks of life—it is sufficient if we point to two things: the breakdown of the ideal of the perfection of the world in the socialist spirit, and the deep crisis in which Western culture finds itself. In the light of all this, a question mark may be added to the subject of this lecture—the significance of HaReAYaH's teaching for our generation! Really? Is it at all possible to speak of the significance of things that were written at such a great qualitative distance?

Among the scholars researching his teachings in our day, one can discern two approaches. As we know, HaReAYaH's teaching includes important and profound chapters of thought in the principles of Judaism, in its values and fundamental concepts. The value of these chapters will remain for generations independently of the situation or the events that occurred in his time. On the one side, his teaching incorporates analyses and commentary to explain the significance of historic events and spiritual movements of his time; explanatory remarks for the character of the generation, its spiritual problems, as well as expectations and forecasts of the development of spiritual, personal, and historical processes; a sort of historiosophy of his contemporary scene. There is an approach that says, Let us put aside the *realia* in HaReAYaH's teachings and leave that to the historians; let us concentrate on those chapters of thought whose value is permanent, for all generations. For them the question is narrowed down: Was the value of those chapters in that they enriched Jewish thought only through their connection with the thought of great Jewish scholars of former generations? Or do they perhaps have a special significance for the perplexed of our times? And there is another approach among scholars devoted to HaReAYaH's teaching. These try to explain all the events of our times and all the problems of our generation according to their formulation in HaReAYaH's teaching eighty years ago. In general, both approaches may be said to suffer from exaggeration.

With regard to the question of the significance of his philosophical teachings for our generation, the answer is absolutely positive. There is a serious grappling in his teaching with most of the problems that preoccupy the modern intellectual man of today. Problems such as faith and heresy, holy and profane, freedom of choice, the chosenness of the people of Israel, *galut*, redemption, the relationship between Israel and the nations of the world, relations between man and society, personal and public morality, the perfection of the individual and the community, the service of the heart (i.e., prayer) and practical mitzvot, spiritual ideals and punctiliousness with regard to the mitzvot, Zionism and the state, Providence and history, law and morality, freedom and compulsion, war and peace, mysticism and realism, vision and reality, faith and science, certainty and assumption, and so on and so forth—all these problems are given rich expression in his deep thinking. And as much as we may think that in matters of opinions and beliefs, it is the intellectual public that is still the dominant one for the greater part of the community, his teaching is nevertheless very significant for a broad general public.

Here we should stress also his constant struggle against the superficial approach in basic concepts of Judaism and his continual cry for deep study of the theoretical part of the Torah, so that a situation should not arise with "generations whose general conceptions have all matured and developed while they have not dealt at all with the section of divine concepts; thus that generation will be left in a lowly and unfortunate situation, and the religious learned people will grow and expand apace" (*Ikve HaTzon,* article on the Service of G-d). These words are especially meaningful in our times, when the educated public is growing and the media go on expanding its knowledge even after it has left school.

It is a common phenomenon that man's first conceptions of the world surrounding him make way, with the expansion of his knowledge, for more developed and more scientific conceptions. How sad it is that in that early chapter there remain also his early concepts associated with Torah, e.g., faith, the unity of G-d, Providence, prophecy, redemption, etc., just as he understood them in his infancy. HaReAYaH speaks with pain of those whose concepts of faith and confidence "are permanently confused in quaint imaginings, just as it all appears to the mind at the beginning of knowledge—because of deserting these high concepts and not occupying themselves with them—in the paths of imagination that are far from the ways of Torah" (*Maamrei Ha-*

ReAYaH, p. 86). Because of this, HaReAYaH never ceased demanding, at every opportunity, increasing study in depth in the field of
beliefs and opinions. It would seem that this demand of his has vital
significance not only for our generation. Our concern and responsibility
for the nation's spiritual future in generations to come oblige us to pay
heed seriously to this demand.

Let us not blind ourselves to the fact that religious Jewry of today
is showing great vitality to flourish and prosper with its "simple religiosity," *"proste frumkeit"* in HaReAYaH's phrase (*Igrot HaReAYaH,*
Vol I, p. 160), without concern for its religious and godly concepts. Let
us not blind ourselves to the presence of scholars among those who are
"returning in *teshuvah"* whose spiritual baggage is limited to the *"Kitzur Shulchan Aruch"* with no interest in religious thought.

I think it would be irresponsible on our part to proceed in the
confidence that there will be no religious crisis in the future arising
from the poverty of religious thought and confused, sometimes childish
conceptions of the principles of faith. Who knows if another generation may not arise for whom it will again be impossible "to explain
simple faith to moderate people except by asserting the heavenly
secrets that are the highest matters of the world" (*Orot HaKodesh*
Vol. I, p. 7).

Also with reference to those sections dealing with the historiosophy
of the present in his teachings, many of them are applicable to our time.
But not everywhere is it possible to separate the historiosophical section
from that of philosophic thought. And there are chapters in his teaching that, in their time, were not completely understood, and even if
they were understood, they did not get the proper echo, nor were they
accorded appropriate importance. Precisely in our days, now, we are
ready and able to understand them in all their depth and to see their
actual and vital significance. I have here chosen a section of his teaching that seems to deal with a general problem with no connection with
the realities of his day. Yet, after careful study, it becomes clear that
it is completely dependent on his nationalist and Zionist perception,
and it has great significance precisely in our time.

I wish to refer here to one of the sections in HaReAYaH's teaching
dealing with an ancient problem: the place and weight of the autonomous duties, that is, the moral duties that a man assumes out of an
inner consciousness and the command of conscience. Rav Saadya

Gaon, Rav Bachaye, and Maimonides have all dealt with it. But while they dealt mainly with the duties included in the 613 commandments and emphasized chiefly the importance of the motivation of the inner conscience, HaReAYaH's teaching deals with the moral duties that were not included in the obligatory halacha. As has already been said, his perception in this matter is dependent on his nationalist and Zionist perception—especially its moral foundations. And as we know, these moral fundamentals are the cornerstone of his nationalist perception. I shall therefore begin with a brief explanation of this perception of his.

2.

The foundation of nationalism in Israel has its source, in HaReAYaH's opinion, in Abraham our father's striving to found a nation. In the words of Maimonides in his *Guide*, "The chief aim of the whole life of the patriarchs was to establish a nation that would know G-d and serve Him" (Part III, p. 51). This striving to establish a nation came really from a universalist aim whose source was in the attribute of loving-kindness that characterized Abraham our father's world; a loving-kindness that was not limited to hospitality to visitors only, or to supplications on behalf of the people of Sodom, but one whose aim was to do good to all mankind. Abraham our father saw the world suffering without end, with persecutors and persecuted suffering equally, and the laws of the forest ruling. He understood that only in keeping the way of the Lord, to do righteousness and justice, was there hope for mankind. Abraham our father understood that mere preaching would not succeed in bringing mankind to the way of the Lord. According to our sages, some attempts of this kind had already been made in the schools of Shem and Eber, but they had not been successful. Therefore Abraham our father longed "to establish a great human community that would 'keep the way of the Lord to do righteousness and justice'" (*Orot*, Chapter 2: The March of Ideas in Israel).

"This is the longing that comes from the clear and mighty awareness and the universal and lofty moral demand to deliver mankind from the terrible suffering of spiritual and material troubles and bring it to a life of freedom full of splendor and happiness illuminated by the divine idea, and to cause all men to prosper. For the fulfillment of this longing, it is really necessary that this society should have a political and social state with its seat of national government, and at the height of human culture, 'a wise and understanding people and a great nation'; and the absolute G-dly Idea should reign there, reviving the people and the Land with the light of its life. By this it will be known that not only wise and special individuals, pious men and Nazirites and holy men, live by the light of the idea of the Divine, but also whole nations, advanced and perfected by all cultural perfections, and politically settled; whole nations including all the various human strata, from the highest artistic intelligentsia, the elites, learned and holy, to the broader social, political, and economic classes, and down to the proletariat in all its groups, even the lowest and earthiest" (Ibid.).

"Two things illumine Israel," writes HaReAYaH, "pure morality in all its strivings in the entire world, in man and in every living creature in the whole of existence; and the knowledge that it all stems from calling on the Name of the Lord" (*Orot Yisrael*, Chaps. 1 and 7). When the people of Israel will succeed in bringing this message to the world, mankind will be healed. This is a long historical process, and for the sake of fulfilling this mission the people of Israel has to pass through many fiery crucibles until it will be fit to have the verse fulfilled: "And many nations shall go forth and say: Come, let us go up to the mountain of the Lord, to the House of the G-d of Jacob, and He will teach us of His ways, and we shall walk in His paths; for the Law shall go forth from Zion, and the word of the Lord from Jerusalem."

This great mission, as much as it appears far off, is what gives reason and significance to Jewish existence; it is this that is planted in the depths of the Jew's inner consciousness; and here is the source of his longing for redemption. In the words of HaReAYaH, "The strength of the desire to be good to everyone in the world without limitation, both in the amount of good to those in need of it, and in the quality of the good—this is the inner seed of the quality of the soul of the Community of Israel. This is its inheritance and the legacy from its ancestors, and this is the secret of the longing for redemption that is in the nation and that gives it strength to live and exist to the wonderment of every thinking person" (Ibid. Chaps. 1, and 4). Note HaReAYaH's expression: "This is the secret of the longing for redemption." Thus, it is not its terrible suffering that is the source of its longing for redemption, but its striving to do good to mankind, for this is the nature of its soul.

And this is how HaReAYaH saw the inner purpose of Zionism in his day. He did not accept Herzl's conception of a haven of refuge for the Jewish people. "It is not the sound of a hated nation going to seek for itself a safe refuge from its persecutors that is fitted to bring life back to this eternal movement" (*Igrot HaReAYaH*, Vol. II, p. 59). He saw the movement for the return to Zion in his days as the "beginning of redemption," that is to say, a process of the fulfillment of the prophetic vision of the return to Zion, a process leading toward the divine mission of the perfection of mankind. "There is no doubt that this great movement is the *atchalta diGeulah* ('beginning of redemption'); may it come speedily, in our days" (*Igrot HaReAYaH*, Vol. II, p. 176).

The motivations for his enthusiastic relationship to the national revival movement we learn from what he wrote in the pamphlet *Needarei BaKodesh:* "If the idea of our national revival were not so high and elevated to the point at which it includes the everlasting vision embracing the whole of mankind and all existence, we would not be able to be connected with it with all our inner soul" (*Maamrei HaReAYaH* Vol. II, p. 417). Here HaReAYaH did not explain why he would not be able to be connected with the movement for national revival without its universal aim. Apparently, he saw it as self-evident, with no need to explain it. But what is not explained here is explained elsewhere in his writings. "There are some righteous men, very great and strong, who cannot limit themselves within the confines of the Community of Israel *(Knesset Yisrael)* alone, but who are always worrying and concerned for the good of the world as a whole. Nevertheless they too are connected inwardly particularly with *Knesset Yisrael*, because *Knesset Yisrael* is the essence of all that is good and most excellent in the world in its entirety, and whatever love and goodness may come to *Knesset Yisrael*, she returns it and envelops all creation with it. These tzaddikim cannot be nationalists in the superficial meaning of the word, for they cannot tolerate any hatred or injustice, or any limitation or shrinking of goodness and loving-kindness; they are good to all, like the attributes of the Holy One, blessed be He, Who is good to all and Whose mercies are over all His works. Yet they wait for salvation with mighty fervor because they know clearly and believe with all the fullness of their pure soul that the salvation of Israel is salvation from the Lord—the salvation of the world and the fullness thereof, of everything in it from the most high to the lowest depths" (*Orot HaKodesh*, Vol. III, p. 349).

But there is a further reason for his emphasizing the universal aim of the idea of revival. HaReAYaH was afraid lest the Zionist idea, based simply and solely on the search for a safe refuge for the people—an idea completely divorced from the prophetic vision of the return to Zion, divorced from the universal moral purpose—was likely to lead to a moral breakdown and to the adoption of the idea of dependence on physical strength. Thus, he writes, "Nationalist feeling is an exalted sentiment for it is moral by its very nature; but when it is not properly directed and turns to a higher goal of overall perfect happiness, it may eventually burst the banks of morality in crossing its boundary, by raising a hand to capture castles that do not belong to it, unjustly, without righteousness and with no holy goal or purpose" (*Olat ReAYaH*, Vol. I, p. 234).

It is worth emphasizing that these things are said with reference to nationalism in Israel; that is, Jewish nationalism that is divorced from the vision of a universal redemption is likely to wither to the point of breaking the banks of morality and to inherit castles that do not belong to it, with no justice or righteousness.

HaReAYaH was also aware of the particular problems from a religious and moral standpoint within a creative sovereign framework: "It is indeed a hard task to make the observance of the general, state law distinctive—a much harder task than the observance of the Torah for the individual. For the Torah and its mitzvot are for the purpose of refining the creatures; but the work of refining society as a whole, a society needing matters of state, is much more complicated than the work of refining each individual for himself as a private person. For behold, in regard even to simple human morality where it is supported by natural justice, our eyes see that while, so far as individuals are concerned, it does at least have some hold on life, humanity as a whole has still not reached a point at which that morality is accepted as a moral obligation in public or party policy. And it is for this reason that, as we know, the same evil inclination that is present in an ordinary private person is many times stronger in a public political person, so that [with him] all the concepts of good and evil, righteousness and wickedness, become entirely lost in the political confusion and the country's seething disorder, which is like a turbulent sea" (*Maamrei HaReAYaH*, Vol I, p. 174).

For this reason, HaReAYaH demands that in this movement in

which we feel the national social flowering, we are duty-bound to raise the moral level and the attachment to our basis of holiness. "It is the strength of our holy Torah that it is the Law of life and the fountain of truth. Far be it from us to think that the stormy waves of political striving are to be permitted to blind our eyes so that we cannot see ahead; and most certainly we dare not permit the separatist party tendency, which may awaken particularly at a time when the political movement is about to be formed, to cause us to act against the attribute of righteousness and truth, of universal and individual human love, of the love of Israel and Israel's special duty of holiness. For our obligation is not only to be men of holiness as individual people but also, and especially, to be a kingdom of priests and a holy nation" (Ibid.).

By this reasoning, HaReAYaH saw it as a vital necessity to emphasize the connection between the national revival movement of his day and the prophetic vision of the return to Zion that incorporated the people of Israel's divine mission to be a holy nation and a kingdom of priests for all mankind.

<h2 style="text-align:center">3.</h2>

Here the question arises: What is that Torah that is to go forth from Zion and that will excite many nations to declare, "Come, let us go up to the mountain of the Lord . . . and He will teach us His ways"? Is the intention only for the laws in the paragraphs of the *Shulchan Aruch Choshen Mishpat?*

Moreover, these laws are obligatory, and that is apparently their strength. The nations of the world were commanded, in the framework of the Seven Noahide Laws, to set up a judicial system of their own according to their own understanding. Will the laws of the *Choshen Mishpat* become mandatory, in time to come, for the sons of Noah also?

Here we return to the question at the beginning of our discussion on the place of the moral duties that a man comes to accept out of an inner consciousness.

To the question Does the halacha include all the duties of a Jew?, Nachmanides has given an answer in his Torah commentary. It is a negative answer, saying that the mitzvot "Ye shall be holy" and "Thou shalt do that which is right and that which is good" are intended to put upon man duties beyond those that he has been commanded: "You must give your mind to do what is good and right in His eyes also in regard to that which He has not in fact commanded you" (Leviticus 19:2; Deuteronomy 6:18).

But while Nachmanides emphasizes the impossibility of detailing everything in the Torah, "Because it is impossible to mention in the Torah all a man's behavior with his neighbors and friends, and all his dealings, and all the orderings of the community and of countries, in their entirety"—HaReAYaH maintains that there is a special purpose in the noninclusion of many duties in the mandatory halacha: There is a special purpose in having these things done out of a free, inner compulsion as a form of free-will offering and the love of kindness. Furthermore, HaReAYaH stresses that "this is the goal of the Torah— that the intellectual understanding should be determined through the practice of love and free will" (*Igrot HaReAYaH,* Vol. I, p. 100). In his view, the ideal is to keep the Torah as the patriarchs kept it, that is, out of a free, inner cognitive awareness, and not because of a heavenly command. And HaReAYaH adds that "this is the basic reason why we always join the covenant of the patriarchs to all the more fundamental matters, and the covenant of *Eretz Yisrael* is joined on because of the rights of inheritance from the patriarchs and the accept- ance of the Torah. The patriarchs indeed kept the Torah out of an inner and free cognitive awareness, and it is fitting that this advantage should not be lacking from a large part of moral existence; and this is the basis of the hidden portions which appear specifically as 'chasidic' attributes (i.e., from piety and love) and beyond the requirement of the law" (Ibid. p. 97). It is the divine balance that watches over the moral development of *Knesset Yisrael* that determined "how much of it should come as the result of law and justice, and how much should issue especially from the goodness of the heart and an inner approval with no outside compulsion at all, not even moral compulsion" (Ibid.). And HaReAYaH adds that if it all came "as mandatory law, people would blur the teaching intended as an ongoing light to the generations of the world, a light to many nations and peoples according to their greatly varying spiritual levels" (Ibid.). In other words, if all the moral duties were to be turned into mandatory halacha, it would spoil the mission of *Knesset Yisrael* to be a light to the nations. The very fact that the people of Israel, by the Torah's guidance, attained to moral paths of life out of an inner and free cognitive awareness will cause many nations to marvel and will move them to go up to the mountain of the Lord. This is the word of the Lord, and this is the Torah that will go forth from Zion and Jerusalem. Moral duties that we are accustomed to define as a way of piety *(chasidut),* and beyond the requirement of the Law, are thus the basis of Torah. And HaReAYaH adds, "One cannot measure the magnitude of the loss that human culture would suffer if these exalted attributes would be fixed in a positive predetermined way. For only that which is more essential to contemporary material and moral life and, if it is weakened, will damage the roots of the future— only this is included in the warning [relating to the observance of the law]; and greater is he who observes [the law] because he has been commanded . . . This is the fate of 'beyond the letter of the law' that will greatly work for good when man's heart of stone will be changed to a heart of flesh" (Ibid.).

And if we ask what is the relative proportional weight of that part that has to be observed out of a free inner cognitive awareness as compared with the obligatory halachic part (of Judaism), HaReAYaH says that "the ethical part that has to be put forward as a voluntary act and as loving-kindness must be in proportion to the general positive moral value—like the free air as compared with the buildings and cultural deeds that fill it; it is impossible that they should not leave it a very broad expanse" (Ibid.).

Note the comparison used by HaReAYaH. The meaning is that the conscience part is ever so much greater than the halachic part. "And know that in the social laws the Torah did not pressure the spirit of the nation to piety, because then general piety [*chasidut*] would have been made into routine and a matter of duty, and the aim of the Torah is for intellectual understanding to function through love and free will. This is the basis of some of the leniencies in Torah law concerning the rules of warfare. As for the elimination of idolatry, this is in keeping with Israel's general mission; and in any case, this was a subject left to the courts to enquire into the moral quality of each cult, since not all cases are identical. Because of our many sins these matters have not been expounded to us in detail, for from the time we lost our national spiritual strength we lacked practical experience in these things, and thus it will remain until G-d, blessed be He, will restore to us our crown of glory; may it be soon, in our days" (*Igrot HaReAYaH,* Vol. I, p. 100).

HaReAYaH here gives a hint that one cannot deduce any lesson from the way wars were conducted in biblical times for our contemporary wars. Those wars were directed against an idolatrous culture that caused great moral damage. And even in biblical times, not all the wars were the same. The court used to weigh up the moral damage caused by the particular idolatrous cult, and the norms for Israel's conduct were prescribed accordingly. A further expression of the importance HaReAYaH ascribed to the moral duties beyond mandated law is to be found in his words defining the term "a righteous nation" in relation to the house of Israel in the text: "Open the gates and let the righteous nation that keepeth faith enter." Righteous nation, says HaReAYaH, means one that executes justice and loving-kindness for every individual and also toward every nation and tongue. Consequently—he adds— "its aim is that its essential conquests also will be with justice and faith. And now, when we are returning to our Land, we are conquering it not with might and not by the sword, but by peaceful means; and we pay with substantial funds for every inch of our Land, despite the fact that our right to the soil of our Holy Land never ceased" (*Maamrei Ha-ReAYaH*, p. 252).

Faithful to this perception, HaReAYaH says also in regard to the law, "And thou shalt love thy neighbor as thy self," which by all principles of halacha refers only to Israel: "It is our desire to observe the command to 'love thy neighbor as thyself' not only with regard to individuals but also concerning the nations, so that the nations of the world also should have no grievance against us" (Ibid.).

Elsewhere, again, HaReAYaH writes, "When we consider the aggadah [homily] that says that in Jerusalem they learned Torah from Sisera's grandsons, and that in Bnai Brak they learned Torah from Haman's grandsons, we penetrate the profundity of the loving-kindness according to which we do not have to be drawn into the stream of hatred even against our worst enemy" (*Orot HaKodesh*, Vol. III, p. 326).

HaReAYaH knows that whoever does not accept his view will be able to clutch on to scattered teachings of our sages. Against such he writes, "The love of fellow man has to break forth from the source of loving-kindness, not as a matter of law, for then the clearest part of its brightness would be lost, but as a mighty inner movement of the soul. And it will have to stand up against very difficult trials, to overcome many contradictions scattered like stumbling rocks in isolated teachings, in the superficiality of several laws and numerous conceptions that arise from the limited expression given to the part of the Torah and the national morality that is revealed" (Ibid. p. 318).

His practical reference to the idea of the love of fellow men is given further expression by him in his call to struggle against spiritual and "physical" hindrances and delays, albeit without explaining their nature. "When the passionate desire to be good to all prevails, then man knows that light has come to him from the upper world. And happy is he if he has prepared a worthy place in his heart, in his mind, in the work of his hands and in all his feelings, to receive the exalted visitor that is greater and higher than all the honored of the land; let him hold on to it and not let it go. And all the hindrances and delays, physical and spiritual, that hinder the acceptance of this holy idea into his very inner self, let them not restrain him; let him fight against all of them and hold fast to his fortress, let him lift up his understanding from afar to seize hold of the attributes of G-d Who is good to everyone and Whose mercies are upon all His works" (Ibid. p. 316).

It would seem that beyond his teaching, something of HaReAYaH's pure personality is here uncovered. "True greatness and genius are joined together in a generous soul to pour a dominion of love, of freedom and honor, onto both man and nation" *(Eder HaYekar)*.

Repentance in Our Days

Rabbi Daniel Tropper

THE GREAT EXCITEMENT that surrounds the phenomenon of repentance ("turning back in *teshuvah*") blinds us against being able to discern a certain problem that accompanies the process. We shall probably be sinning to ourselves if we do not from the outset examine a few points that demand care in this matter of the process of *teshuvah* that is taking place before our eyes. The motivation for raising these points does not come, heaven forbid, from a desire to belittle the importance of the phenomenon. On the contrary, just because of its historic importance there is a duty to bring in also its critical aspects in assessing its value, so that we may do all we can to make it educationally beneficial for the future of the Jewish people. For "if Israel will do *teshuvah*—they will be redeemed" (*Sanhedrin* 97b).

The first problem is that some speak of *teshuvah* today in explosive terms and with an exaggerated optimism. The reason for this talk is obvious. After a period of more than a hundred years of a one-way movement away from religious Judaism, suddenly a two-way stream begins to operate passionately. It is no wonder that religious Jewry is excited by the arrest of the destructive spiritual process of heresy and the commencement of the blossoming of a coming closer to Torah and mitzvot.

But the picture is much more complex than it appears at first sight. If we stop looking at individuals for a moment and turn our eyes to what is happening in society and in the country, we should ask, Do we sense a turning in *teshuvah* on the social and national level? Is our society changing for the better in morals, in volunteering for special units in the IDF, in fairness, in caring, in helping others? It would appear that two opposite processes are taking place today: While *individuals* are coming closer to Judaism, society as a whole is going further away from Jewish morality. This is a phenomenon that invites deep inquiry: Is there a flaw somewhere in *teshuvah*? Is *teshuvah* restricted to the level of ritual, while the moral level remains neglected and forsaken? And is it possible to speak of *teshuvah* marching toward redemption when in the overall assessment of the people of Israel the summing-up is perhaps negative and not positive?

In the wake of this question, there is also another. Does the coming closer of individuals to Torah, or, more correctly, does our behavior in connection with their drawing near to Torah, cause the community as a whole to distance itself? It is no secret that the reactions of many secularists to the phenomenon of the "return in *teshuvah*" border on hysteria. And it is no wonder. For the *teshuvah* phenomenon is an uprooting of the secular foundations that, in the eyes of the secularist, have hitherto stood firm and safe against the threat of religion. And now, suddenly, in the last few years, religion has gone over to the offensive, while the secularists find themselves in an unaccustomed position: on the defensive. It seems to me that the right reaction on our part should have been one of modest reticence. Instead of this, many parade the phenomenon of the *teshuvah* movement publicly and openly display their pride in the change of direction. This behavior demonstrates a lack of sensitivity to a genuine problem of the secularists, and causes the secular public to assume extremist positions. If we add to this phenomenon the fact that most of the work of *teshuvah* today is carried out by the "Charedi" (extreme Orthodox) world— which sometimes is connected with the returnee's separation from his family—then it is no wonder that many secularists have become really worried. This anxiety assumes diverse faces, from a refusal to participate on joint platforms with religious people to a common brutal violence against the religious people and their faith.

In the end, the result of the lack of sensitivity on the part of the

religious public to the predicament of the secularists is a hastening of
the process of removal from Torah and mitzvot. In my view, the
process of *teshuvah* is in a very delicate situation. At one and the same
time, there is both a "bringing near" and a distancing. The final result
will be dependent, among other things, on the sensitivity that the
religious public will show in this area. Without doubt, one of the
central needs for the development and progress of a turning back in
teshuvah is humility, quietness, and restraint on the part of the religionists.

Another face of the problem of returning in *teshuvah* is made clear
through an understanding of the context in which it takes place. *Teshuvah* in our generation stems partly from the existential crisis that
has hit the entire Western world. The Western world suffers today
from a feeling of alienation, isolation, and a loss of direction. Much has
been written on this subject, and there is no need to expand on it. But
what we have to understand is that a process of *teshuvah* that breaks
out by reason of a troubled soul has a danger hidden within it. The man
who suffers from alienation and isolation is open to all kinds of solutions, including Eastern cults and religions. We must beware of a
presentation of Judaism on the level of these alternatives. It is customary today in many organizations to make use of every effective method
of making an impression on a candidate for *teshuvah,* even if this is
connected with a certain lack of intellectual honesty. The end justifies
the means. As a result of this, the Judaism that is presented to secularists does not always stand on a fitting spiritual level. This phenomenon
raises at once questions of principle and education. Is it permissible for
us to twist matters, to change emphases, to exaggerate, to hide, and to
convey part-truths in order to bring an unbeliever to believe in G-d?
And what is the long-term significance of a turning in *teshuvah* linked
with a spiritual concealment?

These questions are connected with a certain distinctiveness of *teshuvah* in our generation. The use of the term "turning back in *teshuvah*" does not really fit the explanation of what is happening in
society today. A man who has been raised from childhood in secularism
and changes to an observance of the mitzvot is not *returning* to any-
place; he is discovering something new. Already in the Talmud *Bava
Metzia* (84a, in the *Tosafot* beginning *"i hadrat bach"*), Rabbenu Tam
objected to the use of the expression "return" for one who has never

kept the mitzvot. This fact raises a basic educational problem that requires clearing up. Should one see the candidate for *teshuvah* as a child who has just begun his studies in school, and who has to go through stages of simple and even veiled thinking until he will acquire sufficient tools for attaining to deep thought? Or should one perhaps use entirely different methods and pass immediately to a spiritual sophistication and depth, because the secularist has already reached intellectual maturity that is open to, and even in need of, profound thinking? It seems to me that the methods used today by certain groups are a mixture of both: a childish program (of studies) with a sophisticated method. I have great doubts as to what lies in store for us in the long term from this system, and I am not prepared to let present successes blind me from seeing the future.

It is not only the concept "returning in *teshuvah*" that is problematic, but also the term *"baal teshuvah"* ("the penitent"). If a man commits a specific transgression and then puts right what he has done, and does not commit that same transgression again, then a clear line can be drawn dividing between his period as a sinner and his new situation as a *baal teshuvah* (i.e., a penitent). But someone who is immersed in a secular world and is far from Torah and mitzvot, and begins to progress toward the observance of mitzvot—when does he come to be described as a *baal teshuvah?* When he is at prayer? Observing Shabbat? Keeping the laws of family purity? Anyone who has dealt with those who are turning in *teshuvah* knows that the progress usually is gradual and not sudden. The use of the concept *baal teshuvah* makes it difficult for us to recognize the complexity of the spiritual stages that operate in a man. The spiritual condition of every man is not static but dynamic. Man's spiritual sensitivity is not the same every day or in every season. Sometimes prayer with devotion comes easily to a man, and sometimes it is bound up with a difficult and drawn-out struggle. Likewise, one who is immersed in processes of *teshuvah* experiences ascents and descents, making it difficult, if not impossible, to fix a clear line showing exactly when he crossed the dividing line between the secular world and the religious world. It is determined not by externals but by an inwardness. Consequently, sometimes even the posing of a correct question at the right moment, even grappling with religious problems, can reflect a spiritual progress. In certain cases, the asker of a question *(baal sheelah)* is a greater *baal teshuvah* (literally, "giver of the answer") than the one known as *baal teshuvah* (literally, "returner in *teshuvah*"). In order to properly appreciate the process of *teshuvah,* we must act from a broad spiritual-religious perception in which Judaism expresses itself in the performance of mitzvot, but is not limited to it.

Finally, it is no secret that much of the *teshuvah* today is linked with extremism. There was a period when I was sharply opposed to this extremism, and I saw it as a plainly negative phenomenon. I must admit that now I have changed ("turned in *teshuvah*") a little in this matter, and I have greater tolerance for those who in "returning" have gone over to complete extremism. What brought me to examine my attitude anew is a passage in the Talmud (Sanhedrin 25b) that raises an interesting question. Usually, *teshuvah* is a private matter belonging to a man's own inner world, and no concern of anyone else. But according to the halacha, there is a specific case when we have to know whether or not a particular man has "turned in *teshuvah*" and this is in regard to the laws of testimony. There are certain sins—for instance, dice-playing (for money)—that disqualify the perpetrator as a witness. What would be the law if a man comes to testify and we disqualify him from giving evidence because he has committed these transgressions, only he pleads, "I have repented and turned in *teshuvah*"? In this case, we are obligated to know if the man is simply pleading a worthless plea, or if he has indeed changed and "turned in *teshuvah.*" The *Gemara* brings a *baraita* that puts forward criteria for deciding the issue:

1. Dice players—i.e., those who play with checkers (polished blocks of wood for the purpose of gambling). And not only with checkers, but even with nut-shells and pomegranate peel. And when are they considered to have repented? When they break their checkers and undergo a complete reformation [*teshuvah*], so much so that they will no longer play as a pastime ("for nothing").

2. A usurer—this includes both lender and borrower. And when are they considered to have repented? When they tear up their bills and undergo a complete reformation [*teshuvah*] so that they will not lend (on interest) even to a non-Jew . . .

3. Pigeon trainers—that is, those who race pigeons (to compete against one another); and not only pigeons, but even cattle, beasts or other birds. When are they deemed to have repented? When they break

up their *pegmas* (i.e., wooden rattles used to spur on the pigeons, etc.) and undergo a complete reformation [*teshuvah*] so that they will henceforth not do it even in the wilderness . . .

4. Sabbatical traders—those who trade in the produce of the Sabbatical (seventh) year. When are they deemed to have repented? When the next Sabbatical year comes round and they refrain from this trading.

The four examples of rehabilitation brought in this *baraita* are presented in a kind of poetic form with four stanzas. Each stanza has two parts—a description of the transgression and a definition of the form of *teshuvah*—linked together by the question "When are they deemed to have repented?" In the first and third stanzas, there is a widening of the definition of the transgression: an extra line that extends the transgression by the expression "even . . ." And with the exception of the last stanza, all the definitions of *rehabilitation* ("return") in *teshuvah*—(the last lines of each stanza) are made up of the initial description plus an addition prefaced by the expression, "When they will undergo a complete reformation *(teshuvah)*—so that they will not do it *even for nothing . . . even to a non-Jew* they will not lend . . . *even in the wilderness* they will not do it again."

These additions in the definition of *teshuvah* are very surprising, for all the acts referred to in the addenda are permitted by the halacha. There is no prohibition to play dice without money (as a pastime), or to race pigeons in the wilderness as a sport (without betting). Similarly, it is permitted to lend money on interest to a non-Jew, as the Torah says, "Unto a foreigner thou mayest lend upon interest; but unto thy brother thou mayest not lend upon interest" (Deuteronomy 23:21). Why then does the *baraita* lay down that a "return in *teshuvah*" does not occur when the sinner merely leaves the sin that he has committed, but only when he forbids himself from doing things that are ordinarily permitted—"Even for nothing they will not do it"? Why is it only then that a man may be seen to have "turned in *teshuvah*"?

This *baraita* teaches us a basic principle in the process of *teshuvah*. In certain stages, the veering to the extreme is a natural—almost vital—characteristic of the penitent. As far as may be seen, sin shocks the soul of the sinner enormously so that he feels an inner need to remove himself completely from the sinning act and to keep himself away from all contact with the action which reminds him of his former deeds, even if, from a halachic standpoint, such action is permitted. In one sentence, the *baraita* teaches us that the tendency to extremism of those who turn in *teshuvah* is natural, and even serves as a way of recognizing the penitent. By this the judge knows that the sinner has repented ("turned in *teshuvah*").

A great and important message is concealed in this passage. Let us not panic because of the polarization to which we are witness in the *teshuvah* movement of our day. This is not a new phenomenon, and maybe it is not entirely negative. The penitent may be in need of extremism. From this point of view, one should not wonder at the surprising success of the Haredim in this field. Many of our friends look with amazement or pain, and sometimes also with anger, at the irony that the *teshuvah* movement that Rav Kook foresaw more than fifty years ago is at last beginning to take on skin and sinews precisely through those who were the greatest opponents of his theory and his methods. But it should be understood that the Haredim may be fulfilling a certain task at this point in history, a task that only they can fulfill. Maybe we have to accept the fact that in the first stages of *teshuvah* the penitent must assume strictness and exaggerations—"Even for nothing they will not do it"—and who is more suited than the Haredim for supplying these strictures?

Yet it must also be remembered that the story does not end here. One day this great page in history will be turned, and it will be followed by great and exalted pages that will dwarf what is happening today as a wave in the ocean that swallows up the previous wave, builds on it, and goes on with greater force. One day the penitents will themselves come out of the intensive closed concentration; they will lift up their eyes to see what is taking place in the Jewish people as a whole; they will begin to understand the meaning of G-d's steps in the history of our times; and they will link their own personal return with the overall return of the people of Israel to Zion.

Symposium

Participants: Professor Rivka Schatz-Uffenheimer, Chairman
Rabbi Menachem Fruman
Dr. Aviezer Ravitzky
Professor Shalom Rosenberg
Professor Nathan Rotenstreich

PROFESSOR RIVKA SCHATZ-UFFENHEIMER:

The subject of this symposium is Rav Kook's contribution to the thought of Jewish Renaissance. In order to locate the problem with this concept, i.e., "Judaism renewed," we must comment on the cultural forces operating in the Land of Israel during the first decade of the twentieth century.

It was the bad fortune of Zionism that it was born under the sign of secularism, i.e., an avowedly antireligious position on the part of many leaders of the *Yishuv,* the Jewish population, the labor movement, and also writers and intellectuals. Secularism virtually became a new religion, for which one ought to go to the barricades. One could almost reach the conclusion that religiosity and renewal were considered inherently contradictory. It did not seem possible to take the religious, spiritual energy of the Jewish people into account in the practical construction of a new society. It suffices to look at the rare pamphlet *Elleh Massei,* which describes Rav Kook's travels in the northern settlements on the eve of World War I, to be impressed by the intense significance of secularism, as it is expressed in his conversations with teachers there.

Secularism itself was a religion. Toward this secular world, from the midst of which Yosef Chayyim Brenner in Jaffa wrote his epic celebrations of crisis and A. D. Gordon his hopeful ones to the "religion of labor," Rav Kook turned his face. First, he sought to understand the nature of the experience of the secular pioneer, its meaning in their lives, the secret of their "sacred" restlessness, and the breaches in their souls and concepts. The legitimation of the secular as representative of the reality of Jewish energy for the generation was therefore the prerequisite for the transformation that he wished that energy to undergo. He did not want to keep secularism out of play: This is his first contribution and perhaps the primary foundation for the metaphysical interpretation that he gave to this reality. Simply put, he might have said, You imagine that you are making history outside of the sacred; in fact the world of the sacred makes history, containing you within it. The tools for the renewal of metaphysical understanding of reality were taken, of course, from the concepts of Jewish tradition; therefore we must grasp the continuum of ideas in their cultural-conceptual context. Hence the relevance of discussions about cultural formulations and the transformation of content (which they underwent) in Rav Kook's work.

My contribution to the symposium will be the presentation of the problem of sacred and profane in its historical depth, not in order to narrate the historical fortunes of the problem but, to the contrary, in order to illuminate the new crossroads at which it has arrived. My discussion will not be historical, but rather at the metaphysical level of Jewish thought. Yet one is obliged to stress that the new historical background is the urgent point of origin of the metaphysics, and is the focus of the problem from which it emerges and to which it returns. It is therefore appropriate to take note of it.

There is no house of study without innovation. Even more so a house of study like Rav Kook's, so completely under the sign of explicit venture, an open call and stormy proclamation to an address that embraces all frameworks of life: an address that seeks to raise matters above the level of historical existence and beyond their agreed ethical status. The question arises, Does this utopian yearning make a man a revolutionary? Was Rav Kook indeed a revolutionary? Is there here a transvaluation? Can one say that the much bandied formula, which arouses much joy and sometimes an incomprehensible shiver, stating that "the old will be renewed and the new sanctified" is merely a nice phrase of encouragement? What are the bounds of the old and what are the rights of the new that is about to be born, who will live and who will die in the battle between the two? Which bills will Jewish tradition present for collection as part of this rejuvenation, what are the solid possessions that none of the temporary injunctions—so favored by Rav Kook—can budge from their place? Are there new criteria by which to measure history? Is that which beckons behind our walls indeed a new highway? Where stand the men on this chessboard, where passes the network of coordinates indicating what is, or is not, possible or permitted? Are there new rules to the game? In simple language, what actually happened to us with the appearance of Rav Kook, about whom we all agree that his stature does not let us sit still?

It seems to me that Rav Kook's awakening is not one that derived from the world of tradition, though he drew the tradition to every place and every front on which conflict occurred. Let there be no misunderstanding, Jewish tradition was Rav Kook's flesh and blood. He did not exist without it even for one moment. But his steadfast struggles were conducted over its head. The true arena was the outside world. In the secular world, events took place, there breaches became apparent. In that world, new answers were given, to which Jews and non-Jewish sages were partners. There, the repute of historical materialism was high; there, it was spoken of biological evolution; there, of the relativity of knowledge; there, the freedom of man was demanded. The secular Jewish world in the Land of Israel entered a high state of Zionist and cultural activity, with a tension and overt rebellion against what was most dear to him. Though Rav Kook's writings set clear boundaries between what is within the tradition and what is outside it, his concern was with extraparliamentary forces, if I may use that phrase. He would use the traditional theological term *forces of the other side*. It is hard to overestimate the importance of the theological and sociological function fulfilled by the powers of "the other side" in Jewish history. We will return to them later.

What is important here is that Rav Kook was a conscious accomplice, even a quite enchanted one, of this external activity. In its name, he became stringent toward what he himself calls Orthodoxy. This means that he contended with whoever was not willing to admit that things were happening of pertinence to the undisturbed serenity of the historical-traditional flow of Jewish life. But our problem is not his "understanding," or coming to terms with the new situations, or his

refusal to ignore them. Our concern is the very bringing of the historical event to the door of theology, and the meaning of its theological
interpretation. The problem is not how real he was in relation to life,
how far he participated in Zionist activity, or what a remarkable man
of character he was. In fact, he was a man of character beyond what
can be imagined.

Let me permit myself to cite a small anecdote, which shook me when
I first learned it. During his rabbinate in Boisk or Zoimel, Rav Kook
wrote an important, interesting book called *Midbar Shur* [still extant
in manuscript]. The book included sermons delivered over approxi-
mately a year and a half to two years. The manuscript was stolen from
his home. He knew the thief, but did not consent to demand of the
man that he return it, to say nothing of calling him to justice or
publicizing the matter. He argued that the man would return it on his
own. Years passed; Rav Kook had died [1935]. In the early sixties, the
manuscript was returned; the matter became public. I recall reading
about it in the newspaper. It said that a certain book (I didn't remember the name then) had been returned. I even recall that it was returned
to the attorney Amdur. I once asked Rav Zvi Yehuda zt'l what had
happened to that book. He leapt from his seat and asked, How do you
know? I told him that I had read about it in the paper some years ago.
Then he told me the story. I asked him what was in the book that so
inflamed that person to steal it. Was it the opinions Rav Kook expressed in it? Rav Zvi Yehuda did not respond. Perhaps he did not
know exactly why. In any event, he said that his father, may he rest
in peace, had said explicitly that the person would return the book and
that he did not consent that he be approached about the matter.
Which brings us back to our discussion.

His theological background led him to a radicalized understanding
of secularism to such an extent that he recognized the inability of
holiness to act as an exclusive power of creation. The holy becomes
dependent, in an absolute way, on the profane, which became an
immediate translation of the "other side." This is the profane that
represented in different ways the creative powers in Jewish mystical
culture. Here, I begin to turn the wheel back.

I do not claim that the holy became red meat to be devoured by the
profane, in Rav Kook's teachings, nor do I argue that he abandoned
his field. He always struggled for the primacy of faith and the religious

interpretation of the profane. But that is the problem: With the strengthening of voices in favor of putting everything under the holy and the slogan appearing throughout Rav Kook's writings—"to triumph over the profane"—one hears the subservience of the holy and the loud chorus of the profane. It is difficult then to believe that the miracle will occur and the proportions will change, especially when the profane often benefits from enviable praise.

Had the entire problem of the secular remained sociological, that is, an admission that Zionism is important and, concomitantly, an element of respect for the secularism of its pioneers, their unyielding will, and the sacrifice they offered to the idea of Jewish political renewal, it would have been an interesting innovation, worthy of note and estimation. But to construct a metaphysics for secularism is a different story— no longer a matter of secularists, but of their ideology of secularism per se. Above, I hinted at the long tradition on the question of good and evil and their metaphysical origins. This is true of all currents in Jewish thought. But it is no secret that the mystical currents, whose logic is dialectical, penetrated deeply their interdependence from the beginning of time or creation. Social mystical currents, like Sabbateanism or Chasidism, included, each in its own way, a legitimation for the introduction of evil or the "other side" or corporeality, whatever we call it, under the aegis of the holy at some level or other. Rav Moshe Hayyim Luzzatto, for example, an original theologian, conceived, in his metaphysics and ethics, of the world as negation and his messianic activism as the turning of evil into good, the mending of all privation and negation, so that being becomes one-dimensional. Buber, for example, stressed the pan-sacramentalism of Chasidism, meaning that all being becomes sanctified. The declaration that all being is sanctified stems from a positive interpretation of the dynamic of forces that would, under other circumstances, be deemed negative, I mean the powers of the other side, the forces of corporeality. Their status has varied with the circumstances, and it is historically important that we grasp this.

Rav Kook does not much dwell upon this mondial moment. Instead, he fought the battle of secular culture that was destined to become sanctified. He confronts this question against a new background and thought about a holy science, a holy aesthetics, and, perhaps most important for us, about historical processes passing over ideas and beliefs that take the barb out of heresy *(kefira)*. This brings us to the heart of the problem. "Heresy" *(kefira)* usurps the place of earlier Kabbalistic, or other, concepts. The actualization of the theory of conversion into holiness—a theory that was prevalent primarily in Chasidism—this conceptual actualization is quite transparent. But it also becomes more radical, with respect to historical life if not the metaphysical plane.

Let me cite two examples from the agenda of spiritual problems facing the Jewish people: biblical criticism and the attitude to Spinoza. These were burning issues at the time. The matters were not publicized, and with respect to Spinoza only that element was aired that did not contain this novelty. I cannot cite verbatim for reasons of space, but this is their gist. With regard to biblical criticism, the notion of heresy is not relevant: There is no genuine friction between science and religion, and "We can walk broadly with all methods of investigation."

What often makes Rav Kook's words difficult is that the exact opposite may appear in the same sentence. In other words, Rav Kook does not accept biblical criticism. In opening his discussion, he states that he rejects biblical criticism. If one cites only part of the text, it is a misrepresentation. What he really meant to claim is that he does not see the need to resort to this method, but that its employment cannot impair faith: New historical data are not liable to harm the Torah as a covenant *(amana);* Rav Kook uses this term because the fulfillment of the Torah does not depend on its historical uniformity (I am paraphrasing here). We have covenanted with whatever is in our power according to the "general consent of the nation." It is comparable to ethical consent that the individual cannot withdraw against society. "The divine link to the Torah is according to the matters that reached us." Meaning that which reached us *post facto,* "and it makes no difference what circumstances pertained until these matters reached us in this form. And since those things that are interwoven in the Torah are included in divine holiness, and if we find the need to be stringent or lenient, it is given to the rabbinical court, *the spiritual center* of the nation cannot be broken in the least."

The conception of the Torah as an agreed-upon text is itself not an ordinary conception. Moreover, the concepts of eternity and sanctity refer, according to Rav Kook, to the fact of the Torah's being a covenant (I hesitate to say, like any constitutional or political contract). So long as the covenant is not abrogated by violating the "spiritual center of the nation," its sanctity remains, whatever opinions are current about the emergence of the covenant. Not the historical uniqueness of revelation dictates its sacred status, but rather the once-and-for-all decision that the Jewish people has taken upon itself. "The people ancient in its covenant" receives the Torah. For Rav Kook, it is not the views of human beings that pull apart the covenant but their heretical intentions—heresy involves the intention of pulling apart!

Let us turn to another point illustrating Rav Kook's confrontation with the issues of the day. I mean what he writes about Spinoza. A short section in *Ikve HaTzon* already carries the imprint of the "corrective" [*tikkun*] that I shall come to below, but because of its brevity in print it is impossible to recognize its full significance.

In the MS version, Rav Kook writes the following: "The Spinozist system, with all its dross, is the complete opposite of the light of Israel. Therefore it was the hand of G-d felt upon the righteous rabbis of Amsterdam to remove him from Israel. It engendered the modern age with all its evils, including anti-Semitism, so that Spinoza and Bismarck are comparable to Bilam and Haman. If he had not been expelled, he would have mingled with the totality of Israel and written major compositions that would have been accepted like the *Guide,* the *Kuzari* and the like. And certainly, along with this, he would have composed some Torah novellae on halacha or aggadah according to his ability and *these would have led to the acceptance of his theological views* [my emphasis, RS] and would, heaven forfend, explode the foundations of Judaism. But these consequences would have been revealed in days to come and many circumstances. Since, with all this, he was of the seed of Israel, there is in his inwardness some fundamental principle that *after much refinement* [my emphasis, RS] should enter the camp that begins to refine him [Next page is missing, apparently pulled out, which presumably described the refinement through history. The next page continues the refinement via Moshe Mendelssohn, who did not finish his *"tikkun"*]. But the Baal Shem Tov "refined" him, without knowing whom he was refining, because he did not need his [Spinoza's] source, because he drew the knowledge from its inner source and refined it [i.e., without direct personal connection to Spinoza] and the work is not yet done, it is gradually being done and when it is finished, he [Spinoza] will emerge from accursed [*arur*] and become blessed [*baruch*]" (obviously punning on the name Benedictus/Maledictus).

The section justifying Spinoza's expulsion is no less interesting than the declaration about the *"tikkun"*: had Spinoza remained within the Jewish people, he would have become an authority in his own right and perhaps as a result of halachic writings, thus his theology would have become a solid possession of Judaism. Rav Kook acknowledges that it is authoritative writing that determines what is accepted into Judaism and what does not. He iterates time and again that Maimonides had stated that he could make peace with the problem of the eternity of the world were it necessary to do so, and this helps him to decide—both regarding biblical criticism and with regard to Spinoza—in favor of the view that no position is absolutely impossible within Judaism. It is not pantheism that is Spinoza's major sin but rather the "loss of yearning for G-d" and submersion in materiality that engenders wickedness. This means the ethics implicit in the writer's intention. He mentions the social function of Spinoza's views and calls him "an evilmaker even if not an evildoer."

Of course, one can pose the obvious question: Is there here a truly revolutionary position with respect to his concept of belief, is everything open and all roads lead to the same place, is everything given to correction and being corrected? If so, there is here a genuine radicalism. Of course, the opposite may be the case: that he forestalls any revolution by preemptive contradiction. Can every negative be turned into a positive, every evil into a good, every profane into holiness? Might it be that just as a torn society expelled Spinoza, so a hopeful society will restore everyone? Is this a happy ending for the Jew who has ceased to fear matter, the physical world, the prohibited, the one-dimensionality of the given, who wishes to awake in a "new culture" as he terms it? Is there a history of the sacred within the profane world, as Moses Hess termed it?

I believe that this problem is Rav Kook's principal, stimulating contribution to the thought of Jewish renewal. As a proposal for my colleagues' discussion, I would say briefly, Where is the revolution, and what is its price in the coin of Jewish tradition?

RABBI MENACHEM FRUMAN:

I will concentrate on one point, which seems to me most timely, I might almost say a political point. In other words, I will attempt to argue that Rav Kook's major contribution to the renewal of Jewish thought is substantially political.

We often heard this from my mentor and teacher the Nazirite. When he taught Rav Kook's thought, he emphasized it very much. Essentially, this doctrine uses words or phrases primarily from the world of Kabbalistic thought for timely or modern needs. This is how Rav Kook defines Maharal, and so apparently he can be defined too.

When I speak of the problem and its resolution, I will try to present it as I see it. I refer to the character of the modern spirit, if one may use this hackneyed phrase. It is a fact that today almost everyone is aware of multiple systems of thought and acquires many contradictory ethical systems.

We are all remarkably broad-minded. We know various cultures, in breadth and depth. Of course, this brings up the problem, at least for me, whether any spirituality remains after all this. Does the spirit still maintain its intensity in the face of the overflow of information, and the fact that one knows that it is possible to posit a proposition and its opposite, and that some have said one thing and others the opposite? In my opinion, this situation threatens the major foundation of the spiritual, the element of truth. That is, how can one believe in something, how is it possible to think that something is true, when you personally know so many things that contradict it? From here we move to the political domain, to which I alluded earlier, not without a tinge of provocation. We see the works of G-d here. How He collected here Jews of all possible types, hailing from virtually all cultures (recently we have even received the Ethiopians). Gathered here are representatives of all kinds of culture and conceptual systems and systems and norms of behavior. And so, let me formulate the question I raised about the political side. Do we possess our truth, the truth of Israel? Is there something that unites us? Have we some line or central point that supports everything? That, I think, is the question. I think that Rav Kook understood it, and attempted to answer it, positively, of course. His basic response: Just as there is a factor that unifies the various divine attributes, so too the various systems of concepts and cultures that we can nonetheless unite into one truth. There is still a truth despite the overflow. It is not a richness that takes revenge on its possessors.

What indeed unifies the divine attributes? Here I must repeat something banal, that is easily said. Sometimes saying it gives you some spiritual sense of it; sometimes not. What unifies all the various attributes is Divinity itself, which is to say, nothingness. It is not a particular thing, a defined thing. Whoever is pleased with this can be quite satisfied with this formula. Whoever is not can say simply that my point about the unifying power of nothing is really nothing. And often when I turn this idea in my mind, I feel that it is nothing, and it is really a question of the psychological atmosphere in which you find yourself, your present spiritual state, whether this talk has something behind it or not. But despite the limitations of this formula, I think that in principle there is no other answer. It is, in principle, impossible. Can this point that is nothing truly unify? What is the difference, what have I added with this talk? If I want to set in one framework all the forces that operate, a framework that gives each one of them its truth within the world of truth, are these forces affected by my pronouncing this formula? That is what I wished to stress, that there is no specific entity that unifies. There is no substratum or compromise or synthesis or material unity that unifies all the various ideas and spiritual and social forces. If I were to propose a substratum, I would be open to criticism as to whether it is good or not. It would be a proposal inviting reaction. But since I make no proposal, and neither, I believe, does Rav Kook— then perhaps nobody can argue against me. Except for the harshest argument, that I am saying nothing.

Nonetheless, I feel that Rav Kook is proposing something, even in the formulation in which he posits nothing as the unifying context of things, perhaps as the strongest thing of all. I can only hint at this, as I have attempted to do. But I would like to move away from this matter and from this plane, to more specific statements in Rav Kook's teaching. Let me stress that I see in these matters that sometimes display self-contradiction expressions of that same matter that I intimated before, that nothingness that is capable of unifying us all. Let me say this, in order that there be in any event something more than silence, as Rav Kook sometimes comments that silence unifies all speech and therefore one man speaks. Thus, Rav Kook speaks. Then there is some speech in this direction of unifying all powers, which is not merely a matter of coalitions, but also gives each of them existence and concreteness.

Let me indicate several ways in which man seeks to sense the realization of the unity. By realization I mean also some element of concreteness. Rav Kook proposes several formulations to realize this unity. I will cite examples, for indeed one can go through his entire output and unify as it were the various ideas and their aspects. The usual, prevalent model is that of completion: One idea completes the other; one force completes the other. The two edges of the table of the House of Israel are Maimonides and Rav Yehuda Halevi in his *Kuzari.* These are two sides of the same table. This formula appears frequently in Rav Kook's writings. A more symbolic formula that Rav Kook pushes, and whose sources are of course not difficult to discover, speaks of all things as limbs of a complete body. The limbs are not separate, but each one reflects completion. Every conception and every outlook is a member of the complete body of truth. As each conception is organic, one can arrive at the manifestation of general perfection. It comes from this ideal of perfection perfected in itself.

Within the framework of completion appear other, virtually psychological, formulations. For example, when Rav Kook discusses Maimonides in his afterword to Rav Zev Javetz's book regarding the arguments raised against the *Guide.* Among other things, he writes that undoubtedly many Jews do not consider the views of the *Guide* likely to affect them for the better. Even if there are many who cannot tie their spirits faithfully to the views expressed in the *Guide,* they are entitled to bind the thoughts of their hearts with the views of great Jewish thinkers who paved for themselves a different way. That is, the way to explain contradictions in the views of great Jewish figures is by referring to the distinctions among people. Each major figure brings someone else closer to the truth. This is an almost pragmatic formulation of the completion model.

There are many other formulations, especially in *Orot HaKodesh,* which seem to intimate a different direction. Let me quote a passage from *Chochmat HaKodesh,* toward the beginning, Section 8: "If these cognitions contradict each other in their inner character, in the psychological power that establishes them and binds them to their inquirer and investigator, the shadows will be denser and darker, and sometimes distorted, and they bring about terrible opposition and contradiction." In other words, every view and every light cast a shadow, and sometimes the shadows are terrible and distorted.

How, then, can one emerge from this, how can one bring it about that matters be unified, what unifies me and a Jew like Avi Ravitzky? Here, Rav Kook does not propose a coalitionary agreement or a common denominator, because this is apparently incorrect, false. He says, "Only in the treasury of the supernal intellect, the glow of the soul at its foundation, does there appear a light that chases away the shadows, to the degree of possibility and the measure of holiness and purity in man, through which the defects are healed that each consciousness casts upon its neighbor's and there is no complete correspondence in the content of the awarenesses." In the content of consciousness, there can be no correspondence between Avi Ravitzky and me. It cannot be. Each has his own truth, and there is no need to obscure this. So where is the harmony? Only "for the Source of wisdom, the Whole of ideas alone, may He be blessed." This means that these lines will meet some day at infinity, as they say. Only for G-d is there a harmony in the content of ideas. And that is what Rav Kook proposes for us: "the inward cleaving unto G-d, which is the foundation of all views, it heals the pressures and wounds that we were smitten by our lovers and His Name is called Peace." He proposes that Avi Ravitzky and I pray to the same point. Not to establish some system in which I am the left corner and he is the right, or something like that, so that together we constitute the table of the House of Israel, as we saw in the previous formulations. Instead, it is the cleaving unto G-d that will unite us.

DR. AVIEZER RAVITZKY:
Yesterday I had the opportunity to speak of more concrete questions, the question of Rav Kook's attitudes to the secularist and secularism, national redemption, repentance. Therefore today I wish to speak on a more theoretical plane, about Rav Kook as a paradigm of the possibility of renewed Jewish thought in our time. For lack of time, I will keep my remarks brief, almost in shorthand.

We have been expelled, to a large degree, from the Eden of classical Jewish medieval thought, both that of the philosopher and that of the mystic. As to the philosopher, we have already learned from medieval thinkers, such as Maimonides, that it is impossible to have a positive, substantial knowledge of G-d, insofar as our knowledge is conditioned by human concepts and is intrinsically tied to matter. It is the nature of our intellect that, when it speaks of divine wisdom, it can only speak of the wisdom of its own experience. Medieval thought, however, taught us that although we cannot attain knowledge of the Creator Himself, we do comprehend His creation, His world, His actions. Physics can teach the very principles of nature, to penetrate the essence and substance of the world to grasp its inner teleology. As all this is G-d's creation, then human cognition is the cognition of G-d's deeds, His attributes of action. Hence the knowledge of nature was endowed a religious significance, the comprehension of His wisdom as revealed in creation—His will as revealed in creation.

Critical philosophy, as represented by Kant and the like, has expelled us from this Eden, has stripped us of this possibility. No longer is it only the Creator alone Who cannot be known; even His creation and His world cannot be known in themselves. From the moment that the cognitive subject was granted a creative power, the world is no longer a given that one photographs; rather, it is within one's power to establish and construct and organize it. The human subject is a mirror. The intellect does not passively receive the world as given, but it plays an active role in the construction of the known object. It organizes the world according to its own categories of thought, of its a priori forms of intuition. Hence I can no longer penetrate to the thing-in-itself; I can penetrate neither to the essence of creation nor to the nature of the Creator. Thus, we were expelled from Eden. Paradoxically, it is precisely the creative status of the human intellect, the constructive status, that took away its religious significance: I comprehend a reality mediated by my concepts and forms rather than the world of G-d in itself.

Something similar happened to Jewish mysticism; if not to all of us, surely to many of us. The mystic too did not know G-d directly but obliquely, mediately. For the mystic, that knowledge came not through the world but through the language of the Torah, the word of G-d, in which each letter intimates hidden worlds, hidden intentions, hidden *sefirot.* The entire Torah, its words, letters, and decorations, consists of the divine revelation and of G-d's Name. Each permutation of the biblical letters represents a different aspect of the supernal, of the infinite overflow. But critical investigations of a different type, not critical philosophy this time, evicted many of us from this Eden as well. Thus, Gershom Scholem confessed that once you no longer understand the concept of Torah from heaven in a fundamentalistic manner, there is already some sort of human mediation and the receiver of the Torah already contributes creatively: From this moment, you can no longer interpret letters and words as the revelation of an infinite afflux. Now, even if one does not follow this critique, he too—for reasons that I cannot now go into—cannot be expected, in most cases, to manifest that sort of creative Kabbalistic power.

Therefore it is precisely the power of construction and mediation "bestowed" upon contemporary man that has propounded for him a problem with respect to the possibility of religiously meaningful knowledge, both in comparison with the medieval philosopher and the medieval Kabbalist. It seems, however, that there remain three domains in which religious knowledge can define itself, despite, or because of, its formative and creative capability. The first area is philosophy of history; the second is human consciousness; the third is halachic thought or the integration of halacha and aggadah.

In order: An outstanding feature of Rav Kook's teachings is the renewed turning of our religious attention to history, to the philosophical meaning of historical occurrences, from ancient days until the present, down until tomorrow. There is here a very serious consideration of the time process and its meaning. There is here an intriguing combination of Rav Yehuda Halevi's attitude to history (contrasted, for example, with the minor place that it occupies in Maimonides' *Guide*) with the Hegelian approach, emphasizing the importance of the history of spirit. Revelation is not, then, first and foremost, cosmological, or even the mystical permutations of words (despite the deep marks of Kabbalah in Rav Kook's world), but rather history. I would say, with a grain of salt, that the terms *history, redemption,* and *revelation,* are often interchangeable in Rav Kook's words. History is the arena of the renascent, constant redemption.

Yesterday I spoke of the process "and I shall give you a new heart to know Me," not as reference to the future world, but as the story of humanity from past to present and from present to future. Time has meaning. Rav Kook believes in the constant elevation of human nature; in a certain sense the myth of the broken vessels and their mending enters history. Much more than other thinkers, Rav Kook devotes great attention to the significance of the event. One might agree with his solutions or disagree with them; that is a personal question. But the turning of our attention to the historical and historiosophical dimension, from a religious perspective, is surely called for, given our reality.

Some trivial comments: In the past generation, several dramatic events have occurred that could shape a Jewish historical myth of biblical proportions. Holocaust on one side; resurrection on the other. I noted before that the attempt to penetrate the secrets of the cosmos has broken down. The approach of mystical permutations has also been undermined for many of us. It seems to me that many historical assumptions implicit in our sources for nineteen hundred years have been undermined for us, to a large degree, as well. We have made assumptions about the way history ought to run. During our Exile, and particularly after the failure of the Bar Kochba revolt, we always assumed that we would indeed be inferior politically to the Gentiles throughout our Exile, but we could survive. The idea that the Jewish people survives, politically inferior, is not only that of Augustine and the church, but to a large extent is home-grown. Take, for example, what is called the conception of the "three oaths." On the one hand, we took the oath not to "go up on the wall," not to press the eschatological end, and not to rebel against the nations. On the other hand, the Gentiles "swore" not to subjugate the Jews too much. The assumption always was that if they overdid it, we would be saved; G-d would intervene and Haman would be hanged.

Therefore one of the holidays that I find difficult is Purim, not only for Ernst Simon's humanistic reasons, but because the Haman of the last generation succeeded in his evil plan respecting a crucial part of the Jewish people of his 127 provinces. I would say, metaphorically speaking, that the Holocaust was the Gentile violation of their oath, the establishment of Israel was our abrogation of our oath as we accepted historical responsibility. The theological equilibrium was thus upset. One may have different opinions about this matter: Anti-Zionist Orthodoxy and religious Zionism have different ideas as to which was the cause and which the effect, i.e., did their violation of their oath release us from ours or vice versa? In any case, the classical theological balance has assumed that "one lamb can survive among seventy wolves." The Talmudic discussion in *Yoma* about "the great, mighty and revered G-d": *mighty* for restraining His anger and permitting the nations to survive, despite what they have done to Israel; *revered* because he enables the lamb of Israel to survive under their yoke. Now in the last generation, all kinds of historical assumptions have changed. For, suddenly, you ask, does a lamb indeed survive among seventy wolves? And it is a dual question: 1) Not all the nations are among the wolves; 2) On the other hand, things have happened that indicate that the lamb cannot survive without teeth. One needs, then, a different philosophy of history. It is difficult to celebrate Purim. All this, I believe, indicates that the dramatic events renewed the question of religious significance of history. To be sure, one can ask whether Rav Kook's optimism can serve us in this age: Is there progress? In any case, there is a primary importance to the historical turn. This is one point I wanted to raise.

A second point is the turn of religious significance to human consciousness. The modern critique of religion, by contrast with earlier critiques, was directed at the image of man that is shaped by religion. It is a criticism of religious life, against religious consciousness, more than an attack on the metaphysical claims of religion. It is the image of the religious human being that is challenged, not the image of G-d or the world. For Nietzsche—slave morality; for Feuerbach—alienated man (for Hegel Judaism represents alienated man); for Marx—passive, drugged man; for Freud—immature man; for Romanticism—man torn from the flow of life.

Rav Kook deals even with theological questions like pantheism and monotheism and with modern scientific developments primarily in terms of the human consciousness that these engender. He did not concentrate on the question of metaphysical validity, as that is a matter with respect to which every human view is partial by definition. Hence his question was what kind of consciousness, what manner of man, what kind of life, does a view generate? E.g., in *Orot HaKodesh*, Rav Kook speaks of tempering sharp, radical monotheism, which generates an unambiguous gap between G-d and man, the monotheism of Maimonides' negative attributes, with a pantheism "purified of its dross." We have just heard (from Professor Schatz) of unpublished writings by Rav Kook that explain what he means by pantheism purified of its dross. In any case, Rav Kook is discussing the most crucial theological question in the history of religious thought—pantheism or monotheism—the central criterion in the light of which he deals with the question is the kind of man who comes into being. Is a fragmented, alienated man created by it, or a unified one? When Rav Kook claims that one should temper monotheism with refined pantheism, his primary consideration is the human consciousness that comes about. I could offer several examples of Rav Kook's internalization of the questions raised by the modern critique of religion, and his efforts to demonstrate that precisely in the light of this critique we can emerge triumphant with the legacy of Kabbalah; i.e., his efforts to demonstrate that Judaism is the religion that does not alienate, and that does not create slave morality but rather a man united with the supernal, etc.

Rav Kook deals with the achievements of modern science in exactly the same way. When he speaks of the innovations of modern thought, the doctrine of evolution (Darwinism), the cosmological revolution (Copernicus; I have located an out-of-the-way text in which he manages to respond to Einstein), he evaluates those theories in light of the same criteria as with the question of monotheism and pantheism. How does this affect man's self-image and his way of seeing his place in the world? Does post-Darwinian man regard himself as more unified, more connected to the cosmic continuum, or less so? Does man's understanding of his descent from the ape lead him to argue, How inferior am I, who am I, what can be demanded of me, if in sum I am only an ape? Or does one say, Whence have I come, how far have I come, how much more can I progress? In other words, from the moment that I abjure knowledge of the thing-in-itself in an absolute and complete manner, so that each human being can attain partial knowledge only, one turns to the human outlook and asks, What manner of consciousness is engendered by each scientific and philosophical doctrine?

The third and last subject is the relation between halacha and aggadah, a grasp of the importance of meta-halacha, of which Rav Amital has already spoken: that there ought not to be a contraction whereby a Jew possesses, from a spiritual point of view, nothing but paragraphs in the *Kitzur Shulchan Aruch.* Rav Kook meant to restore the illumination of prophecy into halacha and vice versa.

In the Lithuanian yeshiva world as well, there has been an attempt to link halacha and aggadah, to bestow upon man creative power. But in the Lithuanian yeshiva world, this meant the introduction of the conceptual analysis into halacha—the depths of *lomdut.* For them, thought is the clarification of the concepts upon which the halacha is founded, which are incarnated in it. Whoever knows Rav Soloveitchik's use of terms like "a priori halacha," "conceptual ideals" will recognize my reference. Here, halacha itself becomes some sort of a platonic idea. These ideas are indeed attractive. Sometimes, however, they seem sterile, and sometimes one senses the danger of contraction because there is no room for meta-halacha, insofar as prophecy and aggadah become the elucidation of concepts within halacha.

Rav Kook resorts to philosophical themes in halacha, but his desire is to integrate halacha and aggadah. There is a passage in *Orot* in which he says that prophecy could grasp the totality, the general values to protest against idolatry, ethical iniquity, but it did not know how to translate this into particular, concrete halachic details, which is why prophecy failed to direct the people, and Israel did not respond. Now came the antithesis, the period of rabbis and sages ("sage is preferable to prophet"), who knew how to define particular halachic norms and succeeded indeed in leading *Klal Yisrael*. However, as is the nature of the world, with the passage of time, "the occupation of the sages has waxed" to the point where the general (the prophetic vision) is swallowed by the particular (halachic details), and we arrive at spiritual contraction. Now, with the return from Exile, synthesis is required— the combination of halacha and prophecy, and prophecy is destined to elevate halacha from within.

As my time is almost over, I would like to end by presenting a section of Rav Kook's text that surveys many of the issues I have covered. These are words as yet unpublished: "I cannot satisfy my soul with that love that stems from the ties of logic, from the search for the divine light through the world, through being that penetrates the eyes." That was my first point—the initial expulsion from knowledge of the world. By contrast, "The Infinite Light is present in the expression of the Name, in the expression of G-d, and in all the names and denominations that the human heart has referred and meditated as his soul levitates on high." Here we learn of the second, rare possibility, of words and names, permutations and intentions. In the next lines, which I will not quote, we learn why, for Rav Kook, the epistemological realm has an ontological significance: If I am torn in my mind from the midst of life, if I am torn in my consciousness from the totality, then something is wrong in the very Being, for I am a portion of the supernal Divine. If something is broken within me, then something is broken within the supernal, and there is a lack of unity. Now Rav Kook goes on to describe his inner experience: "How great is my inner conflict. My heart is full of a lofty, broad spiritual yearning. I desire that the divine pleasantness extend through me, not because of the pleasure of delight in it but because this is what must be, because this only is the status of reality, because this is the content of life . . .

"And my soul becomes more elevated, it rises over all abasement, pettiness and limits, by which the life of nature, the body, the environment and convention limit it, oppress it as with tongs, put it entirely in chains." The soaring soul wishes what is supernal, wishes to pass all bounds. So far the thesis. Now the antithesis: "Now come a flood of obligations," i.e., halacha, "inferences and exactitude without end, complications of ideas and extraction of *pilpul* from the exactness of letters and words, comes and surrounds my white, free, cherub-light soul, pure as the essence of heaven, flowing like an ocean of light, and I have not yet reached that level to envision from beginning to end, to understand the pleasantness of each teaching, to feel the sweetness of every exactitude, to observe the light in the darkness of the world." Of course, we ask, If Rav Kook found it difficult, how hard it must be for us, if he cannot at the moment of writing, who can!? But now comes the quest for synthesis: "I am full of pain and hope for salvation and light, for the supreme loftiness, the appearance of knowledge and lucidity, the dripping dew of life, even in these narrow channels from which I am nourished and satisfied, I will delight in G-d's pleasantness, I will recognize the image of the ideal Will, the lofty hiddenness of supreme power that fills each letter and decoration, every debate and *pilpul,* and I will frolic with Your commandments that I love and converse in Your Law." I believe that we can hear the call to reintegrate prophecy and halacha (I hesitate to venture remarks on the issue of prophecy in Rav Kook's world). Aggadah and halacha, both meditation and details—"I frolic with Your commandments that I love and converse in Your Law."

PROFESSOR SHALOM ROSENBERG:
The Talmud describes Rav Yehuda Hanosi's death as the outcome of a struggle between different angels. Not only do angels lay hold of the great sages. So do scholars, continuers, heirs, and opponents. The "tragedy" of great figures like Maimonides and Rav Kook is that they become the focus for identification, hence mirrors in which many gaze, consciously or unconsciously transforming them into the background for their projections, as if they were human Rorschach blots through which they express themselves. These matters get bound up with the

different styles of writers and scholars. Their work oscillates between two extreme poles, the hysterical pole, full of agitation, and the compulsive pole, full of erudite marginalia.

I think that these comments apply to Rav Kook and his teaching. I do not claim to have the key for an objective understanding of his views and his path. I certainly will not do that today. Here, I will present my Rav Kook, and for me Rav Kook's doctrine is a wager on reality, whose three points I call: anti-alienation, perfection, and dialectic.

Why a wager? To justify this problematic term, I preface two remarks:

1. My point of departure is not historical but philosophical, perhaps existential. In my humble opinion, the historical situation can only present questions but not produce answers. Moreover, in order to understand the historical situation, we must consider the alternatives available within a particular situation. We face today two alternatives, with Rav Kook's teaching at the center of one of them. The choice between them is a wager.

2. For many, a teaching implies an obligation. The normative aspect suffices for them. It may appear egoistical, but I am also concerned with the descriptive question: What correspondence pertains between reality and norm?

The first focus of Rav Kook's teaching I called anti-alienation or, if you will, antignostic. There are two conceptions of revelation. According to the classic conception, an obligation is placed upon me from on high and it is my duty to obey. Obedience for the sake of heaven is the essence of the duty. This conception has attained extreme formulation in the work of Yeshayahu Leibovitz. Against this position arose the Nietzschean critique, according to which such a stance is slavery, for it involves something forced upon me and the demand that I subjugate myself to it.

Against this conception one could posit another, which views the Torah not as a revelation from above but as a creation flowing from me. This was, for example, the stance of Ahad Haam, with respect to the national spirit. This position opened the door to relativism. If the source of the Torah is the spirit of the nation, then it does not obligate me. Between these two positions in confrontation we must locate Rav Kook's first wager, formulated with the aid of the Kabbalistic symbols of the encompassing light and the inner light. There is a correspondence between the encompassing light coming from above and the inner light that derives from it. That is the basis of the first thesis, which I called anti-alienation. It means that the commandment with which I am charged does not contradict the most basic structures of the personality, of the individual, the people, and the human race.

As to the individual: We do not accept the views of the Freudian psychologists who describe the conflict between the hidden will of man and the superego internalizing external values. In the footsteps of Rav Kook, we bet on a humanistic, transpersonal approach to personality. When I say that I bet, I mean that I believe, at least at a pragmatic level, that there is a correlation between the Torah in which I believe, which is normative for me, and the structure of my personality. I will keep this Torah even if it causes me pain, even if have to isolate myself from the world and suffer, and live in another world, a spiritual or physical ghetto, even if every action is one of self-sacrifice. But I do not believe that this is indeed the case.

This is an antignostic position in the strongest sense. By "gnostic" I mean an awareness of coming from another, strange world, that we do not belong to this world. And this wager is connected with our position with regard to the new world. What is our fundamental perspective on it? Do we view it as the creation of the "other side," or perhaps, to the contrary, we must lift to it pan-sacramental eyes, for it too is holy.

The first wager maintains that there is a correlation and not alienation. The second wager claims that the Torah is not the fragmentation of man, but rather his aspiration to perfection. At the center of the human ideal is self-fulfillment, the Maimonidean ideal that must remain in place even after the Kantian critique. But beyond self-fulfillment is an aspiration to transcendence, to a cleaving unto G-d.

Perfection means that there is unity despite problems and contradictions. Let me explain the notion with the aid of an analogy to a lamp. If we lift a lamp, it will illuminate a larger area, but the intensity of light decreases. As I lower it, more light will fall on the pages that I read, but the range will contract. Thus is engendered particular, narrow science. Particular reality is the source of contradictions. But these contradictions can be remedied.

The third wager is that of dialectic, which is an inclusive approach to history and ethics. It is a polysemous concept. Every thinker and each system has a different conception of dialectic. Let me illustrate Rav Kook's approach with his attitude to the controversial figure mentioned earlier, that of Baruch Spinoza. Rav Kook claims, among other things, that a great miracle occurred. The real tragedy could have occurred had Spinoza continued to don his tefillin. Had that been the case, he would not have been excommunicated, and if he had adorned his books with whatever Torah comments, they might have become fundamental works of Judaism without people sensing the great damage that they would have caused. His book indeed was an "outside" work, neither true nor good.

Something basic, radical, had to happen in order for matters to alter and turn about. In fact, a revolution occurred, the corrective was supplied by the modern Hasidic movement, the school of the Besht. In order to grasp Rav Kook's position in this area, we must pass to the second dimension, that which belongs to the compulsive erudites.

I believe that Rav Kook's view should be understood by examining a missing and problematic link. I refer to a theory of Avraham Krochmal, son of Rav Nachman Krochmal. In one of his books, Krochmal proposes the bold, inane notion that the writings of the Kabbalist Rav Adam, which influenced the Besht, were none other than the writings of Spinoza. I do not believe it would be mistaken to assume that Avraham Krochmal's works were available to Rav Kook, including this one. Rav Kook implicitly relates himself to this nexus, except that the historical link never existed, save as a jest or an expression of Krochmal hyper-Hegelianism. In its place, Rav Kook's points to a deeper, and opposite, nexus of ideas. Spinoza was misled by the light he saw, just as Bilam, who wished to see beyond his bound, was blinded. This light finds its corrective only in the doctrine of the Besht.

This is an example of a historical dialectical exegesis interpreting each phenomenon. However, the dialectic applies not only to systems but also to reality. Rav Kook also adopted a dialectical perspective on war. War is sometimes unavoidable (he was not a pacifist), but at a certain stage he believed that we have already passed the era of wars and now have opened a new epoch (see *HaMilchama* in *Orot*, pp. 11–47). In any event, the dialectic must accompany us when we attempt to resolve moral problems. The sin of failing to take it into account precipitates the revenge of reality. This was the great sin of

Christianity, which expressed the great demands of Judaism without taking into account the historical, and also psychological, reality found among the nations and in the human soul.

The last wager is the wager on the totality of the Jewish people *(Klal Yisrael)*. Our struggle with gnosticism implies that we are unwilling to accept a division of our people into good and bad. That means that I bet on *Klal Yisrael*. It is my duty to hear the other in order to understand his self-understanding, but it is my right to see him differently than he sees himself.

I must make room for the other, but I can also allow myself to see the other as part of a total scheme whereby I regard him in terms of the positive in him. "That none be rejected of him" involves a mystical belief with respect to Israel, that each Jew, qua Jew, has a role in the process of world redemption. This is true regarding the Gentiles as well. Hence there is no "other side," because even conflicting views in the world contain a degree of truth. If they had no truth value whatsoever, we could not understand them or arrive at them.

I would like to end with a remark I consider important. There is a position that sees the central principle as Torah for its own sake: This is the approach of Yeshayahu Leibovitz. It is also a principle of the Musar movement and other currents. You can adopt it, but you cannot fulfill it unless you turn Judaism into a very small, limited part of your life.

Rav Kook champions a different principle: "In all your ways, know Him." The difference in positions is so profound that he who follows one principle cannot understand the other. Rav Kook's position implies that all sorts of things in life connected with economics, sanitation (to borrow Leibovitz's usual rhetorical flourish), and the distinctive drives of man, the delight of quest and self-fulfillment, are part and parcel of "In all your ways, know Him." This principle of "In all your ways, know Him" is a wager. It is a wager because I do not know whether Rav Kook is right. I bet that he is. If Rav Kook is right, then I must educate to total openness to all the powers of man. If not, I must develop certain faculties at the expense of others. We do not know the truth, but we have no time to wait. Accepting Rav Kook's approach means that I accept the wager that the world is indeed as he envisioned it.

PROFESSOR NATHAN ROTENSTREICH:

I continue along the lines of my colleagues, though for understandable reasons I do not use the term *wager*. I prefer decision, commitment to a direction, etc.

I want to begin my remarks with a short sketch of the modern philosophical background in the areas that carry weight for our subject, one might say in the issues connected to the foundations of religion and belief. I will emphasize two opposing tendencies, where the second is, by the nature of things, an antithetical response to the first. The first tendency points to identity of human powers and G-d, where the mediation of this identity is reason or the human intellect. Insofar as reason or intellect involve the identity of knower and known, one can turn, or sublate, this identity into an archetype of the essential identity of man and G-d. This tendency was represented by Hegel. He even thought that he had thus given a philosophical interpretation to Christianity. Christianity is founded on an identity of man and G-d, which is only a symbolic or allegorical expression of a more intrinsic identity, for which we must find an appropriate expression in the framework of what is called speculative reason.

As opposed to this there arose, already in the nineteenth century, a tendency to underline the distance between man and G-d. This is either because the inclination of man's heart is evil, or that he is imprinted with original sin, or that man is enclosed by his nature in his four cubits of finitude—the most prominent manifestation of which is death. Many variations of this idea are being formulated, down to the present moment. If we stress the aspect of distance, it is possible that any religious relation or relation of faith is rendered impossible, and if it remains possible that is only through a leap. In that case, man, in the instant, transcends himself and creates a link to G-d that underlines the insufficiency of human spheres, including the ethical, as we find in Kierkegaard. It too cannot succeed in attaining the stage of faith, because the ethical sphere is within the four cubits of human reality, and human reality, when grasped from within, is enclosed within its four cubits.

It seems that it is against this background that one can grasp Rav Kook's thought as an alternative to the two tendencies. Neither an identity between man and G-d nor an unbridgeable gap between man and G-d, but rather a conception primarily based on man's relatedness to reality as a whole. It is not an accident that Rav Kook used two terms with a hierarchical character: the holy and the Holy of Holies; reality itself contains holiness. In common parlance, one might say that reality itself is theophanic, that it reveals G-d. It is not a revelation of the word, but of the structure, which is why I used the Greek derivation *theophany*. Man belongs to this reality. He is, from the outset, beyond himself, and faith involves the confession of this reality, in its proper perspective, and a thanksgiving for this reality, that is, gratitude for the fact that man is not, from the outset, enclosed in his finitude. One of the expressions of this approach is precisely in the sphere of ethics. I highlight and stress this qualification precisely because there are certain approaches to the ethical sphere and its essence that should be seen in this context, and whose relevance will highlight what is distinctive about Rav Kook's position.

There are two types of approaches to ethics. One is that ethics deals with the self-realization of the human telos, perhaps even the cosmic telos. Man is to realize himself, for example, when a being thinks in actuality because he is a thinking being in potential. The second approach is that ethics is not based upon self-realization but on submission to a norm formulated in an abstract, imperative manner, which man must impose upon his actions, normatively, in everyday life. This, for example, is the approach of Kant. Its echoes and resonance can be heard in *Halachic Man* by Rav Soloveitchik, where halacha is ever ideal. Whereas Rav Kook writes in *Orot*, "We link the disconnections of life to the great canvas of life." In other words, there is a great canvas, which can be characterized as relatedness. From the outset, man finds himself within an open reality. He is open to reality, which means that he is open to the other as well. One could phrase it as follows: The concern of ethics is to mold the given structure of the breadth of life, of man's openness to life and to the other, i.e., his fellow man. This ontological status does not necessarily lead to moral shaping, but makes it possible. Hence there is no intrinsic distance between norm and reality, but rather a kind of development of reality toward additional stages, in accordance with the norm or the acceptance of the norm. This is a central point, and Avi Ravitzky already mentioned the pantheistic and monotheistic elements touching each other. We find that this cosmic conception makes possible the transition to the ethical sphere.

At this point, I want to comment on something that came up in the discussions of secularism. I have reservations about the term secularism *(chiloniyut)*. It is a Hebrew neologism that moves from the secular *(chol)* to secularism. Secularity is not connected to the distinction between the sacred and the secular. Secularity means an affirmation of time, of the epoch. I would like this to appear in the Hebrew term as well; perhaps we should give up Hebrew purism for the sake of conceptual lucidity. But the issue is relevant here—and I am continuing a conversation I had with Avi Ravitzky several months ago. Is there indeed a notion of the "cunning of reason" in Rav Kook's thought, as there is in the writings of Hegel? Meaning that the historical process is led on by a kind of legerdemain. By legerdemain a man who seeks power, like Napoleon, is led to world empire, that is, to a type of unity of historical reality. Can one say that, according to Rav Kook, the people called "secularists" serve, against their will and legerdemain, purposes beyond themselves? I think that this reading does not fit Rav Kook's thought because Rav Kook is not discussing in this context motivations that are thresholds of processes, but rather actions. Human actions are integrated in the progression of a broad and inclusive reality. Now action by its very nature takes place in the progression of reality, and becomes part of reality. Thus, it is not a contrast of motivation and goals, but rather the actions themselves that shape the world, thus becoming integrated in the world as a whole, which is not the case when one sees the action alone, and he who thinks the action in the context of its relatedness, as I called it above, and does not see the total sphere but the action alone. On this issue, one might say that precisely he who values the action in itself, whether for ethical reasons or because of the character of Judaism, enriches reality through the actions, thus realizing the total scope of reality.

On this point, one may iterate that there is a distinction between the holy and the Holy of Holies. The holy is spaciousness itself; the Holy of Holies is reality identical with the norm, and this pertains to G-d alone. Therefore we can repeat that within modern Jewish philosophical thought Rav Kook represents an attempt to characterize the nature of faith and correspondingly the nature of that reality to which faith relates itself. Faith is not simply a continuation of reality, but reality does not slap faith in the face, as it were, of which one might say *credo quia absurdum est.* This cannot be the way, neither on the basis of Jewish sources nor the specific perspective from which Rav Kook formulated his thought.

Here permit me one textual remark. Of course, there is reason to seek connections and even influence between Rav Kook's thoughts and trends of modern philosophy. We know that here and there thinkers like Bergson are mentioned. But I do not think that we can get to the core of this special system of thought by emphasizing its relations to various currents. We have here a very individual thinker, who may receive here or there some influences, but is not shaped by them. This has a clear upshot. The influences pass through the refining furnace of Jewish thought.

This leads me to a specific typological note on Rav Kook's thought against the background of Jewish thought in recent generations. We have a combination that seemingly has no parallel, between a submersion in the world of Torah and individual thought. It is not only an attempt to understand the intrinsic themes of commandments or *halachot,* and not only an attempt to grasp the ontological thesis of halacha. It is an attempt to see halacha in its particulars as part of the profile of reality and with this to return to the original themes of faith. These original themes are the normative relationship (both necessary and obligatory) toward reality in its totality. If we consider the classical thinkers of Judaism like Hermann Cohen and Franz Rosenzweig, neither was, for obvious reasons, the combination of complete submersion in Torah and in the individual themes of reflection. This may be a matter of geography, but geography is to some extent accidental. The question is how this molds biography. Thus, it seems to me, one must see here an attempt to define retrospectively a tendency of Jewish thought. If we wish to detach these matters from influences and consequences, what is nowadays called reception, then we must stress this unique synthesis between the nonindividual element of halacha and the individual element of the thinker.

DISCUSSION:

YOSEF OFEK:

I have a question for Rav Fruman. I gathered that the meeting of the two approaches of the different believers will be in the Source of

Wisdom, i.e., the *Ein Sof*. In other words, there is a dichotomy between two types of faith or between the religionist and the secularist.
Even within religion itself, there is a dichotomy, which will be brought
to meeting in the Infinite Source of Wisdom. I have studied the
chapters on belief in *Musar Avicha*. One of the clear criteria that Rav
Kook presents in the last section is that without a relationship to the
Infinite or without the inclusion of the Infinite in our souls, meaning
in the souls of each person, the world of faith is impossible. The
question arises: If there is no relationship to the Infinite in the soul of
every person, and we assume that the encounter is deferred to the
eschatological Source of Wisdom, then we find ourselves, according to
Rav Kook's definition, in a world outside faith. This raises a problem
about Rav Kook's meaning.

Elsewhere in *Musar Avicha,* discussing the traits of the soul, he says
that one must bring all powers from potency to actuality. And again
this actualization is interpreted very broadly. He goes so far as to say
that if we do not actualize our powers, there is a danger of destruction.
The question is what kind of human being we seek to create, and how
to confront a definite conception on the one hand and spirituality and
holiness on the other hand.

RABBI FRUMAN:
The will to unity is a very fine thing. Often, of course, there is a recoil
from the will to unity, because the will to unity will come, as it were,
at the price of compromises or the dulling of the boldness and intensity
of each constituent. I just wanted to say that Rav Kook has formulations about perfection and resolutions and the structure of unity. I
merely wished to indicate, and I did not succeed in achieving a sharper
phrasing, that in the final analysis the inner tendency of things is not
necessarily to the formulations that we know in many areas where each
side holds to his position, but rather the sense that I may neither show
nor see anything specific that brings two things together, and yet there
is something that unifies them. There is, nevertheless, something, even
if it is nothing, that unifies. In this sense, if I understood the question,
I think that every real thing somehow gets integrated, including people
who do not uphold the banner of belief in the Infinite, etc. Certainly
one can introduce them into the framework of Rav Kook's teaching.

PROFESSOR URBACH:

I want to comment on what has been said. First of all I wish to congratulate the initiative for this conference. I have some complaint that it is taking place here. Not because of King David, whom I too respect, but I am not sure that this place fits Rav Kook's image. But let us accept this willingly and gratefully. This session has demonstrated, in my opinion, the contribution of Rav Kook to the renewal of thought. Rightly, it has been renewal of thought, not new thought. Meaning, we are in the process of search and study and investigation. Rav Kook appeared as a figure who showed the way to quest for a renewal of thought and it is certainly difficult to find his like.

I want to comment on some of the things that were said and perhaps to hear some answers. What the chairman, Rivka Schatz, cited with respect to Rav Kook's attitude to Spinoza was not a passing episode. It is an integral part of his historical conception. I would like to point out that Spinoza found many admirers but also one great opponent in Hermann Cohen. Cohen rejected Spinoza in toto, and spoke of him in the sharpest possible language. Rav Kook could not regard Spinoza this way, because he comprehended our entire historical process. Here I reach the point touched upon by Avi Ravitzky, regarding Rav Kook's philosophy of history as a totality. Clearly, he was influenced; I do not care to discuss the influences on him. It is almost Hegelian, more like Nachman Krochmal. He underlined this by locating Hitnagdut, Chasidism, and the Berlin Haskalah, each of which, he claimed, fulfilled a function in the historical process. Spinoza was not ousted from this process, and could not be ousted, because Rav Kook knew (without using this language) that Spinoza was a great man; he did not deny his intellectual stature and also that of his particular style. One may assume that he read Spinoza, for this would cohere with his general outlook.

For Rav Kook stressed that it is a mistake to consider the world to be mended when it is full of dross requiring refinement. To be sure, he added immediately that this lesson has cost us a great deal of tuition, but he does not say that we do not need to pay the tuition. The tuition must be paid.

One point relevant to the problem of belief in Rav Kook. There is a verse in Psalms (51:8) that ought to be mentioned in this discussion: "You desire truth in the kidneys and in the hidden parts You shall inform me of wisdom." Rav Kook wants, first of all, the truth of the kidneys. That means the truth of faith, and from that truth he never swerved. But he awaited the second colon of the verse: "in the hidden parts You shall inform me of wisdom." He believed in wisdom and in human capacity, but did not see man himself as the center; he said this with respect to Maimonides. His harsh criticism of Zev Javetz, who ignored the significance of the *Guide,* has already been mentioned. Rav Kook claimed that the *Guide* prepared the spirit of coming generations. Maimonides deliberately placed the being of the world, not man, at the center. Hence Rav Kook states, when the world underwent crisis with the Copernican revolution that toppled belief in man as the center, we, thanks to Maimonides, who paved the way for future generations, could accept all this.

If we have listened to what was said today, I think we might well say that Rav Kook prepared us, to a certain degree, for many problems that have come up today that we have not discussed.

I have only one request of the organizers of the conference: that our discussions lead to one very important outcome on the scholarly side, and that is the publication of a standard, critical, clear edition of Rav Kook's teachings.

PROFESSOR ROSENBERG:
In one point, I think an important distinction is needed. It is connected to some of Professor Rotenstreich's remarks as well. Let me explain it fully, because I cannot start in the middle.

The question is how Rav Kook evaluates or assesses or looks upon a person who does not seem acceptable to us—how does he receive him? There are three different models in Rav Kook's teaching regarding the evaluation of the negative, the secularist, the antireligious, or the nonreligious.

One model is the one mentioned before, that I will abbreviate as the "Jewish point" that exists, as it were, within the secularist. There is a point, a spark, that acts perpetually.

The second model I call the "dialectic of the conjugation of faces." This maintains that, if AB is ideal, and if there is a negative phenomenon A that is *not B*, e.g., a world alienated from terrestrial existence and from the corporeal, there must appear the dialectically contrary phenomenon, B that is not A. The conjugation of the two should lead to synthesis. This is the way Rav Kook looks upon the appearance of secularism.

The third model is that of the tragedy that occurs in the process or intellectual or mystical elevation. There are people who see very high visions, and what they see is beyond their power to see. This leads to crisis. Rav Kook employs here the model of the broken vessels. The vessels take in more light than they can contain, and consequently shatter. This section of *Orot* is very well known. Some say that it is connected to the figure of Brenner, but without doubt this is the model that he applies, in my opinion, to Spinoza. He says it about Bilaam too, and I think he means Nietzsche. There is a penetration of the light that breaks the man. It is a holy light, but the vessels cannot contain it and bear it, whence the breaking. From all this, it becomes clear that Spinoza cannot be accepted as he is, and that he must be corrected.

I have another comment on Professor Rotenstreich's words, which I think is significant: the description of the man who observes his fellow and hears what he says, and thus gets an account of what the other feels. Thus, too, he receives his knowledge of himself. This is a rational norm, valid perhaps in the Hegelian system, but invalid in Rav Kook's, because Rav Kook had a foundation other than the rational. He worked with a voluntarist foundation. For this reason, Rav Kook is closer to Schopenhauer than to Hegel.

This means that above rationality, man is an active will. His reason attempts to explicate his will, but not always with success. Thus, it may definitely be the case that there are people, religious or nonreligious, who act because of specific drives, who try to subsume under their own rational framework their interpretation of the other. Both the religionist and the secularist may create such interpretations. There is a desire to uncover an unconscious layer in man, and this continues the system of Habad. Let me note that there is a fundamental difference between the unconscious of the Musar movement, which is negative, and the unconscious of Habad and of Rav Kook, which is positive. Man has an unconscious root that comes to expression in the will. The will, by the way, is the *sefira* of *Ayin (Keter)* which is beyond *Chochma* (wisdom). This very clearly means that man acts very clearly in a superrational way, and the rationalization performed afterward is an explanation of what he has done. The secularist rationalizes from within his own activity. It is quite possible that we understand the other better than he understands himself.

PROFESSOR ROTENSTREICH:

First a comment on Professor Rosenberg's last remarks regarding Schopenhauer. Let me suggest that we be very careful in our associations. For Schopenhauer, will is linked to a relation to a world saturated with evil and wickedness. This is not the will that Shalom Rosenberg rightly views as being very important in Rav Kook's outlook and ethic, which is not a will directed to a meaningless world. This is a point that should be noted, and the Asian influence here is worthy of attention.

Let me say something about Spinoza. Professor Urbach rightly referred to Hermann Cohen's evaluation, according to which Spinoza was biographically and systematically defective. The biographical aspect has been illuminated in the work of the late Julius Guttmann. He notes that, according to Cohen, the interpretation of Judaism as a legal-political system, propounded in Spinoza's *Tractatus,* determined Kant's view of Judaism. Judaism is a statutory system, in the words of Kant, and does not come under the rubric of religion. Whether this influence was direct or (ironically) mediated by Mendelssohn's *Jerusalem,* Hermann Cohen held Spinoza responsible for molding Kant's view of Judaism. What nineteenth-century German philosophers called "refined Spinozism" removed the deterministic element and highlighted the dynamic element. In this context, one may say of Spinoza that he is a pantheist who is in fact an acosmist, a negator of the existence of the cosmos. This could not be said of Rav Kook.

To be sure, the famous words of Jean-Paul proclaimed Spinoza as the "G-d-intoxicated philosopher." This is a major point, where we see that the pantheistic conception identifying the world and G-d was interpreted as a conception stressing the total presence of G-d. It is impossible to regard Spinoza as G-d-intoxicated without thus interpreting this aspect of pantheism, i.e., the presence of G-d. From this point of view, there is in fact no secular realm; there is no reality divested of G-d's presence. This perhaps reached Rav Kook through various channels, perhaps through Russian thought, perhaps through Habad. A. D. Gordon is also pertinent to this context. There are different possibilities regarding some intellectual atmosphere, within which we must seek the impressions of this outlook.

DR. AVIEZER RAVITZKY:

I would like to add a note to the subject just discussed. Rav Kook's words have been linked here to names like Hegel, Spinoza, Hermann Cohen. It is astonishing to compare to Hegel the section in *Orot HaKodesh,* to which I have already alluded, regarding the alienation engendered by external monotheistic conceptions. Hegel attacks Judaism, he views biblical Judaism, before Christianity, as a radical monotheism that produces division: G-d is absolutely separated from man. Hegel states that Christianity overcame all this through the Incarnation, whereby there is no longer an infinite gap between G-d and man, between G-d and world.

Rav Kook too critiques the "conventional" monotheism as engendering separation and alienation between man and his Creator. According to him, however, it was Jewish mystical teaching that has overcome this. You penetrate to the inner nature of the Torah when you take pantheism refined of its dross and synthesize it with radical monotheism: This is done on the basis of Jewish mysticism, or, with Rav Kook, "according to the rational approach of modern Chasidism," by which he apparently meant the Habad doctrines. Hegel, thus, had argued that it is Christianity that overcomes the gap engendered by biblical Judaism. Rav Kook says that it is Kabbalah and especially Chasidism, that overcome the separation.

Now let us proceed. When Hegel criticizes Judaism, Spinoza is his model. Spinoza is a Jewish model who is to be negated. For, so he says, the G-d of Spinoza is a cold G-d, an unbridgeable Substance, it is impossible to reach any familiarity with Him, as he puts it, i.e., any closeness; there is no mediation, only alienation and strangeness. Therefore, for Hegel, Spinoza is Jewish exactly because of the impossibility of encounter. That is to say, Hegel already proclaimed of Spinoza, in the name of the Jewish people, "you are our brother," while for Rav Kook, as we heard in the instructive citation brought by Professor Schatz, it will take a number of generations until he finds his remedy and we can say to him—in a new version—"you are our brother." In any event, for Hegel Spinoza is the Jew, creator of a cold Divine Substance. For Rav Kook, by contrast, Spinoza's pantheism plays the opposite role: To the contrary, after his Jewish purification, he is the corrective to radical—that is, alienated—monotheism. Thus, precipitating the encounter between G-d and man, separation passing from the world.

A last note on Hermann Cohen. Normally, Hermann Cohen is truly the classic antagonist of the pantheistic conception. In this manner, he must also be the antagonist of that part of Rav Kook that desires a pantheism purified of its dross. Now we find in Cohen's work on Maimonides' ethics that, in order to protect man's ethical reason, "a measure of pantheism" is sometimes required "to save human reason in the face of G-d." Because G-d the omnipotent, the autonomous legislator, is liable to turn human reason to nothing. In my own language: The extreme monotheistic conception makes it impossible to state "Heaven forfend that You do this thing to kill the righteous with the wicked" [Genesis 18:15], for who am I to speak before G-d. Thus, Hermann Cohen is saying that at times we need a pinch of pantheism to defend human reason from the ultimate monotheism of the Omnipotent, who dominates and turns all to nothing. Precisely here there is a similarity to Rav Kook's words in *Orot HaKodesh* about the way radical monotheism must sometimes be purified of its dross by pantheism, in order to defend human reason or man, for otherwise we would experience total alienation. Thus, it becomes evident that many kinds of circles are closing. Even Hermann Cohen, who in other contexts would oppose Rav Kook's position, here comes to a meeting of the minds with him.

PROFESSOR RIVKA SCHATZ:

In the course of a discussion that is very interesting in itself, in its historical implications, and in the attempt to understand Rav Kook's influences, I prefer to direct my comment in a somewhat different direction. I myself do not believe that Spinoza is Rav Kook's problem as a pantheist. Professor Urbach rightly says that the Spinoza affair is not an episode. I think that Professor Rotenstreich's comments only strengthen this. Meaning that it is not particularly Spinoza, but the whole idea of totality, that is the flesh and blood of Rav Kook's system. I would say that this is his message. He crossed the lines that stood between the transcendent concern as something fine and good that every Jew was aware of, and the world. And I would say that this dichotomy in fact has disappeared. I am not saying that he was the first in Jewish thought to think that way. In my humble opinion, I would add parenthetically, this problem became very acute in the world of Kabbalah, as a result of its dialectical approach, and its complexity and inner conflict already appear in Cordovero, and later in Hasidism. These matters are far from simple, and I do not share the opinion that Spinoza himself is so distant, despite the view he more or less held that all Kabbalah is nothing but gibberish. I truly believe that this integration of G-d and world was virtually axiomatic, if not as an explicit philosophical thesis, then as a sense of life. The experience of G-d's presence, for Rav Kook, took absolute precedence. This is the dominant theme in all his writings. And this is also what drives you to understand the intellectual structures and to analyze them in detail.

The problem that I presented earlier remains nonetheless apparently unsolved. How did he cross these lines so quietly, or perhaps not so quietly, for we see that there was a storm. How did he cross those lines, whereby this superior perfection was possible, as if indeed there were no problem? This is what we asked, and I said that it is something radical, that his attitude to action, to this world, the emphasis, the faith that you can embrace the world, derives from that sense of perfection and from that sense of unity.

How often does the word *unity* appear in his writings? It is a solid rock of his system. I ask how he crossed these lines, when in the history of Jewish thought even those who wished to move toward pantheistic and panentheistic conceptions did not dare to say this openly, univocally. I claim that there is suddenly a stage of development of this idea in the world of Kabbalah to the point where it became totally radicalized in the teaching of Rav Kook.

Professor Rotenstreich said that there is no reality that is separate, from another world, but that is the point, that the act is a realization of reality, and not an act beyond reality that has to be brought to it. Let us stop for a moment and ponder: What are the implications of this bold crossing of the lines, with a sweep that is astonishing? For Rav Kook was not one of those people who did not know what they were about; he knew it very well. Therefore one must accept it as it appears in his writings.

And Spinoza, as I said, does not trouble him. He is troublesome only from the perspective of a shaking of completeness that is generally sociological rather than metaphysical.

RABBI YOCHANAN FRIED:

I want to comment by asking a question or to ask by making a comment. In one of the letters that was studied in one of the workshops, Rav Kook asks Ridbaz, "Are we, G-d forbid, Karaites?" I apply this phrase to the subject discussed here and to the method. Rav Kook left a Written Torah that long and broad, and there are those who enjoy uncovering new faces in it, as new as the morning. Let me tell you that there are another few hundreds of thousands of points that can be discovered in the writings, but there is also an Oral Torah. And I would like to make my comment with an anecdote, a point that is connected perhaps to all that was said here, and by the way to raise a question.

Rav Kook read much of what was written in his time and in previous generations, as we have heard here. Among other things, he read in an area that was not mentioned here, i.e., literature. Now there is a story about Rav Kook's son and interpreter and the poet Saul Tchernichovsky. They met on a ship returning to Israel. Tchernichovsky felt that Rav Zvi Yehuda was keeping his distance. One day Tchernichovsky approached him on the deck; as they gazed at the sea, he said, I heard that your father is an interesting man. Rav Zvi Yehuda responded, Yes, he is an interesting man, and maybe more than that. But, continued the poet, I hear that he has a method, that he elevates the profane to the holy. To which Rav Zvi Yehuda answered quite sharply, True, he elevates the profane to the holy, but not profanity [*tuma*]!

I repeat this because it is my duty, I believe, to ask a question. Rav Kook composed a series of books under the title *Orot HaKodesh,* "Lights of Holiness." Rav Charlop, his great disciple, wrote an essay about him called "His Inner Sanctum" *(Mikdasho haPenimi).* It is appropriate that I use the very words of Rav Kook, who writes that when Maimonides adopted one of the views of Aristotle, he did not do so before he converted it. So writes Rav Kook about Aristotle. And I ask simply as a note, what does it mean that he converted it? Rav Kook was a rabbi; he was an educator. He spoke about holiness. What is the meaning of holiness? This is my question to the colloquium.

PROFESSOR ROTENSTREICH:

The concept of holiness is polysemous. The holy is a separate realm, whose tones resonate in ours as well, "He who separates the holy from the quotidian." The concept appears, for example, in Rudolf Otto's philosophy of religion. The numinous is separate. Among other things, it is ineffable, because it is wholly other. Holiness is understood also as the perfection of the norm, when reality is identical with the norm, as in the holy will of Kant, for example. I propose, for purposes of our discussion, that we distinguish between the holy and the Holy of Holies. This is an important distinction, implying that reality in its breadth, because of its breadth, and because of what is inherent in its breadth, is holy, bears holiness. Holy of Holies refers to a reality in which there is no longer a distinction between the dynamic and the normative, that is, the reality of G-d. This becomes intertwined in one way or another, with the possibility of pantheism.

RABBI FRUMAN:

I think that Rabbi Yochanan Fried has dropped his glove, and I do not want it to remain on the ground. I have the impression that some of Rabbi Fried's expressions (I am not sure if he meant it, but if he didn't, then I do) intended to pose the basic question that I sense at this conference. I do not belong to the academic world, as Shalom described it earlier, and I think that this has something to do with Rav Kook's contribution to reality, to the renewal of thought. That point can serve as a comment on Rabbi Yochanan Fried's words and to Professor Urbach's remark about quoting a verse in Psalms. The point about holiness that was discussed here—and this is essential to Rav Kook's thought—is not just the subject of thought and analysis and investigations about whether the influences come from Kabbalistic sources as I argued, or outside sources, as others suggested, or both. The question is whether you taste in the ideas, in the thought, in the analysis, the flavor of spiritual intensity, of spiritual life, of spiritual truth. That, I believe, is the glove that Rabbi Fried tried to drop. In other words, is there a doctrine to treat or is there also an Oral Torah, something living with which to be concerned? This really raises the issue of whether it is possible to create an expanse of warmth, or whether it is possible to keep warm only by contracting oneself in a corner. I do not mean to imply that the monopoly on warmth in a narrow corner belongs to the Chasidic Shtibel, as one might infer. It is a problem.

I once had a discussion in Dahishe with people from the Bir Zayit University and allied circles. I saw how much narrowness, how much lack of consideration, what limited horizons may exist, which engender a kind of faith, intensity, or something like that. I tried to broaden their horizons. I don't know if I did well.

In other words, I believe that Rav Kook set a challenge, that broad horizons can also possess holiness and intensity, that an academic conference can also have the atmosphere of a yeshiva, that the mood of Elul can be found in the King David Hotel, to borrow another remark from Professor Urbach. That is the problem. Let me tell you that I am suffering at this point. That is the problem here. I do not believe that the answer is easy. When I suggested that Avi Ravitzky and I pray together, and was interrupted in my presentation, I was making a proposal that is found in Rav Kook's statements to jest, to play with ideas, and not in the pejorative sense, but in a very serious sense, that of "Leviathan You created with whom to play." To see in all ideas material for the spirit of man as he writes in that section, "matter for spirit." Here is a question that for me is essential, and I do not believe it is so only for me, as Professor Urbach indicated in his comment to me. I think this is the most essential question that Rav Kook's teaching arouses in me.

REUVEN GARBER:

My question, in fact, will constitute the antithesis to Rabbi Fried's. If he addressed the holy, I wish to address the profane. My question deals with the dual attitude to freethinking, that is, to contemporary secularism. This continues the opening remarks of Professor Schatz, from which we learned about the unmistakable effect on Rav Kook of the secularist movements of his time. In other words, I would like the speakers to sharpen their comments on "postmodern" (in Dr. Ravitzky's definition) secularism or freethinking, with respect to the ideas of human perfection, the motive of faith for postmodern man, the value of secularity in general in connection with the idea of "In all your ways, know Him" stressed by Professor Rosenberg.

PROFESSOR URBACH:

I want to respond to Rabbi Yochanan Fried. I am afraid that he has opened, to some degree, a Pandora's box. This is because the problem of Oral Torah in connection with a specific personality whom we are still chronologically close to, and who has written and published, is a very difficult problem. It reverts to the last point I made about the results of this conference. Rabbi Fried's story, even if he heard it from Rav Zvi Yehuda Kook, I regard as his response and not his father's. It is irrelevant to us. Rav Zvi Yehuda had the right to answer Tchernichovsky as he did. I do not know whether Rav Kook would have given Tchernichovsky the same answer. I do not know that profanity [*tuma*] is the conceptual opposite of holiness, as we know. Thus, it was a riposte, and it is permissible to direct a riposte at an important person. There are ripostes that have led to trouble, and there are nice ones. But it is difficult to ascribe to it the value of Oral Torah, as if he had said it or written it. And let me argue again that the written corpus requires much investigation and work. Hence I take this opportunity to repeat my suggestion for an outcome to this conference.

BENNY LEHMANN:

I want to comment on virtually everything that was said about Spinoza. There are quite explicit statements on this in the essay *Avodat Elokim.* It contains a very clear criticism of the notion alluded to by Professor Rotenstreich, i.e., Spinoza's "G-d intoxication." When he analyzes the will to self, as opposed to cleaving unto G-d, to the divine ideals appearing in the world, Rav Kook states quite explicitly that in Spinoza the will to self is stunning. He criticizes it vehemently, setting it against the alternative, not of cleaving unto G-d, the Divine Substance, but rather cleaving unto His ways, the ways of G-d—as He is merciful, so you be merciful, etc. Here I think it is important to comment on what Professor Schatz has said. That attempt to cross lines and realms toward the pantheistic conception appears in Rav Kook in a very clear way in an adherence to something very substantial that exists within the world. The means to this is *Knesset Yisrael* and the totality of Israel. And this is also connected to what Rabbi Yochanan Fried has said. For the moment one ignores this point, that we are dealing with a cleaving, a reality that exists within the world, one is forsaking of the world, as in all the Habad doctrines that speak of cleaving unto some absolute transcendence that is difficult to adhere to, whereas for Rav Kook this matter is emphasized by means of the concept *Klal Yisrael.* Hence it is so important for those who studied the oral tradition from the mouth of Rav Zvi Yehuda, as I understand. That is explained in the chapter I cited on the service of G-d as the unique quality of Israel, the capacity of revealing matters in concrete existence while cleaving unto G-d's ways. I believe that one should relate to the explicit statements in *Avodat Elokim,* beyond what is quoted here, for there is an absolute, clear critique together with the possibility of refining and elevating the sparks that exist in Spinoza too. But that is in the context of the critique that I mentioned.

PROFESSOR RIVKA SCHATZ:

Let me remark that in my citation there is also a penetrating criticism of Spinoza. Nonetheless, I have the impression—and that is what I called crossing the lines—that the problem is not cleaving unto the divine, as Professor Rotenstreich mentioned by G-d intoxication, it is rather Rav Kook's love to what surrounds, in whatever sense, be it action, secularity, the concrete world. What resounds here is indeed the blurring of boundaries: the intoxication of reality is no less great than that of the divine, be it transcendent according to the concepts of tradition, be it immanent in accordance with the concepts that we today are increasingly close to. So it seems to me.

  Much will not help. Regarding this remark "but not profanity [*tuma*]," let me note that this exactly is the question. If we translate *tuma* as "secular," and declare a distinction between them, then you have not done much. Because even so, the secular ends up in *tuma,* because that was the classical Jewish conception. *Tuma* is not literally something separate, it is a certain continuum or stage; I don't know. What is *tuma* in this case? The prohibited?! He never said that the prohibited can be transformed into the permitted. Unlike Shabtai Zvi, he did not bless "He who looses prohibitions *(issurim)*" in place of "looses prisoners' chains *(asurim)*." This he certainly did not say. But for us, from the viewpoint of fundamental philosophy, we ask precisely, Where do the lines stop?

  For the world of halacha, things are clear: What is prohibited is prohibited; what is permitted is permitted. There is someone to decide. But as a question of principle and philosophy, these lines are the corners of the altar of the entire matter. Where is the delicate limit? Please then, there is a view that says secularity yes, *tuma* no. Why? Because whoever says this wishes, first of all, to exclude the realm of the prohibited from this struggle. He wants to exclude it. He wants to say, Just a moment, ladies and gentlemen, what is completely impure must be counted out. True, there is a rabbinic statement: Why is the pig called *chazir*? Because G-d will restore *(chazir)* it to Israel. Then surely he who cites this as part of his system will maintain, I am radical without veil or curtain; I go all the way; that is my system; unity is unity; stop blurring things. I think it is a wonderful story, which illustrates exactly the point where the problems intensify, and roads diverge.

In the final analysis, this is not a matter of loving the secularists because of their beautiful eyes; rather there are tremendous depths of conception. It did not begin with Rav Kook. About him I only ask which station he is at. I didn't answer; I asked.

DR. AVIEZER RAVITZKY:

Let me say something that is neither philosophical nor theological. Rather something about "Rav Kook's contribution to the thought of Jewish renewal" might be said here. I think the uniqueness of this conference and its power up to the past hour has been its success—for the first time, as memory serves me—in bringing together people sealed with the various stigmas and insignia of two different worlds, for a sincere and genuine encounter, with each side offering its own discipline and outlook. That was its power. I would not want us to go home with the sense that we have lost this achievement.

What do I mean? Let us take the words of Rabbi Yochanan Fried and divide them in two. Regarding one half of what he said, the "oral teaching," I find myself in the camp in which I would be expected to belong according to my uniform. That is, I disagree with him. Respecting the other half, when he speaks of the conversion of a position, that Rav Kook, at the most profound level, converted each position before he embraced it, I identify with him with full enthusiasm. Here I surely do not belong to the camp that I am supposed to belong to, for I truly believe that he did not cross the line.

This is not merely a semantic question. Sometimes those who would criticize Maimonides say that he hellenized Judaism, and those who defend him, that he converted it. These are not questions of semantics. For example, I mentioned earlier Hegel's view that monotheism involves alienation and that Christianity overcomes it, and Rav Kook's view that radical monotheism involves a breach, but that the inner nature of Judaism overcomes the breach. Now if he read Hegel, this is a profound conversion of him; if he did not read Hegel, then there was no need to convert him. However, one finds here parallel spiritual phenomena. Let me formulate it this way. Rav Kook asks many modern questions, which he could not have asked from within the Jewish medieval literature. At the same time, he makes every effort to discover the answers from within, in the classical literature, in what he considered the inner wisdom of Judaism, with all the warmth of which Rabbi Fruman spoke.

In many cases, his problem is modern. But the attempt is to penetrate inward with great intensity for solutions. Therefore it must not happen to us as it does elsewhere where there are only uniforms, insignia, and stigmatization, where questions are not asked, and only masters of response flourish. At the same time, let us not think that answers must involve crossing lines. Certainly not with respect to Rav Kook.

PROFESSOR ROSENBERG:

One word of Oral Torah and one of the Written. I think that some of these matters can be found in the Written Torah. It is not exactly a matter of Oral Torah. There is a classic discussion about the verse "and a shovel you shall have at your side" where Rav Kook says some very harsh things about literature. I do not recall at the moment if he uses the precise term *tuma,* and it doesn't make a difference. It is enough to remember the association connected to the verse. This precisely is the way Rav Kook approaches what we might call a kind of auto-censorship that each person ought to exercise in his literature. He said similar things about Agnon. When he read Agnon, he spoke of a prohibited meat mixed with kosher food in a 1 to 60 ratio, which somehow transforms it into a kosher entity. The same is true of Agnon's writing: Though it contain a measure of contamination, it is annulled by the "ratio of sixty." Thus, I would not be surprised about his criticism of a portion of modern Hebrew literature, including the poetry of Tchernichovsky; I don't know that he used the word *tuma,* but he considered them to be matters best disposed of with "the shovel at your side," that is, buried.

I do not know whether we need to reach a consensus about the next world. At the same time, I think that one thing ought to be clear. We in particular, people coming from the academic world, ought to distinguish clearly between being "Kookians" and being "neo-Kookians," even when we identify with him. Take history, for example. Rav Kook offered a certain interpretation of history, and it may be that we will not be among those who continue his approach. But I am obligated to clarify and distinguish, when I am offering a new interpretation, as Rav Kook may have done with regard to Spinoza, and when I am saying something different. This is, for me, part of intellectual honesty, to clarify whether someone is or is not continuing a certain direction, and how he may be continuing. It may be that there are disciples of Rav Kook who continue his way. And here the question arises whether the teaching of his son, Rav Zvi Yehuda zt'l, continues his or not. This question should be treated in the appropriate manner, not impressionistically.

This point about *tuma* appears to be an interesting example, for it also has implications for the doctrine of the will that I mentioned before. It is true that Schopenhauer has a concept of evil will. Rav Kook says this explicitly through the idea of the blind monster. He claims that there are levels of will, and the will can descend virtually to the lowest level. Thus, he regarded Schopenhauer as one who "descended." But here a question arises, the answer to which I do not believe we know exactly. What is the status of that *tuma* or that evil? The notion is apparently that the secularity he observed in the kibbutzim, in the work of building, is to be sanctified. The phenomenon of sexual license, to which I have no doubt that he referred, which he saw both in literature and in real life, he would explicitly characterize as *tuma*. This is a profanity that cannot attain holiness under any circumstances. If there is another interpretation that can be defended scientifically, I am prepared to change my mind.

PROFESSOR ROTENSTREICH:

I hope that I will not open myself to the suspicion that I am pushing the interests of my "trade union" when I make an additional comment about Spinoza. It is important for our concern. It is an error to attribute to Spinoza the notion that one can attain intellectual love of G-d while leaping over earlier stages. This is the highest level of knowledge, which can be achieved only stage by stage. The term or expression itself, "intellectual love of G-d," is open to different interpretations.

The essential difference between Rav Kook's outlook and that of Spinoza pertains to time. Spinoza saw time as a mode of imagination, what the medieval philosophers called "the imaginative faculty." Rav

Kook, for various reasons, regarded time as an intrinsic dimension of reality in its full breadth. It is possible that, from a systematic perspective, the status of *Knesset Yisrael* is an aspect of a status in time, insofar as *Knesset Yisrael* cannot be grasped as belonging to space. Spinoza distinguished intrinsically between the status of space and the status of time.

Thus, we arrive at a point where modernity is granted importance, because, from a certain perspective, the assumptions of modernity led to the conception that man's world is a temporal world, and is exclusively temporal. Whatever man does is temporal. Whatever he initiates is initiated in time. The alteration of reality, of government, emancipation, the rights of man, progress, all these are components of temporal being. Modernity is characterized by the importance and exclusivity of temporal reality.

Thus, one could say that Rav Kook consents to the integration of reality in time with the essential ontological space, but that by that integration he negates enclosure in time. Thus, we must find here the corrective to Spinoza's view on a most essential issue, a confrontation with the basic assumptions of modernity, and far-reaching reservations with respect to modernity.

I dare say something for which I have no authority. What is *tuma?* It is an error to hold that *tuma* is secular in its orientation, that profanity is secularity. *Tuma*, as I would try to analyze it in my layman's way, is not the absence of ontological status or situation in reality. The "other thing" is not ontologically negated, whatever the laws. The negation is integrating that which is with human behavior. That is the prohibition: to integrate that which ought not to be integrated into the framework of human reality. This should be noted precisely in the outlook that is so open to the various domains of reality, and with respect to the various components of the domains, which distinguishes explicitly or implicitly between the ontological dimension of faith and the axiological one of norm.

RAV WOHLGELERNTER:

There are today among the sacred community of scholars dealing with Rav Kook's teaching two schools concerned with contemporary applications. There are actual problems in halacha, in policy. Several months ago there was a public debate about going up to the Temple

Mount and practical preparations for the construction of the temple. The central question was whether one can base a decision on Rav Kook's view as expressed in the Protocol of the Government Commission of Inquiry in the period of the Mandate, or, as one side argued, must one turn to *Mishpat Kohen* and see how he ruled there. I think that during this blessed, historic conference, the emphasis was on his esoteric teachings, as expressed in *Orot HaKodesh* and *Igrot Ha-ReAYaH*, while the surface of Rav Kook's halachic heritage was barely scratched. This has yet to be publicly aired. As far as I know, Rav Kook did not discuss Talmudic and halachic commentary from a literary-historical perspective. Hence it seems to me that, with respect to matters touched upon today or at other sessions of the conference, which are relevant to practical halacha even in the realm of philosophy and thought, we yet await what will be publicized and discovered as clear halacha. In the final analysis, we shall surely have before us halachic decision on questions of the sort we discussed today.

This conference is certainly very beneficial. But as we prepare to separate, I think we should draw a line and say that we still do not know Rav Kook so long as we do not know his halachic decisions. Hence I ask his disciples here what we can expect in this area in the near future.

PROFESSOR ROSENBERG:

Everyone knows the famous question (*Bava Metzia* 62a) about "two who were on the road and one had a cruse of water. If both drink, both die; if one drinks, he will reach habitation." We know the famous dispute between Ben Petura and Rav Akiva: "Ben Petura taught: Better that they both drink and die, and let one not see the death of his comrade. But then came Rav Akiva came and taught: 'And your brother shall live with you'—Your life takes precedence over your comrade's life!" We know a great deal about this. I would like to mention the nice story told my Agnon about Maharil. When Maharil reached the next world, he was not allowed to enter, because the Tractate *Bava Metzia* protested. That tractate had stated that the decision follows Rav Akiva, while Maharil followed Ben Petura, i.e., he did not want to drink the water but to divide it. Despite any doubts about the source of this legend, it is important and illuminating.

Here, there is a ruling of Rav Kook that is very relevant to what we have heard, and in the military area as well it was, unfortunately, relevant in the disasters that occurred at Tyre, during the Lebanon War, and in several cases. Rav Kook held that it is impossible that both die, and we do not follow Ben Petura. This means that, while it is intolerable that both die, it is absolutely within the halacha that the owner of the water give it away to the other person, without violating Rav Akiva's principle. In other words, according to Rav Kook, Rav Akiva did not impose the egoistic principle (or the principle of justice as Achad Haam saw it), and then completed it with another principle. Rav Kook made the remarkable determination that if your comrade's life is indeed dearer to you than your own, then it is within the framework of the halacha to give the water to him. This is an instance of a halachic ruling that is apparently innovative. I know no source for it. But it is an example of the kind of principled, thoughtful, and ethical reading of Rav Kook, in which halacha and aggadah are intertwined.

PROFESSOR RIVKA SCHATZ:

Thus, we reach the end. I shall not sum up, for we did not reach conclusions. We only began discussions, which I found very interesting. Speaking for myself, as one who has dealt quite a bit with the subject, much became clear to me, both in sweep and implications, the sources from which ideas emerge and where they are headed. In other words, the possible conclusions are plural, as Professor Rosenberg has noted as well. In this matter, the solutions are surely not those of sages but of history. Whoever takes one of the approaches will continue to live with it.

Index

Page numbers marked with an n *refer to footnotes in the text.*